D1308622

The Family, Society, and the Individual

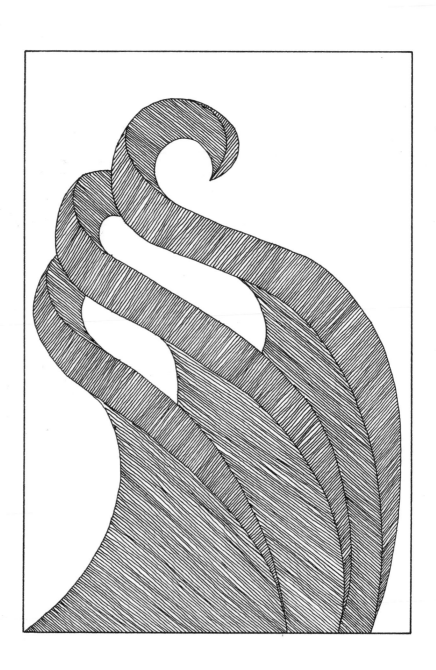

The Family, Society, and the Individual

Fourth Edition

William M. Kephart

University of Pennsylvania

Houghton Mifflin Company   **Boston**

Atlanta   Dallas   Geneva, Illinois   Hopewell, New Jersey
Palo Alto   London

LIBRARY
OF
MOUNT ST. MARY'S
COLLEGE
EMMITSBURG, MARYLAND

All marriages are happy. It's the living together that causes the trouble.

Anonymous

TITLE PAGE AND PART TITLE ILLUSTRATIONS BY GEORGE VOGT.

Copyright © 1977, 1972 by Houghton Mifflin Company. Copyright © 1966, 1961 by William M. Kephart. All rights reserved. No part of this work may be reproduced or transmitted in any form or by any means, electronic or mechanical, including photocopying and recording, or by any information storage or retrieval system, without permission in writing from the publisher.

Printed in the U.S.A.

Library of Congress Catalog Card Number: 76-13094

ISBN: 0-395-24247-9

Contents

Preface

SOME SAY IT was written in the stars, but — whatever the reason — *The Family, Society, and the Individual* has been both criticized and praised. Fortunately, praise has far outweighed criticism, and some 700 colleges and universities have now used the book. Moreover, a large number of teachers and students at these institutions have taken the time to write to me, and I appreciate their many kind words.

In keeping with the trend of the times, a number of readers felt that more space should be devoted to the role of women. Others believed that the time was ripe for an exploration of alternatives to marriage. Accordingly, new chapters or sections dealing with women's liberation and alternative life styles have been added.

Other major changes have also been made; in fact, it would not be much exaggeration to say that *it is change that characterizes this new edition.* The trick, of course, has been to incorporate the new material without altering the readability and flow of the basic book. These have always been essential features of *The Family, Society, and the Individual.* I think I can promise that they remain so in the present edition.

William M. Kephart
Margate, New Jersey

To the Instructor

The Family, Society, and the Individual is designed for one-semester courses in marriage and the family. It is hoped that the
book will afford students a better understanding not only of
their own family system but of the interrelation between the
family and society at large. If all goes well, students may also
gain a better understanding of themselves.

The human family has many dimensions, of course, and for
this reason, *The Family, Society, and the Individual* is eclectic in
its approach. To understand American marriage and family
patterns, for example, it would seem only logical to explore
concomitant behavior in other societies and other times. Accordingly, the initial chapters include both a cross-cultural and
an historical survey. Primary emphasis of the book, naturally, is
on the contemporary scene.

The family is also the province of many different disciplines:
sociology, anthropology, home economics, social psychology,
law, religion, and so on. And while *The Family, Society, and the
Individual* is basically sociological in its orientation, it is also
interdisciplinary. In fact, it is this broad, liberal-arts approach
that has become one of the book's "trademarks."

The new edition contains a number of major changes. In
addition to the sections on women's liberation and alternative
life styles, mentioned previously, new material has been added
on minority family types, experimental family organization,
marriage enrichment, sexual adjustment in marriage, no-fault
divorce, and so on.

The Family, Society, and the Individual includes a number of
instructional aids in both the teaching and research areas. For
instance, the quantity of pertinent research in recent years has
been enormous—and the present edition has incorporated a
multitude of new findings. For more general references, a list of
Selected Readings is included at the end of most chapters. Also—
as an aid to the teacher—an Instructor's Manual has been made
available.

It should be mentioned, finally, that the present edition of

The Family, Society, and the Individual has been immeasurably strengthened by the comments and criticisms of a number of interested persons — both users and nonusers of the text. Special thanks for reviewing the entire manuscript are due to John R. Earle, of Wake Forest University; Lois McCarty-Greene, of Foothill College; Robert C. Sherwin, of Miami University of Ohio; and W. G. Steglich, of the University of Texas at El Paso. Thanks are due as well to those individuals who provided early recommendations for this edition — Shirley Acheson of Grossmont College; James R. George of Kutztown State College; Ben Holeman of Sinclair Community College; and S. C. Lee of Ohio University.

W.M.K.

The Family, Society,
and the Individual

I

The Cultural Setting

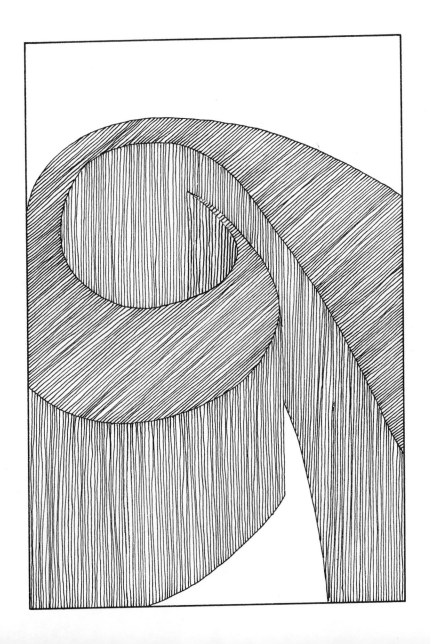

1

Introduction: The Family Field
Approach

THERE ARE MANY ways of looking at the human family, with no
two writers having exactly the same perspective. Traditionally,
for example, the family was thought of in rather simplistic terms:
the interaction of husband and wife and the production and socialization of children. Times change, however, and today's
family textbooks are likely to devote few chapters to the family as
thus depicted. Most texts, for instance, spend a good deal of time
discussing premarital behavior—romantic love, mate selection,
premarital sex codes—as well as such topics as the changing
status of women, divorce and remarriage, social-class differentials, and many others.

These areas are quite important to the study of the family. Just
as the field of criminology is not limited to an analysis of the
criminal, so the family field is not restricted to the study of the
husband-wife relationship. Criminologists are interested in the
causes of crime, the operation of criminal law, the effects of race
and class, the operation of probation and parole, and the like.
Similarly, family sociologists are concerned with sexual behavior,
marriage and divorce laws, minority family patterns, alternative
life styles, and so on. The family, in other words, cannot be studied in a cultural vacuum.

The traditional conception of the family, then, is misleading,
for it does not adequately describe what family sociologists really
study. Supplementing this concept, therefore, let us use the term
"family field" to denote the various cultural, historical, legal, religious, and other institutional and socio-psychological factors
that contribute to a fuller understanding of the human family.
The present volume represents a sociological analysis of the family field rather than of the family proper.

A moment's reflection will show why—at the college level—
the family field approach is so effective. A liberal arts education

should attempt to examine *relationships among phenomena,* and one of the aims of this book is just that: to show the connections among the various sets of factors that have culminated in the present-day family system.

Another aim of scholarly teaching is to give students some appreciation of their cultural heritage and an awareness of both the derivative and contrasting patterns of other societies. Again, one of the aims of the present volume is to place the family within a framework of historical and cross-cultural forces.

THE CHANGING AMERICAN FAMILY

While we are concerned with the family as a social institution, our primary interest centers on the American family. The latter has, on the one hand, been called the backbone of the nation, while almost in the same breath it is said that our connubial system is breaking down, both functionally and morally. One thing seems clear: for better or worse, the modern family is different from that of yesteryear.

Almost 50 years ago, William F. Ogburn, one of the first sociologists to specialize in the family field, contended that the American family had lost many of its traditional functions to other agencies, such as the school, the church, and the state.[1] More recently, John Demos, a historian working with different sets of data, reached a similar conclusion.

> Broadly speaking, the history of the family in America has been a history of contraction and withdrawal; its central theme is the gradual surrender to other institutions of functions that once lay very much within the realm of family responsibility.[2]

In view of the fact that scholars from different disciplines have found the same trend, let us take a further look at the allegedly disappearing family functions.

Economic Function. In the early days of the United States, the American family was an economically producing unit. The first settlers built their own homes, made their own furniture, raised

---

[1] William F. Ogburn and Clark Tibbitts, "The Family and Its Functions," Report of the President's Research Committee on Social Trends in the United States, in *Recent Social Trends in the United States,* New York, McGraw-Hill Book Company, 1934, pp. 661–708.

[2] John Demos, *A Little Commonwealth: Family Life in Plymouth,* New York, Oxford University Press, 1970, p. 183.

The members of a colonial household all worked together to make their family a largely self-sufficient economic unit. Everyone had responsibilities, and the children learned by working alongside their parents. (Brown Brothers)

their own food, and made many of their own clothes. Mother, father, sons, and daughters—all cooperated in the necessary economic endeavors. The early colonial family, writes Demos, "was first of all a business agency of economic production and exchange. Each household was more or less self-sufficient; and its various members were inextricably united in the work of providing for their fundamental material wants. Work, indeed, was a wholly natural extension of family life and merged imperceptibly with all of its other activities."[3]

Gradually, however, with the rise of factories and power machinery, the manufacture of both hard and soft goods passed from the home. Most families—rural as well as urban—no longer raised their own food but bought it. Today there is a minimum of home baking, and what little there is, is likely to be of the instant-mix variety. Foods are seldom preserved for use in winter, since canned or frozen products can be purchased. Practically all clothing, furniture, bedding, and appliances are now bought rather than homemade, and even such activities as cooking, cleaning, and laundering have been greatly facilitated by the use of labor-saving machines.

These changes, as might be expected, have had a marked effect on American domestic life. The family no longer produces

---

[3] *Ibid.*

anything as an economic unit. Since the passage of compulsory-schooling legislation and child-labor laws, children have become economic liabilities instead of assets. It is little wonder that, instead of the large families of yesteryear (the typical family of 1790 had eight children), the one- or two-child family is now the norm.

Educational Function. In the early American family, education was generally considered to be a function of the home. Children were likely to follow their parents' footsteps, and hence the educational process was largely vocational in nature. In later periods some schooling was available, but the terms were short, and for the greater part of the year children were at home, working.

During the nineteenth century, however, it was obvious that the nation was becoming education-conscious. By the twentieth century, free public education had come to be one of the building blocks of American democracy; in fact, the long-term trend in American education can be summed up in one word: more. There are more schools, the number of students and teachers has increased, and the school year has been lengthened. Children start school at an earlier age and leave at a later one. Today, between the ages of 6 and 14, nearly all youngsters attend some kind of school. Most of them graduate from high school, and half or more will probably go on to college.

At all levels—from nursery schools and kindergartens to colleges and graduate schools—various educational services have also increased. Psychologists, psychiatrists, guidance experts, vocational counselors, doctors and nurses, social workers, personnel directors, as well as clubs, workshops, seminars, cooperatives, and in-service training programs—all are part of the modern educational concept. In any event, the process of formal education, both academic and vocational, has long since ceased to be a family function.

Religious Function. Religious training has also come to be largely devoid of any family connotation. In the Colonial period, the home served as a kind of adjunct to the church, with family prayers, Bible reading, teaching of the catechism, hymn singing, and grace before meals. Morgan writes that: "Every morning immediately upon rising, and every evening before retiring, a good Puritan father led his household in prayer, in scriptural reading, and in singing psalms. Whenever they sat down at the table together, he offered thanks to the Lord."[4]

---

[4] Edmund Morgan, *The Puritan Family*, New York, Harper & Row, 1966, p. 136.

Family devotionals, led by the father, were common occurrences in early America. In colonial society, religion and the family reinforced each other's authority. Parents were responsible for the spiritual training of their children and servants, and for their obedience to church doctrine. The church, in turn, taught that the authority of the parents, and particularly the father, was ordained by God. (Historical Pictures Service, Inc.)

Where no church was available, the family often held its own devotionals, led by the father. As time went on and practically all communities had built churches, attendance came to be a family activity. Religion served as an integrating force, one that complemented other institutional controls in the maintenance of a cohesive family system. Even in the late 1800's, Vermont and South Carolina had laws that made church attendance compulsory!

Today, however, the family is neither the dispenser of religious training nor the unit of church participation. During recent years, churchgoing has fallen off—at any rate, it is no longer a family function. In innumerable ways, religion continues as a vital force in the American way of life, but the day has passed when the home was the center of religious activity.

Recreational Function. For the early American family, based as it was on a farm economy, the home was often the center of recreational activities. For one thing, few outside diversions were available; for another, transportation was poor and notoriously time-consuming. Also, the average farm family worked from sunup to sundown and had little time left for recreational pursuits. What entertainment there was usually took place as a family-centered activity—such as visiting, partying, dancing, and participating in games of all kinds.

Mechanization brought many changes, however, one of which was an increase in leisure time. Transportation also improved, and in the twentieth century both recreation and entertainment came to be regarded as things that were bought rather than made. Commercial enterprises offered such fare as theaters, athletic events, bridge clubs, swimming pools, dance halls, racetracks, movies, golf courses, nightclubs, tennis courts, bowling

8

Television has taken over some of the educational functions of the family, and many of its recreational ones. (Peter Travers)

alleys, operas and ballets, symphony concerts, and many other forms of paid entertainment.

Today, catering to leisure time is a giant business, supplying forms of amusement broad enough to meet all demands. For the most part, entertainment is passive in nature; that is, people are spectators rather than participants. As amusement came to be "bought," it was almost inevitable that family participation would be minimized. At the present time, commercialized recreational activities are sufficiently diverse to satisfy the individual needs of all the family members. But as a family function, recreation has apparently played a diminishing role.

Other Functions. The family has lost a variety of other functions, chief of which are those pertaining to security. In the pioneer days it was commonplace for each family to possess firearms for protective purposes. Today, the various governmental services supply police protection. The frontier home was also the chief instrument for medical and health services. Today, this function has been taken over by doctors, nurses, and hospitals. Moreover, the American family of today is likely to be protected by life insurance and casualty and sickness insurance, as well as by a variety of social security programs run by the government. Care of the sick, the aged, and the infirm is no longer the sole responsibility of the family.

OUR PRESENT FAMILY SYSTEM:
WEAKNESSES AND STRENGTHS

The present-day family has not lost all of its functions, of course; some still remain. The family has retained the biological function of procreation. Responsibility for the support and socialization of the child has remained within the family, even though this function is now shared with other agencies. Care for the aged is a family function, though this, too, is often shared. It has also been shown that the extended family still furnishes both psychological and economic assistance for its members. And, of course, it is the family that provides the adult members of society with an approved method for the fulfillment of affectional and sexual needs.

As a matter of fact, not all sociologists would agree with Ogburn's position regarding the disappearing family functions. The dissenters feel that his conclusions were unduly pessimistic and that the colonial family was not the idyllic unit it was purported to be. They also contend that, while the modern family may have

9

lost some functions, it has acquired others—particularly in the realm of companionship and need-satisfaction.[5]

Sociological data being what they are, the argument is far from settled. Whether our family system is in fact disorganized, or whether it is simply being "reorganized," makes a fascinating and serious discussion question and is one that students should endeavor to answer for themselves, not only on the basis of readings, but in the light of daily observations and experience. The following points, which are certainly not exhaustive, will give some idea of the contradictory nature of the evidence.

Weaknesses. One of the disturbing trends in America is the steadily increasing rate of divorce. At present there are more than a million divorces granted annually, giving us not only the highest rate in our history but also the highest rate in the civilized world. Some idea of the magnitude of the current figure can be seen from the fact that in 1867 (the first year for which national figures are available) there were fewer than 10,000 divorces granted!

Interestingly enough, a not insignificant proportion of Americans get divorced more than once, and in a few cases individual divorce histories reach ridiculous levels. Vital statistics records reveal that Mr. Glynn Wolfe was married no less than 19 times! Millionaire Tommy Manville is renowned not only for his 13 marriages, but for the fact that marriage number seven lasted all of 34 minutes![6]

Divorce represents a *legal* severance of the marriage bond and is by no means the only index of marital disruption. In fact, in some areas desertions and informal separations exceed the number of divorces. While there are no nationwide statistics on the subject, the figure undoubtedly runs into the millions.

In view of the large number of divorces, desertions, and separations, some writers have stressed the potentially harmful effects on the children of such broken marriages. Indeed, for a nation that takes pride in its child care, it is difficult to explain the rising tide of juvenile delinquency that has engulfed the nation in recent years. At any rate, to the extent that juvenile delinquency can be attributed to family disorganization, the American family has cause for concern. It might also be mentioned that illegitimacy is much higher than it was 20 years ago.

---

[5] See, for example, F. Ivan Nye, "Emerging and Declining Family Roles," *Journal of Marriage and the Family*, May, 1974, pp. 238–245.

[6] Norris McWhirter and Ross McWhirter, *Guinness Book of World Records*, New York, Bantam Books, 1975, p. 444.

The subject of children, incidentally, raises another problem, for the United States birthrate has recently fallen to an all-time low.[7] Of equal significance is the fact that the expected or *ideal number of children* has also fallen, a phenomenon reported by both the Gallup Poll and the Census Bureau. Gallup reports, for example, that "in the latest survey, 19 percent of the public says the ideal number of children is four or more. Six years ago, the figure was 41 percent. The median response regarding the ideal number of children in a family is two, slightly below the 'replacement level' of 2.1."[8]

Reasons for the declining birthrate are too complex to be discussed here, but what Veevers has termed "The Motherhood Mystique"—the belief that to achieve true happiness women must bear children—is being questioned in some quarters.[9] Also, according to one popular survey the question "Is America a better or worse place to raise children than it was 10 or 15 years ago?" found 64 percent of the respondents answering "worse."[10]

Some observers have blamed our lax marriage and divorce laws for family disorganization, and it must be admitted that these laws and their implementation leave much to be desired. Americans are permitted to marry at extremely young ages. In several states, for example, it is permissible for youngsters to wed as soon as they have reached their fourteenth birthday! Moreover, our marriage laws are so constituted that, if a couple are underage in the state where they reside, there is nothing to prevent them from crossing state lines and marrying in a jurisdiction with a lower age requirement.

Our divorce laws have come in for so much criticism that it is scarcely necessary to repeat the various allegations. Suffice it to say that a good deal of legal mockery is involved; that most divorce cases are cut-and-dried affairs; and that in many states the legal grounds are little more than grab bags into which all manner of marital squabbles are conveniently poured. Again, if the couple desire to expedite matters and travel to one of the

---

[7] U.S. Department of Health, Education, and Welfare, *Monthly Vital Statistics Reports,* Vol. 23, No. 11, January 30, 1975, p. 1.

[8] Gallup Poll syndicated column of April 18, 1974.

[9] See J. E. Veevers, "The Child-free Alternative: Rejection of the Motherhood Mystique," in M. Stephenson (ed.), *Women in Canada,* Toronto, New Press, 1973; "Voluntary Childlessness: A Neglected Area of Family Study," *Family Coordinator,* April, 1973, pp. 199–205; and "The Life Style of Voluntarily Childless Couples," in Lyle Larson (ed.), *The Canadian Family in Comparative Perspective,* Toronto, Prentice-Hall, 1974.

[10] "A Report on the American Family," by the editors of *Better Homes and Gardens,* September, 1972, p. 13.

"quickie-divorce" states like Nevada, there is no legal impediment to stop them.

Finally, a number of writers have pointed with alarm to the increase in obscenity, pornography, and nonmarital sex behavior. American literature, it is contended, has been inundated with tasteless descriptions of both normal and abnormal sexual activities. In this regard, movies have forfeited their claim to being an art form and have lost most of their adult audience. And in the behavioral sphere, it is held that premarital, extramarital, and homosexual activities are so widespread that they are undermining the very structure of marriage.

All in all, a rather pessimistic picture—at least, so the critics contend. Little wonder, they say, that the marriage rate has dropped. Little wonder, they add, that when people were asked in the preceding poll, "Do you feel that family life in America is in trouble?" a resounding 71 percent answered yes.[11]

Strengths. Supporters of the American family system tend to discount the foregoing criticisms. They maintain that the declining birthrate and the rising rate of divorce are merely indications of a more compact, happiness-oriented type of family. They also contend that pornography and nonmarital sex activity, far from weakening the family, may actually strengthen it, by providing an oft-needed safety valve.

However and anon—safety valve or no safety valve—there is no doubt that ours is still a family-centered society. Although the marriage rate has declined somewhat, over 90 percent of both sexes continue to marry. Indeed, the writer would estimate that Americans spend more than $3 billion annually on weddings! Anniversaries are also cherished occasions, and marriages of especially long duration are given special recognition in the newspapers.

> The odds against such a thing happening are 8,750,000 to one, according to the U.S. Commerce Department. But Mr. and Mrs. Ward McDaniel, of Macon, Georgia, have done it. Today they are celebrating their 79th wedding anniversary!
>
> Mr. McDaniel, who is 100, and his wife—who will be 100 in May—live alone. Mrs. McDaniel does all her own housework; her husband takes a daily walk and does all the errands.
>
> Mrs. McDaniel's formula for 79 years of wedded life? "You have to fix your own life, and don't go meddling in other people's business."[12]

---

[11] *Ibid.*, p. 7.

[12] *Philadelphia Evening Bulletin*, January 22, 1969.

(Peter Menzel, Stock Boston)

The rate of home ownership in this country is high, and there can be little doubt that, in terms of material advantages and standard of living, the American family surpasses that of practically any other nation. There are well over 50 million families in our society, and over the years much of our economic strength has been due to the sustained consumer demand on the part of these families.

The concern shown for the American family is reflected in the number and quality of services available, and in this respect it is almost self-evident that ours are among the best-cared-for families in the world. Health centers, child guidance clinics, legal aid societies, marriage councils, family courts, social security and medicare programs, family-life education services, parent-teacher associations, church-sponsored aid societies, social welfare agencies, psychiatric services—all these attest to the continuing high regard for the American family.

On the personal level, also, American marriages apparently have a high happiness rating; at least, questionnaire surveys indicate that, when they are asked to rate their own marriages, most people report themselves as "very happy" or "happy." If they had it to do over again, furthermore, the majority of Americans would not only marry, but would marry the same person.

Special mention should be made here of the position of women in our society. Until fairly recently, wives were more or less subservient to their husbands. Denied the opportunity to work outside the home, forbidden by law to vote or hold public office, deprived of formal education, and with almost negligible legal rights, women were traditionally relegated to second-class citizenship. In some societies, this state of affairs still obtains. In our own culture, however—thanks largely to movements such as woman's rights and women's liberation—inequalities between the sexes have tended to disappear. Today's wife would be highly affronted if it were implied that she is not the equal of her husband.

Children, too, have been accorded legal and educational rights undreamed of a few generations ago. Free public education, child-labor laws, juvenile courts, social and athletic programs, and counseling services are now taken for granted. The most important change, however, has been in connection with *attitudes* toward children. Today there is a sincere conviction that the formative years are crucial in the development of character and personality—and that America's future does indeed lie in the hands of its children.

All things considered, many sociologists have come to the conclusion that, despite the existence of certain points of strain, the American family of today has not only adapted quite satisfactorily to changing economic and social conditions, but has attained a level of democratic operation and personal happiness superior to that of most other societies.

THE INDIVIDUAL-SOCIETAL PERSPECTIVE

One of the difficulties in assessing the weaknesses and strengths of any family system is the fact that the aims and desires of the individual do not always coincide with those of society at large. Certain laws and regulations may well serve the best interests of society while at the same time restricting the freedom of specific individuals or groups. Conversely, unrestricted freedom as regards mate selection, sex behavior, marriage, and divorce would prove to be a bonanza for at least some individuals, whereas for society as a whole it is quite possible that chaos would result.

To illustrate with an example or two, it might seem at first glance that, if a husband and wife are unhappy and want a divorce, they should be entitled to one. Why is it necessary for the law to spell out certain grounds? After all, if the couple are unhappy, whose concern is it but their own? Indeed, it might be that the best interests of this particular man and woman would be served by waiving all legal proceedings and permitting them to go their separate ways. A moment's reflection, however, will reveal some fallacies in a procedure of this kind.

For one thing, if it were recognized and accepted that couples could dissolve their marriages at will, the whole process of mate selection might lose much of its significance. What need to exercise caution and wisdom in selecting a marriage partner if one's mate could be discarded for any reason whatsoever? And if a second marriage proved to be less interesting than anticipated, why not try for number three?

Under such a system, who would provide for the support of children born of these unsuccessful marriages? How would the rules of inheritance operate? What would prevent couples from separating for the most trivial of reasons? Under such a system would it really be possible to uphold the monogamous form of marriage? Or would the matrimonial institution as we know it be in grave danger?

Suppose, on the other hand, that, in order to preserve the institution of marriage, laws were passed stipulating that no one would be permitted to marry unless he or she could pass rigid physical examinations and intelligence tests and that, once married, a couple would be required to stay married and produce a certain number of children in accordance with a quota set by the state. An institutionalized system of this kind would also invite social chaos. What would happen to the sexual and familial needs of all those who failed to pass the qualifying examinations? How could individual desires with respect to the number of children be reconciled with official quotas?

If the above examples seem too extreme, it should be pointed out that within the last two generations both Communist Russia and Nazi Germany actually experimented along these lines. Following the Revolution, Russia instituted a practice that was close to free sexual expression. Marriage was made a private affair, the only requirement being that of official registration. In the case of divorce, even the registration requirement was waived. Gorecki reports that "by 1930, marriages could be terminated by informal mutual agreement, unilateral declaration, or mere desertion without any announcement or agreement whatever." The same author goes on to report that:

> The results of the new sexual freedom were disastrous. The Soviet press reported in the mid-thirties that promiscuity flourished. Stories circulated about men who had as many as 20 wives, and about those who had been registered for marriage 15 times. Women paid dearly for the new freedom, as they were most often the exploited and deserted parties. An even greater penalty, however, was paid by the fatherless and homeless children, who, according to Russian estimates of the early twenties, numbered seven to nine million.[13]

Needless to say, the institution of marriage was soon in such a state that a new set of laws was introduced, placing both marriage and divorce under state regulation.

The Nazi experiment in the thirties and forties was aimed at glorifying the state at the expense of traditional family values. Germans were exhorted to marry for the glory of the Fatherland, and German women were expected to bear children, in or out of wedlock, according to the needs of the state rather than for "selfish" reasons. So much of Hitler's eugenic program was intertwined with religious intolerance and general fanaticism that any meaningful analysis is difficult to make, but the end result was no more successful than that of Russia's family experiment.

The lesson to be learned from these and similar ventures seems clear. When society pulls the institutional strings so tightly as to ignore the needs of the individual, the societal fabric weakens under its own tension. Conversely, when the institutional bonds are loosened to the point where individual desires are indulged at the expense of society at large, institutional breakdown is inevitable. Social institutions are effective as stabilizing forces when they reconcile the needs of society with those of the individual.

Although academic study of the family is largely the province of sociologists, other groups—marriage counselors, psychologists, anthropologists, home economists—have also contributed to our knowledge. Sociologists, however, are the only group who systematically study behavior and social organization from the individual-societal perspective. It is this perspective—within the broader framework of the family field—that is the subject of the present volume.

---

[13] Jan Gorecki, "Communist Family Pattern: Law as an Implement of Change," *University of Illinois Law Forum*, Vol. 1972, No. 1, p. 124.

2

Cross-Cultural Patterns

IT HAS OFTEN been said that one of the most effective aids to an
understanding of one's own society is the study of other societies. This is certainly true in the area of the family, since marital and sexual practices have such a wide range of configurations.
Some societies permit premarital coitus, while others impose severe restrictions. In our own society it is illegal for a person to
have more than one spouse (at a time), yet in a number of cultures plural spouses are quite acceptable. Similarly, child-rearing
patterns, marital interaction, kinship structure, and other elements of family life show substantial variation from one society
to the next.

Along with these cultural variations it is important to recognize the underlying thread of cultural uniformity. For instance,
there are any number of societal variations relating to betrothal
ceremonies, marriage customs, wedding celebrations, and the
like. Underlying all these various rituals is a common purpose,
namely, to impress upon young people the importance of the
institution of marriage. Also, while premarital and extramarital
taboos may vary from one society to the next, _all societies regulate
sex in some manner_ and the most effective regulatory institution,
in this respect, is the family.

THE FORMS OF MARRIAGE

When sexual relationships between men and women are viewed
along a continuum—from free sex to no sex—it is possible to formulate six different types of "interaction."

Promiscuity—no marriage; unrestricted sexual relations
Group marriage—marriage of several women to several
men

Polygamy $\begin{cases} \text{Polyandry—marriage of one woman to several men} \\ \text{Polygyny—marriage of one man to several women} \end{cases}$

Monogamy—marriage of one man to one woman
Celibacy—no sexual relations; no marriage

For the sake of convenience, these six combinations are referred to as the "forms of marriage." Oddly enough, however, only two of them—polygyny and monogamy—have been known to exist with any great frequency. There are specific reasons for the rarity of the others, and it might be well to see whether the ratio of cultural variations to cultural uniformities suggests any principles of marital organization.

Promiscuity. Although the term is often applied to casual or indiscriminate premarital sex affairs, promiscuity literally refers to unbridled sexual interaction, or "sex without rules." In a promiscuous society, every male would be eligible to mate with every female, with blood ties no barrier. Although such a situation is found among most animal species, it simply does not exist at the human level, all cultures having strong rules governing sexual pairings. Most of these rules are based on age and blood relationships, although some preliterate groups have elaborate intra-clan prohibitions.

Actually, promiscuity is incompatible with any known type of human social organization. If people were allowed unlimited sexual freedom, problems involving jealousy and wrangling might be insurmountable. Females would be subject to sexual exploitation. With systematized promiscuity, moreover, it would be hard to maintain an effective child-rearing program. Lacking both family life and a protective environment, children would probably have to fend for themselves at an early age.

Under a system of promiscuity, it is easy to visualize group bedlam; indeed, survival itself would become a problem. The human species can withstand an almost infinite amount of hostility and fighting—from interfamily feuds and tribal clashes to modern warfare—but to insure survival of the species there must be accommodation between the sexes. The accommodative relationship must be enduring enough to provide protection, care, and reasonable security for the offspring. Although the forms of marriage may vary, evidence from small preliterate groups, as well as from our own complex society, indicates that the institution of marriage and the establishment of an integrated family system are of prime importance.

The recently discovered Tasaday tribe is an example of a preliterate monogamous culture with a strong family system. (John Launois, Black Star)

Group Marriage. Earlier anthropologists—Frazer, Morgan, Westermarck, Briffault, and others—wrote extensively about the subject, but it seems unlikely that group marriage has ever existed in any society as the dominant type of marital union. It would almost be more realistic to think of this form as a theoretical construct than as an institutionalized form of matrimony. Even in the rare instances where group marriage has been reported—as among the Toda of India and the Kaingang of Brazil—it has appeared as an atypical pattern or as an expediency stemming from local conditions. For example, the Toda at one time practiced female infanticide, which made for an excess of males. As a result, polyandry (plural husbands) came to be an accepted form of marriage. When the British discouraged infanticide, the proportion of females increased, and occasionally a group of brothers would add plural wives to the one they already shared. Thus, group marriage and polyandry tend to go together.

The practice of wife exchange is reported to have existed among the Comanche Indians, and wife lending is still practiced by certain Eskimo tribes. However, this should not be thought of in the same light as group marriage, for in all instances a specific husband-wife pair constitutes the socially recognized and enduring relationship. Among the Eskimos, wife lending apparently provides a culturally accepted means of sexual gratification for husbands making long treks to distant camps, although it is little wonder that visitors are shocked when they are offered this example of Eskimo generosity.

A moment's reflection will make it clear why, in practice, group marriage is virtually nonexistent. In the first place, it has no advantages over the other marital forms. Problems of jealousy on the part of both sexes would be intensified. Indeed, it is difficult to see how group marriage could ever be institutionalized on any significant scale. Would the incest taboo be enforceable in group families with dozens of children of unknown paternity? How would inheritance, property rights, and lineage be handled?

Although there is a distinct difference between promiscuity and group marriage, in neither case are the advantages great enough to warrant societal adoption, especially since more practicable forms of marriage are always available.

Polyandry. There is no question that polyandry has existed as an institutionalized form of marriage. It is, however, exceedingly rare. There are only a handful of groups—the Toda, Marquesans, Tibetans, Jats, and a few others—in which polyandry has been the prevailing form. The present writer would estimate that, of all the world's societies, a fraction of 1 percent practice polyandry. Indeed, anthropologists are inclined to think of both group marriage and polyandry as "ethnological curiosities." Stephens makes the following observations about polyandry:

> One striking characteristic of polyandrous societies is their general sexual freedom. The Marquesans are probably the most extreme case of sexual freedom on anthropological record. They allowed children and adolescents free access to sex, allowed adults various sorts of extramarital sex liaisons, . . . and sometimes even performed sexual intercourse in public (the only report of this, to my knowledge). . . .
>
> One gets the impression that in these polyandrous societies there is a laissez-faire attitude toward sex. Sex is "cheap" and easy to find. I would guess that there is some sort of causal nexus between co-husbanding, a mild intensity of sexual jealousy, and great sexual freedom. But what the exact connection is, I do not know.[1]

Anthropological reports indicate that polyandry is sometimes associated with hard living conditions. The previously

---

[1] William N. Stephens, *The Family in Cross-Cultural Perspective,* New York, Holt, Rinehart and Winston, Inc., 1963, p. 46.

mentioned Toda, for instance, found it expedient to resort to female infanticide as a method of limiting the population. Polyandry thus served the dual purpose of providing a wife for the excess males and of raising the family subsistence level by utilizing several breadwinners instead of only one.

Aside from the economic factor, it is hard to discern any benefits inherent in polyandry as a form of marriage. Determining paternity becomes a genuine problem, and feelings of jealousy must be kept under constant control. As a matter of fact, in polyandrous matings the plural husbands are often brothers, thus minimizing potential jealousy and friction. In groups where there is no shortage of females, of course, widespread polyandry would leave many women without husbands. Since nearly all societies show a shortage of males rather than females, polyandry would appear to be detrimental to the best interests of both the individual and the larger group.

Polygyny. In a numerical sense, it is true that most societies permit polygyny. At the same time, most *marriages* are monogamous, even in societies that permit plural wives. Obviously, since the number of females in a given population is generally only slightly greater than the number of males, for every man who had two wives another would be consigned to bachelorhood. Practically speaking, moreover, polygyny is an expensive proposition. Whether or not it is culturally acceptable, most men cannot afford to support more than one woman; as a matter of fact, in many groups plural wives serve as visible symbols of prestige for the husband.

Although in some polygynous systems the husbands are more or less free to choose additional wives, many societies restrict the choice to the first wife's sisters, a custom known as the *sororate*. In other cultures, polygyny is actually required, in the sense that a man is obliged to marry the widow of his deceased brother, a practice called the *levirate*. Both the sororate and the levirate are fairly widespread among polygynous societies.

It can be argued, with logic, that the polygynous form of marriage has certain advantages. From a societal view, polygyny seems to be the most satisfactory method of caring for an excess of women, or, to state it differently, of compensating for a shortage of men. Also, from the standpoint of eugenics, a polygynous system would permit superior males to contribute to a larger share of the population.

On the other hand, there are numerous disadvantages inherent in polygyny. While an excess of single females can be reduced under such a system, in most societies there is no serious shortage of men, especially at the marrying age. Polygyny, therefore, tends

21

Polygyny is most likely to be found in preliterate societies in which women outnumber men. Here a chief of the Ukuanjama tribe poses with some of his 18 wives and 38 children. (Alice Mertens from *South West Africa,* Taplinger Publishing Co. by permission)

to permit economically or politically powerful males to acquire plural wives at the expense of their less fortunate fellows. Furthermore, since it takes time for a man to acquire wealth and power, it is likely to be the older men who have plural wives. In consequence, a polygynous system often carries with it the seeds of intergenerational conflict.

Another drawback to polygyny is the fact that the plural wives operate under something of a handicap. Their sex lives, for instance, are necessarily circumscribed. And while bickering and jealousy among such wives are by no means inevitable, they reportedly occur with some frequency in many polygynous systems. After an extensive analysis of the subject, Stephens draws the following conclusions:

> Some co-wives are jealous, and others apparently aren't. There appear to be great differences between societies as well as between individual co-wives within the same society. In most known cases, at least some co-wives suffer rather intensely from jealousy, and a good many of the polygynous families are strife-torn.[2]

---

[2] *Ibid.,* pp. 62–63.

There are other disadvantages to polygyny, including housing problems, child-rearing issues, conflicts over property, and—not least—an all-around social unwieldiness. What is good for one society may not be good for another, however, and in many pre-literate cultures the polygynous form of marriage has worked rather well.

Monogamy. The only form of marriage accepted by *all* societies is monogamy. Even where other forms are permitted, monogamy remains the most common marital practice. Although each society thinks its own particular form of marriage is the most desirable, it is likely that, in an absolute sense, monogamy has more to recommend it than any other form. Under a monogamous system: (1) group members at the normal marrying age have maximal opportunity to find a mate; (2) relatively few members are "left out" of marriage, as compared with the matrimonial residue inherent in polygynous and polyandrous forms; (3) an effective method of sexual gratification is provided for both men *and* women; (4) intra-sex jealousies and quarrels, often a problem in polygamous forms of marriage, are held to a minimum; (5) socio-legal factors involved in inheritance, property rights, and lineage are relatively easy to handle; (6) emotional needs of the spouses—needs associated with primary-group response—are more effectively fulfilled than under any other marital form; and (7) child-rearing practices can be effectively aimed at establishing close emotional ties between parents and children.

While certain of these propositions can be debated, they seem to be borne out by the fact that, in practice, the overwhelming majority of the earth's inhabitants do follow the monogamous form of marriage.

THE EVOLUTION OF MARRIAGE

With the popularization of Darwin's theory of evolution and the attempted application of this theory to social institutions by writers like Herbert Spencer, it was almost inevitable that family scholars would attempt to formulate evolutionary concepts. While the details varied considerably, earlier anthropologists like Bachofen, McLennan, and Morgan conceived of marriage as having "progressed" in some logical fashion. Lewis Henry Morgan, for example, one of the most articulate of the early writers, set forth a universal sequence of marital forms. Since monogamy was well established in civilized society, Morgan reasoned that the original form must have been promiscuity; that is, the opposite of exclusive mating (monogamy) must be indiscriminate mating (promiscuity). After promiscuity came polygamy, which involved more lasting ties between the sexes. Since maternity could always be established, in contrast to paternity, Morgan held that descent was originally reckoned through the mother (*matrilineal*), rather than through the father (*patrilineal*). The final development was monogamy, with descent being figured through both mother's and father's side (*bilateral descent*).[3]

For all its ingenious particulars, Morgan's evolutionary theory has only limited validity. It is true that most animal species are promiscuous, and that Western civilizations practice monogamy. It might further be true that, if all societies were to become "civilized," polygamy would tend to vanish. But with regard to marital forms passing through chronological or linear stages, anthropological reports indicate that monogamy is found among some very backward peoples as well as in civilized societies. In fact, Westermarck, another early authority, was so impressed with the absence of promiscuity and the presence of monogamy among widely scattered primitive groups that he maintained that monogamy, rather than promiscuity, was the original marital form.[4] But this theory, too, is of questionable validity. When the cross-cultural evidence is examined, the case for monogamy is no stronger than for promiscuity.

The truth of the matter seems to be that monogamy and polygamy have existed side by side, the respective causal factors having long since been lost in antiquity. Perhaps, rather than one original form of marriage, there were several, with roughly simultaneous origins. In any case, the question is seldom raised by present-day anthropologists; barring the advent of new methodological instruments, the search for marital origins does not seem particularly rewarding.

CONSANGUINE VERSUS CONJUGAL EMPHASIS

When they visualize marriage, most college students think of a sequence that involves dating, falling in love, a fairly elaborate wedding followed by a reception, a honeymoon, and a fresh start in the new home. This last item has come to signify the break

---

[3] Lewis Henry Morgan, *Ancient Society,* New York, Henry Holt and Company, 1877.
[4] Edward A. Westermarck, *The History of Human Marriage,* New York, The Macmillan Company, 1902.

with parents, for there is a reluctance to marry, in our society, unless the couple can "go it on their own." Families formed in this manner—on the basis of individual mate selection and a "go-it-alone" philosophy—are referred to as *conjugal families*. Some sociologists use the term *immediate* or *nuclear family* in characterizing the husband-wife-children unit. In any case, the strongly developed conjugal system in our society has led most of us to think of "marriage" and the "family" as functionally similar, if not synonymous.

Although the above type of family seems natural to Americans, many primitive societies use a different system of familial organization—a *consanguine* system, in which "marriage" and the "family" are quite distinct from one another. In a consanguine family the stress is on blood relatives. When a couple marry, their allegiance is to their original families; in fact, they may live with or near the husband's or wife's family, depending upon such factors as whether descent is patrilineal or matrilineal. Their children are customarily integrated into the larger kinship group, or the *extended family*, as it is sometimes called.

If we think of the two systems as being extremes, or polar types, a contrasting pattern emerges: the conjugal family system emphasizes individual mate selection, romantic love, sex attraction, independent residence, strong husband–wife ties, and bilateral descent; in the consanguine family system the stress is on mate selection by the respective families rather than by the individuals concerned, *matrilocal* or *patrilocal* residence, unilateral descent, and strong blood ties.

In a structural sense the conjugal family is fragile, since divorce, desertion, illness, or death of a spouse seriously disrupts the household, with a likelihood that the children will be adversely affected. Families based on consanguine relationships, in contrast, can withstand a variety of such stresses and strains. Death and divorce have relatively little effect on a large kinship group. The consanguineal family is better equipped, economically and psychologically, to take care of aged members, a problem that has never been satisfactorily solved in our own society. It is probably true, also, that family adjustment and cohesion are easier under a consanguine system, disputes between siblings apparently being fewer in number than those between spouses.

On the other hand, a consanguine type of family tends to give relatively little heed to the sexual and romantic inclinations of its younger members, a policy which must give rise to numerous frustrations. Consanguine families also tend to grow in size. While it cannot be demonstrated that large families satisfy the

25

CROSS-CULTURAL PATTERNS

LIBRARY
OF
MOUNT ST. MARY'S
COLLEGE
EMMITSBURG, MARYLAND

individual's emotional needs less effectively than small families, one wonders exactly what kind of "family life" there is when the numbers reach 30, 40, 50, or more.

Finally, there is the question of property rights and inheritance. Because the conjugal family is of relatively short duration, there is limited time in which to acquire property and material wealth. Whatever is acquired, moreover, is normally divided among the children every generation. The consanguine family, on the other hand, is well equipped to acquire material wealth and to "keep it in the family"; property and other holdings tend to become cumulative. In many countries consanguineal accumulation of wealth and power has been associated with privilege and titles and social inequalities.

Despite the apparent stresses and strains involved, the conjugal family system seems to be the one most compatible with modern society. If the trend toward urbanism, industrialism, and mobility spreads to other parts of the world, it is just possible that the consanguine type of family organization will tend to disappear—along with polygamy.

THE INCEST TABOO

Whether families are organized on a conjugal or a consanguine basis, all societies maintain strict prohibitions against sex relations and marriage between close blood relatives. This proscription, known as the *incest taboo,* is believed to be the most universal of all mores, even though sex relations between close blood relatives have been permitted or authorized in certain societies. It has been noted, for instance, that among the Azande, a large African tribe, the highest chiefs are required to wed their own daughters. Ethnographic reports have also indicated that at one time brother-sister marriages were permitted or even required in certain royal families, such as the Hawaiian nobility, the Incas of Peru, and the Ptolemies of ancient Egypt. Technically, therefore, incest would have to be defined as sex relations or marriage between persons who are *considered* to be too closely related. It should be mentioned, however, that despite the wide range of marital and sexual customs among the world's peoples, no reports of authorized mother-son marriages have ever been confirmed.

In addition to its universality, the incest taboo is one of the most rigidly enforced of all human behavioral proscriptions. Over the face of the earth, societies have utilized all available controls—formal and informal, sacred and secular—to insure that sex and blood do not mix. These controls have become so effective that most people are repelled by the very thought of an incestuous relationship; indeed, it is difficult for us to visualize a functioning society in which sanctioned incest could coexist with any known type of family organization. In view of the pervasive importance of the incest taboo, it is interesting to speculate on how or why the interdiction arose.

Some of the earlier scholars, such as Hobhouse and Lowie, seemed to feel that there was an innate or instinctive aversion to sexual relations with blood relatives. However, there is no evidence for this belief. No such taboo exists among the other primates. At the human level, siblings reared apart have met as strangers, fallen in love, and married. As a matter of fact, not only does there seem to be no innate sexual aversion to blood relatives, but Freudian psychology is based on the assumption that there is an innate *sexual desire* for the parent of the opposite sex. This assumption, in turn, has been neither verified nor refuted on an empirical basis.

Another proposed explanation for the origin of the incest taboo hypothesizes that close association in the same household tends to discourage sexual attraction. This is a tempting theory, for it is known that the male animals of some species show an increase in their copulatory activity when new females are introduced into the experimental situation. At the human level, also, it would seem that "familiarity breeds indifference" and that adults are readily attracted to persons other than their own spouses. On the other hand, most married couples do maintain a satisfactory sexual relationship over the years. Moreover, if household familiarity does foster sexual indifference or repugnance, it is difficult to explain the cases of incest that are known to occur. Incest occurs, at least sporadically, in all societies; as a matter of fact, it probably takes place more often than most people realize. In our own culture, for instance, it is more-or-less customary to keep such cases out of the newspapers.

Incidentally, in both of the foregoing attempts to account for the origin of the incest taboo—the "innate aversion" and the "close association" theories—it is hard to explain why such powerful regulations would be required for a supposedly self-enforcing restriction!

Still another proposed explanation for the existence of the incest regulation pertains to the necessity of maintaining generational roles and status within the family network. The son of a father-daughter union, for example, would be a half-brother of both his mother and his uncle, the son of his own sister, and the son as well as the grandson of his father! The resultant problems involved in identity, role relationships, and lines of authority are hard to imagine.

One difficulty with this theory is the tendency to project our own role system into the (hypothetical) incestuous family. In the latter, the child of a father-daughter union would have a generational role different from any we are accustomed to. Even the "standard" family nomenclature would be radically different from our own.

A final theory of the incest taboo relates to the so-called harm of inbreeding. It was Westermarck, one of the earlier anthropologists, who championed this viewpoint, but until recently the theory was not taken too seriously. There was no genetic proof that inbreeding was biologically harmful, and in any case primitive people could hardly be expected to understand the mechanism of heredity.

In recent years, however, evidence from a variety of sources indicates that inbreeding may indeed have deleterious effects on the offspring. Animal studies reveal that genetic variability is curtailed, longevity is reduced, and resistance to disease is lowered. Although they are more difficult to come by, studies of human inbreeding tend to be corroborative. Children of incestuous parents, for example, have been found to have a much higher incidence of physical and mental defects than other children.[5]

If the inbreeding theory is correct, those groups that did not impose an incest taboo would have been at a deadly disadvantage. From an evolutionary view, they could hardly have survived. In the course of time, therefore, it was only logical to find the taboo emerging as the cornerstone of the human family system.

Whether the inbreeding theory will be refuted, modified, or substantiated, only time will tell. Certain it is, however, that up to now the origin of the incest taboo has been one of mankind's most fascinating mysteries.

COURTSHIP

Most societies consider the affectional relationship between spouses to be a desirable aspect of marriage. It is true that throughout most of the world romantic love is not accorded so much importance as it is in our own society. It is also true that in

---

[5] For a listing of sources and a pointed discussion of the matter, see Bernard I. Murstein, *Love, Sex, and Marriage Through the Ages,* New York, Springer Publishing Company, 1974, pp. 19–30.

some groups it is the parents who arrange the marriages. But even in these societies the attempt is usually made to match partners who are believed to be mutually congenial.

The Bride-Price. Turning first to those groups where matings are greatly influenced by the parents or families concerned, it should be pointed out that preliterate societies do not generally associate marriage with religion. On the contrary, they tend to look upon matrimony not only as secular in nature, but as involving a *contract* between the two families in question. Like all contracts, the marriage pact involves reciprocity, and it is important to keep this in mind, otherwise the custom of wife-purchase might be misunderstood, since nothing like it exists in our own culture.

Although an occasional society has been reported in which wives can literally be purchased, in most preliterate groups the payment to the girl's family is designed to compensate them for the loss of her services. In the cattle-culture areas of Africa, for example, women are exceedingly important in the tribal economy, since they normally are the ones who tend the cattle. When a daughter marries, therefore, her father is deprived of the services of a valuable herd-tender, and to reimburse him for this loss the husband must hand over a certain number of cattle. This is considered an equitable arrangement inasmuch as the husband procures additional help for his own herds.

The bride-price also serves another function: it tends to assure the wife of favorable treatment throughout her marriage. If the husband should mistreat her, she would be entitled to a divorce—in which case the cattle would not be returned. From the woman's personal position, then, the bride-price serves as a status-gaining transaction: the greater the number of cattle that are offered, the higher her own social prestige becomes. On her part, she is expected to be a good wife and to bear children. In the long run, the husband may actually gain cattle by astute negotiations over his own daughters. (If no children are forthcoming, the wife is assumed to be sterile, whereupon the husband can divorce her and get his cattle back.) Throughout the entire marital procedure the emphasis is on the economic side; while affection and emotional attachments are by no means ignored, they are played down in favor of more practical considerations.

Marriage by Capture. Before turning to conjugal courtship patterns, a word is in order regarding marriage by capture. Some anthropologists of the evolutionary school put great stock in this alleged custom, a few believing it to be the real origin of marriage. Some writers even maintained that our own custom of carrying the wife over the threshold had its origin in the days when wife stealing was practiced. It appears now, however, that earlier reports were greatly exaggerated. So far as is known, no society currently authorizes capture or abduction as a basis for marriage; indeed, it is hard to believe such practices were ever very widespread. It is true, historically, that during tribal warfare women were often taken as part of the spoils of war, but such women, at most, were treated as concubines, not as wives. It is reported, also, that in some primitive groups the man is expected to "abduct" the woman of his choice, with her relatives putting up a "defense" against the foray. In reality, however, all such struggles appear to be mock or sham affairs aimed at dramatizing the loss of the bride to her family. The whole idea of marriage by force involves too many inherent disadvantages—for all parties concerned—to warrant further attention.

Conjugal Courtship. When we turn to mate-selection practices that emphasize the role of the individuals, rather than the role of the respective families, we are on more familiar ground. In all such practices, for example, it is rather common for young people to fall in love, even though the concept of romantic love is not so highly idealized in other cultures as it is in our own.

There is no need to go into details of specific behavior during courtship. Lovemaking is pretty much the same the world over, with the male generally taking the initiative. There are a few societies where romantic activity is apparently less seclusive than it is in our own culture, and in a few groups the practice of kissing is reportedly unknown. But, in general, caressing, kissing, fondling, love talk, and the desire for privacy—maneuvers that might be classified under the heading of "necking and petting" or "making out"—are more nearly the rule than the exception.

In our own society a basic factor in attracting members of the opposite sex is physical appearance, and in other societies this is also true. Our standards of beauty, though, are not necessarily those esteemed in other parts of the world. Anthropologists report that there are few, if any, universal standards of physical attractiveness. Some groups put a premium on thinness; others admire corpulence. Certain groups reportedly stress different traits such as eye color, skin color, or hair texture. In most societies, standards of attractiveness are more likely to be applied to the female than to the male, the latter being judged on such qualities as courage and prowess, rather than on physical appearance.

PREMARITAL SEX STANDARDS

There is no gainsaying the fact, as revealed by numerous cross-cultural surveys, that societies differ sharply in their views on premarital sex. Some groups place an extremely high premium on premarital chastity, while others take premarital intercourse for granted. Although there is no one-to-one relation between cultural level and attitude toward virginity, sanctioned premarital intercourse is more prevalent among primitive groups than among civilized societies. Some groups at the bottom of the cultural ladder, however, do emphasize premarital chastity, especially for the female.

It is well known by now that our own society's views on premarital sex behavior are not shared by a number of other cultures. The account that is most often referred to, in this respect, is Malinowski's description of the Trobriand Islanders.[6]

The Trobriands are a group of islands off the southeast coast of New Guinea. The islanders themselves are a branch of the Oceanic Negroes and are primarily fishermen and farmers. They are well advanced in the arts and crafts, such as woodcarving and basket making, and have a fairly complex social organization. While polygyny is permitted, monogamy is the general practice. The Trobriand Islanders look upon sex as an expression of the personality. They believe it is natural, therefore, to let children begin their sexual activities at an early age. Adults make no attempt to prohibit coitus among the youngsters, although incest taboos are strictly enforced. It is also taboo for adults to have sexual relations with the youth. Children come to take sex for granted, and it is expected that every individual will have a number of affairs prior to marriage.

Eventually, after puberty, each person tends to form a more permanent relationship with someone of the opposite sex, and this soon becomes known in the community. If the association continues, the couple will be expected to marry. Surprisingly, although premarital coitus is quite acceptable, premarital pregnancy is condemned. More surprising still is the fact that the premarital pregnancy rate is quite low, even though contraceptive devices are not used. Malinowski could not explain this phenomenon, although it is now known that among human females *menarche* (the onset of first menstruation) does not necessarily denote the beginning of sustained ovulation.

Inasmuch as sexual behavior of the kind reported for the Trobriand Islanders is foreign to the views of most readers, the

---

[6] References for the Trobrianders and other preliterate groups can be found at the end of the chapter.

question should be raised whether such freedom is advantageous (setting ethical and religious considerations aside for the moment). From the individual viewpoint, a standard permitting premarital intercourse has much to recommend it, especially as far as young people are concerned, since they would then be permitted a legitimate sexual outlet without having to wait for the formalities of marriage. Moreover, by removing the stigma and social culpability attached to premarital intercourse, young people would be free from the guilt feelings and remorse that so often accompany premarital sexual explorations in a society like our own.

For the girl, of course, the possibility of premarital pregnancy is always present and would have to be used as an argument in the other direction—that is, toward upholding the ideal of premarital chastity. With advances in birth control techniques, however, this argument is probably diminishing in importance.

In keeping with the philosophy of this book, any absolute appraisal of premarital standards would have to meet the societal test: assuming that single people would benefit, does the sanctioning of sex before marriage actually benefit society as a whole? In one sense, this may be answered in the affirmative; that is, it can be argued that any activity which promotes the physical and emotional well-being of one segment of the population without infringing on the rights of other segments must be considered advantageous for society as a whole.

In another sense, the premarital sex question may be answered in the negative. If the only sexual activity permitted is *marital* coitus, a basic reason for marrying becomes that of achieving sexual gratification. With *premarital* relations condoned, one of the motivating factors for marriage is thus removed. Since it is to the obvious advantage of society to have the bulk of its members married, premarital sexual latitude might operate against the overall societal interest. In societies where the motivation for marriage is reinforced by economic, cultural, or other considerations, premarital sex privileges might not seriously affect the marriage rate, but in other societies the reverse might be true.

Comparative evaluations of premarital sex patterns throughout the world are hazardous inasmuch as one can never be certain that the units of comparison are reasonably similar. In many preliterate societies, for instance, premarital sex is no great problem since, among other things, the age at marriage is quite low, both sexes marrying shortly after puberty. Then, too, in most civilized societies the overall sex codes are inseparable from the church and the law, both of which, as measures of social control, are often unknown in primitive groups.

In answer to our original question, then, as to whether or not premarital sexual permissiveness benefits society as a whole, there can be no all-inclusive answer. A pattern that tends to stabilize one society might have a disruptive effect on another. While there are some mores pertaining to sexual and marital behavior that have near-universal value, premarital sex regulations probably cannot be included among them.

EXTRAMARITAL SEX RELATIONS

As might be expected, most societies disapprove of adultery. Where it is permitted—as will be explained below—a special situation is usually involved. This general disapproval is understandable, of course, since adultery strikes at the very heart of marriage. If marital fidelity were permitted to be taken lightly, competition over sex partners, jealousies and clashes between spouses, neglect of children, upsetting of homemaking routines—any or all of these disruptive possibilities might be expected to occur; in fact, they often do occur whenever individual cases of adultery are discovered.* As a result of the threat that adultery poses, most societies take measures to insure that marital fidelity is rewarded and that marital infractions are punished.

In some societies, nevertheless, a certain amount of extramarital latitude is permitted. Wife lending among the Eskimos has already been mentioned. Other groups sanction adulterous relationships during ceremonial orgies and fertility dances. These revelries are usually seasonal events, held in connection with tribal rites, such as imploring the gods to look with favor on new crop plantings. Another pertinent custom is the hymen-breaking ritual that occurs among certain primitive groups. Vividly described by the earlier anthropological writers, these rituals often involve defloration and/or sexual intercourse with the bride by someone other than the husband—a tribal chieftain, for instance. This practice represents another example, technically, of sanctioned adultery.

Adultery occurs at least sporadically in all cultures for which reports are available, although how much or how often it occurs is, for obvious reasons, difficult to estimate. In most societies,

---

* It is interesting, Stephens writes, that in the few societies which permit adultery, "the jealousy problem still exists; some people are still hurt when their spouses engage in perfectly proper and virtuous adultery." (Stephens, op. cit., p. 252).

extramarital indulgence on the part of the wife is considered more reprehensible than it is on the part of the husband. In most societies, also, because of this double standard, the incidence of adultery is higher for husbands than for wives.

On a worldwide basis, it seems likely that extramarital intercourse is increasing. This may be a reflection of a more permissive attitude toward behavior in general and toward sex in particular, "swinging" in our own society being a good case in point. The social ramifications of this permissiveness, however, provide an interesting topic of debate.

Some observers believe that a tolerant and flexible attitude toward adultery is a good thing. They contend that so long as the individuals involved remain discreet in their outside affairs, so long as their own marriages are not disrupted—in short, so long as the "scandal" aspects are suppressed—then adultery, at worst, harms no one and in individual cases may actually serve to stabilize the marital relationship.

On the other hand, it can be argued that people tend to live up to and a little beyond the "rules." For example, in a 25-mile-an-hour speed zone drivers tend to go 30 and 35 miles an hour, so that in a sense the law is only partially deterrent. But when the speed limit is raised to 35 miles an hour, it is apparent that drivers start edging up to the 40- and 45-mile-an-hour rates. This analogy may or may not apply to sexual mores, but in the case of extramarital activities one could argue that tolerance leads to increase. It is quite possible that in most societies an overtolerance of sexual relations occurring outside the marital bond would have deleterious effects on the institution of marriage, especially from a long-term perspective.

NONMARITAL SEX BEHAVIOR

The term "extramarital" refers to the relations of a married person with individuals other than his or her spouse; the term "premarital" signifies behavior prior to marriage. Sexual or erotic activities are possible, however, which are not *necessarily* either premarital or extramarital. Such activities can conveniently be classified as "nonmarital" and would include masturbation, prostitution, rape, homosexuality, sadism, masochism, and so on. While some of these phenomena (such as sadism, masochism, and necrophilia) make for interesting reading, they are relatively rare occurrences in all societies and will not be discussed in the present volume. Forcible rape is also a comparatively infrequent occurrence in preliterate cultures and will not be treated here.* Masturbation, prostitution, and homosexuality, on the other hand, involve substantial numbers of people and occur often enough to have some actual or potential effect on marriage.

Masturbation. Whereas in past periods masturbation has been a somewhat condemned form of sex activity in our society, during recent times a more liberal attitude has become apparent. Formerly associated with a variety of afflictions, from bad complexion to mental illness, masturbation is now thought by doctors to constitute a physiologically harmless sexual action. Numerous studies indicate that in our culture masturbation is practiced widely among males, and to a lesser extent among females.

It is somewhat surprising to learn that in most preliterate societies masturbation is a socially disapproved form of sex activity, at least for adults. As a result of their cross-cultural survey, Beach and Ford conclude that "for most peoples masturbation represents an inferior form of sexual activity in which adults should never participate. . . . Even among some of the peoples whose sex mores are very free, masturbation on the part of mature persons is considered undesirable."[7]

The authors go on to point out that most groups have a more permissive attitude toward masturbation on the part of children. With regard to the actual incidence of the activity among adults, Beach and Ford remark that "the cross-cultural evidence suggests that adults in other societies rarely engage in auto-genital stimulation. But . . . informants are likely to underestimate the frequency or to deny the occurrence of behavior that is socially condemned."[8]

The comparative infrequency of masturbation among primitive peoples may be due to the fact of early marriage or because other sexual outlets—especially premarital coitus—are permitted. Whatever the reasons, the low (reported) incidence precludes any cross-cultural analysis of the relationship between masturbation and the overall marriage pattern. The effects of premarital and extramarital intercourse on marriage have been widely discussed—both pro and con—so that perhaps the lack of

---

* In American society, of course, rape is a serious problem. The topic will be covered in Chapter 14.

[7] Frank Beach and Clellan Ford, *Patterns of Sexual Behavior,* New York, Harper & Brothers, 1951, pp. 156–157.
[8] *Ibid.*

anthropological discussion about masturbation is indicative of its unimportance.

Prostitution. Without going into the history of prostitution, it can be stated that the practice of permitting coitus in exchange for monetary considerations is quite old. Houses of prostitution, or brothels, have been permitted by a variety of governments. At the same time, insofar as public opinion is concerned, prostitution has often been a highly condemned type of sex activity. Public criticism was intensified in the sixteenth century, after a serious outbreak of syphilis, and down to the present day, prostitution has often been associated with the prevalence of venereal disease rather than with any infringement of, or danger to, established marital goals.

On a cross-cultural basis, prostitution seems to be rare among primitive peoples. In Kluckhohn's world sample of 193 cultures, "societally tolerated prostitution" was found to exist in only 10 groups.[9] In numerous societies the boy presents the girl with food or minor gifts when he solicits sexual favors, but this is no more (or less) definable as prostitution than is our own courtship pattern in which a certain amount of money is spent on an evening's date.

Whereas prostitution occurs infrequently among preliterate groups, the selling of sex is quite common in many civilized societies and in a number of countries has become virtually institutionalized. In parts of the Orient, in Latin America, and in many Mediterranean areas, much of the male's premarital sex experience is reportedly obtained from prostitutes. One reason for this is the fact that, in these areas, premarital coitus with "respectable" girls is expressly forbidden.

In our own society, organized prostitution has tended to decline. Because marital stability has also declined, some observers see a relation between the two. It is contended that, as premarital and extramarital activity become more widespread, the *need* for prostitution diminishes accordingly. While this is an interesting theory, other societies that have also experienced a decline in marital stability have shown no appreciable reduction in the amount of prostitution. The relationship between prostitution and the state of marriage must remain in the "unknown" category.

---

[9] Clyde Kluckhohn, "Sexual Behavior in Cross-Cultural Perspective," in Jerome Himelhoch and Sylvia Fava (eds.), *Sexual Behavior in American Society*, New York, W. W. Norton & Company, Inc., 1955, p. 341.

Homosexuality. Although the mainsprings of homosexuality have thus far not been identified, certain generalizations can be made in terms of a cross-cultural perspective. For one thing, homosexual activity apparently exists in all societies, even though it is the usual sexual outlet for a relatively small percentage of the population. Secondly, while many primitive groups condone homosexuality for certain individuals (medicine men, for example), the generally accepted and preferred outlet is heterosexual coitus. Social disapproval of homosexual activity reaches its most serious proportions in our own culture: in very few other societies are such severe legal and moral penalties invoked. And finally, anthropologists report that the incidence of homosexuality among females is lower than among males.

Among primitive groups, homosexuality is sometimes interwoven with the custom of *transvestitism,* a practice in which certain males wear women's clothes, assume the role of women, and may even simulate the female's position in making sexual contacts with other males. The transvestite may also be a woman who assumes the role of a man, but this is a rare occurrence. In some preliterate tribes the male transvestite is considered to have supernatural powers and is accorded prestige as a medicine man or shaman, while in other societies the transvestite is tolerated but not granted special status.

Unfortunately for our purposes, cross-cultural data are neither extensive nor accurate enough to permit us to say whether homosexuality is more widely condemned in primitive groups than among civilized societies. Some writers do feel that *condonation* of homosexual practices would weaken the institution of marriage and that this is one reason why human societies prefer and encourage heterosexual relationships. Actually, the effect of sanctioned homosexuality upon marriage would depend in good part on (1) the cause or causes of the condition—that is, whether homosexuality is inborn, acquired, or some combination of both—and (2) the strength of the institution of marriage in a given culture. Since there are so many unknowns in both of these spheres, the relationship between homosexuality and the marital institution represents another area that will probably remain "open for speculation."

DIVORCE

Provisions for divorce are nearly universal and, historically, are of ancient origin, the first written regulation being incorporated into the Babylonian legal code of Hammurabi around 2000 B.C.

This regulation provided that a husband could divorce his wife at will, with no stated reason required. Throughout much of Western history, divorce was considered more of a prerogative for husbands than for wives, although at the present time most Western societies, including our own, accord equal rights of divorce to both spouses. It might be expected that in primitive societies also the male would have greater divorce privileges than the female, but such does not seem to be the case.

Available reports indicate that the majority of societies, both primitive and civilized, permit divorce, although there are exceptions. The African Zulus do not allow divorce for any reason.[10] In Spain, Eire, and some South American countries, there is no provision for divorce. (In the case of an intolerable marriage it is possible to procure a legal separation, but this does not entail the right to remarry.)

Perhaps the most surprising research finding is the fact that the rate of marital breakup in primitive groups is generally high. In fact, ethnographic research over a period of several decades reveals that divorce rates among preliterate peoples are markedly higher than in civilized societies. For some groups—such as the Hopi, the Chukchee, the Alorese, and the Bakweri—between one-third and one-half of all marriages are reported to end in divorce![11]

Why the high rate among primitives? Although the reasons are doubtless complicated, one factor should be mentioned. Generally speaking, preliterate peoples do not consider marriage to be religious or spiritual in nature. They view it simply as a private contract, and when all does not go well in the ensuing relationship, divorce is often a logical alternative.

As might be expected, grounds for divorce vary from one society to the next. In a few groups, divorce is obtainable merely for the asking. Stephens points out, however, that "grounds for divorce are seldom mere incompatibility of husband and wife. Apparently divorce is usually seen as a punishment inflicted on a spouse who has 'done wrong,' that is, violated the marriage contract in some way."[12] A review of the ethnographic literature

---

[10] See Paul Bohannan, *African Outline*, Harmondsworth, England, Penguin Books, 1966; and T. Price, "African Marriage," in Jeffrey Hadden and Marie Borgatta (eds.), *Marriage and the Family*, Itasca, Illinois, F. E. Peacock, Inc., 1969, pp. 101–113.

[11] Stephens, *op. cit.*, p. 234; and Edwin Ardener, *Divorce and Fertility: An African Study*, London, Oxford University Press, 1962, pp. 37–38. See also Remi Clignet and Joyce Sween, "Traditional and Modern Life Styles in Africa," *Journal of Comparative Family Studies*, Autumn, 1971, pp. 188–214.

[12] Stephens, *op cit.*, p. 231.

shows that a few recurrent themes serve as the basis for divorce in most primitive groups; e.g., adultery, sterility, economic incapacity, thievery, impotence or frigidity, desertion, and cruelty. These same grounds would also apply to most civilized societies.

Although most civilized societies and all primitive groups have provisions for divorce, virtually no culture encourages it. The typical attitude seems to be that, while divorce is regrettable and unfortunate, it is sometimes necessary. A number of pre-literate groups have created impediments to divorce, such as imposing fines, prohibiting remarriage, levying alimony charges, or insisting that the bride-price be returned. Civilized societies, of course, employ a variety of stabilizing devices, including religious, economic, and legal pressures. To encourage the continuation of marriage, the one anti-divorce measure that is used by virtually all groups is that of *informal controls*, including censure, gossip, disparagement, condescension, and other seemingly minor but traditionally effective social forces.

SELECTED READINGS

Adams, Bert N., "Doing Survey Research Cross-Culturally: Some Approaches and Problems," *Journal of Marriage and the Family*, August, 1974, pp. 568–573.

Antoun, Richard T., *Arab Village: A Social Structural Study of a Transjordanian Peasant Community*, Bloomington, Indiana University Press, 1972.

Bardis, Panos D., "Synopsis and Evaluation of Theories Concerning Family Evolution," *Social Science*, January, 1963, pp. 42–52.

Beach, Frank, and Ford, Clellan, *Patterns of Sexual Behavior*, New York, Harper & Brothers, 1951.

Burch, Ernest S., "Marriage and Divorce Among the North Alaskan Eskimos," in Paul Bohannan (ed.), *Divorce and After*, New York, Doubleday & Company, Inc. (Anchor Books), 1971, pp. 171–204.

Coser, Rose Laub (ed.), *The Family: Its Structures and Functions*, pp. 1–266, New York, St. Martin's Press, 1974.

Cottrell, Ann Baker, "Outsiders' Inside View: Western Wives' Experiences in Indian Joint Families," *Journal of Marriage and the Family*, May, 1975, pp. 400–407.

Davis, Kingsley, *Human Society*, New York, The Macmillan Company, 1949.

Farber, Bernard, *Comparative Kinship Systems*, New York, John Wiley & Sons, Inc., 1968.

Hendrix, Lewellyn, "Kinship, Social Networks, and Integration Among Ozark Residents and Out-Migrants," *Journal of Marriage and the Family*, February, 1976, pp. 97–104.

Hostetler, John, *Hutterite Society*, Baltimore, The Johns Hopkins University Press, 1974.

Hutchinson, Ira, "The Functional Significance of Conjugal Communication in a Transitional Society," *Journal of Marriage and the Family*, August, 1974, pp. 580–587.

Iro, M. I., "The Pattern of Divorce in Lagos," *Journal of Marriage and the Family*, February, 1976, pp. 177–182.

Kempler, Hyman, "Extended Kinship Ties and Some Modern Alternatives," *The Family Coordinator*, April, 1976, pp. 143–149.

Khatri, A. A., "The Adaptive Extended Family in India Today," *Journal of Marriage and the Family*, August, 1975, pp. 633–642.

Lee, Gary R., "The Problem of Universals in Comparative Research: An Attempt at Clarification," *Journal of Comparative Family Studies*, Spring, 1975, pp. 89–100.

Malinowski, Bronislaw, *The Sexual Life of Savages in Northwestern Melanesia*, 2 vols., New York, Harcourt, Brace and Co., 1929.

Momeni, Djamchid A., "Polygyny in Iran," *Journal of Marriage and the Family*, May, 1975, pp. 453–460.

Morgan, Lewis Henry, *Ancient Society*, New York, Henry Holt and Company, 1877.

Murdock, George, *Social Structure*, New York, The Macmillan Company, 1949.

————, *Outline of World Cultures*, New York, Taplinger Publishing Co., Inc., 1958.

Murstein, Bernard I., *Love, Sex, and Marriage Through the Ages*, New York, Springer Publishing Company, 1974.

Peters, John, and Hunt, Chester, "Polyandry Among the Yanomama Shirishana," *Journal of Comparative Family Studies*, Autumn, 1975, pp. 197–207.

Queen, Stuart, and Habenstein, Robert, *The Family in Various Cultures*, Philadelphia, J. B. Lippincott Company, 1974.

Smith, Raymond T., "The Nuclear Family in Afro-American Kinship," *Journal of Comparative Family Studies*, Autumn, 1970.

Stephens, William N., *The Family in Cross-Cultural Perspective*, New York, Holt, Rinehart and Winston, Inc., 1963.

Sween, Joyce, and Clignet, Remi, "Type of Marriage and Residential Choices in an African City," *Journal of Marriage and the Family*, November, 1974, pp. 780–793.

Vreeland, Herbert, *Mongol Community and Kinship Structure*, New York, Taplinger Publishing Company, 1957.

Westermarck, Edward A., *The History of Human Marriage*, New York, The Macmillan Company, 1902.

Whiting, J. W. M., *Becoming a Kwoma*, New Haven, Yale University Press, 1941.

Yorburg, Betty, "The Nuclear and the Extended Family: An Area of Conceptual Confusion," *Journal of Comparative Family Studies*, Spring, 1975, pp. 5–14.

3

Historical Perspective

IN RECENT YEARS, Americans have shown an unprecedented interest in history. We are, as a nation, taking a closer look at our origins—trying, as it were, to gain a fuller understanding of how we came to be what we are. This inquisitiveness has spread to the family field, where any number of new historical works have been written. As a matter of fact, there are now entire journals devoted to the subject, e.g., *The Family in Historical Perspective* and *The History of Childhood Quarterly*. This is all to the good, certainly, for the American family system has a rich and variegated network of historical roots.

Our legal and moral codes pertaining to sex derive in large part from our Judeo-Christian heritage. Our attitudes toward women and children have been influenced by patriarchal forces starting with the early Hebrews and Greeks and continuing through the Dark Ages and the Renaissance. The concept of romantic love, which has been described as one of our "national problems," can be traced to the Age of Chivalry. Marital symbols, such as the engagement ring, the wedding ring, the marriage ceremony, and the honeymoon, have come to us from a variety of sources. Our religious pronouncements concerning annulment, separation, divorce, and remarriage have been molded by schools of thought that can be traced to the forerunners of both Scholastic and Reformation philosophies. The list of derivatives could be expanded, but—rather than deal with generalities—let us turn to some specifics.

FAMILY LIFE AMONG THE HEBREWS

The history of the Semitic peoples who roamed between Babylon and Egypt before the time of Moses is largely speculative. It was through the personality of Moses that the straggling nomadic tribes became united, and it is roughly from this point—around the thirteenth century B.C.—that Hebrew history takes on meanings that have loomed large for so many of our Western culture patterns. Basic to all Hebrew life, of course, was their rejection of idolatry in favor of the worship of one god, Yahweh.

Over the next millennium the Hebrews were first a pastoral and then an agricultural people. As is so often the case in an outdoor economy, the family was patriarchal in nature. Women were not "free," as we use that term today, but were under the control of their father or husband. Barred from inheriting property, forced to wear veils in public, and generally excluded from commercial and political activities, Hebrew women led a rather restricted existence. They were, in many respects, considered to be part of their husbands' property, as can be seen from the Tenth Commandment: "Thou shalt not covet thy neighbor's house . . . nor his wife, nor anything that is thy neighbor's."

On the other hand, although the Hebrew woman was regarded as property, she was indeed valuable property and was generally well cared for. Unlike her Greek counterpart, she was not isolated and in a few cases managed to achieve some influence. Still and all, the system was—above everything else—patriarchal, and while occasionally a Hebrew woman such as Sarah or Deborah the Prophetess did attain a position of some importance, such cases were exceptional.

Children were also under the control of the father, and their services belonged entirely to him. Though his power was not so absolute as that of the Roman *paterfamilias*, the Hebrew father had the right to handle his children as he saw fit. If he chose, he could sell his daughters into slavery.

Families were large. A man was permitted to have several wives, to say nothing of concubines, slaves, and servants. While most of the patriarchs had but a single wife, some did indeed take advantage of their position. (Solomon is reported to have had 700 wives and 300 concubines!)

If the system described above seems somewhat harsh, it should be explained that the idea of marrying for happiness or for a fuller life is a modern concept and would have had little meaning for the Hebrews or for any of the other groups discussed in the present chapter. Marriage was considered not a privilege but a responsibility, something that was part of the orderly way of life. To marry and have a large family, steeped in religious ceremonials and based on obedience, was as natural to the ancient Hebrews as our own small, happiness-oriented type of family is to us.

43

Betrothal. Turning now to some specific marital practices, the Hebrews required, first, that in order for a marriage to be valid there had to be mutual consent of the two parties involved. This meant that, although the respective parents could *contract* for a marriage, either the boy or the girl could nullify the agreement by refusing to consent. In view of the emphasis on obedience to parents, however, it is unlikely that many sons or daughters ever vetoed parental arrangements.

In keeping with the prevailing practice, Hebrew marriages were normally consummated at an early age. According to the Talmud the legal ages were those at puberty: 12 years for the female and 13 for the male. Marriage prior to these ages was invalid, although there was nothing in the Talmud and little in the way of public opinion to prevent the parents from *contracting* for marriage at any age.

While this contracting-for-marriage, or *betrothal*, was the source of our own custom of the *engagement*, there is a substantial difference between the two. In our society, an engagement is an informal agreement to marry. It is not a legal contract in any sense of the word, the ring being purely symbolic. Among the Hebrews, the betrothal represented an actual contract and was considered to be the beginning of marriage; faithlessness on the part of a betrothed girl was held to be just as serious as adultery, and in both cases the same harsh punishment was inflicted.

At the betrothal ceremony two witnesses were required, and it was customary on this occasion for the boy to give the girl a small coin—to legalize the contract and to symbolize the esteem in which marriage was held. At the close of the ceremony, a benediction was usually pronounced by the girl's father or by a rabbi.

The Marriage Ceremony. The final step was the marriage ceremony itself, which usually took place at least a year after the betrothal. The ceremony, rituals, and wedding procedures have been referred to historically as *nuptials*, although in recent years the term has fallen into disuse. At the wedding, benedictions were pronounced by the bridegroom, a rabbi, or one of the witnesses, after which the affair was concluded with a banquet.

Although benedictions were normally a part of both the betrothal and wedding ceremonies, neither religious pronouncements nor permission of civil authorities were required. Marriage was a private affair between the two families, a pattern which was (and is) widely followed among preliterate peoples. Religious and civil control of marriage did not become prevalent until the end of the Middle Ages.

A final word about Hebrew marriage: the fact that it was in the private domain had absolutely no adverse effects on the marriage rate. There was, essentially, little place in Hebrew society for un-married adults. People were expected to marry, and nearly every-one did. In case of death, both widows and widowers were per-mitted to remarry, and the levirate (described earlier as the obligation of a man to marry his deceased brother's wife) was widely enforced.

Divorce. Although the Hebrews did not look upon marriage from the view of individual happiness or personality develop-ment, instances of marital discord did occur, as indeed they have occurred in all times and among all peoples. The Hebrew hus-band, in this respect, had a free hand. Legally speaking, he could divorce his wife for any reason. Moreover, this right was consid-ered a male prerogative only, practically no provision being made for the wife. Until the advent of the Christian era, further-more, the Hebrew husband was awarded custody of the children in all divorce suits.

In an actual case, a divorced woman would suffer no loss of community status if she were, in fact, innocent of her husband's charges. If she was adjudged guilty, however, she not only was socially disparaged but was forced to relinquish all rights to her dowry. In the event of adultery, the punishment could be much more severe; in fact, both adultery and premarital unchastity could cause her (together with her paramour) to be put to death.

In practice, Hebrew divorce procedure was not nearly so ineq-uitable as it sounds, since group opinion in those days was much stronger than it is today, and any abuse or obvious ill-treatment of the wife would result in severe social condemnation of the husband. Also, the Hebrews did not take kindly to a husband's divorcing his wife for little or no reason, since by so doing he was reneging on his responsibility as protector and provider.

With regard to adultery, it is unlikely that the extreme penalty was often imposed. (There is no case in the Old Test-ament wherein an adulteress was accorded the death sentence.) In fact, so far as is known, relatively few wives actually com-mitted adultery. Of those who did, most cases probably went undetected—even as now. And in the detected cases, there must have been many husbands who, like Joseph and Hosea, simply divorced their wives rather than become involved in a public spectacle.[1]

---

[1] See Bernard I. Murstein, "Hebrew Marriage in the Old Testament," in *Love, Sex, and Marriage Through the Ages,* New York, Springer Publishing Company, 1974, pp. 34–46.

THE GREEK FAMILY SYSTEM

In view of the modern trend toward equality of the sexes, the position held by women in Greek society comes as something of a shock. It was a popular belief in Athens that women were virtually of a different species; at least, their treatment indicates that males considered them to be decidedly inferior. Athenian women were not educated, formally or otherwise. Wives were not allowed to leave their homes without the permission of their husbands, and on the infrequent occasions when they did leave, they were veiled and attended by a slave. In the event of her husband's death, the wife could not even inherit his property!

Within the home, the Athenian woman was expected to remain in her own quarters, and except at mealtimes, when she joined her husband, her social contacts were almost nonexistent. While there were doubtless many couples who shared affection for one another, the husband-wife relationship was characteristically a procreative one, even in this instance the husband

Greek wives were clearly subservient to their husbands and did not partici-pate in their husbands' social activities. Here a drunken husband, returning from a night's festivities, pounds at the door while his fearful wife trembles within. (The Metropolitan Museum of Art, Fletcher Fund, 1937)

being the dominant figure. For example, if the wife were known to have interrupted her own pregnancy without her husband's consent, she could be tried for murder! On the other hand, the husband could, with impunity, order his wife to have an abortion.

Paradoxically, while denying education and social intercourse to wives, the Greeks encouraged and patronized the *hetairae*, a prostitute class who were presumably educated and well versed in civic affairs. Since so much has been written about the *hetairae* (literally translated, "female companions"), the comments of Lewinsohn are revealing.

> The Grecian hetairae are reputed to have bewitched men not by their beauty alone, but also by their wit. This may have been true of some of them. It is reasonable to suppose that the women with whom men like Pericles, Menander, and Epicurus passed long years of their lives must have been of intelligence above the average, interested in things of the spirit and receptive to ideas. . . .
>
> But the women who were capable of combining wit with charm formed, after all, only a small *elite*. They were the exception, even in Athens. The great majority of Greek hetairae were no different in spirit, speech, manners, or ambitions from those of their profession in other lands and other ages.
>
> The prostitute's life is a hard and heavy one which ages prematurely those who lead it, blunts the spirit even of the gifted. . . . There is no time to cultivate the mind, and as a rule, no need, for the customer does not ask for it. Even in Greece, most men did not expect intellectual diversion from a hetaira.[2]

With all the extramarital leeway permitted the husband, it is somewhat surprising to learn that the only sanctioned form of marriage was monogamy. However, public opinion condoned the taking of captured women as concubines, and since warfare was more-or-less continual, concubines were plentiful, as evidenced by their frequent mention in Greek writings.

Not only was the status of wives lower in Greek than in Hebrew culture, but single girls led a severely restricted life; in fact, unlike her Hebrew counterpart, the young Greek girl was not even consulted when it came to marital arrangements. Legally, the consent of neither the girl nor the boy was required in order for the marriage to be valid.

Homosexuality. Despite the reams that have been written about the subject, it seems likely that the incidence of homosexuality in

---

[2] Richard Lewinsohn, *A History of Sexual Customs*, New York, Harper & Brothers, 1958, pp. 54–55.

Greece has been exaggerated. In all probability, as Murstein shows, it was never more than a minor phenomenon.[3] At the same time, it seems safe to say that homosexuality was more prevalent in Greek society than in our own.

At any rate, it has been suggested that Greek homosexuality may have had a somewhat different base; that is, it may have been brought on not so much by a psychological inability to respond to women as by the *cultural role to which women were relegated*. As a consequence, the ancient Greeks may have looked upon a homosexual relationship as more of an emotional than a carnal experience. Murstein pinpoints the issue in the following passage:

> From the social point of view, the situation among Americans and ancient Athenians differs greatly. The American man has the opportunity to marry a woman who, despite discrimination against her, is frequently his equal in education, intelligence, and emotional maturity. The Athenian man had to marry a cloistered girl, often much younger than himself, less experienced in the ways of life, and probably foisted on him by his father. What could he have had in common with such a creature?
>
> The only individuals with the money and freedom of movement, as well as education, to attract adolescent Greek youths were wealthy, older Greek men. Homosexuality, in short, was in no small measure a direct consequence of the vilification of the Grecian wife.[4]

Marriage and Divorce. Like the Hebrews, the Greeks distinguished between betrothal and marriage, the customary procedure being for the girl's father to pledge a dowry at the time of the betrothal. At the marriage ceremony, the bride and groom wore white wedding robes topped with garlands. Sacrifices were made to the gods, a ritual which symbolized the passing of the bride from the father's control to that of the husband. Each of the guests was then given a piece of cake (apparently the forerunner of our own wedding cake), after which a procession moved from the bride's to the groom's home. After a brief mock-struggle, the wife was carried over the threshold by her husband.

In a sense, the circumstances of marriage in classical Greece were similar to our own in that the occasion was a mixture of the festive and the solemn. However, while Greek ceremonies included certain religious observances, the entire procedure, basically, was a private affair. The father himself assumed the role of

---

[3] Murstein, *op. cit.*, p. 56.
[4] *Ibid.*

priest during the sacrificial offerings, and no other religious or civic official was required to be present.

How often divorce occurred is not known, although it must have been infrequent. Public opinion was strongly against it. Technically, a Greek husband could divorce his wife for reasons that were quite petty. In view of the stress placed on family lines, however, a husband who resorted to divorce merely to satisfy a whim would run the risk of social castigation. Also, in the event of a divorce, the husband was required to return the dowry to the wife's father, which fact served as a further deterrent to hasty actions.

There were only two grounds on which the husband could procure a divorce and be assured of public approval—adultery and sterility—and in both instances there was no redress on the part of the wife. The prevailing system was certainly unfair to the Greek woman, since among other things she had practically no rights of divorce herself. Even adultery on the part of the husband was not deemed a sufficient ground. If the wife could prove that the husband's behavior actually endangered the safety and survival of the *family*, she could be granted a divorce, but such instances must have been rare. In reality, about the only recourse a Greek wife had was to try to persuade her husband to give her a divorce.

THE FAMILY IN ROMAN TIMES

In the earlier Roman period (the seventh to second centuries B.C.) the family system was patriarchial in nature and was similar in many ways to the Greek and Hebrew systems. The betrothal, or *sponsalia*, took place at an early age, and in some cases the boy gave the girl a ring instead of the usual coin. Johnston states that "the ring was worn on the third finger of the left hand, because it was believed that a nerve ran directly from this finger to the heart."[5]

Marriage was held in high esteem, with arrangements being made by the parents or by professional marriage brokers. Girls seem to have married in their early teens, boys in their late teens or early twenties. The consent of both parties was required. While matrimony was considered a private matter, the law would not recognize the marriage of a Roman to a foreigner.

---

[5] Harold Johnston, "The Roman Family," in Jeffrey Hadden and Marie Borgatta (eds.), *Marriage and the Family*, Itasca, Illinois, F. E. Peacock Publishers, Inc., 1969, p. 80.

A Roman wedding ceremony, first century A.D. *The bride and groom are shown with hands joined to symbolize their unity.* (Museo Nazionale, Rome: German Archaeological Institute)

Polygyny was not permitted, and although concubinage existed, it was not accorded the same approval that it was in Greece. Divorce was frowned upon and was legally available only to the husband. The Roman wife was not so severely restricted as was her Greek counterpart, and though she was excluded from civic affairs, she was permitted to help entertain her husband's friends and was respected as a homemaker.

The Roman family system differed from that of the Hebrews and Greeks in other ways, one of which was the rather detailed set of regulations pertaining to marriages within and between the various social classes (patricians, plebeians, and slaves). And certainly no account of Roman family life would be complete without mention of the widely quoted *patria potestas*—complete power of the father over his children, a power that lasted as long as he lived. Johnston provides the following description:

> *Patria potestas* was carried to a greater length by the Romans than by any other people, a length that seems to us excessive and cruel. As they understood it, the *pater familias* had absolute power over his children. . . . He punished what he regarded as misconduct with penalties as severe as banishment, slavery, and death. He alone could own and exchange property—all that his descendants earned or acquired in any way was his.
>
> But however stern this authority was theoretically, it was greatly modified in practice. . . . Custom, not law, obliged the *pater familias* to call a council of relatives and friends when he contemplated inflicting severe punishment upon his children, and public opinion obliged him to abide by their verdict.[6]

Under certain conditions, the husband's authority extended over his wife—a form of control known as *manus*. It was only when both husband and wife came from the same social class that the type of marriage entailing *patria potestas* and *manus* could be undertaken.

One of the real strengths of the Roman family stemmed from the fact that ancestor worship was of prime importance. All pious Romans believed that the soul existed apart from the body, not in heaven but at the place of burial. To bring contentment to the soul it was necessary to provide offerings of food and drink on a regular basis. Otherwise, the soul might become an evil spirit. The maintenance of these offerings, writes Johnston, "devolved naturally upon the descendants from generation to generation. Marriage was, therefore, a solemn religious duty, entered into only with the approval of the gods."[7]

In view of the strength and apparent solidity of the Roman family, it is surprising to learn that its demise was but a matter of time.

Disintegration of the Family. Historically, the most fascinating phase of Roman family life was not that of the earlier period described above, but the period from the second century B.C. until the fall of the Empire some 600 years later. This era is of interest to the sociologist because it illustrates the relationship between family decay and societal disintegration. The second century B.C.

---

[6] *Ibid.*, p. 77.
[7] *Ibid.*, p. 76.

is usually chosen as the starting point, since this was the time of the Punic Wars, a conflict against Carthage that stretched over many decades. With the men on the battlefields for extended periods, Roman women began to achieve a measure of independence. Eventually the practice of *free marriage* arose, that is, one without *manus*.

Accompanying the emancipation of Roman women was an influx of wealth, which increased by leaps and bounds as the empire expanded. Slave labor became plentiful, and the myriad of household tasks that formerly occupied the wife came to be taken over by slaves. On the larger estates, the number of slaves would run into the hundreds. Preoccupation with food, entertainment, and gambling—by both men and women—became widespread. Even child-rearing, once so highly regarded by parents, was often given over to servants and tutors.

As *manus* faded into the past, matrimony became more and more a matter of expediency—to be entered into for political reasons, for the attainment of wealth and position, or for the improvement of one's social class. Whereas formerly marriage was considered a civic responsibility, it was now looked upon as an instrument of personal gain. And children, who were once thought of as fulfilling family traditions and sacred obligations, were now increasingly considered a burden.

Inevitably the question came to be, "Why marry at all?" or "Why have children?" And in the hedonistic atmosphere of the times, no satisfactory answer could be found. As a result, the marriage rate fell. Informal sexual liaisons began to flourish, concubinage increased, mistresses multiplied, and general moral laxness spread. According to Livy, "The Romans were able to build a temple to Venus out of the fines paid by adulteresses."[8]

The birthrate fell and childlessness increased to alarming proportions. Infanticide, abortion, and child abandonment came to be more and more common, in spite of the many legal restrictions enacted. Governmental attempts to raise the birthrate through economic incentives were unsuccessful.

Since marriages were often undertaken for mercenary or political reasons, they were necessarily fragile. Divorces not only occurred at the whim of either party (even the calling up of the husband for army service came to be recognized as a ground for divorce!), but many of the most respected Roman officials were themselves involved in unsavory divorce suits. Commenting on

---

[8] See Panos D. Bardis, "Main Features of the Ancient Roman Family," *Social Science*, October, 1963, p. 237.

the high rate of marital breakup among the aristocracy, Bardis writes:

> Of Rome's famous men, Ovidius had three wives, Plinius Caecilius three, Antonius four, Sulla five, and Pompeius five. Other prominent Romans contributed to the high divorce rate as follows: Cato divorced Marcia in order to facilitate her marriage to Hortensius, but when her new husband died and Marcia became a wealthy widow, Cato married her once more.
>
> Cicero divorced Terentia, his wise and virtuous first wife, although they had lived together for thirty years and had two children. . . . His new wife was a very young woman (seventeen), but Cicero divorced her, also. . . .
>
> Julius Caesar married four times. . . . Augustus himself divorced his wife because of an argument which he had with his mother-in-law. Since his new spouse, Scribonia, who had already had two other husbands, seemed ill-tempered, and since he now loved Livia Drusilla, Augustus divorced Scribonia a few hours after she bore their daughter, Julia.[9]

By the fourth century A.D., divorce and marital disruption had reached the stage of public scandal, and both premarital and extramarital sex relations had become sources of official embarrassment. To put it briefly, the meaning had been stripped from marriage.

Looking back on the debacle, it is most ironic to discover that the word "sex" was invented by the Romans.

THE EARLY CHRISTIAN INFLUENCE

As the Roman era drew to a close, the tide of Christianity gathered momentum—and in the year 312 A.D. it was accorded legal recognition throughout the Empire. Essentially, the Christian religion was oriented toward the dignity of the individual and the brotherhood of man, with God the heavenly Father embodying infinite forgiveness and love for all His children.

Worshiping one God, whose spiritual embodiment was revealed through Christ, followers of Christianity believed that marriage was instituted for His purpose rather than for the gratification of sexual desires or the placation of ancestral spirits. And, in the eyes of God, marriage was held to be a permanent relationship between one man and one woman, indissoluble "till death us do part." Unlike the Hebrews, Christians sanctioned

---

[9] *Ibid.*

only monogamy; unlike the Greeks and Romans, Christians condemned all sexual activities outside of marriage; and, unlike so many of the neighboring peoples, Christians preached against divorce.

Beneficial Effects on Family Life. Coming when it did, Christianity had many salutary effects on marriage and the family. Monogamy has already been mentioned. The followers of Christianity had originally been from among the poorer classes, and it is understandable that they would have resented the plural wives of the wealthy Hebrews and the mistresses of the Greeks and Romans. The early Church preached that the Christian ideal entailed marriage between one man and one woman, with premarital chastity and postmarital fidelity. Fornication and adultery were not only severely condemned, but were considered equally culpable for *both* sexes. The Church also spoke out strongly against infanticide.

Jesus taught that divorce was not permissible for any reason (Mark 10:11; Luke 16:18), although there is an inconsistency here, since in two other biblical passages he states that adultery is sufficient cause for divorce (Matthew 5:32 and 19:9). On this point Church leaders have been divided for many centuries.

There were limits to the Christian influence on marriage and divorce, however, since these were still regarded as private matters rather than as affairs of state or church. Indeed, for several centuries Christianity had no patterned or formalized marriage ceremony, the role of the clergy being limited to postmarital benedictions.

Sexual Beliefs. It is also true that while Christianity had a number of beneficial effects on marriage and the family, early teachings with regard to sex were an entirely different matter. For there is no doubt that the early Church founders considered sex per se to be a major evil. As they saw it, most of the immoralities of the day stemmed from the abuse of sex—especially on the part of the upper classes.

> For about three centuries most of the Christians were poor and despised. . . . They were subjected to all manners of humiliating experiences and not infrequently to mob violence. The Emperors Decius, Valerian, and Diocletian sought avowedly to eradicate the whole movement.
>
> Because of this hostility on the part of respectable and powerful elements, it was natural that the Christian codes should condemn many practices of their social "betters" and urge conduct of an

opposite character. Thus there were reactions against easy divorce, "emancipation" of women, and sexual freedom.[10]

The attitudes of the early Christians were also influenced by the Hebrews. The latter, in an effort to set themselves above their Semitic neighbors, such as the Chaldeans and the Canaanites, placed wholesale restrictions on most types of sexual activity. Among the taboos were premarital coitus, adultery, homosexuality, masturbation, and any "unnatural" carnal practices. To this list, the Christians added or emphasized such prohibitions as "contraception, abortion, the reading of lascivious books, singing wanton songs, dancing 'suggestive' dances, bathing in mixed company, and wearing improper clothing."[11] Although it was permitted, remarriage following the death of a spouse was similarly discouraged, the church preferring that both widows and widowers remain continent.

If these "supplements" seem unduly strict, it must be remembered that the early Christian leaders had been reared in a Judaic atmosphere where sex was looked upon as a procreative function. Foremost among the early leaders, of course, were Jesus and Paul, neither of whom ever married. Both were tremendous spiritual teachers, and both took a dim view of the so-called pleasures of the flesh, although Paul—distressed at the laxity he saw as he traveled the Roman road—was the most vituperative of all the apostles.

In light of the prevailing strictures of the early Church, it is little wonder that the idea of virginity came to be held up as a divine state. Sex was a worldly diversion—a carnal obstruction to the attainment of higher spiritual values. Chastity came to symbolize purity of soul and dignity of person. Moreover, in the absence of strong self-control, there was the danger of *internal* sexual contamination. It was not necessary for one to indulge in fornication in order to sin; it was considered lecherous and sinful to have even the desire for sexual relations.

The degradation of sex and, to a lesser degree, of the marital state itself inevitably led to increases in virginity and celibacy. Persons who chose to renounce sex were increasingly considered to be select individuals. Sexual abstinence came to be one of the hallmarks of spiritual dedication, and there were continuing attempts on the part of the Church to prohibit matrimony for bishops, priests, and other ecclesiastics. In fact, centuries later, vows

---

[10] Stuart A. Queen and Robert W. Habenstein, *The Family in Various Cultures*, Philadelphia, J. B. Lippincott Company, 1974, pp. 198–199.
[11] *Ibid.*, p. 217.

of celibacy on the part of the clergy were to become an integral part of the Christian dogma—a development that, in turn, played a significant role in the culmination of the Protestant Reformation.

The Controversy. It is self-evident that the teachings and writings of the early Christian leaders have had a lasting effect on our own sex codes. No one questions this fact. The controversy, from a secular view, is whether this Judeo-Christian influence has had beneficial effects, or whether it has served to foment sexual discord.

A number of modern writers have felt that our own moral and legal codes are still too severe and that the restrictions imposed by the early Christian leaders continue to give rise to a variety of sexual malignancies. These writers point out that under our present system, sex activity is too often accompanied by guilt feelings on the part of the person or persons involved. Masturbation, homosexuality, premarital and extramarital coitus, nudity, and verbal references to the sex act, are all—in varying degrees—looked upon as reprehensible practices.

Other writers, however, contend that the early Christian dogmatics were effective not only in reducing the more flagrant abuses of the day, but also in fostering a societally integrated sexual perspective down to the present. They argue that while the lever of guilt has been the instrument used, pressures brought to bear in order to make people conform *always* involve the threat of either religious or secular guilt. For most people, after all, guilt is simply the realization that they have failed to follow societal convictions of right and wrong.

This is the basic position of writers who feel that our Judeo-Christian sex codes tend to promote and maintain a system of strong family values; i.e., the incentive to marry is increased and the institutional aspects of the family are reinforced by permitting sex relations only between husband and wife.

The controversy over the Judeo-Christian sex codes has by no means been resolved. In recent years, however, it is true that a more tolerant attitude has been shown toward those who do not abide by the codes. Moral indignation has lessened, laws have been lightened or repealed, and sex behavior in general has come more and more to be regarded as a private matter. Many observers feel that the overall results of this permissive trend have been beneficial. Whether or not this assumption is correct is something that readers should attempt to determine for themselves.

THE FAMILY DURING THE MIDDLE AGES

It is difficult to characterize family life during the Middle Ages since there was no single family type as such. The Middle Ages themselves stretched for 1,000 years in time, and during this period there were many changes and variations in family living. Moreover, in the centuries following the Roman collapse, the Empire was overrun by a variety of Germanic tribes—Vandals, Goths, Franks, Lombards, Saxons, and others—each of which settled in a different area; while there was much similarity in their family patterns, there were also differences among the various groups, especially as they developed into sovereign nations. And finally, the rise of feudalism resulted in differing family patterns among the various social classes: marriage and family life among the land-owning nobility was a far cry from that of the serfs. Therefore, rather than attempt to portray family life, as such, during this long medieval period, it will be more feasible to describe some of the recognized forces that helped to shape marital and family values. These influences can be conveniently depicted under three headings: (1) Christianity, (2) feudalism, and (3) chivalry.

The Continuing Effects of Christianity. In the centuries immediately following the fall of the Roman Empire, the Germanic invaders held pretty much to their own marital practices and were little influenced by Christian ideals. The family was patriarchal in form, and there is some evidence that polygyny and wife-capture were practiced among certain Teutonic tribes—actions which might have been a reflection of the incessant warfare characteristic of the period. Though most people married, marriage itself was considered a private matter between the two families, with the ceremonials being nonreligious in nature; in fact, during the Middle Ages it was not unusual for *self-marriage* to take place, in spite of much adverse public opinion. The bride and groom would simply recite the marriage ritual in the presence of one another. The actual words—analogous to "I take thee for my lawful wedded wife"—would be spoken in the present tense *with or without witnesses*. This was the origin of our present common-law marriage; in fact, as it is practiced today in the United States, common-law marriage is almost identical with the self-marriage just described.

But the Church had by no means kept entirely aloof from marital affairs, and little by little, various changes could be seen in the Germanic patterns. The ascendancy of the Church in this period was gradual though unmistakable, and between the fifth and eighth centuries nearly all the Teutonic groups had converted to Christianity. Concubinage was discouraged, and the Church succeeded in erasing the last traces of polygyny. It is interesting that, while polygyny continued to flourish in parts of the Eastern world, the practice never again gained a permanent foothold in Western culture.

By the thirteenth century the Church's control over marriage was virtually complete, the clergy having assumed the function of performing the ceremony.* The father would relinquish control of the bride so that the priest could join the couple in marriage, a procedure that now took place *inside the church*. This assumption of control by the Church is reflected in the present-day religious marriage ceremony, the role of the father being implied by the question "Who giveth this woman to be wedded?" But it is the officiating clergyman who speaks for the Church with the words, "I now pronounce you man and wife."

Not until the Council of Trent (1545–1563) did the Church proclaim, once and for all, that marriage was a *sacrament*, that is, a divine creation, which only the Church, as an instrument of God, could validate by bestowing its blessing. And since marriage was a creation of God, to be performed in the presence of a priest, it followed that the marital bonds were not dissoluble for any reason. This is the Roman Catholic position today.

Although the Church finally succeeded in establishing the principle of the indissolubility of marriage, historical evidence indicates that the ecclesiastical courts in the Middle Ages were liberal in the granting of *annulments*—the declaration that a marriage was null and void because of some condition existing *prior to* the marriage. It is known, for example, that in some instances a distant blood relationship between spouses was sufficient cause for annulment. The Church also reserved the right to grant *divortium a mensa et thoro* (divorce from bed and board), but while this action enabled the husband and wife to live apart it did not permit either to remarry during the lifetime of the other. An annulment gave both parties the privilege of remarrying.

Feudalism: The Class System of the Middle Ages. Because local wars, plundering, and robbery were so common during the Middle Ages, some system was needed that would afford a measure of protection for the average family. Feudalism provided an

---

* The use of the wedding ring also seems to have gained favor during this period, although the specific origins are somewhat hazy. It is likely that the Church encouraged the custom—as part of a continuing effort to underscore the seriousness and permanence of marriage.

answer to the problem, for under the feudal system the land was divided into estates or manors (*fiefs*), each owned by a lord, and by associating himself with one of these the common man could secure protection for his family. In return, he was obliged to perform designated services for the lord of the manor. Society thus came to be divided into a ruling class and a subject class, with a number of gradations in between.

The lowest family in the social-class hierarchy was that of the *serf*, who could not even marry without the lord's permission. Living in a one-room, smoke-filled hut, with infrequent changes of clothing and few bathing facilities, the serf had a most crude family existence. As would be expected, the infant mortality rate was high, and sickness and epidemics were widespread.

Above the serf was the *villein*, whose living conditions were somewhat better and who had certain rights with regard to personal property. Next in the social hierarchy were the middle class, or *freemen*, who owned their own land. Unlike the lower classes, freemen were obligated to perform military services for the lord of the manor. At the top of the class structure were the nobility and royalty, comprising the various earls, counts, viscounts, dukes, princes, and kings.

Family life among the landed aristocracy was strikingly different from that which existed in middle- and lower-class groups. Members of the upper class saw to it that their sons and daughters were steeped in the traditions of their class, and education played an important part in the socialization process. Boys were given in-castle training as pages and squires and were taught riding and swordsmanship. They were trained in the art of warfare, and after they had demonstrated their adeptness, they could ultimately attain knighthood. Girls were taught how to spin and weave, to take care of the sick and wounded, and, perhaps most important, to become thoroughly versed in the customs and good manners of court ladies.

It was during this period that elaborate codes of etiquette were written, and fashion and decorum became the hallmarks of court society; in fact, our modern English words "courtly," "courteous," and "courtship" stem from the propriety and manners that were highly formalized in the medieval court. Women outside the circles of nobility were accorded an entirely different code of conduct, and women in the lower classes were often considered to be "fair game." Indeed, the "right of the first night," or *jus primae noctis*, gave the lord of the manor sexual privileges with the bride of a serf, although it is not known how often he availed himself of these privileges. But the lady of nobility, the upperclass lady of court and castle, was being elevated—in a very special way—to a rather exalted position.

59

Chivalry. Certainly one of the lasting effects of the Middle Ages on family life was a glorification of the "lady" and an idealization of romantic love that crystallized within the framework of chivalry. It was in the twelfth century that the knight came to be obsessed with ideas of undying devotion, bravery, and heroic efforts—all in the service of his chosen lady. On her part, the lady of the castle was not averse to weaving ribbons and fashioning colored plumage to be worn by her knight both in tournaments and in battle. Such glorified interplay between knight and lady came to be idealized by society at large, so that, in spite of the wholesale plundering and widespread oppression characteristic of the times, there developed the concept of romantic love.

The concept captured the imagination of all classes, and, aided by the love songs of the wandering troubadours, Europe was soon engrossed with the diversionary possibilities of romantic love. The latter was not like ordinary love but was held to be an intense, subjective feeling, almost visceral in nature. Romantic love was thought of as an exalted state, *unrelated to the bonds of marriage,* but nevertheless possessing an alluring touch of inevitability. It was the destiny of every lady to meet the knight of her dreams; and for every knight there was one fair lady—somewhere. Such love was viewed as a kind of fate, over which mortal beings had little control. As thus conceived, romantic *amour* was a new concept, one which not only raised the status of women, but which, in an ideal sense, elevated the relationship between men and women beyond the sensual level.[12]

In former periods and in other lands there had probably always been instances of strong emotional attraction between persons of the opposite sex, but not until the Age of Chivalry were such relationships institutionalized. According to our present standards, however, the romantic love of the twelfth and thirteenth centuries would have to be viewed as having a rather unique focus because, according to the tenets of chivalry, romantic love was supposed to occur *after* marriage, with a person *other than one's own spouse!*

Upper-class marriages in those days were largely prearranged, usually for purposes of solidifying social status, and it was not expected that the lord and lady of the manor would be bound by ties of love. For the lady, life in the castle was often boring, and the comings of the troubadours with songs of love were welcomed. The arrival of a battle-tested knight was even more welcome, for now the lady would have a potential opportunity to

---

[12] John C. Moore, *Love in Twelfth-Century France,* Philadelphia, University of Pennsylvania Press, 1972, p. 87.

The idealized relationship between the knight and his lady formed the basis of the concept of romantic love. (Graphische Sammlung, Erlangen)

meet her romantic destiny face to face. The lord of the manor, meanwhile, was fulfilling the role of romantic knight elsewhere, his true love and devotion being shown for a lady other than his wife. Society thus held that both husband and wife had the right to love. Marriage was an obligation, but love was a privilege. And, in keeping with the chivalric codes, neither lord nor lady would pry into the love affairs of the other.

As might be true for most any radical social departure, historians are by no means agreed on the various motivational factors involved in chivalry, and a number of questions remain unanswered. Turner, for instance, raises the following queries:

> Was romantic love, as popularized by the troubadours, a reaction against Christianity, which frowned on eroticism? Was hopeless adoration of woman the result of excessive worship of virginity? Was the cult a literary fashion which came to be taken too seriously? Was it no more than the adulterous art of Ovid adapted to castle society a thousand years later?
>
> Why should lustful adventurers—accustomed to taking what they wanted—have allowed this conception of courtly love to be imposed on them by poets and women? Why should they have succumbed, themselves, into writing verses? . . . Why did they allow the manly sport of knocking each other off horses to be turned into a vying for ladies' favours, with themselves being robed and led into the lists by women, whose gloves and even underclothing they sported as favours? . . . Questions like these may be asked endlessly; for each there are many different answers.[13]

Regardless of the question-and-answer puzzle, it is obvious that, so long as it was merely an extramarital diversion, romantic love could not provide the integrating values necessary for an abiding system of marriage. The romanticism of the twelfth and thirteenth centuries may have filled a class need, but this need could hardly be reconciled with the interests of society at large. With the disappearance of knighthood, therefore, it was predictable that the vine of romantic love would lose its grip and cease to flower.

On the other hand, even within a restrictive, upper-class framework, the impetus of chivalry and the glorification of romantic love were strong enough to affect both the immediate and ultimate course of institutionalized marriage. From the immediate view, chivalry implanted in the minds of men a respect for womanhood that had hitherto been lacking. Also, the possibility was raised that a gratifying emotional relationship between man

---

[13] E. S. Turner, *A History of Courting*, New York, E. P. Dutton and Company, Inc., 1955, p. 32.

and woman could be based on something other than the satisfaction of sexual needs.

From the long-range view, it should be pointed out that, while romantic love ceased to flourish after the Age of Chivalry, the seed had been planted, and all that was necessary for it to take root was the proper climate and nourishment. Although these prerequisites were occasionally found in Europe, they appeared only sporadically, and it was on another continent—America—that the concept of romantic love would begin to thrive, not as an extramarital adjunct, but as a *recognized basis for marriage*.

THE RENAISSANCE AND THE REFORMATION

Toward the latter part of the Middle Ages the feudal system declined. Towns and cities were beginning to emerge, and with the concentration of population in urban areas, the rigid class system gave way to a more personalized existence. There was much work to be done in urban centers, and a serf could normally secure his freedom by remaining in a city for one year. While there were still marked social distinctions among urban dwellers, people had a sense of political equality that was lacking under feudalism.

As time went on, the guild system rose in importance, and trade and commerce flourished. Because of this, there was an influx of wealth and, at least for the upper classes, sufficient leisure to indulge in educational and artistic pursuits. Thus, during the fifteenth and sixteenth centuries, interest in literature, music, architecture, drama, and painting was rekindled after an extended period of intellectual darkness. Historians have termed this scientific and artistic awakening the Renaissance, and a brief marital picture of this period is necessary in order to complete our historical account.

The Renaissance. During the Renaissance it was not unusual for well-to-do families to prescribe a classical education for girls as well as for boys. Also, married women in the upper classes were permitted far more latitude in their social relations than they were during the Middle Ages. These cultural amenities even filtered down, in some degree, to the middle classes. For the masses, educational achievement and cultural refinement remained at a low level, with squalor and illiteracy all too common.

Legally, the position of women remained at rock bottom, irrespective of their social class. Single or married, they had little in the way of property or inheritance rights. In England, for instance, a wife could not bequeath property except with the permission of her husband; in fact, during her own lifetime even such personal effects as her clothing and jewelry belonged legally to her husband!

As in the preceding centuries, marriage during the Renaissance was divided into two parts—the betrothal and the marriage ceremony. The betrothal was held to be a binding contract and was arranged by parents when the children were sometimes quite young; indeed, marriages themselves were consummated at an early age. It was customary for a girl to be married by age 15 or 16, and apparently marriages in which the female was 13 or 14 were fairly common. There is evidence, however, that the men were often in their twenties and thirties at the time of marriage. It is apparent that romantic love played little part in the contractual aspects of betrothal and marriage, although in the middle classes, where there was somewhat more freedom of choice, it is likely that romantic attractions at least occasionally culminated in matrimony.

The marriage ceremony itself was a festive occasion, the degree of festivity and ornateness depending on the social class of the participants. It should be kept in mind that, while the *legal* class distinctions of the feudal period had largely disappeared, society during the time of the Renaissance was sharply stratified according to socio-economic status. It was most difficult in those days for a person to improve his or her class position. After all, upper-class standing was rather carefully guarded, and, since marriages were arranged by parents, it was predictable that cross-class matings would be rare.

Regardless of class position, once the ceremony was over, a wife found herself pretty much under the authority of her husband. And while there were undoubtedly many instances where husband and wife were faithfully devoted to each other, the familiar double standard remained in effect during the entire Renaissance period; i.e., adultery on the part of the wife was severely punished, while the husband's philandering was not regarded too seriously. In the upper classes the age-old custom of keeping a mistress—sometimes referred to as a courtesan—was reportedly quite common.

The Protestant Reformation. The intellectual fervor of the Renaissance was paralleled by a growing restlessness in the spiritual realm. Both Church dogma and clerical practices were being increasingly subjected to criticism, and by the sixteenth century the various dissatisfactions culminated in open revolt. Under the leadership of an Augustinian monk, Martin Luther, the Protestant Reformation had begun. Started in Germany by Luther, the reform movement spread to France, Switzerland, and Scotland, where John Calvin and John Knox led the attack against what they considered to be the abuses of the Church.

In reality, the groundwork for the Protestant Reformation was laid with secular as well as religious ingredients. James gets to the heart of the matter when he states that "the Copernican astronomy and the new learning, the invention of printing and of technical appliances in manufacturing processes, voyages of discovery, the rise of nationalism and of commercial enterprise, had brought about the secularization of society before Luther flung down his challenge at the established ecclesiastical regime."[14]

In any event, although firm in his belief that marriage was the backbone of society, Luther refused to accept the idea that marriage was sacramental in nature. On the basis of his own scriptural interpretation, he maintained that marriage was not a sacrament but was a "temporary and worldly thing which does not concern the Church." It followed, logically, that marriage was a *civil* contract and that the regulation thereof should be under the auspices of the state. There is no doubt that the whole philosophy of civil marriage is primarily attributable to Luther's influence.[15]

65

One of the impelling reasons that led Luther to break with the Church was its position with regard to marriage on the part of the clergy. For several centuries the clergy had been forbidden to marry, and Luther felt that this restriction placed an intolerable burden on the priesthood and led to violations of celibacy. He proclaimed, therefore, that the clergy had the right to marry and supported his contention, again, with a scriptural interpretation.

Luther himself married a former nun, Katherine von Bora (by whom he had six children), though he was not the first reform leader to have entered matrimony. Another cleric, Ulrich Zwingli—the Swiss reformer—had married a year earlier. Referring to Zwingli, Lewinsohn writes: "In April 1524, then forty years of age, he married one Anne Meyer, nee Reinhard, the widow of a judge. No priest of the Roman Church had ventured as much for five hundred years."[16]

The Church bitterly opposed these marital unions, and even some of the Protestants were mildly shocked at the idea of matrimony on the part of the clergy. Eventually, however, the right

---

[14] E. O. James, *Marriage and Society*, New York, John de Graff, Inc., 1955, p. 131.
[15] George Howard, *A History of Matrimonial Institutions*, 3 vols., Chicago, University of Chicago Press, 1904, Vol. I, p. 388.
[16] Lewinsohn, *op. cit.*, p. 147.

of the latter to marry was accepted by all Protestant denominations, and this state of affairs has persisted down to the present.

As the Protestant movement gained headway, with its conception of marriage as civil rather than sacramental, divorce became a growing problem. It followed logically that, if the state could regulate marriage, it could also regulate divorce. Most reformers felt that the prevailing system—whereby divorce was prohibited but annulment permitted—operated to serve the rich and penalize the poor; for the rich had the resources and the influence to establish grounds for annulment, while the poorer classes had no means of escape from an intolerable marriage. King Louis VII of France, for example, was able to have his marriage annulled on the ground that he and his wife, Queen Eleanor, were related in the seventh degree of consanguinity.[17]

Although he disagreed with the principle of marital indissolubility, Luther himself abhorred divorce and held that the only justifications for it were desertion and the "scriptural ground" of adultery. Calvin and other reform leaders were somewhat more liberal in their views toward divorce, and in due time such grounds as cruelty and physical or mental incapacity were accepted.

SELECTED READINGS

Coleman, Emily R., "Medieval Marriage Characteristics: A Neglected Factor in the History of Medieval Serfdom," *Journal of Interdisciplinary History*, Autumn, 1971, pp. 205–219.

Cross, Earle, "The Hebrew Family in Biblical Times," in Jeffrey Hadden and Marie Borgatta (eds.), *Marriage and the Family*, Itasca, Illinois, F. E. Peacock Publishers, Inc., 1969, pp. 60–73.

Demos, John, "Developmental Perspectives on the History of Childhood," *Journal of Interdisciplinary History*, Autumn, 1971, pp. 315–327.

Dudley, Donald R., *The Romans*, New York, Alfred A. Knopf, 1970.

Habakkuk, H. J., "Family Structure and Economic Change in Nineteenth-Century Europe," in Rose Laub Coser (ed.), *The Family: Its Structures and Functions*, New York, St. Martin's Press, 1974, pp. 384–394.

History of Childhood Quarterly.

---

[17] See Nelson Blake, *The Road to Reno*, New York, The Macmillan Company, 1962, p. 18.

Howard, George, *A History of Matrimonial Institutions*, 3 vols., Chicago, University of Chicago Press, 1904.

Johnston, Harold, "The Roman Family," in Jeffrey Hadden and Marie Borgatta (eds.), *Marriage and the Family*, Itasca, Illinois, F. E. Peacock Publishers, Inc., 1969, pp. 73–81.

Laslett, Peter, and Wall, Richard (eds.), *Household and Family in Past Time*, New York, Cambridge University Press, 1972.

Lewinsohn, Richard, *A History of Sexual Customs*, New York, Harper & Brothers, 1958.

Lorwin, V. R., and Price, Jacob (eds.), *The Dimensions of the Past: Materials, Problems and Opportunities for Quantitative Work in History*, New Haven, Yale University Press, 1972.

Moore, John C., *Love in Twelfth-Century France*, Philadelphia, University of Pennsylvania Press, 1972.

Murstein, Bernard I., *Love, Sex, and Marriage Through the Ages*, New York, Springer Publishing Company, 1974.

Patai, Raphael, *Sex and Family in the Bible and the Middle East*, New York, Doubleday & Company, Inc., 1959.

Queen, Stuart A., and Habenstein, Robert W., *The Family in Various Cultures*, Philadelphia, J. B. Lippincott Company, 1974.

Leslie, Gerald R., *The Family in Social Context*, New York, Oxford University Press, 1976. See Part II, "Historical and Theoretical Perspectives," pp. 169–264.

Reiss, Ira, *Family Systems in America*, Hinsdale, Illinois, The Dryden Press, 1976. See Part I, "The Family Systems: Cross-Culturally and Historically," pp. 3–69.

Rosenberg, Charles (ed.), *The Family in History*, Philadelphia, University of Pennsylvania Press, 1975.

Shorter, Edward, "Illegitimacy, Sexual Revolution, and Social Change in Modern Europe," *Journal of Interdisciplinary History*, Autumn, 1971, pp. 237–272.

Stone, Lawrence, "Marriage Among the English Nobility," in Rose Laub Coser (ed.), *The Family: Its Structures and Functions*, New York, St. Martin's Press, 1974, pp. 175–199.

Turner, E. S., *A History of Courting*, New York, E. P. Dutton and Company, Inc., 1955.

Weigand, H. J., *Courtly Love in Arthurian France and Germany*, New York, AMS Press, 1966.

Zimmerman, Carle C., "The Atomistic Family—Fact or Fiction," *Journal of Comparative Family Studies*, Autumn, 1970, pp. 5–16.

67

4

The American Family Heritage

FAMILY LIFE IN the American colonies was shaped in part by the older European traditions and in part by the challenges of an unsettled and unexplored continent. On the one hand, the colonists were steeped in the patriarchal tradition: it was only natural for them to look upon the husband as head of the household and to consider the wife and children as subordinates. Another carryover was the fact that the strict Judeo-Christian sex codes had been handed down almost intact, and sexual activity—except between husband and wife—was equated with sin.

On the other hand, certain circumstances in the colonies operated to bring about changes in the European family system. For one thing, conditions were severe, and the rugged day-to-day living left little time for the niceties of life, particularly in the early Colonial period. For another, some of the colonies experienced a marked shortage of women. European emigration was heavily weighted in favor of males, so that colonial wives were often at a premium. In consequence, marital patterns were altered; women were to have much more choice in the selection of a husband, and the dowry system was to become obsolete. Indeed, before too long, romantic love would come to be a cherished part of the mate selection process.

But let us begin at the beginning. . . .

EARLY HARDSHIPS

A great deal has been written about the suffering and hardships of the English colonists in the first part of the seventeenth century. Readers are probably familiar with the fact that these early settlers—who had left England in quest of religious and personal freedom and economic opportunity—were men and women of courage. They were, however, grossly unprepared to meet the wilderness that faced them. The first settlers at Jamestown, Virginia (1607), the Pilgrims who landed at Plymouth Rock (1620), and the Puritans who settled at Massachusetts Bay (1628) were inept woodsmen and hunters. They were forced to learn by experience, and in the process these early pioneers died by the score.

The Pilgrims unwisely left England in September, and the *Mayflower* did not reach Plymouth Bay until December. By the end of that first New England winter, more than half the colony had died. In fact, during the period of their greatest distress, only a half dozen or so members were in sound health. Little wonder that later historians referred to these early Pilgrims as "babes in the wilderness."

Both the Pilgrims and the Puritans, however, had one advantage over the colonists who had settled along the James River in Virginia: they had brought their wives, whereas Jamestown was an all-male settlement. Despite the bleak New England environment, the Pilgrim and Puritan colonies grew; and despite the relatively mild Virginia climate, the Jamestown settlers became restless and discontented, and the colony was threatened with disintegration. It was not until groups of selected young women sailed from England, to become wives, that conditions in Virginia were stabilized.

And so it was throughout the colonial frontiers: family immigration and settlement made for stability, while all-male migrations carried with them the seeds of discontent.

Housing. The original colonial houses were pitifully inadequate; indeed, they could scarcely be called "houses" at all. Larkin writes that, at first, the settlers dug themselves into caves "or pitched tents which they covered with ship's canvas. When Charlestown in Massachusetts had become a place of streets and houses, people would recall that Captain Green and his friends of 1630 had been glad to lodge in empty casks against the weather. On St. George's River, the settlers simply moved into shelters which the Indians had left behind."[1]

Weslager notes that in Philadelphia some of the colonists lived at first in caves dug into the banks of the Schuylkill River.

> These subterranean hovels were not only unsightly, but caused the new streets to cave in, and the Proprietor was forced to issue orders that the caves be vacated and filled with earth.

---

[1] Oliver Larkin, *Art and Life in America*, New York, Holt, Rinehart and Winston, Inc., 1966, p. 12.

In a land where trees were plentiful, these English and Welsh cave dwellers might have built log cabins, which were more comfortable than damp holes in the earth, but like their conservative countrymen who settled Virginia and New England, they elected not to do so.[2]

This last sentence is most revealing because—contrary to some imaginative modern drawings of both the New England and Virginia settlements—the English apparently did not know how to build log cabins in this early period. Log dwellings were a somewhat later development—a contribution of the Swedes and Finns, both of whom were accustomed to living in heavily forested homelands. The log cabin eventually caught on, however, and—for a variety of reasons—has been termed "the answer to a frontiersman's prayer."

Lynes points out that:

> The obvious reasons for the spread and popularity of the log cabin were the availability of trees, and the fact that the cabin could be built quickly without nails (which were expensive and heavy to carry) and with a single tool. All a man had to have was a stand of timber, an ax, and the skill to use it. . . .
>
> He was as accurate with his ax as a sharpshooter with his rifle. With it, he could build himself and his family a cabin *ten or twelve feet square in a couple of days,* while his wife and children slept in the wagon. How bearable life in a cabin might be depended partly on how well it was built in the first place, partly on whether its occupants were constantly at it to make it behave.[3]

The growth and popularity of the log cabin "complex" are truly amazing. "The frontiersman lived in a log dwelling," writes Weslager, "kept his livestock in a log stable, cured his meats in a log smokehouse, stored his farm implements in a log shed, sent his children to a log schoolhouse, worshipped in a log church, served on a jury in a log courthouse, and sentenced the law infractors of his society to terms in a log jail."[4]

In time, the quality of the houses improved, and eventually well-to-do colonists were erecting strongly built frame dwellings. Occasionally a brick home could be seen, and among the wealthier families the frame houses were two stories high.* In

---

* These houses were not only well made, but hundreds of them built in the 1600's are still standing. The number of houses remaining from the 1700's would run into the thousands.

[2] C. A. Weslager, *The Log Cabin in America,* New Brunswick, New Jersey, Rutgers University Press, 1969, p. 209.

[3] Russell Lynes, *The Domesticated Americans,* New York, Harper & Row, 1963, pp. 23–25.

[4] Weslager, *op. cit.,* p. 316.

Log cabins remained a practical solution to frontier housing problems as late as the end of the nineteenth century, although by then glass windows and shingled roofs often replaced the oiled cloth and sod of earlier times. (Brown Brothers)

general, however, the dwellings of the early colonial farmers and workers were crude, unpainted affairs, and for several decades improvements in structure and design were necessarily slow in making their appearance.

Furnishings. There is abundant evidence to indicate that the typical colonial house of the 1600's was not a cheery dwelling-place. The windows were small, few in number, and—until almost mid-century—made of oiled paper or cloth. One historian has voiced the opinion that, with so few windows, "it must have remained quite dark all the time: perhaps in cloudy weather the settlers were obliged to keep candles burning all day. The low ceilings and dark walls would only have intensified the feeling of oppressiveness. But this, of course, speaks only for our own impressions. The settlers themselves were presumably quite content with such houses."[5]

The fact that the houses were dark, cramped, single-story buildings takes on added meaning when one considers the size

---

[5] John Demos, *A Little Commonwealth: Family Life in Plymouth Colony,* New York, Oxford University Press, 1970, p. 29.

of the average family. It was not unusual for colonial couples to have seven or eight children, and some families were much larger. (Benjamin Franklin came from a family of 17.) In many of the homes there was more overcrowding and congestion than there is in today's tenements. In fact, the question has been raised whether, under such conditions, the concept of privacy had any real meaning.

Like the dwelling-places, household furnishings in seventeenth-century America were cruder than is generally realized. Stools and benches were more common than chairs. Floors were without rugs. The earliest beds were simply wooden frames, with lengths of rope tied to the sides. Wooden platters or "trenchers" often served as dishes, since there was no chinaware. Spoons were plentiful, but knives were rare, and—in Plymouth Colony, at least—numerous inventory lists and excavations have failed to turn up a single fork.[6]

All meals were eaten in the kitchen, where the "dining table" amounted to little more than a few rough planks set on supports. Benches were used as seats, though in some cases people may have eaten standing up. Carson states that, while forks were unknown, "fingers, supplemented by plenty of nappery, met the demands of table manners. In the up-country districts, the trenchers were spoken of as having a 'dinner side and a pie side.' Two persons often ate from the same dish. If a hard-handed beau and his sunburned belle shared a trencher, it was considered that they were betrothed."[7]

The Fireplace. It would be almost sacrilegious not to make special mention of the colonial fireplace. Indeed, the subject is referred to so often in American history that one sometimes gets the impression that the colonists made a veritable career out of the fireplace—an impression, incidentally, that is not wholly incorrect! For, in an almost literal sense, the fireplace was the hub around which the early American family revolved. Referring to the Pilgrims, Chamberlain writes that:

> Their first edifice in the new land was a fireplace, onto which they attached a crude one-room dwelling with a garret and a steep roof. If more room became needed, a similar structure was added to the other side of the house.[8]

---

[6] *Ibid.*, pp. 41–42.

[7] Gerald Carson, *The Polite Americans*, New York, William Morrow & Company, Inc., 1976, pp. 13–14.

[8] Samuel Chamberlain, *Open House in New England*, New York, Bonanza Books, 1968, p. 8.

Winters were long and severe, especially in New England, and, as far as houses were concerned, there was one dominant consideration: heat. And indoor heat came from one source—the open hearth. Whether the dwelling was a single-storied log cabin in the wilderness, or a double-storied frame house in Boston, there was likely to be only one chimney and one fireplace—which in turn meant that there was but one all-purpose room. In addition to being used for heating and cooking, therefore, the fireplace served as the center for social activity.

Early American fireplaces were perhaps the largest that have ever been built, many of them being 10 feet or more in depth and wide enough to hold the largest of logs. Keeping the fireplace lit, however, was another matter, for matches did not make their appearance until well into the 1800's. Gemming notes the following difficulties:

> The fire was kept overnight by carefully raking up the embers and covering them with ashes. If the fire went out, a boy had to run to the neighbor's with a pair of tongs or a metal box and borrow a glowing live coal. And if there were no neighbors, he had to strike a spark with flint and steel, and catch the spark on charred shreds of linen. It took a long time in the bitter morning cold, when the flint was dull and the tinder damp. . . .
>
> In winter, living without a fire was impossible, and it was a good day's work for a man or a boy simply to keep the fire fed.[9]

If they could help it, the early colonists never let the fire go out, most families keeping the hearthstone burning year in and year out!

In 1745 the Franklin stove made its appearance and threatened to supplant the open fireplace. As a matter of fact, the stove—one of Benjamin Franklin's many inventions—actually did alter American eating habits. Muffins, biscuits, flapjacks, and corn bread, for instance, all became popular when the quick-heating stove replaced the slower-heating brick of the fireplace.

But it was the fireplace which somehow captured the spirit of the colonial family, perhaps by symbolizing the hardships that were overcome; and despite the many advantages of the stove, the open hearth remained a hallmark of the American way of life. Even today, when its utilitarian value has been largely eliminated by modern heating methods, the open fireplace can be seen in many homes—a vestigial culture trait, emblematic of the family of an earlier day.

---

[9] Elizabeth Gemming, *Huckleberry Hill: Child Life in Old New England*, New York, Thomas Y. Crowell Company, 1968, pp. 2–4.

The open hearth was the center and symbol of colonial family life. (The Bettmann Archive Inc.)

THE ECONOMIC FUNCTION

It is difficult for modern Americans to appreciate the extent to which the early colonial family was a *socio-economic enterprise.* Hall puts it as follows:

> New England society before 1780 was almost totally lacking in formal organizations for the performance of basic economic and social welfare activities. In the economic realm, there were no banks, no insurance companies, and no corporate enterprises. In the delivery of social services, there were no hospitals, asylums, or orphanages. . . .
>
> The family was the unit through which virtually all major social and economic activities were mediated. Orphans, widows, the insane, and others in need of care were lodged by the towns with families. Vocational training took place under a system of apprenticeship, the trainee taking up residence with his instructor's family. He became, in effect, a member of that family, learning his profession or trade in exchange for a sum of money and his day-to-day labors.[10]

Of necessity, early colonial families were economically self-sufficient units. They cleared the land, constructed the house and barn, and made most of the furniture and farm tools. Every farmer was his own carpenter, builder, and repairman, and it

---

[10] Peter Hall, "Marital Selection and Business in Massachusetts Merchant Families, 1700–1900," in Rose Laub Coser (ed.), *The Family: Its Structures and Functions,* New York, St. Martin's Press, 1974, pp. 226–227.

was common for groups of men to assist one another in the more arduous tasks.

Although women occasionally helped with the heavier farm duties, their role was primarily that of converting the raw materials into usable products. It was the wives who devoted themselves to spinning yarn and weaving cloth for garments and bed coverings, washing and mending the clothes, making candles, cooking and preserving food, and—quite important—running the "infirmary." Since doctors, nurses, drugs, and medicines were all but unknown in this early period, ministering to the sick was part of the housewife's duties.

The home did indeed serve as an apothecary's shop, though how effective the various herbs, roots, and other remedies were is open to question. It must be remembered that, during the Colonial period, the practice of medicine was in a very primitive state. One historian, for example, notes that:

> most births were attended by midwives, whose limited knowledge of medicine may have been an asset. While doctors could use forceps, their feeble understanding of the process of childbirth is illustrated by Dr. Willian Shippen's bleeding mothers just before labor in the belief that women who had not menstruated for nine months had a surplus of bad blood![11]

Children were expected to work side by side with their parents. Girls aided their mothers in household tasks, and boys worked the farm with their fathers. Farm implements—especially plows—were both scarce and crude, and the farmer needed all the human help he could get. It is little wonder that children were considered economic assets. With few schools available and child-labor laws nonexistent, a family with a large number of children was assured of an abundant labor supply.

In the South, a contrasting set of circumstances combined to make the early colonial home quite different from its New England counterpart. The climate was mild. The soil was rich, and tobacco, cotton, and rice were easy to raise. And, of course, slavery provided a seemingly endless supply of labor.

COURTSHIP

Courting in the early colonies was a far cry from today's practice. Colonial courtship was of relatively short duration and was considered as a prelude to marriage rather than as an enjoyable end

[11] J. William Frost, *The Quaker Family in Colonial America*, New York, St. Martin's Press, 1973, p. 71.

LIBRARY OF ST. MARY'S COLLEGE

THE AMERICAN FAMILY HERITAGE

in itself. All of the colonies required parental approval before a specific courtship could begin, although from the records it does not appear that parents often withheld their consent.

Young couples did not have the leeway they have today. There was more group activity and less opportunity for individual pairs to be alone; in fact, there were statutes in Puritan New England whereby a couple could be fined for "riding off together with sinful intent." And while the case can hardly be considered typical, John Lewis and Sarah Chapman were taken to court in 1670 for "sitting together on the Lord's day, under an apple tree in Goodman Chapman's orchard.[12]

It goes almost without saying, of course, that if a courting couple wanted to be alone badly enough they probably found ways to do so, in spite of the watchfulness and chaperonage. The point is that the social atmosphere was far less permissive than it is today.

Parental Approval Versus Romantic Love. Just as parental approval was necessary before courtship could begin, parental consent was a prerequisite to marriage. And there is ample documentary evidence to indicate that parents were shrewd in their matrimonial transactions, especially in the well-to-do families. Colonial court records reveal that detailed contracts were often made for the purpose of specifying the financial terms and property rights of the marrying parties.

While parental approval was required, it was inevitable that some males would attempt to ply their *amours* in spite of objections on the part of the girl's father, and occasionally the latter would take court action in order to check an overenthusiastic suitor. (The offense was known as "inveigling," a misdemeanor defined by law as the courting of a girl without her father's consent.) Generally, though, parents were not supposed to refuse their permission arbitrarily.

Transportation and roads were poor in colonial times, and the choice of eligible mates was often rather limited. As a consequence, courtship usually involved boys and girls who lived near each other and whose families were well known to one another.*

---

* The colonial term "sparking," equivalent to the present "necking," reportedly derived from neighborly observation of chimney sparks. The later the courting couple stayed up, the greater the need of wood for the fireplace. More wood led to more sparks, the significance of which was well understood by perceptive neighbors.

[12] Thomas Wertenbaker, *The First Americans*, New York, The Macmillan Company, 1927, p. 190.

In this eighteenth-century advertisement a bachelor announces his availability. (American Antiquarian Society)

That the problem of "availability" was more pressing in colonial times than it is today can be seen from matrimonial advertisements like the following, which appeared in the *Boston Evening Post* of February 23, 1759:

> To the ladies. Any young lady between the ages of 18 and 23, of middling stature, brown hair, regular features, and a lively brisk eye; of good morals and not tinctured with anything that may sully so distinguishable a form; possessed of £300 or £400 entirely her own; and where there will be no necessity of going through the tiresome talk of addressing parents or guardians for their consent: such a one, by leaving a line directed for A. W. at the King Street Coffee House, will be met with a person who flatters himself he shall not be thought disagreeable by any lady answering the above description.

Profound secrecy will be observed. No trifling answers will be regarded.[13]

What part did romantic love play in colonial courtship? Among the Puritans, as Morgan points out, love was not so much the *cause* as it was the *product* of marriage. Couples were advised to marry, not for love, but for the potentiality of love.

> Thus, when Michael Wigglesworth wished to persuade the pious Mrs. Avery to marry him, he did not lay claim to any violent passion for her. He wrote her a letter carefully listing ten reasons why she should marry him, and answering two objections which she had raised to the match.[14]

Throughout the Southern colonies—which were beyond the sphere of Puritan influence—romantic love was more highly ritualized and interwoven with the threads of chivalry, particularly among the upper classes. The extent to which the Southern belle was placed on a symbolic pedestal can be seen from Morgan's description of a proposal of marriage.

> The lady must be approached with fear and trembling as a kind of saint, the lover prostrating himself either literally or figuratively before her, while she betrayed great surprise and distress at the whole idea. . . .
>   It was never leap year in colonial Virginia, and a self-respecting young woman of quality had to play out the role of aloof and unwilling goddess before she could gracefully take the part of a bride.[15]

The same author states, however, that "money was so proper a consideration in the choice of a mate that the newspapers, in announcing weddings, sometimes stated the sums of money involved. . . . Though marriage was supposed to be connected somehow with love, it was also an investment, and anyone who entered upon it with a good share of capital was expected to take care that his partner should also contribute a proper share."[16]

To get back to our original question, then: what part *did* romantic love play in colonial courtship? The answer obviously is complicated because of temporal and geographical reasons. As time went on and the influence of Puritanism declined, for

---

[13] Quoted in Arthur Calhoun, *A Social History of the American Family,* New York, Barnes & Noble, Inc., 1944, pp. 58–59.

[14] Edmund Morgan, *The Puritan Family,* New York, Harper & Row, 1966, pp. 53–54.

[15] Edmund Morgan, *Virginians at Home,* Charlottesville, The University Press of Virginia (Dominion Books), 1963, pp. 36–39.

[16] *Ibid.,* p. 31.

example, the proportion of marriages that came to be based on romantic love apparently increased. In the early period—of which we are writing—it would appear that, while love was by no means unimportant, economic factors were the dominant consideration. This was especially true among the upper classes.

Bundling. Certainly the most famous—or infamous—courtship practice in the Colonial period was that of bundling. While social historians invariably refer to the custom, very little is known about the incidence, the frequency, or the sexual overtones involved. In view of the widespread interest shown, it is surprising that there has not been more research on the subject.[17]

The custom itself simply involved the couple's going to bed together—with their clothes on. In some instances a centerboard was used to separate the parties, and there are also reported instances where the girl was required to don a "bundling bag."

The origin of bundling is somewhat obscure, although the biblical account of Ruth and Boaz may be pertinent. "And when Boaz had eaten and drunk, and his heart was merry, he went to lie down at the end of the heap of corn; and she came softly. . . . And she lay at his feet until the morning: and she rose up before one could know another"(Ruth 3:7,14).

Since, in the same passage, Boaz says to Ruth, "Tarry this night," bundling is sometimes referred to as "tarrying." Whatever its origin, bundling is known to have occurred in several European countries. In Norway, it was known as *night-running;* in Holland, as *queesting;* in Sweden, as *frieri;* and in Germany, as *windowing* (since the boy entered through the girl's window).[18] But while bundling may not have originated in America, it was certainly in America that it gained notoriety.

Ostensibly, at least, the purpose of bundling was to keep warm. Winter nights were cold, and bundling presumably operated to conserve firewood and candles, as indicated by the following verse, written in 1786:

> Nowadays there are two ways,
>   Which of the two is right?
> To lie between sheets sweet and clean,
>   Or sit up all the night?

---

[17] Interested readers may consult the following booklets: Ammon M. Aurand, Jr., *Little Known Facts About Bundling in the New World,* Harrisburg, Pennsylvania, The Aurand Press, 1938; Henry Reed Stiles, *Bundling: Its Origin, Progress, and Decline in America,* New York, Book Collectors Association, Inc., 1934; and Elmer L. Smith, *Bundling: A Curious Courtship Custom,* Lebanon, Pennsylvania, Applied Arts Publishers, 1969.

[18] Smith, *op. cit.,* pp. 9 ff.

> Nature's request is, give me rest,
>   Our bodies seek repose;
> Night is the time, and 'tis no crime
>   To bundle in our clothes.
>
> Since in a bed a man and maid
>   May bundle and be chaste,
> It doth no good to burn up wood,
>   It is a needless waste.[19]

The reported need to conserve firewood and candles, plus the fact that references to bundling seldom appear in connection with upper-class families, suggests that the custom was practiced principally among the poorer classes. Bundling seems to have died out in the colonies with the close of the eighteenth century, although there is no telling how long individual episodes continued to occur.

The crucial questions, of course, are: (1) How prevalent was the practice? and (2) Was bundling primarily sexual in nature? Unfortunately, neither of these questions can be answered with any certainty. Regarding prevalence, it seems likely that bundling was fairly well known in many colonial areas—even though it was far from general. As to the sexual overtones, all that can be said is that some illegitimate births occurred in areas where bundling is reported to have been practiced. It seems logical to assume that in some instances bundling was motivated by reasons other than fuel conservation. The following verse, written around 1800, would seem to support this assumption:

> Let boars and swine lie down and twine
>   And grunt, and sleep, and snore,
> But modest girls should not wear tails,
>   Nor bristles any more.
>
> Dogs and bitches wear no breeches,
>   Clothing for man was made,
> Yet men and women strip to their linen,
>   And tumble into bed.
>
> Down deep in hell there let them dwell,
>   And bundle on that bed;
> There burn and roll without control,
>   Till all their lusts are fed.[20]

It should be remembered, on the other hand, that there were no sofas in the early Colonial period. Once parents had given

---

[19] Quoted in Stiles, *op. cit.*, p. 97.
[20] Quoted in Smith, *op. cit.*, p. 22.

their approval of the courtship, there was no suitable place for the couple to court during winter months except in bed. Any bundling that took place, furthermore, almost certainly involved pairs who were contemplating marriage. And, finally, the parents were not only in the same house, but were often in the *same room* with the courting couple, so that there was less opportunity for sexual indulgence than there is today in a parked car.

As an early American oddity, bundling is of historical interest; but as far as shedding light on the behavioral patterns of colonial courtship, our knowledge will be increased only when some enterprising person comes up with definitive research.

MARRIAGE

In the Colonial period, marriage was considered an obligation as well as a privilege. People were expected to marry, and they normally did so at a moderately young age. There was little place for the unmarried, who were generally looked upon with disfavor. For a woman, marriage was deemed to be the only honorable state. Bachelors were suspect and in most of the colonies were heavily taxed and kept under close surveillance.

In Connecticut, for example, "every kind of obstacle was put in the way of a bachelor keeping his own house, the assumption apparently being that he would turn it into a brothel. Unless a bachelor had authority to live alone, he was fined £1 a week."[21] In 1683, the Pennsylvania council actually discussed a proposal that would have *required* all men to marry! (The bill was rejected by the assembly.)[22]

Widows and widowers were expected to remarry—and they generally did, usually without much time elapsing. "The first marriage in Plymouth was that of Edward Winslow, a widower for seven weeks, and Susanna White, a widow for 12 weeks. One governor of New Hampshire married a widow of only ten days standing, and the amazing case is cited of Isaac Winslow, who proposed to Ben Davis' daughter the same day he buried his wife."[23]

Widows, incidentally, were considered to be excellent marital choices because of the property inherited from their previous

---

[21] E. S. Turner, *A History of Courtship*, New York, E. P. Dutton and Company, Inc., 1955, pp. 70–71.

[22] Frost, *op. cit.*, p. 150.

[23] Stuart A. Queen and Robert W. Habenstein, *The Family in Various Cultures*, Philadelphia, J. B. Lippincott Company, 1974, p. 300.

marriage. They also would have had valuable experience as homemakers, a qualification that was lacking in the younger, unmarried girls. Of course, remarriages did not always work out as anticipated, a colonial epigram reading as follows:

> Colonel Williams married his first wife, Miss Miriam Tyler, for good sense, and got it: his second wife, Miss Wells, for love and beauty, and had it; and his third wife, Aunt Hannah Dickinson, for good qualities, and got horribly cheated.[24]

It was because the colonists held marriage in high esteem that they made certain it was bolstered by legal, as well as social, sanctions. Not only was parental consent a prerequisite, but the consent had to be given to the town clerk in writing. Throughout the colonies, provision was also made for announcing marital intentions. This was done by posting *banns*—public notice of intent to wed—a certain number of days prior to the marriage. In addition to the notification of consent and posting of banns, it was required that marriages be registered. The registration was done by the town clerk, who also had the duty of recording births and deaths within the township.*

Marriage Rituals. Historians report that no uniform marriage ritual existed in the early Colonial period. Weddings were apparently performed at the bride's home. The wording of the ceremony—whether civil or religious—does not appear to have been standardized. It is likely that in the trying days of the seventeenth century there was neither time nor inclination to make marriage a festive occasion. At the same time, Americans have always had a proclivity for celebrations of all kinds, and before long the "quiet American wedding" had mushroomed into a panorama of relatively large dimensions. Prayers, psalm singing, music, bridal processions, and feasting became commonplace. By the eighteenth century, weddings had become recognized occasions for revelry and merrymaking. Gifts were given, drinking and dancing were on the wild side, muskets were fired, and pranks such as bride-stealing were practiced. For better or worse, the American wedding had come of age.

---

* Recording of divorces presented no problem because there were so few of them. In fact, the Middle and Southern colonies had no general provision for divorce. Some trace of this prohibition carried over to recent times, for South Carolina did not permit divorce *for any reason* until 1949.

[24] Anne H. Wharton, *Colonial Days and Dames*, Philadelphia, J. B. Lippincott Company, 1895, pp. 205–206.

Common-Law Marriage. Not all colonial marriages were cele-brated in the foregoing fashion. Some couples dispensed with all formalities, both social *and* legal. Such marriages were referred to by a variety of terms, such as "handfasting," "self-gifta," "clandestine contracts," and later "common-law marriage." His-torically, these unions have always been a legal and judicial headache. In the Colonial period, matrimonial laws generally pro-vided for consent, banns, officiant, and registration. But what to do with violators? What should, or could, be done when banns were not posted, or when the marriage ceremony was performed by an unauthorized person?

In general, the colonists chose to recognize such marriages as valid, even though a fine might be imposed on the violators. Common-law marriages were treated in the same manner: they were recognized as valid even though the offenders were often fined. Some colonies attempted to invalidate such unions, but the efforts proved ineffective.

It can be argued that, in view of the sanctity attributed to mar-riage, the colonies should have imposed heavier penalties on the violators. Actually, it was *because* matrimony was held in such high esteem that common-law marriages were accepted. After all, once a common-law wife became pregnant, what was to be gained by having the marriage invalidated? Moreover, during Colonial times and throughout much of the nineteenth century the frontier was being pushed westward. Clergymen or author-ized civil officials were frequently unavailable in sparsely settled areas, and common-law marriage was often the only recourse.

Whether or not such marriages serve a worthwhile purpose today is debatable, but in this earlier period the recognition of common-law unions was a functional necessity.

POSITION OF WOMEN

There is no doubt that colonial America was—by modern stan-dards—a man's world. Marriage might be a purely economic arrangement or it might be a love match, but in either case the wife was destined to lead a restricted existence.

Formal education was largely a male province. In some of the colonies, girls were permitted to attend school only during the summer, when the classroom was not being used by boys. Even among the wealthier New England families, education for girls rarely went beyond "reading, writing, and the social graces." As a matter of fact, modern historical research indicates that the majority of New England women were illiterate!

83

An interesting commentary on the alleged perils of women's education is the case of the wife of Connecticut's Governor Winthrop, who lost her mind, whereupon her husband bemoaned the fact that she had gone insane "by occasion of giving herself wholly to reading and writing. Had she not gone out of her way and calling to meddle in such things as are proper for men, whose minds are stronger, she would have kept her wits, and might have improved them usefully and honorably in the place God had set her."[25]

Morgan states that:

> In seventeenth-century New England, no respectable person questioned that woman's place was in the home. . . . The proper conduct of a wife was submission to her husband's instructions and commands. He was her superior, the head of the family, and she owed him an obedience founded on reverence. . . .
>
> She should therefore look upon him with reverence, a mixture of love and fear, not however *"a slavish Fear* . . . but a *noble* and *generous Fear,* which proceeds from Love."[26]

And Carson notes that, among the literate classes in the colonies, "few wives called their husbands by their first names. A love letter from a lady to her absent husband began customarily, 'My dear Mr. Blaine,' or whatever."[27] The same author points out that "above all, silence was enjoined upon women, but not always achieved, as witness this biography-in-brief incised in native granite:

> Here lies as silent clay
> Miss Arabella Young
> Who on the 21st of May
> 1771
> Began to hold her tongue."[28]

There was another side to the picture, however, for while they were subjected to many behavioral restrictions, women were accorded certain rights and protections. Husbands were legally responsible for the support of their wives and for any debts incurred by them. Women also had certain inheritance rights and contractual privileges. Additionally, wives were legally protected against any abuse or maltreatment by their husbands; as a matter of fact, even in Puritan New England, where

---

[25] Calhoun, *op. cit.,* p. 84.

[26] Morgan, *The Puritan Family,* pp. 42–45.

[27] Carson, *op. cit.,* p. 57.

[28] *Ibid.,* pp. 54–55.

public show of affection between spouses was taboo, many husbands were devoted to their wives in much the same manner as they are today. Moreover, as time went on, women gradually achieved greater independence and a more satisfactory personal identity.

On the whole, however, the early New England woman had a circumscribed existence. Legally, both married and unmarried females could own property—and even run a business—but such practices were clearly not encouraged. And while there were undoubtedly many women who would have liked to hold responsible positions, the temper of the times was against them. How much talent was thus wasted will never be known, but—as the subsequent course of events would show—it must have been considerable.

Because of the milder climate in the Southern colonies, women in this region had fewer chores and consequently more leisure. Apparently they were allowed more freedom than New England women. Partly because of the scarcity of females and partly because of the prevailing aristocratic tradition, women in the South were reportedly held in higher esteem than they were in the North. The family was strongly patriarchal, but the prevailing rationale held that the male was the protector rather than the ruler of the female. As a result of this cavalier tradition, there grew up an extensive folklore of Southern chivalry: even today the phrase "Southern gentlemen" is commonplace—and without a Northern counterpart.

How much *actual* difference there was in the treatment of Northern and Southern women is impossible to say, since the legendary aspects of Puritan and Cavalier behavior have become almost indistinguishable from the facts themselves. It is quite possible that in middle- and lower-class families regional differences were minimal. However, this much seems certain: given the contrasting attitudes toward women in the North and in the South, it is easy to understand why the discovery and bestial treatment of "witches" could only have taken place in Puritan New England.

CHILDREN

It has already been mentioned that colonial families were large, and that children were welcomed as an indispensable source of labor. However, the infant mortality rate was much higher than it is today, and in some families half the youngsters died before reaching maturity. As Morgan points out, an infant coming into the world in the early Colonial period "had a good deal more reason to cry about it than one who arrives in any part of the United States today."

> His parents would love him, but since they knew nothing of modern medicine and sanitation, they were woefully unprepared to care for him. They knew nothing about germs and viruses, or how to fight them. Their baby would have to take his chances against diphtheria, diarrhea, and a host of other terrors, and his chances were not very good.
>
> The parents would often be more of a hindrance than a help. They might very well aggravate an illness by administering some potion which today nobody in his right mind would think of drinking himself, let alone giving to a sick child.[29]

In view of their economic value and their high mortality rate, one might expect that the children would have been pampered, but such was not the case. Colonial children may have been loved and wanted, but pampered they were not! On the contrary, childhood was thought of as a period that youngsters simply "went through" in the process of growing up.

To begin with, as Frost demonstrates, colonial children "were believed to be flawed by original sin and, in their natural condition, damned. With the exception of the General Baptists, in no part of Christendom before 1650 was a baby thought of as being innocent at birth, for Adam's sin was considered to have been transmitted to all mankind. Since Augustine's time, most western European Christians had believed that sin was given to a child through the lust in the act of conception."[30]

Puritan parents, furthermore, often used biblical aphorisms to support their views on child-rearing: "Children, obey your parents in the Lord: for this is right" (Ephesians 6:1); "Honour thy father and thy mother, that thy days may be long upon the land" (Exodus 20:12).

One of the keys to colonial child-rearing, particularly among the Puritans, was the concept of "willfulness." As Demos puts it:

> Puritan writings which deal in some direct way with child-rearing share one central theme: The child's inherent "willfulness" must be curbed—indeed, it must be "broken" and "beaten down"—as soon as it begins to appear. All other aspects of character development are dependent on this procedure. Here, for Puritans, lay *the central task* of parenthood; and, in a profound sense, they regarded it as involving a direct confrontation with "original sin."[31]

---

[29] Morgan, *Virginians at Home*, p. 5.

[30] Frost, *op. cit.*, pp. 65–66.

[31] John Demos, "Developmental Perspectives on the History of Childhood," *Journal of Interdisciplinary History*, Autumn, 1971, pp. 320–321.

The Puritans viewed children as being extremely willful, and their methods of discipline were appropriately severe. (The Granger Collection)

In view of all of the above, colonial discipline was understandably strict, and respect for parents was one of the hallmarks of integrated family life. Children often addressed their parents as "sir" or "ma'am" or "esteemed parent." In some families, youngsters were not allowed to sit at the same table with their parents during meals, although this practice was not the general rule.

Both boys and girls were expected to perform rigorous household and farm duties at a young age, and they were supposed to do so willingly and with good grace. Punishment was almost certainly more severe than it is today, Cotton Mather's "Better whipt than Damn'd" philosophy being a case in point. For acts of flagrant disobedience on the part of children, the Puritans prescribed the death sentence, although there is no indication that this penalty was ever imposed.

With regard to formal education, it has already been mentioned that girls were seriously handicapped. And even for boys, schooling, in the sense that we normally use the term, was a relatively unimportant part of the overall training program. Free, coeducational public schools and land-grant colleges—both of which are instrumental in our current educational program—were virtually nonexistent in the pre-Revolutionary period.*

Actually, the most important "education" for the colonial child was to be found outside the school—vocational training at home, religious indoctrination by the church, and "Puritan guidance" by the community at large. But underlying the total child-development process was a certain philosophy, ably expressed in the following extract:

> These, then, were the Puritan assumptions: children were ignorant and children were evil, but their ignorance could be enlightened and their evil restrained, provided the effort was made soon enough. The pious parent therefore was faced with two tasks, instruction and discipline.
>
> There was no question of developing the child's personality, of drawing out or nourishing any desirable qualities which he might possess, for no child could by nature possess any desirable qualities. He had to receive all good from outside himself, from education—and ultimately from the Holy Spirit.
>
> The problem of discipline was to make an evil-natured but at least partly rational animal act against his nature and according to his reason.[32]

It should be mentioned, parenthetically, that colonial fathers retained control over their sons for a much longer period than they do today. In his study of Andover, Massachusetts, Greven found that parental control continued long after the sons were married:

> A fundamental characteristic of most first-generation families was the prolonged exercise of paternal authority and influence over sons. Long after the sons' marriages, which were often delayed until men were in their late 20's, they remained economically dependent upon their fathers, who usually continued to own and control the land on which their sons had settled.[33]

---

* Even when public schools did emerge, they tended to be of the fabled one-room variety. In a typical one-room country school, teen-agers would be studying Latin and Greek in preparation for college; 9- and 10-year-olds would be reading history and geography; still younger children would be trying to master arithmetic and spelling; and at the bottom rung, the beginners were being taught the alphabet! How a single teacher could keep all the students occupied and still maintain discipline remains something of a pedagogical mystery.

[32] Morgan, *The Puritan Family*, p. 97.
[33] Philip J. Greven, Jr., *Four Generations: Population, Land, and Family in Colonial Andover, Massachusetts*, Ithaca, New York, Cornell University Press, 1970, pp. 98–99.

In the last analysis, what can be said about the child-rearing practices of the Colonial era as compared to those of today? Unfortunately, there is no yardstick of comparison available—albeit the results would be most interesting. For the fact is that the colonists were not overly concerned with developing the child's "personality"; indeed, the term had not even been coined at that time. The colonial child was reared on a diet of hard work, respect for authority, love of country, and faith in God. The child of today is more likely to be exposed to a fare of extended formal education, belief in the importance of the individual, respect for the right to personal happiness, and faith in the efficacy of group discussion.

Psychiatrists would probably contend that current child-rearing and educational practices are superior to those of the Colonial period; at the same time, most of our forebears, puzzled by the "freedom" accorded today's children, would probably frown on present practices. Unfortunately, to repeat, there are no clear-cut criteria by which the two systems can be compared. It may be that colonial methods would break down in modern society, and it is quite possible that current child-training concepts would have disrupted colonial equilibrium.

Another interpretation would be that from Colonial times to the present, our society has swung from one extreme to the other: from an excessive preoccupation with discipline to an overemphasis on permissiveness. Fortunately—or unfortunately—there is enough difference of opinion today on "how to raise your child" that parents can utilize the method that best fits their own predilections.

SEXUAL PROBLEMS

If history tells us anything about human sex behavior, it is that all societies, in every stage of development, have had "sex problems"—and colonial America was no exception. In assessing the magnitude of the problem, however, different historians have come up with different answers. Morgan goes so far as to say that "the Puritans became inured to sexual offenses, because there were so many. The impression one gets . . . is that many of the early New Englanders possessed a high degree of virility and very few inhibitions."[34] Other historians, such as

---

[34] Edmund Morgan, "The Puritans and Sex," in Michael Gordon (ed.), *The American Family in Social-Historical Perspective*, New York, St. Martin's Press, 1973, pp. 285–286.

Howard, Calhoun, and Greven—working with legal records involving fornication and illegitimacy—found a much lower incidence of illicit intercourse.[35]

The fact is that only in recent years has sex come to be accepted as a topic of polite conversation. By the same token, sociological surveys inquiring into the intimate details of people's sex lives are also of recent origin. Because sex was neither discussed nor surveyed in the colonies, there is no way of determining what percentage of the population indulged—or how often they indulged—in such actions as fornication, adultery, premarital petting, and other forms of erotic activity that would have been considered immoral.

On the other hand, there is little doubt that the *social climate* in the colonies was far different from today's. Three points, in particular, stand out: (1) those who engaged in nonmarital sex activity were likely to feel guilty about it; (2) sexual immorality, when discovered, was widely publicized; and (3) the individuals concerned were subjected to harsh social and legal penalties.

The colonists also condemned certain activities that are often taken for granted today. Holding hands in public, open displays of affection, and similar acts were frowned upon; in fact, kissing in public was considered a criminal offense. "A classic example," reports Train, "was that of Captain Kemble, who returning home after a long voyage, kissed his wife on the front steps and was promptly lodged in the stocks."[36]

Given the severe moral climate of the day, it hardly seems likely that sex was a major colonial problem. Perhaps a fair overall assessment would be that sexual irregularity was a recurrent headache and, as such, has probably received an undue amount of attention from writers of historical fiction.

From all reports, the servant classes accounted for more than their share of sex problems, one reason being that marriage (or any other kind of sexual outlet) was generally denied them. Under contract for a certain number of years, the "covenant servant" would work until he was financially able to fend for himself.

> Theoretically, no servant had a right to a private life. His time, day or night, belonged to his master, and both religion and law required that he obey his master scrupulously. But neither religion nor law could restrain the sexual impulses of youth, and if those impulses could not be expressed in marriage, they had to be given vent outside marriage.[37]

---

[35] See, for example, Greven, *op. cit.* pp. 113 ff.

[36] Arthur Train, *Puritan's Progress,* New York, Charles Scribner's Sons, 1931, p. 347.

[37] Morgan, "The Puritans and Sex," p. 287.

Colonial court records include any number of sex offenses involving covenant servants, but one of the most bizarre is that reported by Carson, wherein "one Hackett, a servant in Salem . . . was found in buggery with a cow, upon the Lord's day. Man and cow were executed."[38]

Homosexuality was apparently a minor issue, which is somewhat surprising in view of the severe shortage of women in many of the colonial frontier sections. It is possible that the practice was simply cloaked in secrecy and was more prevalent than is commonly realized. Yet it is difficult to believe that the conspiracy of silence would have been almost 100 percent successful. Actually, there were laws against sodomy (anal intercourse), but they were seldom invoked, so that in the absence of other evidence it seems reasonable to suppose that homosexuality was not considered a serious problem.

Prostitution was likewise of little concern to the colonists since, on an organized basis, it was practically nonexistent. Organized prostitution flourishes in large cities, and America had not yet become urbanized. Even as late as 1790, a full 95 percent of the population was rural. In the cities that did exist, the European custom of keeping mistresses was occasionally reported. But even this upper-class practice was rare enough (or so well concealed) that it was of little social concern.

Documentary evidence indicates that the two problems most seriously regarded by the colonists were premarital coitus and adultery.

Premarital Coitus. There were two counterforces at work in the colonies with respect to sex before marriage. On the one hand, rules were strict and were rigidly enforced—and the young people knew it. On the other hand, the custom of *betrothal* meant that the couple were one short step removed from matrimony. This semimarital state offered much temptation, and at least some opportunity, to indulge in premarital sex relations, and it is little wonder that certain couples succumbed.

There are no satisfactory statistics on the incidence or frequency of premarital coitus in the Colonial era. The data that do exist are often difficult to interpret. There also seems to be a substantial variation from time to time and place to place. Howard quotes court figures for Suffolk County, Massachusetts, which indicate that, for the period 1726–1780, fornication cases averaged around 15 a year.[39] In Greven's study of colonial Andover,

---

[38] Carson, *op. cit.*, p. 6.
[39] George Howard, *A History of Matrimonial Institutions*, Chicago, University of Chicago Press, 1904, Vol. II, p. 193.

illegitimacy records and fornication cases suggested a low frequency of premarital coitus "compared to that of other times and places."[40]

In Demos' study of Bristol, Rhode Island, the proportion of couples who had their first child within eight months of marriage ranged from zero percent between 1680 and 1720 to a startling 49 percent between 1740 and 1760.[41]

The Puritans had an almost unwholesome tendency to confess their sexual sins, and records of some of these public confessions have also come down to us. Calhoun reports that "the records of Groton church show that of 200 persons owning the baptismal covenant from 1761 to 1775, no less than 66 confessed to fornication before marriage. . . . At Dedham, for the 25 years before 1781, twenty-five cases of unlawful cohabitation were publicly acknowledged."[42]

In the face of such divergent figures, about all that can be said concerning the incidence of premarital intercourse is that it was prevalent enough to cause some concern in the colonies. As Demos puts it: "There is no way to measure its incidence in quantitative terms, but it happened, and it happened with some regularity."[43] To which one might add: and it happened in spite of strict laws and relatively harsh penalties.

There is no doubt that premarital coitus was severaly dealt with in the colonies. A man who was found guilty of fornication was supposed to marry the woman, but marriage did not absolve either from punishment. The usual penalties were fines or "stripes" (lashes), and these were often imposed on both male and female. Betrothed couples who were found gulity of fornication were given lighter sentences than those who were not under precontract. There are court records, nevertheless, of couples who had been married for many years being punished for prenuptial fornication, such activity having been admitted during a public confessional.

Referring to the penalties imposed by the County Court of Suffolk, Massachusetts, between 1671 and 1680, Howard states that

21 out of 43 single women, and eight out of 13 single men, are sentenced to stripes alone, 19 of them receiving each from 15 to 40 lashes. Out of 20 married couples punished for prenuptial misconduct, 15

---

[40] Greven, op. cit., pp. 113–116.

[41] John Demos, "Families in Colonial Bristol, Rhode Island: An Exercise in Historical Demography," William and Mary Quarterly, Vol. XXV, 1968, p. 56.

[42] Calhoun, op. cit. pp. 133–134.

[43] Demos, A Little Commonwealth, p. 152.

are given the choice of fines or stripes, three are merely fined; and in no instance is whipping alone the penalty decreed.[44]

An interesting case of colonial punishment is the following, cited by Turner:

> In Hartford, Connecticut, in 1639, not only was Aaron Starke pilloried, whipped, and branded on the cheek for seducing Mary Holt, and ordered to pay ten shillings to her father, but he was ordered to marry her when both should be "fit for the condition." The Connecticut Code of Laws included compulsory marriage in its consolidated list of punishments![45]

Adultery and the Scarlet Letter. In some ways, colonial attitudes toward adultery are similar to those of the present era. The colonists considered adultery a more serious offense than premarital coitus, and this tradition has come down to us today. Premarital coitus was more prevalent among the colonists than was adultery, and this variance also persists at present. And finally, although both sexes were severely punished for adultery, women seem to have been more harshly treated than men, and—in a social sense, at least—this is still true.

The Puritans considered adultery a grave offense and they employed legal, as well as religious, sanctions. In almost all of the New England colonies, adultery was originally punishable by death, and court records indicate that several people (of both sexes) were actually executed for the offense.

By 1700, the death sentence seems to have been superseded by whipping, imprisonment, banishment, and branding. Branding was believed to be particularly effective as a deterrent, and the "scarlet letter"—later made infamous by Hawthorne's book of the same name—occupied a prominent place in colonial history. Under the Acts and Laws of Connecticut, to take but one example, we read that:

> Whosoever shall commit adultery with a Married Woman or one Betrothed to another Man, both of them shall be severely Punished, by Whipping on the naked Body, and Stigmatized or Burnt on the Forehead with the Letter *A*, on a hot Iron.
>
> And each of them shall wear a Halter about their Necks, on the outside of their Garments, during their Abode in this Colony, so as it may be Visible. And as often as either of them shall be found without

---

[44] Howard, *op. cit.,* Vol. II, pp. 188–189.

[45] Turner, *op. cit.,* p. 74.

their Halters, worn as aforesaid, they shall, upon Information and Proof of same . . . be Whipt, not exceeding Twenty Stripes.[46]

Unfortunately for those involved, there was no feasible way to atone for adultery once the above penalty was imposed. Branding was permanent, and when the scarlet letter was affixed to a halter or "sewed upon the upper garments," it was presumably to be worn until death. (Pennsylvania had a bizarre set of laws pertaining to adultery. The Great Law of 1682 provided that anyone who "shall defile the marriage bed" be publicly whipped and imprisoned one year for the first offense. For the second offense the punishment was imprisonment for life. But under the Pennsylvania Act of 1705, a third offender was to be marked with an *A* branded on his forehead with a hot iron. Exactly how an adulterer could become a third offender after having spent his life in jail for the second offense is something for the legal mind to ponder!)

In passing, it might be mentioned that the problem of incest gave the colonists some concern. There is no way of estimating how much incest there really was, but the laws were just as severe as for adultery. In most of the New England colonies the only difference was use of the letter *I* instead of *A*. Court statistics indicate that all of the offenders were males; while the number of such cases was small, colonial records are so incomplete that figures mean little. And, of course, a variety of other sex offenses never came before the courts at all.

The Pendulum. There is little doubt that the colonists took a dim view of sexual irregularities. The Puritans believed that the only legitimate sexual outlet was in marriage—and even marital coitus was forbidden on Sunday.* They felt that sexual matters

---

* One of the fears of a colonial couple was that their child might be born on Sunday, for it was commonly held that a child born on Sunday was also conceived on Sunday. Some churches refused to baptize children born on the Lord's day!

If the prohibition against sex on Sunday seems strange to us, it should be remembered that almost everything was banned on Sunday. Even in Virginia—surely not the strictest of colonies—court records reveal indictments for the following "violations on the Sabbath": shelling corn; fetching shoes from the shoemaker; fishing; killing a deer; going on a journey; stripping tobacco; selling cider; driving a cart; dancing; and speaking too loudly in church. (For further details, see Philip Bruce, *Social Life in Old Virginia*, New York, Capricorn Books, 1965, pp. 35–37.)

[46] Howard, *op. cit.*, Vol. II, p. 173.

should not be discussed with children; in fact, the topic was more or less taboo among adults. And, judging by the harsh laws of the period, sexual transgressors were looked upon as a threat to society.

If, in retrospect, the attitude of the colonists seems to have been unduly strict, it should be kept in mind that, historically speaking, our present society has become relatively tolerant. It is only recently that sex education for children has become widespread, that sex has become a respectable topic of conversation, that sexual surveys have become rather common, and that sex outside marriage—in some quarters, at least—has come to be accepted. It is interesting to find that those who attempt to support traditional moral codes are often referred to as "puritanical."

The writer knows from experience that college students tend to look aghast at the severity of the colonial sex codes. But, in all likelihood, the colonists would be equally aghast at our own! For the fact of the matter is that customs and laws which "work" in one historical era may fail in another. The permissive–restrictive pendulum seems to swing back and forth. To be effective, sexual codes must meet the needs of both the individual and society, and each generation tries to decide for itself where the point of balance lies.

SELECTED READINGS

Barker-Benfield, Ben, "The Spermatic Economy: A 19th-Century View of Sexuality," in Michael Gordon (ed.), *The American Family in Social-Historical Perspective*, New York, St. Martin's Press, 1973, pp. 336–372.

Calhoun, Arthur W., *A Social History of the American Family*, 3 vols., New York, Barnes & Noble, Inc., 1944.

Chamberlain, Samuel, *Open House in New England*, New York, Bonanza Books, 1968.

de Mause, Lloyd (ed.), *The History of Childhood*, New York, The Psychohistory Press, 1974.

Demos, John, *A Little Commonwealth: Family Life in Plymouth Colony*, New York, Oxford University Press, 1970.

———, "Developmental Perspectives on the History of Childhood," *Journal of Interdisciplinary History*, Autumn, 1971, pp. 315–327.

Erikson, K. T., *Wayward Puritans: A Study in the Sociology of Deviance*, New York, John Wiley & Sons, Inc., 1968.

Farber, Bernard, *Guardians of Virtue: Salem Families in 1800*, New York, Basic Books, Inc., 1972.

Frost, J. William, *The Quaker Family in Colonial America*, New York, St. Martin's Press, 1973.

Gordon, Michael (ed.), *The American Family in Social-Historical Perspective*, New York, St. Martin's Press, 1973.

Greven, Philip J., Jr., *Four Generations: Population, Land, and Family in Colonial Andover, Massachusetts*, Ithaca, New York, Cornell University Press, 1970.

Hall, Peter, "Marital Selection and Business in Massachusetts Merchant Families, 1700–1900," in Rose Laub Coser (ed.), *The Family: Its Structures and Functions*, New York, St. Martin's Press, 1974, pp. 226–240.

Howard, George, *A History of Matrimonial Institutions*, 3 vols., Chicago, University of Chicago Press, 1904.

Keyssar, Alexander, "Widowhood in 18th-Century Massachusetts: A Problem in the History of the Family," *Perspectives in American History*, Vol. VIII, 1974.

Klein, Randolph S., *Portrait of an Early American Family*, Philadelphia, University of Pennsylvania Press, 1975.

Lantz, Herman; Britton, Margaret; Scott, Raymond; and Snyder, Eloise, "Pre-Industrial Patterns in the Colonial Family in America: A Content Analysis of Colonial Magazines," *American Sociological Review*, June, 1968, pp. 413–426.

Lockridge, Kenneth, *A New England Town The First Hundred Years: Dedham, Massachusetts, 1636–1736*, New York, W. W. Norton & Company, Inc., 1970.

Lynes, Russell, *The Domesticated Americans*, New York, Harper & Row, 1963.

Morgan, Edmund, *Virginians at Home*, Charlottesville, The University Press of Virginia (Dominion Books), 1963.

————, *The Puritan Family*, New York, Harper & Row, 1966.

Reiss, Ira, *Family Systems in America*, Hinsdale, Illinois, The Dryden Press, 1976. See Chapter Six, "Courtship in America," pp. 73–91.

Seward, Rudy Ray, "The Colonial Family in America: Toward a Socio-Historical Restoration of Its Structure," *Journal of Marriage and the Family*, February, 1973, pp. 58–70.

Smith, Daniel Scott, "The Demographic History of Colonial New England," *Journal of Economic History*, March, 1972, pp. 165–183.

————, "Parental Power and Marriage Patterns: An Analysis of Historical Trends in Hingham, Massachusetts," *Journal of Marriage and the Family*, August, 1973, pp. 419–428.

Smith, Elmer L., *Bundling: A Curious Courtship Custom*, Lebanon, Pennsylvania, Applied Arts Publishers, 1969.

Turner, E. S., *A History of Courtship*, New York, E. P. Dutton and Company, Inc., 1955.

Wells, Robert V., "Demographic Change and the Life Cycle of American Families," *Journal of Interdisciplinary History*, Autumn, 1971, pp. 273–282.

Weslager, C. A., *The Log Cabin in America*, New Brunswick, New Jersey, Rutgers University Press, 1969.

Willison, George, *Saints and Strangers*, New York, Reynal and Hitchcock, 1945.

Wright, Louis B., *The Cultural Life of the American Colonies, 1607–1763*, New York, Harper & Brothers, 1958.

Yankelovitch, Daniel, *The New Morality*, New York, McGraw-Hill Book Company, 1974.

II

American Experiments and Minorities

5

Experimental Family Organization I—
The Rappites: No Sex, No Marriage

ALTHOUGH THE PRIMARY emphasis in the present volume is on the mainstream of American family life, there have been any number of "experimental" groups, each with a distinctive type of marital organization. Some of these so-called utopias failed in their endeavors and are no longer part of the American scene. Others are still in existence, even though their family experimentation was a failure. In both instances, the story is a fascinating one.

Within the confines of a standard text, it is not possible to give extensive treatment to all the various experimental groups in question. Instead, two of the more significant examples—the Rappites and the Oneida Community—have been singled out for analysis. They have been chosen because they represent the extremes in family experimentation. The Rappites renounced sex and marriage altogether, whereas in the Oneida Community all men were considered to be married to all women, with full sexual privileges thereof.

Let us turn first to the Rappites. . . .

HISTORY AND GEOGRAPHY

There were a number of Pietist groups that left Germany in the nineteenth century to avoid persecution, and many of them settled in America. Zoar, founded by Joseph Bimeler; Amana, founded by Christian Metz; Harmony, founded by George Rapp—all are examples of utopian "experimentation" made possible by American insistence on religious freedom. Of these groups, Harmony not only was the most unusual but—paradoxically—was the longest-lasting. The Rappites, as they came to be called, endured for a full 100 years, 1805–1905.

Early Beginnings. George Rapp was born in Württemberg, Germany, in 1757. Like his father before him, he operated a small farm. However, he took an early interest in the Bible and before long was preaching on Sundays in his own house to groups of friends and neighbors. So far as the regular clergy were concerned, Rapp's actions amounted to heresy, and both he and his followers were fined and imprisoned on numerous occasions. But in spite of the continued persecution (or perhaps because of it!) the Rappites grew in number. Before the turn of the century, no less than 300 families were listening to the biblical exhortations of "Father Rapp."

Although Rapp taught his followers to obey the law and pay taxes—to the church as well as to the state—he insisted that they had the right to worship when, where, and how they saw fit. As Duss puts it:

> The basic theology of these rebels was the principle of the conscience—that each individual had the potential power of communicating directly with God, and therefore the individual was divinely ordained to judge most things for himself. Like the Quakers, these humble folk saw a spark of the Divine—and Inner Light—in all men. . . .
>
> Their chief objection to attending church was that it did not permit the individual to express himself as the spirit of God moved him. And for this reason they wished to be allowed to worship in their own homes in small groups where all could talk freely.[1]

For spreading these beliefs, Father Rapp was branded a "separatist" by the church hierarchy, a term he was more than willing to accept. At the same time, he came to realize that religious freedom would be found in the New World rather than the Old, and in 1803, accompanied by his son John, he set sail for America.

To the New World. After landing in Baltimore, the Rapps examined sites in Maryland, Ohio, and Pennsylvania, finally settling for 5,000 acres of virgin land just north of Pittsburgh. During the next two years, some 750 Rappites sailed from Germany to join their leader in the wilderness of Pennsylvania.

For the most part, the followers of George Rapp were farmers and mechanics. They were excellent workers and in no time at all had cleared several hundred acres, erected dozens of log houses, put up a church, school, and gristmill, as well as a variety of

---

[1] John S. Duss, *The Harmonists: A Personal History*, reprint ed., Ambridge, Pennsylvania, The Harmonie Associates, Inc., 1970, pp. 10–11.

barns and workshops. It is not known whether their communitarian plans were laid in Germany, but on February 15, 1805, they "formally and solemnly organized themselves into the 'Harmony Society,' agreeing to throw all their possessions into a common fund; to adopt a uniform and simple dress and style of house; to keep henceforth all things in common; and to labor for the common good of the whole body."[2]

There were some economic difficulties, to be sure. At the outset they experienced some severe winters, and their food supply ran low. It was difficult to get credit in Pittsburgh, and at one point the Society had to resort to food rationing. Generally speaking, however, the Rappites did well at their Pittsburgh site. Their communistic economy soon began to flourish, they earned the respect of their neighbors, and they developed strong feelings of group solidarity.

The one major drawback was that they were miles from the nearest river. Since their markets were accessible mainly by water, they decided to move. They bought 30,000 acres of land in the Wabash Valley, Indiana, and in 1814–1815 the entire Harmony Society—now numbering some 800 members—settled in the Hoosier state. As Duss puts it, they "had outgrown their original location."[3]

As at Pittsburgh, they erected scores of houses, barns, and workshops and soon had several thousand acres of land under cultivation. Somehow or other, though, climatic conditions in the Wabash Valley were unsatisfactory; at least, an unduly large proportion of the membership came down with "chills and fever." Also, their neighbors proved to be unfriendly. While the Rappites spoke some English, their basic language was German —and in Indiana, German was looked upon as a foreign tongue. At any rate, in 1824–1825 George Rapp and his followers moved again—for the last time. Their final move took them to Economy, Pennsylvania, not far from their original Pittsburgh site. For their move up the Ohio River, they actually built their own steamship, the *William Penn!*

Economy. Economy not only was their final location, but also proved to be the best of the three. They were now quite close to the Ohio River; the topography was good; and they were back in German-speaking territory. It should be pointed out that

[2] Charles Nordhoff, *The Communistic Societies of the United States,* New York, Dover Publications, Inc., 1966 ed., p. 71.

[3] Duss, *op. cit.,* p. 34.

Pennsylvania was then virtually a German-speaking state. As one historian notes, "Even the laws and school reports were printed in German. The Harmonists did not feel foreign there, and they had friends in many parts of the state—and above all, in the Legislature. Not all these friends were German or of German descent, but most of them certainly were."[4]

The next few decades would see the Rappites reach their greatest level of development. During this period they were known as "the utopia of the nineteenth century." But, in fact, they had already achieved a remarkable record. To repeat an oft-quoted statement, in just over two decades they had cleared three forests and built three towns!

LIFE STYLE

The Rappites lived simply, but well. Aside from the first year or two, there was always plenty of food; clothing was ample; and the houses were reasonably comfortable. For the most part, the life style of the members was marked by uniformity rather than variability. Houses, for example, were all about the same size and were fairly similar in appearance. The only exception was George Rapp's dwelling. The Great House, as it was called, was built especially for him and, since it was used to entertain visitors, was much larger than the others.

(Economy itself was neatly laid out, with the streets running at right angles to the Ohio River. Each thoroughfare was bordered by a brick sidewalk. Houses, workshops, and other buildings were extremely well constructed; indeed, many of them are still standing today. The net impression one receives upon entering the town is that of orderliness, block planning, and quiet strength.)

Although they did not make a fetish of it, clothing styles were also uniform throughout the Society. Knoedler, who was born and raised in Old Economy, writes that "on weekdays the men wore dark trousers, short blue jackets, and tall broad-brimmed hats. Women dressed in dark, heavy skirts and light waists, or in full-skirted clothes, and covered their heads with blue Normandy caps. On Sundays the men donned long coats and the women wore gowns and bonnets."[5]

---

[4] Karl Arndt, *George Rapp's Harmony Society, 1785–1847*, Philadelphia, University of Pennsylvania Press, 1965 revised ed., Rutherford, Madison and Teaneck, Fairleigh Dickinson University Press, 1972, pp. 181–182.

[5] Christiana F. Knoedler, *The Harmony Society, A 19th Century Utopia*, New York, Vantage Books, 1954, pp. 7–8.

Hoover makes this interesting observation:

The shops along the cobblestone street, between the Music Hall and the river, were always busy. It was said in the Society that the tailor looked not at people but saw only what they were wearing, since he was responsible for providing every member with well made clothing of good quality, albeit of exactly the same style. Likewise, the cobbler saw only their shoes, and the hatter what they were wearing on their heads.[6]

The Rappites lived in normal family style, the average household consisting of from four to eight people. Each family did its own cooking, with the women preparing the meals and taking care of the housekeeping, while the men worked in the fields or in the shops. The town itself contained a variety of stores and services, including a bakery, laundry, slaughterhouse, shoemaker, grocery, barbershop, etc. No money changed hands, of course. In true communistic fashion, members were given according to their need, not their ability. Hoover writes as follows:

The Harmony Society store was always a busy place. Each family made out a list of its needs and presented it directly, or through a foreman. Not a cent of money passed hands. Life with the Harmony Society entailed no bills, no rentals, no house payments, no mortgages, no accumulation of money, no lack of money.

The agreement made with Father Rapp was that each member was to contribute his or her service as needed. In turn, each member would be cared for as long as he or she lived. Spiritual as well as material nurture was to be provided by Father Rapp.[7]

The Harmony Society also had its own school, and both boys and girls were taught the traditional "three R's." In addition, the youngsters were given instruction in the German language. It should be kept in mind, however, that the Rappites were basically farmers and craftsmen, and their entire economy rested on these two supports. When a boy reached the age of 14, therefore, he was taught a craft or a trade. While his apprenticeship might last for several years, he was more or less assured of a marketable skill. George Rapp was insistent on this point, believing that if a young person decided to leave the Society—and some did— he should be able to make his own way in the world.

It was Rapp's wish, also, that the Society be totally self-sufficient, a goal that was largely achieved. Every adult did some

---

[6] Gladys L'Ashley Hoover, *River to River,* Rimersburg, Pennsylvania, Pennsylvania Record Press, 1974, p. 58.
[7] *Ibid.,* pp. 58–59.

sort of work *with his or her hands,* and since the workday ran from 6:00 A.M. to 6:00 P.M., the membership was super-productive. They were also thrifty—and ingenious.

> They did not believe in waste of any kind. When there was any grease left over from cooking, it was taken to the factory and used in making soap.
>
> Apple parings were saved for jelly.
>
> In the fall, the sauerkraut would be made. Each household made enough for its own use, but the Society also sold much of it.
>
> On these occasions the kraut would be cut and stomped. Several boys, about 10 to 13 years of age, would be chosen to do the stomping. The women prepared the boys for this task. They were very particular in this respect, as the boys took turns stomping the kraut with their bare feet. . . .[8]

Productivity. The Harmonists not only achieved self-sufficiency but, over the years, were able to produce a variety of goods for sale to the outside. George Rapp's adopted son, Frederick, was in charge of the Society's business component, and he was a truly remarkable man. Indeed, in many ways he and Father Rapp were co-leaders. It was Frederick who was the chief architect and town-planner, and it was he who was responsible for all of the Society's economic and legal transactions. John Duss, who was for many years a trustee in Old Economy, states simply that "as an organizer and executive, Frederick was a born genius."[9]

At any rate, Frederick's master plan called for the Society to develop gradually from an agricultural to a handicraft and then to a factory-type economy. And so successful were the Harmonists that it soon became necessary to hire outside help for their various economic enterprises. Included in their output were cotton and woolen goods, tools, flour, shoes, silk, and a wide variety of agricultural products. Interestingly enough—although they used it sparingly themselves—one of their most famous products was whiskey!

There is no doubt that, contrary to most other communistic experiments of the nineteenth century, the Rappites' economic system was a success. In 1818, a scant dozen years after their founding, they were able—by unanimous consent—to burn their "account book," which recorded the various amounts each family had originally contributed to the communal fund!

As a matter of fact, according to Duss, in several economic areas the Society actually controlled the Pittsburgh market to

---

[8] Knoedler, *op. cit.,* pp. 132–133.

[9] Duss, *op. cit.,* p. 15.

such an extent that charges of monopoly were made by the local press. One paper went so far as to advocate the "total dissolution of the Society by Act of Legislature."[10]

Group Solidarity. In other ways, too, the Harmonists must be regarded as a success. They held together for 100 years, during most of which time they were both liked and respected by their neighbors. Social problems such as crime, delinquency, and alcoholism were unknown in the Society. Yet, as Holloway points out, "These people were obviously not fanatics. They did not find it necessary to torture themselves or to deny themselves beauty and simple joys—and whether or not the picture of bliss is overdrawn, there can be no doubt that they were happy and contented people who lived quietly and pleasantly."[11]

It is true that the Rappites did not start from scratch. Arndt reminds us that:

> Through long acquaintance in Germany they knew each other and their leaders, and knew what would be expected of them. This was not a band of strangers getting together on some untried experiment. . . .
>
> The close intimacy growing out of village life in Würtenberg (and most of them came from small villages in which they and their ancestors had lived for centuries) instilled a sense of confidence in each other.[12]

But it was not their common background alone that accounted for their success. Harmonist success stemmed from a combination of factors: their common background and ancestry; their proclivity for hard work; their belief in God's word as taught by Father Rapp; and their ability to take advantage of the economic opportunities inherent in a free society.

CELIBACY

In 1807, just two years after the Harmony Society was founded, there occurred one of the most curious events in modern social history. The Rappites renounced both sex and marriage! Henceforth, all members would lead a celibate life. Although the full details are not known, the step was apparently taken without

---

[10] Duss, *op. cit.*, p. 72.

[11] Mark Holloway, *Heavens on Earth: Utopian Communities in America, 1680–1880,* New York, Dover Publications, Inc., 1966, pp. 93–94.

[12] Arndt, *op. cit.*, pp. 75–76.

much debate. Holloway states that "no community ever changed from the married to the celibate state with such ease."[13]

Families continued to live together in the same household, as before, but with two striking changes: (1) husband and wife would no longer share the same bed, and (2) it was presumed that no children would be born within the Society. For a time, new families—often with children—were admitted, but, once they had attained membership, husband and wife renounced all sexual claims on each other.

Theoretically, at least, there was no surveillance or checking on the sexual activities of the members. When Nordhoff, who visited the community, asked the question: "What kind of watch or safeguard do you keep over the intercourse of the sexes?" the answer was crystal clear. "None at all," he was told. "It would be of no use. If you have to watch people, you had better give them up. We have always depended on the strength of our religious convictions."[14]

This was the essence of the celibacy stipulation; that is, it was not something imposed by the leadership. It was, rather, a voluntary agreement stemming from the inner convictions of the membership. Indeed, from all accounts, it was the younger members who initiated the celibacy program! Arndt puts it as follows:

> Although celibacy was not a requirement explicitly stated in the constitution or bylaws, there was no doubt that this state was the holier, and that holiness was the goal of the Society. . . .
>
> Those who succumbed to nature's temptation soon began to feel uncomfortable and were subjected to a feeling of inferiority, which usually resulted in their "voluntary" withdrawal from the Society.
>
> Celibacy had become the social custom, and the person who did not live the celibate life felt like the wedding guest who appeared without a wedding garment, even though the invitation did not specify that a "wedding garment" should be worn.[15]

In practice, nevertheless, some problems did arise. When the celibacy program first began, certain members left the Society —and, while some later returned, others did not. Also, there were some "mistakes." That is, there were some children born into the Society—much to Father Rapp's displeasure. These occurrences were infrequent, however, and after 1830 no births were reported.[16]

---

[13] Holloway *op. cit.*, p. 90.

[14] Nordhoff, *op. cit.*, p. 74.

[15] Arndt, *op. cit.*, p. 358.

[16] Duss, *op. cit.*, pp. 27–28.

It should also be mentioned that, while there was no "spying" as such, some controls were placed on the movement of members. Kanter notes that, especially in the early days, "members did not leave without consultation with their leaders, and then only for things unavailable in the community. The night watchman met each train and knew who was to arrive."[17] Muncy also mentions the role of the night watchman and states that:

> Fathers, who retained their positions as heads of households, were responsible for seeing to it that the rules regarding relations between sexes were not violated by members of their own families. The unmarried men and women, however, lived in separate dormitories and were carefully regulated.[18]

No less a person than Father Rapp apparently felt the brushes of temptation; while he never succumbed, he was evidently attracted to one Hildegard Mutschler. The affair has been rather well documented, the following being extracted from Muncy's account:

> George Rapp himself was not past casting an eye at a pretty girl. Hildegard Mutschler was very close to Father Rapp and he showered her with attention. Hildegard also received the attention of one Jacob Klein. Rapp became jealous, ordered Klein to leave Economy, and gave him a hundred dollars. Afterward, Hildegard had an affair with Conrad Feucht and eloped with him
>
> In a lengthy letter, dated September 2, 1829, Frederick Rapp took his father to task for familiarities with Hildegard and for his mourning over her departure, and for his numerous attempts to get in touch with her, unbeknown to her husband. Frederick wrote that he was glad that she was gone, since she was a detriment to the spiritual welfare of the community.[19]

Perhaps the most interesting account of the Hildegard Mutschler episode is contained in Lois Henderson's touching novel, *The Holy Experiment*, wherein the author brings to life the torturous struggle between the flesh and the spirit—as seen through the eyes of both Hildegard and her suitors.[20]

In contrast to the above imbroglio, some observers of the period felt that the appearance of the Rappite women was such as to

---

[17] Rosabeth Moss Kanter, *Commitment and Community: Communes and Utopias in Sociological Perspective*, Cambridge, Massachusetts, Harvard University Press, 1972, p. 85.

[18] Raymond Lee Muncy, *Sex and Marriage in Utopian Communities*, Bloomington, Indiana University Press, 1973, p. 42

[19] *Ibid.*, p. 45.

[20] Lois T. Henderson, *The Holy Experiment*, Hicksville, New York, Exposition Press, 1974.

create sexual *disinterest* on the part of the men. William Faux contended that the women "are intentionally disfigured and made as ugly as it is possible for art to make them."[21] Most writers, however, made no mention of this fact, and it seems likely that —except for their style of dress—Harmonist men and women looked much the same as any other group.

In spite of the problems that undoubtedly occurred, it is clear that the celibacy requirement was generally adhered to. The trouble with the Harmony Society, as we shall see, was not that celibacy failed, but that it succeeded!

Why did the Rappites embark on such a sexually severe way of life, and why did they continue it? The members themselves were fond of saying that celibacy promoted good health and longevity. And, in point of fact, there were any number of octogenarians among them, George Rapp himself living to the age of 90. (Whether sexual abstinence had anything to do with it is another matter.) Harmonists also liked to point out that their Society lasted longer than those communistic groups that permitted sexual relations. Also true. But the real reason for their adoption of celibacy was their religious orientation.

Religious Justification. It was a belief of George Rapp and his followers, adduced from the Bible, that Adam was originally a dual human being, i.e., that he contained both male and female elements ("And God said, Let us make man in our image, after our likeness: and let them have dominion. . . . So God created man in his own image; . . . male and female created he them." Genesis 1:26–27). It was not until later, in the Garden of Eden, that the Lord fashioned a female from Adam's rib. From this sequence, it followed logically—to the Rappites, at least—that celibacy was the path most pleasing to God.

Another Harmonist belief—and one that pervaded their entire way of life—was that the coming of Christ was near at hand. When this occurred, the millennium would prevail, whereby Christ would reign on earth for 1,000 years. Only the chosen few would reap the immediate benefits of salvation (the others would be on probation) and there was no doubt in the minds and hearts of the Rappites that they would be the chosen ones. They would be chosen because they had lived celibate lives, had practiced economic communism, and had otherwise followed the commandments of Jesus.

---

[21] Quoted in Muncy, *op. cit.*, pp. 42–43.

In practice, belief in the millennium softened the impact of celibacy, for, if Christ's return to earth was imminent, then the abstention from sex and marriage was only a temporary phenomenon. Also, it appears that the adoption of celibacy in 1807 grew out of a desire for more self-discipline, particularly on the part of the younger members. This sacrifice of sex, in turn, served to solidify the we-feeling of the group since, in effect, they "were all in it together."

Another feeling that permeated the Society was the conviction that, by practicing celibacy, the members were able to give "all their heart and body" to God. To this end, they were fond of quoting from I Corinthians 7:33, 32—"But He that is married careth for the things that are of the world, how he may please his wife. . . . He that is unmarried careth for the things that belong to the Lord, how he may please the Lord."

111

It should be mentioned that, in spite of their celibacy and in spite of the fact that few children were born into the Society, the Rappites did not proselytize. They never actively sought to convert anyone, even though it was only through conversions that they could survive. In practice, they received applications from all over the world and, *had they desired,* they would have had no trouble expanding. As it turned out, they severely limited their acceptances, and this in turn led to their demise.

The Harmonists had nothing against children, incidentally. Although the Society's birthrate was near zero, a number of youngsters were adopted. On Nordhoff's visit, he found "25 or 30 children of various ages, adopted by the Society and apprenticed to it."[22] All children attended the Harmonist school until they were 14, whereupon they were permitted to choose whatever line of community work appealed to them.

GEORGE RAPP

The leader of the Harmonists was a tall, robust man who, from the start of his career in Germany to his final days in Pennsylvania, remained a controversial figure. Some saw him as a brilliant leader and organizer. Others felt that he was little more than a dictator, who held his followers together through tyrannical methods.

Perhaps the fairest way to describe George Rapp would be to say that he was both an effective leader and an unpredictable

---

[22] Nordhoff, *op. cit.,* p. 68.

The Great House in Old Economy Village, Pennsylvania. (Harmonie Associates)

personality. It may be that the two traits tend to go together. Whether they do or not, the Harmonist leader did have some perplexing qualities. For example, despite the communistic nature of the Society, Rapp's own dwelling—the Great House—was set apart from the others. True, its large size was necessary because of the fact that visitors were housed there. But Father Rapp reportedly wanted the building "set apart from the disturbances of the community" so that he "could keep his line of communication with God clear."[23]

The Harmonist leader's "apartness," however, evidently did not keep him from keeping a close watch on his followers. Kanter reports that he "used a series of underground tunnels to appear suddenly and mysteriously before members!"[24]

George Rapp's escapade with Hildegard Mutschler has already been mentioned. In addition, he also had some serious run-ins with his son John. But irrespective of the importance of the foregoing factors, it does seem that George Rapp brooked no interference with his running of the community. He was the judge,

---

[23] Quoted in Muncy, *op. cit.*, p. 42.

[24] Kanter *op. cit.*, p. 107. Duss, however, denies the report (*op. cit.*, p. 59).

the jury, and the supreme court all rolled into one—and once he had made a decision there was no appeal. As Tyler puts it:

> Father Rapp preached, and to him confession was made by all who desired admission to the colony. No quarrel was allowed to go overnight unsettled, and everyone who had sinned confessed to Rapp before sleeping. It was a patriarchal church, and its pastor looked the part he had created for himself.[25]

On the other hand, dictatorial or not, George Rapp had what is perhaps the most important of all leadership traits: the ability to achieve results. In the last analysis, he attained the goal he had set for himself—the establishment of a successful, communistic, celibate organization. His own Society, furthermore, was without crime, divorce, poverty, and other social problems that plague society at large. And while the Harmonists were not without dissension, there was really but one major schism during the group's 100-year existence.

113

On a personal level, there is no doubt that most of the Harmonists revered George Rapp. The following statements, which were made to Nordhoff on his visit to the Society, speak for themselves.[26]

"George Rapp was a man before whom no evil could stand."

. . .

"When I met him in the street, if I had a bad thought, it flew away."

. . .

"He knew everything—how to do it, what was the best way."

. . .

"He was never idle, not even a quarter of an hour."

. . .

"He was a good man, with true, honest eyes. He always labored against selfishness, to serve the brethren and the Lord."

The last statement is revealing, for it is sometimes forgotten that George Rapp was an extremely devout man. Indeed, religion dominated his entire life. As a staunch millenarian, of course, he was convinced that Christ would soon return to earth, and he often said that he lived only to present his followers to God. Little wonder that, while the Harmonists referred to one another as "Brother" or "Sister," they always referred to their leader as "Father Rapp." Some idea of his indomitable spirituality can be

---

[25] Alice Felt Tyler, *Freedom's Ferment*, New York, Harper & Row (Torchbooks), 1962, p. 124.
[26] Nordhoff, *op. cit.*, pp. 91–92.

seen from the fact that he preached two sermons on the Sunday preceding his death—at the age of 90!

One of the most illuminating statements about the Harmonist leader appeared shortly after his death, when the Pittsburgh papers penned their eulogies. The *Pittsburgh Morning Post* referred to him as "the greatest communist of the age," and added that he had left the world "respected and honored as a truly good man and a most venerable patriarch." The article goes on to say that:

> He was their instructor in morals and religion, their father, the friend in whom all confided and who was worthy of their confidence. Mr. Rapp retained his fine health and extraordinary mental vigor to the last; and has at length departed to a better world, leaving behind him a good name that will be long remembered and honored.[27]

THE "COUNT"

No description of the Rappites would be complete without mention of the one major split that occurred, thanks to the efforts of one Bernhard Muller, who went under the rather pretentious title of Count Maximilian de Leon. An imposing figure and a strong-willed leader in his own right, Count Leon remains one of the most perplexing figures in the history of the communal movement.

A German by birth, Count Leon was no count; in fact, he was an illegitimate child. (His father was a baron, his mother a seamstress.) As he grew up, however, he somehow learned the habits and mannerisms of the nobility. By the time he reached adulthood, he had impeccable manners, a courtly appearance, and a coterie of dedicated followers.

In 1831 Count Leon and his little band of disciples came to America and—under the pretext that they were staunch believers—were royally welcomed into the Harmony Society. There was nothing too unusual about this procedure. Father Rapp had admitted other immigrant groups, and there is every indication that he looked forward to Count Leon's arrival. The latter had scarcely settled in, however, before trouble started.

There are two versions of what caused the trouble. One version—by far the more popular—holds that Count Leon was a schemer and a conniver. No sooner had he gained admission to

---

[27] Quoted in Arndt, *op. cit.*, pp. 579–580.

the Society than he began to undermine George Rapp's leadership. Using his courtly bearing and his eloquence, he persuaded a portion of the "ignorant peasants" that they were entitled to a more interesting, more gratifying way of life. Among the rewards the Count promised them were better living conditions and certain worldly pleasures, including those of the marriage bed.

Count Leon and his followers denied all charges of obstructionism. They were quite ready to leave the Society peacefully, the Count contended, but they were dissuaded by a large number of the Harmonists. The latter, he said, were grossly dissatisfied with George Rapp's dictatorial leadership and economic materialism and looked upon him—Count Leon—as their savior.

One word led to another. The quarreling grew so bitter and the schism so sharp that George Rapp finally called for a vote on the part of the entire Society. When the ballots were counted, the tally showed that 500 members voted in favor of Father Rapp and 250 for Count Leon. Whereupon the Harmonist leader is reported to have proclaimed, from the Book of Revelation: "And the tail of the serpent drew the third part of the stars of heaven, and did cast them to the earth."

Although sharp and bitter, the quarrel lasted only a matter of months. In the summer of 1832 Count Leon and the 250 dissenters left the Society and withdrew to a site 10 miles away, where they set up their own organization. Known as the New Philadelphia Society, Count Leon's group was also based on communistic principles, albeit marriage was permitted.

In retrospect, it is difficult to unravel the pros and cons of the argument. On the one hand, there is little doubt that the Count was a *provocateur* and troublemaker. His title was one that he conferred upon himself, and he evidently had had a spotty record in Europe.

On the other hand, he could hardly have been the scoundrel that many writers made him out to be. Count Leon was, in fact, a well-spoken, knowledgeable person, who evidently could not resist giving his money away to the needy. Furthermore, while the Rappites were working-class people, they were anything but "ignorant peasants," and the fact that 250 of them chose to leave the Society suggests that there was more than mild dissatisfaction within the group.

As a matter of record, prior to the Count's arrival, it had been virtually impossible for a Harmonist to take legal action against the Society and remain a member in good standing.[28] At the

---

[28] Arndt, *op. cit.*, p. 481.

height of the fracas, on the other hand, both the Rappite forces and the followers of Count Leon were filing legal suits against one another. And, while eventually all court actions were withdrawn, George Rapp agreed to give the seceders the sum of $105,000, no small amount in those days.

The Count was a poor businessman, however, and he evidently frittered away the money; at least, the New Philadelphia Society lasted for less than a year. The money gone, Count Leon returned to the Harmonists in an effort to extract more funds, and for a while it appeared that the conflict might be resumed. But in spite of much bombast, the extraction effort failed—and the New Philadelphia Society folded. The Count and a few of his followers took off for Louisiana, where they attempted to establish a new community.

Whether their new venture might have succeeded is conjecturable, for in a matter of months Count Leon was dead of cholera —thus ending the career of a most enigmatic man.

DECLINE OF THE SOCIETY

It might be thought that the Count Leon affair would have had a deleterious effect on the Harmonists, but such does not seem to be the case. It is true that the episode led to some unfavorable publicity, and that the Society lost one-third of its membership. But it was Count Leon, not George Rapp, who bore the brunt of the newspapers' attacks. And those who departed undoubtedly comprised the disgruntled element. In consequence, the Count's foray may have had the unexpected result of strengthening the Society by tightening the bonds of group cohesion.

After Count Leon's group departed, the Harmony Society continued to flourish. Certain natural forces were at work, however, and they could not be denied. Frederick Rapp died in 1834, and—as was mentioned earlier—he was a giant in the community. It was Frederick who designed the buildings and the town layout for all three Harmonist settlements. It was Frederick who composed hymns and, in his father's absence, served as preacher. And, of course, it was Frederick who handled the bulk of the Society's business transactions. He died just short of his sixtieth birthday, and—as time would show—he was irreplaceable.

When his son died, George Rapp was 78 years old, and, although some of his followers may have felt that he would live forever, it was not to be. He passed away in 1847. Thus, in little over a decade the Harmonists lost their two top leaders. The

Society might or might not have survived the loss of one, but with two gone the road ran steadily downhill.

Before he died, Father Rapp had already designated the men who were to succeed him: Romelius Baker and Jacob Henrici. But while both were dedicated men, they lacked the spark and contagion of their former leader—and everybody knew it. By the time of the Civil War, only 200 members remained in the Society.

Lack of leadership was not the only reason for the downfall of the Harmonists. To survive, all groups must have new members, and, so long as the followers of George Rapp practiced celibacy, they were systematically blocking their own future. To compensate for their zero birthrate, they could have concentrated on adding new members, but this they did not do. On the contrary—and for reasons best known to themselves—as time went on they added fewer and fewer members.

Even if the Rappites had made a concerted effort to attract new blood, the results would have been problematical. For the fact of the matter was that attitudes toward sex were changing. In the backwash of the Puritan tradition, it had not been uncommon for sex to be equated with sin, especially where women were concerned. But, as the nineteenth century wore on, sex came to lose some of its sinful connotation, and it is probably no accident that celibate groups such as the Shakers and Harmonists fell by the wayside.

There were other reasons for the group's difficulties. In society at large, the Industrial Revolution was in full swing. The handicraft system was being replaced by assembly-line methods, and the Rappites did not have the facilities to compete with the large factory. Indeed, by the 1870's—with but a score of old people left—"the group could no longer maintain its self-sufficiency: it had to stop manufacturing and start buying."[29]

The Rappites did make some feeble attempts at survival. At one time they corresponded with the Zoarites and the Shakers —hoping, perhaps, to effect a merger—but nothing came of it. Also, toward the end, they accepted some new apprentices. But it was too late. By the 1890's, the end was clearly in sight. The Society was faced with operational difficulties, large debts, and a number of lawsuits by ex-members and would-be heirs.[30] In 1905, after 100 years of existence, the Harmony Society was formally dissolved, thus ending one of America's most unusual social experiments.

---

[29] Kanter, *op. cit.*, p. 145.
[30] *Ibid.*, p. 159.

George Rapp.
(Harmonie Associates)

During the final years—when it became obvious that the Harmonists were simply fading away—could they not have given up the practice of celibacy? The answer is no. As millenarians, they were committed to Christ's imminent return to earth, and their entire life was spent in preparation for the Great Event. As Jacob Henrici, Father Rapp's successor, put it:

> We firmly believe in a visible, personal reign of Christ on earth, and that His second advent will take place before the last member of our Society shall have passed away.[31]

During his visit in 1875, Nordhoff noted that the Rappites seldom discussed the future. When he raised the question as to what would become of the Society, he was told, simply, "The Lord will show us a way."[32]

Epilogue. The Harmony Society has long since gone, but the buildings—and perhaps the memories—still remain. Old Economy Village, as it is known, is situated at its original location, 18 miles northwest of Pittsburgh (Ambridge). The site includes

---

[31] Quoted in Arndt, *op. cit.,* p. 583.
[32] Nordhoff, *op. cit.,* p. 95.

6.7 acres of land and buildings and is administered by the Pennsylvania Historical and Museum Commission. Available for inspection are the Great House of George Rapp, the apothecary shop, church, cemetery, wine cellar, private homes and gardens, and a number of the handicraft shops. Old Economy Village is open seven days a week, all year long.

Several novels and plays have been written about the Rappites, including Gladys Hoover's *Man's Reach* and *River to River,* Lois Henderson's *The Holy Experiment,* and Victor Calverton's *Where Angels Dare to Tread.* The number of scholarly works on the subject runs into the hundreds. Those interested should consult the Selected Readings, which follow.

SELECTED READINGS

Algermissen, Konrad, *Christian Sects,* New York, Hawthorn Books, Inc., 1962.

Arndt, Karl J. R., *George Rapp's Harmony Society, 1785–1847,* Philadelphia, University of Pennsylvania Press, 1965.

Bestor, Arthur E., Jr., *Backwoods Utopias,* Philadelphia, University of Pennsylvania Press, 1950.

Blair, Don, *Harmonist Construction,* Indianapolis, Indiana Historical Society, 1964.

Catton, William R., "What Kind of People Does a Religious Cult Attract?" *American Sociological Review,* October, 1957, pp. 551–566.

Communal Studies Newsletter, January, 1976. (Published at Temple University, under the editorship of John A. Hostetler.)

DeLora, Jack R., and DeLora, Joann S., *Intimate Life Styles,* Pacific Palisades, California, Goodyear Publishing Company, 1975.

Ditzion, Sidney, *Marriage, Morals, and Sex in America,* New York, Bookman Associates, 1953.

Duss, John S., *The Harmonists: A Personal History,* reprint ed., Ambridge, Pennsylvania, The Harmonie Associates, Inc., 1970.

Feldman, Saul D., and Thielbar, Gerald W., *Life Styles: Diversity in American Society,* Boston, Little, Brown and Company, 1975.

Gormly, Agnes M. Hays, *Old Economy: The Harmony Society,* 1910, reprint ed., Sewickley, Pennsylvania, The Harmony Press, 1966.

Henderson, Lois T., *The Holy Experiment,* Hicksville, New York, Exposition Press, 1974.

Hinds, William A., *American Communities and Cooperative Societies*, New York, Corinth Books, 1961.

Holloway, Mark, *Heavens on Earth: Utopian Communities in America, 1680–1880*, New York, Dover Publications, Inc., 1966.

Hoover, Gladys L'Ashley, *River to River*, Rimersburg, Pennsylvania, Pennsylvania Record Press, 1974.

Hostetler, John A., *Communitarian Societies*, New York, Holt, Rinehart and Winston, Inc., 1974.

Kanter, Rosabeth Moss, *Commitment and Community: Communes and Utopias in Sociological Perspective*, Cambridge, Massachusetts, Harvard University Press, 1972.

———(ed.), *Communes: Creating and Managing the Collective Life*, New York, Harper & Row, 1973.

Kephart, William M., *Extraordinary Groups: The Sociology of Unconventional Life Styles*, New York, St. Martin's Press, 1976.

Knoedler, Christiana F., *The Harmony Society, A 19th Century Utopia*, New York, Vantage Books, 1954.

Kring, Hilda, "The Harmonists: A Folk-Cultural Approach," Ph.D. Dissertation, University of Pennsylvania, 1969.

Lockwood, Maren, "The Experimental Utopia in America," *Daedalus*, Spring, 1965, pp. 401–418.

Manuel, Frank E. (ed.), *Utopias and Utopian Thought*, Boston, Houghton Mifflin, 1966.

Muncy, Raymond Lee, *Sex and Marriage in Utopian Communities: 19th Century America*, Bloomington, Indiana University Press, 1973.

Nordhoff, Charles, *The Communistic Societies of the United States*, New York, Dover Publications, Inc., 1966.

Noyes, John Humphrey, *History of American Socialisms*, New York, Hillary House, 1961.

Reibel, Daniel B., *Bibliography of Items Related to the Harmony Society*, Old Economy, Ambridge, Pennsylvania, Pennsylvania Historical and Museum Commission, 1972.

Tyler, Alice Felt, *Freedom's Ferment*, New York, Harper & Row (Torchbooks), 1962.

Wells, J. Gipson, *Current Issues in Marriage and the Family*, New York, Macmillan Publishing Co., Inc., 1975.

Wilson, Bryan R., *Sects and Society*, Berkeley, University of California Press, 1963.

Wilson, William E., *The Angel and the Serpent: The Story of New Harmony*, Bloomington, Indiana University Press, 1964.

6

Experimental Family Organization II—
The Oneida Community: Group Marriage

THE HARMONY SOCIETY and the Oneida Community were alike in some ways, different in others. Both groups had a strong leader; both were communistic; both flourished during roughly the same period; and both experienced a major schism when a "conspiratorial" outsider was admitted.

On the other hand, whereas the Rappites were basically a foreign-born, immigrant group, the Oneidans were strictly "home-grown." The Rappites believed that Christ's second appearing was close at hand, while the Oneidans held that Jesus had already returned to earth. And whereas the followers of George Rapp renounced sex and marriage altogether, John Humphrey Noyes' followers—in a very real sense—glorified the sexual state. As a matter of fact, the Oneida Community may well be the most revolutionary family experiment this country has even seen.

ORIGINS

The story begins at Putney, Vermont, in 1831, where a fierce religious revival was in process. One of those deeply affected was John Humphrey Noyes, a 20-year-old graduate of Dartmouth College, who had been serving his apprenticeship in a local law office. Although Noyes attended the revival meetings with much skepticism, "the result was electrifying." Robertson goes on to state that:

> After four days of wrestling with Satan and the spirit of unbelief, "light gleamed upon his soul," and by nightfall he had decided to devote himself to the service and ministry of God. . . .

As he wrote in his diary, "Hitherto, the world; henceforth, God!" He vowed with all his inward strength that he would live in the "revival spirit and be a young convert forever."[1]

Forsaking the practice of law, Noyes entered the ministry, and upon graduation from Yale Theological Seminary in 1833, he was licensed to preach.

Although he was an avid reader of the Bible and held to what he termed a literal translation, Noyes could not bring himself to accept the orthodox religious teachings of his day. Rejecting the Calvinistic interpretation of the Bible and opposing the "miserable sinner" philosophy, John Humphrey Noyes preached that man was not depraved but was capable of living a sinless life. Basing his belief on certain scriptural passages, Noyes was convinced that Christ, whose second coming was awaited by so many, *had already returned to earth*, so that redemption, or liberation from sin, was an accomplished fact. The doctrine itself—the attainability of the sinless or perfect state—Noyes called "Perfectionism." For the spreading of this alleged heresy, his license to preach was revoked.

A small group had already begun to be attracted to the Perfectionist doctrine, however, in spite of its heterodox nature. Starting as a Bible class in 1839 with Noyes as the pivotal member, this small group of Perfectionists grew both in number and in scope. Their discussions centered on the idea of spiritual equality, a belief that eventually came to embrace both the economic and sexual spheres. In the Kingdom of God, all beings were to love one another equally. The accepted monogamous pattern of one man being married to one woman was looked upon by the Perfectionists as a sign of selfishness.

Carden writes that:

At first, Noyes' theology, comprehensive as it was, did not include the notion of the perfect community. He expected Perfectionism to spread through the regular churches and, eventually, to precipitate serious revisions of orthodox doctrine. However, he gradually realized that those churches would never agree with his conception of the perfect marriage, and that the form of marriage he advocated was impractical except in an isolated community.[2]

---

[1] Constance Noyes Robertson (ed.), *Oneida Community, An Autobiography, 1851–1876*, Syracuse, New York, Syracuse University Press, 1970, p. 3.
[2] Maren Lockwood Carden, *Oneida: Utopian Community to Modern Corporation*, Baltimore, The Johns Hopkins University Press, 1969, p. 16. Copyright © 1969 by The Johns Hopkins Press, Baltimore, Maryland 21218.

Accordingly, in 1846 the Putney Community was formed. Individual members followed a "share-the-wealth" type of economy in which private ownership was taboo. Paralleling their collectivist economy, adult members practiced sexual communism; that is, every adult male had marital privileges with every adult female, and vice versa. As Noyes explained it to outsiders, the Putneyites were simply following the example set by members of the Primitive Church between the time of Christ's ascension and his second appearance, which occurred in the year 70 A.D. Thus, the radical practice of *complex marriage* had its real beginning in New England—an area that had once been the heart of Puritanism!

As the Putney Community grew, Noyes kept busy spreading the Perfectionist gospel elsewhere, through both the printed and the spoken word. In many quarters he was looked upon as a fanatic and a heretic, and rumors soon spread concerning the "sexual promiscuity" of the Putneyites. There were, nevertheless, some converts to Noyes' brand of Perfectionism. As might be imagined, the citizens of Vermont were up in arms, and in 1847 Noyes was arrested and charged with adultery.

Released under bond, he did not wait to stand trial but fled southward. Had he chosen to fight the case in court, the outcome would doubtless have been of socio-historic interest. As it turned out, neither Noyes nor any of his Perfectionist followers were ever to stand trial for their marital practices.

Even as the Putney Community was being broken up, however, Noyes was reassembling his flock in central New York State. The new Community took shape in 1848 on the old Indian lands along Oneida Creek, and henceforth the Perfectionists were known as the Oneida Community. It was here that the most radical of all American marriage systems took root and, for several decades, flourished.

Starting again as a small group—no more than 20 or 30 persons in all—the Oneida Colony was barely able to survive the first few winters. The original members were primarily farmers and mechanics, and while their collectivist economy had certain advantages, they found it difficult to support a growing community solely from their land yields. Fortunately, one of their members, Sewell Newhouse, invented a steel trap, which turned out to be peerless in design. Demand for the product grew, and soon the major part of the Oneida economy came to be based on the manufacture of the now-famous traps. Thereafter, the group was without financial worry.

SOCIAL ORGANIZATION

What was there, in terms of social organization, that held the
Oneida Community together in the face of both internal
problems and external pressures? One integrating element was
the fact that practically the entire membership was housed under
one roof. Although, over the years, there were six different
branches and hundreds of members, the Perfectionists' home
base was at Oneida, New York. It was there that the original
communal home was built in 1849, to be replaced in 1862 by a
spacious brick building known as the Mansion House. In subsequent years, as the membership grew, wings were added as
needed. The building still stands, a striking architectural form
internally as well as externally.

Noyes helped both in the planning and in the actual construction, and while some might question the extent to which physical structure influences social organization, the Mansion House
would seem to be a case in point. That the members were well
aware of the integrating effects of the Mansion House can be
seen from the following Oneida song:

> We have built us a dome
> On our beautiful plantation,
> And we all have one home,
> And one family relation.

The Mansion House in Oneida, New York. (Oneida Ltd. Silversmiths)

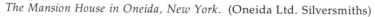

The Mansion House library. (Culver Pictures)

Although each adult had a small room of his or her own, the building was designed to encourage a feeling of togetherness, hence the inclusion of a communal dining hall, recreation rooms, library, concert hall, outdoor picnic area, etc. It was in the Big Hall of the Mansion House that John Humphrey Noyes gave his widely quoted home talks. It was here that musical concerts, dramas, readings, dances, and other forms of socializing were held. Community members were interested in the arts and were able to organize such activities as symphony concerts, glee club recitals, and Shakespearean plays, even though practically all the talent was drawn from the membership.

Occasionally, outside artists were invited, but on a day-to-day basis the Community was more or less a closed group, with members seldom straying very far from home. What might be called their reference behavior related entirely to the group. The outside community was, figuratively and literally, "outside" and was always referred to as The World. It was this system of *cultural enclosure,* sustained over several decades, that served as a primary solidifying force.

It should not be thought that life in the old Community was a continual round of entertainment. The Oneidans built their own home, raised their own food, made all their own clothes (including shoes!), did their own laundry, ran their own school, and performed countless other collective tasks. The following comment was made to the writer by a woman whose childhood had been spent in the Mansion House:

As children, we loved to visit the various departments they used to have: the laundry, the kitchen, the fruit cellar, the bakery, the dairy, the dining room, the ice house, the tailor shop—they even had a Turkish bath in the basement. The thing is that small groups of people worked side by side in most of these places, and they were able to talk with each other as they worked.

It's hard to explain, but my mother used to tell me that no matter how menial the job was, they were so busy talking to each other that the time always flew. It was this sort of thing, year after year, that gave rise to a kindred spirit.

Additionally, adults were subject to self-imposed deprivations whenever they felt the group welfare threatened, and by modern standards "group welfare" was given a most liberal interpretation. For example, although the Perfectionists ate well, meat was served sparingly, pork not at all. Alcoholic beverages were prohibited, as were tea and coffee. Smoking also came to be taboo. The reasoning behind these prohibitions is not always clear, but presumably the Oneidans were dead set against informal distractions of an "anti-family" nature. Thus, dancing was permitted, since it was a social activity, while coffee-drinking and smoking were condemned on the ground that they were individualistic and appetitive in nature. One of the descendants of the Oneida Community—in an interview with the writer—spoke as follows:

I imagine the prohibitions were pretty well thought out. They didn't just spring up, but developed gradually. I know there were some differences of opinion, but the main thing was that certain practices were felt to be bad for group living.

Remember, they were trying to create a spiritual and social brotherhood, and they spent much more time in the art of developing relationships than we do. They had to. After all, hundreds of them were living together as a family, and they worked at it day after day. They were successful, too, for they held together for almost two generations without a major quarrel.

Their unique social organization was not the only thing that held the Oneida Colony together. As the membership increased, three basic principles of Noyes' teaching combined to form the very heart of Perfectionist life style: (1) economic communism; (2) mutual criticism; and (3) complex marriage.

ECONOMIC COMMUNISM

Members of the Oneida Community held equal ownership of all property, their avowed aim being to eliminate competition for the possession of material things. The needs of individual members were taken care of, but there was simply no concept of private ownership, even in the realm of personal belongings such as clothes, trinkets, and children's toys.

Writing of his boyhood, Pierrepont Noyes, a son of John Humphrey, states that "throughout my childhood, the private ownership of anything seemed to me a crude artificiality to which an unenlightened Outside still clung. For instance, we were keen for our favorite sleds, but it never occurred to me that I could possess a sled to the exclusion of the other boys. So it was with all Children's House property." With respect to clothing, the same author writes that "going-away clothes for grown folks, as for children, were common property. Any man or woman preparing for a trip was fitted out with one of the suits kept in stock for that purpose."[3]

In addition to the manufacture of traps, the Oneidians found a ready market for their crops, which they put up in glass jars and cans and which became known for their uniform quality. As their business know-how (and their prosperity!) increased, it became necessary to hire outside help, and eventually the Perfectionists were employing several hundred local workers.

Starting in 1877, the Oneidans embarked on the manufacture of silverware. This venture proved so successful that, when the Community was disbanded, the silverware component was perpetuated as a joint-stock company (Oneida Ltd.), whose product is still widely used today.

How much of the economic success of the group was due to the communistic methods employed, and how much was due to the fortuitous invention of the trap, is difficult to say. On the one hand, collectivist methods probably had certain advantages over competing private enterprise. In tracing the economic history of the Oneidans, for instance, Edmonds notes that "to meet the deadline on an order, the whole Community—including the children—turned out."[4]

On the other hand, the fact remains that the Perfectionists were rapidly becoming bankrupt until Sewell Newhouse's trap, figuratively and literally, "caught on." Pierrepont Noyes states that "by 1860 the Newhouse trap had become the standard of the United States and Canada. Professional trappers would accept no other brand, and for nearly 70 years all the steel traps used by the

127

---

[3] From *My Father's House* by Pierrepont Noyes. Copyright 1937 by Pierreport Noyes. Copyright © 1965 by Corinna Ackley Noyes. Reprinted by permission of Holt, Rinehart and Winston, Publishers. Pp. 126–127.
[4] Walter D. Edmonds, *The First Hundred Years*, Sherrill, New York, Oneida Ltd., 1948, p. 25.

Hudson Bay Company were made at Oneida. Later, Community traps caught sable and ermine in Russia, rabbits in Australia, and nutria in Uruguay. Thus an industrious community became, by force of circumstances, an industrial community."[5]

It is debatable whether the subsequent Oneida industries—including that of silverware—would ever have developed had it not been for the financial windfall brought about by Sewell Newhouse's timely invention. Some idea of the magnitude of the business can be seen from the fact that, in a good year, the Community would turn out close to 300,000 traps!

The economic aspects of both the Rappites and the Oneidans have been mentioned in some detail, since most of the other communistic experiments then under way in America (and there were scores of them) became defunct either partly or largely because of economic difficulties.

Insofar as possible, the various jobs within the Community were rotated from year to year in order to eliminate feelings of discrimination. Members were quick to point out that at one time or another almost everyone took a turn at the necessary menial tasks. Nevertheless, while the jobs were generally rotated, individual variations in ability were recognized, and members were not placed in positions beyond their innate capacities. At the same time, social differentiation by occupational status was played down. If people did their work well, they presumably had equal status whether they were farm laborers or plant superintendents. It was work, rather than a specific type of job, that was held in high regard. As a matter of fact, one of the Perfectionists' most successful innovations was their employment of the cooperative enterprise or *bee*. The latter was

an ordinance exactly suited to Community life. A bee would be announced at dinner or perhaps on the bulletin board: "A bee in the kitchen to pare apples"; or "A bee to pick strawberries at five o'clock tomorrow morning"; or "A bee in the Upper Sitting Room to sew bags."[6]

It should be mentioned that there was seldom any trouble with idlers. On the contrary, a major difficulty was to screen out most of those who made application to join the Community. Relatively few new members were admitted, and those who were accepted had to undergo a long and severe probationary period.

In their efforts to promote equality, all Perfectionists were required to eat the same kind of food, wear the same type of

---

[5] Noyes, *op. cit.*, pp. 14–15.
[6] Robertson, *op. cit.*, p. 103.

Cooperative group activity was a hallmark of the Oneida Community. Here the Community's members participate in a bag bee. (Historical Pictures Service, Inc.)

clothing, and live in the same home. For both sexes, dress was uniformly simple, with jewelry and adornments tabooed. John Humphrey Noyes, incidentally, was responsible for a genuine innovation in the women's clothing style. Dissatisfied with ordinary female attire, he declared in the First Annual Report of the Community (1848) that "woman's dress is a standard lie. It proclaims that she is not a two-legged animal, but something like a churn, standing on castors!" Accordingly, a committee was set up to work on the problem. The costume decided upon—one that was worn forthwith by all the Oneida women—was a short, knee-length skirt, with loose trousers (pantalettes) down to the shoes!

MUTUAL CRITICISM

The Oneida Community had neither laws nor law-enforcing officers, and there was little need for them, major infractions being all but unknown. In any organization, however, no matter how closely knit, conduct problems are bound to occur, and while the Oneidans considered themselves to be Perfectionists, they acknowledged that individual foibles did exist. "Mutual criticism" was the method by which such problems were handled. The system had its inception at Putney, where the original followers of Noyes would subject themselves periodically to a searching criticism by the rest of the group. At Oneida the system was perpetuated—with remarkably successful results.

Whenever a member was found to be deviating from group norms, or whenever a personality or character weakness manifested itself, a committee of peers would meet with the offender to discuss the matter. "The criticisms," according to Edmonds, "were administered in a purely clinical spirit. The subject sat in complete silence while each member of the committee in turn assessed his good points as well as his bad. In cases of unusual seriousness, perhaps involving the violation of a fundamental tenet of their common philosophy, the committee would be expanded to include the entire Community."[7]

From the accounts of the individuals who had undergone criticism, it is evident that, while the experience itself was often an ordeal, the end result was that of a catharsis, or spiritual cleansing. The success of the system probably hinged on the subjects' willingness to accept analysis and also on the fact that, though the criticisms were penetrating, they were offered in a frank, impersonal manner.

Some of those who underwent criticism issued public statements about their experiences. The following comments appeared during 1871–1872 in the *Oneida Circular,* the Community's weekly newspaper:

> I feel as though I had been washed; felt clean through the advice and criticism given. I would call the truth the soap; the critics the scrubbers; Christ's spirit the water.

. . .

> Criticism is adminsitered in faithfulness and love without respect to persons. I look upon the criticisms I have received since I came here as the greatest blessings that have been conferred upon me.[8]

Although the Perfectionists had their share of internal strife, as we shall see, the conflicts were over policy and had nothing to do with deviant behavior. The harmonious living enjoyed by the

---

[7] Edmonds, *op. cit.,* p. 20.
[8] See Harriet M. Worden, *Old Mansion House Memories,* Kenwood, Oneida, New York, privately printed, 1950, pp. 15–16.

group and the virtual lack of pernicious behavior attest to the effectiveness of mutual criticism as an instrument of social control. In fact, as the Colony grew in membership, the technique of mutual criticism came to be employed not so much with errant members but with those who volunteered for purposes of self-improvement.

Carden writes that:

> Noyes was the only person who was not criticized, although he occasionally criticized himself. . . . However, he did not spare his followers. His judgments were sometimes complimentary, often harsh, and always penetrating. That the members did not rebel against this dogmatic treatment attests to the devotion which Noyes inspired and to two outstanding features of his leadership.
>
> First, Noyes was a very good judge of character. He picked out members' faults and strengths with consummate skill. He saw and understood more about them than they knew about themselves. Second, he always judged them in terms of Perfectionist ideals. Thus they could not reject his comments without at the same time rejecting their religion and their whole way of life.[9]

Krinopathy. The Oneidans were so convinced of the effectiveness of mutual criticism that they actually used the technique as a cure for illness! Known as "krinopathy," the criticism-cure was applied to both children and adults and was used for everything from common colds to more serious diseases. The following account appeared in the *Oneida Circular* of December 4, 1863:

> It is a common custom here for every one who may be attacked with any disorder to send for a committee of six or eight persons, in whose faith and spiritual judgement he had confidence, to come and criticize him. The result, when administered sincerely, is almost universally to throw the patient into a sweat, or to bring on a reaction of his life against disease, breaking it up and restoring him soon to usual health.

The Perfectionists not infrequently went to extremes, however, and krinopathy was a case in point. For mutual criticism sometimes continued even after a person had died! Deceased members whose personal effects—letters, diaries, and the like—were thought to be incriminating might find themselves (in the hereafter) being subjected to an "earthly criticism."

In spite of some excesses, nevertheless, there is no doubt that mutual criticism worked. In fact, some observers—including the present writer—feel that mutual criticism was the single most effective method of social control employed by the Community.

---

[9] Carden, *op. cit.*, pp. 72–73.

COMPLEX MARRIAGE

The world does not remember the Oneidans for their economic communism or their mutual criticism, but for their system of complex marriage. Rightly or wrongly, just as the term "Rappites" signifies celibacy, so the name "Oneida" conjures up thoughts about the unique sex practices of the Community. Noyes himself coined the term "free love," although he seems to have preferred the phrase "complex marriage," or occasionally "pantogamy." Realistically, the Oneida marital system can best be described as a combination of communitarian living and group marriage.

From the Putney days, John Humphrey Noyes had no time for romantic love or monogamous marriage. Such practices were to him manifestations of selfishness and personal possession. Romantic love, or "special love" as it was called in the Community, was believed to give rise to jealousy and hypocrisy and, according to Perfectionist doctrine, made spiritual love impossible to attain.

Accordingly, Noyes promulgated the idea of complex marriage: since it was natural for all men to love all women and all women to love all men, it followed that every adult should consider himself or herself married to every other adult of the opposite sex. This collective spiritual union of men and women also included the right to sexual intercourse.

The Perfectionist leader felt strongly that "men and women find universally that their susceptibility to love is not burnt out by one honeymoon, or satisfied by one lover. On the contrary, the secret history of the human heart will bear out the assertion that it is capable of loving any number of times and any number of persons. Variety is, in the nature of things, as beautiful and useful in love as in eating and drinking. . . . We need love as much as we need food and clothing; and if we trust God for those things, why not for love?"[10]

John Humphrey Noyes was a devout person, and the Oneida Perfectionists were a deeply religious group; any assessment of their sexual practices must take these factors into consideration. Insofar as the available information indicates, the Community abided by the doctrine of complex marriage not for reasons of lust, as was sometimes charged, but because of the conviction that they were following God's word.

In practice, since most of the adult men and women lived in the Mansion House, sex relations were easy to arrange. There

---

[10] Quoted in Robert Allerton Parker, *A Yankee Saint*, New York, G. P. Putnam's Sons, 1935, pp. 182–183.

was, however, one requirement that was adhered to: a man could not have sexual intercourse with a woman unless the latter gave her consent. Procedurally, if a man desired sex relations, he would transmit the message to a Central Committee, who would thereupon make his request known to the woman in question. The actual go-between was usually an older female member of the Committee.

The system was inaugurated, as Parker points out, so that the women members "might, without embarrassment, decline proposals that did not appeal to them. No member should be obliged to receive at any time, under any circumstances, the attention of those they had not learned to love. . . . Every woman was to be free to refuse any, or every, man's attention."[11] Although the procedure varied somewhat over the years, if the Central Committee granted approval and the woman in question assented, then the man simply went to the woman's room at bedtime and spent an hour or so with her before retiring to his own quarters.

It must be admitted, apropos of complex marriage, that many of the operational details were never disclosed, and that some writers—both past and present—have taken a questioning look at the sex practices of the Oneidans. Webber, for instance, writes as follows:

> It was commonly declared that a committee of men and women received applications from those desiring certain persons; that if they considered the pairing suitable they arranged the meetings or obtained a refusal which was relayed to the applicant. . . . Thus if there was a refusal there was less embarrassment than if the proposal were made directly.
>
> So much for the rule. One may suspect that is was honored largely, as it were, in the breach. Men and women constantly associated and were free to visit in each other's rooms. It seems unlikely that a burst of romantic feeling might be interrupted while someone trotted off to find a go-between.[12]

Whether, in fact, the Central Committee or the go-between were frequently by-passed must remain a matter of conjecture. One should remember that the Oneidans were a devout group, and that their sexual practices were part of an overall religious system. It is difficult, therefore, for outsiders to assess the sexual motivations of individual Community members.

It is known that Oneidans were presumed to act like ladies and gentlemen at all times. Inappropriate behavior, suggestive

---

[11] *Ibid.*, p. 183.
[12] Everett Webber, *Escape to Utopia: The Communal Movement in America*, New York, Hastings House, 1959, pp. 395–396.

language, overt displays of sexuality—such actions were not tolerated. As a matter of fact, sexual behavior was not openly discussed within the Community, and it is doubtful whether the subject of "Who was having relations with whom?" ever became common knowledge. One male member who became too inquisitive on this score was literally thrown out of the Community, an act which represented the only physical expulsion in the group's history.

Role of Women.   There is no doubt that John Humphrey Noyes had a special place in his heart for the Oneida women—and in this respect he was years ahead of his time. He saw to it that they played an integral part in the day-to-day operations of the Community. The following remarks, made to the writer, provide a good example.

> One thing that most people have overlooked is that Noyes delegated a lot more responsibility to the women here than they ever would have received on the outside. Every committee had women on it. It made a difference, too. All the old folks will tell you it made both men and women respect each other.

In the sexual sphere, also, the Perfectionist leader had advanced ideas about the role of women. Starting in the Putney period, he rejected the idea that sex was simply a "wifely duty"; that is, an act tolerated by the female at the pleasure of the male. Later on, he incorporated his beliefs in the Oneida *Handbook*, as the following passage indicates:

> The liberty of monogamous marriage, as commonly understood, is the liberty of a man to sleep habitually with a woman, liberty to please himself alone in his dealings with her, liberty to expose her to child-bearing without care or consultation.
> The term Free Love, as understood by the Oneida Community, does *not* mean any such freedom of sexual proceedings. The theory of sexual interchange which governs all the general measures of the Community is that which in ordinary society governs the proceedings in *courtship*.
> It is the theory that love *after* marriage should be what it is *before* marriage—a glowing attraction on both sides, and not the odious obligation of one party, and the sensual selfishness of the other.[13]

Although rumors a-plenty were carried by the outsiders, there is unfortunately no published record of the extent to which requested sexual liaisons were vetoed by the Central Committee or

---

[13] *Handbook of the Oneida Community*, Oneida, New York, Office of the *Oneida Circular*, 1875, p. 42.

134

refused by the women themselves. All the evidence is fragmentary. Some individuals, naturally, were more in demand than others. Carden, who has done research on the subject, believes that the women often had more than four different sex partners a month.

> A physician who interviewed a number of ex-members after the breakup, reported that women had intercourse every two to four days. Another report, also by a physician, quoted an obviously discontented older woman who had left the Community. She complained that young girls would "be called upon to have intercourse as often as seven times in a week and oftener.[14]

On the other hand, that there was some rejection can be inferred from Parker's finding—based on a lengthy study—that "this entire freedom of the women to accept or reject the advances of their lovers kept men as alert as during more conventional courtships. Men sought, as always, to prove themselves worthy of the favor of their sweethearts; and that made their life, they confessed, one continuous courtship."[15]

Perhaps the most poignant observation on the subject was that made by Pierrepont Noyes, who spent his early youth in the Community.

> There has survived in my memory an impression, a dim recognition, that the relation between our grown folks had a quality intimate and personal, a quality that made life romantic. Unquestionably, the sexual system inspired a lively interest in each other, but I believe that the opportunity for romantic friendships also played a part in rendering life more colorful than elsewhere.
>
> Even elderly people, whose physical passions had burned low, preserved the fine essence of earlier associations. Child as I was, I sensed a spirit of high romance surrounding them, a vivid, youthful interest in life that looked from their eyes and spoke in their voices and manners.[16]

THE EUGENICS PROGRAM

Child-rearing occupied a special place in the Perfectionist scheme of things. Having familiarized himself with the principles of Charles Darwin and Francis Galton, Noyes was convinced of the feasibility of applying scientific methods to the propagation of the race. He felt that the only people who should have

---

[14] Carden, *op. cit.*, p. 53.
[15] Parker, *op. cit.*, p. 184.
[16] Noyes, *op. cit.*, p. 131.

135

children were those who possessed superior physical and mental abilities. A clear statement of his position appeared in the *Oneida Circular*.

> Why should not beauty and noble grace of person and every other desirable quality of men and women, internal and external, be propagated and intensified beyond all former precedent—by the application of the same scientific principles of breeding that produce such desirable results in the case of sheep, cattle, and horses?[17]

Although the term "eugenics" had not yet been coined, a eugenics program—in which specially chosen adults would be utilized for breeding purposes—was exactly what John Humphrey Noyes had in mind. And, of course, what more logical place to put eugenic principles into actual practice than the Oneida Community? Noyes called his program "stirpiculture" (from the Latin *stirps,* meaning root or stock), and it was not long before the scientific world was discussing the implications of the unique experiment being conducted in central New York State.

For 20 years after founding their Community, the Oneidans had largely refrained from bearing children. They reasoned that procreation should be delayed until such time as the group had the facilities for proper child care. The first two decades, so to speak, merely served the purpose of laying the groundwork for the future growth of the Colony. The birth control technique advocated by Noyes was *coitus reservatus*, i.e., sexual intercourse up to, but not including, ejaculation on the part of the male. Until they had learned the necessary coital control, younger males in the Community were required to limit their sex relations to women who had passed the menopause. Although the technique was claimed by many writers to be incapable of attainment, the record contradicts them.

In any case, by 1869 the group was ready to embark upon its pioneer eugenics program. Couples desirous of becoming parents (stirps) made formal application before a cabinet composed of key members of the Community, Noyes apparently holding the deciding vote. The cabinet, after assessing the physical and mental qualities of the applicants, would either approve or disapprove the requests.* The stirpiculture program was in effect for about a decade before the Community disbanded, and during this 10-year period 58 children were born. Noyes himself

---

* The specific criteria and methods for selecting the stirps have never been revealed. It is known that a cabinet was set up to make the selection, but what system they used remains a mystery.

[17] *Oneida Circular*, March 27, 1865.

fathered upwards of a dozen children, so that evidently he was not averse to self-selection.

Children remained in their mothers' care up to the age of 15 months, whereupon they were gradually transferred to a special section of the Mansion House. Henceforth they would spend most of their childhood in age-graded classes. Although the children were treated with kindness by their parents, sentimentalizing was frowned upon, the feeling being that under Perfectionism all adults should love all children and vice versa.

By their own reports, the children were evidently well adjusted. Recreation, schooling, medical care—all were provided in keeping with accepted child-rearing practices. As a group, the children were remarkably healthy. Mortality comparisons indicated that the products of stirpiculture had a significantly lower death rate than children born outside the Community. Interestingly enough, one of the Oneida children, now almost 100 years old, is still living—in the Mansion House!

That most of the youngsters had a happy childhood can be seen from the following comments, made to the writer:

I was born in the old Community, and the times we used to have! I don't think kids today have the kind of fun we did. There was a ready-made play group all the time, with something always going on. There was some activity in the Big Hall almost every night—plays, musical concerts, entertainment of all kinds. As children, there was always something to look forward to.

. . .

Well, I remember one little girl always wanted her mother. She'd stand outside her window and call to her, even though the mother wasn't supposed to answer. Other than that particular case, all the children seemed happy enough. Everybody was good to us. You knew you were loved because it was like a big family. Also, there were so many activities for the youngsters, so many things to do, well—believe me—we were happy children. Everybody around here will give you the same answer on that!

. . .

We were happy youngsters, and we lived in a remarkable group. Unfortunately, they broke up when I was quite young. I wish I could have lived my whole life with them. . . .

What was the outcome of the stirpiculture program? Were the children actually superior? Many observers thought so. A number of the young people achieved eminence in business and in the professions. And most of them, in turn, had children who were successful. There is one catch, however, in assessing the effectiveness of the program, and that is the fact that the children presumably had an advantageous environment *as well as* sound heredity.

But the really puzzling feature of the Oneida eugenics program was that there were so few children born. With some 100 men and women taking part in the 10-year program, the fact that only 58 youngsters were born is hard to understand, particularly in view of the high birthrate that prevailed during the period. Most of the Oneida females who were selected had but one child. A few had two children, and only two women had three. The only reasonable answer seems to be that Noyes was apprehensive about the effects of multiple childbirth on the health of the women.

THE BREAKUP

As might have been predicted, outside pressures against the Oneida Community were becoming irresistible. Rumblings grew louder against such practices as "free love," "lust," and "animal breeding." Although many of the surrounding townspeople knew the Perfectionists as hard-working, devout individuals, professional crusaders such as Anthony Comstock, self-appointed watchdog of American morals, were successful in creating a storm of adverse public criticism. As a result of this ever-increasing pressure campaign, the Oneidans were forced to give up their practice of complex marriage.

Then, too, in the later years all was not well within the Community itself. John Humphrey Noyes was growing old, and in 1877 he resigned as leader. One of his sons, Dr. Theodore R. Noyes, took over the leadership, but he was in no sense the leader his father was, and factionalism within the Community became rife. In June of 1879—for some inexplicable reason—John Humphrey Noyes left Oneida for Canada, never to return.

In spite of all their woes, the Oneidans might have survived—minus, perhaps, their system of plural marriage—had it not been for the advent of one James Towner, who joined the group in 1874. As in the case of Count Leon and the Rappites, Towner became a divisive force in the Community almost immediately. Charging the Perfectionist leader with being too dictatorial, he attempted to gain control of the organization. While he failed in his attempt, he did manage to sow the seeds of discord.

Like Count Leon, James Towner was a man of some ability. A minister-turned-lawyer, there is no doubt, also, that he found some ready listeners among the Oneidans. In fact, he managed to win over a fair minority of them. Toward the end, his influence declined sharply, and he and some 25 of his followers left for California. (They made no attempt to live communally, Towner himself becoming a county court judge.)

In late 1879, after fearlessly defying public opinion for almost half a century, Noyes sent a message to the Community (from Canada) proposing that they abolish complex marriage and revert to the accepted marital practices. Soon afterward the group disbanded, many of the members becoming formally married. Economically, a joint-stock company was organized and the stock (worth about $600,000) was then divided among the members. Last-ditch efforts to salvage some communal type of family organization failed, thus ending—in rather pathetic fashion—what was probably the most radical social experiment in America.

THE CHARACTER OF JOHN HUMPHREY NOYES

Any attempt to explain either the success or failure of the Oneida Community must take into consideration the character of its leader, John Humphrey Noyes. By all accounts, he was an original thinker with a remarkable sense of dedication, perseverance, and courage. He had tremendous vigor, a vigor that manifested itself in the spiritual, the mental—and the physical. It can be no coincidence that his utopian community included relative freedom of sex expression. At the same time, he strove to keep the behavior of the group on a consistently high plane. The most striking comment on John Humphrey Noyes was the following, made to the writer by a woman whose mother had known the Perfectionist leader quite well:

> I've often wondered about the traits that made him what he was. I just don't know. You might have got an answer 100 years ago. Now, maybe it's too late. I remember asking my mother the same question when I was a young girl. "Why did you live that way? What was there about him?" and I remember her saying, "Don't ask me to explain it. I can't. All I know is that when you were in his presence you knew you were with someone who was not an ordinary man."

Utterly frank in the expression of his innermost thoughts, Noyes wrote a voluminous amount of material dealing with his own particular brand of Perfectionism. He believed that the power of the printed word was stronger than that of the spoken word, and he was the guiding hand for a variety of publications: *The Perfectionist, The Witness, The Spiritual Magazine, The Free Church Circular, The American Socialist, The Oneida Circular,* and so on. By the time of his death in 1886, Noyes had penned

John Humphrey Noyes, in the early 1870's. (Culver Pictures)

140

enough material to keep historians busy for generations.* And while it lasted, the Community itself must objectively be described as successful. Not only were the Oneidans satisfied with their way of life, but the usual social problems—poverty, crime, alcoholism, divorce, and desertion—were virtually nonexistent.

On the other side of the ledger, Noyes was often unpredictable, a trait shared by many zealots. He not only left the group for protracted periods of time, but twice—once at Putney and once at Oneida—deserted when the end appeared imminent. During his reign as leader, moreover, he apparently made no provision for the succession of authority. Had able young men been trained as potential leaders, the factionalism that developed in later years might have been avoided.

---

* Indeed, during the 125 years since its founding, not a single decade had passed—including the 1970's—without new books and articles on the Oneida Community being published!

While he inspired tremendous personal loyalty as head of the Perfectionists, Noyes permitted the group to follow the fate of other dictatorships, which tend to founder when the helmsman becomes irreplaceable. And although the Oneida Community seemed to work well enough while it was in being, the inexorable fact remains that it did not last. Noyes' personal attributes aside, the forces that held the group together and promoted group loyalty were not strong enough to make for survival. It is true that the Colony lacked the usual social problems and that there was a strong measure of social cohesion; in fact, the records indicate that, on the average, only three or four persons "seceded" each year. It is clear, nevertheless, that the existing sentiments, values, and traditions were not sufficiently durable to bring about an integrated, permanent type of social organization.

Perhaps, under the circumstances, it would have been rather surprising if the Oneida Community had endured, for Noyes was attempting to create a society *without marriage and the family* as these terms are commonly understood. The human family seems to be based on sex attraction and exclusiveness, parental child-rearing, and the need for primary-group association, all of which operate as powerful systematizing forces. It is quite possible, in modern society, that some other sort of familial arrangement could be worked out, but it is difficult to conceive of an Oneida-type endeavor as filling the bill. The wonder of it may well be that Noyes' experiment lasted as long as it did.

SELECTED READINGS

Barron, Alfred, and Miller, George (eds.), *Home Talks by John Humphrey Noyes*, Oneida, New York, Oneida Community, 1875.

Bishop, Morris, "The Great Oneida Love-In," *American Heritage*, February, 1969, pp. 14 ff.

Carden, Maren Lockwood, *Oneida: Utopian Community to Modern Corporation*, Baltimore, The Johns Hopkins Press, 1969.

Carmer, Carl, *Listen for a Lonesome Drum*, New York, Farrar & Rinehart, Inc., 1936.

Church, C. C., "Communism in Marriage," *The Nation*, August 11, 1926, pp. 124–126.

Cross, Whitney R., *The Burned-Over District: The Social and Intellectual History of Enthusiastic Religion in Western New York, 1800–1850*, Ithaca, New York, Cornell University Press, 1950.

Ditzion, Sidney, *Marriage, Morals, and Sex in America*, New York, Bookman Associates, 1953, pp. 207–234.

Edmonds, Walter D., *The First Hundred Years*, Sherrill, New York, Oneida Ltd., 1948.

Estlake, Allan, *The Oneida Community: A Record of an Attempt to Carry Out the Principles of Christian Unselfishness and Scientific Race-Improvement*, London, George Redway, 1900.

Handbook of the Oneida Community, Oneida, New York, Office of the *Oneida Circular*, 1875.

Kephart, William M., "Experimental Family Organization: An Historio-Cultural Report on the Oneida Community," *Marriage and Family Living*, August, 1963, pp. 261–271.

McGee, Anita N., "An Experiment in American Stirpiculture," *American Anthropologist*, October, 1891, pp. 324–334.

Nordhoff, Charles, *The Communistic Societies of the United States*, New York, Dover Publications, Inc., 1966.

Noyes, Hilda H., and Noyes, George W., "The Oneida Community Experiment in Stirpiculture," *Eugenics, Genetics, and the Family*, Vol. 1. 1923, pp. 374–386.

Noyes, John Humphrey, *The Berean: A Manual for the Help of Those Who Seek the Faith of the Primitive Church*, Putney, Vermont, Office of the Spiritual Magazine, 1847.

———, *Male Continence*, Oneida, New York, Office of the *Oneida Circular*, 1872.

———, *Essays on Scientific Propagation*, Oneida, New York, Oneida Community, 1873.

Noyes, Pierrepont B., *My Father's House: An Oneida Boyhood*, New York, Farrar & Rinehart, Inc., 1937.

———, *A Goodly Heritage*, New York, Rinehart & Co., Inc., 1958.

Parker, Robert Allerton, *A Yankee Saint: John Humphrey Noyes and the Oneida Community*, New York, G. P. Putnam's Sons, 1935.

Robertson, Constance Noyes, *Oneida Community: An Autobiography, 1851–1876*, Syracuse, New York, Syracuse University Press, 1970.

———, *Oneida Community: The Breakup, 1876–1881*, Syracuse, New York, Syracuse University Press, 1972.

Wayland-Smith, Louis, *Reminiscences*, Kenwood, New York, privately published, 1955.

Webber, Everett, *Escape to Utopia: The Communal Movement in America*, New York, Hastings House, 1959.

Worden, Harriet M., *Old Mansion House Memories*, Kenwood, Oneida, New York, privately printed, 1950.

7

Minority Family Types I—Religion:
The Old Order Amish Family

IF THE FORMER practices of the Rappites and the Oneida Community represent radical family types, the most conservative family type is to be found among the Old Order Amish. The Amish are a branch of the Mennonites, an Anabaptist group that originated in Switzerland during the Reformation conflicts of the sixteenth century. They are named after their founder, Jacob Amman (variously spelled), a Mennonite bishop whose views were too conservative even for the Mennonites. More specifically, Amman felt that his people had grown too lenient in their excommunication practices and too lax in their enforcement of the *Meidung*, usually translated as the "shunning" or "avoiding" of those who have been excommunicated.

Amman believed that the *Meidung* served as the backbone of Mennonite religion and that without rigid enforcement there would be little deterrence for those followers who were tempted to stray from the paths of righteousness. The "shunning" was based on a literal interpretation of the biblical admonition "not to eat" with a person who was under church censure, and, at least as Amman saw it, this admonition carried with it not only religious ostracism but complete avoidance in the social, economic, and domestic (including the marital) spheres. The *"Meidung controversy,"* as it has been called, was a bitter one and led ultimately to a schism within the larger Mennonite group. The followers of Jacob Amman came to be known as the Amish, and to this day the *Meidung* remains an integral part of their religion.

Driven from Switzerland by successive waves of religious persecution, the Amish eventually became part of an ever-increasing stream of American colonists. Largely because of William Penn's promise of religious freedom, the first Amish families settled in Pennsylvania in the early 1700's. Today, Amish settlements can be found in 20 states, as well as in Canada and Central and South America. (There are no Amish settlements outside the Americas.) Although they are usually associated with Lancaster County, Pennsylvania, the Amish actually have a larger settlement in Ohio and one nearly as large in Indiana. The Lancaster County group, however, is the oldest and one of the most conservative of all Amish groups. It is also the group that the writer has had some experience with, and much of the following account stems from personal observations and from conversations with area residents.*

LIFE STYLE

The Amish home is the center of their existence. Work, play, family activities, church services—all take place at home. Amish boys and girls attend the lower grades in public school, but even in the realm of education their real training comes at home. The term "home," however, has a special connotation, for the Amish are entirely a rural people, and their dwelling might more accurately be described as a farmstead.

With very few exceptions, Amish men are farmers.† There are no exact figures, but most estimates indicate that at least 95 percent of the males are agricultural workers. Amish farms are acknowledged to be among the best in the world. In additon to extensive crop acreage, most of their farmsteads consist of large, well-kept barns, stables, springhouses, silos, and storehouses. Also, since Amish people maintain no homes for the aged, a typical farm may include three, four, or even five generations. Additions are made to the farmhouse as they are needed. As we shall see later, the presence of oldsters on the farm serves as a kind of self-perpetuating conservative influence.

The Amish are more than simply conservative. In a very real sense, conservatism is their religion; the Bible is a literal guide, and it has always been so. An Amish boy's life is shaped after his

---

* Customs of Amish groups who live in other parts of the country differ in some respects from those reported herein. Readers who are familiar with the Lancaster County area under discussion will recognize the picturesque names of villages in the heart of Amishland: Intercourse, Fertility, Smoketown, Leola, Compass, White Horse, Bird-in-Hand, Beartown, Paradise, and others.

† The exceptions are an occasional blacksmith, shoe repairman, cabinet-maker, carpenter, harness-maker—practically all of them farm-service occupations.

father's, and the girl's after her mother's. And their children's lives will be similarly patterned. This replication process has been going on for 250 years, life on an Amish farm being much the same today as it was in the early Colonial period. The houses they live in, the clothes they wear, the language they speak (German and Pennsylvania Dutch, some English), the hymns they sing, the beliefs they adhere to—few have changed in any significant way. For the Old Order Amish, major change is looked upon as tantamount to group extinction.

Despite the fact that books, plays, and musical comedies have been written about them, the reader may find it difficult to grasp the extent to which the Amish have resisted the inroads and crosscurrents of modern society. Men's hats—perhaps the most distinctive feature of an Amishman's attire—are of low crown and wide brim. Coats have no collars, lapels, or pockets and are usually worn with a vest. Belts and sweaters, on the other hand, are taboo, as are gloves. (No matter how cold it gets in winter, an Amishman will never be seen wearing gloves.) Trousers are plain, without crease, and are always worn with suspenders. Shirts are also plain and are worn without neckties, the latter being considered useless adornments.

Women's dresses must be a solid color (not necessarily black), and the skirts are required to be near ankle-length. Aprons must be worn at all times. Stockings are black cotton, and shoes are black and low-heeled. Schreiber states that "until a few years ago, high-button shoes for the women were the standard, uncompromised, footgear. Today, however, they cannot be bought anywhere in America. They have completely disappeared, and the Amish do not manufacture their own shoes. Thus, high-button shoes are no longer required."[1]

High-button shoes notwithstanding, it is safe to say that Amish clothes never go out of style, although this is not the principal reason for their standardized and ancient mode of dress. Their attire is based on descriptive biblical passages plus the fact that throughout Amish history their clothing "has always been so." A number of writers have commented on the distinctiveness of Amish apparel, pointing out various functions that are served.

Bachman writes as follows:

Through the maintenance of clothing styles that have remained unchanged for more than two centuries, the Amish seek to show that they are not of this world, with its changing fashions; that they are

---

[1] William Schreiber, *Our Amish Neighbors,* Chicago, University of Chicago Press, 1962, p. 77.

145

146

An Amish family in the 1970's. (Fred J. Wilson)

concerned, not with the outward which man alone sees, but with the inward, which is seen alone by God.[2]

Hostetler, who comes from an Amish background, states that "dress forms a common understanding and mutual appreciation among those who share the same traditions and expectations. Dress keeps the insider separate from the world and also keeps the outsider out."[3]

Smith points out that "the unique appearance of the Amish helps check deviant behavior, because actions unacceptable to the group can be viewed by others."[4]

Along the same lines, the Old Order Amish do not wear jewelry of any kind. In general, whatever is worn must have utilitarian value. An ornamental exception might be the Amishman's beard, though in one sense this has recognition value; that is, prior to marriage the young men are clean-shaven, while married males are required to let their beards grow. (Mustaches are taboo at all times.)

Men and boys wear their hair long, unparted, in a Dutch bob, with an occasional trimming done at home. Women and girls adhere to the age-old custom of parting their hair in the middle, combing it down flat, and knotting it in the back. Following the biblical injunction, Amish women must keep their heads covered at all times ("But every woman that prayeth or prophesieth with her head uncovered dishonoreth her head. . . ." I Cor. 11:5). Both girls and women conform by wearing a small white lawn cap, over which is worn the characteristic black bonnet. When they appear in public, women must also wear shawls and capes.

Amish conversatism goes far beyond their quaint mode of dress; indeed, a list of the modern inventions and devices that they have rejected would read like a technological inventory. Telephones, radios, televisions, automobiles, modern plumbing, furnaces, bathrooms and inside toilets, washing machines, electric lights—all are taboo in an Amish home. Nothing involving electricity is permitted. When it is necessary, an Amishman has no aversion to using a telephone or to riding in a bus, or even in an automobile—so long as it is not his own. In general, modern

---

[2] Calvin G. Bachman, *The Old Order Amish of Lancaster County, Pennsylvania,* Lancaster, Pennsylvania, The Pennsylvania German Society, 1961, p. 89.

[3] John A. Hostetler, *Amish Society,* Baltimore, The Johns Hopkins Press, 1968, p. 138.

[4] Elmer L. Smith, *The Amish People,* Hicksville, New York, Exposition Press, 1958, p. 172.

improvements are considered dangerous to the traditional way of life and their ownership is forbidden.

The automobile is the most talked-about case in point. Some people are under the impression that the Amish use the horse and buggy because automobiles are so much more expensive. (Although inflation affects the Amish, too; buggies now may run as high as $1,000—without horse!) Others maintain that horse-drawn vehicles are used because the animals can supply manure for the farm. To the question regarding his preference for animal-drawn farm vehicles over motor-powered machines, an Amish farmer—in an oft-quoted statement—replied, "Well, if you put gasoline in a tractor, all you get out is smoke."

While there are elements of truth in both of the above contentions, the fact is that the horse and buggy are as much a part of the Amish way of life as the clothes they wear. The Amishman is not an especially articulate individual, and if asked about the ban on autos in favor of the horse and buggy, he would routinely reply, "It has always been so." In reality, the auto represents a threat to his established way of life. Non-ownership of automobiles discourages the young folk from traipsing off to town, and

148

The horse and buggy are an essential part of Amish life, helping to differentiate and perpetuate their unique culture. (Mike Wannemacher)

An Amish barn raising. (Fred J. Wilson)

the older Amish make no bones about their suspicion of the urban way of life.

Attendance at sporting events, movies, bars, and other places of urban entertainment is prohibited. Travel, except for the purpose of visiting, is discouraged. So long as the auto is banned, worldly temptations are minimized. As the Amish see it, acceptance of the automobile might well be disruptive of their whole way of life. An Amishman's place is at home on the farm, and unless he is visiting an Amish neighbor or a relative—in his horse and buggy—the chances are that home is exactly where he will be.

Visiting, incidentally, is something very close to an Amishman's heart. As virtually the only form of adult recreation, it not only gives him something to look forward to, but serves to reinforce the web of Amish relationships. Along the same lines, the Old Order Amish are unstinting in their willingness to offer neighborly assistance. If husband or wife becomes ill, Amish neighbors will take care of the farm or housework. Even the building of new houses and barns is often a joint enterprise in which most of the district men take part. Collective construction is also utilized in the event a fire destroys a member's building. The much-publicized barn raising, as it is called, is an amazing sight to behold. In fact, the writer knows of instances where a large group of Amishmen, working as a team, succeeded in building a complete barn *in one day!* Reciprocal assistance of this type, of course, is essential, since the Amish do not believe in insurance.

AMISH HOMES

An Amishman's home and his farm are tied together in a single way of life. In effect, his home *is* his farm, and there isn't much he doesn't know about farming. While rejecting the use of tractors in the fields, the Amish do maintain some modern farm equipment, including cultivators, sprayers, binders, and balers. A good share of all the farming in Lancaster County is now done by the Amish, who produce some of the world's finest crops in this so-called Garden Spot of America.

Like his farm, an Amishman's house is well kept. It is plain, certainly, and lacking in modern conveniences, but it is clean, in good repair, and sturdy as an oak. By present-day standards the rooms are large, the kitchens enormous. All the furnishings are functional, but at the same time the Amish religion does not forbid the use of color. Walls are likely to be painted blue, dishes are often brightly hued purple, and such things as quilts and towels can be almost any color. Outside the house, there is likely to be a flower garden and a lawn. Fences, landmarks, walls, and posts are often brightly colored.

Much of the furniture is homemade—and massive. The chances are it has been handed down for many generations and will probably be handed down for many more. Floors are uncarpeted, although linoleum may be used. There are no lace curtains, mirrors, photographs, or wallpaper. There are no closets, clothing being hung on hooks and covered with a cloth. As has been mentioned, all electrical appliances are forbidden. Light comes from oil lamps. There are no pictures on the walls. Since the rooms are quite large, when friends or relatives visit—which is often—there is little difficulty in "putting them up."

With the exception of the Bible and hymnal, books are generally lacking, as are magazines and newspapers.* Oddly enough,

---

* The *Ausbund,* the Amish Hymnbook, is believed to be the oldest hymnal used by any Protestant group. First printed in Switzerland in 1564, the *Ausbund* contains a core of some 50 hymns. These tell of early Anabaptist sufferings and were actually written by Anabaptist prisoners awaiting execution. The tunes have been passed down orally ever since, *for the Ausbund contains no notes—only words.*

there is one Amish newspaper, *The Budget,* put out weekly by a non-Amish publisher. *The Budget* carries items of local and regional interest pertaining to visiting, farming, weddings, births, and so forth, and is subscribed to by most Amish families. Aside from *The Budget* and an occasional farm journal, however, the standard news media have little appeal. After all, the topics that are of interest to most Americans—politics, sports, entertainment, business, world affairs—are of little concern in Amishland, hence the apathy toward the printed page. On the other hand, the Amish "grapevine" is amazingly effective, and pertinent news loses no time in making the rounds.

Special mention should be made of the fact that the Amishman's home is also his church. Still adhering to the original Anabaptist custom, the Old Order Amish have no church buildings. All religious services are held in the homes of members, the custom being for the meetings—which are held every *other* Sunday—to rotate among the district membership; in fact, the size of an Amish district is determined largely by the number of persons that can be accommodated at religious meetings. Most districts contain 20 to 30 families and average about 100 members, not including children. When the Sunday services become too crowded because of a local population surge, creation of a new district is not far in the offing.

In any event, the first floor of an Amish home must be spacious enough to seat the entire membership on a given Sunday. This is made possible by the use of double folding doors between the downstairs rooms. If, as occasionally happens, the house is too small, the barn may be used for church services. Each district owns an appropriate number of plain wooden benches, and these are transported from house to house in time for the forthcoming Sunday services. The Amish have no paid clergy, incidentally, the bishops, ministers, and deacons being chosen by lot, after a preliminary nomination ("And they prayed, and said, Thou, Lord, which knowest the hearts of all men, show whether of these two Thou has chosen. . . .And they gave forth their lots; and the lot fell upon Matthias"; Acts I:24,26).

Paid or not, the Amish clergy are a devoutly vigilant group, particularly the bishop. It is he who not only determines right and wrong, but—through the threat of the *Meidung*—serves as enforcement agent. Schreiber writes that:

> The most consistent and the easiest approach for such untrained, rural overlords is to adhere rigidly to the status quo, or "Gebrauch," as they call it, the currently approved manners and morals, and to guard against all changes or innovations. Thus no detail of

life on the farm is too slight to escape the watchful eye of the Amish leaders. The most insignificant or trivial item—a straight pin, a button, the flap of a pocket, a curl in the hair, a tiny glass window in the side curtain of the buggy, a reflector on the rig, a clasp on the horse's harness, the band on the black hat, the trimming of the ragged beard—becomes meaningful. Conformity to the bishop's prescription about such things becomes a behavior essential to salvation. It is easy to see why the leaders exert such tremendous influence in the narrowly confined rural districts when their judgment on conformity or deviation is held to distinguish saint from sinner.[5]

This "watchdog" role of the bishop is a crucial one, and without it Amish society would fall apart. For the strange fact of the matter is that *the Amish keep no written records and have no written rules of any kind.* All of their history, their traditions, and their moral codes are passed down by word of mouth. At any given moment in time it is the bishop who is the symbol of Amish culture, and it is he who is primarily responsible for its continuance.

Sunday services have traditionally been held in German, though more and more Pennsylvania Dutch phraseology is being introduced. Following ancient custom, men and women are seated separately, with the women occupying the rear rows. Amish services are longer than those of most other denominations; in fact starting about 8:30 in the morning, a given service often lasts until noon. The Old Order Amish are a devout people, but since the sermons may be quite lengthy, individuals have been known to doze off during services—as is probably true of church members everywhere

COURTSHIP

Amish youth are much more restricted in dating and courtship activities than are the youth of other groups. For one thing, Amish youngsters are kept busy on the farms and simply do not have the time to "gad about." For another, automobiles are denied them, thus limiting their mobility. Also, because Amish boys and girls do not date the "English" (non-Amish), opportunity for meeting eligible persons of the opposite sex is necessarily circumscribed. And finally, entertainment such as dancing, athletics, and movie-going is forbidden. (Drinking is frowned upon, although some of the youth have been known to indulge.

---

[5] Schreiber, *op. cit.,* pp. 134–135.

Smoking—by men but never by women—is permitted in most districts.)

The most important social outlet for Amish youth is the Sunday night "singing," often held at the same farm that housed the church service. Singings are well attended, and from all accounts the Amish youth enjoy themselves. There are other gatherings for young people, but these are in the form of holidays and special occasions, so that singings are about the only regular social outlet for single people. Outsiders are not welcome at singings; in fact, the writer knows from experience that Amish youth are loath to talk about any part of their courtship activities.

Girls are supposed to remain virtuous until marriage, but to what extent necking and petting would compare with such activity among the "English" cannot be ascertained. It is customary for a boy to drive his date home following the singing, and some of these routes are remarkably circuitous. It is known also that occasionally an Amish boy will "sneak over" to his girl friend's house after dark when the oldsters have retired. And, much to the dismay of the group, premarital pregnancies sometimes do occur. They are infrequent, however, compared with the premarital pregnancy rate among the non-Amish.

From time to time, rumors of bundling crop up, but it is difficult to substantiate them. In the Lancaster County group under discussion, the practice is frowned upon, although it may occur surreptitiously.*

According to custom, young people are free to select a marriage partner of their own choosing. There are two restrictions: (1) marriage must be to some one within the Amish group; and (2) in every case, parental approval is required. The approval is usually granted, and when all parties concerned (including the clergy) are satisfied with the arrangements, banns are posted and the forthcoming marriage is announced at the Sunday services.

Although Amish youth marry at about the same age as the non-Amish, they have nothing that corresponds to an engagement. Not only is there no engagement ring, but serious courtship is supposed to be more-or-less secret. Amish youth seem to be inordinately shy in this respect and they do their utmost to

---

* Elmer Smith, who has made a study of the subject, believes that bundling is by no means uncommon among the Amish, particularly in the more liberal midwestern districts. He states that the Amish themselves refer to the custom as bed-courting rather than bundling, but that—by whatever name—the practice has never created any undue sex problems. (Elmer L. Smith, *Bundling: A Curious Courtship Custom*, Lebanon, Pennsylvania, Applied Arts Publishers, 1969.)

keep their *amours* to themselves. Even their immediate families are not informed until such time as marital approval is requested. Once the couple is "published" in church, however—generally two Sundays prior to the wedding—marriage automatically follows. There is very little interdating or intermarriage with outsiders, and it is a rare day that the Old Order Amish lose one of their fold in this manner. When it does happen, the "grapevine" works overtime.

While courting couples are assumed to have feelings of affection for each other, romantic love is not exalted as it is in society at large. An Amish boy or girl is not expected to fall in love at first sight; in fact, marriage is generally between those who have known one another since childhood. The term "love" to the Amish is more likely to signify a relationship that develops after marriage than a romantic feeling kindled through premarital dalliance. By virtue of training and home experience, Amish boys and girls are aware that their marriage will be a functional relationship, and that the husband, wife, and children will share in the running of the farmstead.

MARRIAGE

Amish weddings are gala occasions; indeed, it is no exaggeration to say that weddings are the most impressive and memorable of all their social events. As was mentioned previously, an Amishman's life revolves around his home. He has relatively few outside interests or activities, and because of this it is easy to see why weddings are of such widespread interest.

"Generally," writes Bachman, "when an Amish minister is asked whether the Amish Church is growing, he will not mention the number of accessions to the Church by baptism, but the number of marriages which took place during the preceding year. The Amish Church is composed of families, rather than of individual members. It is not surprising, therefore, that weddings are occasions of prime importance in the Amish community."[6]

Since it is customary for the entire district membership, plus other relatives and friends, to be invited, weddings generally take place in November after the fall harvest. (It would be rare indeed for an Amishman to marry in June.) Traditionally, marriages are performed on Tuesdays or Thursdays, at the home of the bride. The wedding ceremony is quite lengthy, certain portions of the Old Testament being quoted verbatim. It is a simple

---

[6] Bachman, *op. cit.*, p. 169.

affair, however, as judged by outside standards, since there are no bridal bouquets or floral decorations of any kind. Also notable by its absence is the wedding march or other music. At the close of the ceremony the bride and groom join hands, but in keeping with the Amish ban on jewelry, no wedding ring is exchanged.

The Old Order Amish do not have photographs taken of themselves ("Thou shalt not make unto thee any graven image, or any likeness. . . ." Exodus 20:4), so that—contrary to the popular trend—their weddings are not inundated by a flood of amateur and professional photographers.

If the wedding ceremony is simple, the dinner that follows is most certainly not. Like other rural people, the Amish have remarkable appetites and normally consume large quantities of food at an everyday meal. And the wedding feast is not meant to be an ordinary meal. The writer knows of an Amish bill of fare that included one dozen each of chickens, ducks, and geese; 50 loaves of bread; several bushels of potatoes; vats of assorted vegetables and sauces; 60 pies; a dozen large layer cakes; bowls of mixed fruit; and a seemingly endless supply of fresh milk. With so much food, it is little wonder that belching at the table is accepted by one and all as a sign of appreciation!

Should the reader wonder where all the food comes from, let it quickly be said that an Amishman's appetite, fortunately, is more than matched by his food-raising capacity. In addition to the vast quantities of farm products sold to commercial markets, a ready food supply is kept for home use. In a single season, Amish housewives have been known to put up over 1,000 quarts of preserved fruits and vegetables!

In the actual cooking and serving of the wedding feast, ample help is provided by women of the district. Kitchens are purposely made large so as to contain 8 or 10 cooks at a time, and in most cases the guests are served in shifts. Smith reports that "frequently the same dishes are used without benefit of washing between 'shifts,' and one dish is typically used for many different types of food."[7] Such a system would not appeal to most readers; yet, if some dish-saving procedure were not utilized, things might become unmanageable. It must be remembered that the old-fashioned Amish kitchens have no labor-saving devices. Even at ordinary meals, "saving on dishes" is often a necessity, owing to the large families. Smith goes on to say that:

> When you eat in an Amish home, you are often expected to use one plate for almost everything. This plate is often a large soup bowl, and if the meal starts with chicken noodle soup, you eat the soup

---

[7] Smith, *Amish People*, p. 29.

from this plate, and later, when meat and vegetables or salad are put on the table, you use this same bowl for those foods also.

It is assumed that you will eat everything you put on your plate, for any residue is not only a waste of food but a nuisance, because it has to be taken from the plate to make room for the next course. Further, garbage creates more work, for there is no garbage collection, and the Amish periodically bury it. When the main portion of the meal is completed, home-canned fruit, jello, custard, pie, or whatever is served for dessert is frequently placed on the same plate.[8]

Feast and festivities over, the couple embark on their honeymoon. But, whereas most people visualize the honeymoon as a more-or-less luxurious trip, one aim of which is privacy, among the Amish it is simply an extended series of visits with friends and relatives. As guests on the honeymoon circuit, the couple are the recipients of many wedding presents, usually in the form of practical gifts for the home.

Following the honeymoon, the couple take their place in the community as husband and wife and settle down to the business of farming. In some cases they will live with the husband's parents, gradually taking over the bulk of the farming and household duties, while the parents retire to the addition built onto the house for just this purpose (the "grossdawdy house"). In most cases, however, the couple will live close by their parents' place in a house purchased because of the proximity.

There is an old Amish saying that the children should not move farther away "than you can see the smoke from their chimney," and in actuality the large majority of brides and grooms are born in the same county that their fathers were born in. In fact, about the only time an Amishman moves out of an area is (1) when there is no suitable land available, or (2) when he has had an irreconcilable religious difference with the bishop. And even in these instances, he tends to move to another Amish settlement. It is because of this preference to live among "their own kind of people" that the area they inhabit tends to expand and become rather solidly Amish.

FAMILY AND KINSHIP

Family life among the Old Order Amish is fairly uniform. Both men and women are conscientious workers. They take great pride in their farmstead, and while they have only limited

────────────────
[8] *Ibid.*, p. 99.

association with outsiders, they have the reputation of being completely trustworthy.

They are such excellent farmers and so thrifty in their daily living that even their "English" neighbors believe them to be rather wealthy, although in a monetary sense this is not so. As for property, however, they have some extremely valuable holdings. (Some of their land has sold for as high as $3,000 an acre!) As Hostetler puts it: "A popular notion is that an Amishman has plenty of good hard cash, and that he can dig it out of his pants pocket on demand. This is an unfounded notion, but easy to believe because he often pays his bills in hard cash. The Amishman feeds his family well, but he does not have large investments in commercial enterprises. His money is put back into the land."[9]

The farm is the Amishman's daily concern, and it is little wonder that he customarily has a large number of children to aid in the "corporation." Families with 9 or 10 children are fairly common; in fact, the *average* number is between 7 and 8 per family. To an Amishman, parenthood is quite in keeping with the natural order of things, and so far as is known, birth control is not practiced; it is doubtful whether it is even discussed.

For those interested in kinship structure, the following should be noteworthy: during the Colonial period the number of Amish families immigrating to America was small, and since they do not marry outsiders, they have retained the original surnames. Although there are now thousands of Amish in the area, a dozen surnames—Stoltzfus, King, Beiler, Lapp, Zook, Fisher, Esh, Smucker, Glick, Riehl, Blank, and Petersheim—would just about cover the Lancaster County group. Indeed, approximately half of all the Amish who live in southeastern Pennsylvania have the surnames Stoltzfus, King, or Beiler![10] An oft-repeated story concerns the local Amish one-room schoolhouse in which 39 of the 48 pupils were named Stoltzfus!

To make matters more confusing, Amish families tend to use biblical first names, and it is reported that seven male names—John, Amos, David, Jacob, Samuel, Daniel, and Christian—and seven female names—Mary, Annie, Katie, Sarah, Fannie, Lizzie, and Rebecca—comprise more than half of all the given names![11] As might be expected, anyone who sends a letter

---

[9] John A. Hostetler, *Amish Life*, Scottdale, Pennsylvania, Herald Press, 1973, p. 13.

[10] Elmer L. Smith, *Studies in Amish Demography*, Harrisonburg, Virginia, Eastern Mennonite College, 1960, p. 33.

[11] *Ibid.*, pp. 36–38.

to John Beiler or Mary Stoltzfus with a general rural-delivery address is likely to create a minor community disruption.*

In actual practice, the Old Order Amish are ingenious in their use of nicknames and other identifying family features; indeed, it is doubtful whether any other group even approaches them in this respect. Hostetler writes as follows:

> Name differentiation is achieved by using physical traits of the person, by individual habits, by a humorous happening . . . by occupation, and by place of residence. Chubby Jonas, Curly John, and Shorty Abner are indicative of physical traits. Applebutter John, Butter Abe, and Toothpick John derive from eating habits. Gravy Dan stuck with one Amishman when he poured gravy instead of cream into his coffee. . . .
>
> Jockey Joe is a horse trader, Chicken Elam operates a chicken farm, and Chickie Dan works for him. When my own family moved from Pennsylvania to Iowa, my father was known as Pennsylvania Joe. Nicknames are used in community speech and seldom appear in writing.[12]

Division of labor in an Amish farmstead is clearly demarcated by age and sex. The husband arises around 4:00 A.M., completes his morning chores, and then, aided by his sons, works the fields. His wife, assisted by the daughters, cooks and takes care of the house and garden. During the planting season, however, it is quite common to see what appears to be the entire family in the fields. It should not be forgotten that the Amish are living in much the same manner as the early American colonists, among whom the woman was considered a helpmate, with all that the term implies.

In this connection, there is no doubt that "Papa" has always been the boss. It is he who makes the major decisions. Amish women do not lack for affection and kindness, but theirs is a subordinate status ("But I suffer not a woman to teach, nor to usurp authority over the man . . ."; I Timothy 2:12). They cannot, for example, be considered for the clergy. On the infrequent occasions when the Amish family go to town, it is usually "Papa" who can be seen walking in front, followed by his wife and children. And if perchance you happen to visit an Amish home, the

---

* The postman who delivers mail to Amish families is not the only one facing cognominal difficulties. According to a June, 1974, survey by the Social Security Administration, there are 2,383,000 Smiths in the United States, nearly 2,000,000 Johnsons, more than 1,500,000 Williams, and well over 1,000,000 each of Brown, Jones, Miller, Davis, and Martin!

[12] Hostetler, *Amish Society*, pp. 142–143.

man of the house will do most of the talking. Should a woman forget her place and commence to chatter, her spouse will probably admonish her with a polite but firm "Mama!"

Following the colonial heritage, children also have subordinate status. However, although the Amish are strict, they do not go overboard on discipline, and the writer can attest to the fact that their youngsters have a joyous childhood. Hostetler, the foremost authority on Amish life, writes that:

> Early in life the child learns that the Amish are "different" from other people. Thus he must learn to understand not only how to play the role at home and in the Amish system, but also how to conduct himself in relation to the norms of his "English" neighbors.
>
> He cannot have clothes and toys like the "English" people have. He soon learns to imitate his parents and to take pride in the "difference." The Amish boy or girl is raised so carefully within the Amish family and community that he never feels secure outside it.[13]

Overall, there is a good deal of evidence to suggest that the Amish maintain what is perhaps the strongest and most stable family system in America. They seldom marry outside the group. Their birthrate is unusually high and is not affected by general economic conditions. Illegitimacy is almost unheard of, as is adultery. Desertion is virtually unknown, and no divorces have yet been reported. In brief, practically all the Amish marry, they have large families, and they stay married until death intervenes—and even in this instance, analysis of their death-rate figures indicates an "enviable mortality age."[14]

So far as can be determined, the American record for the largest family is held by an Amishman—John Eli Miller, who died at the age of 95.

> He was survived by five of his seven children, 61 grandchildren, 338 great-grandchildren, and six great-great-grandchildren, a grand total of 410 descendants. . . . At the end of his life, the postman was bringing John Miller word of the birth of a new descendant on the average of once every ten days.
>
> What did he think about his large family? Did it worry him to see it growing so large? Indeed it did. John Miller summarized it in one simple question he constantly repeated: "Where will they all find good farms?"[15]

---

13 *Ibid.*, p. 154.

14 Smith, *Studies in Amish Demography*, p. 96.

15 Glenn D. Everett, "One Man's Family," *Population Bulletin*, 17, No. 8, 1961. See also Garrett Hardin (ed.), *Population, Evolution, Birth Control*, San Francisco, W. H. Freeman and Company, 1963, pp. 47–51.

"OUR WAY OF LIFE"

The question is often raised whether the Amish are a happy people. "How," it is asked, "can a group be content with their way of life when they are still living in the 1700's?" The question is not an easy one to answer. Happiness is a relative term. It is difficult to define and impossible to measure. But in the case of the Amish—a group whose family life is about as different from our own as it is possible for a civilized group's to be—the question warrants consideration.

To begin with, insofar as external signs are concerned, the Old Order Amish would appear to be a thriving group. Economically they are well off. They have good-sized landholdings, which, by the sweat of their brow, they have developed into some of the country's most fertile acreage. There is nothing remotely resembling a millionaire among them, but at the same time there is little or no poverty. No Amishman has ever been on public relief or has accepted any other type of state aid, including old age pensions and other forms of social security; in fact, acceptance of such practices would violate their religious beliefs. (The federal government has agreed to exempt the group from the social security program. Accordingly, the Amish neither pay social security taxes nor receive any of the benefits therefrom.)

The Amish are a rapidly growing group, despite the fact that they make practically no conversions. Yearbook figures in this instance are misleading since only baptized members are counted, thus excluding the younger age groups. Extrapolating from various sources, including the *Mennonite Yearbook,* the

An Amish social gathering. (Fred J. Wilson)

present writer would estimate that the Old Order Amish population in the United States is in the neighborhood of 75,000.

According to those who have lived among them, the Amish are quite content to follow their conservative way of life. They love the soil and are happy in their work. They are well aware that they are different from other people, but this very difference gives them a feeling of closeness to God ("But ye are a chosen generation, a royal priesthood, an holy nation, a peculiar people. . . ."; I Peter 2:9). Their rejection of practically all modern technology is thought of not as a sacrifice but as literal proof that they are following in His footsteps.

Then, too, the fact that all of the membership are following an equally severe path gives the Amish people a powerful feeling of group solidarity. It is this solidarity, plus their communality of interests and rejection of almost all forms of commercialism, that leads them to a genuine enjoyment of one another's company. When a member deviates, the *Meidung* is resorted to, but so deeply does the average Amishman believe in his way of life that this sanction seldom has to be imposed—and when it is, it generally isn't long before the "deviant" repents and is readmitted to the fold.

During a discussion with the late Dr. Charles Spotts, Professor of Religion at Franklin and Marshall College, Lancaster, Pennsylvania, who lived in the heart of the Amish community (Smoketown), the following remarks were made to the writer:

> They probably have more reason to be happy than most other groups in the sense that their areas of tension are not nearly so great. They are not concerned with such things as hot and cold wars or international relations generally. Except on relevant local issues, they rarely vote. They are not concerned with "conspicuous consumption" or "competing" in the secular sense. I don't believe that "envy," as we use the term, has much meaning for them.
>
> They have a feeling of security that comes with being deeply religious. As a matter of fact, most of our so-called social problems are unknown among the Amish. There is practically no alcoholism. Crime is rare, and delinquency is a minor problem. There isn't even much profanity. Sex offenses are few and far between. I never heard of any divorces. The Amish are stone honest and everybody around here knows it. They have placed themselves in God's hands, and His message is derived through Biblical allegories. It is impossible for an Amishman to separate religion from the rest of his life. As it relates to his daily conduct and outlook on life, every day is Sunday.

It would appear, then, on the basis of a variety of evidence, that the Old Order Amish are a relatively contented and well-adjusted people. They have not, obviously, created a utopia.

From time to time, signs of strain appear: tourism upsets daily routine; young people sometimes voice their discontent with the strict way of life; individuals and groups do secede; even suicide is by no means unknown among the Amish.

When the debits and credits are compared, nevertheless, the Old Order Amish come off very well indeed. They are willing to forego personal attainment in exchange for a deeply rewarding system of family and group values. For 250 years the Amish have believed in the primacy of the group over the individual, and in the process they have achieved a life style that harmonizes almost perfectly with their religious beliefs.

THE FUTURE

Whether time will eventually make inroads upon the Amish—in the form of a more liberal way of life—no one can say for sure. Thus far they have shown an almost miraculous resistance to change, and in the writer's opinion, there are indications that they will go right on following their traditional practices.

It is commonly believed that the Amish maintain an inflexible social system, but this is hardly the case. Districts may vary in their degree of orthodoxy, and an Amishman who is not in agreement with the tenets of his own group can move to a district that is more liberal (or more conservative). In some of the more liberal districts, for example, the men's hair is worn shorter, hat brims are narrower, women's skirts are not so long, hymns are sung at a faster tempo, bottled gas may be used; even the horse and buggy may be modernized to include such things as a cigarette lighter, horn, and turn signals.

In the most conservative districts, on the other hand, men actually wear their hair shoulder-length. Not only belts but suspenders are forbidden, trousers being held up by means of drawstrings. Women wear floor-length dresses and "scoop" hats made of straw, similar to those worn by European peasants two centuries ago. Seeming necessities, such as screens for the houses, are completely taboo. Buggies are without springs or dashboard and have a white top.

If the districts in question are not too far apart in their practices, they maintain "full fellowship" with one another; otherwise, there is no interaction. The point is that this hierarchical patterning of the districts from liberal to conservative gives the individual Amish family some choice as to clan affiliation. It should perhaps be mentioned that liberal–conservative gradations continue beyond the Old Order Amish proper; e.g., there are the Church or "Automobile" Amish, the Conservative Mennonites, the Mennonites, the Reformed Mennonites, and various in-between categories.

Paradoxically, the more conservative Amish districts are less likely to lose members than are the liberal groups or those that have established relations with the Mennonites. For instance, the Lancaster County settlement, of whom we have been writing, is quite conservative; yet they are infrequently troubled by dissidents or by splitting off. The district bishops meet periodically to standardize policy, and anyone who disagrees with policy formulations is free to move to another area.

What appears to be "change" to the outsider, therefore, is usually a specific practice by one of the more "liberal" Amish clans. Some of the latter employ only a mild form of the *Meidung* and are fairly modern with respect to their use of farm machinery.

With regard to most of the Old Order Amish settlements, however—such as the *streng Meidung* group of Lancaster County, Pennsylvania—the only changes that have taken place are those involving minor details. In terms of occupation, transportation, housing, rejection of electrical appliances, general attire, religious convictions, moral codes, marital practices, patriarchal emphasis, biblical adherence, pacifism, and general life style, it would be difficult to point to a single major change. There is room in the Amish system for some flexibility, but this relates to differences among districts rather than to significant change within a district.

The attitude of the Amish toward schooling is a well-known case in point. Practically everyone who reads a newspaper is aware of the fact that the Amish do not believe in formal schooling. They agree to send their children to grammar school in order to learn the "three R's," but at the eighth-grade level they draw a line beyond which they will not go.

The Amish feel that their children will be farmers and that what they need is on-the-job training rather than higher education. There is also the fear that high school and college might tend to draw young people away from the farm and away from the Amish way of life. Since the law prescribes compulsory school attendance up to a certain age, the Amish are periodically prosecuted for their refusal to conform. Time and again, parents have gone to jail rather than comply with what they feel are discriminatory statutes. The point is that the conflict has been going on since World War I, and the Amish have not budged from their position—nor is it likely, on a major issue like education, that they ever will.

163

As a matter of fact, it may just be that time is on the side of the Amish. The idea of Amish parents being taken to prison seems inconsistent in a society supposedly noted for its religious tolerance—and both the public and the courts seem finally to be recognizing this fact. When a Wisconsin court convicted Amish parents for refusing to send their children to a local high school, the decision was appealed to the State Supreme Court. In a landmark decision of 1970, the Court overruled the conviction:

> There is no such compelling state interest in two years high school compulsory education as will justify the burden it places upon the appellants' free exercise of their religion. To force a wordly education on all Amish children, the majority of whom do not want or need it, in order to confer a dubious benefit on the few who might later reject their religion is not a compelling interest.[16]

The case was appealed to the United States Supreme Court, and in 1972—in another landmark decision—the Court also ruled in favor of the Amish:

> A State's interest in universal education, however highly we rank it, is not totally free from a balancing process when it impinges on other fundamental rights and interests, such as those specifically protected by the Free Exercise Clause of the First Amendment, and the traditional interest of parents with respect to the religious upbringing of their children. . . .
>   We see that the record in this case abundantly supports the claim that the traditional way of life of the Amish is not merely a matter of personal preference, but one of deep religious conviction, shared by an organized group, and intimately related to daily living. . . . Enforcement of the State's requirement of compulsory formal education after the eighth grade would gravely endanger if not destroy the free exercise of respondents' religious beliefs.[17]

These cases have been quoted in some detail since— from the Amish standpoint— they are perhaps the most momentous decisions ever handed down by American courts. They also attest to the fact that religious freedom in the United States is still a cherished concept.

Another clue to the future lies in the fact that the Amish have a great deal of respect for their old folks, an attitude that in itself may be an indication of a contented people. In any event,

---

[16] Quoted in John A. Hostetler and Gertrude Enders Huntington, *Children in Amish Society*, New York, Holt, Rinehart and Winston, Inc., 1971, p. 99. For an excellent discussion of the issue, see Chapter Seven, pp. 97–104.

[17] Quoted in Gerald Gunther and Noel Dowling, *Constitutional Law and Individual Rights in Constitutional Law*, Mineola, New York, The Foundation Press, Inc., 1974, pp. 434–435.

parents, grandparents, and great-grandparents are likely to be living near their grown children or on the same farm with them. Most Amish farmers are able to retire before they reach 60, so that the length of time they spend near their children is considerable. And any tendency on the part of the young to relax the rules would have little chance of fulfillment so long as the old folks are on hand—which they usually are.

All things considered, it appears that the Old Order Amish have a reasonably bright future in America. It is possible that in certain districts, community problems may flare anew. In other areas, tourism may increasingly upset daily routine. And always, of course, there will be "worldly" trends that must be resisted. On balance, however, the major difficulties of the Amish may be behind them.

165

SELECTED READINGS

Bachman, Calvin G., *The Old Order Amish of Lancaster County, Pennsylvania*, Lancaster, Pennsylvania, The Pennsylvania German Society, 1961.

Budget, The, Sugarcreek, Ohio (newspaper published for Amish readers).

Byler, Uria, *School Bells Ringing: A Manual for Amish Teachers and Parents*, Aylmer, Ontario, Pathway Publishing Company, 1969.

Dyck, C. J. (ed.), *An Introduction to Mennonite History*, Scottdale, Pennsylvania, Herald Press, 1967.

Erickson, Donald A., "The 'Plain People' and American Democracy," *Commentary*, January, 1968, pp. 43–47.

Hostetler, John A., *Amish Society*, Baltimore, The Johns Hopkins Press, 1968.

————, and Huntington, Gertrude Enders, *Children in Amish Society*, New York, Holt, Rinehart and Winston, Inc., 1971.

Jencks, Christopher, "A Reappraisal of the Most Controversial Educational Document of Our Times," *New York Times Magazine*, August 10, 1962, pp. 12 ff.

Kollmorgen, Walter M., *Culture of a Contemporary Community: The Old Order Amish of Lancaster County, Pennsylvania*, Washington, D.C., U.S. Department of Agriculture, 1942

Landing, James E., "The Amish, the Automobile, and Social Interaction," *Journal of Geography*, January, 1972, pp. 52–57.

Madeira, Sheldon, "A Study of the Education of the Old Order Amish of Lancaster County, Pennsylvania," Ph.D. dissertation, University of Pennsylvania, 1955.

Mennonite Yearbook and Directory, Scottdale, Pennsylvania, Mennonite Publishing House (published yearly since 1905).

Mook, Maurice A., "Nicknames Among the Amish," *Mennonite Life,* January, 1962, pp. 33–46.

Redekop, Calvin W., *The Old Colony Mennonites,* Baltimore, The Johns Hopkins Press, 1969.

Redfield, Robert, "The Folk Society," *American Journal of Sociology,* January, 1947, pp. 292–308.

Rice, Charles S., and Steinmetz, Rollin C., *The Amish Year,* New Brunswick, New Jersey, Rutgers University Press, 1956.

Schreiber, William, *Our Amish Neighbors,* Chicago, University of Chicago Press, 1962.

Smith, Elmer L., *The Amish People,* Hicksville, New York, Exposition Press, 1958.

———, *Studies in Amish Demography,* Harrisonburg, Virginia, Eastern Mennonite College, 1960.

———, *Bundling Among the Amish,* Lebanon, Pennsylvania, Applied Arts Publishers, 1969.

Stoltzfus, Grant M., "History of the First Amish Mennonite Communities in America," M.A. thesis, University of Pittsburgh, 1954.

Wenger, John C., *The Doctrines of the Mennonites,* Scottdale, Pennsylvania, Mennonite Publishing House, 1958.

———, *The Mennonite Church in America,* Scottdale, Pennsylvania, Herald Press, 1967.

Yoder, Joseph W., *Rosanna of the Amish,* Huntington, Pennsylvania, Yoder Publishing Company, 1940.

8

Minority Family Types II—Nationality:
The Italian Family

ONE PHASE OF American family life that is sometimes overlooked is the diversity of ethnic subtypes brought about by large-scale immigration. The U.S. Census of 1910, for instance, revealed that 75 percent of the inhabitants of cities such as New York, Chicago, Detroit, Cleveland, and Boston were either immigrants or the children of immigrants. Some groups, such as the Germans and Swedes, assimilated rapidly and within a generation or two had lost much of their ethnic identity. Others, such as the Armenians and Jews, tended to reject the intermarriage process and retained many of their distinctive culture traits.

The Italians, in this respect, fell somewhere in the middle: they assimilated—but not rapidly. They learned to speak English but maintained a working knowledge of Italian. While some moved to "Americanized" neighborhoods, as many, if not more, remained in solidly Italian areas. Some intermarried, but others did not. New loyalties were formed, but not necessarily at the expense of old ones. The assimilation of Italian-Americans is still continuing, and this process—as it affects family behavior—is the subject of the present account. Basic to any understanding of the family life of Italian-Americans, however, is an awareness of their Old-World cultural background.

THE FAMILY SYSTEM IN ITALY

The large majority of Italian immigrants to the United States during the period 1875–1920 came from the provinces south of Rome, including Sicily. For the most part, the men were *contadini* (peasant farmers) and laborers, but almost irrespective of their occupation, they had found it difficult to make ends meet. The land was often poor, taxes were exorbitant, and the ruling classes were insensitive to the needs of the people.

As a matter of record, the history of the region is a sequence of invasion and oppression by such disparate groups as the Phoenicians, Carthaginians, Vandals, Goths, and French, as well as various groups from Northern Italy. And even when there was no invasion as such, exploitation by the landowning classes continued with little interruption. The *contadini* rose up on numerous occasions—against both foreign and native oppressors—but the rebellions were invariably crushed.

That the *contadini* were able to survive at all was due to their ability to form a rock-ribbed family system and to sustain this system irrespective of the outside power structure. A number of writers have commented on this point. As Gambino sees it:

> The unique family pattern of Southern Italy constituted the real sovereignty of that land, regardless of which governments nominally ruled it. If they brought any customs that might strengthen the family system, these were gradually absorbed. But those that were hostile to the family were resisted.[1]

Ianni says simply that "Italy is a nation of families, not of individuals. Throughout Italy the family is the chief architect of the social structure, commanding allegiance above all else. In the north as in the south, the family is inextricably interwoven in business and government."[2]

One of the most eloquent statements is that of Barzini:

> The first source of power is the family. The Italian family is a stronghold in a hostile land: within its walls and among its members, the individual finds consolation, help, advice, provisions, loans, weapons, allies, and accomplices to aid him in his pursuits. No Italian who has a family is ever alone. He finds in it a refuge in which to lick his wounds after a defeat; or an arsenal and a staff for his victorious drives.
>
> Scholars have always recognized the Italian family as the only fundamental institution in the country, adapted through the centuries to changing conditions, the real foundation of whichever social order prevails. In fact, the law, the State, and society function only if they do not directly interfere with the family's supreme interests. . . .[3]

---

[1] From *Blood of My Blood,* copyright © 1974 by Richard Gambino. Reprinted by permission of Doubleday & Co., Inc. Copyright 1972 by Richard Gambino. Reprinted by permission of The Harold Matson Company Inc. Pp. 4–5. See Chapter 1 for an excellent discussion of the subject.

[2] Francis Ianni, with Elizabeth Reuss-Ianni, *A Family Business,* New York, Russell Sage Foundation, 1972, p. 16.

[3] Luigi Barzini, *The Italians,* New York, Atheneum, 1964, p. 2.

The Italian *famiglia* (family) described above was far different from its American counterpart. In the *contadino* tradition, writes Gambino, "the famiglia was composed of all of one's blood relatives, including those relatives Americans would consider very distant cousins, aunts, and uncles, an extended clan whose genealogy was traced through paternity. The clan was supplemented through an important custom known as *comparatico* (godparenthood), through which carefully selected outsiders became to an important extent members of the family."[4]

The same author goes on to say that the family system was the only one to which the *contadino* paid much attention, all the other social institutions being looked upon with attitudes "ranging from indifference to scorn and contempt."

> One had absolute responsibilities to family superiors, and absolute rights to be demanded from subordinates in the hierarchy. All ambiguous situations were arbitrated by the head-of-family, a position held within each household by the father until it was given to—or, in the case of the father's senility, taken away by—one of the sons.[5]

There is an old saying among Southern Italians that, while the father is the head of the *famiglia*, the mother is the center.[6] She was, in other words, the axis around which all family-centered activities revolved. One of her main tasks, in this respect, was the day-to-day care of the children, particularly the daughters. Premarital sex was strongly taboo, and a girl who lost her virginity prior to marriage violated the *onore* (honor) of the *famiglia*.

There were many other facets, of course, to the traditional Italian family, but let us examine these in terms of the *contadino*'s American experience.

THE FIRST GENERATION: CONTINUATION OF *LA VIA VECCHIA*

One wonders—in view of the primacy of their family and their closeness to the soil—why so many Italians left Italy for America. And, indeed, there is a Sicilian proverb that says, "Whoever forsakes *la via vecchia* (the old way) for the new knows what he is

---

[4] Gambino, *op. cit.*, p. 3.

[5] *Ibid.*, p. 5.

[6] Gambino, *op. cit.*, p. 7.

losing, but not what he will find."[7] In his best-selling book about the charms and imperfections of Italy, Luigi Barzini also contends that:

> Not many Italians willingly travel abroad in any direction, north, south, east, or west. They always feel more or less exiled and unhappy in alien lands, and honestly believe the attractions of their homeland to be most satisfying. They are the first victims of the famous charm of Italy, never satiated with her sights, climate, food, music, and life. Familiarity never breeds contempt in them. . . .
>
> Those Italians who travel abroad . . . are usually homesick; they look for caffè espresso, a good Italian restaurant—wherever they go—and sigh for the day of their return.[8]

Whether or not the above can be taken literally, the Italians who immigrated to America did not do so in a spirit of travel and adventure. They came because of the dire economic conditions mentioned earlier. Many of the immigrants came with the idea of returning to Italy once they had accumulated enough money to reestablish themselves in their native land. And many of them did return—millions, in fact. Lopreato writes that "today in Southern Italy, there is scarcely a village where a large percentage (often a majority) of the landowners are not returnees from the United States."[9]

Despite the millions who returned, however, many more stayed in America. Today, Italian-Americans form one of the largest ethnic groups in the country, with a total number running well into the millions. Interestingly enough, Italian immigrants are still entering the United States at the rate of some 25,000 a year—more than from any other country outside the Western Hemisphere.[10]

The *contadini* who came to America during the 1875–1920 period were by no means "united," in either the Old World or the New. On the contrary, different provinces and villages spoke different dialects, and the people of one district often evidenced minor hostility toward residents of another. (Marriages customarily took place *within* rather than between districts.)

As a result, Italians who immigrated to America tended to settle among their *paesani*—kinfolk, friends, and neighbors

---

[7] Quoted in Gambino, *op. cit.*, p. 3.

[8] Barzini, *op. cit.*, p. 2.

[9] Joseph Lopreato, *Italian Americans*, New York, Random House, Inc., 1970, p. 158.

[10] See the U.S. Bureau of the Census, *Statistical Abstract of the United States* (published yearly), for immigration totals. The term "ethnic," as used above, refers to nationality and does not include racial groups.

An Italian family arriving in America in 1905. (Lewis W. Hine, Ellis Island, 1905, International Museum of Photography at George Eastman House)

from the same district in Italy. In the early 1900's it was not uncommon to find certain neighborhoods comprised almost entirely of immigrants from a specific Italian village. Other American groups had little knowledge of the *paesano* principle and were prone to refer to any urban concentration of Italians simply as "Little Italy."

Many of the *contadini* would have been more than happy to settle in agricultural areas, but by the time of their arrival the era of cheap (or free) land had come to an end. The Italians, in this respect, were the first immigrant group not to have easy access to the land. Being a gregarious people, therefore, they settled where they felt the most comfortable—in urban areas as close as possible to their own kind. The major areas of Italian concentration came to be in New York, Philadelphia, Chicago, Boston, Buffalo, San Francisco, Rochester, New Haven, Baltimore, and St. Louis.

Mangione writes as follows on the subject:

Wherever they settled in America, the Italians tried to be as near one another as possible. They were by nature a gregarious people. D. H. Lawrence, the British novelist who once lived in Sicily, observed that the Italians there "hang together in clusters and can never be physically near enough." In their New World, where the immigrants' need to be together was even stronger, the Italians spent most of their free time in a long round of social gatherings with friends and relatives.[11]

Special mention should be made, in this connection, of the Italians' penchant for home ownership. As Lopreato points out, the *contadini* seldom owned land in Italy. Not only were they exploited and their labor controlled, but even their sense of dignity was violated by those in power. Their only secular refuge was their home. "It gave the peasant what little privacy he had, and allowed him to believe he was not absolutely at the mercy of others."[12] Little wonder that, as soon as he could afford it, the Italian immigrant would put a down payment on a house.

Economic Difficulties. The trouble was that economic progress came slowly. Contrary to the Old World rumor, the streets were not paved with gold. As Coleman puts it:

> It was an old superstition, sometimes half believed by the simplest immigrants, that the streets of New York were paved with gold. When they got there, they learned three things: first, that the streets were not paved with gold; second, that the streets were not paved at all; and third, that they were expected to pave them.[13]

Some idea of the economic difficulties experienced by the first-generation Italians can be seen from the following *daily-wage scale*,[14] advertised in New York City newspapers and handbills:

Common labor, white: $1.30 to $1.50
Common labor, colored: $1.25 to $1.40
Common labor, Italian: $1.15 to $1.25

In spite of the fact that the immigrants received communal aid from their own *paesani*, the various urban settlements continued the Old-World pattern of mutual antagonism. Glazer and Moynihan report that "illiteracy seriously hampered the development of these diverse settlements into a single ethnic group, for differences in dialect, which in turn engendered mutual suspicion, tended to endure in the absence of widespread communication."[15] Also, having few skills, the immigrants were shunted to

---

[11] Jerry Mangione, *America Is Also Italian,* New York, G. P. Putnam's Sons, 1969, pp. 53–54.

[12] Lopreato, *op. cit.,* p. 48.

[13] Quoted in Gambino, *op cit.,* p. 101.

[14] Quoted in Gambino, *op. cit.,* p. 77.

[15] Nathan Glazer and Daniel P. Moynihan, *Beyond the Melting Pot,* Cambridge, Massachusetts, the M.I.T. Press and Harvard University Press, 1971, p. 186.

the ranks of day laborers; in fact, many of them took up the pick and shovel just as they had in the old country.

Unfortunately, their peasant background tended to make them suspicious of formal education. In their home villages, schools had been open only to the landowning classes. "Education was for a cultural style of life the peasant could never aspire to. Nor was there an ideology of change. Intellectual curiosity and originality were ridiculed or suppressed. 'Do not make your child better than you are,' runs a South Italian proverb."[16]

Also, there is little doubt that the immigrants considered education to be a threat to *la via vecchia* (the old way) and for this reason they were reluctant to have their children exposed to the "perils" of higher education. Mangione, for example, whose parents were Italian immigrants, reports that "in some families, like mine, parents became so afraid of losing communication with their American-born children that they would not permit English to be spoken in the home."[17]

Resistance to Change.   There is little doubt, also, that the linguistic barrier contributed both to the economic problems of the *contadini* and to their general resistance to New World ideas. The old language and *la via vecchia* seemed to go hand in hand. Lopreato makes the following comment relative to linguistics:

> For the Southern Italian peasant at the end of the nineteenth century, the future rarely extended much further than the next sowing or threshing season. . . . Little wonder that even today the future tense among the group is virtually unknown. . . .
>
> As a result, for a long time the Italians acquired only whatever little English was absolutely essential on the job. For the rest, they relied on the old dialects, which were not always appropriate. . . . New words and conceptualizations had to be developed. There had been no terms in the peasant's language for the English "shop," "store," "refrigerator," "factory," "car," "girlfriend." Thus a special American Italian language developed, heavily interspersed with "shoppa," "storu," "frigidaira," "fattoria," "carru," "gellafrienda," and like terms.[18]

In another connection, Mangione states that the immigrants tended to resist change and "tried to live as they had in Italy. They shopped at stores run by Italians. They went to Italian lawyers, doctors, dentists, shoemakers, and barbers. Nearly all their business and social life was conducted in their native tongue.

---

[16] *Ibid.*, p. 199.
[17] Mangione, *op. cit.*, p. 42.
[18] Lopreato, *op. cit.*, pp. 56–57.

La via vecchia. (Wendy Snyder MacNeill)

This was especially true of the Italian women, who hardly ever encountered Americans. Even when the women worked in factories, as thousands of them did, they were likely to be surrounded by other Italians."[19]

The upshot was that the Italian immigrant tended to create a closed family and community system, with suspicion cast on all *forestieri* or outsiders. This mistrust was often directed not only at the non-*paesani*, but also at the agencies of social control, such as the Church and the law. Indeed, the history of Italian assimilation in the United States is largely a story of their breaking out of these self-imposed bonds of suspicion.

Courtship and Marriage. Most of the immigrants were single, although a fair proportion were married. Nearly all were in the younger age-groups. But their marriages—whether of the Old World or the New—were likely to be arranged or strongly influenced by their parents. Lalli states that the old Italians who survive today—as grandparents and great-grandparents—"often speak of their own marriages as not arranged but exceptional.

---

[19] Mangione, *op. cit.*, p. 42.

This may often be truly the case, but sometimes it seems to be more of a story which the oldsters spin to fit the American expectations of their children. The climax to these stories is the moment of decision at which they told their parents that they would not go through with the arranged marriage but had chosen someone else."[20]

The *contadino* came from a long tradition of severely restricted courtship; as a matter of fact, in the old country it was deemed most improper for a young boy and girl to be alone together. This prohibition, moreover, applied not only to courting couples but to those who were already engaged. According to *la via vecchia*, it was believed that the longer the engagement, the greater the temptation "to give in to the passions. Therefore, the number of assigned chaperons was increased."[21]

It goes almost without saying, of course, that premarital necking and petting were taboo, and for a *contadino* girl to be unchaste at the time of marriage was sufficient grounds for a lasting scandal. Both public opinion and Church edict tended to keep young people in line, and Italian immigrants settling within the various *paesani* groups followed much the same system of social control.

Another consideration—one not faced in the old country—was that Italian boys and girls were forbidden to date non-Italians. And while there were exceptions, to be sure, they were few and far between. In isolated cases, boys and girls were actually "locked in their homes or forcibly sent off to live with faraway relatives to prevent marriages to non-Italian Americans."[22]

Marriage itself was considered by the Italian immigrants to be a most important—perhaps the most important—social institution, another tradition that had its roots in *la via vecchia*. Indeed, one reason for the strong taboo against premarital sex was the danger of a bastard child being born, one that would be without a *famiglia*. In the old country, such a condition was both shameful and pitiful. As Gambino puts it: "To be without a family was to be truly a non-being, *un saccu vacante* (an empty sack) as Sicilians say, *un nuddu miscatu cu nenti* (a nobody mixed with nothing).[23]

Some authorities contend that the Italian immigrants placed so much stress on marriage and the family that the men often

175

---

[20] Michael Lalli, "The Italian-American Family: Assimilation and Change," *Family Coordinator*, January, 1969, pp. 44–48. Copyright © 1969 by National Council on Family Relations. Reprinted by permission.

[21] Gambino, *op. cit.*, p. 197.

[22] *Ibid.*, pp. 200–201.

[23] *Ibid.*, p. 34.

rejected occupational careers that might interfere with the famiglia.[24] However that may be, a good example of family primacy is seen in Mario Puzo's *The Godfather.* Don Corleone, one of the heads of the so-called Mafia, says to his godson, "Friendship is everything. Friendship is more than talent. It is more than government. It is almost the equal of family. Never forget that. . . ."[25]

Insofar as the married life of the Italian immigrant was concerned, there was no serious disagreement about lines of authority. Following *la via vecchia,* the man was the head. It was he who, ostensibly at least, made the major decisions, handled the finances, and otherwise fulfilled the role of respected patriarch.

Although he loved his wife, open displays of affection—in keeping with Old World tradition—were avoided. Family discipline, on the other hand, was quite likely to be witnessed by the neighbors, and, as far as the children were concerned, it was a rare father who "spared the rod." Unlike his American counterpart, the Italian father's domain sometimes included shopping, food buying, and—if only in an advisory capacity—food preparation.*

176

---

* A strong case could be made for the claim that Italians have contributed more to the American cuisine than any other foreign-culture group. The foods that have been introduced and/or popularized by the Italians might include: strega, pizza, gnocchi, hoagies (grinders, heroes), antipasto, minestrone, Italian bread, rolls, and pastries, figs, prosciutto, manicotti, meat balls, veal Parmigiana and scallopini, several types of tomato sauces (including marinara), Italian dressing, capers, anchovies, artichokes, chickpeas, lupine, lasagne, pepperoni, pasta e fagioli, Italian water ice, olives and olive oil, chicken cacciatore, ravioli, a wide variety of Italian cheeses (Parmesan, Locatella, Mozzarella, Romano, Provolone, Gorgonzola, Pecorina, Ricotta), hot peppers, finocchi, Italian sausage, Italian wines, and, of course, a mighty array of *pasta*—macaroni, spaghetti, vermicelli, rigatoni, linguini, fettucini. . . .

The Italians also acquainted Americans with *"caffè espresso,* as well as their own kinds of ice cream, *spumoni* and *biscotto tortone.* They also taught us many ways of adding to the flavor of food, with herbs such as oregano and basil and with garlic. . . . The Italians made Americans aware of many foods they had never known. Mussels was one of them. . . . The Italians also introduced to many Americans such vegetables as broccoli, zucchini, escarole, endive, cardoon, chicory, and dandelion." (Mangione, *op cit.,* p. 98.)

[24] *Ibid.,* pp. 89–91.
[25] Mario Puzo, *The Godfather,* Greenwich, Connecticut, Fawcett Publications (paperback), 1969, p. 38.

Women and Children. The role of the first-generation Italian woman is sometimes misunderstood. It is true that, in a nominal sense, hers was a subordinate position. But, in a very practical way, it was more or less expected that she would be able to manipulate her husband. For example, although the husband was the principal breadwinner, it was customary for the wife to be in charge of the family budget and to do the actual spending.

It was the wife, also, who intervened in the day-to-day imbroglios of the children, a role that is reflected in Italian folk songs and stories. As Lopreato puts it:

> The mother became the child's chief source of comfort, his custodian angel, his staunch defender. In the process, she developed techniques of upbringing that instilled a strong and lasting sense of familial duty in the child. It is not uncommon to hear an Italian mother, wherever she may be, say to her child—whatever his age—that unless he does (or avoids doing) a certain thing, he will surely drive her to her grave.[26]

177

It might be noted that, at a *contadino* wedding feast, the groom would cut "the choicest part of the nuptial meal and ceremoniously serve it to his bride." The latter received the tribute, as Gambino points out, "not as a mere romantic object, but as the symbolic center of the new family."[27]

In this same connection, another observation should be made, namely, that—unlike the Irish, Germans, Scandinavians, and other groups—Italian women did not (and do not) work as domestics. To do so would indicate a division of her *family loyalty*—an intolerable turn of events.[28] Little wonder that the expression "Mamma mia!" is so frequently used by Italians of both sexes, and that the Virgin Mary is their most revered saint.

Discipline was strict in the Italian immigrant family, but this is not to say that youngsters were in any sense downgraded. On the contrary, they were considered to be the heart of the family system. Lalli writes that: "The Italian family in America never was, and probably still is not, one which could be analyzed with sole or great emphasis on the husband-wife relationship. Fifty years ago, as well as during the recent past, the childless couple was regarded as singularly unfortunate. 'For a family to be a family,' an old Italian proverb goes, 'there must be children'."[29]

---

[26] Lopreato, *op. cit.*, pp. 50–51.
[27] Gambino, *op. cit.*, p. 160.
[28] *Ibid.*, p. 14.
[29] Lalli, *op. cit.*, p. 47.

Despite problems of poverty, therefore, the first-generation Italian family was likely to be large. Households with five, six, and seven children were commonplace, while one- and two-child families were relatively scarce.

All in all, the foreign-born Italian family was a remarkably stable unit. Noticeably suspicious of outsiders, family members spent much of their daily living within the kin group. They shared their troubles and clung to one another in time of need; they celebrated together at holiday time. Children were taught to have great respect for the aged. Those who became ill or dependent were not sent to institutions but were cared for by relatives or friends.

Divorce was forbidden, and separation and desertion were rare or—in some neighborhoods—unknown. As far as possible, foreign-born Italians maintained the closely knit, patriarchal type of family organization that had existed in the old country for generations. But as their American-born children grew up, certain changes in *la via vecchia* became inevitable.

THE SECOND GENERATION

Italian-Americans of the second generation made changes in their communal style of living, but at times it must have seemed as though economic progress was slow in coming. Most of the males went into semiskilled occupations, although increasing numbers gravitated toward white-collar jobs. The percentage of Italian youth who went into the professions, however, was quite small. In fact, while skepticism with regard to formal education gradually lessened, relatively few youngsters went on to college. A liberal arts education, after all, emphasized such things as broadening of identity, cultural diversity, membership in the larger society, and other values that were felt to be *contra la famiglia*.[30]

Also, the urban concentrations of *paesani* remained formidable, even though the rejection of "outsiders" softened somewhat. Still, the Palisi study revealed that, as compared with the foreign-born, second-generation Italians had only a slightly greater tendency to participate in outside organizations. In fact, the generational differences were so slight that they were not statistically significant.[31]

---

[30] For a discussion of this subject, see Gambino, *op. cit.*, pp. 245–273.
[31] Bartolomeo Palisi, "Ethnic Generation and Social Participation," *Sociological Inquiry*, Spring, 1965, pp. 219–226.

There were some exceptions, to be sure. In an interview-study of young second-generation Italians—made in the late 1930's —Irvin Child found instances of what he termed "the rebel reaction."

Q. What nationality do you consider yourself?
A. I consider myself an American. I have no leanings and no likes for the old country.
Q. If someone asks you what nationality you are, what do you say?
A. I would say I'm an American. I was born here, but my ancestors were Italian. Because I know we're all American here. America is a melting pot.
Q. Do you ever think of yourself as Italian-American?
A. I have to consider myself Italian-American because I am of the first generation born here. I consider myself a new American. We all try to dissociate, as far as possible, the Italian lineage because we want to become a part of America. I regard the Italians of the old country as a separate race.[32]

The following response was typical of what Child called "the in-group reaction":

Q. If someone asks you your nationality, what do you say?
A. Italian.
Q. Do you ever think of yourself as just American?
A. No.
Q. Why not?
A. I was born in America, but my parents are Italian. I was brought up with Italians, and I always said I would stick to my own kind.[33]

That some Italian youth found themselves caught in a crossfire can be seen from the following dialogue:

Q. If someone asks you your nationality, what do you say?
A. I'd say Italian descent, American born.
Q. Do you ever think of yourself as just American?
A. No. I'd rather call myself Italian-American, because then I wouldn't be hurting nobody. If I said I was American, somebody might say, "Why do you say that, if you're from an Italian family?" If I said "Italian," then they'd say, "Why, since you were born in America?"[34]

Mate Selection and Marriage. One of the first customs to undergo widespread change was that of mate selection. Surrounded as they were by a culture in which free dating was the norm,

---

[32] Irvin L. Child, *Italian or American: The Second Generation in Conflict*, New Haven, Yale University Press, 1943, p. 77.
[33] *Ibid.*, p. 119.
[34] *Ibid.*, p. 152.

young Italians were most reluctant to have their parents choose their mates. (We are talking now, roughly, about the period 1925–1955.) For their part, parents were unwilling to let the decision rest entirely with the children. In effect, a kind of compromise was worked out: young people were permitted to select their own mates, but the latter were supposed to be drawn from among the *paesani*, with parental consent required.

While the young Italians were thus able to date persons of their own choosing, there were still some informal limitations. Dating of non-Italians was frowned upon, and intermarriages were relatively infrequent. In his survey of second-generation intermarriage among nine American ethnic groups, Greeley found the Italian rate to be among the lowest.[35] Lalli has described the courtship pattern during this period as follows:

> The Italian ethnics met, danced, sang, and played at weddings, christenings, patron-saint-day celebrations, first communion feasts, and Christmas. However, these occasions were not solemn, quiet affairs, but gay, filled with music, food, and wine. Because of the nature of the feasts and celebrations, the young people who got to know each other fairly well were limited to those whose parents came from the same village or province.[36]

The same author reports that by World War II the boy-meets-girl pattern had become increasingly secularized. "Sacred holidays, weddings, and christenings were still important, but public dances, school events, and picnics provided more occasions for meetings. Dates were still not specifically arranged. Young men and girls would make their appearance as members of separate groups knowing well exactly who would be there. Although such meetings were 'accidental,' a young man would often have the opportunity of taking a girl home. If the relationship developed to the point where a date or two was arranged in advance, and the young man called at the girl's home—there was a strong presumption in the Italian community that an engagement announcement would soon be made."[37]

Marriages generally involved church ceremonies, and the wedding reception and festivities were usually rather elaborate affairs, with many of the *paesani* attending—and imbibing. Following the marriage, it was not uncommon, especially during the depression-ridden 1930's, for the newlyweds to live with one of the two families until such time as they could save enough to establish their own household. The latter was likely to be in the

---

[35] Quoted in Gambino, *op. cit.*, p. 202.
[36] Lalli, *op. cit.*, p. 46.
[37] *Ibid.*

same neighborhood, with a fair degree of the old-community influence.

Family Living. In the new household some of the old traditions persisted, but others tended to die out. The husband continued to make the major decisions, but he was willing—on most

Among second-generation Italians, the bonds between young and old were strong. (Rick Smolan)

matters—to discuss things with other members of the family. He continued to discipline the children, but was less inclined to use corporal punishment—and he no longer insisted that the youngsters turn their weekly wages over to him. In other words, while the second-generation Italian family remained patriarchal, with the father the presumed head, there was—over the years—less and less attempt on his part to rule the family.

Church ties also weakened during this period, and religious activity often came to be considered the domain of the women. Relatively few Italian males entered the priesthood, and the idea of an Italian girl's becoming a nun was looked upon with some misgiving. The record indicates, in addition, that large numbers of Italians broke away from the Roman Catholic Church.[38]

On the other hand, the second-generation Italian family remained a stable unit. The household was likely to be somewhat smaller in size—with noticeably fewer children—but it was still solid.[39] Divorces and marital separations were infrequent. Children were still considered to be the "joy of the earth," and—quite important—the old folks were still treated with genuine affection and respect. Family friendships and social activities were, for the most part, confined to the ever-present *paesani*.

THE THIRD GENERATION

With the approach of the 1980's, Italian-Americans find themselves at a cultural crossroads. On the one hand, they are proud of their cultural heritage and have no intention of rejecting it. They show little proclivity for changing their names or shedding their ethnic identity. Indeed, Italian is still one of the most commonly spoken foreign languages in the United States.

A sentimental people—Barzini[40] refers to Italy as a "realm of the spirit" rather than as a geographical entity—Italian-Americans of all ages maintain real affection for their *paesini*-flavored urban atmosphere. Their trek to the suburbs has been slow. It is understandable that, when Gans wrote his book on an Italian community in Boston, he called it *The Urban Villagers*. He reports that even after all the community houses and buildings

---

[38] See John V. Tolino, "The Church in America and the Italian Problem," *American Ecclesiastical Review*, January, 1939, pp. 23–32; and Henry J. Browne, "The 'Italian Problem' in the Catholic Church of the United States," *Historical Records and Studies*, United States Catholic Historical Society, XXXV, 1946, pp. 46–75.

[39] See Bartolomeo Palisi, "Ethnic Generation and Family Structure," *Journal of Marriage and the Family*, February, 1966, pp. 49–50.

[40] Luigi Barzini, *From Caesar to the Mafia*, New York, Bantam Books, 1972, p. 93.

had been leveled because of an urban development project, ex-residents "would come back on weekends to walk through the old neighborhood and the rubble-strewn streets."[41]

In Glazer and Moynihan's sociological analysis of the various ethnic settlements in New York City, the authors write that, while the spatial distribution of Jews today bears almost no relation to the pattern of 1920, "the Italian districts are still in large measure where they were."

> Nor are these old Italian neighborhoods only shells of their former selves, inhabited exclusively by the older people. Many of the married sons and daughters have stayed close to their parents. . . . And it is striking how the old neighborhoods have been artfully adapted to a higher standard of living rather than simply deserted, as they would have been by other groups, in more American style.
>
> Tenements that once housed eight families now house half as many. The old houses are rebuilt on the inside (there is always a great amount of skilled building and crafts labor in an Italian community), new furniture is brought into old apartments, new cars line the streets, and even the restaurants reflect quality and affluence, for they serve not only friends and relatives who come back to the neighborhood but also those who never moved away, and who now have an income far greater than the cost and quality of their housing would suggest.[42]

183

In Philadelphia, where the present writer was born and raised, the situation is much the same as it is in New York. Whereas other white minorities have left the city for the suburbs, the Italians remain. Their communities in South and West Philadelphia are still situated in the same neighborhoods as they were 50 years ago. Ninth Street still teems with talkative shoppers searching out food bargains among the mile-long rows of pushcarts, stalls, piled crates, and open-front stores. Externally, the whole area seems to go on, decade after decade, unmindful of social change. Internally, however, many of the homes have been done over and refurnished so lavishly that they compare favorably with those in the suburban areas.

It is easy to demonstrate, in other words, that a fair number of third-generation Italians are reluctant to break away from old-community ties. On the other hand, as Ianni points out, many have discovered that "ethnicity is economically as well as socially retarding."[43] And while there is no doubt that the lure of the

[41] Herbert J. Gans, *The Urban Villagers: Group and Class in the Life of Italian-Americans*, New York, The Free Press of Glencoe, Inc., 1962, p. 304.

[42] Glazer and Moynihan, *op. cit.*, pp. 187–188.

[43] Francis Ianni, "The Italo-American Teenager," in David Goddlieb and Charles Ramsey, *The American Adolescent*, Homewood, Illinois, The Dorsey Press, Inc., 1964, p. 223.

paesani remains strong, there is clear evidence that change is in the making. Traditional feelings of distrust toward the outsider are no longer prevalent. Attitudes toward education have softened, and more and more young Italians are going to college. A goodly proportion of third-generation Italians are also moving up into managerial and professional positions.

Teen-agers have adopted the dating and mating habits of their American schoolmates rather than those of their forbears. Gone are the prearranged group get-togethers. Dating and social activities are no longer restricted to the *paesani*. To make matters worse—in the eyes of the oldsters, at least—many young Italians are marrying non-Italians. (Attitudes toward premarital sex, on the other hand, remain conservative. Of the various ethnic groups questioned in the Greeley survey, Italian-Americans were found to have the most restrictive views about both premarital petting and premarital intercourse.)[44]

Whether or not they are mixed, third-generation marriages are likely to begin with a fresh backdrop. Newlyweds prefer to live some distance away from their parents and indeed may not even live among their *paesani*. Any number of young Italians are starting their own families in non-Italian neighborhoods, substantially removed from the old-community influence.

In the new Italian family the father is still the nominal head of the household, but in practice the roles of husband and wife are likely to be equalitarian. And, as is true in the typical American family, great stress is placed on the personality development of the children. The latter, incidentally, are still welcomed—but in much smaller numbers. Following the national trend, third-generation Italian families are likely to be composed of mother, father, and one or two children. And the chances are that the children will show neither more nor less respect for the aged than in any other American family. Femminella puts the matter succinctly when he says that "third-generation Italian-Americans (middle class, suburban, and upwardly mobile) are familistic only to the degree that others in their class, regardless of ethnicity, may also be familistic."[45]

With regard to religious ties, present-day Italian-Americans seem to be divided. One segment—including, perhaps, most of those who have intermarried—tend to renounce Catholicism or to remain as inactive members, avoiding religious services and sending their children to public, instead of parochial, schools.

---

[44] Cited in Gambino, *op. cit.*, pp. 183–184.
[45] Francis Femminella, "The Italian-American Family," in Meyer Barash and Alice Scourby (eds.), *Marriage and the Family*, New York, Random House, Inc., 1970, p. 138.

184

(Philip Jon Bailey)

Another segment retain their ties with the Church and in some cases become "stronger" Catholics than their parents.

There is still no indication, however, that young Italian-Americans are entering holy orders in any numbers. Of the Roman Catholic priests in the United States, only about 12 percent are Italian-Americans, and of the nuns, only 7 percent. In the higher clerical ranks, Italian-Americans account for only five bishops and one archbishop. There has never been an Italian-American cardinal.[46]

The new Italian-American family is not so stable as its predecessors. It is more democratic in function, but, as is true of other democratic-type families, the divorce rate among third-generation Italians has risen. Kinship ties are no longer so binding, and the once-firm hand of the old folks has lost much of its guiding power.

Whether the old-community structure will eventually die out as a geographical entity or whether the various "Little Italies" will continue to serve as a vitalizing force in the perpetuation of Italian culture patterns, only time will tell. But one thing seems

---

[46] Gambino, *op. cit.*, pp. 232 and 239.

evident: as the Italian family has become assimilated, it has absorbed both the weaknesses and strengths of the American family system.

SELECTED READINGS

Barzini, Luigi, *The Italians,* New York, Atheneum, 1964.

———, *From Caesar to the Mafia,* New York, Bantam Books, 1972.

Browne, Henry J., "The 'Italian Problem' in the Catholic Church of the United States," *Historical Records and Studies,* United States Catholic Historical Society, XXXV, 1946, pp. 46–75.

Campisi, Paul J., "Ethnic Family Patterns: The Italian Family in the United States," *American Journal of Sociology,* May, 1948, pp. 443–449.

Child, Irvin L., *Italian or American: The Second Generation in Conflict,* New Haven, Yale University Press, 1943.

Covello, Leonard, "The Social Background of the Italo-American School Child," Ph.D. dissertation, New York University, 1944.

Dinnerstein, Leonard, and Reimers, David, *Ethnic Americans: A History of Immigration and Assimilation,* New York, Dodd, Mead and Co., 1975.

Femminella, Francis, "The Italian-American Family," in Meyer Barash and Alice Scourby (eds.), *Marriage and the Family,* New York, Random House, Inc., 1970.

Gambino, Richard, *Blood of My Blood,* Garden City, New York, Doubleday & Company, Inc. (Anchor Books), 1975.

Gans, Herbert J., *The Urban Villagers: Group and Class in the Life of Italian-Americans,* New York, Free Press of Glencoe, Inc., 1962.

Gini, Corrado, and Caranti, Elio, "The Family in Italy," *Marriage and Family Living,* November, 1954, pp. 350–361.

Glazer, Nathan, and Moynihan, Daniel P., *Beyond the Melting Pot,* Cambridge, Massachusetts, The M.I.T. Press and Harvard University Press, 1971.

Ianni, Francis, "The Italo-American Teen-Ager," in David Goddlieb and Charles Ramsey, *The American Adolescent,* Homewood, Illinois, The Dorsey Press, Inc., 1964.

———, with Reuss-Ianni, Elizabeth, *A Family Business,* New York, Russell Sage Foundation, 1972.

Kalodny, Ralph L., "Ethnic Cleavages in the United States: An Historical Reminder to Social Workers," *Social Work,* January, 1969, pp. 13–23.

Lalli, Michael, "The Italian-American Family: Assimilation and Change," *Family Coordinator*, January, 1969, pp. 44–48.

Lopreato, Joseph, *Italian Americans*, New York, Random House, Inc., 1970.

McLaughlin, Virginia Yans, "Patterns of Work and Family Organization: Buffalo's Italians," in Theodore Rabb and Robert Rotberg (eds.), *The Family in History: Interdisciplinary Essays*, New York, Harper Torchbooks, 1973.

Mangione, Jerry, *America Is Also Italian*, New York, G. P. Putnam's Sons, 1969.

Musmanno, Michael, *The Story of the Italians in America*, Garden City, New York, Doubleday & Company, Inc., 1965.

Nelli, Humbert S., *The Italians in Chicago, 1880-1930*, New York, Oxford University Press, 1970.

Palisi, Bartolomeo, "Ethnic Generation and Family Structure," *Journal of Marriage and the Family*, February, 1966, pp. 49–50.

Pisani, Lawrence F., *The Italian in America*, New York, Exposition Press, 1957.

Procacci, Giuliano, *History of the Italian People*, New York, Harper & Row, 1971.

Tolino, John V., "The Church in America and the Italian Problem," *American Ecclesiastical Review*, January, 1939, pp. 23–32.

Williams, Phyllis H., *South Italian Folkways in Europe and America*, New Haven, Yale University Press, 1938.

Woods, Sister Frances Jerome, *Cultural Values of American Ethnic Groups*, New York, Harper & Brothers, 1956.

187

9

Minority Family Types III—
Race: The Black Family

ALTHOUGH THE FIELD of race relations has always been one of the cornerstones of sociology, it is only in the last decade or so that the black family has come in for special attention. Until recently, for example, our chief sources of information about the black family were such works as E. Franklin Frazier's *The Negro Family in the United States* (1939) and Kenneth Stampp's *The Peculiar Institution* (1956). In the last few years, however, our knowledge has been enriched by a host of new works.[1]

There are many reasons for this surge of interest, not least of which is the fact that there are now more than 25 million blacks in the United States. During recent decades, furthermore, their proportion in the population has been growing, as the figures in Table 1 indicate.

TABLE 1 *Percentage of Blacks in the U.S. Population, 1790–1980*

YEAR	PERCENTAGE	YEAR	PERCENTAGE
1790	19.3	1920	9.9
1820	18.4	1930	9.7
1840	16.8	1940	9.8
1860	14.1	1950	9.9
1890	11.9	1960	10.5
1900	11.6	1970	11.3
1910	10.7	1980	12+

Source: U.S. Bureau of the Census, *Statistical Abstract of the United States,* published yearly. The 1980 figure is the writer's estimate.

---

[1] For a listing of these materials, see the Selected Readings at the end of the chapter.

It can be seen that the present figure (around 12 percent) is the highest in almost 100 years. And in all likelihood the proportion will continue to increase for some time to come, since reproduction rates are higher for blacks than for whites. Indeed, the main reason for the relative decline in the black population prior to 1930 was that the tens of millions of immigrants who had entered the country were largely whites. Today, immigration is not a major factor, so that unless the law is changed—an unlikely prospect—the population comparison will be between native-born blacks and native-born whites.

As a matter of fact, the 12 percent figure (the present black proportion) is in some ways misleading, for this is a *national percentage*. Local and regional figures are vastly different. In some areas, there are no blacks at all, while in most of the largest cities of the United States blacks make up between 25 and 50 percent of the population. It is this urban concentration—particularly in the ghettos—that has led to the formulation of numerous research projects aimed at a better understanding of the black family.

Any analysis of the black family in the United States, however, must begin where it always begins: with slavery.

SLAVERY

Unfortunately for all concerned, slavery has had a seemingly interminable history. It started at the very dawn of civilization and continued in one form or another until 1962, "when it was outlawed in its last bastion—the Arabian peninsula."[2] In the New World, slavery seems to have begun in 1502 and was considered legal (in Brazil) as late as 1888. In fact, despite the reams that have been written about the Atlantic slave trade, the United States accounted for only 6 percent of the actual slave importation. Most of the captive blacks were taken to Central and South America, Brazil alone accounting for 38 percent.[3]

The arrival of the first blacks in North America has been vividly described by Bennett:

She came out of a violent storm with a story no one believed, a name no one recorded, and a past no one investigated. She was

---

[2] From *Time on the Cross: The Economics of American Negro Slavery* by Robert William Fogel and Stanley L. Engerman, by permission of Little, Brown and Co. and Wildwood House Limited. Copyright © 1974 by Little, Brown and Company (Inc.), p. 13.

manned by pirates. Her captain was a mystery man named Jope, her cargo an assortment of Africans with sonorous Spanish names—Antony, Isabella, Pedro.

A year before the arrival of the Mayflower, and 244 years before the signing of the Emancipation Proclamation, this ship arrived at Jamestown, Virginia, and dropped anchor into the muddy waters of history.

It was clear that she was no ordinary vessel. However, no one sensed how extraordinary she really was. Few ships have unloaded a more momentous cargo. . . .

The ship came from somewhere on the high seas, where she had robbed a Spanish vessel of a cargo of Africans bound for the West Indies.

Why did she stop at Jamestown, the first permanent English settlement in America? No one knows. Claiming that he needed food, the captain offered to exchange his human cargo for "victualle." The deal was arranged. Antony, Isabella, Pedro, and 17 other Africans stepped ashore in August, 1618. The history of the Negro in America had begun.

And it began with a love story. Antony, who had no surname, fell in love with Isabella and married her. Isabella, in 1624, gave birth to the first Negro child in English America. The proud parents named the boy William Tucker in honor of a local planter. . . .[4]

Interestingly enough, these first blacks came not as slaves but as indentured servants—which meant that, after they had worked for a stipulated period of time (usually seven years), they were free men. Throughout most of the seventeenth century, therefore, black colonists worked as farmers and tradesmen, owned land, and voted. Some of them even owned other black servants. And at least one black "imported and paid for a white servant whom he held in servitude."[5] By the close of the century, however, and continuing for over 150 years, nearly all the blacks who were brought into this country were delivered as slaves.

In commenting on the subject, Billingsley states that the importation of slaves from Africa represented a "discontinuity" in the cultural history of the black people.

This total discontinuity had a particular impact on the Negro family, because the family is the primary unit of social organization. Some of the ways in which this culture was disrupted may be briefly stated. First, moving as they did from Africa to the New World, the Negroes were confronted with an alien culture of European genesis. Thus, unlike some of the later migrants, including the

---

[4] Lerone Bennett, Jr., *Before the Mayflower: A History of Black America*, Johnson Publishing Company, 1969, pp. 29–30.
[5] *Ibid.*, p. 36.

Germans, Irish, and Italians, they were not moving into a society in which the historical norms and values and ways of life were familiar and acceptable.

Secondly, they came from many different tribes with different languages, cultures, and traditions. Thirdly, they came without their families and often without females at all. In the fourth place, they came in chains.

These are all major distinctions between the Negro people and all the other immigrants to this country. . . . Negroes were not free to engage in the ordinary process of acculturation. They were not only cut off from their previous culture, but they were not permitted to develop and assimilate to the new culture in ways that were unfettered and similar to the opportunities available to other immigrant groups.

The Negro slaves in the United States were converted from the free, independent human beings they had been in Africa, to property.[6]

191

The Slave Economy. This last sentence by Billingsley is most significant. For, to be understood, the slave system must be seen primarily as an economic institution. The ante-bellum South was a plantation economy, and without an abundant supply of slave labor it would not have been possible to raise (and export) cotton, rice, and tobacco on a competitive basis. And in a strictly economic sense, there seems little doubt that slavery was a profitable venture. It has been estimated that the rate of return on slaves was a "persistent 10 percent."[7]

The planters were well aware of the profitability factor, and many of them kept detailed records of their slaves' productivity. It was customary, in this connection, to rate slaves in terms of "fractional hands." Stampp reports that "children often began as 'quarter hands' and advanced to 'half hands,' 'three-quarter hands,' and then 'full hands.' As mature slaves grew older, they started down this scale. 'Breeding women' and 'sucklers' were rated as 'half hands.' Children sometimes received their training in a 'children's squad,' which pulled weeds, cleaned the yard, hoed, wormed tobacco, or picked cotton. Seldom were many more than half of a master's slaves listed in his records as field hands, and always some of the hands were classified as fractional."[8]

---

[6] Andrew Billingsley, *Black Families in White America*, Englewood Cliffs, New Jersey, Prentice-Hall, Inc., 1968, pp. 48–49.

[7] Fogel and Engerman, *op. cit.*, p. 70.

[8] Kenneth Stampp, *The Peculiar Institution*, New York, Alfred A. Knopf, Inc., © 1956, pp. 56–57.

Contrary to the stereotype that has persisted to this day, the slaves were good workers. In fact, the latest research indicates that "the large slave plantations were about 34 percent more efficient than free southern farms." This advantage, furthermore, was due not to the type of land or equipment, but to the "superior management of planters and the superior quality of black labor."[9]

Another common myth is that slaves were frequently sold and were a major source of profit for the plantation owner. But, according to a study of slave trading in Maryland, total sales amounted to less than 2 percent of the slave population each year. The authors go on to state that, if the same figures were projected to the national level, "total slave sales over the period 1820–1860 averaged about 50,000 per year. In other words, on average, only one slaveholder out of every 22 sold a slave in any given year, and roughly one-third of these were estates of deceased persons."[10]

Some of the sales involved convicted criminals, transactions that further point up the importance of the economic factor:

> It was common to require slaves convicted of crimes to be sold outside of the county or state. This was true even of slaves convicted of capital offenses. Loath to lose the capital value of a slave through execution, the courts frequently commuted the death sentence to a brief (perhaps six months) prison sentence plus whipping, branding, and sale beyond the borders of the state.
> Even in such cases as the Nat Turner rebellion, economic motivation led to the transformation of many of the death sentences into deportation orders.[11]

Still another economic myth that has persisted is the belief that slaves were systematically bred for profit. Exhaustive investigation, however, has failed to uncover any supportive evidence. Fogel and Engerman point out that "the many thousands of hours of research by professional historians into plantation records have failed to produce a single authenticated case of the 'stud' plantations alleged in abolitionist literature. . . . No set of instructions to overseers has been uncovered which explicitly or implicitly encouraged selective breeding or promiscuity."[12]

On the other hand, while they may not have systematically bred slaves, plantation owners certainly encouraged large

[9] Fogel and Engerman, *op. cit.*, pp. 209–210.
[10] *Ibid.*, p. 53.
[11] *Ibid.*, p. 55.
[12] *Ibid.*, pp. 79 and 86.

families and "provided slave women with favorable conditions and attractive incentives."[13] Among the incentives were a lighter workload, special care for expectant mothers, and reduced hours. Also, "women who bore unusually large numbers of children became 'heroes of the plantation' and were relieved from all fieldwork."[14]

That the family system and "incentive" programs were economically effective can be seen from the remarkable increase in the Southern slave population. Census figures reveal that between 1810 and 1860 the number of slaves increased from approximately 1 million to 4 million. (Starting in 1808, importation of slaves from Africa was prohibited by law, and, while there is no doubt that the law was more than occasionally broken, the foregoing gain was due largely to natural increase, i.e., the excess of births over deaths.) At any rate, by 1860 a full 99 percent of the slaves were native-born, with most of them being second-, third-, fourth-, or fifth-generation Americans. In some parts of the South, blacks came to comprise more than 50 percent of the population.[15]

It was during this later period, of course, that the abolitionists were intensifying their efforts to have the South abandon slavery. However, their efforts had little tangible effect. In 1859, only 3,000 slaves were emancipated in the entire South.

Stampp continues as follows:

> Clearly, if the decline of slavery were to await the voluntary acts of individuals, the time of its demise was still long in the distant future. The failure of voluntary emancipation was evident long before the 1830's, when, according to Judge Lumpkin, "the blind zealots of the North" began their "unwarrantable interference."
>
> Judge H. Hammond got at the crux of the matter when he asked whether any people in history every voluntarily surrendered two billion dollars worth of property.[16]

Treatment of Slaves. It is only after the economic basis of slavery is fully appreciated that the question of how the slaves were treated becomes meaningful. From the North came the abolitionist charges of cruel and inhumane treatment. Contradicting these charges were the Southern writers, who painted a picture of kindness and benevolence. In a sense, both sides were partly

---

[13] Stampp, *op. cit.*, p. 251.

[14] Fogel and Engerman, *op. cit.*, p. 85.

[15] *Ibid.*, pp. 23–26.

[16] Stampp, *op. cit.*, p. 235.

right, for practices among individual slaveholders varied tremendously. It is probable that, while cruelty was not nearly so widespread as the abolitionists maintained, it was more prevalent than most Southerners like to believe.

There is little doubt that (1) some plantation owners were cruel men who used cruel punishment, (2) most owners resorted to physical punishment on at least some occasions, and (3) the whip was in evidence on nearly all plantations. The more severe forms of punishment included solitary confinement, the iron collar, stocks, chains, and the death penalty. Castration was also used ("for high spirits") during the eighteenth century, although by the nineteenth century it seems to have been restricted to cases of attempted rape.[17]

On the other hand, as Stampp points out:

> The great majority of owners preferred to use as little violence as possible. Many small slaveholders, who had close personal contacts with their bondsmen and knew them as human beings, found it highly disagreeable to treat them unkindly. Large planters, in their instructions to overseers, frequently prohibited barbarous punishments. Thomas Afleck's plantation record-book advised overseers that the "indiscriminate, constant and excessive use of the whip is altogether unnecessary and inexcusable."[18]

Humanitarian reasons aside, slaves were valuable property, and it must have been the exceptional owner who wished to inflict harm on his own property. For virtually all slaveholders, furthermore, there were too many other alternatives available. Rations could be reduced, passes to town could be withheld, the length of the workday could be increased, privileges could be withdrawn, incorrigibles could be assigned to the more disagreeable tasks, and so on.

Most owners, however, relied more on positive than negative sanctions. Diligent workers were given such rewards as more responsible jobs, better clothing, or plots of land. Many slaves were paid wages, and in a few cases the owners used a profit-sharing system. Once in a great while, a slave could earn enough money to buy his own freedom. (The cost of a prime slave was likely to be $1,000 or more.)

In view of the above factors, it is little wonder that even whipping—the most commonly used form of physical punishment—seems to have been used in moderation. Although reliable

---

[17] Eugene Genovese, *Roll, Jordan, Roll: The World the Slaves Made*, New York, Pantheon Books, 1974, pp. 67–68.
[18] Stampp, *op. cit.*, pp. 178–179.

records on whipping are extremely limited, the one series that has come down to us, from the diary of a Louisiana planter, indicates that "over the course of two years, a total of 160 whippings were administered, an average of 0.7 whippings per hand per year. About half the hands were not whipped at all during the period."[19] (The planter was Bennet Barrow, who was known for his harsh discipline. His plantation numbered about 200 slaves, 120 of whom were in the actual labor force.)[20] It should perhaps be mentioned that during the seventeenth and eighteenth centuries whipping was a common form of punishment for whites as well as blacks.

It should also be mentioned that not all slaves worked on plantations. Hundreds of thousands were employed in cities, in factories, and as domestics. In addition, by 1860 there were approximately a quarter of a million so-called free Negroes in the South, some of whom owned slaves.

Abolitionists were prone to emphasize the squalid living and working conditions of the slaves. Plantation owners were quick to answer that the slaves had a higher standard of living than the great mass of workers in other civilized countries. But both sides seem to have missed the point: it was not so much in the material realm that the slave suffered. It was in the psychological realm, in the crippling of the human spirit.

This point was emphasized by W. E. B. Du Bois, the eminent black scholar, who conceded that the living conditions of the slaves compared favorably with those of other laborers. Writing in the mid-1930's, he asked:

What did it mean to be a slave? We think of oppression beyond all conception: cruelty, degradation, whipping and starvation, the absolute negation of human rights; or we may think of the ordinary worker the world over, slaving 10, 12, or 14 hours a day, with not enough to eat, compelled by his physical necessities to do this and not to do that, curtailed in his movements and his possibilities; and we say, here, too, is a slave called a "free worker," and slavery is merely a matter of name.

But there was in 1863 a real meaning to slavery different from that we may apply to the laborer today. It was in part psychological, the enforced personal feeling of inferiority, the calling of another Master; the standing with hat in hand. It was the helplessness. It was the defenselessness of family. It was the submergence below the arbitrary will of any sort of individual. It was without doubt

---

[19] Fogel and Engerman, *op. cit.*, p. 145.
[20] *Ibid.*

worse in these vital respects than that which exists today in Europe and America.[21]

One final—and very important—word on the subject of slave deprivation. It is not true that the slaves were uniformly relegated to the ranks of field hand and unskilled laborer. Many had reasonably good jobs in the crafts and trades. In fact, documentary evidence indicates that "over 25 percent of the males were managers, professionals, craftsmen, and semiskilled workers."[22] Even on the plantation, more than 70 percent of the overseers were slaves.[23]

On the other hand, the fields that were closed to the slaves would read like a *Who's Who* of the professions. To begin with, slaves were prohibited from owning land, which meant that they could not amass property or become farm owners. They could not become businessmen in any meaningful sense. They could not aspire to political position. The legal and medical professions were closed. No learned slave—and there were some with considerable erudition—could hope for an appointment to the faculty of a Southern University. At most, such a man could hope for the job of tutor to the children of the plantation owner.[24]

As Fogel and Engerman point out, "It was on the talented, the upper crust of slave society, that deprivation hung most heavily." Little wonder that this group, rather than the field hands, was the first to flee northward as "Yankee advances corroded the Rebel positions."[25]

Marriage and Family. In a strictly legal sense, slaves—as chattels—could not make contracts. Marriages between them, therefore, were not binding. There was no official marriage license or marriage certificate. Legally there was no such thing as bigamy, adultery, fornication, or bastardy. Generally speaking, neither public opinion nor the law was very much concerned with the moral life of the slave.

In practice, rules and procedures governing courtship and marriage among slaves were left pretty much up to the master, and as was true in so many other areas of behavior, there was considerable variation from one plantation to the next. Most planters, however, certainly found it to their advantage to maintain as cohesive a family system as possible among their slaves.

---

[21] W. E. B. Du Bois, *Black Reconstruction in America*, New York, 1935, pp. 8–9.
[22] Fogel and Engerman, *op. cit.*, p. 40.
[23] *Ibid.*, p. 211.
[24] *Ibid.*, pp. 153–154.
[25] *Ibid.*

Most plantation owners encouraged the maintenance of a stable and cohesive family system among their slaves. (Brown Brothers)

This was true in both an economic and a sociological sense. After all, both male and female slaves were more likely to be productive workers if they were contented than if they were sullen, and a responsive family relationship served to bolster the morale of both husband and wife. Then, too—as has been mentioned—it was to the owner's advantage to have a high birthrate among his slaves, a condition best achieved through the operation of a stable family system.

There was also the matter of keeping peace on the plantation. As Blassingame puts it: "A black man who loved his wife and children was less likely to be rebellious or to run away than would a 'single' slave. The simple threat of being separated from his family was generally sufficient to subdue the most rebellious 'married' slave. Besides, there was less likelihood of fights between slaves when monogamous mating arrangements existed."[26]

In any case, most plantation owners encouraged slave marriages, despite the fact that they were not recognized by state law. In some cases, the master would perform a simple ceremony at the conclusion of which the couple would jump over a broom,

---

[26] John W. Blassingame, *The Slave Community: Plantation Life in the Antebellum South,* New York, Oxford University Press, 1972, p. 80.

thereby sealing the marriage. In other cases, the marriage ceremony was taken more seriously; i.e., a slave preacher or a white clergyman would preside, a wedding feast would be held, and a variety of small gifts would be given to the newlyweds. A fair number of the ceremonies were apparently performed in churches.

While most planters preferred their slaves to marry someone from the same plantation, they raised no real objection to "outside" courtship. The following case is quoted by Bernard:

> Mr. Jack Tabb would let us go a-courting on other plantations near any time we liked, if we were good. And if we found somebody we wanted to marry, and she was on a plantation that belonged to one of his kinfolks or a friend, he would swap a slave so that the husband and wife could be together.[27]

198

Some masters, unfortunately, were not so accommodating. Some required that their consent be obtained before a given marriage could take place. Others—unlike Mr. Jack Tabb, above—refused to make the trades necessary to permit the slave couple to live together. This gave rise to the establishment of 'broad wives—wives who lived "abroad" on other plantations—a fairly common occurrence throughout the South. "In such cases," reports Genovese, "the men generally got passes to visit their wives on weekends; many for Wednesday night also; some, whose wives lived on a neighboring farm, nightly."[28]

A few slaveholders actually "assigned" husbands to women who had reached marrying age. In fact, Genovese estimates that forced marriages constituted perhaps 10 percent of all slave marriages, a practice that brought forth "considerable protest from the blacks."[29]

Mostly, however, the slave couple lived on the same plantation, with the owner's blessing. Normally, there was one slave family per cabin, with an average of 5.3 persons per household (U.S. Census figures). According to the survey by Fogel and Engerman, the cabins compared favorably with those of free workers of the period.[30]

Issues of food and clothing also seem to have been adequate. Food consumption, in particular (again, according to U.S. Census data), was of the same order as that of the whites.[31] In addition to the rations issued by the plantation owner, slaves

---

[27] Jessie Bernard, *Marriage and Family Among Negroes*, Englewood Cliffs, New Jersey, Prentice-Hall, Inc., 1966, p. 77.
[28] Genovese, *op. cit.*, pp. 462, 472–473.
[29] *Ibid.*, p. 464.
[30] Fogel and Engerman, *op. cit.*, pp. 115–116.
[31] *Ibid.*, pp. 109–115.

augmented their diet by fishing, hunting, and cultivating their own gardens.

Did not "sexual problems" occur among the slaves? Indeed they did, although there is no way of knowing the extent or the seriousness of the problems. Premarital sex relations certainly took place, and so did adultery, albeit to a much lesser extent. But, rumors to the contrary, slaves were not promiscuous. Most plantation blacks married for reasons of love and affection, with the spouses demonstrating a genuine fondness for one another. Concomitantly, as Genovese observes, they evidenced a definite "hostility toward adultery."[32]

More significant than sexual problems—from the view of family stability, that is—were the problems associated with separation and "divorce." Marital breakups among the slaves are known to have occurred with some frequency, though systematic records are not available.

199

Some marriages were also broken through the practice of slave-trading, although this figure seems to have been exaggerated. Data from the New Orleans sales records, which cover thousands of transactions over many decades, reveal that a very small percentage of slave marriages were ever broken by the auctioneer's gavel.[33] Theoretically, of course, as Stampp points out: "Every slave family had about it an air of impermanence, for no master could promise that his debts would not force sales, or guarantee that his death would not cause divisions."[34]

For years, sociologists—the present writer included—have been accustomed to thinking of the slave family as a structurally weak unit. Recent research, however, has indicated otherwise. While much more investigation is needed, it now appears that—under the circumstances—the slave family evidenced a surprising strength and resilience. It is to the credit of the men, women, and children involved that they managed to preserve their familial integrity in the face of what must have seemed to be a lost future.

Miscegenation. For some reason, the subject of miscegenation—interbreeding between blacks and whites—has held a fascination both for historians and for the general reader. Understandably, however, the evidence has been difficult to interpret. In the case of the plantation, Northern visitors certainly *reported* that sex relations between white planter and female slave were commonplace—and they pointed to the presence of mulatto chil-

---

[32] Genovese, *op. cit.*, p. 471.
[33] Fogel and Engerman, *op. cit.*, p. 49.
[34] Stampp, *op. cit.*, pp. 344–345.

dren as evidence. But the question is whether these sexual episodes were common occurrences that were rarely reported, or rare
occurrences that were commonly reported. Even the matter of
mulatto children is open to varying interpretations.

The reports themselves—and some came from Southern as
well as Northern sources—are somewhat contradictory. On the
one hand, it is alleged that the master (or male members of his
family) used seductive and/or forcible methods to gratify his
illicit sexual desires. On the other hand, it is held that the female
slave willingly bestowed her sexual favors upon the owner, in return for preferential treatment. What is one to make of the
various reports?

To begin with, there is absolutely no doubt that sex relations
between slave and master did occur—and that they did cause
concern in some quarters. There is no doubt, also, that in certain
instances the master used both threats and coercion, while in
others the female slave was more than willing. Some of the white
fathers rejected or were indifferent to their mulatto children;
others treated their youngsters with loving kindness. In some
cases, the identity of the father may have been uncertain.

On the other hand, sex relations between master and slave
could hardly have been "commonplace," as alleged by some.
There were too many counteracting forces. Public opinion was
dead set against the whole idea. To the extent that miscegenation
occurred, it occurred in spite of scathing criticism.

Moreover, since it was to the planter's own self-interest to
maintain a strong family system among his slaves, it would have
been illogical for him to permit disruptive sexual practices to
develop. And sex relations between master and slave were indeed potentially disruptive. As Genovese observes, "Many black
women fiercely resisted such aggression, and many black men
proved willing to die in defense of their women."[35]

Also, of course, such actions were likely to cause rifts in the
planter's own family, since sexual relations between master and
slave were difficult to keep secret. All things considered, the
slaveholder who embarked on a sexual escapade had to be
prepared to pay the price.

How, then, to account for the mulattoes? According to the 1850
census, 7.7 percent of the slaves were mulattoes. But, as Fogel
and Engerman point out, the fact that after 23 decades of black-
white contact (1620–1850) only 7.7 percent of the slaves were mulattoes suggests that in any given year a very small proportion
were fathered by white men.[36]

200

---

[35] Genovese, *op. cit.*, pp. 422–423.
[36] Fogel and Engerman, *op. cit.*, p. 132.

By 1860, the percentage of mulatto slaves had risen to 10.4. However, it should be mentioned that mulatto children arise not only as a result of black-white matings. Two mulatto parents can have a mulatto child, and so can two parents who are each only one-eighth white.

The mulatto puzzle is further complicated by the fact that (1) not all the African slave imports had black skin in the first place, and (2) skin color itself is probably a poor index of the proportion of white genes in an individual.

Thus far, of course, we have been discussing miscegenation in terms of plantation whites and plantation slaves. But there were other types of interracial sex liaisons. For example, approximately three-fourths of all Southerners owned no slaves, and Stampp states that "men of the non-slaveholding class were responsible for much of the miscegenation. Masters often complained that whites in the neighborhood interfered with their slave women."[37]

Miscegenation also occurred between whites and the so-called free Negroes. In fact, mulattoes came to be concentrated in the cities and among the freedmen. There are indications that even today the proportion of white genes in the black population of urban centers such as New York and Detroit is much higher than it is among the blacks in rural Georgia.[38]

At any rate, it would seem that most of the miscegenation that took place did so elsewhere than on the plantations. Indeed, on the basis of modern genetic research, it is estimated that the proportion of black children fathered by plantation whites "probably averaged between one and two percent."[39]

RECONSTRUCTION

Slavery is a familiar topic, and most Americans seem to have some idea of the plantation system. But our thoughts about the period following emancipation have somehow never crystallized—perhaps because this era has so seldom served as the background for novels or motion pictures. What actually did happen to the slaves when they obtained their freedom? How did they react? How did they manage to live and survive? What happened to their family life? The Reconstruction period, as it has

---

[37] Stampp, *op. cit.*, p. 353.
[38] Edward Reed, "Caucasian Genes in American Negroes," *Science*, August, 1969, pp. 762–768. See also Laura Newell Morris, *Human Populations, Genetic Variation, and Evolution*, San Francisco, Chandler Publishing Company, 1971.
[39] Fogel and Engerman, *op. cit.*, p. 133.

been called, has not received attention commensurate with its importance, for the effect on blacks was drastic.

"Freedom."   To the ex-slave, freedom meant—above all else— the right to move, and he took full advantage of that right. Donald states that "the Negro just released from slavery changed his name and wandered away from his plantation, setting out along the road. His movement was an aimless migration. . . . Groups and gangs of Negroes were passing and repassing and moving restlessly to and fro, some with bundles, some with none. In the summer of 1865, a visitor in South Carolina met, on a moonlight night, streams of Negroes, each carrying his bundle and making his way to Charleston and the coast, where perhaps freedom was supposed to be freer."[40]

As might be expected, some of the freedmen took to the road because they were fearful of being re-enslaved if they stayed where they were. Occasionally their fears were justified, as the following case, cited by Meltzer, indicates.

> I worked for Massa 'bout four years after freedom, cause he forced me to. Said he couldn't afford to let me go. His place was near ruint, the fences burnt, and the house would have been, but it was rock. . . .
>
> Massa says, "You son of a gun, you's supposed to be free, but you ain't, 'cause I ain't gwine give you freedom." So I goes on working for him till I gits the chance to steal a hoss from him. The woman I wanted to marry, Govie, she 'cides to come to Texas with me. Me and Govie, we rides that hoss 'most 100 miles, then we turned him a-loose and give him a scare back to his house, and come on foot the rest of the way to Texas. . . .[41]

In most cases, however, there was little attempt at forcing blacks to stay on the plantations. Some owners offered to keep their slaves and in effect guaranteed them lifetime jobs. And some blacks, particularly the older ones, gratefully accepted. Other freedmen, once they had experienced the maelstrom of the outside world, became disillusioned and voluntarily returned to the safety and security of the plantation.

Once they were emancipated, though, the great bulk of the slaves left their masters permanently and set out to explore the perimeters of freedom. The catch was (1) they had no education, (2) they had no political power, and (3) they had no money.

---

[40] Henderson H. Donald, *The Negro Freedman*, New York, Henry Schuman, 1952, p. 1.

[41] Quoted in Milton Meltzer, *In Their Own Words: A History of the American Negro, 1865–1916*, New York, Thomas Y. Crowell Company, 1965, pp. 3–4.

Despite severe social and economic handicaps, some blacks in the post-Reconstruction era were able to rise into the middle class. (Frances B. Johnston, "A Hampton Graduate at Home," plate from an album of Hampton Institute, 1899–1900. Platinum print, 7½″ × 9½″. Collection, The Museum of Modern Art, New York, Gift of Lincoln Kirstein.)

There was one other handicap that soon became apparent: ex-slaves were not about to be welcomed into white society with open arms. On the contrary, they found themselves rejected on all sides. Even the abolitionists—those who had fought the hardest against slavery—refused to accept the doctrine of equal opportunity. It is difficult, of course, to delineate "public opinion" of the period, but for many whites, in the North as well as in the South, the idea of treating blacks as equals was incomprehensible. Prejudice, economic discrimination, social and political inequality —such things became hallmarks of what can best be described as a split culture.

The federal government, fortunately, provided help. Military camps were authorized to issue rations free of charge to ex-slaves. The U.S. Treasury Department provided aid, as did a number of benevolent societies. In 1865, the Freedmen's Bureau was established by an act of Congress, the purpose being to "conduct relief work, promote education, regulate labor, and administer justice. . . . In time, it became a complete government over the 4,000,000 Negroes in the South."[42]

While the Freedmen's Bureau provided genuine help, some emancipated blacks came to believe—quite erroneously—that the government was going to distribute free land to them. Presumably the lands were to be appropriated from their former masters, and each ex-slave was to get "40 acres and an old gray mule."

The work of the Freedmen's Bureau was discontinued in 1869, and in 1877 the last federal troops were withdrawn from the South. Long before this, however, it had become clear to the ex-slave that he was not going to get his 40 acres. Furthermore, despite his illiteracy, he was going to have to compete in the open job market.

Some of the freedmen were able to find employment in the semiskilled and skilled trades, but most of them turned to the occupation they knew best—agriculture. Over the years, a fair number of blacks managed to buy and farm their own lands, but the great bulk of those who stayed in the South became general field laborers, tenant farmers, or sharecroppers.

Consequences of Reconstruction. The effects of geographical and cultural displacement on black family life were drastic. In some cases, it was not easy to determine who was married to whom. As ex-slaves, blacks had no marriage certificates, and in the period immediately after Emancipation, marital unions were often of the common-law variety. The Freedmen's Bureau did issue a set of rules aimed at legitimatizing black marriages, and eventually the licensing procedures prevailed. But problems of desertion, illegitimacy, and squalid living conditions persisted. As Donald puts it: "Living conditions in the homes of the freedmen generally were unsatisfactory. . . . The family did not assemble around the table at meals, because there were no meals."[43]

It is only in the last few years that systematic research on the Reconstruction period has been undertaken. And while the findings are thus far only tentative, they suggest that the material

204

---

[42] Donald, *op. cit.*, p. 4.
[43] *Ibid.*, pp. 70–74.

conditions of the blacks were worse after slavery than before!
Fogel and Engerman report as follows:

> It appears that the life expectation of blacks declined by 10 percent
> between the last quarter-century of the antebellum era and the last
> two decades of the 19th century. The diet of blacks deteriorated.
> Sickness rates in the 1890's were 20 percent higher than on slave
> plantations.
>
> The skill composition of the black labor force deteriorated. Blacks
> were squeezed out of some crafts in which they had been heavily
> represented during the slave era, and were prevented from entering
> the new crafts that arose with the changing technology.
>
> The gap between wage payments to blacks and whites in compa-
> rable occupations increased steadily from the immediate post-Civil
> War decades down to the eve of World War II. It was only with
> World War II that this trend reversed itself.
>
> How could it have happened? . . . . That the proposition seems
> absurd is due partly, as we have tried to show, to an exaggeration of
> the severity of slavery. But it is also due to an exaggeration of the ex-
> tent of the moral reform sought by the antislavery crusaders. Few of
> the antislavery critics had equality of opportunity for the races as
> the goal of their crusade. . . .
>
> What antislavery critics generally objected to was not the fact
> that slavery constrained the opportunities open to blacks, but the
> form which these constraints took. While physical force was not
> acceptable, legal restrictions were. Thus many one-time crusaders
> against slavery sat idly by, or even collaborated in passing various
> laws which served to improve the economic position of whites at the
> expense of blacks.
>
> Licensure laws helped to squeeze blacks out of some crafts. Edu-
> cational restrictions helped to exclude them from others. Mean-
> while, taxation and fiscal policies were used to transfer income from
> blacks to whites, perhaps more effectively, certainly more elegantly,
> than had been possible under slavery.[44]

205

URBANIZATION AND SEGREGATION

Although some ex-slaves headed North after Emancipation, the
northward trek was slow in getting underway. By 1900, around
90 percent of the blacks still lived in the South. Changes were
afoot, however, and with the turn of the century the northward
migration accelerated. By the time of World War I, blacks were
streaming into Northern cities by the tens of thousands. By

---

[44] Fogel and Engerman, *op. cit.*, pp. 261–263.

TABLE 2 *Indexes of Negro Residential Segregation for Selected Cities*

Akron, Ohio	88.1	Milwaukee, Wis.	88.1
Alexandria, Va.	87.8	Minneapolis, Minn.	79.3
Annapolis, Md.	80.9	Montgomery, Ala.	94.7
Atlanta, Ga.	93.6	Muncie, Ind.	92.1
Atlantic City, N.J.	89.2	Nashville, Tenn.	91.7
Baltimore, Md.	89.6	Newark, N.J.	71.6
Birmingham, Ala.	92.8	New Orleans, La.	86.3
Boston, Mass.	83.9	New York, N.Y.	79.3
Buffalo, N.Y.	86.5	Norfolk, Va.	94.6
Camden, N.J.	76.5	Omaha, Nebr.	92.0
Charleston, S.C.	79.5	Peoria, Ill.	86.7
Charlotte, N.C.	94.3	Philadelphia, Pa.	87.1
Chester, Pa.	87.4	Phoenix, Ariz.	85.6
Chicago, Ill.	92.6	Pittsburgh, Pa.	84.6
Cincinnati, Ohio	89.0	Portland, Oreg.	76.7
Cleveland, Ohio	91.3	Providence, R.I.	77.0
Dallas, Tex.	94.6	Raleigh, N.C.	92.8
Daytona Beach, Fla.	96.7	Richmond, Va.	94.8
Denver, Colo.	85.5	Riverside, Calif.	85.5
Des Moines, Iowa	87.9	Roanoke, Va.	93.9
Detroit, Mich.	84.5	Rochester, N.Y.	82.4
Erie, Pa.	86.9	Saginaw, Mich.	87.5
Flint, Mich.	94.4	St. Louis, Mo.	90.5
Fort Lauderdale, Fla.	98.1	St. Petersburg, Fla.	97.1
Fort Wayne, Ind.	91.7	Salt Lake City, Utah	68.9
Harrisburg, Pa.	85.7	San Antonio, Tex.	90.1
Hartford, Conn.	82.1	San Diego, Calif.	81.3
Huntington, W.Va.	88.8	San Francisco, Calif.	69.3
Indianapolis, Ind.	91.6	Savannah, Ga.	92.3
Jackson, Miss.	94.2	Seattle, Wash.	79.7
Jersey City, N.J.	77.9	Shreveport, La.	95.9
Kansas City, Mo.	90.8	South Bend, Ind.	85.8
Knoxville, Tenn.	90.7	Spartanburg, S.C.	87.5
Las Vegas, Nev.	91.8	Spokane, Wash.	80.1
Little Rock, Ark.	89.4	Springfield, Ill.	86.9
Los Angeles, Calif.	81.8	Springfield, Mo.	81.2
Louisville, Ky.	89.2	Springfield, Ohio	84.7
Miami, Fla.	97.9	Washington, D.C.	79.7

Source: Reprinted by permission from Karl E. and Alma F. Taeuber, *Negroes in Cities* (Chicago: Aldine Publishing Company); copyright © 1965 by Karl E. and Alma F. Taeuber. Table 1, pp. 32–34.

World War II the number had reached well into the millions, and today there are probably more blacks living outside the South than there are in the South.

It should also be pointed out that blacks are not evenly distributed throughout the United States population. Some states have less than 1 percent, others have more than 30 percent. Black

Americans, however, are heavily concentrated in urban areas, both North *and* South. In fact, the writer would estimate that between 1900 and 1980 the black population will have changed from 80 percent rural to 80 percent urban. It is in the very large cities, moreover, that the concentration is most noticeable.

The sequence of black urbanization is well known by now. In nearly all cases, the migrants were forced to settle in slum or near-slum areas. And while urban redevelopment and a rising standard of living have led to improved housing conditions in recent years, it is still true that blacks are concentrated in the poorer areas of most cities.

It is also well known that urban blacks are, in a residential sense, highly segregated. The extent of this segregation, however, is not fully understood, even by some of the specialists in the field of race relations. In an attempt to quantify the degree of residential segregation in various cities, Karl and Alma Taeuber, working with decennial census data, have compiled "indexes of segregation" for various cities.

The figures in Table 2 represent the percentage of blacks who would have to relocate within the city in order to bring about an even, unsegregated distribution of the population. *The higher the index, the greater the degree of segregation:* 100 would represent total residential segregation; zero, total integration.

Commenting on the high segregation indexes obtained in their survey, the Taeubers make the following observations:

> Negro protest groups often seek publicity with claims that their city is the most segregated in the nation, and Southerners often allege that residential segregation is greater in Northern than in Southern cities. However, systematic study of the block-by-block patterns of residential segregation reveals little difference among cities. A high degree of racial residential segregation is universal in American cities. . . .
>
> This is true for cities in all regions of the country and for all types of cities—large and small, industrial and commercial, metropolitan and suburban. It is true whether there are hundreds of thousands of Negro residents, or only a few thousand. Residential segregation prevails regardless of the relative economic status of the white and Negro residents. It occurs regardless of the character of local laws and policies, and regardless of the extent of other forms of segregation or discrimination.[45]

---

[45] Reprinted by permission from Karl E. and Alma F. Taeuber, *Negroes in Cities* (Chicago, Aldine Publishing Company), copyright © 1965 by Karl E. and Alma F. Taeuber, pp. 2, 32–34, 35–36.

THE BLACK FAMILY IN THE 1980's

The foregoing account of the black experience during slavery, Reconstruction, and ghettoization has been given in some detail, since the current (and future) picture can be understood only in the light of these historical forces. What seems to have happened is that black Americans have developed norms that are closely related to the social-class structure. This is also true of white families, with one difference: relatively speaking, lower-class blacks comprise a much larger group than lower-class whites.

It is the lower-class black family—largely concentrated in urban ghettoes—that has given rise to the stereotype of conjugal fragility among blacks. And it is true that the ghetto family has been characterized by high rates of divorce, desertion, illegitimacy, and delinquency. Rainwater, who is the country's leading authority on lower-class culture, writes that "lower-class Negroes know what the 'normal American family' is supposed to be like. . . . .Many of them make efforts to establish such families but find it impossible to do so either because of the direct impact of economic disabilities, or because they are unable to sustain in their day-to-day lives the ideals which they hold."[46]

It is this ghetto-type family, also, that is so often matriarchal in nature and that turns up on census enumerations as "married, spouse absent." Writing on the homemaking procedures followed in the matriarchal family, Rainwater reports that:

> Because men are not expected to be much help around the house, having to be head of the household is not particularly intimidating to the Negro mother if she can feel some security about income. She knows it is a hard, hopeless, and often thankless task, but she also knows that it is possible.
>
> The maternal household in the slum is generally run with a minimum of organization. The children quickly learn to fend for themselves, to go to the store, to bring change home, to watch after themselves. . . .
>
> In this culture there is little of the sense of the awesome responsibility of caring for children that is characteristic of the working and middle class.[47]

In contrast to the matriarchal, ghetto-type family described above, black middle- and upper-class families tend to be similar to their white counterparts. In his study of 400 stable black families *above* the lower class, for example, Scanzoni found "many

---

[46] Lee Rainwater, "Crucible of Identity: The Negro Lower-Class Family," *Daedalus,* Winter, 1966, pp. 182–183.

[47] *Ibid.,* pp. 195–196.

(Harvey Stein)

basic similarities with what we know of white families located at
comparable status levels." The same author continues as follows:

MINORITY FAMILY TYPES III

The clear trend within black family structure is toward convergence with family patterns existing in the dominant society. This is not necessarily planned, nor is it because the dominant family forms are deemed "better." It is simply because family forms (black or white) in modern society are a response to the exigencies and demands of that kind of society.

The overwhelming majority of black Americans have made a value judgment; i.e., they want to participate in the economic benefits of modern society. Inevitably, as a result of this goal, their family form takes a certain shape. As they increasingly enter into the dominant society economically, they also enter it conjugally. . . .

There are more similarities than differences in black and white conjugal relations, and if blacks are permitted to participate more fully in the economic system, any existing differences will probably diminish in significance. Already . . . there is considerable movement toward a convergence of black-white behavior patterns.[48]

There is every reason to believe that the size of the large lower-class black population can be reduced. Census data reveal that "Negroes are more likely than ever before to be earning decent incomes, holding good jobs, living in better neighborhoods, and completing their education."[49] The same source indicates that there has been a significant improvement in the occupational level of employed blacks.[50] Even the ratio of black income to white increased between 1950 and the early 1970's.[51]

Most sociologists would agree with Eshleman, who—after examining the available data—concludes as follows:

Evidence seems to suggest a change in conditions among the black families from a submerged group at the bottom of the social-class structure to the development of a small, able working class and the emergence of a larger middle class. Generally, as Goode and others suggest, as economic conditions improve, the incidence of family disorganization decreases, family life becomes increasingly stable, there are higher aspirations for children, and there is greater conformity to the sexual mores of society.[52]

[48] John H. Scanzoni, *The Black Family in Modern Society*, Boston, Allyn and Bacon, Inc., 1971, pp. 264–265.

[49] *Current Population Reports*, "Recent Trends in Social and Economic Conditions of Negroes in the United States," Department of Labor, Series P-23, No. 26, July 1968, p. v.

[50] *Ibid.*, p. 16.

[51] U.S. Bureau of the Census, *Current Population Reports*, Series P-20, No. 85, Washington, D.C., 1972, p. 34.

[52] J. Ross Eshleman, *The Family: An Introduction*, Boston, Allyn and Bacon, Inc., 1974, p. 219.

On the other hand, there is no gainsaying the fact that, while it may not be as large as it once was, the economic and educational gap between blacks and whites remains formidable. To close the gap completely will take a concerted effort on the part of all thoughtful Americans.

SELECTED READINGS

Battalio, Raymond, and Kagel, John, "The Structure of Antebellum Southern Agriculture: South Carolina, A Case Study," *Agricultural History*, January, 1970, pp. 25–37.

Bernard, Jessie, *Marriage and Family Among Negroes*, Englewood Cliffs, New Jersey, Prentice-Hall, Inc., 1966.

Billingsley, Andrew, *Black Families in White America*, Englewood Cliffs, New Jersey, Prentice-Hall, Inc., 1968.

Blassingame, John W., *The Slave Community: Plantation Life in the Antebellum South*, New York, Oxford University Press, 1972.

Curtin, Philip D., *The Atlantic Slave Trade: A Census*, Madison, University of Wisconsin Press, 1969.

Dietrich, Katheryn, "A Reexamination of the Myth of Black Matriarchy," *Journal of Marriage and the Family*, May, 1975, pp. 367–374.

Elkins, Stanley, *Slavery*, Chicago, University of Chicago Press, 1964.

Engerman, Stanley, and Genovese, Eugene (eds.), *Race and Slavery in the Western Hemisphere: Quantitative Studies*, Princeton, Princeton University Press, 1974.

Farley, Reynolds, *Growth of the Black Population*, Chicago, Markham Publishing Co., 1970.

Filler, Louis, *Slavery in the United States of America*, New York, Van Nostrand, 1974.

Fogel, Robert W., and Engerman, Stanley L., *Time on the Cross: The Economics of American Negro Slavery*, Boston, Little, Brown and Company, 1974.

Frazier, E. Franklin, *The Negro Family in the United States*, New York, The Dryden Press, 1951.

Genovese, Eugene, *Roll, Jordan, Roll: The World the Slaves Made*, New York, Pantheon Books, 1974.

Heiss, Jerold, *The Black Family: A Sociological Inquiry*, New York, Columbia University Press, 1975.

Henri, Florette, *Black Migration: Movement North, 1900–1920*, Garden City, New York, Doubleday & Company, Inc. (Anchor Books), 1974.

211

Lammermeier, Paul J., "The Urban Black Family of the 19th Century: A Study of Black Family Structure in the Ohio Valley, 1850–1880," *Journal of Marriage and the Family*, August, 1973, pp. 440–456.

Liebow, Elliot, *Tally's Corner*, Boston, Little, Brown and Company, 1967.

Moynihan, Daniel, *The Negro Family—The Case for National Action*, Office of Policy Planning and Research, U.S. Department of Labor, Washington, D.C., 1965.

Meier, August, and Rudwick, Elliott (eds.), *The Black Community in Modern America*, New York, Atheneum, 1969.

Meltzer, Milton, *In Their Own Words: A History of the American Negro, 1865–1916*, New York, Thomas Y. Crowell Company, 1965.

Morgan, Edmund S., *American Slavery—American Freedom*, New York, W. W. Norton, Inc., 1975.

Morris, Laura Newell, *Human Populations, Genetic Variation, and Evolution*, San Francisco, Chandler Publishing Company, 1971.

Rainwater, Lee, "Crucible of Identity: The Negro Lower-Class Family," *Daedalus*, Winter, 1966, pp. 172–216.

———, and Yancey, William (eds.), *The Moynihan Report and the Politics of Controversy*, Cambridge, Massachusetts, The M.I.T. Press, 1967.

Scanzoni, John H., *The Black Family in Modern Society*, Boston, Allyn and Bacon, Inc., 1971.

Schultz, David, A., *Coming up Black*, Englewood Cliffs, New Jersey, Prentice-Hall, Inc., 1969.

Stampp, Kenneth, *The Peculiar Institution*, New York, Alfred A. Knopf, Inc., 1956.

Staples, Robert, "Research on Black Sexuality: Its Implication for Family Life, Sex Education, and Public Policy," *Family Coordinator*, April, 1972, pp. 183–188.

Taeuber, Karl E., and Taeuber, Alma F., *Negroes in Cities: Residential Segregation and Neighborhood Change*, New York, Atheneum, 1969.

Washington, Joseph R., *Marriage in Black and White*, Boston, Beacon Press, 1970.

Weinstein, Allen, and Gatell, Frank (eds.), *American Negro Slavery: A Modern Reader*, New York, Oxford University Press, 1973.

Yetman, Norman R. (ed.), *Life Under the "Peculiar Institution": Selections from the Slave Narrative Collection*, New York, Holt, Rinehart and Winston, 1970.

10

The Changing Status of Women:
Woman's Rights and Women's Liberation

THE READER MAY wonder why a chapter on women is included in that section of the book dealing with minorities. Yet, in many respects, American women have indeed been discriminated against over the years. In her provocative article, "Women as a Minority Group," Hacker points out many of the specifics: educational inequality, social and legal impediments, job discrimination, unequal pay, and so on. The same author comments on the relevance of Louis Wirth's definition:

> A minority group is any group of people who, because of their physical or cultural characteristics, are singled out from the others in the society in which they live for differential and unequal treatment, and who therefore regard themselves as objects of collective discrimination.[1]

Times are changing, of course, and nowhere is this fact clearer than in the area of women's rights. Courtship, marriage, sex behavior, education, the job market—practically every traditional "sphere of restriction" has been liberalized. And while the results have proved beneficial to all concerned, the struggle for equal rights has been long and hard; indeed, it is still going on. The story of the various changes—culminating in the present women's liberation movement—is the focus of the present chapter.

CHANGES IN COURTSHIP

As was shown in Chapter 4, matrimony in the Colonial period was looked upon as an economic necessity. Marriages were often

---

[1] Nona Glazer-Malbin and Helen Youngelson Waehrer (eds.), *Woman in a Man-Made World*, Chicago, Rand McNally & Company, 1972, p. 39.

influenced by the wishes of the respective families, while the importance of romantic love was played down. Courtship itself was not regarded as an integral part in the lives of young people, and much of it was highly formalized, parental approval being necessary before a specific dating relationship could begin.

Irreversibly, however, the twin processes of urbanization and industrialization altered the existing social structure. When the first census was taken in 1790, for example, there were only 33 cities in the United States, none of which was as large as 100,000. Today, our *fiftieth* largest city (Tampa, Florida) has a population of well over 250,000.

In any case, by the first half of the nineteenth century, certain changes were already discernible. The use of dowries, never as prevalent in America as they were in Europe, soon ceased altogether. Parental permission to begin courtship was no longer a strict necessity, and the custom of precontract became extinct. While parents still had a fair measure of control over the marriages of their sons and daughters, love matches were clearly growing in favor. Furthermore, a rapidly increasing urban population meant that young people had more leeway in the choice of mates. It was no longer necessary to marry the boy or girl on a nearby farm simply because of the dearth of available partners. Indeed, it became customary for a girl to have more than one suitor.

Although dating was becoming more liberal, it should not be thought that the nineteenth century was an age of amatory laxness and premarital frivolity. On the contrary, up to the time of World War I, courtship customs were fairly restrictive. Even though young people had a relatively free hand in choosing a mate, the selection process itself followed a prescribed course.

The "Pedestal." One of the characteristics of the period, especially among the propertied classes, was that of gallantry. Women were placed on a pedestal and, in true chivalric fashion, were presumed to be morally and spiritually superior to men. The fair sex was believed to be endowed with a sense of dignity and purity, and the function of the male was that of protection. Escorts were not only obliged to protect the good names of their ladies, but in many quarters a couple could not attend social events without the proper surveillance. Schlesinger states that, as late as the turn of the century, "chaperonage was so generally observed in the East that a girl would not venture to combat it without the risk of sharp criticism from alien tongues."[2]

---

[2] Arthur M. Schlesinger, *The Rise of the City, 1878–1898*, New York, The Macmillan Company, 1933, pp. 122–123.

Social gatherings, as they were called, included church affairs, concerts, community dances, picnics, home parties, and—somewhat later—athletic events. Boys were not supposed to lay hands on the girls they escorted, and many a young lady supposedly remained unkissed except by her fiancé.

Naturally there were lapses, as there are under any social code. That kissing, hugging, and fondling did occur is suggested by the now-defunct expressions "sparking" and "spooning." But insofar as community attitudes were verbalized, and to the extent that such attitudes were expressed in the public media— newspapers, magazines, novels, speeches, and sermons—courtship in the last century was held to be a *prelude to marriage* and as such was regarded with a seriousness worthy of the marital state.

On their part, ladies were exhorted to act like ladies. They were presumed to hold an exalted moral position, and their behavior was supposed to reflect that position. They were expected to act in a dignified manner, to be gracious in social situations, and never to be forward in their relations with men. It goes almost without saying that girls were forbidden to smoke or drink or use coarse language.

Women of the period were even loath to use realistic terms when referring to the human body. Thus, arms and legs were alluded to as "limbs." Frost reports that "American women described their bodies from head to waist as stomach, and from there to the foot as ankles. They refused to mention specific parts of the body even to doctors. . . . Some expectant mothers refused to have doctors attend them during childbirth, preferring to use midwives. And husbands were barred from the sight of a birth."[3]

The methods by which a young lady was supposed to protect her "fair name" seem rather amusing, in the light of modern custom. In a talk given in 1891, Anna Potts, M.D., a noted lecturer of her day, declared:

> If a young man does not leave by half-past ten or eleven at night, the lady should give him a gentle hint by opening the door and remarking, "It is a very pleasant evening!" Under such suggestions, any young man should surely take up his walking stick and hat, and depart. But if he does not, again open the door, and let it stand unclosed. Speak more emphatically, "It is a very pleasant evening!" The young woman would do well after this to invite him to depart.
>
> Gentlemen should be watchful for all such slight suggestions, and prevent a more stern command. There is no good arising from these long night visits; they are injurious to both health and morals.

---

[3] J. William Frost, *The Quaker Family in Colonial America*, New York, St. Martin's Press, 1973, p. 180.

Parents should advise their daughters against such improprieties. And any well-bred man would admire and love a girl the more for not permitting them, and would have more confidence in her mother.[4]

Feminine Attire.   One of the hallmarks of the 1800's was the attire of the lady—modest to an extreme. In pointed prose, Leuba reports that "she covered herself from top to toe with numerous layers of clothing and an abundance of fluff and ruffles. Her body was not only concealed, it was made almost impregnable: it was a fortress with outworks of crinoline and an inner citadel protected by a tightly laced corset through which ran strips of bone or steel. The perfect young lady was one who moved and dressed in a manner that would not reveal the existence of her body."[5]

216

The excessive use of body coverings was aimed at lessening the sexual appetite of the male. According to the rules of the game, women were permitted to attract men, but not by any such direct approach as revealing portions of their bodies. In fact, the reader may be surprised to learn that in the early days of our seashore resorts, men and women were not permitted to go swimming together. One beach was used by the gentlemen bathers, while a separate one was reserved for the ladies! As late as the World War I period, "at Atlantic City, where women once wore corsets when they entered the water, the city employed viewers equipped with tape measures to check on the legality of the exposed epidermis."[6]

The "System."   How did the ladies attract the male animal? Since they were supposed to be passive and retiring in their relations with men, women attempted—theoretically, at least—to capitalize on these very qualities. They were gracious, dignified, and ladylike. They were supposed to exude goodness and respectability. Also, if we can believe the literature of the period, women were adept at the use of flattery and were skillful in the exploitation of their "helplessness." In brief, women were presumably able to appeal to the so-called gallant side of man's nature.

The above portrayal represents an idealization, of course, and one suspects that there were many behavioral exceptions. Any

---

[4] Mrs. Anna Longshore Potts, *Love, Courtship, and Marriage,* privately published, Paradise Valley Sanitarium, National City, California, 1891, p. 39.
[5] Clarence Leuba, *The Sexual Nature of Man,* New York, Doubleday and Company, 1954, p. 5.
[6] Gerald Carson, *The Polite Americans,* New York, William Morrow & Company, 1966, p. 233.

In the nineteenth century, women were viewed by many as weak, helpless, and in need of protection by men. (Marburg—Art Reference Bureau)

number of women must have resented the rather insipid role accorded them. And on some occasions, at least, the resentment took unladylike form:

> The guardians of public morality were originally disturbed by the fact that motion pictures would require dark, dark rooms in which to project. What vulgarities would men and women perform under the curtain of blackness?

One prudent operator separated the men and the women in his audience, seating them on opposite sides of the aisle to protect them against temptation. He was severely beaten by one respectable married lady who resented the protection![7]

The Modern Era. Following World War I it became obvious that courtship customs were changing, and by World War II the era of the dainty lady had become a distant memory. In spite of dire warnings by the older generation, young women began to smoke, drink, use male vocabulary, listen to risqué jokes, engage in athletic activities, and in general repudiate the retiring demeanor that had characterized their grandmothers.

As the ladylike role was abandoned, it was almost unavoidable that women's fashions would change. It was time for the modern woman to wear modern clothes. Little by little the various layers of petticoats were pared away. Bustles disappeared and corsets were left off. As the armor was removed, feminine clothing took on a more functional look. Frills and ruffles were replaced by a simplicity of design. Dresses no longer contained yards of bulky material. Necklines became lower, sleeves and hemlines were shortened.

On the social front, dating activities often started at an extremely young age. And whereas in earlier generations, courtship was normally initiated with matrimonial aims, now it was often undertaken *as an end in itself.* Dating, in other words, was no more likely to be used as an instrument of mate selection than it was as a means of spending an enjoyable evening.

Parents had only moderate control over their daughters' dating behavior and almost none at all over their sons'. It was often difficult for mothers and fathers to keep abreast of their children's latest dates. From time to time, boys and girls became secretly engaged without their parents' knowledge; and in some cases young people would even marry without their parents' permission. (Historically, the circle had come full turn—in reverse. Whereas it was once customary for parents to marry off their children without the latter's consent, it was now quite easy for children to marry without their parents' consent!)

What factors were responsible for these rather pronounced changes? Urbanization and industrialization have already been mentioned, but along with the movement from farm to city went commercial amusements such as movies, athletic events, dance halls, and, of course—bars. Opportunities for meeting young people of the opposite sex increased rapidly, and dating came to

---

[7] Jerry Stagg, *The Brothers Shubert*, New York, Random House, Inc., 1968, p. 93.

denote activities of the solitary *couple* rather than *group* participation, as formerly.

Still other factors contributed to the change in courtship procedures, and for want of a more precise term these elements are often referred to as a "decline in the authoritarian tradition." Between the two world wars, new child-rearing methods were astir, and the old philosophy of "spare the rod, spoil the child" was being reversed. Parents were told not to overdiscipline their children, and in the interests of personality development youngsters were given more and more free rein.

The church, too, seemed to have waned in influence. Attendance declined, and in some areas clergymen were discovering that their sermons were being heard largely by older people. Society in general was adopting a more permissive attitude toward the youth of both sexes. For better or worse, behavior that once would have been considered shocking was now commonplace. Boys and girls held hands and put their arms around one another in public. Terms like "flirting" and "spooning" gave way to "necking," "petting," and "making out." Kissing lost all matrimonial significance, and personal intimacies were indulged in by most people of dating age.

Most surprising of all—at least in the eyes of the older generation—was the fact that the new system of courtship actually seemed to work. Despite the fact that women were no longer exalted and placed on a pedestal, romantic love flourished as never before, and the marriage rate remained high. Indeed, one of the distinctive features of modern matrimonial selection is the priority accorded romantic love. Financial obstacles, parental opposition, housing problems, religious or social-class differences— according to popular notion, such things can be worked out. The only indispensable prerequisite to marriage, presumably, is love.

CHANGES IN THE SEX MORES

Throughout the 1800's, sexual codes in the United States remained strict. It is true that the extreme penalties imposed by the colonists—flogging, the scarlet letter, the death sentence—were no longer in effect. But nineteenth-century America was not in a mood to take sex lightly. Spiritually and morally, women had been placed on a pedestal, and woe betide the female who brought discredit to the fair name of womanhood. A girl who indulged in premarital coitus not only suffered the loss of reputation but was often marked for life, especially if she had an illegitimate child (in which case the child was similarly stigmatized).

To single womanhood, virginity was a cherished value, and, in view of the torrent of societal scorn that was directed against the unchaste, it is little wonder that premarital coitus was sometimes referred to as "a fate worse than death." Unmarried males, on the other hand, were allowed much more leeway, and the age-old double standard of "boys will be boys" prevailed; in fact, during the nineteenth and early twentieth centuries prostitution flourished in most large cities, and it was quite common for young men to avail themselves of this opportunity. Although it may seem strange by modern standards, boys could thus "sow their wild oats" and at the same time preserve their respect for the purity of womanhood, since prostitutes were considered to be of lower-class origin or to be "fallen women."

Behavioral Changes. As the twentieth century dawned, however, the same forces that tended to liberalize courtship customs served to weaken the existing sex mores; indeed, it is difficult to separate the two. The emancipation of women, accelerated urbanization, the decline in secular and religious controls, a more permissive attitude on the part of the public—all were involved. Three additional factors should be mentioned apropos of the changing sex codes: (1) the automobile, with its phenomenal growth following World War I; (2) the increased availability of contraceptive devices; and (3) a relatively quick and simple cure for venereal disease, which became generally available after World War II.

Although attitudinal and behavioral changes in sexual conduct made their appearance gradually, World War I seems to have been a major dividing line between the old and the new. As was true in the case of courtship patterns, the 1920's witnessed a severe break in the sexual dam. Necking and petting became widespread—and remain so today. Premarital coitus increased greatly, especially on the part of engaged or almost engaged couples. In the convenient privacy of the automobile, and with the ever-increasing availability of birth control measures, the issue often was not whether the girl should permit a goodnight kiss, but whether the couple should engage in sexual intercourse. Organized prostitution, on the other hand, seems to have declined sharply—in part, no doubt, because of the general increase in sex activity on the part of single girls, and in part because of the association that prostitution came to have with civic corruption and crime.

Changes in Attitude. While there have been significant changes in American sexual behavior during the past decades, equally important from the sociological viewpoint have been the manifold changes in attitudes. Most of the changes have been gradual, and many of them, on the surface at least, appear unrelated. In effect, however, they are related in the sense that they have all been in the same direction—namely, toward a more permissive set of regulations pertaining to sex. It might be added that our current attitudes seem quite natural to the younger generation, and it is only when these views are compared with those of the nineteenth century that the contrast becomes apparent.

The American woman of an earlier period, ideally at least, held a position of refinement and dignity. Sex was presumed to be abhorrent to her, and even after marriage, myth had it that any sexual response on the part of the wife was unladylike. Gradually, however, as the emancipation movement gained headway, marital coitus came to be regarded as an activity that was pleasurable for wife as well as husband. Terms like "sexual compatibility" and "sexual adjustment" began to be heard, and impotency on the part of the husband was incorporated as one of the grounds that could be used by the wife in a divorce suit. Today, of course, *mutual* pleasure in the sexual realm is held to be an important factor in overall marital happiness, and a variety of marriage manuals are available to instruct newlyweds in the art of coital techniques.

About the same time that wives were becoming sexually emancipated, there was a gradual but steady increase in the number of words and phrases that were permissible in polite company. Whereas prior to World War I, sex was a subject deemed unfit for feminine ears, the succeeding decades witnessed a let's-bring-sex-out-in-the-open philosophy. And as a result, people in all walks of life—males as well as females—came to have a better understanding of the subject.

THE WOMAN'S RIGHTS MOVEMENT

Although female emancipation was clearly evident in such areas as wearing apparel, courtship, sexual behavior, and the like, there were more important changes in the offing. It must be remembered that, throughout the Colonial period, women were accorded *inferior status in virtually all walks of life*. While they were protected by law from severe verbal and physical assaults, and while they were generally loved and respected by their husbands, colonial wives found themselves in a subordinate position—socially, legally, and economically. This condition persisted well into the nineteenth century.

As late as 1850 a wife had no legal control over her own personal property; all her belongings were legally in the hands of her husband, to dispose of as he saw fit. Her services also belonged to him, and she had no legal right even to the custody of her own children. Women were not permitted to vote, nor was their education taken very seriously. Female wage earners and career women were looked upon with suspicion and were sometimes excluded from social functions. In general, a woman had little alternative but to marry and fulfill her childbearing and homemaking "destiny."

The above inequalities, of course, are clearly incompatible with democratic concepts, and it was inevitable that a protest movement should arise. This was known as the woman's rights movement. In 1848 the momentous first convention was held in Seneca Falls, New York, and a declaration of sentiments was adopted. The basic objectives were threefold: (1) to free the persons and property of married women from the absolute control of their husbands and to establish the wife as a legal personality, (2) to open the doors of higher education to all women, and (3) to procure full political rights for women.

The booming factory system was also instrumental in raising the status of women. Cheap labor was needed, and what better source than young farm girls? In spite of abominable conditions, it soon became apparent that the girls were excellent workers. It was also shown that, given a chance, women could support themselves. Once women were freed from their strict economic dependence, the cry for legal and educational equality grew louder. As might be expected, there was serious opposition to the woman's rights movement from both press and pulpit. Many men denounced the whole idea; indeed, slight remnants of such opposition can still be found. Once the first gains had been made, however, the woman's rights movement surged ahead on all fronts.

Legal and Political Gains. It would not be much exaggeration to say that throughout most of American history, women were veritable legal ciphers. The following cases provide good examples:

> In 1873 a woman in Massachusetts slipped and fell on the ice. Being a woman, she was unable to sue for damages. Her husband, however, was awarded thirteen hundred dollars by the courts as compensation for his loss of her labor—money he could spend as he pleased—without consulting his wife.
>
> One man who failed in business was supported for years by his wife, who established a successful milliner's shop. Eventually he

Winning the right to vote was a major accomplishment of the woman's rights movement, but repeal of discriminatory economic laws was an equally important achievement. (Brown Brothers)

died, leaving her shop and her savings, legally his own, to somebody else. Had he died in debt, everything she had would have been sacrificed to pay off his creditors—although the law did allow her to keep her own clothes, a single table, six chairs, six plates, six knives and forks, one sugar bowl, and twelve spoons.[8]

Over the years, however, inequities of the above type were removed, as the various states amended their married women's property laws. Today—without going into detail—the wife is legal owner of the property she possessed prior to marriage. She can negotiate contracts, run her own business, and keep her earnings. Inheritance laws generally give both husband and wife equal status, a principle that also applies to child custody and guardianship.

Politically, also, women have been granted equal rights, although it was not until 1920 that they were accorded the right to vote by the Nineteenth Amendment to the Constitution. In years to come, women will probably become more influential,

---

[8] Olivia Coolidge, *Women's Rights: The Suffrage Movement in America*, New York, E. P. Dutton & Co., 1976, pp. 9–10.

since (1) there are more women than men in the population, and (2) the imbalance is increasing.

In addition to their voting power, women in recent periods have held a wide variety of political and administrative offices, such as Treasurer of the United States, Secretary of Labor, Secretary of Health, Education, and Welfare, Director of the Passport Office, Director of the Mint, head of the Interstate Commerce Commission, Assistant to the President for Consumer Affairs, Director of the Bureau of Public Assistance, and so on. Several women have been elected to the post of state governor and lieutenant governor. Women have also run—albeit unsuccessfully—for the presidency of the United States. At the present time there are 18 women serving in Congress.[9] And at the local level, women have held virtually every elective and appointive office that men have held.

Educational Advancement. In the Colonial period it was deemed neither practical nor prudent to expose young women to serious education. Even in the nineteenth century, antifeminists stoutly protested against providing girls with "boys' education." Historical documents reveal a variety of bizarre reasons for this position. It was held, for example, that education would affect the female's health, make her nervous, teach her to be dissatisfied, to run away from home, or to be treacherous. Perhaps the chief objection was to the effect that formal education would weaken the female's role as homemaker.

In spite of varied protests, the nineteenth century saw the admission of girls into elementary schools and eventually into secondary schools. In 1833, feminine education scored a gain when Oberlin College admitted women as well as men. In 1837 Mount Holyoke Seminary for Girls was established in Massachusetts, thanks to the pioneering efforts of Mary Lyon. Vassar opened its doors in 1865, followed by Smith College in 1871, Wellesley in 1877, and Bryn Mawr in 1880. The University of Michigan had meantime admitted women in 1870, and by the turn of the century coeducational colleges and universities were becoming commonplace. Today, the large majority of the more than 2,000 institutions of higher learning in the United States are coeducational, including practically all professional schools.

In 1890, the date of the first official report, women were the recipients of less than 20 percent of the undergraduate college degrees granted. Today, the figure has grown to nearly 45 percent.

---

[9] For details, see the Citizens' Advisory Council on the Status of Women, *Women*, Washington, D.C., U.S. Government Printing Office, May, 1975.

Anti-feminists of yesteryear would also be surprised to discover that females are more likely to complete high school than are males!

Economic Improvement. Unless they were employed as servants, colonial women had little opportunity in the occupational sphere. Even during the early 1800's, after certain types of jobs had been opened to women, the female wage earner continued to be stigmatized by inferior social status.

The first large-scale influx of women workers took place in the New England factories. Most of the workers were unmarried farm girls, some of them little more than children. They were welcomed, nevertheless, since they were not only conscientious employees but would work for low wages.

225

> Mill workers at Lowell, Massachusetts, who were supposed to enjoy model conditions, testified in 1846, *while agitating for a ten-hour day,* that they lived six to a room and two to a bed in company boarding houses, and that their wages after deduction for board were about two dollars a week![10]

During the Civil War an increasing number of occupations were opened to women, a phenomenon that was to be repeated in the First and Second World Wars. During World War II, women were employed as welders, mechanics, machinists, taxi drivers, and streetcar operators; in fact, with the exception of heavy-duty laboring jobs, females could be found in virtually every branch of industry. It should also be mentioned that, because of their excellent record, women have been made a permanent part of the armed forces.

Today there are some 36.5 million women in the work force, which is approximately 46 percent of all women who are of working age. Of those not in the labor force, the large majority are not looking for a job—by virtue of age, home responsibilities, and so on. From a long-range perspective, the following figures reported by the Department of Labor will be of interest. In 1900, women comprised 18 percent of the labor force. By 1940, the figure had risen to about 25 percent. Today—as we approach the 1980's—the figure has risen to approximately 40 percent![11]

Over and above their widespread employment in factories, women have come to be utilized more and more in white-collar, managerial, and professional occupations. Women now serve as

---

[10] Coolidge, *op. cit.*, p. 10.
[11] Bureau of Labor Statistics, U.S. Department of Labor, *U.S. Working Women: A Chartbook*, Washington, D.C., U.S. Government Printing Office, 1975.

Today women can be found in occupations previously restricted to men. (Left, United Press International; right, Daniel S. Brody, Stock Boston)

business executives, bank presidents, scientists, editors and publishers, doctors, college professors, lawyers and judges, engineers, and clergy. The role of women in literary, artistic, and entertainment fields is well known, and, of course, in the area of fashion and design they hold a superior position. In brief, women have entered practically all the employment fields, including those that in an earlier period were reserved "for men only."

WOMEN'S LIBERATION

In one sense, "women's liberation"—which got underway in the 1960's and is still continuing—is a sequel to the woman's rights movement, described above. That is, there was a growing feeling that, while women had indeed made gains in the educational, political, and economic spheres, the gains were not only insufficient but in many ways amounted to little more than "tokenism." Both governmental figures and private surveys bore out what was already self-evident.

Working with U.S. Census data, Hecht et al. were able to show that as late as 1970, American colleges graduated 128,000 more males than females. At the graduate level, the imbalance was even more pronounced, with some 23,000 males earning their doctorate as against 3,500 females.[12]

---

[12] Marie Hecht, Joan Berbich, Salley Healey, and Clare Cooper, *The Women, Yes!* New York, Holt, Rinehart and Winston, 1973, pp. 15–17.

In the political realm, discrimination against women was also apparent. In a survey of a large Northeastern city by Babchuk, Marsey, and Gordon, it was found that women played a relatively insignificant role in the power structure of the community.[13] At the national level, the picture was found to be much the same, Glazer-Malbin and Waehrer reporting as follows:

> Women have little political power as office-holders. No woman has ever been President of the United States (or Vice President), and only two have even occupied major cabinet posts. No woman has ever been appointed to the Supreme Court. Few women are elected to the Congress, or to state legislatures, or to the office of governor or mayor. The listing is seemingly endless, and probably continues to the local dog-catcher.[14]

In the economic sphere, figures indicated—not surprisingly—that women were likewise underrepresented in the better-paying jobs. In a survey by Epstein, for example, the author reports that:

> During the past half-century, women have entered many upper-level occupations and positions from which they were once excluded, and their general level of involvement in the labor force has risen. But their participation in the occupations of highest rank—among them the professions of law, medicine, teaching in higher education, and the sciences—has not kept pace with these developments, nor has their access to the elite levels of the professions been greatly improved.[15]

Using U.S. Census data, the same investigator notes that women comprised only 19 percent of the college professors, 6.8 percent of the doctors, 3.5 percent of the lawyers, 8.6 percent of the chemists, 5.8 percent of the clergy, and less than 1 percent of the engineers.[16] Blitz, in a study reported in the Department of Labor's *Monthly Labor Review*, also found women drastically underrepresented in such occupations as doctor, lawyer, social worker, and clergy.[17]

[13] Nicholas Babchuk, Ruth Marsey, and C. Wayne Gordon, "Men and Women in Community Agencies: A Note on Power and Prestige," in Nona Glazer-Malbin and Helen Youngelson Waehrer (eds.), *Woman in a Man-Made World*, Chicago, Rand McNally & Company, 1972, pp. 248–253.

[14] *Woman in a Man-Made World*, p. 245.

[15] Cynthia Epstein, "Encountering the Male Establishment: Sex-Status Limits on Women's Careers in the Professions," in Athena Theodore (ed.), *The Professional Woman*, Cambridge, Massachusetts, Schenkman Publishing Company, Inc., 1971, pp. 52–54.

[16] *Ibid.*

[17] Rudolph Blitz, "Women in the Professions, 1870–1970," *Monthly Labor Review*, May, 1974, pp. 34–39.

227

Granted that the women's liberation movement of the sixties and seventies uncovered and publicized inequities of the type mentioned above, the question remains: Was the movement successful in actually *improving* political, economic, and educational conditions for women? The answer is a resounding yes, and these improvements will be discussed in the concluding section. Before doing so, however, a word is in order with respect to another dimension of women's liberation.

Sociological Aspects. It is difficult to pinpoint the exact beginning of the women's liberation movement, but certainly the publication of Betty Friedan's *The Feminine Mystique,* in 1963, played an important part. In her travels across America and her interviews with housewives from every social stratum, Friedan detected a kind of shadowy unrest. Despite obvious material comforts and—oftentimes—a relatively high plane of living, wives were evidencing a sense of purposelessness and discontent. In the very first chapter, the author begins as follows:

> The problem lay buried, unspoken, for many years in the minds of American women. It was a strange stirring, a sense of dissatisfaction, a yearning that women suffered in the middle of the twentieth century in the United States. As she made the beds, shopped for groceries, matched slipcover material, ate peanut butter sandwiches with her children, chauffeured Cub Scouts and Brownies, lay beside her husband at night, she was afraid to ask even of herself the silent question: "Is this all?"[18]

As Betty Friedan saw it, this was indeed not all; or at least it did not *have* to be all. She then proceeded to enumerate certain plans and alternatives for women, such as: (1) marriage has been oversold, and not all women, certainly, should marry; (2) motherhood has also been greatly oversold, and not all women should have children; (3) in order to prevent unwanted births, both contraceptive methods and abortion should be made readily available to those women who want them; (4) women should press for specific social and economic changes that would make the female role a more rewarding one.

Although Friedan's "platform" was greeted with derision in some quarters, large numbers of people—particularly in the younger age groups—agreed with her position. Slowly at first, then more and more rapidly, women's liberation groups made their voices heard. Demands were made for more and better

---

[18] Betty Friedan, *The Feminine Mystique,* New York, W. W. Norton & Co., Inc., 1963.

jobs, equal social and athletic facilities, child-care centers, legalized abortions, equal educational opportunities—especially at the graduate and professional level, and so on. In brief, whether the issue at hand was economic, political, social, or sexual, the demand was loud and clear: *down with the double standard.* It soon became apparent, furthermore, that women's liberation was more than a slogan, more than a fad. It was—demonstrably—an idea whose time had come.

THE PRESENT SCENE

While women have by no means reached parity with men, most of the signs seem encouraging. Thus Title VII of the Civil Rights Act prohibits discrimination in employment based on sex as well as on race and religion. The Federal Minimum Wage and Hour Law applies equally to males and females. And the Equal Pay Act requires identical remuneration for men and women "in the same establishment performing substantially equal work."[19]

Also encouraging is the educational scene. For, while women still lag substantially behind men, the trend is clearly toward equality. For instance, of all the college and university degrees granted today, well over 40 percent are awarded to women. (In 1900 the figure was 17 percent, and as recently as 1950 it was only 24 percent.)[20]

Most encouraging of all, perhaps, is the trend in graduate and professional training. In the Parrish survey, it was found that in all eight professional fields—architecture, dentistry, engineering, law, medicine, optometry, pharmacy, and veterinary medicine—female enrollment percentages had either doubled or tripled in recent years.[21] The present writer would estimate that, in contrast to some figures cited earlier, first-year female enrollment in most of the above fields now runs as high as 20 to 25 percent. (In 1960, corresponding figures ranged from 1 to 5 percent.) Parrish himself writes that:

> Recently, women in this country have been moving into professional training in increasing numbers, both absolutely and relative to men. In this regard, more change has occurred in the last few years than in the previous half century. . . .

---

[19] See U.S. Department of Labor Leaflet 55, *A Working Woman's Guide To Her Job Rights,* Washington, D.C., 1975, pp. 4–12.

[20] See Blitz, *op. cit.,* p. 38.

[21] John Parrish, "Women in Professional Training," *Monthly Labor Review,* May, 1974, pp. 41–43.

First-year enrollment figures indicate that the rise in the proportion of women in professional training is likely to continue. . . . The evidence suggests that rigid sex stereotyping of many U.S. professions may well become blurred in the future.[22]

Effects on Marriage. It is reasonable to suppose that the woman's rights movement and women's liberation have had an effect on marriage and the family. After all, 60 percent of all women workers in the United States are married and living with their husbands.[23] Some 40 percent of all women workers have children under 18, and while most of the youngsters are of school age, the most recent figures reveal that "about six million were below regular school age, requiring other arrangements for care in their working mothers' absence."[24]

Granted that the women's movement has affected marriage, has the overall effect been positive or negative? This is a complicated question, and there are arguments both pro and con. On the one hand, there is no doubt that the marriage rate has fallen and the divorce rate has risen. Part of the decline in the marriage rate may be due to the fact that women now have viable alternatives to marriage—alternatives that were formerly closed to them. Similarly, the rise in the divorce rate is probably related to the fact that, since jobs are now available to them, women no longer feel "strapped in" to an unhappy marriage.

In certain respects, on the other hand, the women's movement has probably strengthened marriage. Education, for instance, has certainly established an additional bond between husband and wife. It is no longer necessary for husbands to be condescending, or for wives to feel inferior. Also, women's improved occupational status has strengthened marriage in an economic sense; that is, wives have often reinforced or even preserved marriages through their financial contributions. In fact, the Department of Labor reports that "both husband *and wife* are earners in nearly half of the husband-wife families."[25] Where the wife works full-time, furthermore, she contributes close to 40 percent of the family income.[26]

Public opinion polls elicit an interesting response to questions pertaining to the women's movement. To the question, "Do you think the dominant role of the husband in the American family is declining in importance?" 79 percent of the respondents in one

---

[22] *Ibid.*

[23] U.S. Department of Labor, *Chartbook*, pp. 23 ff.

[24] *Ibid.*, p. 29.

[25] *Ibid.*, p. 39.

[26] *Ibid.*, p. 40.

Rather than assigning household tasks solely on the basis of traditional roles, some couples are experimenting with a more flexible division of family responsibilities. (Philip Jon Bailey)

popular poll answered yes, 21 percent answered no. In the same poll, the question, "All in all, do you feel that the movement for women's rights is a force for the better?" found 55 percent answering yes, 45 percent answering no. To the latter question, however, only 43 percent of the high school graduates answered yes, compared with 56 percent of the college graduates, and 69 percent of those who had done graduate work. The greater the educational level, in other words, the greater the tendency to view women's liberation as a positive force.[27]

The responses of college females themselves are also quite revealing. In both the Watley survey[28] and the Epstein-Bronzaft study,[29] women college students were asked whether in looking ahead they were planning "marriage only," "career only," or

---

[27] *A Report on the American Family*, by the editors of *Better Homes and Gardens*, September, 1972, pp. 19 and 41.

[28] Donivan J. Watley, "Career or Marriage: A Longitudinal Study of Able Young Women," in Theodore, *op. cit.*, pp. 260–274.

[29] Gilda Epstein and Arline Bronzaft, "Female Freshmen View Their Roles as Women," *Journal of Marriage and the Family*, November, 1972, pp. 671–672.

"marriage with career." In each study the clear preference was for "marriage with career." In a survey of his own students undertaken by the present writer in 1975–1976, no less than 77 percent of the women reported that they intended to combine marriage and a career. One respondent wrote as follows:

> My sister is nine years older than I am, and I kind of feel sorry for her. She's married and has three small children—and has nothing to look forward to. I mean, she should have gone to medical school. She was a biology major, and graduated Phi Beta Kappa. She was a natural. She would have made a brilliant doctor. . . .
>
> But in her day, marriage was the "in" thing. If a girl didn't have a prospect by the time she graduated, she was likely to feel something was wrong with her. Anyway, my sister married right after commencement.
>
> Not me. I have a good job lined up as a sales representative. It involves traveling, and I'm looking forward to it. I have nothing against marriage—but as I see it, there's no reason I can't do both.

This last statement drives home a very pertinent point. What the recent women's liberation movement has done is *to provide women in all walks of life with a choice.* Those who wish to do so can still select the "marriage only" option. But, for others, the temper of the times now makes it possible to explore career possibilities without sacrificing a rewarding matrimonial relationship. If as a consequence the marriage rate falls somewhat, the price would seem to be a reasonable one—in keeping with the precepts of a free society.

SELECTED READINGS

Benet, Mary K., *The Secretarial Ghetto,* New York, McGraw-Hill Book Co., 1973.

Blitz, Rudolph, "Women in the Professions, 1870–1970," *Monthly Labor Review,* May, 1974, pp. 34–39.

Bradshaw, Thomas, and Stinson, John, "Trends in Weekly Earnings: An Analysis," *Monthly Labor Review,* August, 1975, pp. 27–32.

Brogan, Donna, and Kutner, Nancy, "Measuring Sex-Role Orientation: A Normative Approach," *Journal of Marriage and the Family,* February, 1976, pp. 31–40.

Bureau of Labor Statistics, U.S. Department of Labor, *U.S. Working Women: A Chartbook,* Washington, D.C., U.S. Government Printing Office, 1975.

Campbell, Frederick, "Family Growth and Variation in Family Role Structure," *Journal of Marriage and the Family,* February, 1970, pp. 45–53.

Carson, Gerald, *The Polite Americans*, New York, William Morrow & Company, 1966.

Chafe, William H., *The American Woman: Her Changing Social, Economic, and Political Roles*, New York, Oxford University Press, 1972.

Clavan, Sylvia, "Women's Liberation and the Family," *Family Coordinator*, October, 1970, pp. 317–323.

Coser, Rose Laub (ed.), *The Family: Its Structures and Functions*, New York, St. Martin's Press, 1974, especially Part 9, "Changing Roles of American Women," pp. 471–531.

Decard, Barbara, *The Women's Movement: Political, Socioeconomic, and Psychological Issues*, New York, Harper & Row, 1975.

Epstein, Gilda, and Bronzaft, Arline, "Female Freshmen View Their Roles as Women," *Journal of Marriage and the Family*, November, 1972, pp. 671–672.

Freeman, Jo (ed.), *Women: A Feminist Perspective*, Palo Alto, California, Mayfield Publishing Company, 1975.

Friedan, Betty, *The Feminine Mystique*, New York, W. W. Norton & Co., Inc., 1963.

Frost, J. William, *The Quaker Family in Colonial America*, New York, St. Martin's Press, 1973.

Ginzberg, Eli, and Yohalem, Alice (eds.), *Corporate Lib: Women's Challenge to Management*, Baltimore, The Johns Hopkins Press, 1973.

Glazer-Malbin, Nona, and Waehrer, Helen Youngelson (eds.), *Woman in a Man-Made World*, Chicago, Rand McNally & Company, 1972.

Handbook on Women Workers, Washington, D.C., The Women's Bureau of the U.S. Department of Labor, 1974.

Hecht, Marie; Berbich, Joan; Healey, Salley; and Cooper, Clare; *The Women, Yes!* New York, Holt, Rinehart and Winston, 1973.

Huber, Joan (ed.), *Changing Women in a Changing Society*, Chicago, University of Chicago Press, 1973.

Janeway, Elizabeth (ed.), *Women, Their Changing Roles*, New York, Arno Press, 1973.

LeMasters, E. E., "The American Mother," in *Parents in Modern America*, Homewood, Illinois, The Dorsey Press, 1974, pp. 106–123.

Parrish, John, "Women in Professional Training," *Monthly Labor Review*, May, 1974, pp. 41–43.

Pivar, David J., *Purity Crusade: Sexual Morality and Social Control, 1868–1900*, Westport, Connecticut, Greenwood Press, Inc., 1973.

Seward, Georgene, and Williamson, Robert C. (eds.), *Sex Roles in Changing Society*, New York, Random House, Inc., 1970.

Theodore, Athena (ed.), *The Professional Woman,* Cambridge, Massachusetts, Schenkman Publishing Company, Inc., 1971.

U.S. Department of Labor, *A Working Woman's Guide to Her Job Rights,* Washington, D.C., Government Printing Office, 1975.

Wells, J. Gipson, *Current Issues in Marriage and the Family,* "Men's and Women's Roles," pp. 116–154, New York, Macmillan Co., Inc., 1975.

234

III

Premarital Behavior Patterns

11
Mate Selection I

PERHAPS THE MOST intriguing question in the entire family field is the baffling "Who marries whom and why?" Surely for the college student there can be no more pertinent topic. After all, it is logical to assume that marital unhappiness is caused not so much by issues arising *after* marriage as by the *imperfect choice of a partner*. For most college students there seems to be an adequate supply of potential mates. Which particular one is chosen is obviously a decision that will have important and lasting consequences.

The supply of partners is not limitless, of course. On the contrary, mate selection in all societies operates within formal or informal circumscriptions. An American youth, for instance, is expected to marry someone in the same age category. It is presumed, further, that he or she will marry within the same race and, to a lesser extent, within the same religion and socioeconomic class. Young Americans are thus faced with a neat interplay between societal expectations and individual freedom of choice.

College students are sometimes prone to question the need for any type of "restrictions" governing mate selection, yet it is difficult to conceive of a reasonable alternative. As Eckland puts it:

> One possible way of illustrating the conserving or maintenance function of social homogamy in mate selection is to try to visualize momentarily how a comtemporary society would operate under conditions of *random* mating. Considering their proportion in the population, Negroes actually would be more likely to marry whites than other Negroes; Catholics more often than not would marry Protestants; and a college graduate would be more apt to marry a high school dropout than to marry another college graduate.
>
> In a like manner, about as often as not, dull would marry bright, old would marry young, Democrats would marry Republicans, and

Casual acquaintanceships first formed at a neighborhood dance can be the basis of more lasting relationships. (Derrick TePaske)

teetotalers would marry drinkers. What would be the end result of this kind of social heterogamy? A new melting pot, or chaos?[1]

PROPINQUITY

Propinquity refers to nearness in place, or proximity, and for more than 40 years one of the truisms in sociology has been that young people tend to marry those who live near by. The original propinquity study was done by Bossard in 1932. Transcribing street addresses from 5,000 consecutive marriage licenses issued in Philadelphia, he discovered that one-sixth of the applicant-pairs lived within a block of each other, one-third lived within five blocks, and more than half lived within 20 blocks of each other. As the author aptly concluded: "Cupid may have wings, but apparently they are not adapted for long flights."[2]

In the last four decades, dozens of replication studies have been undertaken in such diverse cities as Columbus, Ohio; New Haven, Connecticut; Nashville, Tennessee; Seattle, Washington, and others. Rural as well as urban areas have been investigated,

---

[1] Bruce Eckland, "Theories of Mate Selection," *Eugenics Quarterly,* June, 1968, p. 79.
[2] James Bossard, "Residential Propinquity as a Factor in Marriage Selection," *American Journal of Sociology,* September, 1932, p. 222.

as have such far-away places as Oslo, Norway, and Karachi, Pakistan. And while research design has been amplified and sharpened, Bossard's original findings have been basically substantiated. Cherished notions about romantic love aside, it appears that, when all is said and done, the "one and only" may have a better than 50–50 chance of living within walking distance!

In the Catton-Smircich survey of Seattle, the investigators found much the same ecological distribution as in previous investigations; that is, most of the applicant-couples were found to live within a relatively short distance of each other.[3] Instead of stopping with these findings, however, the researchers applied mathematical models in an attempt to impart meaning to the Seattle figures. Why, they ask, does propinquity operate? Why, indeed, in view of the fact—as they point out—that the number of potential mates actually *increases with the distance away from one's residence!* Before continuing with the investigators' analysis, it is necessary to turn to some additional dimensions of mate selection.

239

THE AGE FACTOR

Age is another element that tends to circumscribe the choice of a marriage partner. In the first place, most people in our society marry within their own age range. There are exceptions, especially in the case of remarriages and older people, but it is more or less expected that first marriages will involve two individuals whose ages are relatively close.

A second consideration is the fact that women customarily neither date nor marry men who are younger than themselves; in fact, government figures reveal that in only 15 percent of American marriages are wives older than their husbands. On the average, husbands are two to three years older than their wives.

The implications here are greater than is generally realized, for in point of fact the expected age differential greatly reduces the number of eligible partners for both sexes. To illustrate, if the customary marital age range were three years in either direction, a 22-year-old person could choose a mate in the 19–25 bracket, *provided it made no difference which sex was older.* Since the expectation is that a man will at least be no younger than his bride, the

---

[3] For a bibliography of studies on propinquity—as well as an excellent discussion of the subject—see Wesley R. Burr, *Theory Construction and the Sociology of the Family*, New York, John Wiley & Sons, 1973, pp. 90 ff.

hypothetical 19–25 age range is almost halved, with the actual span shrinking to 19–22 for the man and 22–25 for the woman.

In the college situation, age differentials have a significance that is all too clear to students. On an age basis, the freshman girl can date virtually any boy in college. By the time she is a senior, this marriage market has shrunk to one-quarter of its original size. In the case of the boy, the situation is reversed, for on an age basis a college senior has four times as much opportunity as he had when he was a freshman.

A final age-limiting factor is the American custom of early matrimony. The age at marriage in the United States has fallen since the turn of the century. In 1900, the average (median) age at first marriage for men was 26, and for women, 22. Corresponding figures at the present time are 23 for men and 21 for women. The downward trend seems to have leveled off, however; in fact, the figures are slightly higher today than they were a decade ago. (The average age at marriage for college graduates—both men and women—is a year or two higher than that of the general population.)

On a cross-cultural basis, Americans seem to marry young, at least as compared with other civilized societies. Although the median age at first marriage in India is 20 for males and 14.5 for females, other nations evidence relatively high figures; e.g., England (25.2 for males, 21.8 for females), France (26.0 and 22.6), Norway (27.9 and 24.4), Japan (25.8 and 23.1), Switzerland (27.2 and 24.5), and Austria (26.6 and 24.0). The highest medians have been those of Ireland—31.4 for males and 26.5 for females.[4]

Is There a "Best" Marrying Age? In view of the tendency toward early marriage in the United States, some young people feel that life is passing them by if they do not have a definite prospect of matrimony by the time they are in the 23–25 age range. The degree to which this feeling acts as a circumscribing factor in mate selection can only be conjectured, but in all likelihood it assumes significant proportions. If it were required by law that all persons wait until age 30 before getting married, one might speculate about the percentage of people whose chosen mate would have been the same one selected, say, 8 or 10 years previously!

At any rate, from the 1930's to the 1970's, a number of studies have explored the relation between age at marriage and such phenomena as marital happiness, frequency of divorce, and the

---

[4] Population Reference Bureau, Washington, D.C., *Population Bulletin*, 17, June, 1961. For a comprehensive discussion of age at marriage, see F. Ivan Nye and Felix Berardo, *The Family: Its Structure and Interaction*, New York, The Macmillan Company, 1973, pp. 225–244.

like.[5] Irrespective of the criteria used, the studies are virtually all in agreement that early marriages have a relatively poor prognosis. Lasswell, who has made a survey of the various findings, writes as follows:

> Getting married in the teen years is unquestionably the worst time to marry, not only in terms of the stability of the marriage, but in terms of the reported satisfaction.
>
> The divorce rate is correlated with age at marriage, and the older the couple is at marriage, the greater likelihood that the marriage will succeed. For men, there is a point of diminishing returns at about age 31. . . . For women, the divorce rate declines with each year they wait to marry until a gradual leveling off at about age 25.
>
> From the standpoint of marriage stability, then, men who marry between 27 and 31, and women who marry at about 25 seem to have waited long enough to maximize their chances at a durable relationship. This is more than three years, for both men and women, past the average age at first marriage in the United States currently.[6]

MARITAL STATUS

Sociologists have long been aware that marital status itself tends to act as an influencing factor in mate selection; that is, single persons are likely to marry other single persons, widowed tend to marry widowed, and divorcés tend to marry divorcées. Jacobson's figures indicate that this marital-status phenomenon occurred at least as far back as the turn of the century.[7]

The tendency has persisted down to the present, studies by the Census Bureau, the National Vital Statistics System, the Metropolitan Life Insurance Company, and private researchers all yielding the same results. "Previous marital status" figures have

---

[5] See, for example, Lewis Terman, *Psychological Factors in Marital Happiness*, New York, McGraw Hill Book Co., 1938, pp. 180–181; Ernest Burgess and Leonard Cottrell, *Predicting Success and Failure in Marriage*, Englewood Cliffs, New Jersey, Prentice-Hall, Inc., 1939, p. 116; Harvey Locke, *Predicting Adjustment in Marriage*, New York, Henry Holt and Co., 1951, p. 102; Thomas Monahan, "Does Age at Marriage Matter in Divorce?" *Social Forces*, October, 1953, pp. 84–85; Paul Glick, *American Families*, New York, John Wiley & Sons, Inc., 1957, pp. 56–58; Lee Burchinal," Trends and Prospects for Young Marriages in the United States," *Journal of Marriage and the Family*, May, 1965, pp. 243–254; Paul Glick and Arthur Norton, "Frequency, Duration, and Probability of Marriage and Divorce," *Journal of Marriage and the Family*, May, 1971, p. 315. See also Paul Glick, "A Demographer Looks at American Families," *Journal of Marriage and the Family*, February, 1975, pp. 15–26.

[6] Marcia E. Lasswell, "Is There a Best Age to Marry?: An Interpretation," *Family Coordinator*, July, 1974, p. 240.

[7] Paul Jacobson, *American Marriage and Divorce*, New York, Rinehart & Co., Inc., 1959, p. 67.

been remarkably consistent over the years. Tabulations indicate that more than 9 out of 10 single (never married) persons marry single persons, and that more than 5 out of 10 widowed or divorced persons marry within their respective group. For each marital-status class—single, widowed, divorced—the largest number of marriages occur between brides and grooms of the same class.[8] A recent study by Kuzel and Krishnan indicates that marital-status similarity is also true for Canada.[9]

ENDOGAMY

Anthropologists use the term *endogamy* to signify marriage within the tribe or other social unit, as contrasted to *exogamy*, or marriage outside the group. Sociologists have come to apply these terms to intra- and intermarriage with respect to broad groupings such as race, religion, nationality, and social class.

Race. It seems to be sad but true, apropos of national marriage and divorce statistics, that the things people are most interested in are those about which we have the least information. This is certainly true in the area of interracial and interreligious marriage. In the case of interracial marriage, for example, we do not have—and never have had—satisfactory national figures on the subject. We do have data based on U.S. Census samples, and also some information gleaned from the vital statistics of certain states. Both types of data involve some well-known methodological limitations, and in view of this fact we are fortunate in being able to make at least some generalizations.

To begin with, the interracial marriage rate—no matter how it is computed—has been increasing. Virtually all the studies are in agreement on this point; for example, there are surveys by Monahan,[10] Aldridge,[11] and Heer,[12] based on a number of individual states, and a data-analysis by Heer, based on decennial census samples.[13]

---

[8] See the yearly reports on *Marriage*, issued by the National Vital Statistics System, Department of Health, Education, and Welfare, Washington, D.C.

[9] Paul Kuzel and P. Krishnan, "Changing Patterns of Remarriage in Canada," *Journal of Comparative Family Studies*, Autumn, 1973, pp. 215–224.

[10] Thomas Monahan, "Interracial Marriage: Data for Philadelphia and Pennsylvania," *Demography*, August, 1970, pp. 287–299; "Are Interracial Marriages Really Less Stable?" *Social Forces*, June, 1970, pp. 461–473; "Interracial Marriages in the United States: Some Data on Upstate New York," *International Journal of Sociology of the Family*, March, 1971, pp. 94–105; "Interracial Marriage and Divorce in Kansas," *Journal of Comparative Family Studies*, Spring, 1971, pp. 107–120; "Marriage Across Racial Lines in Indiana," *Journal of Marriage and the Family*, November, 1973, pp. 632–640.

Despite the increase, however, the ratio of interracial marriages to total marriages remains quite low, a conclusion borne out, again, by all of the above studies. Indeed, one of the reasons for the increase is the fact that the black-white marriage rate started a generation or so ago from a base of near zero. Jacobson reports that in 1939, interracial marriages accounted for 0.08 percent of all U.S. marriages.[14] (Up to 1967, interracial marriages were illegal in some 20 states. In that year, the Supreme Court ruled that such prohibitions were unconstitutional.) The present writer would estimate that, even at the present time, less that 1 percent of U.S. marriages are between blacks and whites.

Since blacks comprise around 12 percent of the population, it is apparent that the practice of racial endogamy serves to delimit mate selection for both races. As Eshleman puts it: "Despite scientific findings and the removal of legal barriers, the restrictions concerning interracial marriages still remain the most inflexible of all the mate-selection boundaries."[15]

What of the future? Will the interracial marriage barriers ultimately break down? The point can be argued either way. On the one hand, people are reportedly taking a more tolerant view toward such marriages, a view that seems especially pronounced on the part of younger people and those with a college education. The latest Gallup Poll figures[16] in answer to the question "Do you approve of marriage between blacks and whites?" are as follows:

	APPROVE (%)	DISAPPROVE (%)	NO OPINION (%)
National	29	60	11
Men	32	58	10
Women	26	63	11
Whites	25	65	10
Blacks	58	21	21
18–30 years	44	44	12
30–40 years	28	60	12
50 and over	19	72	9
College	45	46	9
High School	24	64	12
Grade School	20	68	12

[11] Delores Aldridge, "The Changing Nature of Interracial Marriage in Georgia," *Journal of Marriage and the Family*, November, 1973, pp. 641–642.

[12] David Heer, "Negro-White Marriage in the United States," *Journal of Marriage and the Family*, August, 1966, pp. 262–273.

[13] David Heer, "The Prevalence of Black-White Marriage in the United States, 1960 and 1970," *Journal of Marriage and the Family*, May, 1974, pp. 246–258.

[14] Jacobson, *op. cit.*, p. 62.

[15] J. Ross Eshleman, *The Family: An Introduction*, Boston, Allyn and Bacon, Inc., 1974, p. 312.

[16] Released for publication November 19, 1972.

On the other hand, opinion polls to the contrary, there does not appear to be any concerted effort to boost the interracial marriage rate. From a mate-selection view, blacks and whites seem almost compartmented into two groups. Times change rapidly, of course, and no one can say just what the future will bring.

For reasons that are by no means fully understood, interracial marriages much more often involve a black male and a white female rather than the other way around. Also, on the basis of one or more studies, there is a suggestion that interracial marriages (1) show a relatively high rate of prior divorce on the part of one or both partners, (2) involve couples who marry at a comparatively late age, (3) involve a white female who is foreign-born or of foreign parentage, and (4) produce fewer children than other marriages.[17]

With regard to the last point, it is often alleged that black-white marriages are fragile and that children add to the fragility by creating a "difficult situation." This is an extremely important consideration, and the whole matter of interracial marital stability will be discussed in Chapter 21.

Religion. The extent of religious endogamy in the United States depends largely on the particular religion or denomination being considered. Among the Old Order Amish, mate selection outside the group is virtually nonexistent. On the other hand, intermarriage among the various Protestant denominations—Episcopalians, Baptists, Presbyterians, Lutherans, Methodists, and others—is quite common. If, in Protestant households, husband and wife are usually of the same denomination, it is not because of endogamous mate selection but because one party frequently "converts" after marriage.[18]

When questions are raised concerning religious intermarriage, however, what is usually meant is the pattern involving Protestants, Catholics, and Jews, and we are fortunate in having some excellent studies available. Special mention should be made, in this connection, of Dr. Thomas Monahan, who—more than any other sociologist—fought for the inclusion of both race and religion on vital-statistics registration forms. Without such information, our knowledge of the intermarriage process would be severely limited.

[17] See especially Monahan and Heer, *footnotes 10, 12, and 13.*
[18] See Nicholas Babchuk, Harry Crockett, and John Ballweg, "Changes in Religious Affiliation and Family Stability," *Social Forces*, June, 1967, pp. 551–555; and Andrew Greeley, "Religious Intermarriage in a Denominational Society," *American Journal of Sociology*, May, 1970, pp. 949–952.

Although intermarriage rates seem to be rising for all major religious groups, most people continue to marry within their own faith. (Owen Franken, Stock Boston)

It is common knowledge that all three major religious groups encourage their members to marry within the fold, although there is some variation in respective church attitudes. The most flexible are the Protestants, the most rigid are the Jews, with the Catholics falling in between. A Catholic priest will marry a Catholic and a non-Catholic, provided certain stipulations are met, but most rabbis will not marry a Jew and a non-Jew. Wise men know, however, that the marriage market sometimes makes its own rules.

It should not be forgotten that Jews and Catholics represent minority religions in the United States, so that young people of both faiths are overexposed, statistically speaking, to the larger Protestant group. In certain areas the proportion of Catholics or Jews is so small that the forces of religious exogamy have been almost irresistible. "There is strong evidence," writes Burchinal, "that the proportion of a religious body in a community is probably the single most influential factor for predicting interreligious marriage rates."[19]

The Jews have a special problem apropos of numbers. While they are traditionally an endogamous people, they comprise a

---

[19] Lee Burchinal, "The Premarital Dyad and Love Involvement," in Harold Christensen (ed.), *Handbook of Marriage and the Family*, Chicago, Rand McNally & Co., 1964, p. 651.

bare 3 percent of the U.S. population. If they adhered to strict religious endogamy, the Jews would be excluding themselves from 97 percent of the larger market. In practice, they have been increasingly active in the larger market, although their intermarriage level varies from place to place—from less than 5 percent in Providence, Rhode Island, to more than 50 percent in Indiana.[20] Overall, however, a number of studies have been undertaken in different parts of the United States, as well as in Canada, and the increase in the Jewish intermarriage rate is unmistakable.[21]

On the basis of the available evidence, the writer would estimate that somewhere in the area of 30 percent of current Jewish marriages are mixed. While religious endogamy is still a significant force in Jewish mate selection, it is not so pervasive as it once was.

Numerically, the most significant interreligious marriage pattern is that involving Protestants and Catholics. There are in excess of 50 million Catholics in the United States; hence, if religious endogamy prevailed, both groups—Catholics and Protestants—would face sizeable restrictions in terms of mate selection. However, as in the case of the Jews, a wide array of studies indicates that Catholic intermarriage has been heading upward.

The evidence also suggests that the smaller the proportion of Catholics in an area, the greater the likelihood of intermarriage occurring. Overall, research findings indicate that a third or more of present-day Catholic marriages in this country are mixed. In some areas, the figure is reported to exceed 50 percent.[22] It should be added, however, that while both Jewish and Catholic intermarriage has been increasing, substantial numbers of both groups remain opposed to the idea.*

---

* In Prince's study of Catholic college students, "approximately 70 percent of the women and 51 percent of the men agreed with the statement that one should marry within one's faith." (A. J. Prince, "Attitudes of Catholic Students Toward Intermarriage," *International Journal of Sociology of the Family*, May, 1971, pp. 99–126.) And in Cavan's survey of Jewish college students, 43 percent of the Reform males and 51 percent of the females, and 61 percent of the Conservative males and 79 percent of the females, stated that they would be unwilling to marry outside their faith. (Ruth Cavan, "Attitudes of Jewish College Students Toward Interreligious Marriage," *International Journal of Sociology of the Family*, May, 1971, pp. 84–98.)

[20] See Thomas Monahan, "Some Dimensions of Interreligious Marriages in Indiana," *Social Forces*, December, 1973, pp. 195–203.

[21] In addition to Monahan (footnote 20), see Erich Rosenthal, "Studies of Jewish Intermarriage in the United States," *American Jewish Year Book*, Vol. 64, pp. 3–53; Sidney Goldstein and Calvin Goldscheider, "Social and Demographic Aspects of

Sociologists have also been interested in studying the *characteristics* of the intermarried. Jewish males, for instance, are much more likely to be involved in mixed marriages than are Jewish females. In the case of Protestant-Catholic marriages, no parallel tendency has been ascertained. The following will give some idea of the findings that have been reported in one or more studies.[23]

As compared with those who marry within their own faith, persons who intermarry are likely to have:

1. Weak religious and familial ties.
2. A high rate of prior divorce.
3. A civil rather than a religious marriage ceremony.
4. Parents who were involved in a mixed marriage.
5. A high rate of premarital pregnancy.
6. An urban background.

There seems to be no doubt that (1) interreligious marriage has been increasing in the United States, and (2) persons who intermarry have certain social characteristics that differentiate them from those who marry within their own faith. Of equal significance is the fact that public opinion on the subject is also softening, as evidenced by Gallup Polls taken over the years. The most recent figures indicate that less than 15 percent of the respondents were opposed to marriages between Jews and non-Jews, or between Protestants and Catholics.[24]

Jewish Intermarriage," *Social Problems*, Spring, 1966, pp. 386–399; Eugen Schoenfeld, "Intermarriage and the Small Town: The Jewish Case," *Journal of Marriage and the Family*, February, 1969, pp. 61–64; Erich Rosenthal, "Divorce and Religious Intermarriage: Effect of Previous Marital Status upon Subsequent Marital Behavior," *Journal of Marriage and the Family*, August, 1970, pp. 435–440.

[22] Monahan, "Interreligious Marriages in Indiana," p. 197.

[23] See Larry Barnett, "Research in Interreligious Dating and Marriage," *Marriage and Family Living*, May, 1962, pp. 191–194; Alfred Prince, "A Study of 194 Cross-Religion Marriages," *Family Life Coordinator*, January, 1962, pp. 3–7; Jerold Heiss, "Premarital Characteristics of the Religiously Intermarried in an Urban Area," *American Sociological Review*, February, 1960, pp. 47–55; Lee Burchinal and Loren Chancellor, "Factors Related to Interreligious Marriages in Iowa," *Research Bulletin 510* of the Iowa State University's Agricultural and Home Economics Experiment Station, November, 1962, pp. 672–695; Harold Christensen and Kenneth Barber, "Interfaith Versus Intrafaith Marriage in Indiana," *Journal of Marriage and the Family*, August, 1967, pp. 461–469; Erich Rosenthal, "Divorce and Religious Intermarriage"; Thomas Monahan, "Some Dimensions of Interreligious Marriages in Indiana."

[24] The actual breakdown was as follows: marriage between Jews and non-Jews: 67 percent approve, 14 percent disapprove, 19 percent no opinion; marriage between Protestants and Catholics: 72 percent approve, 13 percent disapprove, 15 percent no opinion. Gallup Poll released for publication November 19, 1972.

It is true that a substantial majority of American youth—perhaps between 65 and 85 percent, depending on the religious group involved—continue to marry within their own faith. But while it is hazardous to predict the future, indications are that the forces of religious endogamy will continue to weaken.

Nationality. Since by definition Americans are immigrants or descendants of immigrants, nationality has played a significant role in their political, economic, and social life. Americans are more conscious of their ethnic origins than are the inhabitants of most other countries, even though large-scale immigration stopped shortly after World War I. In recent decades the number of new arrivals has been reduced to a trickle, and today the foreign-born are a very small proportion of the population. Many writers expected, therefore, that as time went on nationality would become less and less of a "problem." The Americanization process, interethnic marriage, internal migration—all these forces of assimilation, it was felt, would combine to obliterate nationality lines.

Like many other untested theories, however, the "melting pot" concept, as it was called, failed to materialize—at least, to the degree anticipated. This is not to say that the assimilation process failed in the 1920's, 1930's, and 1940's. Far from it. The public school system, common recreational and social activities, and the intermeshing of jobs and personalities in the giant labor market tended to soften the shell of ethnic rigidity. At the same time, urban groups such as the Italians, Greeks, Armenians, and Poles, and rural groups like the Swedes and Finns, maintained their ethnic identity to a surprising degree.

In the 1930's a study by Bossard of some 70,000 marriage records in New York State revealed that nationality lines were still being preserved.[25] Kennedy's New Haven survey in the 1940's disclosed that the "Irish, Italians, and Poles marry mostly among themselves, and British-Americans, Germans, and Scandinavians do likewise. . . ."[26]

During the same decade, Nelson, studying some 900 marriages in rural Minnesota, discovered that in two-thirds of the cases husbands and wives were of the same nationality group (e.g., Finns, Swedes, Germans).[27] Reporting in 1950 on a later New

---

[25] James Bossard, "Nationality and Nativity as Factors in Marriage," *American Sociological Review*, December, 1939, pp. 792–798.

[26] Ruby Jo Reeves Kennedy, "Single or Triple Melting Pot? Intermarriage Trends in New Haven, 1870–1940," *American Journal of Sociology*, January, 1944, p. 339.

[27] Lowry Nelson, "Intermarriage Among Nationality Groups in a Rural Area of Minnesota," *American Journal of Sociology*, March, 1943, pp. 585–592.

Haven study, Hollingshead wrote that "ethnicity within a religious group has been a very potent factor in influencing the mate selection process in both the parental and the present generation, but it was stronger a generation ago than it is now."[28]

In the 1960's several studies attested to the fact that nationality was far from a dead issue. Bugelski found that more than half the Poles and Italians in Buffalo were still marrying within their own nationality.[29] Working with U.S. Census data, Bogue discovered that "there is clearly a tendency for people in the same ethnic group to marry each other. . . . Persons of Puerto Rican, Irish, Polish, USSR, and Italian extraction have a very strong propensity to marry within their own group. Persons from Northwest Europe, if they do not marry other persons of the same national origin, have an affinity for marrying other people from Northwest Europe or Canada."[30] The same author found that certain interethnic marital combinations were quite rare, for example: USSR and Irish; Polish and Irish; Italian and German; Canadian and USSR; Canadian and Polish; Italian and USSR; Italian and United Kingdom.

In the 1970's, it appeared that nationality was still a factor in mate selection. In their widely read *Beyond the Melting Pot*, Glazer and Moynihan note that long after mass immigration stopped, "the ethnic pattern is still strong in New York City." The same authors go on to present a most provocative theory:

> The fact is that in every generation, throughout the history of the American republic, the merging of the varying streams of population *has seemed to lie just ahead*—a generation, perhaps, in the future. This continual deferral of the final smelting of the different ingredients into a seamless national web, as it is to be found in the major national states of Europe, suggests that we must search for some systematic and general causes for this American pattern of subnationalities; that it is not the temporary upsetting inflow of new and unassimilated immigrants that creates a pattern of ethnic groups within the nation, but rather some central tendency in the national ethos which structures people, whether those coming in afresh or the descendants of those who have been here for generations, into groups of different status and character.[31]

[28] August Hollingshead, "Cultural Factors in the Selection of Marriage Mates," *American Sociological Review*, October, 1950, p. 624.

[29] B. R. Bugelski, "Assimilation Through Intermarriage," *Social Forces*, December, 1961, pp. 148–153.

[30] Donald Bogue, *Principles of Demography*, New York, John Wiley & Sons, Inc., 1969, pp. 358–359.

[31] Nathan Glazer and Daniel Moynihan, *Beyond the Melting Pot*, Cambridge, Massachusetts, The M.I.T. Press and Harvard University Press, 1971, pp. 290–291. (Italics added.)

Members of ethnic groups often tend to choose marital partners from within their own group. (UPI Photo)

And now—with the 1980's upon us—what is the picture? Ethnic endogamy, certainly, is not so significant as it once was. Young people of different nationalities do seem to be paying less and less attention to ethnic lines. The foreign-born are comparatively few in number, with many reaching an age where, statistically, they are dying off at a rapid rate.

Still and all, the "melting pot" continues to simmer, with many of the ingredients remaining clearly visible. And therein lies the puzzle. To rephrase Glazer and Moynihan's analysis of the intermarriage process: "The final smelting of the different ingredients into a seamless national web always seems to lie just ahead—a generation, perhaps, in the future." To which we can only add: time will tell.

Social Class. During recent decades sociologists have spent a good deal of time analyzing the so-called class structure in the United States. Although concepts and definitions vary somewhat, one commonly used set of class criteria refers to occupation, income, education, and residence. On this basis, do young people tend to choose mates within their own social stratum, or is class exogamy the rule? Is the class system in America becoming more rigid or more flexible? While these two questions are not identical, they are doubtless related, and—at least insofar as the mate-selection process is concerned—we are fortunate in having a number of empirical studies available. Incidentally, the question whether the American class system is becoming more rigid or more fluid has divided social scientists for many years, and while the information included herein does not solve the problem, mate-selection data are certainly germane to the issue.

In his classic study of Elmtown, a small Midwestern city, Hollingshead found that in the 1940's social-class endogamy was clearly the rule:

> Elmtowners will tell you that "love alone" is the thing; "it brings young people together." They will argue that people marry when "Miss or Mr. Right comes along," and not before. But in a very large number of cases Miss and Mr. Right belong to families who are members of the same class grouping in the community. If we include the immediately adjacent classes, then almost all cases are included. In short, the romantic complex operates, in large part, within the confines of the class system.[32]

Another well-known study, by Centers in the late 1940's, involved a national cross section of the population. Dividing occupations into broad groupings of (1) business executive, (2) professional, (3) small business, (4) white-collar, (5) skilled manual, (6) semiskilled, and (7) unskilled, Centers found that both men and women were more likely to marry partners of their own occupational stratum than of any other single stratum. It was found that while there was a substantial amount of occupational exogamy, cross-class marriages for the most part involved adjacent occupational groupings.[33]

In a later study by Hollingshead, it was found that 58.2 percent of the marriages in New Haven involved partners from the same residential social stratum, and that when marriages involving "a partner from an adjacent class area were added to the first group the figure was raised to 82.8 percent."[34]

Throughout the 1950's and 1960's a wide variety of investigations reaffirmed the principle of social-class endogamy, and in

---

[32] August Hollingshead, "Class and Kinship in a Middle Western Community," *American Sociological Review*, August, 1949, p. 475.

[33] Richard Centers, "Occupational Endogamy in Marital Selection," *American Journal of Sociology*, May, 1949, pp. 530–535.

[34] August Hollingshead, "Cultural Factors in the Selection of Marriage Mates," *American Sociological Review*, October, 1950, p. 624.

the 1970's several analytical accounts appeared.[35] Not all the studies have been in agreement, to be sure. In the Dinitz–Banks–Pasamanick survey, the investigators found a decline over the years in both maximally endogamous and maximally exogamous marriages, with a somewhat broader middle-class range.[36]

Nevertheless, the evidence seems clear that for several decades young Americans have had a pronounced tendency to marry within their general socio-economic level. Eckland estimates that between 50 and 80 percent of the marriages in the United States are endogamous for social class, "the exact figures depending on the nature of the index used and the methods employed to calculate the rate."[37]

The College Situation. In view of the tendency of Americans to marry within the same social class, the dating "exposure" inherent in the college situation is of particular relevance; in fact, it appears that college is playing an increasingly important role in the dynamics of mate selection. For one thing, more and more young people are attending institutions of higher learning, a trend that will probably continue. For another, more and more colleges have become coeducational, and there is almost no likelihood that this direction will be reversed.

It would be expected, therefore, that many college students select mates who attend the same college or university, and scattered references suggest that this is indeed the case, although there have been no recent studies on the subject.

There is more inclination, also, for young people to marry while they are still in college. At one time it was not uncommon

[35] See A. Philip Sundal and Thomas McCormick, "Age at Marriage and Mate Selection: Madison, Wisconsin," *American Sociological Review,* February, 1951, p. 46; National Office of Vital Statistics, *Special Reports,* Vol. 45, No. 12, September 9, 1957, p. 287; Robert Coombs, "Reinforcement of Values in the Parental Home as a Factor in Mate Selection," *Marriage and Family Living,* May, 1962, pp. 155–157; Simon Dinitz, Franklin Banks, and Benjamin Pasamanick, "Mate Selection and Social Class: Changes During the Past Quarter Century," *Marriage and Family Living,* November, 1960, pp. 348–351; U.S. Bureau of the Census, *Women by Number of Children Ever Born,* PC (2) 3A, United States Census of Population, 1960, Washington, D.C., U.S. Government Printing Office, 1964; Robert Garrison, V.E. Anderson, and Sheldon Reed, "Assortative Marriage," *Eugenics Quarterly,* June, 1968, pp. 113–127; Zick Rubin, *Liking and Loving,* New York, Holt, Rinehart and Winston, Inc., 1973; J. Ross Eshleman, *The Family: An Introduction,* Boston, Allyn and Bacon, Inc., 1974, pp. 298–304; Richard Rockwell, "Historical Trends and Variations in Educational Homogamy," *Journal of Marriage and the Family,* February, 1976, pp. 83–95.

[36] Dinitz, Banks, and Pasamanick, *op. cit.*

[37] Eckland, *op. cit.,* p. 78.

for colleges to prohibit undergraduates from marrying, and "headstrong youths" who broke the rules were expelled. Today, the rule has just about disappeared; in fact, while they are still the exception, marriages on the part of undergraduates are by no means uncommon.

In dating their "peers," do college students follow a pattern of social-class endogamy? The answer seems to be, "Yes, but—" And the qualification lies in the fact that the stratification system which exists on the campus is not the same as that which exists in the community. In the Coombs survey of married college students, for example, it was found that 83 percent of the marriages were endogamous when both parties lived at home, compared with a figure of 61 percent when neither lived at home.[38]

In another study, by Reiss, two hypotheses were tested: (1) serious dating on campus will be in line with an existing campus stratification system, and (2) campus dating will reflect the parental class system. Statistical results strongly supported the first hypothesis. Hypothesis 2 was also supported, although the author states that "the evidence is more suggestive than conclusive."[39]

While some educators may bemoan the trend, it seems likely that college will continue to play an important role in the process of mate selection. As one student irreverently put it, "The beauty of the system is that you can also pick up some education on the side." In a more serious vein, the fact remains that college does provide an excellent opportunity for young people to meet partners with similar backgrounds and interests under conditions that facilitate marital assessment.

INTERLOCKING ASPECTS OF ENDOGAMY

Thus far, we have discussed race, religion, nationality, and social class as factors that circumscribe or influence the selection of a marriage partner. It should not be thought, however, that these

---

[38] Coombs, op. cit., pp. 155–157.

[39] Ira Reiss, "Social Class and Campus Dating," in Jeffrey Hadden and Marie Borgatta (eds.), Marriage and the Family, Itasca, Illinois, F. E. Peacock Publishers, Inc., 1969, pp. 234–244. Two other studies should be mentioned. Little or no endogamy was found in Leslie and Richardson's survey of married college students. ("Family Versus Campus Influences in Relation to Mate Selection," Social Problems, October, 1956, pp. 117–121.) Pronounced endogamy was found in a later study by Eshleman and Hunt. (Reported in Eshleman, op. cit., 1974, p. 299.) When all the studies are considered collectively, the weight of the evidence confirms the existence of social-class endogamy on the part of college students.

elements operate independently of one another. Studies indicate that nationality and religion are often related, so that a marriage which is endogamous for religion may also be endogamous for nationality. Similarly, it is known that there is a relation between nationality and religion on the one hand and social class on the other, so that it is quite possible for a given marriage to be endogamous in terms of all three factors.

From this vantage point, it is easier to understand why *residential propinquity*, discussed at the beginning of the chapter, plays such an important part in the mate-selection process. Racial and nationality groups often tend to live within rather well-defined areas. This is also true in terms of social class and, to a lesser degree, of religious groupings. The relationship between propinquity and endogamy, however, involves more than meets the eye.

Katz and Hill, who were the first to integrate the various propinquity distributions and to synthesize the results, have developed what they term a *norm-interaction theory*, which includes the following assumptions:

1. That marriage is normative; i.e., mate selection is restricted by cultural considerations. Every individual has a field of eligibles among whom he or she selects a marital partner.
2. That the cultural groups (nationality, social class) that comprise the field of eligibles are residentially separated.
3. That within the field of eligibles, the probability of marriage varies directly with the probability of interaction.[40]

Catton and Smircich, on the other hand, pose a different theoretical explanation.[41] Rather than viewing mate selection normatively; that is, in terms of endogamous pressures that combine to bring about propinquitous marital selection, these authors suggest that cause and effect may operate the other way around. Perhaps people of similar religion, nationality, or social class marry one another not because of presumed cultural pressures but because of proximity. It may be, for instance, that the Irish tend to marry the Irish, not because of ethnic and religious endogamy, but simply as a result of living in the same neighborhood.

Whether endogamous factors cause propinquity, or whether propinquity accounts for endogamy is a tantalizing question, the

---

[40] Alvin Katz and Reuben Hill, "Residential Propinquity and Marital Selection: A Review of Theory, Method, and Fact," *Marriage and Family Living*, February, 1958, pp. 27–35.

[41] William Catton and R. J. Smircich, "A Comparison of Mathematical Models for the Effect of Residential Propinquity on Mate Selection," *American Sociological Review*, August, 1964, pp. 522–529.

implications of which have often been overlooked. It may well be that the two factors reinforce each other. Whatever the matrix, it is doubtful whether the endogamous components of mate selection can be satisfactorily understood without a basic understanding of the role of propinquity.

HOMOGAMY

There have been scores of studies dealing with the homogamy-heterogamy problem, that is, the tendency of "like to marry like" versus the inclination of "opposites to attract." It is beyond the scope of this volume to list even a major portion of the studies or to discuss the various methodological problems involved. It will, however, be worthwhile to include the major areas of study, together with some possible conclusions. In the present context, *homogamy* refers to a similarity of physical or psychological traits, while *endogamy*, covered previously, refers to group similarities, such as race, religion, nationality, and social class.

Intelligence. It has already been shown that individuals tend to select mates with an educational level equal to their own. Studies based on I.Q. tests reveal a similar tendency toward intellectual homogamy. During the past 50 years, dozens of studies have been undertaken in an effort to establish the relationship between the intelligence test scores of husband and wife. While there is some variation, both in study design and statistical findings, the correlations between spouses have been found to range from about .32 to .55, which approaches the same relationship as that found between siblings. The fact that husband and wife are fairly similar in I.Q. seems to have been established beyond reasonable doubt, and in recent years a number of investigators have turned their attention to other facets of marital homogamy.

Physical Characteristics. With regard to physical traits such as height, weight, complexion, head shape, hair color, facial type, and general health, findings from a number of anthropological studies over the last several decades indicate, again, that a homogamous tendency between spouses is in evidence. In Spuhler's extensive survey, for instance, 29 out of 43 physical traits measured were found to be homogamous.[42]

---

[42] J. N. Spuhler, "Assortative Mating with Respect to Physical Characteristics," *Eugenics Quarterly*, June, 1968, pp. 129–137.

Although the figures vary somewhat from study to study, the overall correlation between spouses' physical traits is on the order of .20 to .30 which suggests that physical likeness plays a less important role in mate selection than does intellectual similarity.

Social Attitudes. In a number of studies the investigator has attempted to measure the extent to which couples agree or disagree on political, economic, social, and religious issues. Most of the studies seemed to show a trend toward homogamous social attitudes, although convergence scores differed according to the particular attitude being measured.

One difficulty with most of the studies on similarity of attitudes is the inability to pin down causal factors. Assuming that mates tend to have a somewhat similar outlook on social issues, would not this similarity of viewpoint arise as a sort of by-product of endogamy? If an engaged couple, for example, had the same religious, nationality, educational, and socio-economic background, would they not be expected to evidence a similarity of viewpoint on, say, political or economic issues?

To test this possibility, Schellenberg compared the social attitudes of a group of engaged or married couples with a *group of artificial couples,* i.e., men and women who remained unknown to each other but who were matched on paper with respect to religion, nativity, socio-economic background, and the like. Results indicated that both groups were homogamous with regard to the social and political values that were measured! The real couples, nevertheless, had significantly higher convergence scores than the artificial couples.[43] Apparently, similarity of background (endogamy) does not entirely account for attitudinal homogamy.

Personality and Temperament. When people raise the question "Does like marry like or do opposites attract?" it is probable that they are referring primarily to temperament and personality. If there is a secret to the mate-selection process that would explain why we marry one particular person, it probably lies within the cavernous vault of personality. No one has yet found the key, if indeed a single key is all that is involved. "Personality" is a

---

[43] James Schellenberg, "Homogamy in Personal Values and the 'Field of Eligibles'," *Social Forces,* December, 1960, pp. 157–162. For more extensive coverage, see Bernard I. Murstein (ed.), *Theories of Attraction and Love,* New York, Springer Publishing Company, Inc., 1971; and Ted L. Huston (ed.), *Foundations of Interpersonal Attraction,* New York, Academic Press, 1974.

256

PREMARITAL BEHAVIOR PATTERNS

tremendously complex notion. It is not easy to define, let alone measure or understand. Social scientists are by no means in agreement on the subject, and it is hardly surprising to find that the various studies do not lead to any definite conclusion.

Taken as a group, the studies do seem to show more support for homogamy than for heterogamy, though one is struck by the long series of low correlations. At any rate, the personality riddle in mate selection has thus far withstood all attempts at solution, although sociologists and psychologists have developed some provocative theories. It is to these theories that we turn in the next chapter.

SELECTED READINGS

Aldridge, Delores, "The Changing Nature of Interracial Marriage in Georgia," *Journal of Marriage and the Family*, November, 1973, pp. 641–642.

Bean, Frank, and Aiken, Linda, "Intermarriage and Unwanted Fertility in the United States," *Journal of Marriage and the Family*, February, 1976, pp. 61–72.

Burr, Wesley R., *Theory Construction and the Sociology of the Family*, New York, John Wiley & Sons, Inc., 1973.

Eckland, Bruce, "Theories of Mate Selection," *Eugenics Quarterly*, June, 1968, pp. 71–84.

Elder, Glenn, "Appearance and Education in Marriage Mobility," *American Sociological Review*, August, 1969, pp. 519–533.

Garrison, Robert, Anderson, V. E., and Reed, Sheldon, "Assortative Marriage," *Eugenics Quarterly*, June, 1968, pp. 113–127.

Glick, Paul, *American Families*, New York, John Wiley & Sons, Inc., 1957.

_____, "A Demographer Looks at American Families," *Journal of Marriage and the Family*, February, 1975, pp. 15–26.

Heer, David, "Negro-White Marriage in the United States," *Journal of Marriage and the Family*, August, 1966, pp. 262–273.

_____, "The Prevalence of Black-White Marriage in the United States, 1960 and 1970," *Journal of Marriage and the Family*, May, 1974, pp. 246–258.

Hollingshead, August B., *Elmtown's Youth and Elmtown's Youth Revisited*, New York, John Wiley & Sons, Inc., 1975.

Huston, Ted L. (ed.), *Foundations of Interpersonal Attraction*, New York, Academic Press, 1974.

Kuzel, Paul, and Krishnan, P., "Changing Patterns of Remarriage in Canada," *Journal of Comparative Family Studies,* Autumn, 1973, pp. 215–224.

Laswell, Marcia E., "Is There a Best Age to Marry?: An Interpretation," *Family Coordinator,* July, 1974, pp. 237–242.

Lewis, Robert A., "A Longitudinal Test of a Developmental Framework for Premarital Dyadic Formation," *Journal of Marriage and the Family,* February, 1973, pp. 16–25.

Monahan, Thomas, "Are Interracial Marriages Really Less Stable?" *Social Forces,* June, 1970, pp. 461–473.

————, "Marriage Across Racial Lines in Indiana," *Journal of Marriage and the Family,* November, 1973, pp. 632–640.

————, "Some Dimensions of Interreligious Marriages in Indiana," *Social Forces,* December, 1973, pp. 195–203.

Murstein, Bernard I. (ed.), *Theories of Attraction and Love,* New York, Springer Publishing Company, Inc., 1971.

Parelius, Ann P., "Emerging Sex-Role Attitudes, Expectations, and Strains Among College Women," *Journal of Marriage and the Family,* February, 1975, pp. 146–153.

Reiss, Ira, "Social Class and Campus Dating," in Jeffrey Hadden and Marie Borgatta (eds.), *Marriage and the Family,* Itasca, Illinois, F. E. Peacock Publishers, Inc., 1969, pp. 234–244.

Rockwell, Richard, "Historical Trends and Variations in Educational Homogamy," *Journal of Marriage and the Family,* February, 1976, pp. 83–95.

Rosenthal, Erich, "Studies of Jewish Intermarriage in the United States," *American Jewish Year Book,* Vol. 64, pp. 3–53.

————, "Divorce and Religious Intermarriage: The Effect of Previous Marital Status upon Subsequent Marital Behavior," *Journal of Marriage and the Family,* August, 1970, pp. 435–440.

Rubin, Zick, "Do Americans Marry Up?" *American Sociological Review,* October, 1968, pp. 750–760.

————, *Liking and Loving: An Invitation to Social Psychology,* New York, Holt, Rinehart and Winston, Inc., 1973.

Spuhler, J. N., "Assortative Mating with Respect to Physical Characteristics," *Eugenics Quarterly,* June, 1968, pp. 129–134.

Stuart, Irving, and Abt, Lawrence, *Interracial Marriage,* New York, Grossman, 1972.

Washington, Joseph R., Jr., *Marriage in Black and White,* Boston, Beacon Press, 1970.

Yaukey, David, and Thorsen, Timm, "Differential Female Age at First Marriage in Six Latin American Cities," *Journal of Marriage and the Family,* May, 1972, pp. 375–379.

12

Mate Selection II

SINCE MATE SELECTION in our culture is circumscribed by such factors as age, marital status, propinquity, race, religion, nationality, and social class—as well as by certain physical and mental traits—it is tempting to argue that the final selection of a marriage partner is closer to a "forced draw" than it is to a bona fide choice. In practice, as most American youth are fully aware, our mate-selection process is anything but a forced draw; in fact, there are few societies where young people have the free hand in marital selection that is accorded them in the United States.

It must be admitted, however, that—within the field of eligibles—exactly "who marries whom" has proved to be an exasperating question to answer. Some earlier scholars believed that for each man there was a particular woman and that a kind of "instinct" guided them to one another. Jung, for instance, felt that falling in love was tantamount to being caught by one's "archetype"—a mental image every man carried in his genes. The image was that of a particular female, and when the right female came along, said Jung, you were immediately "seized."*

Another early theory of mate selection was the psychoanalytic view. Stated simply, this theory assumed that people were guided in their choice of a mate by a "parental image," i.e., an image of the parent of the opposite sex. Boys would thus be drawn (unconsciously) toward someone who resembled their mother, and girls to someone who resembled their father.

Later theorists focused on broad personality traits, in an attempt to determine whether "like marries like" (homogamy) or "opposites attract" (heterogamy).

---

* And afterward, Jung acknowledged, you may find out that "it was a hell of a mistake!" (See R. Evans, *Conversations with Carl Jung*, Princeton, New Jersey, Van Nostrand, 1964, pp. 51–52.)

Simplistic theories such as the above, however, have been more or less discarded. There is no "archetype." Empirical research has failed to substantiate the psychoanalytic concept of "parent image." And the homogamy-heterogamy approach to personality attraction turned out to be a surprisingly complex phenomenon.

Today, mate-selection theories—and their supporting investigations—have taken a more sophisticated turn, with emphasis placed on such things as social roles, values, need gratifications, and sequences. And while there is still no final solution to the problem of who marries whom, several of these modern theories do show genuine promise.

BASIC THEORIES OF MATE SELECTION

Role Theory. One of the most commonly used terms in sociology, "role" refers to a set of social expectations that are appropriate for a given position or status. These expectations serve as behavioral guidelines, reminding the individual what he or she should and should not do by virtue of being a male, female, employer, college student, and the like. Most people find it more rewarding to fulfill the roles society has set forth than to "buck the trend." In modern society, nevertheless, there is enough disagreement on roles to evoke a fair amount of social conflict.

As applied to mate selection, persons would tend to choose partners on the basis of courtship and marital role agreement. It would be unlikely, according to the theory, for a man who believed that woman's place is in the home to marry a career woman. Nor would it be likely for a woman who thinks men should be active in community affairs to marry a laissez faire man.

Note that it is not the roles themselves, but the agreement on role playing that is the important factor. A compatible couple would be one in which both spouses play the expected or agreed-upon roles, almost irrespective of what these roles actually are.

Role theory has been extensively analyzed by sociologists, although its application to mate selection is a relatively new development. As we shall see, however, several investigators have incorporated the concept of role into their own theories of marital selection. Whatever the final answer may turn out to be, it is likely that "role" will prove to be one of the ingredients.

Values. Values refer to ideals, customs, or behavior patterns about which people have such strong emotional feelings that they think of them as "good," "bad," "right," or "wrong."

Coombs, who has written extensively on the subject, believes that values are so important to those who hold them that "they are accepted without question." Indeed, because values are so central to a person's mode of conduct, Coombs feels that mates tend to be chosen on the basis of similarity of values. "For therein," he writes, "lies emotional security."

> The thesis is that value consensus fosters mutually rewarding interaction and leads to interpersonal attraction. It is reasoned that the sharing of similar values, in effect, is a validation of one's self which promotes emotional satisfaction and enhances communication.
>
> This is not to deny the possibility that a binding relationship may develop between dissimilar persons, but to suggest that such a relationship is less likely to occur as spontaneously or persist as permanently. Although dissimilar persons can provide new information, be unpredictable and therefore exciting, and at times give a more objective and accurate appraisal of the self, they also create more uncertainty about one's status and esteem, and anxiety over acceptable conduct and speech.[1]

Coombs is also of the belief that endogamous factors such as race, religion, and social class operate largely as a function of values. For example, a person may wish to marry someone of the same religion, not only because marrying a member of "the Church" may be an important value in itself, but because individuals with similar backgrounds will probably develop similar value systems—thus setting the stage for mate selection.

This theory has the advantage of simplicity and also seems to be borne out by common observation. In fact, Coombs' own research study, based on a college dating situation, did tend to support the theory of value consensus.[2] Whether similarity of values is in fact central to the mate-selection process—and if so, precisely which classes of values are involved—will have to be determined by continued research.

Exchange Theory. Another theory of mate selection conceives of all social behavior as a kind of "exchange." Exchange theory, according to Huston, assumes not only that human actions are goal-oriented, but that "social transactions are regulated by the interactants' desire to derive maximum pleasure and minimum pain from others." Huston adds that "more formally, exchange theory suggests that individuals are most attracted to persons who provide the highest ratio of rewards to costs."[3]

---

[1] Robert Coombs, "Value Consensus and Partner Satisfaction Among Dating Couples," *Journal of Marriage and the Family*, May, 1966, pp. 166–173.

[2] *Ibid.*

[3] Ted L. Huston, *Foundations of Interpersonal Attraction*, New York, Academic Press, 1974, p. 20.

Although a number of social scientists have commented on the theory, Edwards' explanation remains one of the clearest:

> Individuals are impelled to enter into association with one another in order to accomplish their desired ends . . . but the attainment of one person's goals entails an investment and cost on the part of the other.
>
> A very common situation of this sort is where one party gives a certain portion of his time and labor for which he receives from the other party a certain amount of appreciation and esteem. The resources exchanged in a social situation need not be of the same kind. What is important . . . is the mutually held expectation that reciprocation will occur.[4]

The same author goes on to say: "It is further assumed that each party to a transaction attempts to maximize his gains and minimize his costs. Over the long run this means actual exchanges tend to become equalized, particularly in view of the operation of the principle of reciprocity. Structural conditions, however, sometimes make equalization difficult. If one party clearly possesses more power, the other party is at a distinct disadvantage, his cost in the transaction exceeding the potential gain."[5]

The above excerpts represent only a small part of social exchange theory, but they will be sufficient to provide a background for the application to mate selection, as proposed by Edwards:

1. Within any collectivity of potential mates, a marriageable person will seek out that individual who is perceived as maximizing his rewards.
2. Individuals with equivalent resources are most likely to maximize each other's rewards.
3. Pairs with equivalent resources are most likely to possess homogamous characteristics.
4. Mate selection, therefore, will be homogamous with respect to a given set of characteristics.[6]

Edwards does not attempt to classify the resources that will be perceived as equivalent, and in this sense exchange theory, as applied to mate selection, can hardly be called definitive. On the other hand, the theory has the advantage not only of explaining why homogamous tendencies "work," but also of serving as a

---

[4] John Edwards, "Familial Behavior as Social Exchange," *Journal of Marriage and the Family,* August, 1969, pp. 518–526. Copyright © 1969 by National Council on Family Relations. Reprinted by permission.

[5] *Ibid.,* p. 519.

[6] *Ibid.,* p. 525.

(Stephen G. Williams, Black Star)

foundation or steppingstone for the development of a more precise theoretical formulation.

Complementary Needs. Although the idea that mate selection may be a function of personality need-fulfillment is fairly old, it remained for Winch to formulate a definitive theory of the subject and put the theory to empirical test. According to Winch, an individual chooses for a mate someone who provides him or her with maximum need-gratification. However, maximum gratification occurs when the specific need-patterns of the man and woman are *complementary rather than similar*. Among the specific need-complements that Winch posits are hostility–abasement, dominance–deference, nurturance–succorance, achievement–vicariousness, and others. For purposes of simplification, Winch offers the following hypothetical illustration:

> Let us assume that there is a chap by the name of Jonathan, and that Jonathan's most distinguished characteristic is a need to be dominant in interpersonal relationships. We shall assume further that among his acquaintances are two girls, Jean and Jennifer. Jennifer is like Jonathan in being dominant and in being intolerant of differences in viewpoint, whereas Jean does not have strong convictions and is used to being governed by the judgments and wishes of others. If we are informed that Jonathan is about to marry one of these women, and if on the basis of the information cited above we are asked to guess which one, probably we should agree that Jean would be the more likely choice for Jonathan to make. . . . Thus Jonathan should see Jean as a "truly feminine, tractable, agreeable young lady who knows when and how to help a man," whereas to Jean, Jonathan might well appear as a "vigorous and decisive tower of strength." I should expect further that Jonathan would be repelled by Jennifer and would see her as bossy, unfeminine, and probably shrewish.[7]

Winch does not assume that all aspects of complementarity necessarily register at the conscious level. It may be that in those areas where the couple do not consciously recognize the complementary factors, both parties are more comfortable if they do not have to acknowledge the arrangement. Winch continues: "Let us assume that Jennifer, the bossy woman, marries a passive, compliant chap—say, Herbert. . . . Because the pattern of dominance, although complementary, would run counter to the conventional conceptions of sex roles (she being a 'masculine' woman and he a 'feminine' man), it seems likely that neither party would wish to admit to himself or to anyone else that this pattern of dominance was a bond between them"[8]

Winch's own research confirmed his general theory, but subsequent investigations failed to provide corroboration.[9] A number of methodological difficulties are involved, however, and Winch himself has suggested that the incorporation of *role compatibility* might strengthen the theory.[10] Other researchers

----

[7] Robert Winch, *Mate Selection,* New York, Harper & Brothers, 1958, p. 97.
[8] *Ibid.*
[9] For a critique and discussion, see Wesley Burr, *Theory Construction and the Sociology of the Family,* New York, John Wiley & Sons, Inc., 1973, pp. 98–102.
[10] Robert Winch, "Another Look at the Theory of Complementary Needs in Mate Selection," *Journal of Marriage and the Family,* November, 1967, pp. 756–762.

have proposed corollaries, and it may be that the theory of complementary needs will undergo further modification.[11]

Whether the theory turns out to be basically correct or basically incorrect, only time will tell. But whatever the outcome, Winch's efforts—coming when they did—served to revitalize much of the socio-psychological thinking on the subject of mate selection.

SEQUENTIAL THEORIES OF MATE SELECTION

Although the theories discussed in the previous pages are, obviously, all different from one another, they do have one thing in common; namely, they concentrate on a *single set of factors* such as roles, values, or needs. In a conceptual sense, however, it is quite possible (or even probable) that *different sets of factors operate at different stages of courtship*. These stage-theories we have termed "sequential," and several of them are worthy of serious consideration.

The Filter Theory. In an attempt to integrate or combine some of the above-mentioned approaches to mate selection, Kerckhoff and Davis have hypothesized that certain social attributes and personality relationships operate differently, depending on the particular stage of courtship; e.g., perhaps agreement on values is paramount at one stage and need-complementarity at another. To test this hypothesis, the investigators made a longitudinal survey of a group of engaged or "seriously attached" couples. The couples were studied at the beginning and again at the end of the school year. Statistical results tended to support the idea that value consensus operates in the early stages of courtship and need-complementarity later on.[12]

The Kerckhoff-Davis theory points to a sequence of screening or "filtering" factors that operate in the mate-selection process. In the very beginning, endogamous factors such as religion and social class narrow the field of eligibles. Subsequent courtship (among eligibles) is not likely to progress very far, or very satisfactorily, unless agreement on values is reached. In the final

265

---

[11] See Burr, *op. cit.*; and Ellen Karp, Julie Jackson, and David Lester, "Ideal-Self Fulfillment in Mate Selection: A Corollary to the Complementary Need Theory of Mate Selection," *Journal of Marriage and the Family*, May, 1970, pp. 269–272.
[12] Alan Kerckhoff and Keith Davis, "Value Consensus and Need-Complementarity in Mate Selection," *American Sociological Review*, June, 1962, pp. 295–303.

stages, the presence or absence of need-complementarity determines whether a permanent mating will result. The mate-selection sequence thus appears to be one of endogamy–homogamy–heterogamy.

The above explanation is somewhat oversimplified; in fact, not all of the statistical findings fell into precise sequential slots. Furthermore, the one replication study that has been made (by Levinger, Senn, and Jorgensen) failed to support the Kerckhoff-Davis theory.[13] Nevertheless, the filter theory was the first to integrate homogamy–heterogamy attributes on a time basis, and thus it represents a genuine contribution to the field. It is hoped that further replication studies—conceptually sharpened—will be undertaken.

The Process Approach. Most of the foregoing theories assume that mate selection hinges on certain personal or social attributes of the two individuals involved. A radically different approach, by Bolton, looks at mate selection from the view of the *developmental process itself*. While the process approach does not ignore endogamous or homogamous-heterogamous elements, the implication is that interpersonal transactions have their own course of events (escalators) and that one interactive phase, being *sui generis*, shapes another. For this reason, the process approach is classified among the sequential theories.

> Seen from this viewpoint, the development of a mate-selection relation is a problematic process. By "problematic" is meant that the outcome of the contacts of the two individuals is not mechanically predetermined either by the relation of their personality characteristics or the institutional patterns providing the context for the development of the relation—though these are both certainly to be taken into account—but that the outcome is an end-product of a sequence of interactions.
>
> These interactions are characterized by advances and retreats along the paths of available alternatives, by definitions of the situation which crystallize tentative commitments and bar withdrawals from certain positions, by the sometimes tolerance and sometimes resolution of ambiguity, by reassessments of self and other. . . . In short, the development of love relations is problematic because the product bears the stamp of what goes on between the couple as well as what they are as individuals.[14]

---

[13] G. Levinger, D. Senn, and B. Jorgensen, "Progress Toward Permanence in Courtship: A Test of the Kerckhoff-Davis Hypothesis," *Sociometry*, Vol. 33, 1970, pp. 427–443.

[14] Charles Bolton, "Mate Selection as the Development of a Relationship," *Marriage and Family Living*, August, 1961, pp. 235–236.

The above passage does not make for easy reading, since the process approach represents a fairly high level of abstraction; in fact, one of the problems of the researcher is to develop terminology that is appropriate to the complexity of the process phenomenon. Thus, Bolton talks of "pressuring for commitment," "retreating under stress," "escalators," "turning points," and "isolation of problem areas."

In an intensive process analysis of the type just described, Bolton found that among 20 married couples there were no less than five different types of development process: personality meshing, identity clarification, relation centered, pressure centered, and expediency centered. The investigator remarks that "the great difference in these types makes clear the necessity of having multiple rather than monolithic explanations for mate selection." In his concluding statement, Bolton adds that:

> If it is true that the heart of the process approach is the view that transactions between human subjects are determinants in the outcome of social encounters, then it becomes imperative to gather information on what actually transpires between people in building up their social acts as well as information on what initially composes the situation.[15]

The process theory thus represents another approach that seems to hold promise for future development.

Stimulus–Value–Role Theory. One of the most interesting and comprehensive of all mate-selection theories is the three-stage sequence proposed by Murstein.[16] Stimulus–value–role (SVR) theory holds that in a relatively free-choice situation most couples go through three stages prior to marriage.

1. In the first or "stimulus" stage, one individual is drawn to another because of his perception of the other's "physical, social, mental, or reputational attributes, and his perception of his own qualities that might be attractive to the other person." Although attraction is based on visual and auditory cues, rather than on interaction, the first stage involves a great deal more than simply "good looks." A young man may have appeal, for example, not

---

[15] *Ibid.*, pp. 237 and 240.
[16] Bernard I. Murstein, "Stimulus–Value–Role: A Theory of Marital Choice," *Journal of Marriage and the Family*, August, 1970, pp. 465–481. Copyright © 1970 by National Council on Family Relations. Reprinted by permission. Unless otherwise noted, all the quotations in this section have been taken from the Murstein article.

because of his looks but because he is known to be an intern or because he comes from a wealthy family.

Murstein points out that, as a result of his previous experiences, a person builds up an image of his attractiveness to the opposite sex. "If he sees himself as highly attractive, he is more likely to approach a highly attractive partner than if he sees himself as unattractive. . . ." Utilizing social-exchange terminology, the author adds that:

> A man who is physically unattractive (liability), for example, might desire a woman who has the asset of beauty. Assuming, however, that his non-physical qualities are no more rewarding than hers, she gains less profit than he does from the relationship and, thus, his suit is likely to be rejected. Rejection is a cost to him because it may lower his self-esteem and increase his fear of failure in future encounters; hence, he may decide to avoid attempting to court women whom he perceives as much above him in attractiveness.
>
> Contrariwise, he is likely to feel highly confident of success if he tries to date a woman even less attractive than himself where he risks little chance of rejection (low cost). However, the reward value of such a conquest is quite low, so that the profitability of such a move is also low. As a consequence, an experienced individual is likely to express a maximum degree of effort and also obtain the greatest reward at the least cost when he directs his efforts at someone of approximately equal physical attraction, assuming all other variables are constant.
>
> During the first moments of contact, the individual may attempt to supplement his visual impression of the other with information regarding the other's role in society, professional aspirations, and background. Persons attracted to each other, thus, are likely to be balanced for the total weighted amalgam of stimulus characteristics even though, for a given trait, gross disparities may exist. Men, for example, tend to weigh physical attractiveness in a partner more than women do, whereas women give greater weight to professional aspiration in the partner; accordingly, although physical attraction may play a leading role, it is hypothesized that the weighted pool of stimulus attractions that each possesses for the other will be approximately equal if individuals are to progress into the second stage of courtship.

The first or "stimulus" stage has been described in some detail, because of its cruciality to SVR theory. For unless there is mutual attraction, as defined above, a courting relationship will normally fail to materialize.

2. Assuming that there has been a mutual "stimulus" attraction—say, at a "mixer" dance—and that the couple sit down to talk, "they are now entering the second stage, that of 'value comparison'." Murstein goes on to state that:

Unlike the "stimulus" stage in which attributes of the partner are evaluated without any necessary interpersonal contact, the value comparison stage involves the appraisal of value compatibility through verbal interaction. The kinds of values explored through discussion are apt to be much more varied than those possible in the "stimulus" stage. The couple may compare their attitudes toward life, politics, religion, sex, and role of men and women in society and marriage. The fact that the couple are now interacting also permits more continuous and closer scrutiny of physical appearance as well as other important factors such as temperament, "style" of perceiving the world, and ability to relate to others.

It is possible that closer appraisal of physical qualities and temperament will lead to a changed opinion regarding the desirability of the partner, and this may result in an attempt to terminate the contact as soon as gracefully possible. If contact has been made on the basis of strong stimulus attraction, however, it is more likely that the couple will remain in the second stage, continuing to assess the compatibility of their values.

Should the couple find that they hold similar value orientations in important areas, they are apt to develop much stronger positive feelings for each other than they experienced in the "stimulus" stage. One reason for this is that when an individual encounters another who holds similar values, he gains support for the conclusion that his own values are correct; his views are given social validation.

Further, many values are intensely personal and are so linked to the self-concept that rejection of these values is experienced as rejection of the self, and acceptance of them implies validation of the self. Providing we have a reasonably positive self-image, we tend to be attracted to those persons whom we perceive as validating it. Also, perceived similarity of values may lead to the assumption that the other likes us, and there is empirical evidence that we like those individuals whom we think like us. . . . In sum, the holding of similar values should be a major factor in drawing two individuals together.

3. Whether or not a couple progress to the "role" stage usually depends on their similarity of values, though not always. "A beautiful woman," writes Murstein, "may be desirable even if her values depart somewhat from those of the man. Conversely, an unusually strong satisfaction derived from similarly held values may offset the fact that the physical appearance of the partner is only minimally satisfying."

In some cases, a couple may decide to marry on the basis of the first two stages—stimulus attraction and value congruence—but for most people it is also necessary to *function in compatible roles*.

The role of the husband, for example, may be perceived by the wife as embodying tenderness and acceptance of her. This role, however, does not necessarily clash with another role of the husband, that of ability to aggressively maintain the economic security of the family. There are, in short, a multiplicity of roles for the different kinds of situations that one encounters.

In the premarital phase, however, the partner's ability to function in the desired role is not as readily observable as his verbalized expression of views on religion, economics, politics, and how men should treat women. Knowing, for example, how much emotional support the partner will give when the individual fails a history examination presupposes an advanced stage of intimacy. It is for this reason that the "role" stage is placed last in the time sequence leading to marital choice.

The above explanation of SVR theory is by no means complete and is offered here merely to acquaint the reader with some of the highlights. It should be mentioned, however, that Murstein distinguishes between "open" and "closed" fields.

> An "open" field encounter refers to a situation in which the man and woman do not as yet know each other or have only a nodding acquaintance. Examples of such "open field" situations are "mixers," presence in a large school class at the beginning of the semester, and brief contacts in the office. The fact that the field is "open" indicates that either the man or woman is free to start the relationship or abstain from initiating it, as they wish.
>
> The contrary concept is the "closed field" situation in which both the man and the woman are forced to interact by reason of the environmental setting in which they find themselves. Examples of such situations might be that of students in a small seminar in a college, members of a law firm, and workers in complementary professions such as doctor-nurse, and "boss"-secretary.

The point is that the SVR theory described in the preceding paragraphs pertains to the "open field" situation. The effect of a "closed field" is to "weaken the influence of stimulus variables on marital choice and to maximize the influence of the second-stage or verbal-interaction variables; thus, the individual who might never have been approached in an 'open field' because she is of modest physical attraction may become quite attractive to her co-worker in the office as a result of luncheon conversations in the cafeteria which reveal her intelligence, sensitivity, and the similarity of her value-orientation to his own."

SVR theory is one of the most recent of all mate-selection theories, and as yet there has been no attempt at empirical verification. From all the signs, however, Murstein has made a valuable contribution to the literature, and it is to be hoped that the work he started will be continued. If the theory seems unduly complicated, here is what the author himself—in a later work—has to say:

Perhaps no simple theory will account for marital choice because the latter is an extremely complex, multidetermined act. To the layman, the complex nature of marital choice is hidden under the catch-all rubric of "love." To say that individuals marry for love, however, is to say little because "love" covers all kinds of rationales. When it accounts for everything, it accounts for nothing.[17]

THE DATING SYSTEM

One diffculty with the foregoing theories of mate selection is that they may appear to the reader to be overly serious. That is, the mate-selection process is often made to seem like a series of encounters or contests—a running "battle of the sexes," as it were. In point of fact, however, a good deal of dating takes place outside the periphery of mate selection. Casual dating, dating for fun or for social convenience, or for sexual purposes—the American dating game seemingly has its own *raison d'être* and its own rules.

Innumerable accounts have been written about our dating system, but the most interesting—certainly the most provocative—is that penned by Geoffrey Gorer, in his *The American People: A Study in National Character.* Departing from textbook seriousness for a moment, we would like to quote extensively from Gorer. Whether or not you agree with his analysis, you must admit that he had made some telling observations.[18]

According to Gorer, the date begins as an invitation from the boy to the girl for an evening's entertainment, "typically at his expense." The boy "should call for the girl in a car" (unless he be particularly young or poor) and should take her back in the car. The entertainment itself depends on the boy's means—anything from an ice cream soda to a lavish meal—but it is usually in a public place and generally involves eating and dancing.

Although "showing the girl a good time" is essential, it is not the primary object of the date. The real object, says Gorer, is for the young man to prove that he is "worthy of love, and therefore a success." And while being a good dancer helps, the necessary signs of approval—predictably—are elicited by talk. "Once again, the importance of words is paramount."

It often happens that on first dates the couple are comparatively unknown to each other. Therefore, Gorer contends, "a

[17] Bernard Murstein (ed.), *Theories of Attraction and Love,* New York, Springer Publishing Company, Inc., 1971, pp. 145–146.
[18] Geoffrey Gorer, *The American People, A Study in National Character,* rev. ed., New York, W. W. Norton & Company, Inc. 1964, p. 114.

certain amount of autobiography is necessary in the hope of establishing some common interest." These life-stories are rather similar to those accompanying any meeting between strangers, except for the "persiflage, flattery, wit, and love-making which was formerly called a 'line' but which each generation dubs with a new name."

Most young men are acutely aware of their "line" and can describe it in great detail. The girl's task, of course, is to parry the "line." "To the extent that she falls for the 'line' she is a loser in this intricate game; but if she discourages her partner so much that he does not request a subsequent date she is equally a loser. To remain the winner, she must make the nicest discriminations between yielding and rigidity."

The young man is the winner, says Gorer, if he "is able to get more favors from the girl than his rivals," the proving time being the return trip to the girl's home. "A good-night kiss is almost the minimum repayment for an evening's entertainment," but how much more depends on such things as the expertise of the young man and the attitude of the girl.

The love-making remains emotionally uninvolved, even though the linguistics and behavior are quite similar to genuine love-making. The young man should "prove that he is worthy to be loved by pressing for ever further favors, but the girl who yields too much, or too easily, may well be a disappointment, in exactly the same way as too easy a victory in tennis or chess may be a disappointment. . . . It would be a paradox, but not too great a one, to say that the ideal date is one in which both partners are so popular, so skilled, and so self-assured that the result is a draw."

PROBLEMS OF DATING

In the contemporary (1970–1980) period, dating is an activity in which nearly all young people participate. Participation, furthermore, commences at a rather tender age. In the writer's study of college students, it was found that more than half of both sexes had had their first date before they were 14 years old. In fact, without going into detail, it can be stated that the historical trend in the United States has been toward (1) earlier dating and (2) more dating.

The development of an extensive dating system seems to be a modern-American innovation. In the absence of historical and cross-cultural precedents, therefore, it is only natural to find that the codes have not fully crystallized. Lacking standards of right

The single's bar—one of the more modern methods of meeting partners and socializing. (Rick Smolan, Stock Boston)

and wrong, propriety and impropriety, and in the absence of institutionalized patterns of behavior, dating couples have been more or less forced to "make up the rules as they go along." Consequently, dating behavior is often marked by uncertainties and difficulties, not only on the part of the couples involved, but also for parents and other adults charged with the responsibility of regulating conduct norms.

Not all of the difficulties involved in dating stem from the lack of behavioral guideposts. In all ages and in all cultures the socialization of youth has been recognized as a problem involving time and patience. Also, interaction between the sexes—youthful or otherwise—is seldom characterized by total harmony, and it is hardly to be expected that dating relations would be an exception. All things considered, when these "natural" difficulties are augmented by a scarcity of behavioral rules, it is little wonder that problems arise. While it is by no means exhaustive, the following summary is probably representative of the kinds of issues that have come to be associated with the American dating system.

Parental Influence. There can be no doubt that parents exert a fairly strong influence on the dating and courtship activities of their children. Numerous studies in the last 30 years all confirm the fact. There is also no doubt that this influence leads to a measure of conflict between young people and their parents, particularly in the case of teen-agers. In the present writer's study of 1,079 college students, the question "Have you ever had arguments or conflicts with either of your parents regarding persons you have dated?" revealed that over 50 percent of the females and nearly 40 percent of the males answered in the affirmative.

Whether parents should or should not express their feelings on the subject is an open question, although certainly one could argue that failure to voice an honestly held opinion may be just as harmful as voicing one. In practice, most parents do feel impelled to speak out, and many young people feel just as impelled to resent the "intrusion." As a matter of fact, modern movies—which routinely seem to side with the young people—are likely to depict parental advice as "interference."

In everyday life, however, do parents really exercise poor judgment concerning their sons' and daughters' choice of a mate? Or is their advice likely to be sound? Findings based on empirical investigation indicate that the judgment of parents is beneficial rather than harmful, although in recent years there has been a paucity of research aimed at answering the question. But, irrespective of the evidence, it is likely that conflict between parents and children over dating and marital selection will remain. Such conflict must be written off as one of the prices of a relatively free dating system.

Interreligious and Interclass Dating. Closely related to the problem of parental influence is the question of dating persons of a different faith or of a different socio-economic level. If young people were entirely free in the matter of dating and marital selection, it is likely that problems relating to religion and social class would be minimal. But the fact of the matter is that parents and relatives do exert influence, and in most cases they take a dim view of so-called exogamous marriages.

Parents who caution their children against dating someone from a lower social stratum are not necessarily being snobbish, and mothers and fathers who remonstrate with their children on the dangers implicit in interreligious dating are not necessarily bigoted. In both instances, parents may be motivated by a sincere belief that exogamous marriages are not successful. They may feel that, once two people have fallen in love it is usually too late to do much about it, and hence the logical thing is to refrain from interdating in the first place.

Young people are usually more liberal than their parents insofar as the above-mentioned factors are concerned, so that it is almost inevitable that interreligious and interclass dating should lead to a certain amount of conflict within the home. Over the years, it would be expected that such conflict might diminish, since theoretically the liberal attitudes of youth should persist as they grow older. What seems to happen, though, is that the views of young people become less and less liberal as they grow older, and by the time they themselves are parents it is likely that they, too, will take a dim view of exogamous marriages.

275

The Lack of Physical Attractiveness. Throughout the world, physical appearance is of some importance, even though it may not be considered so crucial as intelligence or personality. In a society that exalts romantic love, however, physical attractiveness is of special significance, particularly in the case of young people, whose very marriageability often depends on "looks." With the faces of glamorous stars beaming from movie and television screens, with newspaper ads, magazine covers, and billboards flooded by pictures of handsome men and beautiful women, a social historian might well characterize the present era as the age of The Face. And whatever the impact on society at large, it can hardly be doubted that young people are susceptible to the veritable onslaught of physical charm. Whether adults like it or not, the daydreams of youngsters are quite likely to involve physical attributes of handsomeness and beauty.

Since men are more readily influenced by physical attractiveness than are women, "good looks" have become a fetish with many an American girl. And, in view of the value our culture places on beauty, this particular feminine emphasis may not be entirely misplaced. Figuratively, and in some ways almost literally, the pretty girl in our society is accorded the role of queen.

But what society giveth with one hand it taketh away with the other, for, if the pretty girl is placed on a pedestal, the unattractive girl is likely to find herself shunned. By adult standards, young people are often cruel in their social treatment of others, and nowhere is this fact more apparent than in the dating situation. With our cultural emphasis on The Face, young people— boys especially—have a tendency to overlook the underlying facets of personality and character, even though in a formal sense they may have been taught otherwise. Lack of physical attractiveness, therefore, is one of the most serious of our dating problems; indeed, from the point of view both of the number of individuals affected and the extent to which they are affected, it may well be the most serious.

While girls may be penalized more than boys, neither sex can escape the humiliation that too often accompanies homeliness, facial deformity, bad complexion, defective teeth, and the like. Individuals so afflicted sometimes retreat from the dating front altogether, rather than suffer continued—and in their own view unjust—rejections. Young people have a need for emotional security (more so, perhaps, than at any other time in life), and it is unfortunate that our dating system sometimes hinders rather than helps the situation.

Like most of the other difficulties associated with dating, there is no ready solution to the problem. One possible, if unlikely, solution would lie in a change of emphasis in our mass media, whereby The Face would be considered less important than The Person. More societal emphasis in this direction, certainly, would help to alleviate a chronic problem associated with dating.

Social Awkwardness. It is a common observation that most youth, especially those in their early teens, are somewhat awkward and ill at ease in their associations with the opposite sex. The boys may be loud and gesticulatory, and the girls may giggle and laugh continually, but these are often signs of tenseness rather than composure, however much the participants try to give the appearance of poise. In fact, research findings indicate that young people of both sexes are keenly aware of the problem.

All things considered, it is perhaps a wonder that teen-agers do as well as they do. Many adults are by no means at ease on social occasions, and at some time or another practically *all* adults have difficulty thinking of an appropriate remark to make. At any rate, it is easy to understand why young people have conversational difficulties, and why solitary dating couples so often run out of things to talk about. Conversational adeptness hinges in part on the scope of personal experience, and one of the reasons adults are better conversationalists than young people is that the former have a fund of knowledge and a storehouse of personal experiences to draw from. Also, the art of conversation, like other social graces, takes practice. And if, in this respect, dating situations are sometimes painful, they are seldom traumatic. While it may seem disheartening at the time, social awkwardness can hardly be considered a major problem.

276

(Burk Uzzle, Magnum Photo)

Sexual Involvements. Although many adults have succeeded in closing their eyes to the fact, sex has become an important part of the general dating pattern. While the goal of dating may not be primarily sexual, it is probably safe to say that there are relatively few dates wherein the sex problem does not make itself felt in one way or another.

If the couple indulge in some sort of sexual activity, there may be feelings of remorse and guilt. If they abstain altogether, there may be feelings of frustration. If they have intercourse, there is always the possibility of pregnancy. Verily, it would seem that all roads lead to some sort of conflict.

The whole question of sex during dating represents something of a paradox. On the one hand, it has become almost customary to shut our eyes to the issue and to pretend that no problem exists; at least, the subject is rarely mentioned in polite company. On the other hand, as judged by the number of words written about it in books and magazines—to say nothing of the number of plays and films on the subject—the premarital sex problem is of extreme importance. It will probably be many, many decades before societal views on the subject have become crystallized to the point where a consensus can be said to exist. In the meantime, the premarital sex issue will continue to plague a fair percentage of dating couples.

ASSESSMENT OF THE DATING AND
MATE-SELECTION SYSTEM

It should not be thought that the American dating and mate-selection system is all pain and no pleasure. Far from it. The beneficial features, in fact, are self-evident: dating serves as an aid in the general process of socialization and personality development at a most important time in life; the system provides young people with opportunities for learning to get along with the opposite sex; and, of course, while dating is enjoyable for its own sake, it also establishes a measure by which a marriage partner is ultimately chosen; in fact, although social scientists are still grappling with the socio-psychological intricacies of the mate-selection process, young people themselves apparently have little difficulty in making sound choices, particularly at the college level.

Interestingly enough, the personal characteristics that young people look for in the opposite sex—dependable character, emotional stability, pleasing disposition, and so on—seem to be

278

(R. P. Angier, Stock Boston)

TABLE 3 *Abbreviated Rank Order of Desired Personal Characteristics in Mate Selection, by Year and Sex*

	MALE RANKING				FEMALE RANKING			
	1939	*1956*	*1967*	*1975*	*1939*	*1956*	*1967*	*1975*
1. Dependable character	1	1	1	2	2	1	2	2
2. Emotional stability	2	2	3	1	1	2	1	1
3. Pleasing disposition	3	4	4	5	4	5	4	3
4. Mutual attraction	4	3	2	3	5	6	3	4
5. Good health	5	6	9	4	6	9	10	5
6. Desire for home/children	6	5	5	7	7	3	5	7
7. Refinement	7	8	7	6	8	7	8	6

remarkably stable over the years. Table 3 shows the rank order of desired traits, as reported by both college males and college females, over a period of more than 35 years.

Hudson and Henze, who ran the initial comparisons shown in Table 3, make the following summary statement:

> The charge that young people have departed from traditional values and are less serious about mate selection is not given support by the present study. Indeed, the findings suggest that youth's values regarding the importance of personal characteristics in mate selection are much the same today as they were a generation ago.
>
> It might be said in conclusion that social change in the area of mate selection has not been as great as indicated by the press, feared by the parent, and perhaps hoped by the youth.[19]

From an overall view, what assessment can be made of our dating and mate-selection system? It is the writer's opinion that the system has worked out reasonably well; indeed, given the American style of life it is difficult to conceive of any better method. True, there are certain acknowledged difficulties, but as far as the average young person is affected, none of them seems to be traumatic in nature. Boys and girls today appear to be quite content to play the dating game. From all accounts, they generally enjoy themselves. And so long as romantic love remains a concomitant of mate selection, dating seems to be an effective method whereby young people can indulge in the quest for romantic attainment.

---

[19] John Hudson and Lura Henze, "Campus Values in Mate Selection: A Replication," *Journal of Marriage and the Family*, November, 1969, pp. 772–775. Copyright © 1969 by National Council on Family Relations. Reprinted by permission. The 1939 data were gathered by Reuben Hill, the 1956 data by Robert McGinnis, and the 1975 data by the present writer. See the Hudson-Henze article for the detailed rank-order listings and complete citations. See also Zick Rubin, "From Liking to Loving: Patterns of Attraction in Dating Relationships," in Huston, *op. cit.*, pp. 383–402.

From the societal point of view, also, there is no evidence that our dating and marital system is unsatisfactory. The marriage rate has remained high, and research studies reveal that a substantial majority of couples report themselves as happily married. If the divorce rate also remains high, it is probably because of a complex set of factors associated with space-age civilization rather than because of a defective system of mate selection.

SELECTED READINGS

Adams, Thayla W., "Understanding and Communication," *The Family Coordinator*, January, 1976, pp. 87–89.

Burr, Wesley, *Theory Construction and the Sociology of the Family*, New York, John Wiley & Sons, Inc., 1973.

Byrne, Donn, and Clore, Gerald, "A Reinforcement-Affect Model of Attraction," in Ted Huston (ed.), *Foundations of Interpersonal Attraction*, New York, Academic Press, 1974, pp. 143–150.

Centers, Richard, "Attitude Similarity-Dissimilarity as a Correlate of Heterosexual Attraction and Love," *Journal of Marriage and the Family*, May, 1975, pp. 305–312.

Coombs, Robert, "Value Consensus and Partner Satisfaction Among Dating Couples," *Journal of Marriage and the Family*, May, 1966, pp. 166–173.

Coser, Rose Laub, *The Family: Its Structures and Functions*, New York, St. Martin's Press, 1974. See Part 4, "Marital Selection," pp. 175–240.

DeLora, Jack R., and DeLora, Joann S., *Intimate Life Styles*, Pacific Palisades, California, Goodyear Publishing Company, Inc., 1975. See Part One, "Dating and Mate Selection," pp. 1–52.

Eckland, Bruce, "Theories of Mate Selection," *Eugenics Quarterly*, June, 1968, pp. 71–84.

Edwards, John, "Familial Behavior as Social Exchange," *Journal of Marriage and the Family*, August, 1969, pp. 518–526.

Gorer, Geoffrey, *The American People: A Study in National Character*, New York, W. W. Norton & Company, Inc., 1964.

Homans, George C., "Attraction and Power," in Bernard I. Murstein (ed.), *Theories of Attraction and Love*, New York, Springer Publishing Company, Inc., 1971, pp. 46–58.

Huston, Ted. *Theories of Interpersonal Attraction*, New York, Academic Press, 1974.

Kephart, William M., "The Dysfunctional Theory of Romantic Love: A Research Report," *Journal of Comparative Family Studies*, Autumn, 1970, pp. 26–36.

_____, "Evaluation of Romantic Love," *Medical Aspects of Human Sexuality*, February, 1973, pp. 92–112.

Levinger, George, "A Three-Level Approach to Attraction: Toward an Understanding of Pair Relatedness," in Ted Huston (ed.), *Theories of Interpersonal Attraction*, New York, Academic Press, 1974, pp. 99–120.

Murstein, Bernard I., *Theories of Attraction and Love*, New York, Springer Publishing Company, Inc., 1971.

Nye, F. Ivan, and Berardo, Felix M., *The Family, Its Structure and Interaction*, New York, The Macmillan Company, 1973. See Part II, "Prelude to Marriage," pp. 109–244.

Parelius, Ann P., "Emerging Sex-Role Attitudes, Expectations, and Strains Among College Women," *Journal of Marriage and the Family*, February, 1975, pp. 146–153.

Reiss, Ira, *Family Systems in America*, Hinsdale, Illinois, The Dryden Press, 1976. See Part II, "The Sociology of the Courtship Institution."

Rubin, Zick, *Liking and Loving: An Invitation to Social Psychology*, New York, Holt, Rinehart and Winston, Inc., 1973.

Scanzoni, Letha, and Scanzoni, John, *Men, Women, and Change*, New York, McGraw-Hill Book Co., 1976. See Chapters 2, 3, and 4.

Spanier, Graham B., "Measuring Dyadic Adjustment," *Journal of Marriage and the Family*, February, 1976, pp. 15–28.

Udry, J. Richard, *The Social Context of Marriage*, Philadelphia, J. B. Lippincott Company, 1974, pp. 152–199.

Wells, J. Gipson, *Current Issues in Marriage and the Family*, New York, Macmillan, 1975. See Parts One and Two, pp. 14–114.

281

13

Romantic Love

ROMANTIC LOVE OCCUPIES a special place in the hearts of most Americans. In no other society and in no other period—including the Age of Chivalry—has an emotion been so nearly institutionalized. As one French writer noted, over a generation ago: "America appears to be the only country in the world where love is a national problem." In words that seem as true today as when first written, De Sales went on to say that "the great majority of Americans of both sexes seem to be in a state of chronic bewilderment in the face of a problem which they are certainly not the first to confront, but which—unlike other people—they still refuse to accept as one of those gifts of the gods which one might just as well take as it is: a mixed blessing at times, and at other times a curse or merely a nuisance."[1]

It is no accident that the foregoing quotation was written, not by a social scientist, but by a professional writer. Relatively few quotable statements on romantic love have come from the pens of social scientists, the reason being, evidently, that the latter are primarily analysts—and romantic love is one subject that tends to suffer in the light of factual dissection. Moreover, being an emotion, love lends itself descriptively to emotional language rather than to the somewhat formal presentation of textbook writers; hence, it is only natural that the most memorable romantic lines have come from novelists, dramatists, and poets.

DEFINITION

Any attempt to define romantic love is fraught with difficulties. As Moore puts it:

---

[1] Raoul De Roussy De Sales, "Love in America," *Atlantic Monthly*, May, 1938, p. 645.

Whatever love is, it has aroused the curiosity of the men and women of Western civilization as has no other subject. Love is something people do or enjoy, something that happens to them, something they fall into. It is something people think about. . . .

But ancients and moderns alike have failed to agree about what love really is. The disagreement is not surprising. Like truth and beauty, love is one of the great intangibles.[2]

Not only is love one of the great intangibles, but until quite recently empirical research on the subject has been almost entirely lacking. Rubin, one of the pioneers in the field, says that "the index to my edition of Bartlett's *Familiar Quotations* lists 769 references to 'love,' second only to 'man' with 843. But whereas the nature of love has long been a prime topic of discourse and debate, the number of behavioral scientists who have conducted empirical research on love can be counted on one's fingers."[3]

The folklore about romantic love tells us nothing—or tells us everything—as can be seen from such conflicting aphorisms as "Out of sight, out of mind" and "Absence makes the heart grow fonder." In fact, one writer contended that "love is such a tissue of paradoxes, and exists in such an endless variety of forms and shades, that you may say almost anything about it that you please, and it is likely to be correct."[4]

Lexicography is also of limited help. *The Random House Dictionary of the English Language* lists no fewer than 24 meanings for "love." Americans, it would seem, apply the term to just about everything, animate and inanimate. Thus, one can love baseball, music, beer, dogs, dolls, parents, children, sweethearts, spouses, and God. It is even claimed that some individuals can be in love with love; however that may be, there is little doubt that love has a variety of connotations. The specific brand of love that we are concerned with, however, is romantic love, the love that is glorified by songwriters and poets. And, in order to arrive at a more definitive concept, let us first eliminate those aspects of love with which we are *not* presently concerned.

Studies indicate that when spouses are questioned directly, the average American husband and wife report that they love

---

[2] John C. Moore, *Love in Twelfth-Century France*, Philadelphia, University of Pennsylvania Press, 1972, p. 1.

[3] Zick Rubin, *Liking and Loving: An Invitation to Social Psychology*, New York, Holt, Rinehart and Winston, Inc., 1973, p. 211.

[4] H. T. Finck, *Romantic Love and Personal Beauty*, New York, Macmillan, 1891, p. 244. Quoted by Ellen Berscheid and Elaine Walster, "A Little Bit About Love," in Ted Huston (ed.), *Foundations of Interpersonal Attraction*, New York, Academic Press, 1974, p. 356.

each other. If we assume that they do, and further assume that their love is a deep and abiding one, the fact remains that this is not romantic love. Love between spouses may be a richer and more rewarding experience than the highly emotionalized love that characterizes premarital attraction, but it is the latter rather than the former which is under scrutiny.

Along these same lines, it is also clear that the feeling most parents have for their children is love in the purest sense; at least, the self-sacrificing nature of parental love is probably unparalleled. Yet, however selfless, it is obviously not romantic love.

It is sometimes said that the sexual embrace is the acme of love, but though it may be a more intense emotion and a more sensual experience than romantic love, sexual love is *not* romantic love. And, finally, most of us are visually attracted from time to time by persons of the opposite sex whom we deem to be appealing—and whom we generally do not meet. For most people, apparently, the sands of time obliterate the memory of dozens or even hundreds of such incidents. But visual attraction is not romantic love, though it may be one of the ingredients thereof; that is, "attraction" is in good part a function of the beholder and in this sense is often a prelude to love.

But what *is* romantic love? It is tempting to say that if you have been in love you know what it is, and if you have not, a definition is not likely to convey very much. Perhaps so, but underlying most definitions are the following: (1) a strong emotional attachment toward a person of the opposite sex; (2) the tendency to think of this person in an idealized manner; and (3) a marked physical attraction, the fulfillment of which is reckoned in terms of touch.

Because love is a highly personalized experience, it cannot be said that the foregoing ingredients apply to everyone. But, for most people, the essence of romance would seem to be physical attraction, emotional involvement, and idealization. In this sense, it would not be misleading to say that romantic love is what the songwriters and poets say it is.

Most people, furthermore, seem to have little difficulty in recognizing love as it relates to their own experience. In the writer's study of college students, based on 1,079 questionnaires, respondents were asked whether they thought they knew what love was. Close to 90 percent replied in the affirmative, as the following results indicate.[5]

---

[5] For findings relative to the writer's study, see William M. Kephart, "Evaluation of Romantic Love," *Medical Aspects of Human Sexuality*, February, 1973, pp. 92–112.

	Males	Females
I'm sure I know what love is	25%	36%
I think I know what love is	59	54
I don't think I know what love is	12	8
I'm sure I don't know what love is	4	2
	100%	100%

Some authors try to differentiate between love and infatuation, yet such a distinction must be hairline. Infatuations are usually thought of as brief, adolescent affairs, quickly built up and—balloonlike—even more quickly punctured. But the question that is most difficult to answer is, "How does love differ from infatuation *during the period of infatuation?"* Notice that whenever individuals speak of their infatuations it is nearly always in the past tense. In the writer's survey of college students, for example, very few individuals reported themselves as being currently infatuated, yet at a given time a fair number considered themselves to be in love. What apparently happens is that when love affairs terminate, especially those of relatively short duration, they tend to become viewed in retrospect as infatuations.

One could almost say: "What is, is love; and what was—with perhaps one or two notable exceptions—was infatuation." At any rate, it is romance that gives us some of our happiest—and some of our most miserable—moments, and whether the heartaches and joys are attributed to love or infatuation seems to matter not a whit.

Our three-part working definition of romantic love seems self-explanatory, though perhaps a few words are in order regarding

285

(Lyn Gardner, Stock Boston)

the matter of idealization. From the Age of Chivalry, it has been held that idealization of the love partner is of maximal importance in the romantic concept. Not only in literature but in everyday life it is contended that love is blind. A person who is "head over heels" in love is presumably incapable of making a rational assessment of the character and personality of the beloved. Instead, it is held that the lover is prone not only to overlook faults and magnify virtues, but actually succeeds in creating what amounts to an unreal picture of the loved one. Many authors have written descriptively—and eloquently—about the idealization process.

While it can hardly be doubted that idealization is involved in virtually all love affairs, evidence from several studies indicates that the process may operate at a somewhat lower altitude than has been supposed. For example, to the question, "Does your head rule your heart, or does your heart rule your head?" 60 percent of the respondents in the writer's survey answered "Head rules."

It is possible, as some writers contend, that over-idealization of the beloved is the mark of a lover who feels insecure in the love relationship. The interplay between personality balance and romantic love is extremely important and will be considered later in the chapter.

FREQUENCY

Rare is the person who lives out his or her life without experiencing love, as we are using the term. Yet, aside from the fact that some people seem to be more "vulnerable" than others, very little is known of the frequency with which the average American falls in love. In this connection, more is known about sexual intercourse than about love! Some empirical evidence on the latter point is available, although the subjects have been college students, whose love patterns may or may not parallel those of the noncollege group. Next to nothing is known of the love frequencies of the adult population.

In the writer's survey, it was evident that the respondents were no strangers to romance. On the average, students reported that they had been infatuated six or seven times and had been in love once or twice. To repeat, current affairs were nearly always reported as love, while infatuations were relegated to the past.

Such studies, of course, reveal the number of romantic episodes *reported as of the time the questionnaire was filled out.* Since love affairs that occurred subsequently could not be reported, the above frequencies must be viewed as minimal. It seems reasonable to assume, therefore, that the average college student has around eight romantic experiences prior to marriage.

An interesting sidelight to the above study was the fact that about half of the respondents stated that at some time in their lives they had been infatuated or in love with two persons at the same time!

Accounts of the love frequencies of older persons must remain largely speculative, at least for the present, although it is logical to assume that married people fall in love less frequently than the single. For one thing, while our society condones—and, in a sense, even encourages—falling in love on the part of single people, once they are married they are somehow supposed to resist further romantic attractions.

Insofar as the middle and older age groups are concerned, attractiveness itself is a factor. Whether we like it or not, aging detracts from physical appeal. Bald heads, dentures, wrinkles, and double chins are hardly conducive to romance. True, older men sometimes fall in love with young girls, but nonreciprocal love is a frustrating experience, and the majority of oldsters seem content to let romance remain the province of the young.

Most people, of course, take marriage seriously and presumably have little desire to jeopardize the relationship by actively seeking new love partners. Also, the job of running a home and supporting a family is often a full-time task, and for many married people new romantic experiences would be almost out of the question. It can be hypothesized further that since romantic love is an emotion, and since an emotion denotes glandular response, it might be that the *capacity* for such response decreases with advancing age.

Logical or not, however, the foregoing analysis is largely speculative. It is quite possible that the older, married segment of our population experiences more in the way of romantic love than is commonly realized. For example, in the Knox survey, the investigator measured attitudes toward romantic love on the part of three age groups: (1) high-school seniors, (2) persons married less than five years, and (3) persons married more than 20 years. Surprisingly enough, both the high-school group *and* those married more than 20 years were found to have a more romantic conception of love than the group that was married for less than five years.[6]

---

[6] David Knox, "Conceptions of Love at Three Developmental Levels," *Family Coordinator*, April, 1970, pp. 151–157.

A not unrelated finding has to do with the extent of adultery in our society. A generation ago, Kinsey discovered that some 50 percent of the husbands and 26 percent of the wives in his sample acknowledged that they had had extramarital coitus, figures which at that time were far greater than had been expected.[7] In the modern era—with the advent of wife swapping or "swinging"—it seems likely that the figure is even higher. Could it be that the incidence of extramarital love would also be above expectations? Here, certainly, lies a ready-made research project for someone!

SEX DIFFERENCES

Popular impression has it that girls fall in love more often (and more deeply) than boys. This belief apparently stems from the notion that females are more emotional than males and therefore more inclined to be involved in romantic affairs. However, if females really are the more emotional sex, it is only in a superficial way; in fact, there is evidence to suggest that, on the whole, females have more stable personalities than males.

In collegiate circles, it does seem as though girls are more prone to discuss their romances than are boys. The latter, on the other hand, seem more likely to discuss (and exaggerate?) their sexual exploits. And, again, this verbal difference makes it *appear* that the female is more "love-prone" than the male.

Empirical evidence on the subject is somewhat fragmentary, although there seems no doubt that it is the male who *is attracted more readily*. Various studies, undertaken over a span of several decades, all show the same results. The question asked in the present writer's survey was: "Do you think it has been easy or difficult for you to become attracted to the opposite sex?" Almost twice as many males as females checked "very easy," while at the other end of the scale females were more likely than males to check "difficult."

On a somewhat related question, several surveys have shown that females are less likely than males to show a real interest in their partner at the time of the first date.[8] A number of studies

---

[7] Alfred Kinsey, Wardell Pomeroy, Clyde Martin, and Paul Gebhard, *Sexual Behavior in the Human Female*, Philadelphia, W. B. Saunders Company, 1953, p. 437.

[8] See, for example, Emily Strong, William Wallace, and Warner Wilson, "Three-Filter Date Selection by Computer," *Family Coordinator*, April, 1969, pp. 166–171.

have also shown that males are more romantic than females, as measured by various "romanticism scales."[9]

In the present writer's questionnaire study, the average (median) number of romantic experiences (both infatuation and love) for the female was seven, while the corresponding figure for the male was a little less than six. But it should be remembered that girls mature much earlier than boys. They have more extensive dating and romantic experience at an earlier age than boys; in fact, over one-fifth of the males reported that they had not yet been in love, as compared with only one-tenth of the females. In contrast to the males, furthermore, the majority of the females in the sample were actually in love at the time of the survey.

In brief, males and females are on a different time span with regard to romance. Girls start earlier, but they also marry earlier and thus remove themselves from the romantic scene several years before the boys. In the writer's survey, the college women were certainly much closer to the end of their premarital love experience than were the men. If both sexes could be questioned *at the time of marriage,* it is quite possible that the male figure would equal or exceed that of the female. At any rate, the writer's study led him to conclude that:

> Contrary to rather strong popular impression, the female is not pushed hither and yon by her romantic compulsions. On the contrary, her romanticism seems to be more adaptive and directive than that of the male. Apparently she is able to exercise a greater measure of control over her romantic inclinations, adapting them to the exigencies of marital selection.[10]

Assuming that males are as much or more "love-prone" than females, which sex falls in love more deeply? This is a different question entirely, and the few studies we have do not necessarily point in the same direction. In the Kanin-Davidson-Scheck survey it was found that males consistently developed love feelings in the relationship earlier than females. However, with regard to the actual love experience itself, these investigators found that both idealization of the partner and feelings of euphoria were more likely to be associated with the female.[11] Fengler, on the other hand, discovered that "males generally tend to become more romantic and females less romantic with

---

[9] See, for example, Zick Rubin, "From Liking to Loving: Patterns of Attraction in Dating Relationships," in Ted Huston (ed.), *op. cit.,* p. 398.

[10] Kephart, *op. cit.,* p. 100.

[11] Eugene Kanin, Karen Davidson, and Sonia Scheck, "A Research Note on Male-Female Differentials in the Experience of Heterosexual Love," *Journal of Sex Research,* February, 1970, pp. 64–72.

increased involvement in courtship."[12] And, in a study by Eslinger, Clarke, and Dynes, it was found that the females were less
willing than the males to break off their current dating relationship.[13] Each of these studies had a different focus, and it will
doubtless take a much more extensive research effort before
various pieces of the romantic edifice can be put together.

NOBLE OR NEUROTIC?

Because romantic love is so typically American, it is little wonder
that the theme is heavily underscored in our novels, movies, and
television. Love, in these media, is nearly always portrayed as a
noble virtue, and who can doubt that this portrayal influences
Americans of every age?

Insofar as the movies are concerned, love apparently overshad-
ows all the other virtues. Not only do individuals fall in love with
amazing rapidity, but they often do so with a seeming disregard
for the character and personality of the other party. According to
the Hollywood formula, it is almost obligatory to maintain loyalty to the loved one even though the latter may possess more
than his or her share of reprehensible qualities.

While the "love is blind" theme is much more characteristic of
the movies than of real life, most of us have known instances
where romantic love has played havoc with the assessment of
personality and character. At any rate, because of the presumed
"blind" nature of love, and because of the rapidity and frequency with which some individuals are romantically attracted,
the question has been raised whether susceptibility to love may
be, if not a neurotic symptom, at least a highly emotionalized
and possibly a defective personality trait.

The issue is obviously of some importance, inasmuch as the
charge strikes at the very heart of the American marriage system. In any case, several researchers—Dwight Dean, Graham
Spanier, the present writer—have conducted empirical surveys
on this topic. Speaking generally, none of the studies found a
positive relationship between romanticism and neuroticism, or
between romanticism and marital maladjustment. Spanier, for

---

[12] Alfred P. Fengler, "Romantic Love in Courtship: Divergent Paths of Male and
Female Students," *Journal of Comparative Family Studies*, Spring, 1974, pp.
134–139.

[13] Kenneth Eslinger, Alfred Clarke, and Russell Dynes, "The Principle of Least
Interest, Dating Behavior, and Family Integration Settings," *Journal of Marriage
and the Family*, May, 1972, pp. 269–272.

example, concludes that "romanticism does not appear to be harmful to marriage relationships in particular or the family system in general, and is therefore not generally dysfunctional in our society."[14]

In the present writer's survey, scores made on the Bell Adjustment Inventory were correlated with such factors as the number of times the subjects had been infatuated, the number of times they had been in love, and the age at which they had their first romantic experience. Major conclusions were as follows:

> Although the results are perhaps not clear-cut, findings suggest that romantic love is not a manifestation of emotional dysfunction. Students with inferior personality test scores did not fall in love or become infatuated more often than those with superior scores. As compared with the latter, the poor scorers were not more readily attracted to the opposite sex; they did not start dating at an earlier age; they did not date more often; they did not have their first infatuation at an earlier age; they did not have their first love experience at an earlier age.

> On the other hand, there is a suggestion that those students—particularly males—with the very highest number of romantic experiences (12 or more) were overrepresented among the inferior personality test scorers. Also, males who were romantically involved with two females at the same time were overrepresented among the inferior scorers.

> It is the writer's interpretation that becoming infatuated and falling in love are part of the normal maturation process. The fact that American youth have multiple romantic experiences may simply be a reflection of the fact that (a) certain components of personality undergo developmental change; (b) there is widespread—and constantly varying—premarital association of the sexes; and (c) romantic love has traditionally held an exalted—some would say over-exalted—position in our culture.

> It may be true that hyper-romanticism—as evidenced by an excessive number of infatuation and love experiences, or by becoming romantically involved with two persons simultaneously—is a manifestation of some emotional dysfunction. But this obliquity should not obscure the larger, more important picture; namely, that periodic romantic attractions seem to be part of the normal youth response in a culture which more or less encourages freedom of marital choice. Although far from being in the "proved" category, this conclusion appears to be supported by the handful of pertinent research studies thus far undertaken.[15]

---

[14] Graham B. Spanier, "Romanticism and Marital Adjustment," *Journal of Marriage and the Family*, August, 1972, pp. 486–487.

[15] William Kephart, "The 'Dysfunctional' Theory of Romantic Love: A Research Report," *Journal of Comparative Family Studies*, Autumn, 1970, pp. 26–36. See also Berscheid and Walster, *op. cit.*

(Joel Gordon)

In brief, while love may have its "blind" aspects, it appears that the irrationality component has been exaggerated. Movies and television to the contrary, American youth do not habitually fall in love with unworthy or undesirable characters. In fact, it is the writer's personal observation that college students usually make rather sound choices. Moreover, for most people love is an enriching experience, which, for all its heartaches and unevenness, provides the individual with an emotional insight and a sense of self-sacrifice not otherwise attainable.

One of the questions included in the preceding study was this: "On the basis of your total infatuation and love experience, would you say this experience has made you a happier person, unhappier, or neither?" The results—which speak for themselves—are as follows:

	Males	Females
Happier	70%	75%
Unhappier	5	4
Neither	25	21
	100%	100%

INTRODUCTION SERVICES

Most young Americans have ample exposure to members of the opposite sex, and all that seems necessary for Cupid to operate is to let nature take its course. Some individuals, however, do experience difficulty. These would include the excessively shy, the physically or socially handicapped, older people, those who are geographically isolated, and others for whom romantic love has limited applicability. For such individuals, a number of formalized services are available—marriage brokers, lonely hearts clubs, matrimonial agencies, dating bureaus, and the like—and no discussion of American mate selection would be complete without some mention of these rather unusual enterprises.

Marriage Brokers. Professional matchmaking seems to have originated in the Near and Far East, and from all accounts it is a very old profession, one instance being mentioned in the Old Testament. The custom spread to Europe, and during the Middle Ages marriage brokerage was a recognized profession. Among Jewish groups, for instance, the *shatchen* (a go-between or matchmaker) was a respected personage. In the United States the *shatchen* performed the role of marriage broker, arranging introductions for individuals of both sexes who had some difficulty in finding a suitable mate.

293

While the *shatchen* has largely disappeared from the American scene, marriage brokers continue their operations. They have their own organization, the Association of Marriage Brokers of the United States, which holds periodic meetings and claims a growing membership. The brokers strive for respectability and, according to their own code, are not supposed to arrange matches without investigating the background of both parties. The fees vary, incidentally, some brokers charging a flat rate, others utilizing a sliding scale based on the socio-economic status of the client.

Lonely Hearts Clubs. Whereas marriage brokerage dates back several thousand years and is of Old World origin, lonely hearts clubs are an American innovation of fairly recent vintage. The first clubs were established in the 1890's, although it was not until after World War I that they became widespread. As they are generally set up, lonely hearts clubs operate as introductory clearing houses, supplying lists of names and addresses to all who become club members, a "member" being defined as anyone who pays the membership fee, usually from three to five dollars. Subsequent lists of names call for additional fees, although "subscriptions" can be had at a cut rate.

The club member, or subscriber, not only obtains lists of names of the opposite sex, but also gets his or her name entered on candidate lists. Enterprising individuals can (and do) join several clubs, hoping that their names will thus receive wider circulation. However, it is now common practice for many of the organizations to circulate master lists, so that a person who joins half a dozen different clubs may receive the same list of names from all six.

It is standard practice, also, for the lists to contain descriptions of the physical and social characteristics of the participants:

294

> Betty: A perfectly gorgeous, shapely young lady. Gorgeous auburn hair. VERY LONESOME and very eager to meet a nice young man like YOU!

. . .

> George: Masculine type. Age 25. Holds respectable job, and is not stingy. Brown hair, brown eyes, and looking for sincere companionship.

. . .

> MY NAME IS MARY: "I live in Ala. Am 21 years old, 128 lbs, 5'6, Baptist. Am considered pretty and also kind."

In addition to descriptions of this type, some of the more progressive clubs include pictures as well. From all reports, male members outnumber female members by a wide margin, estimates ranging from 2:1 to 5:1.

Although most of the better-known periodicals are reluctant to accept them, some magazines routinely carry full pages of advertisements from lonely hearts clubs, such as Friendship World, Starlight Lodge, Olde Southe Clubbe, Rainbow Service, Club Cordially Yours, the "400" Club, and Destiny League. A typical lonely hearts ad might read as follows:

ARE YOU LONELY?

> Cheer up! Let us help you find a mate. That certain some one. Mail $3.00 and open Destiny's Door. Starlight Club, Box 29E.

Some ads are rather optimistic in nature:

MEN! MEN! MEN!

> Our women are screaming to meet you! Tell us what kind you want. In a week you'll start receiving letters. Don't forget our slogan: "No man is any good without a woman!" Janis Lynn. P.O. Box 1100

It is understandable, in view of the many extravagant claims made, that lonely hearts ads and operations are routinely checked by U.S. postal inspectors, and that from time to time local police are called upon to investigate the more unscrupulous clubs. The sad fact of the matter is that, although their business is marriage, lonely hearts clubs need no license to operate, and no specific laws control them. Little wonder that the number of such clubs is so large, and that their reputation is somewhat tarnished.

On the other hand, it can be argued that lonely hearts clubs do serve a purpose; in fact, it is difficult to judge their overall effect. While there undoubtedly is some exploitation, it is also true that the reputable clubs provide marital opportunities for many individuals whose chances might otherwise be near zero.

295

Matrimonial Agencies. Although there are some similarities, matrimonial agencies tend to differ from lonely hearts clubs in that they generally perform their services through personal contacts rather than through the mails. Of necessity, therefore, matrimonial agencies are usually local in nature and are generally set up in metropolitan centers such as New York City. Matrimonial agencies are quite similar to marriage brokers, about the only real difference being one of size. The smaller (one-person) agencies are referred to as marriage brokers, while the larger ones are called "matrimonial bureaus," "marriage agencies," and the like. In recent years the tendency has been to drop the term "marriage broker" and use such terms as "service," "agency," and "enterprise."

The larger agencies may occupy suites of rooms and employ several interviewers. Some attempt is made to match clients on the basis of age, religion, educational level, interests, and other factors that the agency deems relevant. While some agencies appear to be "scientific" in their matching of client traits, no published figures have been forthcoming. Nevertheless, the fees charged are fairly high, prices in the $300 range being fairly common. Just how successful matrimonial agencies are in finding mates is open to question. The agencies themselves report a high rate of success, but, again, no published figures have been made available.

Computerized Services. The latest innovation in formalized introduction has been the employment of computerized methods. Both males and females fill out lengthy questionnaires—dealing with family background, attitudes, interests, and so forth—and the computer then proceeds to "match" specific individuals, usually on the basis of homogamous tendencies. This method does have the advantage of analyzing a large number of variables in an impersonal manner. Also, unlike the matrimonial agencies and lonely hearts clubs, computerized services have some appeal for college students; in fact, computerized dating on a nonprofit basis has been tried on some campuses, with moderate success.

On the other hand, while they have sometimes "accepted" computerized introductions, college students retain a healthy skepticism of the system. A number of students have informed the present writer that questionnaire answers are, in many cases, deliberately falsified. Also, the computer system has a built-in flaw inasmuch as the important ingredient of physical attraction is ignored. As a matter of fact, simple homogamy—which is the basis of most computerized matching—is far from being established as a primary basis for successful mate selection.

Strong and Wilson, who conducted a research survey based on college students matched via the computer, contend that "computerized dating is at least as efficient as blind dating, chance meetings on campus, and the other avenues that are commonly used." But the same authors also state that:

> To those who ask, "Is computer dating successful?" the researchers would answer, "What are your expectations?" A majority indicated that they found at least one satisfactory date among the three names. For those who think of computer dating as a novel diversion, it will be perceived as fun. A few will marry, and a few will feel defrauded. Those who are looking for a magic box to produce Miss or Mr. "Right" will very likely be disappointed.[16]

The Future of Introduction Services. It is doubtful whether formalized introduction services, including the computer variety, can count on much future growth in the United States. That is to say, there seems to be little likelihood that such services will achieve greater acceptance than is now accorded them. For whether they are in the form of a lonely hearts club, a matrimonial agency, or a computerized system, the fact remains that there is an artificiality about them that is somewhat distasteful to most young Americans. Romantic love and dating have become integral parts of our mate-selection system, and when introductions and meetings become structured, most of the sparkle is removed. As a matter of fact, there is some tendency to be skeptical not only of the services themselves but of the people who patronize them.

---

[16] Emily Strong and Warner Wilson, "Three-Filter Date Selection by Computer," *Family Coordinator*, July, 1969, p. 259.

The chances are that, in spite of a certain amount of exploiting, formalized services will continue to operate, the more reputable ones probably benefiting certain classes of people. But insofar as the bulk of the population is concerned, it is likely that these services will continue to be looked upon as little more than tragicomic enterprises. For better or worse, American youth seem to be in foursquare agreement with the philosophy of modern romanticism: no love, no marriage.

SOCIETAL IMPLICATIONS OF ROMANTIC LOVE

Formalized introduction services aside, the question should be asked whether romantic love serves a societal, as well as an individual, function. For the fact is that, in a competitive, technological society like our own, marriage is not always the wisest "economic" choice to make. As Greenfield points out, marriage often requires individuals to dissipate rather than accumulate income and to do so in ways that are non-prestige-gaining, such as paying for repair, maintenance, and medical services.

> What appears to be necessary for American culture in its present form then, is a special mechanism that would induce these generally rational, ambitious, and calculating individuals—in the sense of striving to maximize their personal achievement—to do what in the logic of their culture is not in their own personal interest. Somehow they must be induced—we might almost say in spite of themselves—to occupy the positions of husband-father and wife-mother. . . .
>
> But how can an entire population . . . be induced to behave in a manner that can be considered abnormal and irrational, and like it?
>
> What we are suggesting is that the romantic love complex in middle-class America serves as the reward-motive that induces individuals to occupy the structurally essential positions of husband-father and wife-mother.
>
> A person who falls in love and marries comes to believe that he or she is "doing the right thing" and takes understandable pride in doing so. This feeling is then given group support and validation by friends and relatives. The sentiments involved thus may be compared with those of the person in a kin-oriented society who has made a "proper marriage"—a person, for example, who marries a cross-cousin in a society with a pattern of prescriptive cross-cousin marriage. This is the right thing, and both the involved parties and those around them know it and rejoice in the feeling that goes with what is right.[17]

---

[17] Sidney Greenfield, "Love and Marriage in Modern America: A Functional Analysis," in J. Ross Eshleman (ed.), *Perspectives in Marriage and the Family*, Boston, Allyn and Bacon, Inc., 1969, pp. 346–362.

(Frank Siteman, Stock Boston)

Whether a system other than romantic love—one based, say, on an extended kin involvement—would "work" in our society is highly problematical. It must be remembered that Americans place a high value on individual choice; in fact, in the one empirical study that has been done, the investigators found that "as parents began to interfere more in a relationship, the couples appeared to fall more deeply in love. When the parents became resigned to the relationship, and interfered less, the couples began to feel less intensely about one another."[18]

In terms of the current value pattern, at any rate, it would probably have to be shown that our romantic method is much weaker than it seems to be before any other system of mate selection would be considered. And in the last analysis, whatever else it may be, our romantic syndrome is anything but dull. For a large number of people it provides a breath of fresh air, of real or

---

[18] Berscheid and Walster, *op. cit.,* pp. 369.

vicarious excitement, in an otherwise monotonous routine of daily living. All things considered, furthermore, most of us show few ill effects from the "system."

Let us end the chapter as we began it, with a statement by the French writer, De Sales: "There is no reason to suppose that love in America will not cease to be a national problem, a hunting ground for the reformer, and that it will not become, as everything else, a personal affair very much worth the effort it takes to examine it as such. All that is necessary is for someone to forget for a while love as Hollywood—or the Professor—sees it, and sit down and think about it as an eternally fascinating subject for purely human observation."[19]

SELECTED READINGS

Altman, I., and Taylor, D. A., *Social Penetration: The Development of Interpersonal Relationships*, New York, Holt, Rinehart and Winston, Inc., 1973.

Bardis, Panos, "Erotometer: A Technique for the Measurement of Heterosexual Love," *International Review of Sociology*, March, 1972, pp. 71–77.

Berscheid, Ellen, and Walster, Elaine, "A Little Bit About Love," in Ted Huston (ed.), *Foundations of Interpersonal Attraction*, New York, Academic Press, 1974, pp. 355–381.

Brogan, Donna, and Kutner, Nancy, "Measuring Sex-Role Orientation: A Normative Approach," *Journal of Marriage and the Family*, February, 1976, pp. 31–40.

Byrne, Donn, *The Attraction Paradigm*, New York, Academic Press, 1971.

Dean, Dwight, "Romanticism and Emotional Maturity: A Preliminary Study," *Marriage and Family Living*, February, 1961, pp. 44–45.

DeRougemont, Denis, *Love in the Western World*, New York, Harcourt Brace, 1940.

De Sales, Raoul De Roussy, "Love in America," *Atlantic Monthly*, May, 1938, pp. 645–651.

Eslinger, Kenneth; Clarke, Alfred; and Dynes, Russell, "The Principle of Least Interest, Dating Behavior, and Family Integration Settings," *Journal of Marriage and the Family*, May, 1972, pp. 269–272.

Fengler, Alfred P., "Romantic Love in Courtship: Divergent Paths of Male and Female Students," *Journal of Comparative Family Studies*, Spring, 1974, pp. 134–139.

---

[19] De Sales, *op. cit.*, p. 651.

Fromm, Erich, *The Art of Loving*, New York, Harper & Brothers, 1956.

Greenfield, Sidney, "Love and Marriage in Modern America," in J. Ross Eshleman (ed.), *Perspectives in Marriage and the Family*, Boston, Allyn and Bacon, Inc., 1969, pp. 346–362.

Harlow, H. F., "The Nature of Love," *American Psychologist*, Vol. 13, 1958, pp. 673–685.

Hobart, Charles, "The Incidence of Romanticism During Courtship," *Social Forces*, Vol. 36, 1958, pp. 362–367.

Huston, Ted (ed.), *Foundations of Interpersonal Attraction*, New York, Academic Press, 1974.

Kanin, Eugene; Davidson, Karen; and Scheck, Sonia, "A Research Note on Male-Female Differentials in the Experience of Heterosexual Love," *Journal of Sex Research*, February, 1970, pp. 64–72.

Kephart, William M., "The 'Dysfunctional' Theory of Romantic Love: A Research Report," *Journal of Comparative Family Studies*, Autumn, 1970, pp. 26–36.

————, "Evaluation of Romantic Love," *Medical Aspects of Human Sexuality*, February, 1973, pp. 92–112.

Klinger, E., *Structure and Functions of Fantasy*, New York, John Wiley & Sons, Inc., 1971.

Knox, David, "Conceptions of Love at Three Developmental Levels," *Family Coordinator*, April, 1970, pp. 151–157.

Kunz, Philip, "Romantic Love and Reciprocity," *Family Coordinator*, April, 1969, pp. 111–116.

Leslie, Gerald R., *The Family in Social Context*, New York, Oxford University Press, 1976. See Chapter 13, "Premarital Involvement," pp. 447–494.

Moore, John C., *Love in Twelfth-Century France*, Philadelphia, University of Pennsylvania Press, 1972.

Murstein, Bernard I., *Theories of Attraction and Love*, New York, Springer Publishing Company, Inc., 1971.

Reik, Theodore, *A Psychologist Looks at Love*, New York, Henry Holt and Company, 1944.

Rubin, Zick, *Liking and Loving: An Invitation to Social Psychology*, New York, Holt, Rinehart and Winston, Inc., 1973.

Shorter, Edward, *The Making of the Modern Family*, New York, Basic Books, Inc., 1976.

Spanier, Graham B., "Romanticism and Marital Adjustment," *Journal of Marriage and the Family*, August, 1972, pp. 486–487.

Strong, Emily; Wallace, William; and Wilson, Warner, "Three-Filter Date Selection by Computer," *Family Coordinator*, April, 1969, pp. 166–171.

Udry, J. Richard, *The Social Context of Marriage,* Philadelphia, J. B. Lippincott Company, 1974. See Chapter Seven, "Love," pp. 131–151.

Walster, Elaine, "Passionate Love," in Bernard I. Murstein (ed.), *Theories of Attraction and Love,* New York, Springer Publishing Company, Inc., 1971, pp. 85–99.

Wilkinson, Melvin, "Romantic Love: The Great Equalizer? Sexism in Popular Music," *Family Coordinator,* April, 1976, pp. 161–166.

14

Premarital Sex Codes

IF THERE IS one subject that Americans are likely to find themselves in disagreement on, that subject is premarital sex. From a historical view this is somewhat surprising; indeed, earlier texts dealing with the family did not even include the topic. Not only was the incidence of premarital sex much lower than it is today, but the subject itself was by no means acceptable as a basis of either conversation or publication.

During the 1930's, however, it became evident that premarital sex was a problem to be reckoned with. The old taboos were weakening, and the younger generation was getting restless. Books, magazines, plays, and movies either reflected the trend of the times or—as some would say—"led the parade." In any case, the premarital sex theme became part of the standard literary and theatrical repertoire, with concepts like "free love" and "trial marriage" being endlessly embroidered.

By the 1950's, it was obvious that premarital sex was not just a passing fad; on the contrary, as judged by the attention given it, the subject was more popular than ever. Terms like "hot" and "cold" became routine sexual adjectives, and words like "necking" and "petting" became so common that dictionaries included them. A number of factual surveys on the subject—based on personal interviews or questionnaires—revealed what everybody suspected: there was a good deal more premarital sex than there was supposed to be.

By the 1970's further changes were in evidence. Young people came more and more to feel that premarital sex was a personal matter and not something to be regulated by outside agencies, a view that was championed by the movies and other mass media.

And now, with the advent of the 1980's, there is every indication that the trend is continuing. Public opinion polls, sex studies, attitude surveys—all indicate (1) a softening of views

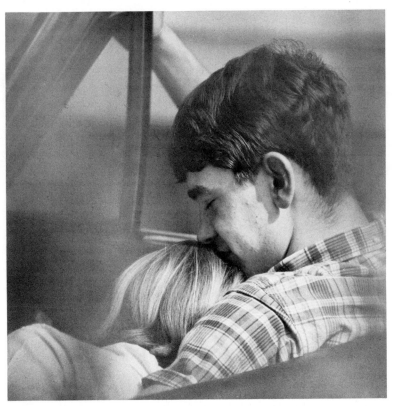

(Burk Uzzle, Magnum Photo)

concerning premarital sex, and (2) an increase in the actual incidence of premarital coitus. With different varieties of the Pill being developed and made available to young people, the trend toward premarital permissiveness would seem to be irreversible.

At the same time, there continues to be a good deal of public resistance to the whole idea of sex before marriage. Movies, for example, have come to be largely shunned by adult segments of the population. Major relogous and civic organizations are by no means ready to endorse the principle of premarital sex. Many parents, surely, are against the idea.

In brief, it appears that we are in the throes of a divided society on the premarital sex issue. And although, obviously, neither the writer nor anyone else can "solve" the problem at this point in time, it is hoped that the following pages will perhaps sharpen some of the dimensions.

LEGAL SANCTIONS

As legal scholars have pointed out, American sex laws are based on the Judeo-Christian moral codes, modified or influenced by Roman law and the sex codes of the English ecclesiastical courts. Reflecting the seriousness with which sex was regarded in the Judeo-Christian heritage, our present laws are outgrowths of the reproductive concept; that is, sex outside marriage is held to be illegal. Hence, fornication, seduction, prostitution, incest, and adultery are punishable by law. There is no denying the fact that some of our American sex laws are strict and far-reaching. They were meant to be.

It goes almost without saying that in many instances the sex laws work hardships, especially in the case of the unmarried, the widowed, and the divorced—none of whom can very well conform to the legal requirement of sex within marriage. Because of this seeming injustice, there are those who advocate a repeal, or at least a softening, of the existing sex codes. These observers would endorse legal principles that are not only more humane, but are more in keeping with the realities of the situation.

There are others who believe that sex laws should not be enacted so as to fit the needs of certain individuals or groups, but should embody those principles that are best suited to society as a whole. While recognizing the many injustices under our current system, these individuals are convinced the institution of marriage is so important that any weakening of it in the form of legalizing nonmarital sex would ultimately have adverse societal effects.

Premarital Petting.   There are no laws in the United States against premarital necking or petting or "making out," despite the fact that such behavior often involves erotic arousal, sometimes to the point of orgasm. It is interesting to contemplate the reason for this seeming omission in what is otherwise a strict legal code. It may be that at the time the sex laws were being codified, necking and petting were hardly considered important enough to warrant legislative consideration. As a matter of fact, it was only with the advent of the automobile that the terms "necking" and "petting" came into prominence, presumably as a result of the amorous and erotic opportunities which the automobile afforded. Stated simply, it is difficult to legislate against forms of behavior that have no name.

This is not to say that individuals are not sometimes prosecuted for petting. They are, albeit infrequently. Petting in public, or petting involving a girl under the age of consent, sometimes

304

results in police action, and if the case is flagrant enough, charges may be brought on the basis of disorderly conduct, public indecency, or some other convenient ground.

Also, some of the specific techniques involved in petting are punishable under various state laws. Genital manipulation between the sexes is apparently illegal in some states, and behavior involving mouth-genital contact between male and female is punishable as a felony in most states. In the very nature of such cases, of course, legal evidence is hard to come by. Arrests and prosecutions are few and far between, and convictions are even fewer.

Regardless of whether or not specific types of petting behavior are punishable by law, most participants are probably unaware that any illegality is involved. And even if they were, it is doubtful—in the present social climate, at least—whether any substantial behavioral modification would result.

Premarital Coitus. In legal terminology, premarital coitus is usually referred to as *fornication*. Generally speaking, fornication is illegal in the United States. It is defined as a crime in most states, and in the others it is often punishable under such catch-all terms as lewd and obscene behavior, disorderly conduct, and lascivious indecency. Some states define fornication as a single act of intercourse on the part of two unmarried persons, while other states refer to it as a "continuing relationship." (Fornication is not considered a criminal offense in most European countries.)

Occasionally there is some confusion between *fornication* and *adultery*. True, the former refers to premarital coitus and the latter to extramarital coitus, but what is it when one party is single and the other married? In most states, the single person would be guilty of fornication, the married partner guilty of adultery. The distinction has, upon occasion, proved to be important, since the crime of adultery carries a heavier penalty than that of fornication.

Regardless of how it is defined, the crime of fornication seldom results in prosecution. It is not only a fairly difficult type of case to prove, but the various police departments are simply not interested. Both the police and the district attorney's office are cognizant of the fornication statutes, but neither takes them too seriously. And even if they did, the effect on premarital sex behavior is questionable. Enforcement of the fornication laws *without the support of the various informal social controls* would, in all likelihood, have limited effect.

Rape. Legally, rape is defined as sexual intercourse with a woman, other than the offender's wife, forcibly and against her will. As thus defined, rape cases are highly publicized in the newspapers, for a rapist on the prowl is a menace to the community. Less publicized is the fact that once in a great while a woman is found guilty of rape. This comes about when a female, as an accessory, assists a man in the raping of another woman. It is also legally possible for a husband, as an accessory, to be convicted in the rape of his own wife.

Reflecting public opinion, the various state legislatures have decreed penalties for rape up to and including death or life imprisonment. It is probable, however, that less than half the defendants are found guilty, since forcible rape charges are fairly difficult to prove. Among other things, the female must give evidence of having displayed "utmost resistance." Once the proof is forthcoming, of course, the law speaks in no uncertain terms, and there is usually little sympathy for the convicted.

As will be shown later in the chapter, the incidence of (voluntary) premarital coitus has increased in the United States. One would expect, therefore, that the number of forcible rape cases would be on the decline. Oddly enough, however, the opposite seems to be true. Department of Justice figures, shown in Table 4, indicate that both the number and the rate have about tripled in a little over a decade!

TABLE 4 *Forcible Rape Cases in the United States*

YEAR	NUMBER	RATE
1963	17,650	9.4
1965	23,410	12.1
1967	27,620	14.0
1969	37,170	18.5
1971	42,260	20.5
1973	51,400	24.5
1975	56,090	26.3

Source: From the United States Department of Justice, *Uniform Crime Reports,* Washington, D.C., issued yearly. The rate is per 100,000 inhabitants.

In many rape cases the female *consents to intercourse,* but for one reason or another the consent is not recognized by law. Such reasons would include the female's being drugged, drunk, mentally deficient, insane, or underage. These cases are all classed as *statutory rape,* and while nationwide figures are not available, they would add considerably to the totals shown in Table 4.

The philosophy behind statutory rape is that, even though the female consents to intercourse, her condition is such as to invalidate the consent. It is these nonforcible varieties of rape that have led some lawyers to advocate a softening, both of the statutory definitions and the penalties. For example, while the statutory age for females in most states is 16 or 18, the actual range is from 12 to 21! For a male to be convicted of rape when his (consenting) female friend is 20 years of age would seem to be a legal parody. It has also happened that males have been convicted of statutory rape for having sex relations with teen-age prostitutes!

Finally, mention should be made of the fact that in some states it has become legally possible to charge an adult female with statutory rape if she is known to have had intercourse with an underaged male.

Seduction. The crime of seduction, in essence, is the persuading of a female, by deceptive methods, to surrender her virginity. About three-fourths of the states have seduction laws, and in most of them the specific method of seduction is defined as a promise by the male to marry the female in the near future if she agrees to premarital coitus now. The promise to marry must be specific and not implied; the fact of an engagement ring would not be sufficient legal grounds for prosecution. Some states also require that the woman be under a designated age. Of course, if the man actually goes through with the marriage, the case normally will be dismissed.

Situational factors and the nature of the proof are such that seduction cases are only occasionally brought to court; in fact, many states will not convict on the uncorroborated testimony of the female. When indictments and convictions are secured, however, the penalties for seduction may be severe.

Legal Implications. Rape and seduction have been included here not only to give the reader some idea of the legalities involved, but also to show the seriousness with which certain extreme facets of sex are regarded. While our chief concern is with the statutes involving premarital coitus, there can be little doubt of the striking power of the law insofar as cases involving nonconsent or quasi consent are concerned.

Laws prohibiting *voluntary* premarital coitus are another matter. Some authorities feel that, since these laws are difficult to enforce and have limited deterrence value, they should be repealed. Other authorities feel that if our society is genuinely desirous of curtailing premarital sex indulgence, the use of legal provisions is a justifiable measure in the overall process of social control.

Generally speaking, however, premarital sex in the United States is a *sociological rather than a legal issue.* That is, acceptance or rejection of sex before marriage will depend not on the law but on such factors as the attitude of the church, public opinion, effects of the mass media, and the like. Let us examine these factors separately.

ATTITUDE OF THE CHURCHES

From all indications, religion exerts a considerable influence on the morals of many young people. This influence operates not only directly, but also indirectly; that is, boys and girls are influenced by their parents, by teachers, and by other adults who, in turn, may have had *their* attitudes shaped by religious teachings. At any rate, a discussion of premarital sex codes should logically include some analysis of the viewpoints of the three major religious groupings in our society.

Roman Catholic. The Roman Catholic Church is unequivocally opposed to premarital coitus, an act that is held to be a mortal sin and that would be not permitted in any circumstances. Whether or not the couple are engaged, or whether the individuals are older people, or whether conditions are such as to work a hardship on the couple—none of these would serve as mitigating factors. According to the Catholic Church, premarital sexual intercourse represents a violation of the Sixth Commandment: Thou shalt not commit adultery. This commandment is interpreted to mean not only adultery, but any kind of sexual activity outside of marriage.

From the Roman Catholic view, it follows that if premarital coitus is sinful, activities that might lead to premarital indulgence are also morally wrong. Erotic necking, petting, passionate kissing, and other manifestations of sex are expressly forbidden at the premarital level, whether or not the couple are engaged.

This is not to say that all expressions of affection outside marriage are prohibited. On the contrary, affectionate behavior is recognized as quite normal. What is prohibited is behavior of an *erotic* nature, and since individuals are known to differ in their arousal capacity, no hard-and-fast rules are laid down in this respect.

As in most other areas of morality, then, the position of the Roman Catholic Church regarding premarital sex activities is crystal-clear: such activities are considered morally wrong, and there are no extenuating circumstances. Furthermore—and in the present context, quite importantly—the Catholic clergy are unanimous in their pronouncements. A Catholic boy or girl asking a question about premarital sex would receive the same categorical answer from a priest anywhere in the United States. As we shall see, this same unanimity of pronouncement does not necessarily apply in the case of Protestant ministers and rabbis.

Protestant. In spite of the fact that there is some denominational variation, as well as differences of opinion among ministers of the same denomination, the overriding conclusion to be drawn from any survey on the subject is that, as a group, the Protestant clergy in the United States are against premarital coitus. Of special interest in this connection is the survey by Phillips of the sex education programs of the major Protestant denominations (Episcopal, Presbyterian, Lutheran, Methodist, Baptist).

> Among the sexual issues confronted, the one receiving by far the most attention is that of premarital sex. Uniformly, the denominations' stance on this issue is clearly and strongly that of chastity.
>
> The support for this position is neither that of moralistic legalism nor is it judgmental. The traditional negative supports—conception, infection, detection—receive comparatively little attention, although in the name of realism they are not ruled out as legitimate considerations. The primary supports, however, are scriptural, rational, and positive.[1]

Phillips' finding on the premarital sex issue is of more than usual importance, since the churches represented in the survey had a "combined membership of approximately 40,000,000, and a church school enrollment of over 21,000,000."[2]

As a group, the Protestant clergy are also opposed to "petting," "making out," and other forms of premarital activity that lead to erotic arousal. However, while most ministers continue to condemn premarital sexual activity per se, a minority do take a more permissive view; in fact, a few are quite outspoken on the subject. It is not that these men advocate a *general acceptance* of premarital coitus. Their position is rather that, while premarital sex relations are morally wrong, there may be certain

---

[1] John Phillips, *Sex Education in Major Protestant Denominations*, New York, National Council of Churches, 1969, p. 10.

[2] *Ibid.*, p. 2.

circumstances calling for religious extenuation. These men would contend, in other words, that one cannot give a blanket yes-or-no answer to questions relating to premarital sex.

When all is said and done, however, it should not be thought that Protestant clergymen are divided on the issue. A clear majority are agreed that in the Christian way of life sex should be reserved for marriage, exceptional cases notwithstanding. One minister, in speaking with the writer, made the following comments:

> No, I don't believe you would find much difference of opinion on the part of the clergy. Premarital sex relations are sinful. They are counter to God's word. When young people question me about the problem—which, unfortunately, is not very often—that is the answer they get.
>
> It may be true that some of my colleagues won't go so far as to say premarital sex is unalterably wrong under all possible circumstances. There may be medical or legal factors which should be taken into consideration. But don't think there is a general division among the clergy on the subject. There isn't. Sex is sinful outside of marriage. That's the Christian view. It always has been and it always will be.

Jewish. Most rabbis are also against premarital coitus, a finding that was confirmed by Miller's recent survey.[3] At the same time, it appears that of the three groups discussed here—Catholics, Protestants, and Jews—the Jews are the most liberal on matters pertaining to premarital sex.

Rabbinical attitudes differ markedly among the Orthodox, Conservative, and Reform groups. Miller found that, whereas 90 percent of the Orthodox rabbis and 70 percent of the Conservative rabbis were opposed to premarital coitus, only 30 percent of the Reform rabbis were opposed. Those rabbis who "approved" of premarital intercourse generally did so in reference to a special situation, e.g., one involving an engagement or commitment on the part of the couple involved.

Rabbis who opposed premarital coitus did so because they felt that it would demean the status of marriage, and because such action was contrary to Jewish law. In the words of one Conservative rabbi:

> Premarital relations would destroy the sanctity of the Jewish home and family. The natural desire for physical intimacy, which increases as a relationship grows, should be saved for marriage.

---

[3] Beverly Miller, "Rabbinical Attitudes Toward Premarital Sex," unpublished paper (23 pp.), University of Pennsylvania, Sociology 4, 1975.

310

Rabbis who took a more permissive view toward premarital coitus did so "in response to a changing society." These respondents felt that such a view did not contradict Talmudic law. As one rabbi put it:

> The laws laid down by Judaism are viewed not as legalities, but as guidelines. Each person must carefully consider and decide upon his own sex ethic.

With regard to premarital petting, "making out," and the like, Orthodox, Conservative, and Reform rabbis all take a relatively permissive attitude. Miller found that, in spite of a fairly wide range of opinion, only 20 percent of the rabbis took a negative view. At the same time, there was a feeling that premarital intimacies of any kind should be reserved for a "serious type" of relationship.

311

PUBLIC OPINION

Since premarital coitus is frowned upon by both the church and the law, the general societal attitude would be expected to be negative—and such is indeed the case, at least with respect to adult segments of the population. Nationwide public opinion surveys conducted over the past 35 years all indicate a negative reaction. At the same time, the latest Gallup Poll figures reveal that a substantial change in attitude has been taking place:

> Although a majority of the American people support the Supreme Court's recent ruling which calls for tougher guidelines on obscene literature, far fewer today than in 1969 say they would be offended by pictures of nudes in magazines—55 percent compared to 73 percent. Those who would object to actors and actresses appearing in the nude in Broadway plays have declined from 73 percent to 44 percent, while the proportion who would be offended by topless nightclub waitresses has declined from 76 percent in 1969 to 59 percent in the latest survey.
>
> In terms of attitudes on premarital sex, two out of every three Americans in 1969 held the view that premarital sex relations are "wrong." Today, the public is closely divided, with 48 percent believing sex before marriage is wrong and 43 percent holding the opposite opinion.
>
> Evidence of a "generation gap" is seen in the fact that only 29 percent of young persons, 18 to 29, believe that premarital sex is wrong.
>
> While attitudes on nudity and premarital sex have become more liberal, the Puritan ethic continues to have a strong hold on the thinking of most Americans. A large majority of people over the age

of 30 continue to believe premarital sex is wrong. In addition, large majorities of the over-30 group say they would be offended by nudity in magazines, in the theater, and by topless waitresses.[4]

Generally speaking, pollsters have found that conservatism on sexual matters increases with age and decreases with educational level. It has also been found that women are more conservative than men. With respect to religious differences, the Gallup Poll cited above reported that Catholics now hold more liberal views on premarital sex than do Protestants. An earlier poll indicated, however, that "Jews are by far the most liberal of all major religious groups."[5]

SOME COUNTER FORCES

It should not be thought that the various facets of public opinion are all arrayed against premarital sex permissiveness. Far from it! Common observation indicates that there are influential forces pulling in the opposite direction, with the result that young people often find themselves caught in the middle.

The Mass Media.   There is little doubt that, taken collectively, modern movies, novels, and plays are exceedingly permissive in their treatment of sex outside marriage. Whether the theme is that of adultery or premarital coitus, the persons involved are likely to be portrayed in a sympathetic light, while the activity itself is seen as a more-or-less natural manifestation of man's inexorable nature. As a corollary, society is pictured as a repressive force, against which free men (youth) must struggle. It is easy to understand, in this connection, why movies have become largely the province of young people.

It is sometimes charged that the mass media are waging a deliberate campaign to "undermine" traditional moral codes, but this contention would be difficult to support. After all, novelists and playwrights are hardly the kind of people to become part of an organized propanganda venture. The fact is that these writers sincerely believe our present sex codes are not only outmoded but unduly restrictive of the human spirit. Their writings are for the most part genuine reflections of honest beliefs. It is also true, of course, that any number of lesser writers embellish the sexual theme because of anticipated financial profit.

---

[4] Princeton, New Jersey, Gallup Poll release of August 12, 1973.
[5] Princeton, New Jersey, Gallup Poll release of May 20, 1970. The 1973 Poll did not contain figures on Jewish response.

(Ellis Herwig, Stock Boston)

Family Specialists. Those who specialize in the family field—including textbook writers, marriage counselors, and teachers of family courses—are by no means in agreement on the premarital sex issue. Some are quite permissive in their views; others take a more restrictive approach. However, it is probably safe to say that, as a group, these men and women are more permissive in their beliefs than, say, the average American parent. The reason for this is not hard to find, for the family specialist has a great deal more personal contact with young people than does the average adult.

The marriage counselor, for example, spends a good many of his working hours counseling young people. He knows full well that a fair percentage of them—particularly engaged couples—are participating in some sort of sexual activity. Knowing of this activity and of the persistent temptations that produce it, the counselor finds it most difficult to adopt a moralistic tone. This same difficulty is also experienced by some teachers of marriage and family courses.

Attitudes of Young People.   As debate over the premarital sex issue continues year after year, what is the attitude of young people themselves? As the public opinion polls show—and as anyone who has been around college students knows—young people are much more likely than adults to hold permissive attitudes toward premarital sex. The idea of unmarried couples living together, for example, is considered reprehensible by most adults, yet many young people accept the practice as a matter of course.

It should be added, however, that college students and others who voice approval of premarital sex relations do not generally approve of indiscriminate indulgence. They feel, rather, that sex is a private matter rather than a concern of church or community and that, if two people have genuine feeling for one another and are willing to accept responsibility for their actions, then premarital sex participation is a legitimate and natural component of the courtship process.

THE EXTENT OF PREMARITAL SEX ACTIVITY

As the reader can well imagine, it is not easy to gather valid figures relating to premarital sex behavior. Some individuals "cover up" their activities, others tend to exaggerate. At best, the available figures refer only to *reported* behavior; hence, all statistics on the subject should be regarded as approximations of fact with an as-yet-undetermined margin of error. In brief, (1) we do not know the extent to which reported behavior reflects actual behavior; and (2) even assuming the margin of error to be small, we do not know whether the behavior of those who are *willing to report* is representative of the larger group.

It is difficult, also, to compute meaningful figures on premarital coitus because of the differential rates of indulgence. It is one thing for a researcher to discover that half of those interviewed on a given campus admit to having premarital intercourse, but the significance of this figure changes when, to take a hypothetical situation, it is further discovered that most of those involved have had but a single experience! Also, in the very nature of premarital necking and petting, virginity is, in a sense, a matter of definition. It is possible that some "technical virgins" have had more sexual experience than those who make no claim to chastity.

Methodological difficulties notwithstanding, it would seem that—because of the age-old double standard—American males have more extensive premarital sex experience than do the females. This statement is based not only on common knowledge but on a variety of interview and questionnaire surveys. Data from the latter suggest that somewhere between 65 and 90 percent of American males indulge in coitus before marriage, the specific figures varying according to educational level. For male college students the proportion is around 65 percent, a figure that has remained relatively constant for several decades.[6]

Premarital sex figures for females have always received more "publicity" than those for males, and over the years a number of cross-sectional and segmental studies have been undertaken. Earlier figures—reported by several investigators in the 1940's and 1950's—suggested that about 50 percent of American females were engaging in coitus before marriage.[7]

In the large-scale survey by Zelnik and Kantner, reported in the 1970's, it was found that 14 percent of the females had had premarital intercourse by age 15, 27 percent by age 17, and 46 percent by age 19.[8] Only the age group 15 to 19 was surveyed, but

[6] For a résumé of earlier studies, see Erwin Smigel and Rita Seiden, "The Decline and Fall of the Double Standard," *Annals of the American Academy of Political and Social Science*, March, 1968, pp. 6–17. For later findings, see Eleanor Luckey and Gilbert Nass, "A Comparison of Sexual Attitudes and Behavior in an International Sample," *Journal of Marriage and the Family*, May, 1969, pp. 364–379; Gerald Wiechmann and Altis Ellis, "A Study of the Effects of Sex Education on Premarital Petting and Coital Behavior," *Family Coordinator*, July, 1969, pp. 231–234; Gilbert Kaats and Keith Davis, "The Dynamics of Sexual Behavior of College Students," *Journal of Marriage and the Family*, August, 1970, pp. 390–399; Ira Robinson, Karl King, and Jack Balswick, "The Premarital Sexual Revolution Among College Females," *Family Coordinator*, April, 1972, pp. 189–194; Charles Hobart, "Sexual Permissiveness in Young English and French Canadians," *Journal of Marriage and the Family*, May, 1972, pp. 292–303; Arthur Vener and Cyrus Stewart, "Adolescent Sexual Behavior in Middle America Revisited," *Journal of Marriage and the Family*, November, 1974, pp. 728–735. See also Lura Henze and John Hudson, "Personal and Family Characteristics of Cohabiting and Noncohabiting College Students," *Journal of Marriage and the Family*, November, 1974, pp. 722–727; and Graham B. Spanier, "Sexualization and Premarital Sexual Behavior," *Family Coordinator*, January, 1975, pp. 33–41.

[7] See Smigel and Seiden, *op. cit.*

[8] See Melvin Zelnik and John Kantner, "The Probability of Premarital Intercourse," *Social Science Research*, September, 1972, pp. 335–341; and "The Resolution of Teenage First Pregnancies," *Family Planning Perspectives*, Spring, 1974, pp. 74–80. See also Ira Reiss, "Heterosexual Relationships Inside and Outside of Marriage," *University Programs Modular Studies*, Morristown, New Jersey, General Learning Press, 1973, pp. 15 ff.; and J. Richard Udry, Karl Bauman, and Naomi Morris, "Changes in Premarital Coital Experience of Recent Decade-of-Birth Cohorts of Urban American Women," *Journal of Marriage and the Family*,' November, 1975, pp. 783–787.

it seems evident from the last figure that well over half of American females are indulging in premarital coitus.

Surveys relating to the incidence of premarital coitus among American *college females* have been more or less continual, and the findings are extremely interesting. A dozen or so studies in the 1950's and 1960's showed that, depending on the institution surveyed, between 13 and 28 percent of college females reported having premarital coitus.[9] The average figure for all these studies would probably work out to a little over 20 percent.

The most recent surveys, however—those reported in the 1970's—reveal a significant increase in the figures for college females. In the Kaats and Davis study of a large Western university, the investigators found a premarital coital rate of 41 percent. In their study of a large Eastern university, Bell and Chaskes found a figure of 39 percent. In the Robinson–King–Balswick survey of a Southern university, the premarital figure was 37 percent, and in Hobart's Canadian study it was 44 percent.[10]

On the basis of a number of recent studies, then, it appears beyond a reasonable doubt that a permissive trend has been developing, which involves both attitudes and rates of indulgence. The significance of this development is of great interest to family scholars everywhere.

THE FUTURE

Although it is difficult to predict the future, there is little indication that the permissive trend will reverse itself. Premarital permissiveness has increased rather consistently in the last decade or so and appears to be part of a worldwide trend. At the same time, it is doubtful that—as some critics contend—young people are going hog wild over sex. As a matter of fact, there seems to be a genuine attempt to associate sex with feelings of affection. For example, to a Gallup Poll question on the subject, only 19 percent

[9] See footnote 6.

[10] Robert Bell and Jay Chaskes, "Premarital Sexual Experience Among Coeds," *Journal of Marriage and the Family*, 1970, pp. 81–84. For all the other sources listed above, see footnote 6. See also James Teevan, "Reference Groups and Premarital Sexual Behavior," *Journal of Marriage and the Family*, May, 1972, pp. 283–291; Donald Carns, "Talking About Sex: Notes on First Coitus and the Double Sexual Standard," *Journal of Marriage and the Family*, November, 1973, pp. 677–688; Graham B. Spanier, *op. cit.*; and John Edwards and Alan Booth, "Sexual Behavior In and Out of Marriage: An Assessment of Correlates," *Journal of Marriage and the Family*, February, 1976, pp. 73–81.

of American youth stated that they felt premarital sex was permissible "even if the parties concerned were not in love."[11]

But if the trend continues, is it not likely that the 19 percent figure will get larger? Perhaps so. (In Sweden the figure is twice as large—38 percent.)[12] It should be pointed out, however, that youth tend to become more conservative on sex and other matters as they get older. Reiss, a well-known authority on the subject, writes as follows:

> There are two basic institutions that are of key importance for the development of premarital sexual attitudes and behavior—courtship and the family. The fundamental orientation of the *participant-run* courtship institution is one of relatively high premarital sexual permissiveness. In a related manner, the orientation of the *adult-run* family institution is one of relatively low premarital sexual permissiveness.
>
> As the individual matures in American society, the relative strength of influence of these two institutions varies in accord with his role positions, and his premarital sexual attitudes vary accordingly. . . .
>
> The basic tendency in a participant-run system is for the participant, due to his role position, to increase his permissiveness during courtship and to somewhat reverse his views after marriage and parenthood.[13]

Special mention should also be made of the religious factor. Sexual morality has been an integral part of Western ethics for many centuries. If the major American church bodies maintain their present position, it is unlikely that the coitus-before-marriage pattern will receive general societal acceptance. If they change their position, of course, then a permissive premarital sexual standard may well be forthcoming.

If the writer were to venture a prediction, it would be that American opinion on premarital sex will become "trolarized," that is, divided along three different lines. The first line will include those who feel that premarital coitus is wrong under any circumstance. The second line would include those who accept premarital relations only when the couple evidence mutual love and affection. The third line would include those who accept sex before marriage with no qualifications other than that of mutual consent.

---

[11] Princeton, New Jersey, Gallup Poll release of August 12, 1973, p. 4.

[12] *Ibid.*

[13] Ira Reiss, *The Social Context of Premarital Sexual Permissiveness,* New York, Holt, Rinehart and Winston, 1967, pp. 165–167. Italics added.

Which view will become the *dominant* one, only time will tell. But today's college generation may eventually find itself in the position of playing a decisive role in the outcome.

SELECTED READINGS

Carns, Donald, "Talking About Sex: Notes on First Coitus and the Double Sexual Standard," *Journal of Marriage and the Family,* November, 1973, pp. 677–688.

Clayton, Richard, *The Family, Marriage, and Social Change,* Lexington, Massachusetts, D. C. Heath and Company, 1975.

DeLora, Jack R., and DeLora, Joann S., *Intimate Life Styles,* Pacific Palisades, California, Goodyear Publishing Company, 1975.

Edwards, John, and Booth, Alan, "Sexual Behavior In and Out of Marriage: An Assessment of Correlates," *Journal of Marriage and the Family,* February, 1976, pp. 73–81.

Eshleman, J. Ross, *The Family: An Introduction,* Boston, Allyn and Bacon, Inc., 1974.

Henze, Lura, and Hudson, John, "Personal and Family Characteristics of Cohabiting and Noncohabiting College Students," *Journal of Marriage and the Family,* November, 1974, pp. 722–727.

Hobart, Charles, "Sexual Permissiveness in Young English and French Canadians," *Journal of Marriage and the Family,* May, 1972, pp. 292–303.

Jedlicka, Davor, "Sequential Analysis of Perceived Commitment to Partners in Premarital Coitus," *Journal of Marriage and the Family,* May, 1975, pp. 385–390.

Kaats, Gilbert, and Davis, Keith, "The Dynamics of Sexual Behavior of College Students," *Journal of Marriage and the Family,* August, 1970, pp. 390–399.

Kirkendall, Lester, *Premarital Intercourse and Interpersonal Relationships,* New York, The Julian Press, 1961.

Luckey, Eleanor, and Nass, Gilbert, "A Comparison of Sexual Attitudes and Behavior in an International Sample," *Journal of Marriage and the Family,* May, 1969, pp. 364–379.

McCary, James L., *Freedom and Growth in Marriage,* Santa Barbara, California, Hamilton Publishing Company, 1975.

Macklin, Eleanor, "Heterosexual Cohabitation Among Unmarried College Students," *Family Coordinator,* October, 1972, pp. 463–472.

Miller, Beverly, "Rabbinical Attitudes Toward Premarital Sex," University of Pennsylvania, Sociology 4, unpublished paper (23 pp.), 1975.

318

Phillips, John, *Sex Education in Major Protestant Denominations,* New York, National Council of Churches, 1969.

Reiss, Ira, *The Social Context of Premarital Sexual Permissiveness,* New York, Holt, Rinehart and Winston, 1967.

———, "Premarital Sex as Deviant Behavior: An Application of Current Approaches to Deviance," *American Sociological Review,* February, 1970, pp. 78–87.

Robinson, Ira; King, Karl; and Balswick, Jack, "The Premarital Sexual Revolution Among College Females," *Family Coordinator,* April, 1972, pp. 189–194.

Schultz, David A., and Rodgers, Stanley F., *Marriage, the Family, and Personal Fulfillment,* Englewood Cliffs, New Jersey, Prentice-Hall, Inc., 1975.

Seward, Georgene, and Williamson, Robert C. (eds.), *Sex Roles in Changing Society,* New York, Random House, Inc., 1970.

Smigel, Erwin, and Seiden, Rita, "The Decline and Fall of the Double Standard," *Annals of the American Academy of Political and Social Science,* March, 1968, pp. 6–17.

Spanier, Graham B., "Sexualization and Premarital Sexual Behavior," *Family Coordinator,* January, 1975, pp. 33–41.

Tavuchis, Nicholas, and Goode, William J., *The Family Through Literature,* New York, McGraw-Hill Book Company, 1975.

Teevan, James, "Reference Groups and Premarital Sexual Behavior," *Journal of Marriage and the Family,* May, 1972, pp. 283–291.

Thomas, John, *Looking Toward Marriage,* Notre Dame, Indiana, Fides Publishing, Inc., 1966. See Chapter Nine, "Of Men and Women," pp. 153–178.

Udry, J. Richard, *The Social Context of Marriage,* Philadelphia, J. B. Lippincott Company, 1974.

———; Bauman, Karl; and Morris, Naomi, "Changes in Premarital Coital Experience of Recent Decade-of-Birth Cohorts of Urban American Women," *Journal of Marriage and the Family,* November, 1975, pp. 783–787.

Vener, Arthur, and Stewart, Cyrus, "Adolescent Sexual Behavior in Middle America Revisited," *Journal of Marriage and the Family,* November, 1974, pp. 728–735.

Wells, J. Gipson, *Current Issues in Marriage and the Family,* New York, Macmillan Publishing Co., Inc., 1975.

Zelnik, Melvin, and Kantner, John, "The Probability of Premarital Intercourse," *Social Science Research,* September, 1972, pp. 335–341.

———, "The Resolution of Teenage First Pregnancies," *Family Planning Perspectives,* Spring, 1974, pp. 74–80.

15

Socio-Legal Aspects of Marriage

320

IN THE NOT-TOO-DISTANT past, marriage was considered a private affair, arrangements being made between the families of the participants. In some primitive groups this concept is still recognized. Among civilized societies, however, it has become increasingly apparent that the state must take an active part in the regulation of matrimony. However much these regulations would seem to impinge on the rights of the participants, it is clear that society cannot adopt a laissez faire attitude toward the institution of marriage. There is too much at stake.

In modern society, where property rights and inheritance are so important, formal regulation of marriage becomes a necessity. The state is also charged with the prevention of bigamy and incest, acts that might disrupt the entire marital system if allowed to go unchecked. Additionally, the state is concerned with prohibiting child marriages, with regulating licensing procedures, with spelling out the grounds for divorce and annulment, and so on. Historically speaking, therefore, it was inevitable that the private system of marriage give way to one of public regulation.

As one sociologist put it:

> We want dependability and predictability of conduct. Such being the case, our marriage regulations do not seem excessive; on the contrary, they appear very few in number and relatively mild in form. The individual yields his privilege of acting impulsively on matters important to the group, thus relinquishing a measure of personal freedom but getting in return a compensating measure of personal security and social stability. A few may not be happy to make the trade, but it must be made nevertheless; for the group believes its welfare is at stake, and in the long run a clash between the individual will and group will can end in only one way—the group's way.[1]

[1] Ray Baber, *Marriage and the Family*, New York, McGraw-Hill Book Company, 1963, p. 49.

The present chapter will aim at presenting some of the more important legal regulations of marriage, together with a sociological interpretation of these regulations, as they affect both the individual and society.

VOID VERSUS VOIDABLE MARRIAGE

Whereas the state regulates marriage by setting up statutory provisions, the interpretation and enforcement of these provisions raise some ticklish problems, one of which involves the distinction between void and voidable marriages. Some marriages are void from the moment they are entered into, and neither the wishes of the participants nor the fact of living together can change the situation. Other marriages, despite the fact that they were entered into illegally, are allowable; they are voidable—that is, they may be invalidated by court action—but, until and unless the court so decrees, these marriages are legal and binding.

Let us look at some fictitious illustrations. Arthur, a traveling salesman, has been married for several years. Unable to get along with his wife, he asks for a divorce. His wife refuses. Arthur packs his belongings, leaves the city, and marries a girl whom he had met in the course of his travels. The second marriage, of course, is bigamous and, as such, is void. In many states it is not even necessary to go to court to have the action invalidated, since in the eyes of the law there never was any marriage. The fact that Arthur and his new "wife" have lived together and consider themselves married has no bearing on the case. The second marriage was void from its inception. The parties thereto are criminally liable. And the children, should there be any, can be declared illegitimate.

Tom and Pauline have had several dates. Pauline fancies herself in love with Tom, and although he is not in love with her, he acts as though he were. Some time later, she discovers that she is pregnant and righteously demands that Tom marry her. He refuses. Pauline's father brings pressure to bear, of the so-called shotgun variety, whereupon Tom decides to marry the girl. This marriage is not void, though it is certainly voidable. If he takes the case to court, the chances are—on the basis of the evidence as stated—that the court will grant an annulment. If the case is not taken to court, however, the marriage is legitimate. Note, also, that if Tom had merely succumbed to *verbal* pressure on the part of the girl or her relatives, it is doubtful whether most courts would grant an annulment. In such cases, the sympathies of the court favor the girl.

Fraud. Voidable marriages are those involving fraud or misrepresentation of some kind. The catch is that not all fraudulent marriages are voidable, as the following case illustrates. Susan and Ralph have been going steady for some time, and while Ralph is somewhat reluctant, Susan is eager to get married. In due course, they commence to have premarital sex relations. A few months later Susan announces that she is pregnant and tearfully asks Ralph to marry her. He reluctantly agrees. Time proves, however, that Susan is not pregnant, and upon questioning she admits her deceit. In such instances, many courts have refused to grant an annulment. Their reasoning is, apparently, that while fraud is evident, it is not blatant enough—in view of the male's willingness to engage in premarital coitus—to relieve him of his marital obligation.

322

On the other hand, let us suppose that Martha and Bob are going steady and plan to marry. Bob has normal sex desires, but Martha is inclined to look upon all sexual matters with disgust, a fact she carefully hides from her fiancé. She is highly desirous of marriage but has no intention of permitting sexual intercourse. After the wedding, Bob discovers to his sorrow that he is married to a frigid woman. Amatory attempts to no avail, he goes to court in an effort to have the marriage annulled. In such cases, the courts are inclined to side with the male. Unless there is a prior agreement to the contrary, the marriage contract is held to imply normal sex relations, and failure to live up to these contractual implications on the part of either spouse is generally sufficient grounds for annulment.

Sociological Significance of Void Versus Voidable Marriage. It can be seen that there is a clear-cut difference between marriages that are void (as in the instance of a bigamous relationship) and those that are merely voidable (as in the above case of sexual fraud). In the event of a void marriage, there is likely to be a blanket rule over which neither the participants nor the court have much control. In the case of voidable marriages, on the other hand, the outcome is by no means inevitable. Whether a particular marriage is terminated may depend on the wishes of the spouses or on a ruling of the court. The question arises, then, why there should be a difference between the two. Why is the void marriage so inflexibly "wrong," while the voidable marriage may or may not be held invalid?

The answer hinges on who is being hurt, the individual or society. Generally speaking, if the overall societal interest is at stake, the illegal marriage is held to be void. If the illicit marriage victimizes one of the participants, the matrimonial venture is merely voidable. In the case of bigamy, for example, it is clear that the societal rather than the individual interest is at stake. Society must wield an iron hand in this instance since, if the practice of bigamy were to get out of hand, the entire marriage system would be in jeopardy. Marriages involving fraud, on the other hand, such as a false claim of pregnancy, do not threaten the societal interest; hence the legal flexibility that has developed.

Admittedly the distinction between the individual and societal interest is sometimes a matter of opinion, and this point has been reflected in the varying state laws. Also, by the very nature of the distinction between void and voidable marriages, we should expect to find comparatively few grounds for the former, and such is the actual case. There are any number of ways in which the individual participants to a marriage may be aggrieved through fraud, but society considers its interests threatened only in the case of marriage between close relatives, bigamy, and other "gross impediments."

323

CONSANGUINITY

Consanguinity refers simply to blood relationship and should not be confused with the term *incest*, which refers to sexual intercourse between close relatives as defined by law. The reason the two terms are sometimes confused is that the law prohibits both the marriage of close relatives and coital activity among relatives.

The various state laws are fairly uniform regarding the prohibition of marriages among immediate family members. All states prohibit the marriage of mother and son, father and daughter, brother and sister, grandmother and grandson, grandfather and granddaughter, aunt and nephew, uncle and niece. In addition, more than half of our states prohibit the marriage of first cousins. Some states also forbid the marriage of second cousins, as well as marriage to a grandniece or grandnephew.

More than half of the states prohibit marriage to a half brother or half sister, and in some states this prohibition extends to half cousins, half nieces, and half nephews. As a matter of fact, although such laws fall under the heading of *consanguinity,* approximately half of the states have marital restrictions pertaining to *affinity,* a term used to denote a relationship through marriage, as distinguished from a blood tie. For example, many states prohibit marriage between stepparents and stepchildren, between mother and son-in-law or father and daughter-in-law, and between a woman and her husband's father or grandfather (or between a man and his wife's mother or grandmother).

The laws prohibiting marriage to a close relative—mother, father, brother, sister—are clear enough in design. The state is desirous of perpetuating the conjugal system of marriage and will not brook any interference. When the prohibition is extended to include first and second cousins, half nieces and half nephews, some writers are of the opinion that the law is carrying things too far. And when the prohibitions relate to affinity—stepparents and stepchildren, for instance—a number of critics are of the belief that the law has gone completely overboard. They fail to see any purpose in a state law that prohibits the marriage of a man to his son's widow, or of a woman to her deceased daughter's husband, or of a person to an aunt or uncle by marriage. It is argued that such situations seldom arise and that, when they do, no significant harm can result from an impending marriage.

It must be realized, however, that incest and consanguineous marriages are of vital concern to society. Prohibition, in this respect, is not something to be taken lightly. Laws pertaining to consanguinity are designed not only to prohibit marriage between close relatives, but *to prevent or discourage familial jealousies.* An older husband, for example, is put on notice that his stepdaughter's amative charms can never—legally—displace those of his own wife. And while such situations are not common, they arise more often than most people realize, as court officials and lawyers can attest.

No matter how one argues the merits of the various state laws, however, some of the differences between states are remarkable. States such as Connecticut, Michigan, North Carolina, and Oregon simply declare that "relatives nearer than first cousins may not marry." Maryland, Massachusetts, Rhode Island, West Virginia, and Washington, D.C., on the other hand, employ a much more complicated phraseology. To illustrate, the law of Washington, D.C., prohibits the marriage of a man to his grandmother, grandfather's wife, wife's grandmother, aunt, mother, stepmother, wife's mother, daughter, wife's daughter, son's wife, sister, granddaughter, wife's son's daughter, son's son's wife, daughter's son's wife, wife's daughter's daughter, and niece.[2]

---

[2] Readers interested in specific laws pertaining to marriage and divorce should consult the statutes of their own states, inasmuch as the laws are subject to change. For a general treatment of the subject, see the *Legal Almanac Series* of Oceana Publications, Dobbs Ferry, N.Y.; the yearly *World Almanac and Book of*

MISCEGENATION

Miscegenation (from the Latin *miscere,* to mix, and *genus,* race) refers to sex relations or interbreeding between races, although the term is more commonly used to denote interracial marriage. At one time, more than 40 states had laws prohibiting the marriage of whites and nonwhites; in fact, as late as the mid-1960's miscegenation laws were still in effect in some 20 states. Categorical prohibitions varied from state to state, and at one time or another there were laws forbidding the marriage of whites with Negroes, mulattoes, persons of African descent, nonwhites, Mongolians, American Indians, half-breeds, Malayans, Hindus, Chinese, Japanese, or—as it was expressed in some statutes—"people of color."

In many of the states having miscegenation laws the marriage of a white and nonwhite was considered void rather than merely voidable. As time went on, however, most states repealed their miscegenation laws, so that persons who wished to marry across racial lines could usually do so; i.e., if their home state did not permit such marriages, the couple could simply move to a state that did.

But whereas the first miscegenation law in colonial America was enacted in 1661, it was more than 300 years later that the United States Supreme Court consented to rule on the issue. On June 12, 1967, the Court swept away all legal barriers to intermarriage. In a unanimous decision, the Supreme Court asserted that: "Under our Constitution, the freedom to marry or not to marry a person of another race resides with the individual and cannot be infringed by the state."

325

THE LEGAL AGE OF MARRIAGE

In the Judeo-Christian heritage, early marriage was the rule rather than the exception. According to Talmudic law, the permissible ages coincided with puberty—12 for the female and 13 for the male. Under the agricultural system that prevailed, youthful marriages worked no great hardship, either on the participants or on the group as a whole. In modern society, obviously, the age at marriage must be considered in a different light. Children of 12 and 13 are considered to be—children. The

Facts, Newspaper Enterprise Association, Inc., New York City; and "There Ought to be a Law" section of *The Family Coordinator* (a publication of the National Council on Family Relations). See also the *Family Law Quarterly,* published by the American Bar Association, Section of Family Law.

idea of permitting such youngsters to marry would strike most of us as wrong. Our culture emphasizes such things as emotional maturity, education, and wage-earning ability, and it is felt that marriage should not be undertaken until family responsibilities can be met. In short, there is little question that our society must regulate the age at which individuals may marry.

The "Four Ages." The Constitution left the regulation of marriage and divorce to the individual states, hence it is not surprising to find considerable difference in the various age laws. Insofar as the statutes are concerned, the legal age of marriage in the United States actually ranges from 13 to 21. This range includes four classifications: (1) the age at which a boy may marry provided he has parental consent; (2) the age at which a girl may marry provided she has parental consent; (3) the age at which a boy may marry without parental consent; and (4) the age at which a girl may marry without parental consent. In New York State, for example, the four ages are:

	Without Parental Consent	With Parental Consent
Male	21	16
Female	18	14

In California, the corresponding age requirements are:

Male	18	18
Female	18	16

The most common age with consent is 18 for the male and 16 for the female, while the age without consent is generally 21 for the male and 18 for the female. There is considerable variation, however, and in New Hampshire it is still possible for a 13-year-old girl to marry, provided she has the necessary consent. In Montana, on the other hand, both parties must be 19 even though they have parental consent.

It is also possible, in a number of states, for a couple to be allowed to marry even though one or both of the individuals are below the minimum age. This comes about when the girl is pregnant or has borne a child by the husband-to-be. In such cases, a judge or other authorized official may waive the age requirements.

An interesting sociological question has been raised apropos of the age factor; namely, is the minimal legal age for marriage generally too low in the United States? Almost all the states permit a 16-year-old girl to marry, and more than a dozen states grant the same right to a 16-year-old boy. An additional dozen states will permit 14- and 15-year-olds to marry.

At first glance, these age minimums do seem rather low. It should be remembered, however, that these ages require parental consent, and that many youths in this age bracket are equipped for marriage *as judged by the standards of the group in which they live.*

Our society, like others, encourages marriage. The purpose of our laws is not to discourage matrimony but to regulate it in such a way as to minimize irresponsibility. The fact of the matter is that youthful marriages are anything but a rarity; indeed, there are millions of women in the United States who were between 14 and 16 when they married. Were the minimum-age requirements to be raised, it is difficult to see what overall purpose would be served; in fact, it is questionable whether such laws would be enforceable.*

On the whole, we seem to be in an era of rather early marriage. Young people are maturing more quickly nowadays, and many of them are desirous of early matrimony. And while the research evidence does indicate that very early marriages have less chance of success than later-age ventures, it is doubtful whether the advantages to be gained from raising the minimal age would outweigh the disadvantages. If there is a solution to the problem of early marriage, it would seem to lie in the educational rather than in the legal sphere.

The Penalties. One of the arguments against a general raising of the legal marriage age pertains to the matter of enforcement. As court officers are well aware, enforcement of the present age requirements—low as they may seem—is no easy matter; in fact, there is some question as to how meaningful our current laws really are. A couple who are underage in their home state can journey to a nearby state having lower age requirements, get married, and return home with legal impunity. Their marriage is a valid one and normally will not be annulled.

Common belief has it that underage marriages can, through court action, be annulled by the parents, but such annulments are the exception rather than the rule. To illustrate: in Tennessee the legal age of marriage without parental consent is 21. Betty and John, residents of the state, are each 18 years of age. They desire to marry but cannot secure parental approval. They cross the state line to North Carolina—where the age without consent is

---

* In any number of countries the minimal age of marriage is 14 for the male and 12 for the female. In other countries the minimal age requirement is listed simply as the "age of puberty." In still other countries there is no prescribed minimum age for marriage.

18—get married, and return home. Does this procedure constitute a legal marriage? The answer is yes. They are husband and wife, and there isn't much the parents or anybody else can do about getting the marriage annulled.

As a matter of fact, Betty and John would not necessarily have had to leave the state of Tennessee to marry. Conceivably, they might have falsified their age, and if the local official had issued the license without checking their birth records, they could have been married in Tennessee. And, again, it is unlikely that the court would grant an annulment or that Betty and John would be legally punished in any way. Generally speaking, such marriages are neither void nor voidable.

If underage marriages are generally not voidable, and if the courts make no effort to penalize the participants, what, then, is the purpose of the age laws? Actually, these statutes are not so ineffective as they seem. In the first place, while the couple are not penalized, the licensing officials may be punished for their failure to verify or investigate the facts. In some states the penalty may include the person performing the ceremony. Secondly, age laws are effective for those who marry under the *minimum legal age*. Had Betty and John been 15 years of age, for example, there would have been little difficulty in getting the court to declare an annulment, since the minimal age (age with parental consent) in North Carolina is 16 for both sexes.

Finally, of course, it is to be presumed that the age laws are effective in that most people obey them. While it is known that a considerable number of underage marriages do occur by one method or another, most young people are law-abiding citizens, and rather than leave their home state or lie about their age, they are willing to wait until their marriage can be consummated without the shadow of illegality.

Our age laws leave something to be desired, and from time to time critics have voiced some reasonable proposals. In view of the various state laws and differing court interpretations, the age factor will continue to present problems. Nevertheless, the law cannot be blamed for all the difficulties. Under the best of laws, lackadaisical officials can make a farce of the age requirements. Conscientious officials can do a good deal to implement existing laws.

PROCEDURAL ASPECTS OF MARRIAGE

While the marriage procedure varies somewhat from state to state, there are certain legal requirements that generally must be met. These include procurement of the marriage license and the recording of the marriage certificate, as well as the physical examination, waiting period, and marriage ceremony.

Licensing and Recording.   Although marriage is a contract, it differs in many ways from an ordinary civil contract. A regular contract can be modified or broken by mutual consent. This is not true of marriage. A civil contract can be drawn for two parties irrespective of their marital status and blood relationship, but, as we have seen, this is not necessarily true of the marriage contract. In brief, a civil contract is a *private* contract between the two parties involved, whereas the marriage contract involves the state as well. It is evident, therefore, that the state must have an administrative procedure to insure that the designated marital requirements are being met. And the most practicable method of handling the situation is through a licensing system.

The marriage license is the cornerstone of the system and as such it serves three vital functions: (1) it serves as written proof to state officials that all legal requirements have been met; (2) for

The marriage license not only is an integral part of the national vital statistics program, but also provides both partners with a legal proof of marriage. (Daniel S. Brody, Stock Boston)

the two parties involved, the completed marriage certificate serves as legal proof of matrimony, which is often necessary in terms of inheritance, social security, or insurance rights; and (3) it provides the nation at large with a potentially rich source of statistical information about marriage.

Marriage licenses are issued by the county marriage license bureaus of the various states, to both residents and nonresidents. Once issued, the form must be used *within* the state *within* a certain period of time. Note that the issuance of a license does not signify that the couple are married. The license must be taken to a person authorized to perform the ceremony (a clergyman or a civil official). After the ceremony is over and the officiant has signed the marriage license, the license becomes a marriage certificate and represents legal evidence that the couple are married.

330

Although details vary from one state to the next, the central feature is that the marriage certificate is kept by the couple, with a duplicate being mailed back (by the officiant) to the local office of issuance. The local office forwards an abstract to the state Vital Statistics System. While a few states do not maintain central files of marriage records, most of the others forward data to the National Vital Statistics System (NVSS) in Washington, D.C. It is from NVSS that we get the publications containing national marriage (and divorce) information.

Physical Examination. In 1913 Wisconsin passed the first law requiring (for males only) a premarital examination for venereal disease. It was not until the 1930's that other states began to adopt similar legislation, and it was only after World War II that the idea of premarital blood tests for both sexes became widespread. Today, the large majority of states have a blood test provision. The usual requirement is for the couple to furnish a medical certificate attesting to the fact that neither party has syphilis, or that the disease is not in communicable form. Without the medical certification, a marriage license will not be issued. Predictably, there is a good deal of variation among the states.

In a few jurisdictions, an affidavit is all that is required. In a few others, the law requires a blood test for both parties, but, if syphilis is discovered, the marriage license will be issued anyway! (All that is required is that the couple be informed of the presence of the disease.) And, of course, thousands of individuals continue to get married every year without a blood test or certification of any kind simply because their home state or jurisdiction (Maryland, Minnesota, Washington, Nevada, South Carolina, and the Virgin Islands) lacks such a requirement.

Even in those states requiring the standard blood test, there are legal ways of getting around the provision. Several states have laws permitting the serological test to be waived for "good cause," e.g., in the case where the prospective wife is pregnant or has already borne a child by the husband-to-be. Blood tests may be waived for members of the armed forces, where time and distance often present a problem. Also, the blood test can be legally avoided simply by going to a state that has no such requirement. Common-law marriage represents still another method of evading the blood test provision. In fact, should the marriage license—through some clerical negligence—be issued without the necessary medical certification, the ensuing marriage would still be a valid one.

In addition to the blood test requirement, a number of states have other medical prohibitions. A few states prohibit individuals with infectious tuberculosis from marrying. Under Pennsylvania law, no one may marry who has a communicable disease. Mental defectives, epileptics, psychotics—even alcoholics—are prohibited from marrying in some states, and all jurisdictions have legal provisions for annulling a marriage in which one of the parties was mentally incapable of "understanding" at the time the marriage was performed.

Waiting Period. It used to be that, if a boy and a girl decided on the spur of the moment to get married, all they had to do was to procure a license and get an authorized officiant to perform the ceremony. The couple could be on their honeymoon in a matter of hours. In recent periods, however, the law has made it harder and harder for these "quickie" marriages to be undertaken. For one thing, the blood test itself may take time, and this serves as a brake on hasty marriages. Also, more and more states have instituted a waiting period between the time of application and the actual issuance of the license.

The required waiting period varies from one to five days, although most jurisdictions have settled on a three-day rule. A few states have stricter waiting requirements for nonresidents than for residents. Delaware, for instance, requires a one-day waiting period for residents and a four-day period for nonresidents. About a dozen states have no waiting period at all, and in the others it is possible to procure waivers for the same emergency situations that apply in the case of the blood test.

The aim of the waiting period is to prevent spur-of-the-moment, ill-advised marriages, although just how effective the requirement is can be debated. It is true that a number of

332

(Cary S. Wolinsky, Stock Boston)

marriage license applicants never return, after the waiting period, to pick up their licenses. In fact, some couples, upon discovering the waiting-period requirement, leave the marriage license bureau without even bothering to fill out the application form!

On the other hand, a determined couple can usually find a reasonably quick way of getting married. Nevada, for example, has the dubious distinction of requiring neither a blood test nor a waiting period. Also, in some of the states with a blood test requirement but no waiting period, the serological examination is completed in jig time. The fact that so many of our states recognize common-law marriage acts as a further aid to those couples who, for reasons of their own, desire to short-cut the usual matrimonial procedures.

The Marriage Ceremony. There is very little regulation of the marriage ceremony itself. In most states either civil or religious officiants may preside, although Delaware still requires the marriage to be solemnized by a clergyman—a carry-over from the colonial South, when matrimony was considered a religious rather than a civil affair.*

All states provide that any ordained clergyman, regardless of faith or sect, may perform the ceremony, although a few states require clergymen to be registered or licensed before they can officiate. In most states, authorized officials would include judges, mayors, recorders, justices of the peace, magistrates, and—in some jurisdictions—even notaries. Most Americans prefer a religious ceremony, NVSS figures indicating that four out of five marriages are presided over by a clergyman. Some civil officiants, however, do a staggering amount of business.

The states generally make no attempt to regulate the specific form of the ceremony or the actual words that must be spoken by the officiant. The details of the marriage ceremony are considered to be a private matter. So long as the two parties mutually and solemnly affirm that they take each other as husband and wife, and so long as the declaration is made before an authorized officiant and in the presence of witnesses, the ceremony is valid and the marriage legal.

GRETNA GREEN MARRIAGE

The term "Gretna Green" derives from the name of a well-known town in Scotland, just across the border from England. In the days of Queen Victoria, young couples who were determined to marry in spite of parental objection often traveled to Gretna Green, where, because of the lax Scottish laws, marriage could be accomplished in a matter of hours, with no questions asked.

---

* And even Delaware permits one secular exception: the Mayor of Wilmington is authorized to perform the marriage ceremony. West Virginia requires the marriage to be solemnized by a clergyman, although "judges of a court of record" may also serve as officiants.

Weddings in establishments providing easy access to marriage ceremonies may lack some of the solemnity of those performed in more traditional surroundings. (Donald Dietz, Dietz-Hamlin)

There was no waiting period, and, since the couple had only to take the marriage vows in front of two witnesses (a clergyman was not required), the popularity of Gretna Green was assured. While the enactment in 1876 of a 21-day waiting period resulted in a curtailment of the marriage trade, the town's reputation has endured, and the term "Gretna Green" is still used to refer to a marriage-market town or marriage mill.

Because of our different state laws, it was almost inevitable that marriage mills would spring up, and over the years scores of Gretna Greens have flourished in various parts of the United States. Reno and Las Vegas, in Nevada, and Elkton, Maryland, have been targets of nationwide publicity and have become veritable symbols of the "quickie" marriage. In fact, in its heyday some 25,000 marriages a year were being performed in Elkton, a figure more than three times the town's population!

The attractions of a Gretna Green are obvious—no waiting period, minimal age requirements, no blood test, "round-the-clock service," and so on. Surprisingly enough, some couples are attracted to a Gretna Green because of the so-called glamour involved. Older couples, who have no special desire to evade the age, blood test, or waiting-period requirements, sometimes elope to a Gretna Green for no apparent reason other than the offbeat measures involved in such a marriage. For example, despite the fact that the introduction of a waiting period and other requirements have eliminated most of the matrimonial reasons for journeying to Elkton, the town still averages some 6,500 marriages a year!

The question has often been raised: "Why aren't the various Gretna Greens eliminated altogether?" The fact is that, because of tighter laws, many of them have been put out of business. Others continue to flourish, however, for elimination has been a piecemeal process. Las Vegas, for instance, averages more than 50,000 marriages a year! Few sociologists would question the desirability of doing away with marriage mills, but, in view of the constitutional rights accorded the individual states, the specific method of elimination is subject to much debate. This debate will be the topic of the concluding section.

COMMON-LAW MARRIAGE

Thus far, the term "marriage" has denoted mutual consent, licensing, and a ceremony that duly solemnizes the matrimonial union. This is the only type of marriage that most of us are familiar with. But there is another variety—common-law marriage —that rests almost solely upon the consent of the two parties. A valid common-law marriage requires neither license nor ceremony, blood test nor witnesses. If an unmarried couple are of age and are not too closely related, all that is necessary for a common-law marriage to take place is a private agreement. The agreement may take place anywhere—in an automobile, at a baseball game, or in the aftermath of a New Year's Eve party!

The surprising thing is not only that such marriages occur, but that they are recognized as valid in so many jurisdictions. The following states and territories permit common-law marriage:

Alabama	Kansas	Rhode Island
Colorado	Montana	South Carolina
Georgia	Ohio	Texas
Idaho	Oklahoma	Washington, D.C.
Iowa	Pennsylvania	Virgin Islands

A dozen or so additional states will recognize the validity of a common-law marriage if it was entered into prior to a certain date (the date on which the statute was enacted outlawing all *subsequent* common-law unions). And even those states that specifically prohibit common-law marriages will recognize them if they were valid in the state where they were contracted.

While many courts have insisted that the couple live as husband and wife in the eyes of the community before a common-law marriage is recognized, the basic prerequisite continues to be that of mutual consent. In essence, the couple "must accept one another as husband and wife as of this moment." In a legal sense, it is almost as if the right hand of the state were in opposition to what the left hand is doing. That is to say, through its statutory provisions the state says: "You must take a physical examination. You must procure a marriage license. And you must have the license validated by a duly authorized officiant in front of witnesses."

But the same state also says: "You really need not comply with any of these provisions. So long as you take one another, in the present tense, as husband and wife, we will consider you to be validly married."

Why, asks the mystified reader, do such marriages continue to be recognized? Why, in fact, were they ever recognized in the first place?

The unfortunate fact is that common-law marriage has both legal and religious roots. As was pointed out in an earlier chapter, it was customary among ancient peoples, such as the Hebrews and Romans, to permit marriage at the age of puberty: 12 for the girl, and 13 or 14 for the boy. And since marriage in those days was a private affair, under the control of neither church nor state, little more was required than a spoken pledge of matrimony on the part of the individuals involved.

During the Middle Ages, self-marriages were rather common. The Christian Church recognized these nonsolemnized marriages, even though the ceremonial form was preferred. It was not until 1563, at the Council of Trent, that the Church ruled that the marriage ceremony must henceforth be performed by a priest in the presence of witnesses. Thereafter, in Roman Catholic countries, common-law marriages were abolished; in Protestant countries, they continued.

When the colonists settled in America, common-law marriage was accorded legal recognition, a decision that could be defended on grounds of expediency. Under pioneer—and later under frontier—conditions, it was frequently impractical and sometimes impossible to hold a ceremonial wedding. Settlers often lived far from a religious or civil officiant—and even farther from a marriage license office. Rather than postpone marriage and rather than "live in sin," with the possible stigma of illegitimate children, common-law unions were sometimes resorted to. As thus practiced, such marriages filled both an individual and a societal need.

But, while tradition often embodies a cumulative wisdom and thus serves as a binding force between generations, custom per se cannot turn wrong into right. The fact of the matter is that common-law marriage has long since outlived its usefulness. It has no place in modern society and should have been abolished in the United States long ago, for the following reasons:

1. So long as the licensing procedure is permitted to be bypassed, society loses much of its control over specific marital prohibitons. State legislatures have prescribed laws that spell out in detail marriage qualifications. Included in these laws are specific provisions about blood tests, communicable diseases, and other physical and mental prerequisites. In this sense, recognition of common-law marriage is little more than a blanket invitation to unregulated matrimony, extended to those who do not measure up to the rules laid down by the group.

2. One of the functions of a licensed, ceremonial marriage is to provide both the participants and society with an authorized record of the event, so that in questions pertaining to property rights, inheritance, and so forth, the courts have a recognized basis for making equitable decisions. Common-law marriages—devoid as they often are of documentary proof—tend to snarl the machinery of the courts. This is especially true in decisions involving inheritance rights, one of the best-known

examples being that of Abe Erlanger, the multimillionaire theatrical king. After his death, it took several months of hearings—including 149 witnesses, 834 exhibits, and some 7,000 pages of testimony—before the court ruled that the woman Erlanger had been living with (sans marriage certificate) was his wife and not his mistress. It is probably no coincidence that, at its next meeting, the New York State legislature promptly abolished common-law marriage.

In contrast to the foregoing case, there have been innumerable instances where common-law widows, unable to establish the fact, have been deprived of property, social security benefits, insurance payments, and other inheritance rights. Indeed, one might wonder why so many women jeopardize their legal position by entering into marriages of the common-law variety.

3. Finally, our licensing and recording procedures enable us to compile valuable statistical information regarding marriage and divorce in the United States. The prevalence of common-law marriage upsets—to an unknown degree—all of the available figures, since a nonlicensed marriage is neither recorded nor reported.

Both from an individual and a societal viewpoint, there can be little doubt that common-law marriage is a social evil. It is difficult to think of any benefit that is gained by the continued recognition of such marriages. Even the so-called legitimatizing of children—which is sometimes held up as a reason—is questionable, in view of the fact that the court must first establish the authenticity of the alleged marriage. In due time, perhaps, such marriages will be outlawed by all the states. Lawyers and bar association groups have been advocating such a measure for many years, and social reformers continue to predict that it is just a matter of time. Unfortunately, marriage laws are not noted for their speed of change.

THE POSSIBILITY OF UNIFORM MARRIAGE REQUIREMENTS

Aside from the specific legal and procedural deficiencies noted in the foregoing pages, there remains the important question of uniform marriage legislation. So long as the various states go their own ways and enact their own marriage laws, and so long as one state generally recognizes as valid a marriage performed in another state, the conditions are ripe for marrying couples to circumvent the law. And, of course, this is exactly what has been happening.

The sad fact of the matter is that under existing procedures a handful of states can spoil it for the rest. Conceivably, 49 states might adopt a reasonably strict marriage code, with requirements for waiting period, physical examination, marriage license, and so on, and yet one state that had lax marriage laws or permitted common-law marriage could go a long way toward neutralizing the efforts of the other 49. The answer to the problem has puzzled both legislator and social scientist; indeed, no real solution has yet been found.

One possibility is the adoption of a federal marriage and divorce law. Theoretically, this is perhaps the most effective remedy, for a federal law would preclude the possibility of a few holdout states neutralizing the efforts of the others. A national marriage and divorce law—with a provision outlawing common-law marriage—would virtually eliminate the confusion and evasion that now occur. Also, a federal law would reduce the number of court cases, thus saving the taxpayer money. And finally, such a law would help provide improved statistical information—information that is sorely needed for a better understanding of the very factors that make for marital adjustment and maladjustment.

Unfortunately, the objections to a federal law are also rather telling. For one thing, such a law is probably unconstitutional and would call for an amendment authorizing Congress to regulate marriage and divorce. A proposed amendment has been introduced in the Senate on several occasions, but support has been negligible. A number of legislators have been of the opinion that states' rights should be upheld as a matter of principle, and that a national law on marriage and divorce would be a step in the wrong direction. Also, there is no gainsaying the fact that the specific provisions of a federal law might run counter to the customs of a particular region or locale. For these and other reasons the enactment of national legislation on marriage and divorce seems a rather remote prospect.

Another possibility would be to establish a so-called model act, such as was done in the case of juvenile delinquency. In the latter instance, interested lawyers and criminologists fashioned a model act, with the expectation that the various states, in enacting legislation, would pattern their law along the lines of the model act. Unfortunately, minimal progress has been made in the area of marriage legislation.

One difficulty with the model act approach has been the relative indifference shown by so many social scientists. As a consequence, the various commissions that have been set up to formulate a model act have been dominated by lawyers—with less than satisfactory results. Legal practitioners, understandably, have limited understanding of the various sociological problems involved in marriage and divorce. As Thomas Monahan—one of the few sociological activists—puts it:

> Lawyers should not be given exclusive priority in designing our marriage and divorce laws. Also, it should be realized that sound law should rest on sound facts, and adequate provision should be made for the collection of statistics on marriage, divorce, desertion, and other family matters, without invasion of anyone's privacy.[3]

It is the present writer's opinion that, in spite of many obstacles, a model act approach offers the most realistic solution to the problem. If correctly formulated—and adopted—a model act would do much to bring uniformity to our marriage laws, thus reducing the evasive actions that are now so prevalent. One can only hope that, as time goes on, more social scientists will interest themselves in the problem.

Meanwhile, the present jumble of marriage laws will probably continue. For it is not only the social scientists who have evidenced a lack of concern, it is also the general public. It is not so much that the public thinks of the marriage and divorce situation as unimportant; the feeling seems to be, rather, that there are so many other things that are more important and that are in need of legislative attention.

SELECTED READINGS

Andrews, Ernest E., *The Emotionally Disturbed Family*, New York, Jason Aronson Book Publishers, 1974.

Berman, Claire, *We take This Child: A Candid Look at Modern Adoption*, Garden City, New York, Doubleday & Company, Inc., 1974.

Callahan, Parnell, *The Law of Separation and Divorce*, Dobbs Ferry, New York, Oceana Publications, Inc., 1970.

Chester, Robert, "Official Statistics and Family Sociology," *Journal of Marriage and the Family*, February, 1976, pp. 117–126.

Dubin, Murray, "Elkton Marriage Mill Grinds Slower," *Philadelphia Inquirer*, October 1, 1973.

---

[3] Thomas P. Monahan, "National Divorce Legislation: The Problem and Some Suggestions." *Family Coordinator*, July, 1973, p. 356.

Glendon, Mary Ann, "Is There a Future for Separate Property?" *Family Law Quarterly*, Fall, 1974, pp. 315–328.

Glick, Paul C., "A Demographer Looks at American Families," *Journal of Marriage and the Family*, February, 1975, pp. 15–26.

Goldstein, Joseph, and Katz, Jay, *The Family and the Law*, New York, Free Press of Glencoe, Inc., 1965.

Harper, Fowler V., and Skolnick, Jerome H., *Problems of the Family*, New York, The Bobbs-Merrill Company, Inc., 1962.

Hazard, G. C., "Interdisciplinary Courses in Law and Social Work," *Family Law Quarterly*, Winter, 1972, pp. 423–440.

Kuchler, Frances W., *Law of Engagement and Marriage*, Dobbs Ferry, New York, Oceana Publications, Inc., 1966.

Levy, Robert J., "Comments on the Legislative History of the Uniform Marriage and Divorce Act," *Family Law Quarterly*, Winter, 1973, pp. 405–412.

MacNamara, D. E., "Sex Offenses and Sex Offenders," *Annals of the American Academy of Political and Social Science*, March, 1968, pp. 148–155.

Monahan, Thomas P., "National Divorce Legislation: The Problem and Some Suggestions," *Family Coordinator*, July, 1973, pp. 353–357.

Nichols, William C. (ed.), *Marriage and Family Therapy*, Minneapolis, National Council on Family Relations, 1975.

Ploscowe, Morris, *Sex and the Law*, Englewood Cliffs, New Jersey, Prentice-Hall, Inc., 1951.

Polak, A. Laurence, "Family Law: A Doctrinaire or a Rationalistic Approach," *Family Law*, May–June, 1973, pp. 86–91.

Resnicoff, Samuel, *M.D.A.—Marriage, Divorce, Annulment*, New York, Pageant Press, Inc., 1968.

Rogers, W. Horton, "Sham Marriages," *Family Law*, January–February, 1974, pp. 4–7.

Rondell, Florence, and Murray, Anne-Marie, *New Dimensions in Adoption*, New York, Crown Publishers, 1975.

Schafrick, Frederick, "Protection of Putative Father's Parental Rights," *Family Law Quarterly*, Spring, 1973, pp. 75–111.

Schur, Edwin, *Law and Society: A Sociological View*, New York, Random House, Inc., 1968.

Sheehan, Thomas, "Selected Community Property Problems of the Migrant Spouse," *Family Law Quarterly*, Winter, 1973, pp. 433–451.

Sonne, John C., "On the Question of Compulsory Marriage Counseling as a Part of Divorce Proceedings," *Family Coordinator*, July, 1974, pp. 303–305.

Stotter, Lawrence, "A Proposal for a Family Law Self-

Assessment Program," *Family Law Newsletter,* Spring, 1974, pp. 1 ff.

Tully, Leo, "Family Responsibility Laws," *Family Law Quarterly,* December, 1971, pp. 32–62.

Weiner, Richard, "A Proposal for Individual Contracts and Contracts in Lieu of Marriage," *Family Law Commentator,* May–June, 1975, pp. 5–7.

Wells, J. Gipson, "A Critical Look at Personal Marriage Contracts," *Family Coordinator,* January, 1976, pp. 33–37.

342

IV

Marital Interaction

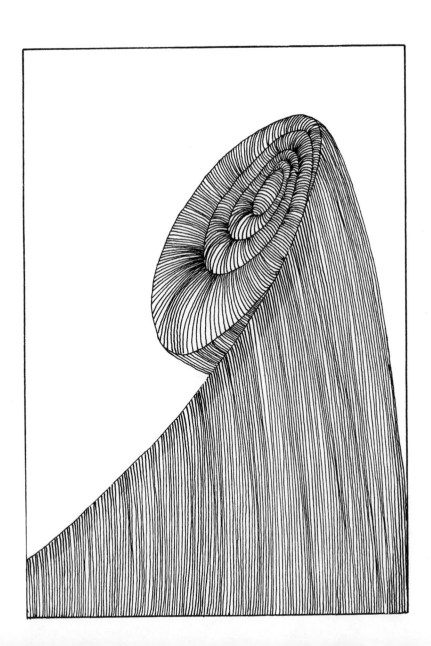

16

The Physiological Basis of Marriage

ALTHOUGH MOST FAMILY courses are taught by sociologists, the family itself has any number of dimensions, e.g., religious, historical, legal—and physiological. Ideally, it would be better if family sociologists restricted their teaching to the sociological aspects, leaving the historical parts to historians, the physiological areas to physiologists, and so on. Usually, however, there is but one course in the family available to undergraduates, and for this reason most family texts are necessarily eclectic in their approach. The present chapter, therefore, will be devoted to a generalized description of the physiological aspects of marriage. Such a chapter should fit the needs of most students taking the family course. As a minimum, students should know the names and functions of the various organs involved in sexual behavior and reproduction. It is hoped, also, that a knowledge of the genital differences between male and female will help the reader understand the problem of marital sex adjustment, discussed in the next chapter.

MALE SEXUAL ANATOMY

The genital and reproductive apparatus of the human male constitutes a centralized and highly dynamic sexual system. The system is also rather complex, and for present purposes it will be necessary to limit our discussion to the following organs: testes, vas deferens, prostate gland and seminal vesicles, epididymis, and penis.

The testes take their name from the Latin root of the word for "witness" or "testify," recalling an ancient custom whereby the man solemnly placed his hands on his genitals when taking an

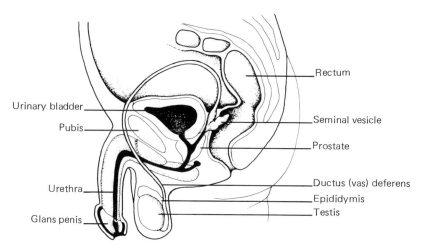

Urinary bladder —
Pubis —

Urethra —

Glans penis —

Rectum

Seminal vesicle

Prostate

Ductus (vas) deferens
Epididymis
Testis

346

The male reproductive system.

oath.[1] Also known as male gonads, or sex glands, the testes have a primary function of manufacturing sperm and a secondary function of secreting male sex hormones. Because abdominal temperature is too high to permit sperm manufacture, the testes are normally carried on the outside of the body, in a skin pouch called the scrotum. In about 85 percent of all males, the left testis is lower than the right.

Within the testes are hundreds of *seminiferous tubules*, the organs that actually produce the sperm. (The aggregate length of these tubules in both testes is about one mile!) Beginning at puberty, the tubules begin to manufacture immense quantities of *spermatozoa*, the structures that contain all the hereditary material—in the form of chromosomes and genes—that is transmissible to the offspring. The process of sperm manufacture (spermatogenesis) continues for many years, in some cases throughout the entire life span of the male; at least, there are authentic records of 80- and 90-year-old men who have become fathers. In most cases, however, sperm manufacture apparently slows down in later years, although not a great deal is known about this phase of human reproduction.

Scattered among the seminiferous tubules are groups of *interstitial cells*, which release the sex hormones—the androgens and the estrogens. These hormones are responsible for such secondary sex traits as pitch of voice, body and facial hair, and musculature. While both men and women produce both types of sex

[1] Herant Katchadourian, *Human Sexuality*, San Francisco, W. H. Freeman and Company, 1974, p. 2.

hormone, males produce a much greater quantity of androgen, females a much greater quantity of estrogen.

Along the side of each testis lies an *epididymis,* a coiled, tube-like organ that serves as the storage place for the ripened or nearly ripened spermatozoa. From the epididymis, spermatozoa pass into the *vas deferens,* a tube that carries the sperm to the penis, whence they are expelled through the urethra.

While most people are aware that the human sperm is an actively moving or motile organism, it is not so well known that, for all its whiplike capacity, the sperm is largely inactive until it mixes with the fluids secreted by the prostate glands and the seminal vesicles. It is the secretions from these glands, plus the spermatozoa, that make up the substance commonly referred to as seminal fluid, or semen.

The sudden physical release or expulsion of semen through the urethra is known as the male ejaculation, and the subjective sensation accompanying ejaculation is called orgasm. In the case of preadolescent males, orgasm may occur without ejaculation, a situation which also applies to adult males who are afflicted with ejaculatory impotence. So far as is known, however, no male can experience ejaculation without also experiencing orgasm.

It might also be mentioned that there is no necessary relationship between *virility* and *fertility,* even though these terms are sometimes used interchangeably. Fertility, in this connection, refers primarily to the male sperm count. Males with a deficient sperm count, of course, cannot become fathers. These same men, however, may be quite virile; that is, they may be masculine or manly and evince a normal sex drive with complete coital powers. It must be kept in mind that the testes have a dual function: the manufacture of spermatozoa and the release of male sex hormones. Apparently there is no one-to-one relationship between these two functions.

The male sex organ, the *penis,* is the instrument of seminal implantation, and as such it must have the capacity for erection. This is brought about through a rather intricate combination of physical and psychological factors. Physiologically, the penis not only contains an elaborate network of spongy tissue, but also includes constricting bands of muscles and a rich supply of blood vessels. In addition, the external surface is covered with a special set of sensory nerve endings.

In times of sexual excitation—facilitated, as it were, by the size and location of the penis—nerve impulses flow to the muscle fibers. The blood vessels thereupon become engorged, the erectile tissue enlarges, and the entire sex organ becomes extended and takes the form usually referred to as erection. This erectile

347

process is sometimes called *tumescence,* and the reverse process —which sets in after ejaculation has occurred or after sexual excitation has passed—is known as *detumescence.*

Throughout the ages, much superstition has surrounded the male sex organ, one authority writing as follows:

> The penis is the subject of a rich folklore. At various times and places, it has been the object of religious veneration as a fertility symbol. . . .
>
> While such practices have ceased to exist in their original forms, preoccupation with the penis continues. One fallacy involves the size. A flaccid penis, usually three to four inches long, enlarges to about six inches when erect, while its diameter increases between ¼ and 1¼ inches. However, perfectly adequate penises can be considerably smaller, and penises larger than 13 inches have been reported.
>
> The size and shape of the penis have very little to do with the competence of the man in giving or receiving sexual satisfaction. Size and shape are not related to his body build, skin color, or sexual experience, and are no more significant than the size and shape of his nose.[2]

From the view of species perpetuation, the human male sex organ is surely one of nature's ingenious devices. On the basis of its size, location, cell structure, nerve endings, and blood supply, it is easy to see why sexual excitability among males runs high, particularly at the younger age levels. In fact, not only is penile erection commonly observed in baby boys, but—as Kogan points out—"the male infant is quite capable of having an erection even before his umbilical cord is cut."[3]

Masters and Johnson report that "erection normally develops with extreme rapidity in young males. The penis may reach full erection from an unstimulated flaccid state within three to five seconds of the onset of any form of sexual stimulation."[4] Most amazing of all, perhaps, is the case reported by Pomeroy of a 63-year-old man who "was able to masturbate to ejaculation in ten seconds from a flaccid start."[5]

Erectile capacity in the male probably hinges as much on psychological as physiological factors. If they lack any other kind of sexual outlet, for instance, most males experience nocturnal

---

[2] Katchadourian, *op. cit.,* p. 7.

[3] Benjamin A. Kogan, *Human Sexual Expression,* New York, Harcourt Brace Jovanovich, Inc., 1973, p. 1.

[4] William Masters and Virginia Johnson, *Human Sexual Response,* Boston, Little, Brown and Company, 1966, p. 251.

[5] Wardell B. Pomeroy, *Dr. Kinsey and the Institute for Sex Research,* New York, The New American Library, Inc., 1972, p. 129.

sex dreams, replete with ejaculation and orgasm. While such experiences are infrequent among older men, teen-age boys report these "wet dreams" to be monthly or even weekly occurrences.

FEMALE SEXUAL ANATOMY

Unlike the male, the female's sex organs are for the most part internal rather than external. The *labia majora* and *labia minora* (the outer and inner lips of the female genitalia) are external, although the labia majora contributes little to the sexual response of most females. The labia minora is a highly sensitive area, as is the *clitoris*, which is the counterpart of the male penis. The labia majora, the labia minora, and the clitoris together make up the *vulva*.

349

The clitoris is a small organ—a fraction of an inch long—whose function is sexual rather than reproductive. Although it is partly imbedded in tissue, the clitoris, like the penis, is richly endowed with nerve endings and blood supply. During sexual excitation, the organ enlarges somewhat and becomes engorged with blood. However, unlike the penis, there is no such thing as a clitoral erection.

The female organ of copulation is the *vagina*, a muscular, cylindrical tube extending into the body at an upward angle. Normally in a collapsed state, the vagina is only three to four inches long; however, the tubular walls are highly distensible—as indeed they must be to meet the exigencies of childbirth. It should

The female reproductive system.

be mentioned, in this connection, that the vagina is largely devoid of nerve endings.

At birth, the vaginal opening is bordered by a membrane, the hymen, which partially closes the entrance to the vagina. The hymen is usually ruptured during the initial sexual intercourse, although for other reasons it may be broken earlier. Interestingly enough, the hymen has no known sexual or reproductive function and may simply be a vestigial organ. In some lower animals, for example, the vaginal opening is covered by a membrane except during the rutting period.

Since they possess neither prostate gland nor seminal vesicles, females do not produce seminal fluid—which means that they do not ejaculate. Most females do experience orgasm, however, although there seems to be some question whether there is a difference between a clitoral and a vaginal orgasm. In the widely quoted Masters and Johnson study, the researchers discovered but one type of orgasmic response. In a more recent survey, however, Fisher reported that the females in his sample could indeed distinguish between the two types.[6]

Insofar as sexual response is concerned, Fisher's study also indicated that the modern American wife leads a rather active sex life.[7] The capacity for vaginal lubrication is apparently present at a very early age,[8] and, while there are still significant behavioral differences in the sex lives of men and women, cultural factors are believed by most sociologists to be largely responsible. (These factors will be discussed in the next chapter.)

The female sex glands—corresponding to the male testes—are the *ovaries*, which, like the male gonads, have a dual function: (1) the production of ova (eggs), and (2) the manufacture of the female sex hormones. This latter process is more complicated than the corresponding testicular activity, since in addition to estrogen (responsible for the female secondary sex traits) *progesterone* is also secreted. Progesterone is the hormone that facilitates the prenatal development of the child and the subsequent parturition (childbearing) process.

The ovaries—rounded structures about an inch in diameter, located on each side of the pelvis—are functionless until puberty (roughly 11 to 14 years of age), at which time *menarche*, or first menstruation, occurs. This is generally an indication that ova are

350

---

[6] Seymour Fisher, *The Female Orgasm*, New York, Basic Books, Inc., 1973, pp. 7–8.

[7] *Ibid.*, p. 201.

[8] Kogan, *op. cit.*, p. 1.

being produced, a cyclic function that will continue until menopause sets in some three decades later.

About as big as a dot, the human egg is just large enough to be seen with the naked eye, and hence is many times larger than the sperm. All the transmissible hereditary traits of the mother are carried in the ovum. Normally, an egg is released every 28 days, one ovary functioning one month, the other ovary the next month, and so on. Following ovulation, the egg is usually, though not always, "captured" in the Fallopian tube, or oviduct, the upper end of which contains a fingerlike expansion designed to receive ripened ova. (There is no direct connection between ovary and oviduct.) The egg has no power of self-locomotion but is pushed through the oviduct by ciliary action and wavelike muscular constrictions.

If the egg has been fertilized (in which case it is known as a zygote), it is carried through the oviduct to the uterus, a pear-shaped structure approximately three inches in length. The zygote eventually affixes itself to the uterine wall, an area richly supplied with blood vessels, and the process of prenatal development begins. Approximately nine months after conception this developmental process is completed, whereupon the uterine muscles contract and parturition commences.

If the egg has not been fertilized, it disintegrates and is sloughed off, together with the unused uterine lining. This, of course, is the process known as menstruation.

351

THE MENSTRUAL CYCLE

Like all female mammals, the human female is so constituted that her reproductive process is cyclic in nature. An egg is ovulated, it passes through the oviduct, it is eliminated. Another egg ripens in the other ovary, it is ovulated, and so on. This recurrent process is known as the menstrual cycle and corresponds to the estrous cycle of lower animals, although there are differences.

Over the years, there has been much misunderstanding about the human reproductive cycle, both on the part of primitive groups and among civilized societies. Some primitive peoples regard the female as unclean during menstruation and impose strict taboos against associating with her during this period. Civilized societies, while generally recognizing menstruation as a normal biological function, have not always understood the relation between ovarian phases and fertility. Although not all of the details are known, research has uncovered the basic physiological principles governing the cycle of reproduction, and these facts should be understood by students of the family.

One of the keys to an understanding of the human menstrual cycle is the realization that *nature intended the egg to be fertilized.* During the process of ovulation, the ovarian follicle secretes certain hormones (estrogen and, later, progesterone), which act upon the lining of the uterus. A cellular growth takes place and the mucous membrane that lines the uterus is expanded. Concurrently the uterine blood supply is increased, and the lining is structurally changed in preparation for the zygote, or fertilized egg. If the egg is not fertilized, these uterine changes have been for nought. Consequently, the newly prepared lining breaks down and peels off from the wall of the uterus. The subsequent discharging of the unused lining and the "ready" blood supply, plus the sloughing off of the unfertilized (and now disintegrated) egg, constitutes menstruation. In a very real sense, therefore, the direct cause of menstruation is the nonfertilization of the ovum.

Menstruation lasts for several days, with varying degrees of discomfort experienced. Most women evidence emotional variations—crankiness, irritability, or depressions—that correspond to certain phases of the menstrual cycle and about which, unfortunately, nothing much can be done.

Women have also recognized that fluctuations in sexual desire occur during various phases of the menstrual cycle. Most often mentioned as being the peak periods of sexual receptivity are the days immediately preceding and following menstruation. However, some knowledgeable writers have reported that the peak period tends to correspond with the time of ovulation.[9] About all that can be said with certainty is that there is much variation among women.

The Cultural Interpretation. Most treatises on sex eduation take pains to point out that menstruation is a normal biological process, experienced by women the world over. This is an involved point, however, and whether menstruation is indeed a "natural" process is a matter of interpretation. Menstruation does occur among women everywhere and is a natural consequence of nonfertilization. On the other hand, it can be demonstrated that menstruation is, in one sense, a *cultural* phenomenon!

[9] See Julia Sherman, "What Men Do Not Know About Women's Sexuality," *Medical Aspects of Human Sexuality*, November, 1972, pp. 138–151; and John Cavanagh, "Cyclicity of Female Sexual Desire," *ibid.*, p. 170.

Among lower animals, where there are no cultural restrictions, whenever an egg is produced, it is normally fertilized. Exceptions would occur in areas where there is an extreme shortage or absence of males, or in the case of captive or domesticated animals where the sexes are purposely separated. If *Homo sapiens* lived as a creature of the wild, it is quite likely that fertilization would generally follow ovulation. Man does not live like an animal, however; he has developed a family system and a complex culture, and in all societies there are cultural restrictions that preclude indiscriminate coitus.

In primitive groups there are rules prescribing mating behavior, and taboos relative to sexual intercourse. And in civilized societies there are severe restrictions on sexual matters. Within our own culture, premarital coitus is limited and premarital pregnancy is frowned upon. Furthermore, most American wives practice some sort of birth control. Both phenomena—premarital restrictions and the utilization of birth control—are culturally determined.

Menstruation does not occur in other species, and in the absence of cultural regulations it might well be considered "unnatural" by the human animal. One could almost say—if it weren't for the play on words—that "menstruation is natural but it is cultural"; that is, it is natural, given the present cultural setting.

Fertility Period. Although the average length of the menstrual cycle is about 28 days, individual women have reported cycles as short as 20 and as long as 60 days. In the normal 28-day cycle, the period of maximal fertility is roughly the midpoint of the cycle; in fact, it is not generally realized that conception must occur within a narrow period of time. The human egg starts to disintegrate shortly after it leaves the follicle, and sperm motility is reduced in a matter of hours, although in both instances exact figures are hard to come by. Most authorities doubt whether the egg can be fertilized more than 12 to 24 hours after it leaves the follicle. Human sperm apparently lose their penetrating power after 48 hours.

Menopause. Just as menarche, or first menstruation, denotes the beginning of a woman's fertile period, menopause marks the end. Like other aspects of the female's reproductive process, menopause shows some individual variation. After age 40, as the climacteric approaches, most women evidence irregular menstrual periods. At some time between the ages of 40 and 50, menstruation stops altogether, though exceptions do occur. Reported pregnancies after age 47 are rare, however, and after 50 they can be considered freaks of nature. There are two authenticated cases, nevertheless, where women have given birth to infants at the age of 57![10]

It should be pointed out that menopause does not necessarily denote the cessation or diminution of sexual desire. Some women do find themselves less desirous of coitus after menopause has been reached, but just as many or more seem to notice no significant change. Some women even experience an increase in sexual desire following menopause, presumably because the fear of pregnancy has been removed.

Whether human males undergo any experience comparable to the female climacteric is still being debated. There is no male menopause in the sense of sperm production ceasing abruptly at a given age. Most males, as they get older, do experience some decline in virility, and perhaps in fertility, although the diminution is apparently more gradual than in the case of the female.

CONCEPTION

Fertilization is a function of the gametes, the name applied to the egg or sperm. A great many more human gametes are produced than are actually used, especially in the case of the male—a phenomenon that is quite common throughout the animal world. The ovaries of a human female contain thousands of ova, but they are in an immature state, the normal process being for one egg to ripen each menstrual cycle from puberty to menopause. Precisely which ovum ripens—out of the large supply available—is apparently a matter of chance.

By comparison, the number of male spermatozoa dwarfs the female supply, for in the course of his life the human male produces *billions* of mature gametes. As a matter of fact, there are more than enough sperm in a single human ejaculate to produce a population twice the size of the United States! And in a month or so, one human male produces sufficient numbers of spermatozoa to populate the earth at its present density. All of these gametes, incidentally, could fit in a space about the size of a needle. Out of this prodigious supply, exactly which sperm, if any, fertilizes the egg is again presumably a matter of chance.*

---

* Although there are from 300 to 500 million sperm in an ejaculate, the human male is dwarfed by the males of other species. There are 12 to 13 billion sperm in the ejaculate of a male stallion, and some 85 billion in that of the wild boar!

[10] See the account in the *Philadephia Inquirer*, November 25, 1972.

Students have sometimes raised the question "What difference does it make which sperm fertilizes which egg?" The answer is that it makes a great deal of difference. All the gametes—male and female—differ in their genetic content, and the child's physical features, native intelligence, and the presence or absence of hereditary defects all hinge on the crucial meeting of particular sperm and particular egg.

Other questions have also been raised: How do the spermatozoa locate the egg at exactly the right spot? Why isn't the egg fertilized in the ovary rather than the oviduct? Why is only *one* egg ovulated at a time, and why does only a *single* sperm penetrate the egg? And if only one ovary and oviduct function at a time, what would prevent the spermatozoa from heading toward the "wrong" ovary?

To take these questions singly, conception normally takes place in the upper portion of the oviduct. It cannot take place below this point—in the uterus or vagina, for example—because the ovum would have disintegrated. Conception can take place *above* the oviduct (i.e., in the space between ovary and oviduct). Fertilization in this area is infrequent, however, for among other things the spermatozoa are likely to lose their motility (striking power) before this point is reached. Even if the egg is fertilized above the oviduct, the chances are that it will descend in normal fashion and implant itself in the uterine wall. Very occasionally, however, an egg fertilized above the oviduct escapes into the abdomen, with an abdominal pregnancy resulting.

Once the spermatozoa are deposited in the vaginal tract, they head in all directions. Some never leave the vagina, and some do not get past the uterus. On a probability basis, one-half of the remainder would be expected to move toward the wrong (inoperative) ovary since, so far as is known, there is no chemical attraction between sperm and egg. (Under a slide, a sperm will swim past an egg, although admittedly this situation would not necessarily obtain under natural conditions.) In any event, that conception occurs at all is due to the fact that the number of ejaculated spermatozoa is so large. In all likelihood, relatively few male gametes survive to reach the upper portion—the fertilization area—of the oviduct. And even here, the diameter of the oviduct is relatively large compared with the size of the gametes, and it is probable that some spermatozoa by-pass the egg.

To repeat an old saying, however, "it takes only one" sperm to effect fertilization, and though the odds are certainly against conception during any one coital act, the fact is that most people who want children experience no undue difficulty in having them. In fact, amazing as it may seem, "there have been cases in

355

which a woman missing a tube on one side and an ovary on the other side has nevertheless become pregnant!"[11]

As to why only *one* sperm fertilizes an egg, the answer seems to hinge on the chromosomal allotment of the species. Every species has its own number of cellular chromosomes (the diploid count), the human number being 46. However, the gametes produced in the ovaries and testes have only 23 chromosomes, the haploid count. When sperm and egg meet, the 23 chromosomes from each gamete unite to form the zygote, so that each of us starts life as a single cell with a full complement of 46 chromosomes.

If more than one sperm penetrated an egg, the "extra" chromosomes would either be unusable or, possibly, would complicate the diploid count, perhaps with dire consequences to the offspring. Therefore, as soon as one sperm enters the egg a protective membrane or coating is formed, thus preventing further penetration.

Multiple Pregnancies. Human conception normally involves one egg and one sperm, with subsequent development inside a single placental sac in the uterus. Occasionally, plural ovulation takes place—more than one egg is ovulated from the same ovary or from different ovaries—in which case multiple conception may occur. The resultant offspring are usually termed fraternal or two-egg twins. Fraternal twins may or may not be of the same sex, they develop in separate placentae, and are no more alike genetically than siblings. Identical twins, on the other hand, are the product of one sperm and egg, with the original zygote splitting and ultimately forming two separate individuals. Identical twins are always of the same sex, usually share common fetal membranes, and are genetically indistinguishable. Fraternal twins, incidentally, occur about twice as often as identicals.[12]

Twin births—both fraternals and identicals—while relatively infrequent, are by no means rare. Speaking very generally, they occur about once in 90 births, although the figure varies from time to time and place to place. Spain has a twin rate of one in 110 births, while Denmark has a rate of one in 71.[13] Scheinfeld also points out that:

> On a racial basis, the highest rate of twinning is among Negroes; the next highest rate among Whites, and the lowest among Mongolians, such as Japanese, Chinese, and American Indians. The

[11] Katchadourian, *op. cit.*, pp. 9–10.
[12] Amram Scheinfeld, *Twins and Supertwins*, Philadelphia, J. B. Lippincott Company, 1967, p. 63.
[13] *Ibid.*, pp. 68–69.

world-record twinners are African Negroes, with a rate in many tribal groups of about one twin pair in 40 pregnancies, and reported as reaching the astounding average of one twin pair in 22 pregnancies among the Yorubas of Nigeria. (Negroes in the United States, who are of considerably mixed ancestry—African and White, with some Indian—have a twinning rate now averaging about one pair in 73 births.) At the opposite extreme, the Japanese average only one pair in about 160 births, and even lower rates have been reported for other Mongoloid groups.[14]

The cause of twinning is by no means understood, although a hereditary factor is believed to be present, at least in the case of fraternals. It is known that the chances of having twins increase with the age of the mother. In recent years, however, modern drugs have tended to cloud the statistical picture. On the one hand, birth control pills serve to depress the figures, while fertility pills—those which *stimulate* ovulation—tend to increase the incidence of twins. Many of the "supertwins" of recent years—the triplets, quintuplets, and sextuplets—have been born of mothers who had been taking fertility pills.*

Unfortunately, there is a high mortality rate among twins and supertwins. Among the smaller animals there is little danger, for the uterus is designed to hold large numbers. The tiny field mouse, for example, has six or more litters a year, each one containing a dozen or so offspring. But in the larger animals, including man, the uterus is geared for a single embryo, and when there are two—or four or six—prenatal conditions become somewhat "crowded." In the case of quintuplets or sextuplets, for instance, it is most unlikely that all the offspring will be born alive and live to adulthood.

Another danger stems from the possibility of incomplete twinning in the case of identicals. The splitting of the zygote apparently can be stopped—for reasons unknown—at almost any state of twin development. The later the stage of arrestment, the more fully separated will be the individual twins. Early arrestment may result in freaks, such as two-headed babies, while later arrestment may result in so-called Siamese twins. Note the following unfortunate case, reported by Scheinfeld:

> The worst freaks occur where an early embryonic division is only partial, for this may result in a monster with four arms and four

* The record for human multiple births was set on June 12, 1971, when a 29-year-old Australian housewife, who had been under fertility treatment, gave birth to nine children within a period of 35 minutes. Only two of the nine were stillborn. All told, there were four girls and five boys.

[14] *Ibid.,*. p. 62.

legs, or with two heads, or with various other duplications, internally and externally. The most spectacular example was that of the Russian coalescent twins who had two heads, one torso, four arms, and two legs, and—if that weren't enough—a rudimentary tail as well. Born in 1937, they lived for a year. Fortunately, all but a few of such monstrosities perish before birth. . . .[15]

Fetal Development. Returning now to the subject of normal conception, the subsequent development of the zygote is a truly remarkable process. At the end of the first month the embryo is approximately one-quarter of an inch in length, having increased its original weight several thousand times. Even at this early stage of development, close examination will reveal the beginnings of body, head, arms, and legs. At the end of three months the fetus has grown to some three inches in length: bones and teeth have begun to develop, sex can be determined, and spontaneous movements are occasionally made. By the fifth month the fetus is nearly a foot long and weighs about one pound. Fingernails and toenails are well developed and head hair has begun to grow.

By the seventh month the weight has increased to about three pounds, and fetal movements can easily be felt by the mother. Should birth occur at this time the child would have a chance for survival.* By the ninth month—the full term—the weight is in the area of seven pounds and the length some 20 inches. From the moment of conception until full-term birth, the fetus increases in size and weight several million times!

To provide for this tremendous increase, the uterus also increases to many times its original size and weight. Within the placenta, nourishment and oxygen pass from mother to offspring by a process of membranous absorption (osmosis). Note, however, that there is no direct connection between the two blood streams. The baby makes its own blood and does not, as is sometimes believed, receive its supply from the mother. Nor is there a neural connection between mother and offspring. The common superstition that a prenatal experience on the part of the

---

* Exactly how premature a baby could be, and still live, is debatable. Infants born prematurely and weighing 10 ounces or less are known to have survived. At the other extreme, the largest baby ever born weighed a full 26½ pounds! This birth occurred in Teheran, Iran, in 1972. (Associated Press report, *Philadelphia Inquirer,* February 13, 1972.)

[15] Amram Scheinfeld, *The New You and Heredity,* Philadelphia, J. B. Lippincott Company, 1961, p. 136. See also Eric Golanty, *Human Reproduction,* New York, Holt, Rinehart and Winston, Inc., 1975.

358

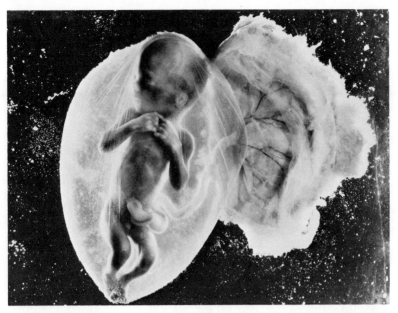

A four-month fetus. At this stage, the baby is already well developed. (Lennart Nilsson, L. Nilsson, *A Child is Born* [New York, Seymour Lawrence (an imprint of Dell Publishing Co.), 1967])

mother—a so-called "maternal impression"—can in some way affect the unborn child is simply a superstition. There is no known method by which such impressions can be conveyed to the fetus. The dietary condition and general physical and emotional well-being of the mother, however, may play an important part in the overall sequence of prenatal development.

It might be mentioned that, whereas the average pregnancy lasts 9 months, or approximately 273 days, there is a remarkable range of variation among human females. Some "successful" pregnancies last less than 7 months, while the longest one ever recorded lasted just over 13 months![16] Calcified fetuses have been carried in the uterus for much longer periods.*

Among the lower animals the pregnancy, or gestation, range is truly prodigious. At one mammalian extreme is the opossum—a mere 10 to 13 days. At the other is the elephant, with a gestation

---

* In the spring of 1976, an Alabama woman was found to have carried a calcified fetus in her abdomen for a quarter-century! (Associated Press report, *Philadelphia Inquirer*, May 13, 1976.)

[16] A picture of the mother and son, from Wolverhampton, England, appeared in an Associated Press report (*Philadelphia Inquirer*, June 16, 1975).

period of nearly two years. Generally speaking, the larger the animal, the longer the gestation. None of the largest animals normally have plural offspring.

INFERTILITY: CAUSES

While most people who want children experience no particular difficulty in having them, and although some persons who do not desire children become parents in spite of themselves, the fact remains that a certain proportion of married couples are unable to have children, even though they may want them very badly. In former years, such involuntary childlessness was referred to as "sterility," but as more and more research findings have accumulated, it has become apparent that all people cannot be divided into "sterile" and "fertile" groups. Fertility appears to be a relative matter on the part of both male and female—that is, some individuals are highly fertile, others relatively infertile, and still others are so low on the scale as to be classed as sterile. Merely for the sake of convenience, we shall refer to the condition of involuntary childlessness as infertility.

For obvious reasons, the percentage of couples who are unable to have children is not known with any exactness. Some 15 to 20 percent of the married couples in the United States live their lives without having children, and perhaps half of these entail involuntary childlessness.[17]

At one time it was customary to blame childlessness on the wife ("barrenness," it will be remembered, was one of the traditional grounds on which a husband could procure a divorce), but in recent years it has been recognized that either husband or wife may be infertile. As a matter of fact, modern medical and biological research has revealed that the causes of infertility are much more numerous, and in some ways more complex, than has generally been realized. Let us look at some of the more prevalent causative factors.

Age. One of the most obvious factors affecting fertility is age. The female's reproductive span begins at puberty and ends with

---

[17] As J. E. Veevers—who has done the most work on the subject—points out: "The research available concerning the phenomenon of childlessness is very limited, especially when compared with the voluminous literature which has been directed toward other facets of human reproduction." For an excellent discussion, see his "Factors in the Incidence of Childlessness in Canada: An Analysis of Census Data," *Social Biology,* Vol. 19, No. 3, 1974, pp. 266–274.

menopause, roughly a period of 35 years. Conception cannot occur after menopause, of course, since ovulation has ceased. Less obvious is the fact that even prior to menopause, a woman's fertility often declines as she gets older. As she passes from the twenties to the thirties and forties, each succeeding decade may mark a lowering of the chances for conception.

The age factor also affects fertility in the male. It has been commonly held that production of spermatozoa declines with age, but the research studies in this area have been insufficient either to support or to refute this belief. It is known, though, that male potency (the erectile capacity for coitus) diminishes with age, and that coital frequency on the part of married couples drops off markedly with advancing years.

Physical Disability. A number of organs—penis, vagina, oviducts, vas deferens, prostate gland—come into play before fertilization occurs, and should any of them be defective the chances of conception and successful pregnancy would be appreciably lowered. Common among reproductive disorders are blocked tubes, acidity in the vaginal tract, malfunctioning of the prostate gland, displacement of the uterus, cervical obstructions, and malformation of the male and female genital organs.

General body health seems also to be related to fertility, a number of authorities holding to the belief that such factors as physical and mental strain, faulty metabolism, hormonal imbalance, and inadequate nutrition tend to reduce the possibilities of conception. It is known that germ diseases such as syphilis and gonorrhea may result in lowered fertility, for both male and female, and under certain conditions the same would hold true for cancer. The effect of most other diseases on fertility has not been established.

Probability. One of the causes of involuntary childlessness stems from the statistical probability—or improbability—of sperm meeting egg. Even if we assume that large numbers of spermatozoa are deposited in the vaginal tract around the time of ovulation, there is little guarantee of fertilization. The ovum is tiny, and the spermatozoa are minute, and the chances of conception resulting from any particular coital act must be relatively small.

In the case of many couples, furthermore—especially those with little knowledge of female fertility cycles—there is no necessary reason to suppose that coitus coincides with ovulation; indeed, the reverse might well be true. To take a hypothetical illustration, suppose Mrs. J. has a regular menstrual cycle and ovulates on the fourteenth day of every period. Assume, further, that ovulation begins around 6:00 A.M., and that the ovum remains in the upper portion of the oviduct for about 12 hours. If Mr. and Mrs. J. are like most couples and confine their sexual activity to nighttime, the chances of conception are quite slim— even though both may be highly fertile. Many married couples engage in sexual intercourse only sporadically, so that, if daytime ovulation occurs with anything like regularity, the chances of conception—even over a relatively long period—remain problematical.

Deficiencies in Sperm and Semen. It cannot be emphasized too strongly that even in the case of fertile males the chance of conception resulting from a particular coital act is not great. Assuming the egg to be in a fertilizable position, the spermatozoa are confronted with a series of natural obstacles. Not only is the distance relatively long, but female body heat tends to kill off large numbers of sperm, as does the acid condition of the vaginal tract. It can be seen, therefore, that when the spermatozoa themselves are defective, the chances of conception may drop to near zero. As a matter of fact, spermatic deficiencies may well be the single most important cause of involuntary childlessness.

At one time it was felt that sterility in the male involved simply the absence of spermatozoa. Later it was believed that "infertility," as it came to be called, was not necessarily the absence of spermatozoa but the production of the latter in insufficient numbers. More recent research has indicated that male fertility involves at least five components: (1) the *morphology*, or structure of the spermatozoa; (2) the *density*, or number of spermatozoa per ejaculate; (3) the *motility*, or movement of the spermatozoa; (4) the *viability*, or life span of the spermatozoa; and (5) the *quantity* and *quality* of the seminal fluid. Infertility in the male apparently stems from defects in any or all of these five components.

INFERTILITY: CURES

It is safe to say that involuntary childlessness is more likely to be cured today than at any previous time. In former periods, infertile couples were prone to turn to adoption, but nowadays, while thousands of adoptions still take place every year, there are simply not enough infants available to meet the demand. Involuntary childlessness is still a very real problem, although advances in medical research are holding out promise of help in cases that once might have been considered hopeless.

Advances in surgery have made it possible to alleviate many structural disorders of the genital and reproductive tracts. Hormonal deficiencies can often be remedied. Much more is known about the female menstrual cycle, and tests are now available for determining with remarkable accuracy the time of ovulation.

Also, modern diagnosis can pretty well determine whether the husband or wife is the infertile partner. For the wife, fertility pills which stimulate ovulation have been widely used for some time now. Corresponding pills for the husband—that is, pills that would increase spermatogenesis—have not yet been developed.* Research has shown, however, that sexual abstinence for several days on the part of the male will aid in the building up of a more adequate sperm count.

In general, the whole problem of infertility is less shrouded in mystery than it was a few decades ago. Today there is much less tendency for spouses to blame one another, and more willingness to consult a physician. There is every reason to believe, furthermore, that medical advances will continue to be made.

Artificial Insemination. A "new" cure for infertility—and one which doubtless will continue to make headlines—is artificial insemination, the process whereby seminal fluid is deposited in the female reproductive tract by nonsexual means. Actually, this method is by no means new, artificial inseminations being reported in the eighteenth and nineteenth centuries, but only in recent times have significant numbers of such cases been reported. Estimates vary widely as to how many children are conceived by this method. However, it seems safe to say that tens of thousands of living Americans were conceived via artificial insemination. Some writers believe that the numbers run into the hundreds of thousands.[18] But, if the estimates seem large, it must be remembered that as yet there is no wonder drug that would enable a subfertile male to raise his sperm count to the necessary

---

* Nor, despite persistent rumors to the contrary, has there been any drug developed that would increase the male or female sex drive. As an aphrodisiac, the so-called Spanish fly—known chemically as *cantharidin* —is evidently ineffective. Unfortunately, there have been several instances where Spanish fly is known to have caused death.

[18] For a comprehensive discussion of the matter, see Neal Weinstock, "Artificial Insemination—The Problem and the Solution," *Family Law Quarterly*, September, 1971, pp. 369–402. See also Mary Ann Oakley, "Test Tube Babies," *Family Law Quarterly*, Winter, 1974, pp. 385–400.

level. The only recourse for such males is adoption—or artificial insemination of the wife.

Artificial insemination has been referred to as *homologous* when the husband's seminal fluid is used and *heterologous* when the semen of a donor other than the husband is employed. Homologous insemination has raised no special medical or legal problems, so, unless otherwise stated, the term "artificial insemination" will refer to the controversial heterologous variety.

When a donor is used, great care is taken to insure that his identity is kept secret. He, similarly, is not informed of the name of the recipient. Donors are carefully chosen on the basis of physical and mental qualifications, and insofar as possible, a specific donor is selected on the basis of his physical resemblance to the husband. The doctor attempts to determine the time of ovulation, whereupon the donor's semen is deposited, by instrument, in the wife's reproductive tract.

From all reports, the rate of conceptions following artificial insemination is quite high. Equally as important is the fact that, as reported by doctors at least, the children are treated by their parents without emotional qualms. Because of the understandable secrecy involved, however, no large-scale sociological study has been undertaken regarding the attitudes and emotional configuration of such families. Since artificial insemination is supposed to be employed only in those cases where *both* husband and wife express their willingness, it is unlikely that the "test tube" children would be adversely affected, although in the absence of a controlled empirical study, no definitive statement can be made.

The practice of artificial insemination has provoked a good deal of controversy in recent decades. On the one hand, it has been hailed as a humanitarian blessing for childless couples; on the other hand, it has been condemned as adultery. Eugenicists have seen in artificial insemination a method for improving man's hereditary qualities, while certain religious groups—such as the Roman Catholic Church and the Church of England—condemn the practice as patently immoral. Many lawyers and doctors hail artificial insemination as a cure for childless marriages, but many others rebel against the idea. Some medical associations condone the practice, others do not. And so it goes.

Even the legal status of artificial insemination remains unsettled. Lower courts have ruled both ways, and the United States Supreme Court has not made a direct decision as to whether artificial insemination constitutes adultery. As a result of the uncertainty, legal battles will, in all likelihood, continue to be fought. Before the outcome is finally settled, it may be that a method for increasing sperm count will be discovered. In the meantime, because of legal and medical opposition, many doctors are loath to handle artificial insemination cases. It is unlikely, therefore, that the immediate future will see any great upsurge in the rate of artificially conceived infants.

CONTRACEPTION

In spite of the reams that have been written on the subject, it may come as a surprise to learn that contraceptive techniques are age-old. Historical records indicate that most of our so-called modern methods, in principle at least, have been used for several thousand years. The oldest known contraceptive recipe is found on a papyrus dating from the period 1850–1550 B.C. Ancient records show quite clearly that, while many of the devices were magical in nature (the wearing of charms, the eating and drinking of ingenious concoctions), others were designed specifically for preventing the union of sperm and egg. However unwieldly and insanitary, membranous sheaths were used to cover the male organ, and a variety of materials were employed as vaginal insertions or pessaries—gum arabic, honey, ground leaves, elephant dung, plant extracts, oils, and the like. Some of these substances—those that were gummy or acid—probably acted as a sperm deterrent, but others that were alkaline had the unlooked-for effect of increasing sperm motility!

Having but limited success with the crude contraceptive techniques that were available to them, the ancients were much more likely to resort to abortion and infanticide in an effort to keep their population within the bounds of the existing food supply. The term "contraception," however, refers to the voluntary prevention of conception and does not include abortion and infanticide. In recent years, terms such as *conception control, family planning, birth control, prevenception, fertility limitation,* and *planned parenthood* have come to be virtually synonymous with the word "contraception." Whatever the term employed, the topic itself has been a center of controversy for almost 150 years.

Areas of Controversy. Birth control has not only been a controversial subject, but the *focus of argument* has shifted over the years. It will be worthwhile, therefore, to examine separately the major areas of disagreement.

1. *Medical-legal.* In the United States, the first booklet on birth control seems to have been Robert Dale Owen's *Moral Physiology,* published in 1830. "Two years later, Dr. Charles Knowlton, a

Massachusetts physician, published anonymously a further treatise on contraceptive methods, curiously entitled *Fruits of Philosophy*. Knowlton eventually served a term of imprisonment for his part in publishing this book, and later it was the subject of a celebrated English trial."[19] Throughout most of the nineteenth century, both in Europe and the United States, contraceptives were generally associated with prostitution and sexual immorality; in fact, the birth control movement did not begin to achieve respectability until after World War I—and even then there were many hurdles to clear.

When the late Margaret Sanger started the modern birth control movement in 1912, she was met by a torrent of abuse. Religious leaders, doctors, law-enforcement agents—and a considerable portion of the public—combined to make her early career a thorny one. But her experience as a nurse on New York's Lower East Side had convinced her that one of the greatest tragedies of the day was the fact that thousands of lower-class wives continued to bear children in the midst of squalor—because contraceptive devices were not available. So, in spite of numerous court battles and a jail sentence, Margaret Sanger persisted in her crusade to make birth control acceptable, both legally and medically.

Eventually she won the fight. Today, birth control has been accepted by both the medical profession and the public at large, with family planning centers now available in virtually every part of the country. With regard to the college population, Scarlett's survey indicated that 96 percent of the undergraduates "agreed on the desirability of limiting family size."[20]

2. Protestant-Catholic. As the medical-legal battle waned, the argument over birth control came to revolve around Protestant–Catholic differences. The Catholic Church has held that all forms of birth limitation, other than the rhythm method, are contrary to natural law. Granted the basic tenets of the Roman Catholic Church, this viewpoint is logical and consistent, and it is regrettable that some non-Catholic writers have been rather intolerant in their approach to the subject.

Proponents of contraception, on the other hand, have argued that birth control is an economic blessing to poorer families, that child-spacing patterns are improved, and that population growth

[19] Norman St. John-Stevas, "History and Legal Status of Birth Control," in Edwin Schur (ed.), *The Family and the Sexual Revolution*, Bloomington, Indiana University Press, 1964, pp. 333–348.
[20] John A. Scarlett, "Undergraduate Attitudes Toward Birth Control: New Perspectives," *Journal of Marriage and the Family*, May, 1972, pp. 312–314.

is reduced. From a secular view, this position is also a logical one, even though certain Catholic writers have refused to accept the legitimacy of the arguments.

While it is hardly likely that Protestants and Catholics will reconcile their views on birth control completely, the argument in recent years has tended to subside. Each side has become more tolerant; in fact, it now appears that a substantial majority of Catholic wives are using some sort of birth control other than the rhythm method.

3. *Methods and techniques.* Modern contraceptive techniques fall into several categories: (1) mechanical or chemical obstructions—such as condoms, pessaries, intrauterine devices (IUD's), and foam tablets—aimed at preventing the union of egg and sperm; (2) surgical methods, e.g., closing off the male or female gamete-carrying tubes; (3) coitus interruptus; (4) the rhythm method; and (5) oral contraceptives.

While each of these methods continues to have its advocates, the oral contraceptive—generally referred to as the Pill—has emerged as the most popular American form of birth control. The extent to which the Pill has harmful side effects is still being debated. But, while the Pill is probably here to stay, new contraceptives may be forthcoming. These would include capsules that are implanted under the skin, hormonal injections, vaccines, and chemicals that impede the manufacture of sperm. In any event, the best available evidence indicates that the long-term decline in the birthrate will probably continue.

SELECTED READINGS

Berman, Claire, *We Take This Child: A Candid Look at Modern Adoption,* Garden City, New York, Doubleday & Company, Inc., 1974.

Burr, Wesley; Mead, D. Eugene; and Rollins, Boyd C., "A Model for the Application of Research Findings by the Educator and Counselor: Research to Theory to Practice," *Family Coordinator,* July, 1973, pp. 285–290.

Cochrane, Susan, and Bean, Frank, "Husband-Wife Differences in the Demand for Children," *Journal of Marriage and the Family,* May, 1976, pp. 297–307.

Fink, Paul J., and Hammett, Van Buren O., *Sexual Function and Dysfunction,* Philadelphia, F. A. Davis Company, 1969.

Fisher, Seymour, *The Female Orgasm,* New York, Basic Books, Inc., 1973.

Golanty, Eric, *Human Reproduction,* New York, Holt, Rinehart and Winston, Inc., 1975.

Goldman, G. D., and Milman, D. S. (eds.), *Modern Woman: Her Psychology and Sexuality,* Springfield, Illinois, Charles C Thomas, 1969.

Gross, Leonard (ed.), *Sexual Issues in Marriage,* New York, Spectrum Publications, Inc., 1975.

Katchadourian, Herant, *Human Sexuality: Sense and Nonsense,* San Francisco, W. H. Freeman and Company, 1974.

———, *Fundamentals of Human Sexuality,* New York, Holt, Rinehart and Winston, 1975.

Kephart, William M., *The Family, Society, and the Individual,* Boston, Houghton Mifflin Company, 1972, 2d ed. See Chapter Two, "Biological Foundations of the Family," pp. 15–48.

Kinsey, Alfred; Pomeroy, Wardell; Martin, Clyde; and Gebhard, Paul, *Sexual Behavior in the Human Female,* Philadelphia, W. B. Saunders Company, 1953.

Kogan, Benjamin A., *Human Sexual Expression,* New York, Harcourt Brace Jovanovich, Inc., 1973.

Liu, William T. (ed.), *Family and Fertility,* Notre Dame, Indiana, University of Notre Dame Press, 1967.

Masters, William, and Johnson, Virginia, *Human Sexual Response,* Boston, Little, Brown and Company, 1966.

McCary, James Leslie, *Human Sexuality,* New York, D. Van Nostrand Company, 1973.

———, *Human Sexual Inadequacy,* Boston, Little, Brown and Company, 1970.

Movius, Margaret, "Voluntary Childlessness—The Ultimate Liberation," *Family Coordinator,* January, 1976, pp. 57–63.

Oakley, Mary Ann, "Test Tube Babies," *Family Law Quarterly,* Winter, 1974, pp. 385–400.

Parkes, A. S., "The Biology of Fertility," in Roy Greep (ed.), *Human Fertility and Population Problems,* Cambridge, Massachusetts, Schenkman Publishing Company, Inc., 1963, pp. 23–42.

Pomeroy, Wardell B., *Dr. Kinsey and the Institute for Sex Research,* New York, The New American Library, Inc., 1972.

Scarlett, John A., "Undergraduate Attitudes Toward Birth Control: New Perspectives," *Journal of Marriage and the Family,* May, 1972, pp. 312–314.

Scheinfeld, Amram, *Twins and Supertwins,* Philadelphia, J. B. Lippincott Company, 1967.

Sherman, Julia, "What Men Do Not Know About Women's Sexuality," *Medical Aspects of Human Sexuality,* November, 1972, pp. 138–151.

Shuttleworth, Frank, "A Biosocial and Developmental Theory of Male and Female Sexuality," *Marriage and Family Living,* May, 1959, pp. 163–170.

St. John-Stevas, Norman, "History and Legal Status of Birth Control," in Edwin Schur (ed.), *The Family and the Sexual Revolution,* Bloomington, Indiana University Press, 1964, pp. 333–348.

Van Vleck, David B., *The Crucial Generation,* Charlotte, Vermont, Optimum Population Inc., 1973.

Veevers, J. E., "Factors in the Incidence of Childlessness in Canada: An Analysis of Census Data," *Social Biology,* Vol. 19, No. 3, 1974, pp. 266–274.

Wendt, Herbert, *The Sex Life of the Animals,* New York, Simon and Schuster, 1965.

Weinstock, Neal, "Artificial Insemination—The Problem and the Solution," *Family Law Quarterly,* September, 1971, pp. 369–402.

Wilson, Edward O., *Sociobiology: The New Synthesis,* Cambridge, Massachusetts, Harvard University Press, 1975.

369

17

Husband-Wife Relationships

IT WOULD HAVE been difficult for our forebears to envision a book that contained a chapter on "husband-wife relationships." Traditionally, marriage was so closely woven into the agricultural fabric of American life as to be taken almost for granted. The roles of husband and wife were clearly defined—and seldom questioned. The man was expected to be the breadwinner, and woman's place was clearly in the home. Once they were married, furthermore, a couple would almost certainly stay married "until death did them part."

If the husband proved to be shiftless or the wife incompetent as a homemaker, there would likely be trouble in the family. But "compatibility," "communication," "sexual adjustment," or "marriage enrichment"—such things had little place in the sunup to sundown existence of a pioneer, agrarian people.

It is abundantly evident, however, that times have changed. No longer do we visualize marriage and the family as a system of roles and statuses, institutionalized procedures, rights and responsibilities of husband and wife. Increasingly, matrimony has come to be thought of in terms of sharing, need-fulfillment, and emotional security. If these goals are not achieved, a husband and wife are likely to feel that their marriage is unsuccessful.

There is probably no real point in comparing today's marital system with that of yesteryear. Each age, perhaps, develops a system that best fits its own perceived needs. But this much seems certain: over 90 percent of Americans will marry—and most of them hope and expect to have happy marriages. A majority will find their expectations fulfilled. A substantial minority will not. The present chapter will attempt to touch on some of the features of the husband-wife relationship, as seen by the sociologist.

WHY MARRY?

In earlier times it was unlikely that young people paused to ask themselves the question, "Why do I want to marry?" since the alternative—bachelorhood or spinsterhood—was a rather grim one. Today the question has real meaning, and most young people are aware of that fact. For several years the writer has routinely raised the question ("Why marry?") for class discussion. From the students' view, the reasons mentioned most often include love, companionship, economic security, sexual gratification, the stigma attached to the unmarried, and a desire for children. To make things interesting, the writer tries, half in jest, to refute the arguments or reasons for marriage. For what they are worth, the usually proposed reasons—and the "refutations"—follow. The specific question is: "Why do you want to marry?"

1. *Love.*   If there is such a thing as a prime motivating factor in American marriage, romantic love must be it. As one student put it, "Well, you fall in love and marry. It's as simple as that." Whether or not falling in love is a simple matter can be debated; nevertheless, there is no denying the fact, as married couples will attest, that the romantic love experienced before marriage is, by its very nature, not the kind that lasts very long after marriage. Romantic love is an emotion, and like all emotions it is difficult,

(Rick Smolan)

if not impossible, to sustain. Married love may be more satisfying than premarital romance, but the former seems to be an all-encompassing term, involving companionship, security, sex, and so on, and these points must be defended on their own merits. As far as romantic love is concerned—as more than one writer has pointed out—marriage is likely to bring it to a fairly abrupt end.

2. *Companionship.* Admittedly, many husbands and wives are companions in a very meaningful sense, but it is also common observation that many are not. Despite the fact that sex roles are—fortunately—less rigid than they used to be, they have not entirely disappeared. There are still some conversational spheres that tend to interest females, while others are "male-oriented." The decline in sex-role stereotyping is of fairly recent origin, and there is probably some distance to go before companionship in marriage can be said to be the norm.

3. *Economic security.* It may well be, in today's society, that marriage *lessens* economic security. At a yearly salary of $12,000 to $20,000, a single man can lead a reasonably comfortable life. With a wife, two or three children, and a home, this same man could hardly be characterized as free from economic worries. The same is true for a woman. An unmarried woman with a salary in the $12,000 to $20,000 range can live rather well. But if she were to marry and bear children, either she would have to work or her husband would have to earn more than twice that amount to provide the level of living to which she was accustomed. In either case, "economic security" would be hard to substantiate as a rationale for marriage.

4. *Sexual gratification.* Although most men and women do have sexual needs, is it really necessary in this day and age to *marry* in order to achieve this need-gratification? As a matter of fact, could it not be argued that marriage is a rather expensive method of attaining sexual satisfaction? Some individuals, furthermore, would prefer a variety of partners, a practice that is neatly blocked by monogamous marriage.

5. *Stigma attached to the unmarried.* At one time, no doubt, the unmarried were looked upon somewhat askance, especially in the case of women. But cultural norms have changed markedly. Today, social stigma attaches neither to the unmarried nor to the divorced. Indeed, with more and more wives entering the labor market—many in responsible positions—one could argue that

the unmarried career woman is being emulated rather than stigmatized!

6. *Children.* Most people want children, true, but they seem to be wanting them in smaller and smaller numbers. This is hardly surprising when one considers that, according to government figures, it costs around $45,000 to raise a child from birth through college. The same figures also show that, by having one or more children, the "mother who might have worked" lost even more income than the net cost of the offspring.

Expense notwithstanding, how much do children contribute to overall marital adjustment? In the review of a decade's research literature, Hicks and Platt found that—blow of blows—"Perhaps the single most surprising finding to emerge from research is that children tend to detract from, rather than contribute to, marital happiness!"[1]

When confronted with the "refutations" listed above, most college students are somewhat taken aback. Their attitude is one of good-natured disbelief in the instructor's arguments. "What's the catch?" they want to know. "You've poked fun at our answers, but now tell us, *what is* the reason for marriage? But there is no catch, really. The refutations are oversimplified and somewhat exaggerated, but, taken piecemeal, each of them contains more than a germ of truth.

The reason that "anti-marriage" arguments prove disconcerting is that many students have never had occasion to think along such lines. Conditioned as they are to envision matrimony in terms of personal happiness, students sometimes fail to realize that there are two sides to the picture, i.e., that, along with personal pleasures, there are also displeasures and responsibilities. Maintaining a house, raising children, dealing with in-laws—such things call for an infinite amount of patience on the part of both husband and wife. Understandably, society tries to "sell" marriage to its young people, for if a substantial number of persons did not marry and reproduce, society itself would be threatened. The catch seems to be that some young people are oversold.

Before leaving the "Why marry?" question and the various refutations, a few counterarguments are in order. In the first place, although sex gratification can certainly be attained outside

---

[1] Mary W. Hicks and Marilyn Platt, "Marital Happiness and Stability: A Review of Research in the Sixties," *Journal of Marriage and the Family*, November, 1970, p. 569.

wedlock, society continues to frown on indiscriminate premarital sex. For a practical and acceptable method of sexual gratification, marriage appears to be the most satisfactory answer.

In the second place, though it is true that romantic love tends to vanish after marriage, the ties that bind happily married couples are deeper and more enduring than those experienced either at the premarital level or among friends of the same sex. Many—perhaps most—friendships are not long-lasting. As we move from adolescence to middle years, our circle of companions tends to change. Old friendships peter out and new ones are formed. In happy marriages, however, the spouses do not outgrow each other.

In the third place, though the unmarried are no longer seriously stigmatized, the fact remains that our adult social life is geared to the needs of the married, not the unmarried. Dances, dinners, bridge parties, and other social events tend to be based on the participation of *couples* rather than of single individuals. It

(Gabor Demjen, Stock Boston)

is not that single people are purposely excluded; the simple fact is that the extra person presents social difficulties.

Finally, of course, the desire for children seems to be deep-seated. Granted that youngsters are sometimes unappreciative, often rebellious, and always expensive, most parents would still not be without them. In many respects, ours is a child-centered culture, and for most adults the prospect of childlessness would be a bleak one indeed.

In short, there are any number of sound reasons for marriage, as most married couples can attest. Most couples can also attest that matrimony entails a certain loss of personal freedom even as it bestows a measure of security, and that marital privileges must be balanced against marital responsibilities. All too often, young people see only the points of privilege, and in this sense they may expect too much from marriage. As a wise man once said—or should have said—if people expected less, they might actually receive more.

MARITAL PREDICTION STUDIES

As their name implies, marital prediction studies are more concerned with the *predictive* aspects of marriage than with the fine points of marital adjustment. The studies generally involve the use of two groups of people: a happily married group and an unhappily married group. The latter is selected from divorce court records, through self-ratings, or through ratings by friends of the couple; the happily married group is selected by self-ratings or ratings of others.

Having made the selection of the two groups, the next step is to search out—through personal interviews or questionnaires —premarital *background* differences between the groups, e.g., religious orientation, social class affiliation, home environment.

After exploring a large number of background factors, the final proceeding is to formulate a set of items that *differentiates* between the happily and the unhappily married groups. The assumption is that these discriminating items, in the form of a schedule or test, can be administered to those contemplating marriage, and that the results can be taken by the latter as suggestive of their eventual level of marital happiness. Couples with extremely poor scores might wish to reconsider their plans for marriage; others could undertake matrimony with a measure of confidence.

The following items have been found in one or more studies to have predictive value and are illustrative of the kinds of items that are utilized: happiness of parents' marriage, length of acquaintance, age at marriage, educational level, childhood happiness, adaptable personality, behavioral conventionality, emotional stability, parental approval of marriage, good health, no undue conflict with mate before marriage, and number of friends.

CRITICISMS OF PREDICTION STUDIES

A number of marital prediction studies have been made in the United States, many of them involving years of painstaking work and massive statistical computation.[2] These studies succeeded in demonstrating that quantitative techniques could be applied to the study of marital adjustment. They also focused attention on predictive variables, and in the postwar period some progress was made toward building a fund of knowledge. Perhaps the most important contribution of the prediction studies was the remarkable interest they evoked on the part of both the social scientists and the public. It was these studies that gave major impetus to the family field as an area of scientific endeavor.

On the other hand, there were certain drawbacks to the marital prediction approach. It was difficult to set up *criteria* of marital adjustment. Happiness ratings—by the couples themselves or by their friends—were of questionable validity. Practically speaking, furthermore, marital happiness is a relative matter. That is to say, a given marriage must be judged not only on the basis of the adjustment or happiness of the spouses, but also on the basis of *alternative arrangements.* Bernard has written as follows on the subject:

> From this relativistic point of view, two criteria may be set up: (a) a marital relationship is successful if the satisfaction is positive; that is, if the rewards to both partners are greater than the cost; and (b) a marital relationship is successful if it is preferable to any other alternative. . . .
>
> An example of the first situation would be this: A and B do not like one another; they get on one another's nerves; the costs of remaining married are great. But the rewards are great also: together they can afford a lovely home; they have high status in the community; the children are protected, etc. . . .
>
> An example of the second criterion would be the marriage of a dependent woman to, let us say, an alcoholic, in which the costs in misery were much greater than the rewards in security and status.

---

[2] For a listing of these studies, as well as a comprehensive discussion, see Gerald R. Leslie, *The Family in Social Context,* New York, Oxford University Press, 1976, pp. 541–582.

But the spread between costs and satisfactions would be much greater if she left him. She would then be alone; she would not have the protection of the status of marriage; she would not have even the occasional sober companionship of a husband, etc. Bad as it is, therefore, her marriage seems better *than any alternative.*[3]

The marital prediction approach can also be criticized for treating the husband's and wife's personalities as separate entities rather than within the context of a *relationship.* Murstein and Glaudin comment as follows:

> Among the questions which baffle the student of marriage is the relative importance of the individual personalities of the partners in contrast to their relationship as a social dyad. To what extent is success predicated on "readiness," "maturity," "mental health," and the like, compared to "compatibility," "right choice," or "good fit?"
>
> Undoubtedly, some people could not get along with a saint because of unstable, selfish, hostile personalities. Is this the main problem? On the other hand, perhaps the commonness of marital distress indicates that people with adequately functioning personalities, considered individually, are frequently mismatched.
>
> If unhappy marriage is, in the main, a function of the misfitting of essentially sound men and women, there is no reason to expect that the primary personality characteristics of distressed mates should be drastically different from those of happily married ones. Contrariwise, if marital adjustment is more prominently a reflection of the basic *inadequacy* of one or both partners rather than their *incompatibility*, we would expect that a study of unhappy mates by personality tests would reveal various areas of marked deviancy.[4]

In an attempt to resolve the issue, the authors compared a group of unhappily married couples (undergoing counseling) with a control group who were not undergoing counseling. Both groups were given a personality test. Results indicated that for men, marital adjustment was not related to personality factors, while for women, there was only a moderate relationship in 3 out of the 13 personality factors measured.[5] And while this type of research is only in its infancy, there is a real suggestion that marital adjustment may depend more on a *fitting* of the two personalities than on the personalities themselves.

A final criticism of the prediction study approach—and one of the most important ones—is this. How can marital happiness be

337

[3] Jessie Bernard, "The Adjustment of Married Mates," in Harold Christensen (ed.), *Handbook of Marriage and the Family,* Chicago, Rand McNally & Company, 1964, pp. 732–733.

[4] Bernard I. Murstein and Vincent Glaudin, "The Relationship of Marital Adjustment to Personality: A Factor Analysis of the Interpersonal Check List," *Journal of Marriage and the Family,* February, 1966, p. 37.

[5] *Ibid.,* pp. 37–43.

meaningfully predicted on the basis of *static* background factors such as educational level, age at marriage, length of acquaintance, and the like, when it is self-evident that marriage is a *dynamic, developing* relationship? The relational process is hardly the same during the first year of matrimony as it is, say, during the tenth. Different marriages, furthermore, seem to develop in different directions, with one spouse—more than occasionally—outgrowing the other.

In view of the above criticisms, it is easy to see why the traditional marital prediction type of study has given way to a more dynamic approach. Modern studies of marital adjustment no longer stress static background factors or isolated personality components, but instead focus on relational and developmental aspects.

CURVILINEAR ASPECTS OF MARITAL ADJUSTMENT

In line with the developmental aspects referred to above, there are four possible patterns of marital adjustment. Couple A, after a comparatively happy beginning, may go steadily downhill. Couple B, after an initial period of maladjustment, may reconcile their problems to the point where their marriage becomes more rewarding with the passing of time. Couple C may experience an up-and-down pattern over the years. Couple D may report no significant change.

Of the four patterns, which is the most common? It would be encouraging to be able to report that marriages tend to improve with time, but such does not seem to be the case—despite the fact that most couples begin matrimony with the best of intentions. A fair proportion of all marriages now end in divorce. The temporal or "curvilinear" aspects of those that survive have been studied rather extensively.

A number of earlier studies—by Udry, Nelson, and Nelson,[6] Luckey,[7] Blood and Wolfe,[8] and Pineo[9]—reported that marital

---

[6] J. Richard Udry, Harold Nelson, and Ruth Nelson. "An Empirical Investigation of Some Widely Held Beliefs About Marital Interaction." *Marriage and Family Living*, November, 1961, pp. 380–388.

[7] Eleanore Braun Luckey, "Number of Years Married as Related to Personality Perception and Marital Satisfaction," *Journal of Marriage and the Family*, February, 1966, pp. 47–48.

[8] Robert Blood and Donald Wolfe, *Husbands and Wives*, New York, Free Press of Glencoe, Inc., 1960, pp. 263–264.

[9] Peter Pineo, "Disenchantment in the Later Years of Marriage," *Marriage and Family Living*, February, 1961, pp. 3–11; and "Development Patterns in Marriage," *Family Coordinator*, April, 1969, pp. 135–140.

satisfaction declined with the passing of time. Luckey, for example, writes of the "process of disillusionment that takes place." Blood and Wolfe refer to the "corrosive influence of time." And Pineo makes the following interesting observation:

> Why is it that the unforeseen changes result in loss of marital satisfaction rather than gain? The answer lies in the fact that mating occurs by personal choice. If it were by random pairing, as many gains in the "fit" between husband and wife would occur as losses. But marriage by personal choice implies that a marrying group, at the time of marriage, has a self-contrived high degree of fit between the individuals involved.
>
> Individuals do not marry unless, to some extent, they feel they have more basis for union than would have occurred if their mating were determined by chance. The fit between the two is maximized before marriage will occur. Subsequently, a regression effect occurs.[10]

379

Later studies, using a different statistical approach, added some new dimensions to the problem. Burr found that when specific aspects of marital satisfaction were considered—such as companionship, sex adjustment, and finances—fluctuations rather than declines were reported.[11] Surveys by Rollins and Cannon[12] and by Spanier, Lewis, and Cole[13] found some evidence for a so-called U-curve, with the marital satisfaction rating declining during the first few years, then leveling off, and finally—in the later years—improving. The U-curve, however, was not pronounced.

What is one to make of this array of findings? Although they are obviously not all in agreement, certain findings do stand out: (1) none of the studies shows an increase in marital adjustment over the years; (2) virtually all of the studies show a decline in marital adjustment during the first few years; (3) the studies, by definition, do not include cases of separation and divorce—and since the majority of the latter occur in the early years of marriage, the implication is strong that the immediate postmarital period is the most hazardous in terms of marital adjustment.

[10] *Ibid.*

[11] Wesley Burr, "Satisfaction with Various Aspects of Marriage over the Life-Cycle: A Random Middle-Class Sample," *Journal of Marriage and the Family*, February, 1970, pp. 29–37.

[12] Boyd C. Rollins and Kenneth Cannon, "Marital Satisfaction over the Family Life Cycle: A Reevaluation," *Journal of Marriage and the Family*, July, 1974, pp. 271–282.

[13] Graham B. Spanier, Robert A. Lewis, and Charles L. Cole, "Marital Adjustment over the Family Life Cycle: The Issue of Curvilinearity," *Journal of Marriage and the Family*, May, 1975, pp. 263–275.

What are the practical implications of the above? Surely it is not time itself that is the culprit. More likely, as Burr theorizes, it is the role strains that accompany certain phases of the family life cycle.[14] Rollins and Cannon have made the following pointed observation:

> The consistent but weak relationship between family life cycle and marital satisfaction might only be an indirect indication of the relationship between role strain and marital satisfaction. . . .
>
> If developmental family life cycle changes associated with decreases or increases in marital satisfaction is the limit of our knowledge, then in a practical sense all we can do is either stop the clock or prepare for the storm. However, if we understand the role dynamics of marital satisfaction and the high risk stages of the family career in terms of these dynamics, then alternative preventive strategies seem promising.[15]

Final word on the subject is not yet in, and it is hoped that further research will clarify some of the developmental issues in marital adjustment. In the meantime, couples should realize that marriage is a dynamic rather than a static relationship. It cannot be taken for granted. The writer has observed that college students often work harder at making their courtship a happy one than they do at making their marriage a success. The fact of the matter seems to be that spouses change and their roles change. And unless both husband and wife make a conscious effort, they are likely to find that the change has sent them in different directions. If they remain aware of the developmental phenomenon, however, it is quite possible for most couples to use it to their advantage.

SEXUAL ADJUSTMENT AND MALADJUSTMENT

Although it might not always have been so, sexual intercourse today is looked upon by both husbands and wives as an integral part of marriage. For most young people, certainly, the prospect of marriage without sex would be a grim one indeed. Under such conditions it is problematical as to what proportion of single males would actually propose, or what percentage of the females would accept.

A generation or two ago, sex was likely to be thought of as an obligation or duty insofar as the wife was concerned. Sexual gratification was felt to be a prerogative of the husband rather than

---

[14] Wesley R. Burr, *Theory Construction and the Sociology of the Family*, New York, John Wiley & Sons, Inc., 1973, pp. 218–233.
[15] Rollins and Cannon, *op. cit.*, pp. 281–282.

as a joint venture of both husband and wife. The latter was presumed to "submit" to the desires of her mate, and if in the process she received any gratification herself, the fact was likely to be kept secret, since sex was neither written about nor discussed as it is today. And if, in the process of satisfying her husband's passion, the wife was left sexually unsatisfied, it was unlikely that she would voice her complaints, since any manifestation of her sexual needs or desires was considered unladylike.

Today, conditions have changed, and it is recognized that women as well as men have sexual needs. Indeed, unless this fact is recognized by the couple, the chances of a happy marriage may be materially reduced. As a working definition of sexual adjustment, therefore, we will consider a married couple to be sexually adjusted when the frequency of coitus and the physical and psycho-emotional responses involved are mutually satisfactory. It is recognized that this definition depicts an ideal type, and that in reality sexual adjustment is more likely to be a matter of degree rather than a question of black or white.

The Seriousness of Sexual Maladjustment.   From all accounts, sexual discord is fairly widespread in the United States. Research findings from a variety of sources—divorce courts, clinics, marriage councils, questionnaire and interview surveys—have all shown sexual difficulties to be among the most often listed marital complaints. Masters and Johnson—perhaps the two best-known practitioners in the field of sex therapy—go so far as to state that one-half of the marriages in this country are either "presently sexually dysfunctional," or will be so in the future.[16]

But while there seems little doubt about the frequency of sexual complaints, it is more difficult to assign a specific weight to the *importance* of the sexual factor. For example, if husband and wife cannot agree on how often to have intercourse, it is likely that this disagreement will adversely affect the day-to-day congeniality of the spouses. Conversely, if the day-to-day congeniality of the spouses were at a low level, it seems likely that their sexual adjustment would be hampered, even assuming an otherwise equal interest in sex relations.

Marriage counselors, clinicians, and lawyers who handle divorce cases are often of the belief that sexual discord is the most important single cause of marital unhappiness. This belief is also shared by many doctors and clergymen. Most family researchers, however, while conceding the importance of the sexual factor, would hesitate to label it the number one culprit. Masters and

381

---

[16] William Masters and Virginia Johnson, *Human Sexual Inadequacy*, Boston, Little, Brown and Company, © 1970, p. 369. Reprinted by permission.

Johnson say, simply, that "very few marriages can exist as effective, complete, and on-going entities without a comfortable component of sexual exchange."[17] The present writer would certainly agree. On the basis of his own research in the divorce court, as well as a general familiarity with the sociological literature, he would judge that sex is about as important a part of marriage as any other single factor.

There is no need to go into detail regarding the specific sexual complaints that are heard—premature ejaculation on the part of the husband, failure of the wife to reach orgasm, disagreement on coital techniques, lack of affection on the part of one spouse—they have all been well publicized in both the clinical and the popular literature. There is a real need, however, to take a careful look at some of the proposed solutions to the problem of sexual maladjustment.

SOME PROPOSED SOLUTIONS

The Clinical Approach. Couples with serious sexual problems are frequently advised to go to a marriage clinic, where professional guidance by physicians, psychiatrists, and counselors is available. The Reproductive Biology Research Foundation (St. Louis), for example—the site of the Masters–Johnson studies—includes a clinic for the treatment of human sexual dysfunction. The Foundation has developed the concept of "conjoint marital-unit therapy."

> Isolating a husband or wife in therapy from his or her partner not only denies the concept that both partners are involved in the sexual inadequacy, but also ignores the fundamental fact that sexual response represents interaction between people. . . . The Foundation's basic premise of therapy insists that, although both husband and wife in a sexually dysfunctional marriage are treated, the marital relationship is considered as the patient.[18]

The Foundation also operates on the assumption that the marital unit can be treated most effectively by a *male-female team* of therapists rather than by a single individual.

> Controlled laboratory experimentation in human sexual psychology has supported unequivocally the premise that no man will ever fully understand woman's sexual function or dysfunction. The exact converse applies to any woman. . . . She, too, learns to conceptualize

---

[17] *Ibid.*, p. 15.
[18] *Ibid.*, pp. 2–4.

male sexual functioning and dysfunctioning, but she will never fully understand the basics of male sexual response because she will never experience ejaculatory demand nor seminal fluid release. . . .[19]

First, communication is developed across the desk between patients and cotherapists. Within a few days, verbal exchange is deliberately encouraged between patients. The cotherapists are fully aware that their most important role in reversal of sexual dysfunction is that of catalyst to communication.

Along with the opportunity to educate, there exists the opportunity to encourage discussion between the marital partners wherein they can share and understand each other's needs. . . .

With detailed interchange of information, and with interpersonal rapport secured between marital partners, the dual-sex therapy team moves into direct treatment of the specific sexual inadequacy.[20]

While space precludes a description of the various therapeutic measures employed, the Foundation has had a remarkable record of success. Despite the fact that some extremely difficult cases were handled—both male and female—a five-year follow-up revealed a failure rate of only 20 percent.[21]

What are the drawbacks to a clinical-type approach, such as that described above? There are two major ones. In the first place, there are simply not enough clinics to go around. Following the Foundation pattern, clinics would require a physician on each therapy team—and physicians are in short supply. Referring to their own situation, Masters and Johnson point out that, even if the caseload were quadrupled, "no discernible reduction would be made in the level sea of clinical demand for treatment of human sexual inadequacy."[22]

A second drawback to the clinical approach is the fact that, even if a sufficient number of clinics could be established, the incidence of sexual incompatibility would remain high. A clinical approach, by definition, aims at curing existing problems rather than preventing them. To be of maximal individual and societal value, therefore, programs aimed at reducing sexual discord must embody a preventive philosophy.

The Marriage Manual Approach. Marriage manuals are small, inexpensive booklets, which advise married couples on the fine points of sexual adjustment. Although there are scores of such booklets in stores and on newsstands, in virtually every case the

383

---

[19] *Ibid.*
[20] *Ibid.*, pp. 14–15.
[21] *Ibid.*, see pp. 364–369.
[22] *Ibid.*, p. 369.

"message" is the same. In capsule form it is as follows: because of a variety of background factors and because she has been conditioned to be reserved in sexual matters, the wife is ordinarily slower in reaching sexual climax than her husband. To achieve sexual happiness, therefore, the wife must be willing to throw off her reserve and cooperate fully with her spouse, while the husband must endeavor (1) to slow down his own responses and (2) to become proficient in the art of lovemaking. If these principles are followed, there is little reason why orgasm cannot be a matter of mutual attainment.

According to the marriage manuals, therefore, sex adjustment is primarily a matter of specific sexual *techniques,* with the male assuming both the major role and the major responsibility. In a survey of the more popular manuals, Brissett and Lewis found that "between three and four times as many prescriptions for behavior are directed to the male as to the female."[23]

In recent years—as might have been predicted—marriage manuals have been heavily criticized, for the fact of the matter is that sexual adjustment is much more than a simple game of genital skillo. For example, the manuals do not take into consideration the great range of individual differences in human sex drive. Some individuals are highly sexed, others experience feelings of sex desire infrequently. And for the latter group, it is unlikely that recourse to erotic techniques would alter the basic sexual pattern.

In this same connection, both husbands and wives bring a lifetime of experiential values to the marriage bed, and, if these attitudes and beliefs are not in keeping with the techniques advocated in the marriage manuals, it is possible that an attempt to apply them will do more harm than good.

And finally, in the case of many couples who otherwise enjoy sexual intercourse even though the wife does not regularly experience orgasm, the advice given in the marriage manuals may (1) cause her to feel that something is wrong with her sexuality and (2) engender feelings of inadequacy on the part of the husband, because of the failure of his wife to achieve orgasm.

Commenting on the problem of the husband, Brissett and Lewis write as follows:

> It is our contention that the manuals are espousing an ideal of sexual activity that is extremely difficult to attain, particularly for the male. An attempt to measure up to the guidelines of the manuals may indeed be a source of certain sexual difficulties in marriage.

[23] Dennis Brissett and Lionel Lewis, "Guidelines for Marital Sex: An Analysis of Popular Marriage Manuals," *Family Coordinator,* January, 1970, p. 42.

384

We are also dubious about the very nature of sexual activity depicted as ideal by these manuals. To achieve the highly organized, extremely rational kind of sexual life they propose does not appear to be necessarily idyllic. It seems questionable that people should continually have to constrain, control, and suppress their emotions, impulses, and passions, in order to achieve a satisfactory sex life.[24]

With regard to the problem for the wife, Fisher—on the basis of his own exhaustive research—writes that:

> One is struck with the finding that orgasm consistency is not correlated with either intercourse rate or preferred intercourse rate. The ability to reach orgasm, as such, is probably not a prime determinant of how much a woman wants or engages in intercourse.[25]

Actually, the Fisher study—probably the most intensive yet made on female sexuality—revealed a number of facts that conflict with the message of the marriage manuals. These findings will be discussed in the concluding section. There is little doubt, however, that the manuals place undue stress on sexual techniques and coital positions; in fact, many of the booklets convey the idea that physical love and intercourse are luridly mechanical processes, as the following composite table of contents reveals:

Lurid or not, there is no doubt that marriage manuals are big business. In the Brissett and Lewis content-survey, the authors reported that sales of the leading manuals ran into the millions.[26]

A Sociological Approach. Basic to any sociological approach is the premise that, like so many other aspects of marriage, sexual adjustment is a fairly complex phenomenon that cannot be solved by recourse to a few simple maxims. To begin with, the sociologist is quite cognizant of the existence of individual differences. Practically all the research surveys have revealed wide differences in individual sex drive, and an understanding of

385

---

[24] *Ibid.*, p. 47.
[25] From *The Female Orgasm: Psychology, Physiology, Fantasy* by Seymour Fisher, © 1973 by Basic Books, Inc., Publishers, New York, p. 217.
[26] Brissett and Lewis, *op. cit.*, p. 42.

such differences on the part of the couple concerned would seem to be a prerequisite to sexual compatibility.

Over and above the matter of individual differences, the sociologist would also consider sexual adjustment as inextricably linked with the total personality interaction of the two spouses. Sexual discord is often held up as the cause of marital unhappiness, and all too seldom is it realized that marital difficulties may *precede* sexual maladjustment. In the case of a husband who drinks incessantly and is otherwise rude and inconsiderate, it is unlikely that his wife would show much enthusiasm in the sexual realm. The futility of the marriage manual approach in such a case becomes obvious. It seems likely that the better the all-around adjustment of a couple, the easier it will be to achieve sexual harmony. But, in any case, before attributing sexual incompatibility to strictly sexual factors, the sociologist would want to know more about the overall level of marital adjustment.

Within the sexual realm itself, there is one factor that has caused a good deal of controversy, namely, orgasmic response on the part of the wife and the various correlates associated with it. On the one hand, it is well established that some wives attain multiple orgasm during intercourse, a capability beyond that of their husbands. On the other hand, repeated research studies have shown that around 30 percent of all married women never or rarely attain orgasm. Fisher goes on to state that "these findings have been interpreted by some to mean that a large segment of women in our culture do not get aroused by, or really enjoy, sexual stimulation. Observations from the writer's studies would argue that this is an overstatement. The women in our samples did generally value sexual stimulation and did assign considerable importance to it in their lives, despite their not infrequent difficulties in achieving orgasm."[27]

It is on this specific aspect of sexual adjustment that many marriage manuals—and some clinicians—are guilty of oversimplification. For, insofar as the wife is concerned, sexual adjustment cannot be explained solely in terms of orgasm attainment. Fisher writes as follows on the matter:

> Years of marital intercourse seem to have rather unimpressive effects on orgasm attainment. For example, the writer noted that number of intercourse positions and length of foreplay had only chance correlations with orgasm consistency. A primary deduction to be made from such material is that the ability to be sexually responsive cannot be learned by an adult woman in the way that she learns other motor skills. . . . Beyond a moderate level of

---

[27] Fisher, *op. cit.*, p. 396.

knowledge concerning primary erogenous zones, the factors facilitating sexual arousal seem to be largely interpersonal, involving feelings of intimacy and closeness. . . .[28]

The same author goes on to outline some of the needed areas of research on the subject—research correlating female sexual response with such factors as prior role of mother and father, family crises, and role of the husband. This last aspect may be of particular importance, since in the final analysis sexual adjustment involves a marital *relationship*. Fisher suggests that it would be important to determine the wife's feeling about her husband's "dependability as a love object. . . . One would want to evaluate the husband with respect to traits such as conscientiousness and ability to identify with his wife, and one would also want to ascertain how much confidence she had in him."[29]

While there are a number of approaches to the problem of marital sex adjustment, most sociologists would be inclined to stress the advisability of research. Sex is no longer the hush-hush topic it used to be, and there is every reason to believe that, as time goes on, more and more worthwhile surveys—such as the Fisher study quoted above—will be undertaken. Findings from these surveys, in turn, should be of help to those couples with sexual problems. In the past, unfortunately, advice to couples has sometimes outstripped the factual information available at the time.

SELECTED READINGS

Aldous, Joan, "The Making of Family Roles and Family Change," *Family Coordinator*, July, 1974, pp. 231–235.

Anderson, Wayne J., *Challenges for Successful Family Living*, Minneapolis, T. S. Denison & Company, 1974.

Bernard, Jessie, "The Adjustment of Married Mates," in Harold Christensen (ed.), *Handbook of Marriage and the Family*, Chicago, Rand McNally & Company, 1964, pp. 732–733.

Blood, Robert, and Wolfe, Donald, *Husbands and Wives*, New York, Free Press of Glencoe, Inc., 1960.

Brissett, Dennis, and Lewis, Lionel, "Guidelines for Marital Sex: An Analysis of Popular Marriage Manuals," *Family Coordinator*, January, 1970, pp. 41–48.

Burr, Wesley R., *Theory Construction and the Sociology of the Family*, New York, John Wiley & Sons, Inc., 1973.

---

[28] *Ibid.*, p. 440.
[29] *Ibid.*, pp. 441–442.

Fineberg, Beth L., and Lowman, Joseph, "Affect and Status Dimensions of Marital Adjustment," *Journal of Marriage and the Family*, February, 1975, pp. 155–160.

Fink, Paul J., and Hammett, Van Buren O., *Sexual Function and Dysfunction*, Philadelphia, F. A. Davis Company, 1969.

Fisher, Seymour, *The Female Orgasm: Psychology, Physiology, Fantasy*, New York, Basic Books, Inc., 1973.

Glenn, Norval D., "Psychological Well-Being in the Postparental State: Some Evidence from National Surveys," *Journal of Marriage and the Family*, February, 1975, pp. 105–110.

Harry, Joseph, "Evolving Sources of Happiness for Men Over the Life Cycle," *Journal of Marriage and the Family*, May, 1976, pp. 289–296.

Heller, Peter, "Familism Scale: A Measure of Family Solidarity," *Journal of Marriage and the Family*, February, 1970, pp. 73–80.

Hicks, Mary W., and Platt, Marilyn, "Marital Happiness and Stability: A Review of Research in the Sixties," *Journal of Marriage and the Family*, November, 1970, pp. 553–574.

Hutchinson, Ira W., "The Significance of Marital Status for Morale and Life Satisfaction Among Lower-Income Elderly," *Journal of Marriage and the Family*, May, 1975, pp. 287–293.

Kinsey, Alfred C.; Pomeroy, Wardell B.; Martin, Clyde E.; and Gebhard, Paul H., *Sexual Behavior in the Human Female*, Philadelphia, W. B. Saunders Company, 1953.

Le Masters, E. E., *Parents in Modern America*, Homewood, Illinois, The Dorsey Press, 1974.

Leslie, Gerald R., *The Family in Social Context*, pp. 459–494, New York, Oxford University Press, 1973.

Luckey, Eleanore, and Bain, Joyce, "Children: A Factor in Marital Adjustment," *Journal of Marriage and the Family*, February, 1970, pp. 43–44.

McConnell, Lawrence, "An Examination of the Counselor's Skills When Counseling Clients with Sexual Problems," *Family Coordinator*, April, 1976, pp. 183–188.

Masters, William, and Johnson, Virginia, *Human Sexual Inadequacy*, Boston, Little, Brown and Company, 1970.

Medical Aspects of Human Sexuality, published monthly by Hospital Publications, Inc., 609 Fifth Ave., New York, N.Y.

Orthner, Dennis K., "Leisure Activity Patterns and Marital Satisfaction over the Marital Career," *Journal of Marriage and the Family*, February, 1975, pp. 91–102.

Otto, Herbert A., "Marriage and Family Enrichment Programs in North America—Report and Analysis," *Family Coordinator*, April, 1975, pp. 137–142.

Petras, John, *Sex: Male/Gender: Masculine,* Port Washington, N.Y., Alfred Publishing Co., 1975.

Pineo, Peter, "Development Patterns in Marriage," *Family Coordinator,* April, 1969, pp. 135–140.

Rodman, Hyman, "Marital Power and the Theory of Resources in Cultural Context," *Journal of Comparative Family Studies,* Spring, 1972, pp. 50–69.

Rollins, Boyd C., and Cannon, Kenneth, "Marital Satisfaction over the Family Life Cycle: A Reevaluation," *Journal of Marriage and the Family,* July, 1974, pp. 271–284.

Spanier, Graham B.; Lewis, Robert A.; and Cole, Charles L., "Marital Adjustment over the Family Life Cycle: The Issue of Curvilinearity," *Journal of Marriage and the Family,* May, 1975, pp. 263–275.

Terman, Lewis M., *Psychological Factors in Marital Happiness,* New York, McGraw-Hill Book Company, 1938.

_____, "Correlates of Orgasm Adequacy in a Group of 566 Wives," *Journal of Psychology,* October, 1951, pp. 115–172.

Wagner, Nathaniel, *Perspectives on Human Sexuality,* New York, Behavioral Publications, 1974.

Wallin, Paul, "A Study of Orgasm as a Condition of Women's Enjoyment of Intercourse," *Journal of Social Psychology,* Vol. 51, 1960, pp. 191–198.

Wells, J. Gipson, *Current Issues in Marriage and the Family,* pp. 1–11, New York, Macmillan Publishing Co., Inc., 1975.

18

Social-Class Variations

ALTHOUGH THE DOMAIN is by no means entirely his, it is the sociologist who has been the driving force behind the study of social class. Whether the area involved is sex behavior, crime, political affiliation, or general life style, the sociologist, more than any other social scientist, has come to look for explanatory factors in terms of socio-economic status. It would be expected, therefore, in the marriage and family area, that an investigation of social-class factors would prove to be rewarding, an expectation that has been borne out by the facts. Scores of studies have revealed significant differences among upper-, middle-, and lower-class families.

While there is still disagreement over the concept of social class, sociologists often "stratify" a population on the basis of such factors as occupation, income, and educational level.[1] Adjudged by these criteria, the precise number of classes becomes somewhat arbitrary. However, a convenient classification is the five-way breakdown into upper, upper-middle, middle, working, and lower classes. Mention will be made of all five strata, but primary emphasis in the present chapter will be placed on the family perspective as seen from the top, the middle, and the bottom levels.

THE UPPER-CLASS FAMILY

Although by far the smallest of the various social classes, the upper class is a tremendously powerful and influential segment

---

[1] For a comprehensive review of the subject, see Luther B. Otto, "Class and Status in Family Research," *Journal of Marriage and the Family*, May, 1975, pp. 315–332.

of the population. Sometimes classed as the "upper-upper," "established upper," or "elite," they show little tendency either to relinquish or to share their influence. Despite criticism from the middle and lower strata, upper-class families remain substantially endogamous. Goode comments on this point as follows:

> Ultimately, any stratification system is based on some pattern of *evaluation*. In the early Middle Ages, class position was based in part upon property ownership and in part upon religious learning. In the period just prior to that, courage and skill in war played a very great part in establishing a family in high place. In Imperial China, movement upward was based upon a knowledge of the classics, calligraphy, philosophy, and general humanistic learning.
>
> However, no matter what the basis for the stratification—skill, honor, courage and success in war, technical and scientific knowledge, etc.—by definition the upper social strata have more of it than do the lower. That is indeed how one defines lower and upper classes. . . .
>
> One consequence of this is that upper-class families actually have more to lose, and spend much more energy on training their young, and on controlling their adults by group pressures. They must maintain greater group cohesion in order to keep from falling in class position. At the same time, they have more *resources* with which to control the young who might marry wrongly.[2]

It is this relative *impermeability* that sets the upper class apart from other social strata. By and large, the American class structure is fairly fluid; at least, education, drive, and the accumulation of wealth usually lead to an improvement in one's class position. Failure in these spheres tends to bring about a loss of social status. This fluidity, however, does not extend to the upper class. Families neither enter nor leave this privileged group solely on the basis of economic criteria.

The Kinship System. Although it is obvious that the upper stratum is a moneyed class, pride in family name is also their hallmark. Thus, while names such as Morgan, Vanderbilt, Wanamaker, Mellon, Astor, Biddle, Harriman, Du Pont, Carnegie, Drexel, and Rockefeller are readily identified as centers of enormous financial power, the fact is that these families also reach back through generations of American history. They are *historical families* and place great emphasis on ancestral respect and generational accomplishments. In this sense, therefore, the upper stratum is perhaps more akin to a caste than a class.

---

[2] William Goode, *Family and Mobility*, A Report to the Institute of Life Insurance, 1964, pp. 21–23.

Class or caste, the upper stratum perpetuates itself through a vast kin network. Significantly, it is difficult for an outsider to comprehend the kinship system, embodying as it does nuclear units interlocked through blood ties, marriage, and joint ownership of property. Since kinship ties extend through many generations, the upper class tends to become clanlike in structure. Cousins, uncles, aunts, siblings, in-laws, nieces and nephews, parents and grandparents—all combine to form an imposing *range of familiarity*.

This upper-class range is solidified not only through extensive business and personal relationships but through systematic encouragement of endogamous marriage. Cousin marriages, particularly the second- and third-cousin variety, are commonplace. In a given locality, therefore, it is easy to see how a particular family can exert considerable influence. It is also easy to understand why the same names appear over and over in the Social Register. In writing of the Du Pont family, for instance, Baltzell notes that:

> The Social Register listed some 73 Du Pont adults, compared to 31 Mellons, 28 Harrimans, 27 Rockefellers. Down through the years the number of consanguine marriages has been unusually high. One *paterfamilias* was forced to issue an edict against the practice. Yet Pierre Samuel Du Pont, the last of the patriarchial rulers of the family, married his own mother's niece.[3]

Geographically, the upper class tends to be rather stationary, in contrast to the middle class. Whereas the middle-class family head is likely to move several times in the course of his occupational career, the upper-class male generally "stays put." The chances are that he will be born, live, and die in the same community, along with the rest of his kin. This nonmobility explains why certain upper-class names are associated with specific areas, e.g., the Du Ponts in Wilmington, the Lowells in Boston, the Biddles in Philadelphia, and the Rockefellers in New York.

The concentration of specific upper-class families within a community, plus a strong affiliation with the kin network, leads to a respect for the elderly that is unparalleled in other strata. Cavan writes as follows:

> The elderly heads hold somewhat the same position that the elders hold in primitive societies. In their youth they knew members of at least two preceding generations whose lips repeated the legends of still earlier generations. Family victories are thus preserved—sometimes family defeats. Children are compared to earlier members of

---

[3] E. Digby Baltzell, *The Protestant Establishment: Aristocracy and Caste in America*, New York, Random House, Inc., 1964, p. 251.

(Philip Jon Bailey)

the family, and expectations are established that these children will equal or surpass the feats of their ancestors. Admired personality traits of the ancestors are held before children in their impressionable years. . . . Thus, as with primitives, the elders of the upper class are the repository of legend and wisdom for both the social class and the particular family group.

The elders wield great power over both adult and youthful descendants, often determining such matters as type and place of education, occupation, and selection of the spouse. If, as often happens, they hold the joint family property and wealth, they possess an enormous authority since they may control the amount of income of younger members. Thus middle-aged men who, in other social classes, would be independent heads of their small families and control their own social and economic destinies, in the upper class may still play the role of dependent sons to their old parents.[4]

Courtship and Marriage. Predictably, courtship in the upper stratum is rather circumscribed, especially for girls. Dating outside the class is frowned upon, and considerable pressure is

---

[4] Ruth Cavan, *The American Family*, New York, Thomas Y. Crowell Company, 1969, pp. 88–89.

brought to bear on deviators. Contrary to the Hollywood stereotype, however, upper-class boys and girls are far from eager to "kick over the traces." Through the years, they have been quite content to date and marry within their own class; in fact, given their social status and style of life, it would be strange indeed if they were to seek matrimony outside the group.*

It should not be forgotten that many of their social relationships are of the *intra-class variety,* so that in most cases all that is necessary is for dating (and nature) to take its course. True, there are exceptions, and these do cause concern in the families involved, particularly when a "wrong" marriage results. In general, though, the problem of exogamous marriages has not been a major one—for, in the last analysis, the upper-class youth who marries outside the group is well aware that the spouse may not be admitted to class membership.

394

There are indications that a relatively high proportion of upper-class members marry, although—compared with other social strata—they marry at a somewhat later age. It also appears that very few upper-class women renounce marriage in favor of a career. In fact, in the Blumberg–Paul sample, a relatively small percentage of the upper-class women mentioned any occupation at all.[5]

Available sociological evidence suggests—contrary, perhaps, to the Hollywood stereotype—that upper-class marriages are probably happier than those of the middle and lower strata. Marital prediction studies reveal a positive correlation between class position and marital adjustment. Also, as will be shown in a later chapter, divorce rates are much lower in the upper strata. Desertions, as might be expected, are virtually unknown. Marital disputes do occur, of course, and when they are serious they are likely to be reported by the press. Nevertheless, of the various social strata in the United States, the upper-class family is evidently the most stable.

---

* It should be mentioned that, while the description herein refers largely to those persons listed in the Social Register, not all members of the upper class are Registerites. Research findings suggest that a substantial amount of intermarriage occurs between these two upper-class elements—with most of the (intermarrying) non-Registerites subsequently being listed. (See Lawrence Rosen and Robert Bell, "Mate Selection in the Upper Class," *Sociological Quarterly,* Spring, 1966, pp. 157–166. See also Paul Blumberg and P. W. Paul, "Continuities and Discontinuities in Upper-Class Marriages," *Journal of Marriage and the Family,* February, 1975, pp. 63–77.)

[5] Paul Blumberg and P. W. Paul, *op. cit.,* p. 73.

The reasons for upper-class stability can only be conjectured. Educational and economic advantages undoubtedly serve as influencing factors, though other considerations are probably involved. Since upper-class couples are at the apex of the social hierarchy, they need not concern themselves with the status aspirations that characterize so many middle-class families. Then, too, the upper stratum has more commitment to "family," per se, than do the other classes. That is, marriage is thought of not only as a *husband-wife relationship* but as *an interlocking part* of a broader kin network, which includes both in-laws and blood relatives.

Life Style. Basic to an understanding of the upper-class way of life is the fact that (1) since members are already established at the top of the social ladder, there is no striving for status; and (2) there are generally no financial problems. Since status and wealth (preferably inherited wealth) are taken for granted, there is no need for ostentatious living. Upper-class families live comfortably—very comfortably—but they shun any display of opulence. Thus they live in large houses, but not large *new* houses. They dress well, but probably not so well as the upper-middle class. They may buy an expensive new car, or they may not, depending on their mood or fancy. They probably own precious jewelry, but wearing it is something else again. In brief, to exhibit one's wealth—or even to talk about it openly—is considered crass and ill-mannered.

Upper-class families travel a great deal both here and abroad. They usually have a summer home and almost certainly have an extensive (intra-class) social life. As Kahl notes, "The upper class in any local community is, relative to other strata, small and cohesive; it is an *organized social group,* not merely a statistical category of similar people. In this sense, it is qualitatively different from the other classes."[6]

Traditionally, upper-class families have sent their children to private schools and on to Ivy League colleges, though the college pattern is not nearly so strong as it used to be. Still strong, however, are the interlocking relationships on the boards of large corporations. The influence of the upper class is also keenly felt in the private men's clubs that cater to top corporation executives. Indeed, the private upper-class men's clubs in our large cities are perhaps the most exclusive organizations in America.

---

[6] Joseph Kahl, *The American Class Structure,* New York, Rinehart & Company, Inc., 1958, p. 188.

It should not be thought that upper-class family life is totally without problems. Personality conflicts, disputes, arguments with in-laws—such discord occurs in all social strata. Moreover, there are certain kinds of difficulties that arise primarily at the upper-class level. Le Masters describes three in particular:

1. "The shadow of the ancestor" often haunts the children of illustrious parents. John D. Rockefeller, Jr., describes how he left the business world because he knew he could not compete with the reputation of his father—the world's first billionaire. The son eventually achieved a meaningful life in the field of philanthropy, establishing the Rockefeller foundation. . . .

Middle and lower-class children can surpass the accomplishments of their parents. This is usually not possible at the upper-class level.

2. Wealthy parents have always had the problem of not spoiling their children. This is one reason for the spartan characteristics of the upper-class boarding schools—small rooms; modest food; early rising; and stern schoolmasters.

A related problem of upper-class parents is that of motivating their children to "do something" in this world, when the children already have everything that most people spend their lives struggling for.

3. Finally, upper-class members face the problem of notoriety—the merciless glare of publicity that hovers over them from cradle to grave. One of the writer's students was the daughter of the state governor. She talked at length about newspaper photographers and reporters following her car, some of them hoping for material that could be used against her father politically.[7]

The Future of the Upper Class. The upper class faces another generic problem that should be mentioned: recurrent censure and hostility from critics. Writers of American fiction, from F. Scott Fitzgerald to John P. Marquand and James Cozzens, have long satirized the upper class. But in recent years nonfictional writers like George Lundberg, Edmund Wilson, C. Wright Mills, Cleveland Amory, William Domhoff, Stephen Birmingham, and Digby Baltzell have come up with some penetrating criticisms of certain upper-class practices. Baltzell, for example, contends that a "crisis in moral authority" has developed largely because of the upper class's unwillingness to absorb "talented and distinguished members of minority groups into its privileged ranks."[8]

---

[7] Reprinted with permission from Le Masters, *Parents In Modern America* (Rev. Ed.; Homewood, Ill.: The Dorsey Press, 1974c.), pp. 83–84.

[8] Baltzell, *op. cit.*, p. x.

Criticism of the upper class does not necessarily mean that it is in fact weakening. In every society the upper stratum has been subjected to sharp criticism. Baltzell maintains, however, that the American upper class is indeed weakening—*through the courtship system.*

> Today, the debutante ritual is still in full force in most of our major cities. Yet it has *far less meaning for the debutantes themselves,* especially for those with the ability and ambition to go to one of the better colleges. They now take their education seriously, and as a result the campus community, on the whole but not entirely, has come to displace the local community with its country clubs and the debutante balls as the major upper-class courting environment.
>
> What seems to be happening is that a scholastic hierarchy of campus communities governed by the values of admissions committees is gradually supplanting the class hierarchies in local communities which are still governed by the values of parents. And by and large, the higher the scholastic standing of the campus the more the students will be attracted to one another on the basis of intellectual interests as against the traditional affinities of caste and class.[9]

In the latest study, by Blumberg and Paul in 1975, the authors also found certain points of "weakening" in the upper-class structure. Basing their findings on an analysis of marriage announcements in the Sunday *New York Times,* they discovered an increase in the percentage of Social Registerites marrying non-Registerites. They also found a decrease in the percentage of Registerite men who had gone to an elite private school and an Ivy League college and a decrease in the percentage of Registerite women who had made debuts and who had gone to one of the Seven Sister colleges. There was clear evidence, in other words, of a "deconcentration and dispersion" on the part of the upper class.

But, in spite of these developments, the authors conclude, "a great theme of continuity runs through these largely upper-class marriages. Although tremendous forces have shaken American society in the past generation, the upper class has maintained itself remarkably intact, and, having done so, is perhaps the most untouched group in American life." In more detail, the same authors write that:

> In our study, just as in the one 30 years ago, conventional church weddings prevail. And though there seem to be more Catholic marriages announced than heretofore, the class churches, especially Episcopalian, continue to predominate. As before, an education at a prestigious Eastern private school is typical of the men. As before,

---

[9] *Ibid.,* pp. 350–351.

husbands have followed their fathers into business and professional occupations. As before, the brides mention affiliation with clubs and organizations such as the Junior League.[10]

Will the democratization process and the changing pattern of American courtship make for modifications in the upper-class structure? Will the latter eventually lose its castelike impermeability? Only time will tell. Thus far, there has been no pronounced tendency to "let down the bars." At the same time, social change takes place slowly at the upper-class level, where the stakes are very high indeed. But if there is a change—surely a big if—it may well occur, as Baltzell contends, through Cupid's perambulations on the college campus.

THE MIDDLE-CLASS FAMILY

The middle stratum in American society presents some problems in classification, and not all sociologists employ the same nomenclature. Just below the upper class, described above, are those well-to-do families in which the father is usually a professional man or a business executive. This group is variously referred to as the "lower-upper" or "upper-middle" class. The next lower stratum in the social hierarchy is the middle-class proper, families of moderate means in which the husband is in the white-collar—clerical or sales—category. The line between middle and upper-middle is not always clear-cut. Men in the higher administrative or sales positions, for example, tend to merge into the upper-middle class. As a matter of fact, while the middle stratum has some identifiable characteristics, the so-called middle-class way of life—as we shall see—has been greatly oversimplified.

The Kaleidoscopic Class.   For all its written-about simplicity, the middle-class family is a veritable kaleidoscope. It looks different, depending on the light and the angle, and no two people seem to see the same design. Bensman and Vidich maintain that:

> Going to church, taking pride in property, being neat and orderly, and showing a capacity for moral indignation against corruption are the chief elements of the middle-class legacy.[11]

---

[10] Paul Blumberg and P. W. Paul, "Continuities and Discontinuities in Upper-Class Marriages," *Journal of Marriage and the Family*, February, 1975, pp. 75–76.
[11] Joseph Bensman and Arthur Vidich, "The New Class System and Its Life Styles," in Saul Feldman and Gerald Thielbar (eds.), *Life Styles: Diversity in American Society*, Boston, Little, Brown and Company, 1975, pp. 136 ff.

Le Masters points out that some observers feel the middle class is in a rather unenviable position:

> They lack the pride of the old blue-collar aristocracy; they make less money; they have less skill to sell; and they lack job security. At the same time, they tend to identify with the more highly educated and prosperous groups above them.[12]

Kahl writes of the middle class as follows:

> They are the people who seldom make basic decisions about their work, yet carry out the instructions with intelligence, technical understanding, and considerable initiative. They accept many of the career values of the upper-middle class, and are constantly striving to get ahead; *yet most never will get very far, and after they have outlived the romantic dreams of youth, they know it. . . .*
> Middle-class people cannot cling too strongly to career as the focus of their lives, for their jobs do not lead continuously upward. Instead, they tend to emphasize the respectability of their jobs and their styles of life.[13]

It is probably true that most middle-class workers, after a spell, realize that they will not move ahead. Yet enough of them apparently do get ahead to disprove the notion that the middle class is invariably a dead-end road. Cavan writes that middle-class families generally do not have heirlooms, family portraits, or written records of prior generations. Any possessions that were inherited have probably been worn out by constant use.

> The true middle-class family, however, is content with its independence, with its relative freedom from the past and from collateral kinship groups, and with the opportunity for upward mobility within the class.[14]

Clearly the white-collar job, with its combination of rewards and frustrations, is central to an understanding of middle-class people. It must be remembered that these people are perched squarely in the middle of the socio-economic ladder, and it is temptingly American to look up rather than down. This tendency to identify with the upper rather than the lower strata is probably a major reason for the white-collar workers' reluctance to unionize. Attempts to unionize white-collar employees have been made for several decades now, with a noticeable lack of success.

But if the middle-class worker does not take to the idea of unionizing, he most certainly embraces other American culture traits, such as the belief in education, a respect for hard work,

---

[12] Le Masters, *op. cit.*, p. 79.
[13] Kahl, *op. cit.*, p. 203.
[14] Cavan, *op. cit.*, p. 113.

and a high regard for the power of personality. In Arthur Miller's *Death of a Salesman*—one of the memorable American plays—there is a scene between Willy Loman and his son Biff. Willy, a pathetic figure as a fading salesman, tries to prime the boy for a business interview.

WILLY: But don't wear a sport jacket and slacks when you see Oliver.
BIFF: No, I'll—
WILLY: A business suit, and talk as little as possible, and don't crack any jokes. . . . Remember, start big and you'll end big. Ask for fifteen. How much you gonna ask for?
BIFF: Gee, I don't know—
WILLY: And don't say "Gee." "Gee" is a boy's word. A man walking in for fifteen thousand dollars does not say "Gee!"
BIFF: Ten, I think, would be top though.
WILLY: Don't be so modest. You always started too low. Walk in with a big laugh. Don't look worried. Start off with a couple of good stories to lighten things up. It's not what you say, it's how you say it—because personality always wins the day.[15]

In the short space of a few sentences, poor Willy has completely reversed himself—and he is not even aware of it, so eager is he to move his stagnant son to right action. For Willy is convinced that the road to socio-economic success is paved with personality. It is interesting that many middle-class workers, in real life, seem to have the same idea; e.g., one of the contentions of small merchants and salespeople is that they "enjoy meeting people and learning about human nature."

One of the most poignant statements about the "personality" approach to sales is found in C. Wright Mills' classic *White Collar*:

The employer of manual services buys the workers' labor, energy, and skill; the employer of many white-collar services, especially salesmanship, also *buys the employees' social personalities.* . . . In a society of employees, dominated by the marketing mentality, it is inevitable that a personality market should arise. . . .

One knows the salesclerk not as a person but as a commercial mask, a stereotyped greeting and appreciation for patronage. . . . Kindness and friendliness become aspects of personalized service or of public relations of big firms, rationalized to further the sale of something. With anonymous insincerity the Successful Person thus makes an instrument of his own appearance and personality. . . .

Many salesgirls are quite aware of the difference between what they really think of the customer and how they must act toward her.

---

[15] *Death of a Salesman*, in *Arthur Miller's Collected Plays*, New York, The Viking Press, 1957, pp. 168–169.

The smile behind the counter is a commercialized lure. . . . In the normal course of her work, because her personality becomes the instrument of an alien purpose, the salesgirl becomes self-alienated.[16]

But are the actions and reactions of people like Willy Loman and the salesgirl really *typical* of middle-class behavior? Kahl is of the belief that modern writing has tended to emphasize the extremes of middle-class life. He adds: "Must we judge each group by its extremes? For many . . . the middle-class way of life is quietly satisfying; it connotes the accomplishment of moderate education and moderate occupational achievement; it means successful Americanization from not-too-distant ethnic roots; it brings a strong, stable, family-centered life; and in the smaller towns and cities, it brings a degree of public recognition as solid citizens."[17]

We have presented several quotations purporting to describe middle-class life. Which one represents the true picture? The answer is that they probably all do. The middle class is larger than either the upper or lower strata and covers a much broader social spectrum. This spectrum is variegated and at times appears inconsistent. Social scientists can depict patterned behavior for the upper or the lower strata much more readily than for the diversiform middle class. It is easy to see why the latter is truly "kaleidoscopic."

Dominant Values. There are certain values that pervade the middle class, although the above caution should be kept firmly in mind. The present capsuled account will merely serve to show certain contrasts between the middle class and those at the upper and lower ends of the social hierarchy.

To begin with, "respectability" looms large in the eyes of the middle-class family. The latter may be uncomfortably close to certain elements of the lower class, and respectability sometimes represents the line of division. Middle-class parents, for example, would be heartbroken to learn that their son had been apprehended by the police, a happening that may be taken in stride by lower-class parents. It is the affirmation of respectability that makes middle-class parents fearful of permitting their children to associate with lower-class boys and girls.

There are certain outward signs of respectability, which middle-class families take some pains to observe. Home owner-

---

[16] C. Wright Mills, *White Collar*, New York, Oxford University Press, 1953, pp. 182–184 (italics added).

[17] Kahl, *op. cit.*, pp. 204–205.

(Vicki Lawrence, Stock Boston)

ship is important, and long-term mortgages are clearly preferred over the usual alternative—apartment living. Moreover, it is not just home ownership that is involved, but the endless trappings, such as interior and exterior improvements, alterations, attractive furniture, electrical appliances, and—of course—an automobile.

This particular style of living thus presents something of a problem. Whereas the family would dearly like to save some money for a rainy day, they are reluctant to scrimp on the middle-class status symbols. And since the necessary purchases—home, car, appliances—must frequently be made on a time basis, there is often little money left over for saving. In fact, at any given moment, the middle-class family is likely to have a fair amount of debt. It is the debt factor that prompts so many of the wives to seek employment.

There is one cause for which middle-class parents try their very best to save: a college education for the children. Most middle-level parents sincerely want their children to improve on their (the parents') socio-economic position, and a college degree is widely believed to be the instrument of improvement. While the upper and upper-middle classes may send a greater proportion of their children to college, it is the middle class that makes the most sacrifices. Among the lower strata, as we shall see, the concept of higher education is not particularly meaningful.

In addition to the expense involved, the middle-class stress on college education sometimes produces unexpected results—in the form of conflict within the home. Eshleman makes the following observation:

> Many state universities are comprised of a large proportion of students from this (middle class) background. Frequently parents make major sacrifices to see their children receive a formal education, with the result that the educational goals they set for their children result in values that lead them away from the family.
>
> Thus a self-defeating prophecy is at work. The parents work to provide an education for their children, which in turn introduces the children to a set of values frequently in conflict with those of the parents.[18]

Religion is another hallmark of middle-class persons. The latter are, as Kahl indicates, "probably the most regular church-goers in our society (although the upper-middle may have a greater proportion who maintain a formal church membership)."[19] And even though much literary cynicism has been directed toward "middle-class morality," it is nevertheless true that the middle class is a major influence on matters pertaining to sexual behavior, attitudes toward divorce, obscenity and pornography, personal ethics, and other moral considerations.

THE LOWER-CLASS FAMILY

Just below the middle class is the large working class—factory workers, electricians, bus drivers, and others in the "blue-collar" category. *Below the working class,* occupying the bottom

---

[18] J. Ross Eshleman, *The Family: An Introduction,* Boston, Allyn and Bacon, Inc., 1974, p. 252.
[19] Kahl, *op. cit.,* p. 203.

rung of the socio-economic ladder, is the lower class—unskilled workers, day laborers, the erratically employed, and the chronically unemployed. These are the poor, and in recent periods they have been the focus of much sociological research. While we shall refer to the working, or blue-collar, class from time to time, our primary concern here is with the lower class—the bottom rung.

The exact size of this class depends on how the term is defined. Recent U.S. Census data place the figure "below the poverty line" at around 12 percent of the population, though some authorities feel the real figure is higher.[20] But, whatever the figure, the problems involved are immense, both from a societal and an individual perspective. A Senate subcommittee, in referring to the lower class writes as follows:

> Being poor is not a choice for these people; it is a rigid way of life. It is handed down from generation to generation in a cycle of inadequate education, inadequate homes, inadequate jobs, and stunted ambitions. The poor citizen lacks organization. . . . A spirit of defeat often pervades his life.[21]

The lower-class person is well aware that he or she is on the bottom rung of the socio-economic ladder and, more important, realizes that the position is not likely to change. This lack of upward mobility is even characteristic of the working class. In one study of marriage among blue-collar workers, a husband was asked, "Does your wife take an interest in your job?" He replied, "I don't take much interest in it myself, so I wouldn't expect her to."[22]

Husbands and wives in the lower class are at a loss to explain their position. On the whole, they do not consider the world a friendly or predictable place. They are wary of outsiders and tend to be suspicious regarding the motivations of others. In terms of the developing chain of events, they are fatalists: they do not feel they have much control over things. Uncertain and lacking self-confidence, lower-class individuals expect the worst to happen, and the chances are that it will. Unforeseen events just seem to

---

[20] See Catherine S. Chilman, "Families in Poverty: Rates, Associated Factors, Some Implications," *Journal of Marriage and the Family*, February, 1975, pp. 49–60.

[21] U.S. Congress, Senate, Select Subcommittee on Poverty, *The War on Poverty: Economic Opportunity Act of 1964*, 88th Cong., 2d sess., 1964, pp. 35–36.

[22] Mirra Komarovsky, *Blue-Collar Marriage*, New York, Random House, Inc., 1964, p. 152. See also Melvin L. Kohn, "Social Class and Parental Values," in Rose Laub Coser (ed.), *The Family: Its Structures and Functions*, New York, St. Martin's Press, 1974, pp. 334–353.

(Joel Gordon)

crop up, and the first thing you know the husband is out of a job again.

Most lower-class men and women have a genuine desire to assume the role of good family members. The men like to be considered good husbands and fathers, and the women want to feel that they make dutiful wives and mothers. But—in the very nature of things—these roles are made difficult. The lower-class person, for example, is a poor planner. When he has money he is likely to spend it impulsively, shutting out thoughts of tomorrow. Because of this tendency to live each day for what it is, lower-class couples are likely to become embroiled in arguments and bickering.

From the societal view, also, lower-class families are overrepresented in the "social problem" area. As Eshleman puts it, the lower class "has the highest rates of divorce, psychoses, and physical disabilities, the least amount of health and dental care, the largest proportion of people on public welfare, the greatest rejection rate from the armed forces, the greatest amount of premarital sexual experience, the highest crime rate, the largest number of children, the highest rate of venereal disease, the most unemployment, the lowest level of income, and as perceived by many middle-class persons, 'the most of the worst'."[23]

---

[23] J. Ross Eshleman, *op. cit.*, pp. 260–261.

Courtship. As was mentioned in earlier chapters, courtship for the middle and upper classes is a fairly elaborate sequence of events. Dating starts at an early age, dozens of persons are dated, attractions are numerous, and infatuations or love affairs are far from infrequent. This premarital screening, or trial-and-error process, is extensive enough to permit the formulation of *marital criteria*. The final selection of a mate, after years of experience, is anything but a hit-or-miss proposition. Lower-class youth, however, marry at a significantly younger age, and they often give the impression of just having drifted together. Instead of the extensive dating and trial-and-error procedures, there is a pattern of drift and a philosophy of "what will happen, will happen."

Rainwater, an authority on lower-class culture, states that lower-class youth "do not often show a great deal of enterprise in seeking or choosing marriage partners. Rarely do they express strong feelings about the decision to marry." He adds that "although it is unlikely that these people would have gotten married without some sense of personal meaningfulness to each other, it does seem that conscious choice and planning play a much smaller role than among middle-class men and women." For example:

> I met him over on Lafflin Street. There's a place I used to go to dance with a gang of us girls. I saw my husband lots of times before I went around with him. . . . I don't know exactly how it happened; we got to going to the beach at night and fooling around some, and then we decided it would be best to get married right away.

> . . .

> He stayed . . . close to where I lived. I'd known him off and on for a year or two. I don't know how it come about, we just got married.[24]

It is also apparent that many lower-class boys and girls are themselves anxious to escape from an unhappy home life. They are inclined, therefore, to rush courtship procedures and—as compared with the higher classes—to short-cut the mate-selection process. In the study of blue-collar marriage referred to earlier, the author writes of the "marriage as liberation" syndrome and records the following comments:

---

[24] Lee Rainwater, *And the Poor Get Children,* Chicago, Quadrangle Books, 1960, pp. 62–63. Excerpts on pp. 406, 408, 410 from *And the Poor Get Children* by Lee Rainwater. Copyright © 1960 by Social Research, Inc. Reprinted by permission of New Viewpoints division of Franklin Watts, Inc. See also Alan P. Bates and Joseph Julian, *Sociology: Understanding Social Behavior,* Boston, Houghton Mifflin Company, 1975, pp. 137–159.

I got out from under. . . .

. . .

One reason I got married at 16 was to get away from home. My parents would tell us kids that they stayed together for our sake—that made us feel real good. . . . I got married to get away from it all, but I got out of the frying pan into the fire.[25]

Family Living. A host of surveys indicate that the lower-class family is reluctant to participate in community or social activities. In one of the pioneering surveys, conducted during the mid-1920's, the Lynds discovered that in Middletown 47 percent of the lower class had no intimate friends, in contrast to only 16 percent of the upper class.[26] More recent studies have reported similar findings; that is, the lower the position on the social-class scale, the less the participation in civic and religious affairs, the fewer the number of organizational activities, the less entertaining done at home, and so on.

In the widely read *Workingman's Wife*, the authors report that lower-class wives "have difficulty feeling themselves to be full-fledged members of the wider society." For example, to the question, "Are you a member of any clubs or other organizations?" typical responses were:

I'm not in any clubs because I don't know anyone who belongs to introduce me.

. . .

I've never been asked. Nobody ever talked to me about anything.

. . .

I'm just a common ole girl.[27]

Even the practice of entertaining at home is minimal. In the blue-collar marriage study, the author reports that "joint social life with friends is far from being the important leisure-time pursuit that it is in higher socio-economic classes. This applies to exchange of home visits as well as to joint visits to public recreation places. . . . A few of our respondents appear hardly aware of the pattern of entertaining at home. Thus, an older woman said

[25] Komarovsky, *op. cit.,* pp. 25–26.

[26] Robert S. Lynd and Helen M. Lynd, *Middletown,* New York, Harcourt, Brace and Company, 1929, p. 272.

[27] Lee Rainwater, Richard Coleman, and Gerald Handel, *Workingman's Wife,* New York, MacFadden Books, 1962, pp. 51–52, 129.

that such a custom may have existed in the past but must have gone out of fashion because no one she knew followed it."[28]

A number of surveys have shown that the satisfaction of affectional and sexual needs is a common problem among lower-class spouses. For example, a comparative analysis of marital sexuality among the lower classes in England, Mexico, Puerto Rico, and the United States revealed that sexual adjustment was generally poor. Wives tended to have a negative attitude toward sex, and both husbands and wives were likely to feel that "sex is a man's pleasure and a woman's duty." The author goes on to say that "in all of these lower-class sub-cultures, there is a pattern of highly segregated conjugal role relationships. Men and women do not have many joint relationships; the separation of man's work and woman's work is sharp, as is the separation of man's and woman's play."[29]

In Rainwater's study, the author found that lower-class wives felt isolated from their husbands without knowing exactly why. They were also unsure of their spouses, and for many of the wives "holding one's man" had become a major objective. In effect, they were willing to settle for what they had because they were of the opinion that "nothing better was to be had from a man."

> Until things become impossibly bad, they simply resign themselves; if the situation is unbearable, the wife is justified in leaving. The middle ground of negotiation, give-and-take, and mutual understanding requires too much faith in the basic goodness of men and too much assertiveness on the woman's part to be really considered.[30]

Lower-class men, according to Rainwater, find the world around them confusing and chaotic. Since women are part of that world, it is difficult to figure them out. They are emotional, demanding, and argumentative. They cry without reason and always act hurt. Furthermore, women are "clinging" and insist on their men being affectionate.

On their part, the husbands often employ blustering and aggressive tactics "in order to gain the gratifications they want and at the same time have the woman keep her proper distance. Each likes to think of himself as master of the house, and he plays on his wife's capacity to be intimidated by aggressive actions and threats to withdraw. . . ."[31]

---

[28] Komarovsky, *op. cit.*, pp. 311–312.
[29] Lee Rainwater, "Marital Sexuality in Four Cultures of Poverty," *Journal of Marriage and the Family*, November, 1964, pp. 462–463.
[30] Rainwater, *And the Poor Get Children*, pp. 72–77.
[31] *Ibid.*, pp. 77–81.

Children.   Children represent something of a special problem in lower-class families. For one thing, the birthrate is noticeably higher than in the upper classes. Birth control measures are imperfectly understood by many lower-class couples. In brief, those who can least afford them have the largest number of children.

Scholastic difficulties present another recurrent problem. Lower-class boys and girls find it difficult to accept the middle-class values purveyed by the school system. Troubled, perhaps, by poor grades, conduct problems, or by sexual involvements, these youths too often become the dropouts. Sooner or later, it is the lower-class juvenile who is most likely to run afoul of the law.

Lower-class boys and girls also appear to have more than their share of personality problems. Earlier sociological works gave the impression that the various neuroses were more likely to be associated with middle-class children, the "strivers." However, findings from more recent research studies have pointed to the opposite conclusion.

It may or may not come as a surprise to learn—in view of the difficulties listed above—that physical punishment is much more common in lower-class families than in the higher strata. McKinley's survey disclosed that "lower-class families are more likely to punish for offenses, more likely to punish with ridicule or by inflicting pain." The punishment is evidently symptomatic of underlying tension between the children and their father:

> The father's role is more highly associated with class than is the mother's. Thus, the mother is about as severe as the father at the upper levels but the father becomes increasingly more severe at the lower levels. . . .
>
> Data from this study and other studies show that the father loses authority in the family at the lower levels as a consequence of his social and occupational inadequacy. In the upper levels of society the father's occupation provides him with prestige and motivational resources that allow him to exercise benevolent authority.
>
> The father's deprived social position in the lower levels of society also results in a greater hostility toward and a reduced involvement in the emotional life of the adolescent son.[32]

Although not so deep-seated, the rift between lower-class children and their mother also creates problems. Shostak writes that "many blue-collar mothers regard the behavior of their children as mysterious and almost beyond understanding. Believing the

---

[32] Donald McKinley, *Social Class and Family Life,* , New York, Free Press of Glencoe, Inc., 1964, p. 243. Of tangential interest is George Rosenberg and Donald Anspach, "Sibling Solidarity in the Working Class," *Journal of Marriage and the Family,* February, 1973, pp. 108–113.

child to be inherently mischievous, these mothers endlessly threaten or cajole, but seldom discuss or reason with, their offspring. Discipline tends to be impulsive, inconsistent, and sharp, though it rarely entails the threat to withdraw love, a practice more common among many white-collarites."[33]

Bright Spots.   In many ways the lower-class family presents a rather grim picture, but it is far from a hopeless one. As a matter of fact, in view of the many economic, educational, and social handicaps suffered, perhaps the wonder of it all is that the lower-class family is as stable as it is. Fundamentally, these men and women have a sincere desire to be good husbands and wives and to fulfill their family obligations, and *most of them manage to succeed.* Overbalancing the comments reported in the previous pages are examples like the following, quoted from Rainwater:

> I don't know what to say; I think you can describe him as just good. He's kind and considerate. We don't always have enough money to go around, but we have enough love. . . .
>
>   . . .
>
> He's a friendly type person and real easy to live with. He gets along well with the children, and I know you won't believe this but we've never had a bad argument.
>
>   . . .
>
> He has a wonderful personality; he's handsome and a wonderful father to the kids. He plays with them and always has time to spend with them. . . . I'm very happy and wouldn't trade married life for anything.[34]

A number of writers have pointed out that the lower class has certain advantages not enjoyed by the other social strata. Keeping up with the Joneses, status striving, economic competition, and other phases of the "rat race" are relatively unimportant to lower-class couples. Riessman notes the following "positive dimensions" of lower-class culture:

> The cooperativeness and mutual aid that mark the extended family; the avoidance of the strain accompanying competitiveness and individualism; the equalitarianism, informality, and humor; the freedom from self-blame and parental protection; the children's enjoyment of each other and lessened sibling rivalry. . . ; the enjoyment of games, sports, and cards; the ability to express anger; the

---

[33] Arthur Shostak, *Blue-Collar Life,* New York, Random House, Inc., 1969, pp. 129–130.
[34] Rainwater, *And the Poor Get Children,* p. 76.

freedom from being word-bound; and finally, the physical style involved in learning.[35]

The above list may seem a little "far out" to some readers, but it must be remembered that most college students have been exposed to middle-class values. In this respect, Rodman contends that what the middle-class person thinks of as being typical problems of the lower-class family may—from the latter's purview—be more accurately described as *solutions* to the many problems faced in day-to-day living.[36]

Another bright spot is the fact that sociologists have been devoting considerable time to the study of lower-class families. At one time, research projects dealing with the lower class were few and far between. In recent years, this dearth has been corrected. And while research, per se, will not solve the problems of lower-class families, it is hardly likely that the problems will be solved *without* a solid research foundation.

Also, while the birthrate continues to be higher in the lower classes, there are indications that the latter now have a genuine desire to limit the number of offspring. Whether a comparable reduction in the lower-class birthrate actually materializes remains to be seen, although it is a likely possibility—particularly in view of the increasing popularity and availability of oral contraceptive methods.

And, finally, social workers who deal with lower-class children and their families are in a better position to provide help than formerly. Rodman states that:

> Historically, social workers started out with a moralistic approach to lower-class behavior, and it is only recently that they have become more psychiatric in their approach. This, of course, has paralleled the fact that more and more social workers are being professionally trained.
>
> One of the most significant approaches . . . is best symbolized in the social work literature by such phrases as "hard-to-reach," "hard-core," and "multiproblem" families. This approach recognizes that many lower-class clients are difficult to work with, and it emphasizes the need to understand and accept lower-class families before making any attempts to reform them.[37]

The problems of the lower-class family will not be easy to solve. The stakes, however, are staggeringly important. From the

[35] Frank Riessman, "Low-Income Culture: The Strengths of the Poor," *Journal of Marriage and the Family*, November, 1964, p. 419.

[36] Hyman Rodman, "Middle-Class Misconceptions About Lower-Class Families," in Arthur Shostak and William Gomberg (eds.), *Blue-Collar World*, Englewood Cliffs, New Jersey, Prentice-Hall, Inc., 1964, p. 65.

[37] *Ibid.*, p. 63.

411

lower-class individual's view, family members are neither partaking of cultural activities nor enjoying cultural benefits. From the societal view, the lower-class family too often represents a lost human resource. A multipronged attack by the government, by local schools and agencies, and by social scientists would seem to offer the best chance of coping with the problem.

SELECTED READINGS

Bahr, Stephen; Chadwick, Bruce; and Stauss, Joseph, "The Effect of Relative Economic Status on Fertility," *Journal of Marriage and the Family*, May, 1975, pp. 335–343.

Baltzell, E. Digby, *The Protestant Establishment: Aristocracy and Caste in America*, New York, Random House, Inc., 1964.

Bates, Alan P., and Julian, Joseph, *Sociology: Understanding Social Behavior*, Boston Houghton Mifflin Company, 1975. See Chapter Six, "Social Stratification," pp. 137–159.

Bensman, Joseph, and Vidich, Arthur, "The New Class System and Its Life Styles," in Saul Feldman and Gerald Thielbar (eds.), *Life Styles: Diversity in American Society*, Boston, Little, Brown and Company, 1975, pp. 129–143.

Blumberg, Paul, and Paul, P. W., "Continuities and Discontinuities in Upper-Class Marriages," *Journal of Marriage and the Family*, February, 1975, pp. 63–77.

Burt, Nathaniel, *First Families*, Boston, Little, Brown and Company, 1970.

Chilman, Catherine S., "Families in Poverty: Rates, Associated Factors, Some Implications," *Journal of Marriage and the Family*, February, 1975, pp. 49–60.

Cutright, Phillips, "Income and Family Events: Marital Stability," *Journal of Marriage and the Family*, May, 1971, pp. 291–306.

Domhoff, G. William, *The Higher Circles*, New York, Vintage Books, 1971.

Elder, Glen H., *Children of the Great Depression: Social Change in Life Experience*, Chicago, University of Chicago Press, 1974.

Glenn, Norval; Alston, Jon P.; and Weiner, David, *Social Stratification: A Research Bibliography*, Berkeley, California, The Glendary Press, 1971.

Hodges, Harold, *Social Stratification*, New York, Harper & Row, 1971.

Hollingshead, August B., *Elmtown's Youth and Elmtown's Youth Revisited*, New York, John Wiley & Sons, Inc., 1975.

Kelly, John R., "Life Styles and Leisure Choices," *Family Coordinator*, April, 1975, pp. 185–190.

Kohn, Melvin L., *Class and Conformity: A Study in Values*, Homewood, Illinois, The Dorsey Press, 1969.

Komarovsky, Mirra, *Blue-Collar Marriage*, New York, Random House, Inc., 1964.

Kriesberg, Louis, *Mothers in Poverty: A Study of Fatherless Families*, Chicago, Aldine Publishing Company, 1970.

Le Masters, E. E., *Parents in Modern America*, Homewood, Illinois, The Dorsey Press, 1974. See Chapter Five, "Parents and Social Class," pp. 68–85.

Mortimer, Jeylan, "Social Class, Work and the Family," *Journal of Marriage and the Family*, May, 1976, pp. 241–256.

Otto, Luther B., "Class and Status in Family Research," *Journal of Marriage and the Family*, May, 1975, pp. 315–332.

Rainwater, Lee, *And the Poor Get Children*, Chicago, Quadrangle Books, 1960.

———, *Behind Ghetto Walls*, Chicago, Aldine Publishing Company, 1970.

Rodman, Hyman, "Middle-Class Misconceptions About Lower-Class Families," in Arthur Shostak and William Gomberg (eds.), *Blue-Collar World*, Englewood Cliffs, New Jersey, Prentice-Hall, Inc., 1964.

Rosenberg, George, and Anspach, Donald, "Sibling Solidarity in the Working Class," *Journal of Marriage and the Family*, February, 1973, pp. 108–113.

Schulz, David A., *The Changing Family*, Englewood Cliffs, New Jersey, Prentice-Hall, Inc., 1972.

Seligson, Marcia, *The Eternal Bliss Machine: America's Way of Wedding*, New York, William Morrow & Company, Inc., 1973.

Simmons, Roberta, and Rosenberg, Morris, "Functions of Children's Perceptions of the Stratification System," *American Sociological Review*, April, 1971, pp. 235–249.

Tumin, Melvin M., *Patterns of Society*, Boston, Little, Brown and Company, 1973. See Chapter Seven, "The Class System: Life Chances, Styles, and Consciousness," pp. 103–118.

19

Parent-Child Interaction

DURING THE THOUSANDS of years that the human race has been on earth, people should perhaps have discovered—simply on the basis of trial and error—the best way to raise children. Obviously, however, this is not the case. Children are as difficult today as they ever were. Indeed, when conduct problems and delinquency rates are considered, it would seem that our child-rearing procedures are less effective than formerly, although the use of other criteria might lead to a more optimistic conclusion. Nevertheless, the inexorable fact remains that the desires and aims of children are often a far cry from those of adults, and it is unlikely that this conflict of interests will ever be completely resolved.

While the problems of child-rearing remain great, the present era has seen the rise of two interrelated phenomena that are, in every sense of the word, new. The first of these has been the popularization of the belief that childhood experiences are the crucial determinants of adult personality. The formative years, as they are called, have come to be regarded as a sort of personality mold. Psychiatrists and child guidance centers have reported an almost limitless number of case histories attesting to the needs and need-deprivations of children. Based on these case histories, as well as on derivative child-centered theories of personality formation, literally thousands of books, pamphlets, and articles have been published, read, and widely discussed. As a result of this "parent education program," the needs and problems of children, as well as techniques for the solution of these problems, have become a permanent part of the American ethos.

The second development has been the widespread and sustained interest in the study of children on the part of academicians. Anthropologists have surveyed child-rearing practices in other societies; sociologists have studied relationships between childhood experiences and delinquency, crime, alcoholism, and mental illness; psychologists have conducted empirical surveys on intelligence testing, rewards and punishments, motivation, and so on, as well as on the personality manifestations stemming from specific child-raising techniques. Based in good part on the implications of these studies, courses in child psychology and in the sociology of child development have come to be offered in many of our colleges.

In the short space of a generation or two we have truly become a child-centered society, and there is little indication that the situation will change. Public and professional interest in child study shows no sign of wearing off. On the contrary, interest in the subject seems to be increasing. As students of the family, therefore, let us examine this phenomenon of childhood, which has so fascinated our culture.

HISTORICAL STATEMENT

In view of the current interest in child study, it is difficult to realize that throughout most of human history, childhood was not considered a very important phase of life. Medieval painters, for example, made no attempt to portray childhood. If a scene called for children, the artist would simply paint adult men and women on a reduced scale. This "miniaturizing" of adults, as Ariès points out, was due not to the incompetency of the artist but to the fact that childhood had no place in the medieval world. The same writer goes on to state that:

> No one thought of keeping a picture of a dead child. . . . it was thought that the little thing which had disappeared so soon in life was not worthy of remembrance: there were far too many children whose survival was problematical. The general feeling was that one had several children in order to keep just a few. *People could not allow themselves to become too attached to something that was regarded as a probable loss.*[1]

The point that Ariès emphasizes is that, while individual children were treated with affection, the *concept of childhood* was generally lacking:

> In the Middle Ages, children were mixed with adults as soon as they were considered capable of doing without their mothers; in other words, at about the age of seven. They immediately went into

---

[1] Philippe Ariès, *Centuries of Childhood*, New York, Alfred A. Knopf, 1962, pp. 29–33. (Italics added)

the great community of men, sharing in the work and play of their companions, old and young alike. . . .

The great event was the revival, at the beginning of modern times, of an interest in education. Henceforth it was recognized that the child was not ready for life, and that he had to be subjected to a special treatment, a sort of quarantine, before he was allowed to join the adults. This new concern about education would gradually install itself in the heart of society, and transform it from top to bottom.[2]

By the seventeenth and eighteenth centuries, the philosophy of treating children as "little adults" had long since passed. Children were recognized as children. The problem was how to prepare them for adulthood. To this end, child-rearing was geared to obedience, industriousness, and dependability. In looking over letters and documents of the Colonial period, one is struck by the repeated use of terms like "obedient," "faithful," "hardworking," "humble," "earnest," and "God-fearing."

Discipline was strict, and punishment could be severe. Lack of respect on the part of children was considered a serious matter, which pattern was in keeping with the patriarchal nature of the colonial family. Interestingly enough, parents did not consider themselves to be overly strict with their youngsters. And de Tocqueville, writing of the early 1800's, contended that "the several members of a family stand upon an entirely new footing toward each other; the distance which formerly separated a father from his sons has been lessened; and paternal authority, if not destroyed, is at least impaired."[3]

One wonders what de Tocqueville—probably the most famous observer of American society—would say of the discipline problem in America today? For the fact is that, by present standards, colonial parents were indeed strict. As was mentioned in Chapter 4, the Puritans prescribed the death penalty for flagrantly disobedient children, even though the penalty was never actually imposed. But while they were strict, there is absolutely no basis for the belief that the colonists did not love their children. It was the manifestation of parental love that was different.

Nothing seems more natural today than for parents to want to raise happy children and to shower them with love and attention in an effort to bestow happiness. Colonial parents were apparently less demonstrative in their show of affection, and the term "happiness" did not play such a vital part in the daily routine of living. Parental love, as the early settlers must have seen

---

[2] *Ibid.*, pp. 411–413.

[3] Alexis de Tocqueville, *Democracy in America*, New York, Schocken Books (paperback edition), 1961, p. 229.

Not all children were given the opportunity to enjoy their childhood in the nineteenth century. Despite a growing emphasis on the importance of a child's early years, economic realities sometimes took precedence. (Culver Pictures)

it, reflected itself in the imparting of skills, rules of conduct, industriousness, a belief in God, and ethical and economic values that were in accord with an agricultural, primary-group type of society.

As conditions changed, as the urban rather than the rural way of life came to dominate the American scene, child-rearing patterns also changed. Families became smaller, formal education increased in importance, the patriarchal nature of the family group changed, and discipline and respect for authority came to be something less than cornerstones of the good life. During the nineteenth century such changes came slowly. As late as the First World War the old adage "Children should be seen and not heard" was in a fairly common usage, even though fewer and fewer children seemed to abide by it.

Following World War II, however, child-rearing practices changed rapidly—for the better, according to some; for the worse, according to others. But, for better or worse, results of the change were to be felt for many decades. This change in the philosophy of child-training was caused by no single event nor by any single person; yet if one name were to be selected as having the most lasting influence, the name would probably be that of Sigmund Freud.

THE FREUDIAN IMPACT

More than any of his predecessors, it was Freud who emphasized the importance of infancy and childhood as determinants of adult personality. Working with his own patients, Freud was convinced not only that neuroses were rooted in sexual conflicts, but that the roots of these conflicts developed very early in life. In the first stage, said Freud, the infant achieves sexual pleasure from the exploration of the *erogenous zones* (oral, anal, genital) of his body—hence the term "autoeroticism." By the age of five these explorations become localized in the genital region. During this first stage the infant also acquires pleasure from being nursed by his mother, and Freud held that this, too, is a sexual gratification; in fact, he believed that this physical and emotional contact develops into a love attachment for the mother. Such an attachment, however, is prohibited by a strong societal taboo against incest. And since the father loves the mother, the child is confronted with a rival; hence, the emergence of the Oedipus complex, in which the child loves his mother and hates his father.

By the age of six or so, society's dictates having won out, the Oedipal phase gives way to a second stage, one of so-called *latency*. During this period between infancy and puberty, the love attachment the child had for his mother is severed, the child comes to identify himself with his father, and spends much of his time with companions of his own sex. The onset of adolescence marks the beginning of the third stage, a period when sex interest re-emerges and is directed toward members of the opposite sex.

Freud contended that both sexes *normally* pass through these three stages, but that in individual cases the normal process may not occur; that is, a person may *fixate* on the second stage and develop a degree of homosexuality, or a child who is rejected by his playmates may *regress* to the comforting relationship he once had with his mother (first stage) and later on in life may have serious difficulty in adjusting to girls. Freud made no bones about the fact that his theories were based on sex, albeit in some of his writings sex was defined in general as well as specific terms.

(As might be expected, Freud's beliefs shocked both laymen and scientists. Reared in the Victorian tradition, neither group could at first accept the view that infants and children had a sexual nature. Nevertheless, because of the heated controversy engendered by Freudian theory, the entire concept of childhood—particularly childhood sexuality—came in for a much closer examination.)

One of the cornerstones of Freudian theory is the reality of the *unconscious*, a powerful force that constitutes the mainspring of so many human actions. And between the conscious and the unconscious there is likely to be strife. The following case history, for example, would seem to illustrate the Freudian point of view:

> Albert T., a young man of 26, was under intensive psychiatric treatment, having complained of a number of disturbing symptoms. Among the latter were recurrent nightmares, excessive perspiring, and the compulsion to wash his hands 15 or 20 times a day. When asked why he washed his hands so often, he replied that the city air contained poisonous microbes.
>
> Psychoanalysis revealed that when Albert was 15 years old his father had caught him masturbating in the bedroom. Overcome with shame and embarrassment, he had succeeded in "forgetting" the incident. Not long afterward, however, his hands began to appear dirty to him, and he took to washing them at frequent intervals. About the same time he began to have nightmares, and for no apparent reason would perspire heavily during the day.
>
> The psychoanalyst was successful in his treatment of Albert. After a series of psychoanalytic sessions, the masturbatory incident which had been pushed back to the unconscious was brought to light, and with the recall of the traumatic boyhood scene with his father, the above-mentioned symptoms disappeared.

In cases such as this, Freud and his followers would routinely subject the patient to a lengthy and intensive soul-searching, or psychoanalysis, the purpose of which was to bring the unconsciously rejected event, usually sexual in nature, back to conscious experience, thereby bridging the gap in the divided personality. Thus, in the case of Albert, the disturbing symptoms disappeared with the recall of the precipitating experience. Generally speaking, Freudians would contend that a person is abnormal, or neurotic, to the extent that his unconscious controls his conscious. The task of the psychoanalyst is to help rid the patient of this unconscious control.

The importance of infancy and childhood in the Freudian scheme of things now becomes clear. It is during these formative years that sexual conflicts tend to arise, that acceptance or rejection by parents is most keenly felt, and that the child's personality, in an almost literal sense, is being molded. This being the case, Freud implicitly warned against the overuse of punishment with children. Aware of the possible effects of so-called traumatic experiences during infancy and childhood, Freud showed in many of his writings that parental love was a vital ingredient in the child's personality development. And while Freud certainly cautioned that there was a distinct danger in the excessive loving of one's children, the general effect of his writings led to a concern over too little love rather than too much. Some of Freud's more ardent followers, as a matter of fact, tended to reject the notion of discipline altogether and to maintain that there was no such thing as loving a child too much.

In passing, it should be mentioned that Freudian teaching received unlooked-for support from the doctrines of John B. Watson and John Dewey, exponents of behaviorism and progressive education, respectively. It was Dewey whose philosophy led to many of the modern concepts of education, with emphasis on personality development and training of the "whole child," rather than on discipline, drill, and the inculcation of the three R's. And it was Watson's behaviorism that focused sociopsychological attention on the *conditioning* process, which hitherto had been the province of Pavlov and his followers. In his *Behaviorism*, Watson contended as follows:

> Give me a dozen healthy infants, well-formed, and my own specified world to bring them up in and I'll guarantee to take any one at random and train him to become any type of specialist I might select—doctor, lawyer, artist, merchant-chief, and yes, even beggarman and thief, regardless of his talents, penchants, tendencies, abilities, vocations, and race of his ancestors.[4]

But whereas many of the ideas of Dewey and Watson have failed to stand the test of time, Freudian doctrine is still in vogue and, however debatable, continues to exert a powerful influence on American thought.

RESEARCH FINDINGS ON FREUDIAN THEORY

It was predictable that such a revolutionary theory as Freud's would be sharply challenged. Taken collectively, Freudian

---

[4] John B. Watson, *Behaviorism*, New York, W. W. Norton & Company, Inc., 1924, p. 82.

Aspects of Freud's theory of child development remain controversial, but its influence has been pervasive in American society. Nowadays infants rarely are forced to adhere to rigid feeding and toilet training schedules, and there even has been a renewed interest in nursing. (Vicki Lawrence, Stock Boston)

contentions regarding the unconscious, the Oedipus complex, latency periods, dream analysis, the primacy of sexual factors, the etiology of mental illness, the importance of infancy in personality development, and so on, gave rise to intellectual cries of anguish the likes of which have seldom been heard. Long and bitter academic arguments ensued—and the end is not in sight. The Freudian controversy, however, will not be solved by intellectual arguments but by research, and in this area there is factual information to report.

If Freudian theory is valid, it follows that infants raised under Freudian precepts—breast feeding, gradual weaning, "mothering," late toilet training, and so on—will, as they grow older, manifest superior personality traits as compared with those children reared by non-Freudian methods. However, what Baumrind calls "an avalanche of studies" have now been carried out—studies that involve the comparison of children reared by

Freudian as against non-Freudian methods—and the results have rather consistently failed to support Freudian precepts.[5]

The researchers, in this instance, admittedly have a difficult task. Parents are often inconsistent in their child-rearing practices; that is, permissiveness may be used in some situations, restrictiveness in others. Also, personality is not easy to measure. Children who are tested at one stage of development may evidence different results when tested at a later stage. For these and other reasons, research on the subject continues.

Thus far, however, in spite of the case-history-based claims of his followers, Freud's child-rearing theories have not stood up under empirical investigation, and no amount of talk can change this fact. On the other hand, anti-Freudians are wrong when they claim that Freudian theory has been disproved. Difficult as it seems to be for experts to take a neutral stand on the matter, the fact is that Freudian theory has not been disproved. It has simply not been proved.

Parents who wish to follow Freudian precepts have a perfect right to do so, in spite of the lack of empirical validation. Practically all of our behavioral philosophy is based on faith rather than science, and there is no reason to except the area of child-training. As a matter of fact, many clinicians who deal with problem children continue to make effective use of Freudian theory, at least as reported in individual case histories.

One could argue that, over and above the validity or nonvalidity of his theories, Freud performed a service in focusing attention on the formative years of childhood. If, however, the formative years are *not* so important in personality formation, then psychiatrists and social scientists have spent an unwarranted amount of time in studying childhood at the expense of other areas, such as the role of adolescence and young adulthood in personality development.

In the corridors of time there have been few more original thinkers than Sigmund Freud, and in the last analysis it may be that many of his theoretical constructs will be vindicated. It is unfortunate for all concerned that his theories tended to split the intelligentsia into two opposing camps, with claims and counterclaims far outweighing objective analyses. The behavioral sciences are still in their infancy, and theoretical contributions are badly needed, as are the concomitant empirical checks. There is

---

[5] Diana Baumrind, "Effects of Authoritative Parental Control on Child Behavior," in Robert Winch and Louis Goodman, *Selected Studies in Marriage and the Family*, New York, Holt, Rinehart and Winston, Inc., 1968, pp. 299–317. See also F. Ivan Nye and Felix Berardo, *The Family: Its Structure and Interaction*, New York, The Macmillan Company, 1973, Chapter 15, "The Socialization of Children," pp. 273–404.

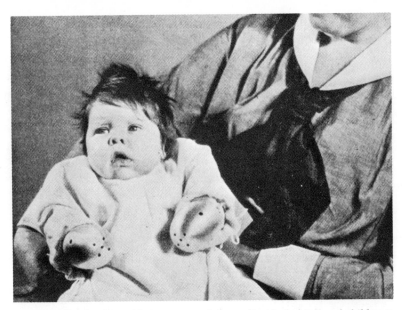

In the 1920's thumb-sucking was regarded as a "nasty habit," and child-care manuals advocated extreme measures to prevent gratification of such instincts. This infant is wearing aluminum mitts.

no place in the present scheme of things for factional strife of the kind that catches the public in the middle.

THE CHILD-REARING "PENDULUM"

In the absence of a validated system of child-rearing, American practices seem to operate in terms of fads and cycles. For example, in 1914 the government published the first edition of *Infant Care*, a book that has gone through umpteen editions and sold tens of millions of copies. As the various editions have been published, however, there have been some remarkable changes of advice given to mothers.

In the 1920's, thumb-sucking and masturbation were looked upon as dangerous impulses that must be curbed. As late as 1938 the book showed a stiff cuff that would stop the baby from bending its arm, thus preventing thumb-sucking. Yet in 1942, readers were told that masturbation and thumb-sucking were harmless. In 1951 the caution was voiced that too much pampering might result in the child's becoming a "tyrant."[6]

---

[6] Martha Wolfenstein, "Trends in Infant Care," *American Journal of Orthopsychiatry*, Vol. 33, 1953, pp. 120–130.

In the present decade, *Infant Care* has taken a markedly permissive attitude toward such things as weaning, masturbation, thumb-sucking, and toilet training. However, as was pointed out in the Gordon survey, the interesting point is that now *Infant Care* has adopted a permissive attitude when "the popular periodicals seem to be shifting toward greater restrictiveness."[7] And so it goes.

Perhaps the most remarkable thing about the child-rearing pendulum is not the changes in advice that have taken place since 1914, but the fact that these fluctuations have actually been occurring in the United States since at least as far back as 1800! A number of excellent studies show clearly that advice on weaning, feeding, discipline, and other topics ebbed and flowed like the tides themselves.[8] Prior to 1800, child-rearing literature was imported from England; and while no one has analyzed these imports, it is quite possible that the advice pendulum was in motion —in both England and America—even before 1800.

Reasons for the Pendulum. The reason that child-rearing advice varies—both from one period to another and from one magazine or book to another—is that a comprehensive and valid body of knowledge about children has failed to materialize. Much research has been done—the bi-monthly *Child-Development Abstracts* summarizes over 1,000 studies a year—and in the future it is almost certain that the quantity will increase. Yet the researcher is faced with some formidable obstacles. In addition to those mentioned earlier:

1. Obviously, all children are different. They differ not only in temperament, aptitude, and intelligence, but in their rates of physical and mental maturation. Child-rearing techniques that might be effective for one child might have a totally different effect on another.

2. In parallel fashion, parents also differ from one another, and methods successfully employed by some parents might be ineffective when used by others. Statistical studies often tend to gloss over such differences.

---

[7] Michael Gordon, "Infant Care Revisited," *Journal of Marriage and the Family,* November, 1968, p. 583.

[8] For an interesting discussion of the topic, as well as a bibliography, see Jerry J. Bigner, "Parent Education in Popular Literature," *Family Coordinator,* July, 1972, pp. 313–319. See also Paul Rosenblatt and Robert Phillips, Jr., "Family Articles in Popular Magazines," *Family Coordinator,* July, 1975, pp. 267–271.

3. It is often difficult to experiment with children. Researchers can hardly expect parents to lend their children for certain experimental purposes. In studies dealing with the effect of rewards and punishments, for example, is it reasonable to ask parents to let their children partake in an experiment (especially as part of the "punishment" group) that conceivably might have some effect on the youngster's personality?

4. Certain kinds of child study can best be carried on in the home or in a normal family setting; in fact, some investigators feel that one should not attempt to study the child without also studying the larger family group. But there are two difficulties involved: (1) how to gain access to families that, let us say, were selected by random sampling methods; and (2) assuming access, just how does the researcher conduct the investigation or observation without in some way disrupting the very thing that is supposed to be observed? This dilemma has by no means been solved.

5. In the final analysis, what criterion should be used in evaluating the results of specific child-rearing techniques? *Should not group welfare be considered as well as the child's own?* Certain permissive techniques might well be conducive to need-gratification on the part of the individual involved, yet play havoc with overall group welfare. This particular problem has been raised by sociologists, but in all likelihood it will be some time before consensus is reached.

The above difficulties have been mentioned simply to give the reader some idea of the kinds of problems involved in child-training research. The list is by no means exhaustive. In view of both the depth and extent of the problems, however, one might expect that published advice on "how to raise your child" would be (1) scarce, and (2) treated with skepticism by the public. Paradoxically, just the opposite is true. Popular writing on the subject of Your Child has reached flood proportion, and all the signs indicate that the public is eager for more.

PARENT EDUCATION

On the one hand, the fact that child-rearing advice has reached such large dimensions is surprising, since a fund of validated research information has yet to be established. On the other hand, it is perhaps not so surprising when one considers that much of

(Peter Menzel, Stock Boston)

the advice in other behavioral areas (personality testing, retirement planning, educational programming) rests on a similarly thin foundation of substantiated fact. The point of the matter seems to be that Americans accept not only those things that have demonstrated worth, but also that which looks good, or sounds good, or is well advertised, or which otherwise has some emotional appeal.

And so it is in the area of child-rearing. Most Americans are vitally interested in their children, and as parents they want to do what is "right" (or what is said to be "right" by the experts). So if the advice sounds reasonable or if it appears to be "scientific," the chances are good that some parents will accept it. In economic terms, there is a ready-made and inexhaustible supply of consumers, which, in turn, calls for a continuing high level of production. This production of child-rearing information is channeled through newspaper articles and columns, magazines, books, monographs and pamphlets, radio and television programs, study groups, child guidance centers, medical and nursing personnel, lectures, filmstrips, school offerings, and other educational programs.

The Effects of Parent Education. It is easy to demonstrate that a voluminous amount of child-rearing material is beamed regularly at a very large number of parents. Indeed, at the present time the number of newspaper columns, books, magazines, and pamphlets devoted to child care probably runs into the tens of thousands. The question is: Does it all have any effect? In spite of numerous research studies on the subject, no one has come up with a satisfactory answer. Arguments about the value of parent education continue to be voiced, however, along the following lines:

1. *Positive arguments.* On the one hand, it can be argued that the overall parent education program has had a number of beneficial effects. In the area of child health, for instance, there is no doubt that parents are better informed than ever before. The dissemination of information ranging from the proper care of children's teeth to the necessity of polio immunization has been instrumental in raising the general level of child health.

In the area of child behavior, parents have been made more aware of the specific problems involved. Regardless of the paucity of factual information, the tremendous flow of printed material has probably served to focus attention on an area of needed research. In this respect, the public has become acquainted with at least some of the research that has been done in the child-rearing field.

Parents have also had an opportunity to hear what some of the leading scholars are saying with respect to controversial child-study areas. This, in turn, probably encourages parents to discuss their child-training problems with one another and thus perhaps to gain a measure of self-confidence.

It is also likely that some of the written or spoken advice *has* helped certain parents by giving them insights they might not otherwise have attained. Many parents who read newspaper or magazine articles dealing with child-training information adopt the "if the shoe fits, wear it" philosophy, and if certain advice happens to fit in the case of their own child, the result is all to the good. It might be added that, in the last analysis, it is not the writers or counselors but *parents* who raise children. No one forces the parents to accept written or spoken advice, and if they do so it is of their own free will.

2. *Negative arguments.* It can also be argued, and quite eloquently, that the parent education program has had some harmful effects. Basic to this view, of course, is the unalterable fact that there is currently no scientific body of knowledge on the subject of child-rearing, occasional claims to the contrary notwithstanding. Furthermore, most of the child-training "education" stems not from researchers in the field but from persons who often have no interest in or awareness of the research that is being done.

While it is true that no one forces parents to accept the so-called educational material, it is also true that many parents stand in awe of the printed word and are inclined to accept it as established fact. Along the same lines, while some parents have undoubtedly been helped by child-care education, others have probably been hurt. This would almost have to be the case, since many of the articles on child-rearing not only conflict with one another, but also tend to change in keeping with the guiding philosophy of the moment. One wonders, for instance, what the overall effects have been of the many writings that cautioned parents against the use of punishment for the child. Whether, in this respect, the total effects have been for ill or for good there is no way of knowing.

The Balance Sheet. It should be apparent from the above arguments that the parent education movement is neither as beneficial as its protagonists contend nor as harmful as its detractors claim. The question must not only be asked, "Does parent education do more harm than good?" but also "Is parent education better or worse than *no parent education?*" If the public had to wait until such time as a scientific body of child-rearing knowledge appeared, they would be in for a long wait, indeed. In the meantime, it would seem reasonable to familiarize parents with the results of the research that is being undertaken.

Unfortunately, the present parent education movement goes far beyond this modest goal. Popular advice by the carload is based either on segmental research studies or, more often, on no studies at all. And since the purveyors of such advice are often unwilling (or unable) to reveal the basis from which their "knowledge" is derived, the wise parent should endeavor to assess the advice for what it really is—namely, an array of value judgments, frequently perceptive, but often based neither on research nor on wide experience. Viewed in this light, the bulk of today's child-rearing information would probably compare favorably with the opinion advice offered in a variety of other behavioral areas.

THE PERMISSIVE VERSUS THE
RESTRICTIVE PHILOSOPHY

Of all the problems of child-raising, perhaps the one that most concerns parents relates to the freedom that should be accorded the child on the one hand, versus the necessary discipline on the other. This is a crucial area, and one wishes there were definitive research evidence that could be used as a guide. But until such time as a factual body of knowledge accumulates, parents will have to rely largely on their own experience and common sense, plus such assists from the authorities as are deemed reasonable. The following brief account is presented for the purpose of describing the problem rather than solving it.

The Permissive School. Proponents of the permissive school of thought lean toward the view that the formative years are crucial insofar as personality development is concerned. They feel that the child has certain needs, or "rights," such as the need to be attended, to be loved, and to be accorded freedom of self-expression. Particular stress is placed on the child's need to feel secure, and it is held that this feeling is best engendered through fondling, caressing, and ample physical contact with the mother.

As the child gets older:

> The permissive parent attempts to behave in a nonpunitive, acceptant, and affirmative manner toward the child's impulses, desires, and actions. She consults with him about policy decisions and gives explanations for family rules. She makes few demands for household responsibility and orderly behavior.
>
> She presents herself to the child as a resource for him to use as he wishes, not as an ideal for him to emulate, nor as an active agent responsible for shaping or altering his ongoing or future behavior.
>
> She allows the child to regulate his own activities as much as possible, avoids the exercise of control, and does not encourage him to obey externally defined standards. She attempts to use reason and manipulation, but not overt power, to accomplish her ends.[9]

Although proponents of the permissive school do not reject discipline, their emphasis is on love, affection, understanding, and the satisfaction of the child's needs, rather than on the inculcation of respect for authority. Some extremists do reject the use of discipline entirely, feeling that any repression tends to thwart the child's personality development. Neill, for instance, states bluntly: *"I believe that to impose anything by authority is wrong. The child should not do anything until he comes to the opinion—his*

429

---

[9] Baumrind, *op. cit.*, p. 301.

own opinion—that it should be done." [10] However, this view does not fairly represent the permissive philosophy.

On the basis of common observation, most American parents seem to be rather permissive in their child-raising practices. Whether this permissiveness reflects the bias of the "experts," or whether—as some writers have contended—Americans are simply soft-hearted, is a matter of debate.

The Restrictive School. Those who believe in a nonpermissive, or restrictive, philosophy of child-rearing hold that such practices as extensive fondling, mothering, and caressing tend to result in a spoiled child. It is felt that permissiveness, by definition, encourages non-respect for the rights of others and hence in the long run is detrimental to the best interests of society. Proponents of the restrictive school believe in furthering the child's personality development, but they feel strongly that personality formation hinges not so much on physical affection and freedom of self-expression as on the development of character and self-respect. These latter traits, it is held, can best be developed through the cultivation of discipline, respect for authority, awareness of property rights, and other aspects of group order. Restrictive parents would thus be less reluctant to impose physical punishment than would permissive parents.

Advocates of the restrictive approach by no means reject parental affection as an insignificant factor—any more than the permissive school rejects discipline—but in terms of *emphasis* it is held that discipline and respect warrant more consideration than do the physical manifestations of parental feeling. Restrictive parents, in other words, would be more inclined to express love for their children through imbuing them with an awareness of responsibility and order, rather than through a catering to immediate needs. Some extremists do reject entirely any display of physical affection or open manifestation of love and instead try to "force" their children through the various stages of development, but this position is not typical of restrictive philosophy. Dr. William Dewees, for instance, author of "the most famous of the early American textbooks in pediatrics" (1826), went so far as to tell his readers that infant bowel-and-bladder control could be attained by the age of one month![11]

In the last generation or so, the restrictive approach to child-rearing has not been very much in evidence. And yet in the past

[10] A. S. Neill, *Summerhill*, New York, Hart, 1964 (italics Neill's).
[11] Cited in Bernard Wishy, *The Child and the Republic*, Philadelphia, University of Pennsylvania Press, 1968, p. 40.

few years—as juvenile crime has risen and youthful conduct has "erupted"—some calls have been sounded for a more restrictive action program. For example, to the question "Are most parents these days too permissive with their children?" 85 percent of the respondents in one popular survey answered yes. In the same poll, the question "Do you think children should be disciplined by physical punishment?" found 65 percent answering in the affirmative.[12] Whether any real change will take place is a matter of conjecture. From a historical view, however, a reasonable prediction would be that the child-rearing pendulum is due for a swing to the restrictive side.

An Assessment. Readers may ask, "Is it really necessary for parents to follow one school of thought or the other? Why not combine the best of both philosophies?" And, in practice, it is likely that many parents do, or try to do, just that. Interestingly enough, international surveys reveal that German youngsters rate their parents more highly than do American youth, despite the fact that German parents impose greater discipline. The explanation may lie in the fact that the German children also receive greater affection—and are under less pressure for achievement.[13]

It is the present writer's view that the real danger in child-rearing lies not in which philosophy is followed, but in the application of *extreme* measures of either school of thought. The child who is not only loved but is pampered and coddled, whose need-satisfactions become the dominant part of parental action, and whose misdeeds remain consistently unpunished—this child may well become *persona non grata* to both children and adults. Such a child has received little in the way of preparation for responsible adulthood, however much love was bestowed by the parents. Granted that childhood needs are important, it is also true that such needs are not the center of the universe, and the child who does not learn this fact at home is likely to suffer some hard knocks later on. Character, responsibility, respect for the feelings of others—all of these form part of the necessary ingredients of personality, and parents whose permissiveness prompts them to disregard these factors would seem to be doing their children a disservice.

431

---

[12] *A Report on the American Family*, by the eidtors of *Better Homes and Gardens*, September, 1972, pp. 99–101.

[13] See Edward Devereux, "Authority and Moral Development Among German and American Children: A Cross-National Pilot Experiment," *Journal of Comparative Family Studies*, Spring, 1972, pp. 99–124.

432

Disciplining a child is part of a parent's love, although a child may not always see it that way. (Peter Vandermark, Stock Boston)

On the other hand, a child who has been reared in an atmosphere where obedience, discipline, and respect for the rights of others are stressed at the *expense* of physical love and demonstrated affection—this child also may find himself handicapped in a society where emotional warmth, expressiveness, and love are cherished values. Children who have been overly disciplined and from whom physical displays of love and attention have been withheld are not likely as adults to look back with fondness on their childhood memories. And if, as the Freudians maintain,

Expressions of parental love and attention enrich the experience of childhood.
(Burk Uzzle, Magnum Photo)

emotional security hinges in good part on the physical love and affection received in childhood, the withholding of such love would certainly have adverse effects on adult personality structure.

In terms of the permissive-restrictive controversy—a debate that perhaps has aroused social scientists more than parents—no one can say with certainty just where the stress, if any, should fall. In the absence of more research information, perhaps the safest course of action for parents to follow is to hew to the middle of the line.

SEX EDUCATION

Sex education, it seems, is always in the news. On the one hand, most parents apparently favor some sort of formal program for their youngsters. In the previously mentioned poll, for example, to the question "Should sex education be taught in school?" 79 percent of the respondents answered yes.[14] On the other hand, in many localities resistance to sex education has been heated. And even those who agree on the desirability of such a program are likely to find themselves in disagreement on the content.

In a historical sense, neither the church nor the school showed much enthusiasm for the subject of sex education. Nominally, at least, instruction in sexual and reproductive matters was the province of the home. Although no explicit policy was involved, when children were old enough to know about such things, they were presumably instructed in the "facts of life" by their parents.

It was rather evident, however, that in actual practice one of two things happened: (1) by the time the parents felt that the children were old enough, the latter had already received a variety of sexual information—from dubious sources; or (2) because of embarrassment or the lack of an adequate vocabulary, parents simply ignored the topic of sex education altogether, trusting that the children would somehow acquire the necessary information from books, biology classes, or other competent sources.

Research evidence has confirmed the above picture. Any number of surveys—from the 1940's through the 1970's—have revealed that American youth are ill-informed on topics of sex and reproduction.[15] And, as the present writer can attest, this inadequacy extends to the college as well as to the noncollege population.

It appears that a large proportion of American youth are not only ill-informed on sexual matters, but that much of the so-called sex education is of the "informal" variety. As Gagnon and Simon point out, the fact that the primary source of sex information is the peer group has been shown by studies going back as far as 1915![16]

Sex "education," in brief, too often comes from the street and involves the use of obscene language. The upshot is that the whole concept of sex in America has come to have lewd connotations—as evidenced by the hush-hush attitude in the home, pornographic inscriptions in public places, the snickering attitude toward nude art forms, the endless supply of "dirty" jokes, and so on.

[14] *A Report on the American Family*, p. 75.

[15] See, for example, Melvin Zelnik and John Kantner, "The Resolution of Teenage First Pregnancies," *Family Planning Perspectives*, Spring, 1974, pp. 74–80.

[16] John H. Gagnon and William Simon, *Sexual Conduct: The Social Sources of Human Sexuality*, Chicago, Aldine Publishing Company, 1973, p. 115.

Deploring this state of affairs, many educators have advocated a fairly comprehensive sex education program, starting in the lower grades and continuing through high school. Some schools already have programs that include such topics as human reproduction, menstrual cycles, sexual anatomy, and childbirth. The major Protestant denominations have also instituted a fairly elaborate sex education program. It should perhaps be added that in most sections of the country illustrated booklets and pamphlets are now available to parents, giving the whys and wherefores of sex questions that are likely to be asked by young people. But whether the advocated sex education program is in the home, the church, or the school, the goal is the same: to take sex out of the gutter, so to speak, and frame it in such a manner as to promote healthier and more wholesome attitudes.

Basic to this philosophy is the belief that, when a child is old enough to ask a meaningful question, a meaningful answer should be provided. Thus, when a child asks, "Where do babies come from?" (often asked at age four or five), the recommended answer is: "From the mother's stomach." To the question, "How did it get there?" an acceptable reply is, "The father planted the seed." More involved questions can be answered effectively with the aid of published diagrams and pictures.

Educators are probably correct in maintaining that when a child asks a relatively simple question such as, "Where do babies come from?" it is not necessary to involve the child in an elaborate discussion of the sexual and reproductive processes. Detailed explanations, supplemented by pictures and anatomical diagrams, should be reserved for a somewhat later age. It is contended, however, that by junior high school the boy or girl should be in possession of (1) the basic facts concerning sex and reproduction, (2) a vocabulary large enough to converse and read intelligently on sexual topics, and (3) an attitude toward sex that is wholesome enough to permit reading or discussion of the subject without embarrassment or shame.

A number of educators urge that parents supplement the sex education program by treating nudity as more or less natural within the home—that is, by permitting themselves to be seen in the nude with no attempt made to "cover up" or otherwise to show concern. The assumption is that sooner or later the growing child will be exposed to nudity—in both sexes—and that in terms of mental hygiene the healthiest place to handle the problem is in the home.

Some Considerations. While there is perhaps nothing intrinsically wrong with a sex education program such as that outlined above, certain considerations are involved, and these should be examined before any conclusion is reached. For instance, while the aim of the sex education program—to engender healthy attitudes toward sex in the minds of children—seems reasonable enough, is there a danger that these attitudes may become too "healthy?" Does the sex education program contain any built-in safeguards that would restrict youthful exploitation of an otherwise rational policy?

Do the available books, pamphlets, and filmstrips, at the same time that they straightforwardly present sexual material, also point out the prevalent attitude of the community toward sex? Are today's teachers really qualified to impart sexual information to young children? Are sex education programs being offered *at the expense* of basic courses in English, science, and mathematics?

Let us examine one or two of the above items in more detail. The question concerning teacher qualification poses some real problems. In the Malfetti–Rubin survey of teachers' colleges, only 8 percent of the colleges were found to be offering courses "intended to prepare teachers to teach sex education." And of the institutions that did not offer such courses, only 3 percent "had plans to do so in the future."[17]

No less an authority than Margaret Mead states that "the serious problem in sex education is the tremendous shortage of persons who by their background, training, and experience are able to teach the subject properly."[18] And in an excellent historical survey of the subject—covering a period of more than 50 years—Carrera reports that not only is there a "pressing need" for sex educators, but that "the critical nature of this need has been recognized throughout the history of sex education."[19]

Another question raised above—"Is there a danger of children's attitudes toward sex becoming too healthy?"—also involves more than meets the eye. Would not a sex education program encourage some youngsters to indulge in sexual activities that violate community standards? We do not know, certainly, although it is known that *changes in attitude* do take place. In one study of 10- and 11-year-old children, for example, it was found that a sex education program resulted in attitude changes "from lesser to greater permissiveness relevant to such aspects of

[17] James Malfetti and Arline Rubin, "Sex Education: Who Is Teaching the Teachers?" *Family Coordinator*, April, 1968, pp. 110–117.
[18] Margaret Mead, "Teacher Shortage in Sex Field Noted," *New York Times*, October 11, 1969, p. 26.
[19] Michael Carrera, "Preparation of a Sex Educator: A Historical Overview," *Family Coordinator*, April, 1971, p. 106.

sexuality as masturbation, same-sex behavior, nudity, love-making, touch-talk, and gender identity."[20]

As might be imagined, it is on just these moral issues that the community at large often splits on the subject of sex education. It must be kept in mind that the entire boy-girl relationship has changed. It is anything but the formal, stand-offish arrangement of yesteryear. Our culture, in effect, now encourages the sexes to associate at a very young age. Because of this free association and day-to-day contact, therefore, some parents have questioned the implementation of certain sex education programs.

Sociologically speaking, a *balanced program* of sex education, in which individual learning privileges are made to mesh with community goals, might well prove advantageous to all concerned. A short-sighted program in which the interests of one group are stressed at the expense of the other, might in the long run prove less effective than no program at all. Much would depend on the way the undertaking was designed and administered. Before a specific sex education program is adopted, therefore, it would seem only reasonable to inquire whether all interests—the children's, the parents', and the community's—are adequately represented.

437

SELECTED READINGS

A Report on the American Family, by the editors of *Better Homes and Gardens,* September, 1972.

Ariès, Philippe, *Centuries of Childhood,* New York, Alfred A. Knopf, 1962.

Baumrind, Diana, "Effects of Authoritative Parental Control on Child Behavior," in Robert Winch and Louis Goodman (eds.), *Selected Studies in Marriage and the Family,* New York, Holt, Rinehart and Winston, Inc., 1968.

Bigner, Jerry J., "Parent Education in Popular Literature," *Family Coordinator,* July, 1972, pp. 313–319.

Brofenbrenner, Urie, *Two Worlds of Childhood, U.S. and U.S.S.R.,* New York, Russell Sage Foundation, distributed by Basic Books, Inc., 1970.

Carrera, Michael, "Preparation of a Sex Educator: A Historical Overview," *Family Coordinator,* April, 1971, pp. 99–108.

Carton, Jacqueline, and Carton, John, "Evaluation of a Sex Education Program for Children and Their Parents," *Family Coordinator,* October, 1971, pp. 377–386.

---

[20] Jacqueline Carton and John Carton, "Evaluation of a Sex Education Program for Children and Their Parents: Attitude and Interactional Change," *Family Coordinator,* October, 1971, p. 377.

de Mause, Lloyd (ed.), *The History of Childhood,* New York, The Psychohistory Press, 1974.

Demos, John, and Demos, Virginia, "Adolescence in Historical Perspective," in Michael Gordon (ed.), *The American Family in Socio-Historical Perspective,* New York, St. Martin's Press, 1973, pp. 209–221.

Devereux, Edward, "Authority and Moral Development Among German and American Children: A Cross-National Pilot Experiment," *Journal of Comparative Family Studies,* Spring, 1972, pp. 99–124.

Gagnon, John H., and Simon, William, *Sexual Conduct: The Social Sources of Human Sexuality,* Chicago, Aldine Publishing Company, 1973.

Gecas, Viktor, and Nye, F. Ivan, "Sex and Class Differences in Parent-Child Interaction," *Journal of Marriage and the Family,* November, 1974, pp. 742–749.

Gunter, B. G., and Moore, Harvey, "Youth, Leisure, and Post-Industrial Society: Implications for the Family," *Family Coordinator,* April, 1975, pp. 199–207.

Hendrickson, Norejane J.; Perkins, Deborah; White, Sylvia; and Buck, Timothy, "Parent-Daughter Relationships in Fiction," *Family Coordinator,* July, 1975, pp. 257–265.

History of Childhood Quarterly, 2315 Broadway, New York, N.Y.

Kerckhoff, Richard, and Habig, Myrna, "Parent Education as Provided by Secondary Schools," *Family Coordinator,* April, 1976, pp. 127–130.

Klausner, Samuel, *Two Centuries of Child-Rearing Manuals,* Technical Report Submitted to the Joint Commission on Mental Health of Children, 1968.

Libby, Roger, "Parental Attitudes Toward High School Sex Education Programs," *Family Coordinator,* July, 1970, pp. 234–247.

Malfetti, James, and Rubin, Arline, "Sex Education: Who Is Teaching the Teachers?" *Family Coordinator,* April, 1968, pp. 110–117.

Nye, F. Ivan, and Berardo, Felix, *The Family: Its Structure and Interaction,* New York, The Macmillan Company, 1973, Chapter 15, "The Socialization of Children," pp. 273–404.

Rapson, Richard, "The American Child as Seen By British Travelers, 1845–1935," in Michael Gordon (ed.), *The American Family in Socio-Historical Perspective,* New York, St. Martin's Press, 1973, pp. 192–208.

Rosenblatt, Paul, and Phillips, Robert, Jr., "Family Articles in Popular Magazines," *Family Coordinator,* July, 1975, pp. 267–271.

Scanzoni, Letha, and Scanzoni, John, *Men, Women, and Change,* New York, McGraw-Hill Book Company, 1976.

Steinmann, Anne, and Jurich, Anthony, "The Effects of a Sex Education Course on the Sex Role Perceptions of Junior High School Students," *Family Coordinator,* January, 1975, pp. 27–31.

Walter, James, and Stinnett, Nick, "Parent-Child Relationships: A Decade Review of Research," *Journal of Marriage and the Family,* February, 1971, pp. 70–111.

Weiner, Florence, *Help for the Handicapped Child,* New York, McGraw-Hill Book Company, 1973.

Zelnik, Melvin, and Kantner, John "The Resolution of Teenage First Pregnancies," *Family Planning Perspectives,* Spring, 1974, pp. 74–80.

V

Family Disorganization and
Reorganization

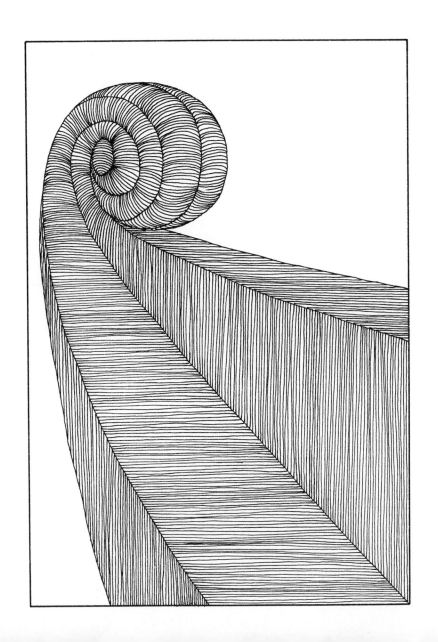

20

Marital Breakup I—
Socio-Legal Aspects

IN SPITE OF the seemingly endless controversy over divorce, the
basic issue can be summed up by asking two conflicting sets of
questions: (1) If a married couple are clearly unhappy, why must
they stay married? Why not permit them to get divorced, simply
and inexpensively? (2) But if divorce were made available "on demand," would not one party be tempted to leave for trivial
reasons—at the expense of both the other party and the children?
Would not the institution of marriage itself be undermined?
Scholars have grappled with these questions for decades, with
the end nowhere in sight. The purpose of the present chapter is
to discuss and analyze some of the areas of controversy.

SOCIO-HISTORICAL BACKGROUND

In the pre-Christian era, divorce was generally available only to
the husband. Among the Greeks and Hebrews, for example, a
husband could divorce his wife for almost any reason, whereas
the wife had virtually no grounds available to her. However,
public opinion, group pressures—and the primacy of the
family—tended to keep husbands from abusing their divorce
privilege.

Under Christianity, divorce per se was eventually abolished.
Marriage came to be regarded as sacramental in nature; hence it
was dissoluble only through death. The Church recognized,
however, that under certain conditions married life might become intolerable, and therefore the ecclesiastical courts sometimes granted a *limited divorce,* which permitted the spouses to
live apart but did not permit them to remarry. Even in this instance, a limited divorce (divorce from bed and board) was
authorized only for grave and serious reasons, e.g., "cruelty
which doth threaten life and health." Cruelty, in other words,

was used in the literal sense and was looked upon as a method whereby wife and children could escape the ravages of a brutal husband. It should be noted that a limited divorce signified relief from a wrong action: one spouse was deemed to be good, the other bad, and the ensuing separation was an attempt to make life tolerable for the good spouse, even though remarriage rights were denied both partners.

The Protestant Reformation led to a repudiation of the sacramental theory of marriage. Responsibility was transferred from church to state, thereby paving the way for a recognition of absolute divorce. The Protestant reformers, however, rejected the concept of divorce by mutual consent, holding that, while marriages could be dissolved and remarriages permitted, the grounds must be serious (adultery, cruelty, desertion) and clearly demonstrable in the legal sense. In brief, divorce was to be granted to the innocent party as a relief from the gross wrongdoing of the spouse adjudged to be guilty. Throughout most European countries the verdict as to whether one party really was innocent and the other guilty came to be determined in a court of law.

In the United States, most state legislatures came to adopt these traditional principles: (1) that divorce should be granted only for grave and serious reasons and (2) that one party, and one party only, should be "guilty." In a number of states, these principles hold true today. Most states, for example, include grounds that are obviously of a serious nature: cruelty, desertion, neglect, criminality, adultery, habitual drunkenness, and insanity. Moreover, the courts are empowered to represent the interests of the state.

The state does not necessarily oppose the granting of a divorce. However, since society has some stake in the preservation of marriage, the legislative philosophy has been to ascertain that the residence requirements have been fulfilled, that the alleged grounds are valid, that the testimony—so far as can be determined—is factual, that no frivolity is involved, and so on.

During recent years the question has repeatedly been asked: Granted the necessary societal interest in the matter, why the continued insistence on the "guilt-and-innocence" concept of divorce, with one party the plaintiff and the other the defendant? Cannot society's interests be served without putting the spouses through an expensive legal maze?

At times it has seemed that no two legislators could agree on an answer, and indeed even today each state has its own particular divorce code. Starting with California in 1970, however, the concept of "no-fault" divorce—wherein the whole idea of blame or guilt is eliminated—has received growing recognition. But while many states have adopted no-fault provisions, others have not, the upshot being that we are really operating under a dual system.

THE FAULT SYSTEM OF DIVORCE

This system has deep roots. It is based on the age-old guilt and innocence concept, mentioned previously. It is also based on the theory of *contest;* that is, the belief that justice can best be attained by having each party present his own side of the case—through his attorney—to the best of his ability. However, any resemblance between a divorce "contest" and a genuine lawsuit is illusory.

Under the fault system, one of the spouses—usually the wife—sues for divorce on the legal ground that is most applicable, the "applicability" often being determined by the plaintiff's attorney. In court, the plaintiff assumes the role of the innocent and good spouse, while the partner is painted various shades of evil. Witnesses are seldom called, and rarely does the court delve into the realities of the situation. And, perhaps most important, the defendant usually is not in court to defend himself. He has been notified of the hearing, but he generally does not bother to attend. Since he is not in court to refute the allegations made by the wife, the court assumes him to be guilty and the divorce is granted.

Occasionally the divorce suit is a real contest, with both spouses represented by their lawyers. But in at least 90 percent of fault cases, the spouses have more or less agreed beforehand which party will be the plaintiff, what the grounds will be, and that the defendant will not contest the suit—despite the fact that such an agreement is prohibited by law.

The following is an example of court dialogue:

LAWYER: And as a result of this [cruelty] . . . how did you feel?
PLAINTIFF: I felt bad. It didn't bother my husband any, though.
LAWYER: I mean, how did it affect you physically? Did it affect your health?
PLAINTIFF: Oh, yes! My health got to be very bad.
LAWYER: Were you able to eat properly?
PLAINTIFF: No, I lost my appetite. *He* ate like a cannibal.
LAWYER: Were you able to get the proper amount of sleep at night?
PLAINTIFF: Not usually. Often I would toss and turn the whole night.
LAWYER: Did you lose any weight?
PLAINTIFF: Oh, yes, a great deal.

LAWYER: About how much did you weigh when you were married?

PLAINTIFF: About 125.

LAWYER: And what did you weigh when you were separated?

PLAINTIFF: Less than 105.

LAWYER: As a result of all this . . . did you experience any nervousness?

PLAINTIFF: Yes. I was jumpy all the time. I used to get headaches and crying spells.

LAWYER: Prior to your marriage did you ever have spells like this?

PLAINTIFF: No, never.

COURT: Actually how serious was the state of your health as a result of your husband's actions?

PLAINTIFF: Well, toward the end I had to go to my family doctor almost every week, my nerves were so bad.

COURT: Who is your family doctor?

PLAINTIFF: Dr. Ralph Peterman, on Goren Street.

COURT: What did Dr. Peterman say to you?

PLAINTIFF: He said I shouldn't live with my husband any more; that I should leave him before I was a total wreck.

Note that the lawyer in this instance is merely trying to establish that his client's life "has been made intolerable" insofar as the legal meaning of the term is concerned, and, of course, this process entails the plaintiff's cooperation. Note, also, that while the court inquired into the doctor's opinion, no attempt was made to have him put on the witness stand and actually testify. What it all amounts to is that throughout the entire range of American law, fault-divorce litigation is the only instance where the defendant does not try to keep the plaintiff from succeeding!

Understandably, fault divorce has come in for heavy criticism over the years. Sociologists, clergymen, reporters, screenwriters —almost everyone, it seems, has castigated the "system." Especially heavy criticism has come from within the legal profession itself, the feeling being that the fault procedure—with its obvious hypocrisy—breeds disrespect for the law. Also, it is no secret that the divorce lawyer has a rather low status within the legal profession, even though the status ascription may seem unwarranted. Nevertheless, most of the top lawyers in this country have traditionally shunned divorce cases. One result is that in many cities a large share of all divorce suits are handled by a small group of lawyers.

THE NO-FAULT SYSTEM

As conceived by its designers, the purpose of no-fault divorce was quite clear: to eliminate the adversary aspects, the hypoc-

Divorce has always been viewed as a painful proceeding, as can be seen in this nineteenth-century poster showing a child at her parents' divorce court hearing. (The Bettman Archive Inc.)

risy, and the legal folderol that had characterized the typical divorce case. Accordingly, California—the first state to act on the matter—coined the phrase "irremediable breakdown" to apply to those marriages that could be legally severed under the no-fault concept. If the matrimonial ties were irremediably broken, as affirmed by the spouses, then the court was obligated to dissolve the marriage.

No longer would it be necessary for one spouse to accuse the other of a real or imagined wrongdoing. No longer would it be necessary to attend protracted court hearings to answer inane questions. Even the pleadings were changed from the former *"Helen Brown* v. *George Brown"* to *"In re the marriage of George and Helen Brown."* As a matter of fact, the California legislators went so far as to abolish the term "divorce" entirely, substituting instead the term "dissolution of marriage." (Technically, at least, there is no divorce in California.)

Following the pioneer efforts of California, a number of other states adopted no-fault provisions. Sometimes the phraseology was different: "irremediable breakdown," "irreconcilable differences," irretrievable breakdown," "no reasonable likelihood" of preserving the marriage, and so on, but it looked as though (finally) the fault concept of divorce was on its way out in the United States.

Before long, however, certain cracks began to appear in the no-fault edifice—or at least so it seemed to the critics. For one thing, the divorce rate in states like California increased noticeably. It was charged that many persons were getting divorced for trivial reasons, and since most divorces involved minor children, the best interests of youngsters were being disregarded. There were also complaints about alimony and property settlements.

One of the chief criticisms of the no-fault system pertains to the matter of definition. Exactly what do terms like "irremediable breakdown" and "irreconcilable differences" mean? It is one thing when the couple *agree* that the differences have become insurmountable, but what happens when they *disagree?* According to California law, the general principle has been that, if one party wants the divorce, he or she is entitled to it—despite any objections by the other party. In Wheeler's words, "As the law has been applied, if one person says the marriage has broken down and the other says it has not, that in itself may be considered an irreconcilable difference." The same author points out that:

> It is no longer necessary to point the finger of fault at one spouse or the other, so either can start a proceeding to dissolve the marriage. Thus a man or woman who is having an affair can initiate a divorce, while under traditional notions of law, he or she would be considered "at fault," and thus be barred from doing so.[1]

---

[1] Michael Wheeler, *No-Fault Divorce,* Boston, Beacon Press, 1974, pp. 20–22. Copyright © 1974 by Michael Wheeler. Reprinted by permission of Beacon Press.

Because of trepidations about the above points, some states have refused to adopt no-fault provisions. And while such states are clearly the exception, *only a dozen or so states have no-fault provisions only*. Strange as it may seem, most jurisdictions have a divorce system that embodies both fault and no-fault provisions!

GROUNDS FOR DIVORCE

It is difficult to appreciate the jumble of divorce laws in the United States until one checks the statutes of the individual states.[2] Several states have but a single ground (irretrievable breakdown), but just as many have a dozen or more grounds. Although the wording of the various statutes makes it difficult to arrive at a precise figure, there appear to be close to 50 legal grounds in the various states and territories:

Abandonment
Adjudication of mental incompetence
Adultery
Any cause rendering the marriage void
Application following decree of divorce from bed and board
Attempt to corrupt son or prostitute daughter
Attempt to murder spouse
Bigamy
Consanguinity
Conviction of a felony
Crime against nature
Cruel and inhuman treatment
Desertion
Deviant sexual conduct
Drug addiction
Force, menace, or duress in obtaining the marriage
Fraud
Gross misbehavior and wickedness
Habitual drunkenness
Idiocy
Impotence
Imprisonment
Incapability of procreation at time of marriage
Incest
Incompatibility
Incurable physical incapacity
Indignities
Infection of spouse with communicable venereal disease
Insanity
Intolerable severity
Irremediable breakdown of marriage
Membership in sect believing cohabitation is unlawful
Mental cruelty
Mental incapacity at time of marriage
No reasonable likelihood of marriage being preserved
Nonsupport
Physical incompetence at time of marriage, continued

---

[2] For a summary of divorce grounds in the various states and territories, see Doris Jonas Freed, "Grounds for Divorce in the American Jurisdictions," *Family Law Quarterly*, Winter, 1974, pp. 401–423.

Proposal to prostitute wife
Refusal by wife to move with husband to this state
Seven years' absence, absent party not being heard from
Sodomy or buggery
Treatment seriously injuring health or endangering reason
Unnatural sexual intercourse with person of the same sex or of a different sex or a beast

Vagrancy by husband
Voluntary separation
Wife being pregnant by another man at time of marriage without knowledge of husband
Wife being prostitute prior to marriage without knowledge of husband
Willful neglect

Interestingly enough, in spite of the wide array of available grounds in the United States, the large majority of them are seldom used. Adultery, for example, is probably used in less than 1 percent of all divorce suits, widespread publicity to the contrary. Three grounds—incompatibility or "irreconcilable differences," cruelty (variously defined), and separation or desertion—would account for perhaps 90 percent of all divorce cases in this country.

DEFENSES AGAINST DIVORCE

In most divorce cases—both fault and no-fault—the actual proceedings are rather cut-and-dried affairs. In the no-fault cases, the intent of the law clearly is to facilitate divorce, so except for the affirmation of "irreconcilable differences" and the certification as to residency, the hearings are routine. In California, for instance, "most cases take only a few minutes of the court's time."[3] In fault divorce, the spouses have presumably agreed upon a convenient ground—usually cruelty or desertion—and at the hearing the defendant ordinarily does not appear. And if the technical requirements are fulfilled, the chances are that the divorce decree will be signed in quick order.

Occasionally, in a fault case, one of the spouses does *not* agree to the divorce, and a genuine contest—and much trouble—develops. The writer would estimate that less than 10 percent of all divorce suits are *really* contested. Those that are, can be long, drawn-out affairs and are likely to be headaches for all concerned. It would not be much exaggeration to say that it is as difficult to win a contested case as it is easy to win an uncontested one. The following defenses have been commonly employed in fault divorce suits.

---

[3] Wheeler, *op. cit.*, p. 24.

450

Recrimination. Stated simply, the principle of recrimination means that if one party is guilty a divorce may be granted, but if both are guilty neither one is legally entitled to a divorce. To illustrate: Herbert is guilty of adultery; the evidence is incontrovertible. Nevertheless, he can block the divorce if he is able to prove that his wife, Joan, has also had extramarital sex relations. However quaint the legal reasoning is on this point, the fact remains that recrimination is still in force in a number of states and over the years has been one of the defenses most often used in divorce actions.

Recrimination is by no means limited to adultery. Betty, the plaintiff, accuses her husband, Jack, of desertion—which he cannot deny. Jack in turn accuses her of mental cruelty, and if he can make the charge stick, Betty's plea for divorce may be denied. The prevailing rule has been that no matter what the demonstrated guilt of the defendant might be, if the plaintiff can be shown to be guilty of any of the statutory grounds of the state, the divorce can be effectively blocked.

451

Collusion. In nontechnical language, collusion means simply that the spouses have cooperated in getting their divorce (under fault procedures). Since fault law stipulates that a divorce suit must be a legal *contest,* collusion represents any method whereby the element of contest is subverted. Generally speaking, collusion may take one of three forms.

1. The parties may agree to submit false evidence regarding an offense that was actually not committed. "Hotel adultery" is a good example of the submittal of false evidence. Not only is the wife well aware of the fact that her husband is not having an adulterous affair with another woman, but she—the wife—is notified when and where the extramarital escapade is to take place so that the proper witnesses, detectives, and photographers can be on hand.

2. An offense may be committed by one of the parties for the sole purpose of facilitating the agreed-upon divorce. The husband may, for example, "desert" his wife and "refuse her pleas" to return home. At the divorce hearing, an agreed-upon leave of absence is then blown up into a full-fledged case of desertion. And so long as the defendant does not put in an appearance or contest the suit, the divorce will nearly always be granted.

3. A legitimate defense may be suppressed by the defendant. Mabel sues for divorce on the ground of cruelty, claiming that

her husband, Ted, struck her repeatedly. The contention is true, but what the court doesn't know (and doesn't want to know) is that Ted's behavior was provoked by Mabel's drinking and her refusal to perform normal household duties. Since both want the divorce, they agree that Ted will not appear in court to tell his side of the story. This agreement is open-and-shut collusion.

While no one can tell for certain what the exact percentage is, it is rather obvious that a substantial majority of all fault-divorce suits are collusive in nature. If the court discovers that it has, to use a legal phrase, been imposed upon, the divorce will be denied, or, if already granted, may be revoked. In reality, however, collusive practices infrequently come to light, for the simple reason that nobody wants to rock the boat.

Connivance.   Connivance is a kind of half-relative of collusion and is usually found in adultery cases. Let us suppose that Ralph and Trudy are married—but not happily. Ralph is a business executive, and after a high-pressured day at the office he feels the need for a relaxed home environment and a quiet cocktail. Trudy, however, can hardly wait until he gets home before she burdens him with her latest troubles. Finally, Ralph takes to staying away from home as much as possible and eventually he meets someone more to his liking. He asks Trudy for a divorce, but his wife turns him down pointblank.

In desperation, Ralph not only hires a detective to spy on Trudy but—to help matters along—he arranges for a handsome suitor to shower her with attention. Eventually Trudy succumbs to the suitor's advances, at which point the detective charges in for some choice photographs, the case for adultery thus being established.

Ralph may be in for a surprise, however. If the court finds out about his involvement in the affair, his plea for divorce will be denied, for this is a crystal-clear case of connivance.

Condonation.   Where one spouse has committed an unprovoked wrongdoing—desertion, cruelty, adultery—the other is entitled to a divorce. But the law has inserted an "if." The plaintiff is entitled to a divorce *provided* he or she has not forgiven the wrongdoing. Such forgiveness is known in the courts as "condonation" and is generally an effective defense in fault-divorce suits.

Condonation is usually assumed where the spouses have cohabited or have indulged in sex relations subsequent to the wrongdoing. If, for instance, a husband deserts his wife and stays away for several years, his wife cannot effectively sue for divorce on the ground of desertion if it becomes known that she had sex relations with her husband, let us say, just before filing the suit.

Some states limit condonation to those cases involving specified grounds—adultery, for example—but nearly all states follow the letter of the law where the case is applicable. In fault-divorce suits, therefore, one question has been routinely asked by the court: "When did you last have sex relations with your spouse?"

Alimony. In recent years the defenses of recrimination, collusion, connivance, and condonation have been widely criticized, and a number of states have eliminated them in whole or in part, although in other states they are still recognized. However, the controversy over these traditional defenses is as nothing compared with the wrangling that has taken place over alimony.

On the one hand, it can be argued that in a period of increasing equality between the sexes the idea of alimony is clearly anachronistic. As Clark points out: "Legal principles devised by Solomon and administered by Oliver Wendell Holmes could not mitigate the hardship caused by divorce to families in the middle and lower-income ranges. The hardship is made even more acute when the husband remarries, as he frequently does, and acquires a new family to support. In that event, an income barely adequate for one family must be stretched to provide for a husband, a wife, an ex-wife, and two sets of children."[4]

On the other hand, it is argued that if a woman has been a devoted wife and mother for many years, she is certainly entitled to compensation—in the form of alimony—if her husband decides to divorce her. This is especially true in those cases where the wife has been out of the labor market during her most economically productive years.

In any case, it can be seen that the threat of alimony—though not a defense against divorce in the same sense as recrimination, collusion, connivance, and condonation—has probably prevented more divorces than all the foregoing defenses combined!

Some states have been fairly liberal in their awards of alimony, while others tend to look with disfavor on the whole idea. In a few states, such as Pennsylvania and Texas, alimony has been abolished altogether. Some courts will not award alimony in those cases where the husband is the plaintiff. But where the wife is plaintiff, some courts have awarded huge sums of money,

---

[4] Quoted in Wheeler, *op. cit.*, p. 66.

regular payments being required until she dies or remarries. One New York court awarded the wife $90,000 a year!

Remarriage of the husband does not relieve him of his alimony obligations, although some courts consider this just cause for a reduction in the size of payments. Some states place a limit on the amount of the payments; in fact, most of the alimony awards in the United States are fairly modest, many of them not exceeding $150 a month. It should be kept in mind, also, that most divorce suits *do not involve alimony*. The writer would estimate that alimony is awarded in perhaps 10 to 15 percent of all divorce suits, although property agreements and out-of-court settlements would tend to increase this figure.

Most courts will include the following factors in considering alimony awards: length of marriage; earning potential of the wife, as based on education and experience; age of the wife; ability of the husband to pay; and wife's income, if any. Thus, an older woman who has been married for many years to a wealthy man will receive more consideration from the court than a young woman, recently married, who is an experienced secretary.

The majority of alimony cases are presumably handled in an equitable manner, but there is no doubt that some husbands have been saddled with exorbitant payments. And once the judge signs the court order—just or unjust—alimony must be paid or the husband faces a prison sentence. As one attorney puts it, "Debtor's prisons have been outlawed in the United States, except in divorce cases!"[5]

Wheeler cites the following episode:

A Vermont man who owed his family $2500 in temporary support was found in contempt of court and served more than five years in jail. After he was finally released, the state indicated that it was considering imprisoning him again unless he paid the additional $20,000 which had mounted up while he was in jail.[6]

The same author points out that imprisonment is a rather expensive method of enforcement. "Once a man is in jail, he certainly cannot earn enough money stamping out license plates to make up what he owes; it costs the state more to keep him locked up than it would to support him and his family in a welfare program."[7]

Can wives be ordered to pay alimony to their ex-husbands?

[5] Stanley Rosenblatt, *The Divorce Racket,* Los Angeles, Nash Publishing Corporation, 1969, p. 43.
[6] Wheeler, *op. cit.,* pp. 54–55.
[7] *Ibid.,* p. 55.

The answer is generally no—but sometimes yes. Wheeler writes that "many states will not order a woman to pay alimony to her former husband no matter what the circumstances are."[8] Occasionally, however, because of a special situation, wives have been required to pay alimony. In fact, a judge in California "awarded one man $30,000 a year in spousal support."[9]

LIMITED DIVORCE

The concept of limited divorce springs from canon law and from the action of the ecclesiastical courts, and hence is religious in origin. While they rejected the notion of absolute divorce, the ecclesiastical courts sometimes authorized husband and wife to live apart in cases where continued cohabitation was grossly intolerable. Neither party, however, was permitted to remarry, for the simple reason that the bonds of matrimony were still intact. In both a figurative and literal sense the divorce was from "bed and board" only, a term that is still used.

In America the various state legislatures were divided on the question of limited divorce: some looked upon it as a sensible alternative to an intolerable marriage; others rejected the idea on the ground that it served no real purpose, their argument being that, since the parties could neither remarry nor live together as man and wife, they were left in a highly unnatural state of existence. The upshot was that some states provided statutory grounds for limited divorce, others did not, and this dichotomy still exists. In those states providing for limited divorce, it is referred to by a variety of terms—judicial separation, partial dissolution, divorce from bed and board, limited divorce, and *separatio a mensa et thoro*. All of these terms contrast with absolute divorce (*divortium a vinculo matrimonii*).

Under a limited divorce decree neither party may remarry within the lifetime of the other, the husband is still responsible for the support of his wife and children, and (in most states) the couple may not live together without express permission from the court. Should the couple disregard the court order and cohabit, and should the wife give birth to a child, the latter would be presumed to be illegitimate. Should either husband or wife have sexual intercourse with someone else during the period of judicial separation, he or she could be adjudged guilty of adultery.

---

[8] *Ibid.*, p. 57.
[9] *Ibid.*, p. 60.

Although there are some differences among the states, the legal grounds for limited divorce are rather similar to those for absolute divorce—for example, desertion, cruelty, adultery, conviction of a crime, nonsupport, habitual drunkenness. In general, a limited divorce is available to either party, although in the large majority of cases the wife institutes action.

The question must be raised, "Exactly what purpose does a limited divorce serve?" The most common answer is that it permits couples who have religious or moral scruples against divorce to live apart. Such couples can live apart, however, without going to the trouble and expense of procuring a judicial separation.

In a number of states, a limited divorce serves as one of the grounds for a final divorce. That is, a certain period of time after a legal separation is granted—generally one, two, or three years, depending on the state—the separation may be converted to a final divorce. In these cases the judicial separation serves a real function, namely, that of providing a "cooling-off" period for the couple before they take the final step toward marital severance.

In some states, limited divorces are often used by wives who, although they do not morally believe in divorce, have been mistreated by their husbands. A judicial separation in these instances may be the only practicable safeguard short of criminal proceedings.

Generally speaking, however, limited divorces have a rather restricted usage in the United States. The writer would estimate that they comprise only 1 or 2 percent of the total divorce actions. For some reason, they have been accorded much wider acceptance in European countries.

Interlocutory Decrees. These decrees should not be confused with limited divorce. An interlocutory decree (*decree nisi*) is part of an absolute divorce in a number of states and simply serves as a *preliminary decree*. In these states it is not until some time after the interlocutory decree is issued that the divorce becomes final and the parties are free to remarry. The time required between the preliminary or interlocutory decree and the final decree varies, depending upon the state, from one month to one year. Utilization of the interlocutory decree has the advantage of discouraging hasty divorces and encouraging reconciliation. Theoretically, also, the court is given time to investigate possible collusion and connivance, although at present such investigations are seldom undertaken.

ANNULMENT

Like limited divorce, the concept of annulment has its roots in the canon law of the Catholic Church. The latter has taken the position that marriage is indissoluble except by death, a premise that, until 1857, was also held by the Church of England and the English ecclesiastical courts. Both the Catholic Church and the Church of England, however, have always permitted annulment—the declaration that, because of premarital impediments, the marriage itself has been null and void from the time of its inception. Parties to a religious annulment are free to remarry because, in the eyes of the Church, the marriage is considered never to have existed. Our own family laws, greatly influenced by canon law, have come to include the concept of annulment, and today most states—though not all—have statutory provisions by which marriages can be annulled.

457

A commonly held distinction between divorce and annulment is that a divorce dissolves the marriage as of the date the decree is signed, whereas an annulment is legal recognition that a valid marriage never took place. In one sense this distinction is a real one, but in another it is simply a play on words. Frank marries Helen, and two years later she has twins. For reasons that need not concern us now, Frank goes to court and sues for an annulment, which is granted. However, the law of the state provides that in such instances the children are deemed legitimate, and Frank must therefore pay for their support. The court, furthermore, orders Frank to pay alimony to Helen. What does it really matter if the annulment decree, in all legal elegance, announces that a valid marriage never existed? *In effect,* how does such an annulment actually differ from a divorce? The answer is that it differs very little, if at all. And while the foregoing illustration is hardly typical, some states do award alimony in annulment cases.

Perhaps the most realistic distinction between divorce and annulment pertains to the *time of the cause.* The cause or reason for an annulment must generally precede the marriage, whereas the ground for a divorce supposedly occurs after the marriage has taken place. Thus such typical causes of annulment as impotence, existence of a prior marriage, being under age, or being too closely related by blood are all factors that existed before the marriage. Cruelty, desertion, irreconcilable differences—the usual grounds for a divorce—involve behavior that arose after the marriage.

The most common ground for annulment, and the one that is the most difficult to interpret, is fraud—that is, a "serious misrepresentation" by one party prior to the marriage. Originally, fraudulent actions included such things as concealment of a premarital pregnancy (caused by another man), a premarital history of prostitution or homosexuality, and so on. Unless it could be shown that the plaintiff was aware of the condition, an annulment would normally be granted.

Like divorce, however, annulment suits have shown a marked discrepancy between the law on the books and the law in practice, and the "serious" part of the misrepresentation has often been winked at. Annulments have actually been granted because the husband had exaggerated the extent of his salary; because the wife had held herself out to be a virgin (which she wasn't); because the husband reneged on his promise to have a religious ceremony following the civil proceedings; because the husband had certain character defects prior to marriage, and so forth.

It should also be mentioned that at one time annulments were common in those states where the divorce law was strict, but today the "strict" states have just about disappeared.* As a consequence, annulments are probably declining in number, and at the present time they seem to be almost as infrequent as legal separations.

THE FORMULATION OF DIVORCE POLICY

Divorce has been a problem for thousands of years. Policy has varied from age to age and from country to country. Even today, divorce practices vary tremendously. Some European and South American countries prohibit divorce entirely, while one or two permit divorce by mutual consent. Unfortunately, it is difficult to formulate matrimonial principles on the basis of a cross-cultural comparison, for laws and public policies that are effective in one society may have different consequences in another.

In a sociological sense, divorce may well represent another area where the needs of the individual and those of society do not coincide. From the individual's view, a system of free divorce might seem to be the most satisfactory answer. A person marries. He or she tries to make a success of the marriage. But, if the marital relationship is an unhappy one, why not grant that

---

* Prior to 1949, South Carolina did not permit divorce for any reason. And prior to 1967, the only recognized ground for divorce in New York State was adultery.

person the right—quickly, easily, with no undue legal and financial involvement—to procure a divorce, thus providing another chance at matrimony, hopefully with a more suitable partner?

Society, however, would seem to have a stake in the maintenance of a viable family system, and to that end it can be argued that at least some restrictions on divorce might be beneficial. For example, would not the imposition of a waiting period (with reconciliation services available) encourage some couples to solve their problems? Should not a divorce code contain provisions for looking after the best interests of the innocent parties, particularly children? Does not the presence of legal and procedural impediments tend to discourage hasty marriages on the part of young people?

These are all questions that both legal practitioners and social scientists have grappled with for many years. And while our present hodgepodge of divorce laws is hardly a satisfactory solution, this very diversity is an indication that some states are willing to experiment. Unfortunately for all concerned, the various socio-legal experiments have been accompanied by a noticeable increase in the divorce rate. The cause of the increase, in turn, is still a matter of debate. It should be pointed out, however, that in the most recent survey of the various state laws, in

459

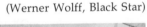

(Werner Wolff, Black Star)

1975, Stetson and Wright found a positive relationship between permissiveness of divorce and divorce rates.[10]

Some observers feel that our society should adopt certain features of the European system. Most European countries, for example, recognize two classes of divorce: absolute and relative. Those that are absolute are spelled out in the statutes; if the facts of the case are in accord with the statutes, a divorce must be granted, the judge having little discretionary power. But if the grounds are relative, the judge has the authority to *grant or deny* the divorce, no matter how conclusive the evidence. The decision, in this instance, will depend largely on whether the judge feels the marriage is beyond repair.

The difficulty is that the European divorce rate is low compared with that of the United States. In most of our states, the time (and money) required for judges to involve themselves in divorce suits would be prohibitive.

Whatever the answer, it will probably not be found until we know more about the sociological factors associated with divorce. We need to know much more about the characteristics of divorced persons and about the conditions under which divorce flourishes. It would be desirable, also, to know more about the effectiveness of the therapeutic approach to divorce—reconciliation services, marriage counseling, and the like. In brief, we need to spend more time investigating the various factors underlying marital discord, and less time debating the advisability of loosening or tightening the legal provisions. It is to some of the sociological aspects of marital discord that we now turn.

SELECTED READINGS

Anspach, Donald, "Kinship and Divorce," *Journal of Marriage and the Family*, May, 1976, pp. 323–330.

Bohannan, Paul (ed.), *Divorce and After*, Garden City, New York, Doubleday & Company, Inc. (Anchor Books), 1971.

Callahan, Parnell, *The Law of Separation and Divorce*, Dobbs Ferry, New York, Oceana Publications, Inc., 1970.

Clark, Homer H., Jr., *The Law of Domestic Relations in the United States*, St. Paul, Minnesota, West Publishing Co., 1968.

---

[10] Dorothy Stetson and Gerald Wright, "The Effects of Laws on Divorce in American States," *Journal of Marriage and the Family*, August, 1975, pp. 537–547.

Family Law Quarterly, published by the American Bar Association, Section of Family Law, Chicago, Illinois.

Family Law Reporter, published by the Bureau of National Affairs, Inc., Washington, D.C.

Fisher, Esther Oshiver, *Divorce—The New Freedom*, New York, Harper & Row, 1974.

Freed, Doris Jonas, "Grounds for Divorce in the American Jurisdictions," *Family Law Quarterly*, Winter, 1974, pp. 401–423.

Goldstein, Joseph, and Katz, Jay, *The Family and the Law*, New York, Free Press of Glencoe, Inc., 1965.

Krantzler, Mel, *Creative Divorce*, Bergenfield, New Jersey, New American Library, 1974.

Martin, John R., *Divorce and Remarriage*, Scottsdale, Pennsylvania, Herald Press, 1974.

Mayer, Michael, *Divorce and Annulment in the 50 States*, New York, Arco Publishing Company, Inc., 1967.

Monahan, Thomas, "American Divorce: Legal Dilemmas and Social Realities in the 1970's," (mimeo), Villanova University, Pennsylvania, Fall, 1971, 20 pp.

National Council on Family Relations, "Task Force Report on Marriage and Divorce Reform," Minneapolis, Minnesota, October, 1973.

O'Neill, P. T., "Divorce: A Judicial or an Administrative Process," *Family Law*, March–April, 1974, pp. 71–72.

O'Neill, William L., *Divorce in the Progressive Era*, New Haven, Yale University Press, 1967.

Resnicoff, Samuel, *Marriage, Divorce, Annulment*, New York, Pageant Press, Inc., 1968.

Rheinstein, Max, *Marriage Stability, Divorce, and the Law*, Chicago, University of Chicago Press, 1972.

Robbins, Norman N., "To Condone or Condemn Condonation," *Family Coordinator*, January, 1971, pp. 74–76.

Rosenblatt, Stanley, *The Divorce Racket*, Los Angeles, Nash Publishing Corporation, 1969.

Schur, Edwin, *Law and Society: A Sociological View*, New York, Random House, Inc., 1968.

Shover, Neal, "Responses to Divorce Law Reform," (mimeo), Department of Sociology, University of Tennessee, February, 1972, 31 pp.

Sonne, John C., "On the Question of Compulsory Marriage Counseling as a Part of Divorce Proceedings," *Family Coordinator*, July, 1974, pp. 303–305.

Stetson, Dorothy, and Wright, Gerald, "The Effects of Laws on Divorce in American States," *Journal of Marriage and the Family*, August, 1975, pp. 537–547.

461

Turner, J. Neville, "Comments on Family Courts," *Family Law*, March–April, 1974, pp. 39–44.

Weiner, Richard, "Inflation and Alimony in New York," *Family Law Commentator*, November–December, 1973, pp. 1–2.

Wells, J. Gipson, "A Critical Look at Personal Marriage Contracts," *Family Coordinator*, January, 1976, pp. 33–37.

Wheeler, Michael, *No-Fault Divorce*, Boston, Beacon Press, 1974.

462

21

Marital Breakup II—

Sociological Aspects

THROUGHOUT THE PRESENT volume, much attention has been paid
to the various research studies undertaken by social scientists.
Government agencies are another source of pertinent information. Special mention should be made of the Division of Vital
Statistics, which issues regular reports dealing with marriage
and divorce in the United States. These reports, together with
census data and sociological research findings, shed valuable
light on the problem of marital disruption, particularly with
respect to such questions as: Is the divorce rate rising or falling?
Who are the divorce-prone groups in our society? What geographical areas show the highest (and lowest) rate of divorce?
During what period of married life is divorce most likely to
occur? What proportion of divorced persons remarry, and what
are their characteristics? What percentage of divorces involve
minor children? Can anything be said about the real—as opposed to the legal—causes of divorce?

While not all of these questions can be answered definitively, a
fairly respectable body of information has now been compiled.
Material in the following sections may be taken as illustrative of
this information.

DIVORCE IN THE UNITED STATES: AN OVERVIEW

The Divorce Rate. During the Colonial period, divorce was a
rare phenomenon; in fact, up to the time of the Civil War, the
problem was not considered important enough to warrant the
collection of national figures. In the mid-1800's, as a concomitant
of the woman's rights movement, divorce laws were liberalized,
and by the 1860's various groups, fearful that family values were
being undermined, demanded that national divorce figures be

tabulated. The initial tabulations, published by the Census Bureau, were for the year 1867. The total number of divorces in that year was 9,937. One hundred years later—in 1967—the number had increased to over a half-million. And at the present time, there are well over 1 million divorces granted annually in the United States!

There are any number of ways of computing a divorce rate,[1] but irrespective of the method used, the long-term trend in the United States is upward (see Table 5).

TABLE 5 *United States Divorce Rate for Selected Years*

YEAR	NUMBER OF DIVORCES	DIVORCES PER 1,000 POPULATION
1867	9,937	0.3
1887	27,919	0.5
1900	55,751	0.7
1910	83,045	0.9
1920	170,505	1.6
1930	195,961	1.6
1940	264,000	2.0
1950	385,144	2.6
1960	393,000	2.2
1970	715,000	3.5
1975	1,026,000	4.8

Source: See the regular reports issued by the Division of Vital Statistics, U.S. Department of Health, Education, and Welfare, National Center for Health Statistics, Rockville, Maryland.

Perhaps the figures in Table 5 will be more meaningful in the light of the following information. In 1867, the population of the United States was approximately 37 million; by 1975 the figure had grown to some 215 million—roughly a six-fold increase. During the same period, however, the yearly number of divorces rose from 9,937 to 1,026,000—a 100-fold increase. In other words, divorces increased more than 17 times as fast as the population!

It now appears as though there will be roughly 10 million divorces granted during the present decade (1970–1980). Indeed, on the basis of the latest figures reported by the Vital Statistics Division, the writer would estimate that more than one-third of the marriages in this country are ending in divorce! As we shall see, however, the probability of divorce varies depending on such factors as race, religion, social class, and geographical area.

---

[1] See, for example, J. Lynn England and Phillip R. Kunz, "The Application of Age-Specific Rates to Divorce," *Journal of Marriage and the Family*, February, 1975, pp. 40–46.

The Duration of Marriage. In addition to charting the trend of the divorce rate, sociologists are also interested in the *time patterns* involved. How long, on the average, do unsuccessful marriages last? During what year of married life is a divorce most likely to occur? Is there, as popular writers have contended, a "dangerous fourth year"?

A number of studies have shown that marriages that end in divorce are generally of short duration. The modal, or *most likely*, time of separation is the one- or two-year period immediately following marriage, with the figures showing a subsequent yearly decline. There is no "dangerous" fourth, sixth, or tenth year; in fact, the longer a marriage lasts, the less the likelihood of a divorce. It is true that some couples get divorced even after 40 years of marriage, but such cases are few and far between. The average (median) elapsed time from marriage to separation is around five years. Because of the legal procedures involved, however, average elapsed time to the issuance of the divorce decree is about six and a half years.

465

Geographical Variations. Although specific figures are lacking, indications are that divorce is relatively more frequent in urban than in rural areas. Vital statistics gathered over many decades also reveal that divorce rates tend to increase as one moves from east to west. New England and the Middle Atlantic states have the lowest rates, the Midwest has intermediate rates, while the Pacific Coast has the highest divorce rate. The Pacific Coast, for example, has a divorce rate more than twice as high as the Northeast.

There are a number of explanations for this regional differential. For one thing, a "frontier" area is generally less conformist than the longer-established sections of the country. Differences in the ethnic, racial, and religious composition of an area also affect the rates; e.g., one reason for the low prevalance of divorce in the Northeastern and Middle Atlantic regions is the large Catholic population. It must be admitted, though, that all the reasons for the regional divorce differentials are not known. If they were, we would be in a much better position to understand the problem of divorce causation.

Migratory Divorce. It is often thought that geographical differences in divorce rates are due to the easy residence requirements in certain states, but this is not so. True, Nevada has a divorce rate more than three times as high as the national figure, but the state grants a relatively small number of divorces. Vital

eveal that, out of the million-odd divorces that take
ally in the United States, Nevada grants only about
less than 1 percent of the total.

vada is not the only "quickie" state, it is doubtful
a numerical sense migratory divorce is very signifi-
s not more than 1 or 2 percent of American divorces
in nature, and the figure has been declining in re-
fter all, (1) divorce laws have become much more
..., so that the necessity to "migrate" is reduced; (2) travel is
becoming more and more expensive; and (3) the legal entangle-
ment of an out-of-state divorce continues to act as a deterrent.

Children and Divorce. One of the most important—and most
publicized—aspects of divorce is the effect on children. Sociologists have also been interested in the reverse problem: the effect
of children on divorce. That is, does the very presence of children
tend to militate against divorce? Family researchers have given a
good deal of thought to both of these problems.

In days gone by, a substantial majority of divorces were those
in which children *were not involved.* Thus in 1922 only 34 percent
of the divorce actions involved minor children. More recently,
however, the figure has increased to over 60 percent. And since
the divorce rate itself has risen drastically, the actual number
of children affected has reached staggering proportions. Whereas
in 1922 there were 93,000 children affected by divorce, the figure
has now passed the million-children-a-year mark! Clearly, children are no longer the deterrent to divorce they used to be.

What about the effect of the so-called broken home on children? Unfortunately for all concerned, the answer does not seem
to be clear-cut; at least, researchers have not yet come up with a
definitive conclusion. There is some suggestion, however, that
unhappy, unbroken homes may have a more harmful effect on
children than do broken homes, and that both types may affect
children adversely as compared with normal, happy homes.

Remarriage. It stands to reason that, as the divorce rate increases, remarriage becomes more of a factor in the total marital
picture. As Schlesinger, an authority on the subject, points out:
"Remarriage is a social institution; that is, it is an established
pattern of operating which serves both public and private interests in an orderly, accepted, enduring way."[2] And while the subject of remarriage has been "underinvestigated," there have

---

[2] Benjamin Schlesinger, "Remarriage as Family Reorganization for Divorced
Persons," *Journal of Comparative Family Studies,* Autumn, 1970, p. 101.

Parental responsibilities do not end after the dissolution of a marriage, but adjusting to new roles and arrangements can strain parent-child relationships. (Frank Siteman, Stock Boston)

been a sufficient number of studies to permit the following generalizations:

1. A substantial majority of divorcees eventually remarry. Referring to U.S. Census data, Glick reports that "according to the latest information available, about four out of every five of those who obtain a divorce will eventually remarry."[3]

---

[3] Paul C. Glick, "A Demographer Looks at American Families," *Journal of Marriage and the Family*, February, 1975, p. 17.

2. Remarriage rates (including both the widowed *and* the divorced) are noticeably higher for men than for women.
3. Most divorcees not only remarry, but they do so rather quickly. In the latest vital statistics survey, Williams and Kuhn note that "25 percent of the divorced brides and grooms remarried within four to five months after divorce, 50 percent remarried within slightly more than one year, and 75 percent remarried within approximately three years."[4]
4. Remarriages (involving the divorced as well as the widowed) are fairly common. At the present time, 25 percent or more of all marriages are those in which one or both parties had been married previously. The figure is probably increasing.
5. As Williams and Kuhn point out, "Far more divorced than widowed persons are involved in remarriages—and the upward trend reflects the trend for the divorced, not the widowed."[5]
6. Americans who remarry show a marked tendency to marry those in a similar marital-status category; i.e., divorced persons tend to marry divorced persons, and widows tend to marry widowers.
7. Remarrying couples are much more likely than those marrying for the first time to have a civil ceremony. This tendency is more pronounced for the divorced than for the widowed. Both groups are much less likely than first marriages to include such "hoopla" as presents, reception, or honeymoon.
8. Divorcees who remarry show a tendency to marry someone of a different religion. Rosenthal notes that "this tendency is so pronounced that previous divorce must be considered a major contributing factor in the formation of religious intermarriages."[6]

INTERRACIAL MARRIAGE

The divorce rate among blacks, in the United States, appears to be higher than among whites, although there is much regional

---

[4] Kristen M. Williams and Russell P. Kuhn, Division of Vital Statistics, *Remarriages: United States,* DHEW Publication Number (HRA) 74-1903, Series 21, Number 25, December, 1973, p. 13.

[5] *Ibid.,* p. 1.

[6] Erich Rosenthal, "Divorce and Religious Intermarriage: The Effect of Previous Marital Status upon Subsequent Marital Behavior," *Journal of Marriage and the Family,* August, 1970, pp. 435–440.

variation.[7] However, in view of the increasing rate of interracial marriage, attention has come to be focused on the *outcome* of such marriages. Do black-white marriages have a greater or lesser chance of "surviving" than do racially homogamous unions? It is laborious work for a researcher to gather enough cases to make a representative study. Most of the surveys, therefore, have been segmental in nature. Nevertheless, in view of their social significance, it is important to scrutinize the results.

Forty years ago Baber did a study of mixed marriages and found that of all the combinations—interracial, interreligious, and internationality—mixed black-white marriages had the lowest happiness rating.[8] The results of the study were quoted for many years. Actually, however, Baber's sampling procedure was inadequate; in fact, there were only 25 black-white couples included in the survey.

Three other surveys of interracial marriage—reported in the 1950's and 1960's by Golden,[9] by Smith,[10] and by Pavela[11]—are also mentioned in the literature. All were based on careful interviews and involved three different cities: Philadelphia, New York, and Indianapolis, respectively. While the three studies differ in design, they make it clear that interracial marriages do experience difficulty in such areas as parental relations, housing, job discrimination, being stared at in public, and patterns of friendship.

On the other hand, findings indicated that in some ways external pressures were not as severe as anticipated, with many of the couples making a satisfactory adjustment. Again, however, one drawback to these interview-studies was the small number of cases involved. The Philadelphia sample had 50 couples; the New York sample, 22 couples; and the Indianapolis sample, 9 couples.

469

---

[7] See, for example, Phillips Cutright, "Income and Family Events: Marital Stability," *Journal of Marriage and the Family*, May, 1971, pp. 291–306; and Division of Vital Statistics, *Divorces: Analysis of Changes*, DHEW Publication Number (HSM) 73-1900, Series 21, Number 22, April, 1973, pp. 11–13.

[8] Ray Baber, "A Study of 325 Mixed Marriages," *American Sociological Review*, October, 1937, pp. 705–716.

[9] Joseph Golden, "Characteristics of the Negro-White Intermarried in Philadelphia, *American Sociological Review*, April, 1953, pp. 177–183.

[10] Charles Smith, *Negro-White Intermarriage, Metropolitan New York—A Qualitative Case Analysis*, New York, Columbia University Teachers College, 1961, cited in Gerald Leslie, *The Family in Social Context*, New York, Oxford University Press, 1976, p. 513.

[11] Todd Pavela, "An Exploratory Study of Negro-White Intermarriage in Indiana," *Journal of Marriage and the Family*, May, 1964, pp. 209–211.

A later study—by the Seattle Urban League in the late 1960's—utilized questionnaires rather than interviews, and again a variety of responses emerged. Some couples encountered problems with their own parents, with friends, with discriminatory practices in housing and employment. Other couples seemed to experience a minimum of outside hostility. Of special interest, perhaps, was the general finding regarding the children of racially mixed couples:

> The myth that an interracial couple and their children will be rebuffed by both races, and by their neighbors and relatives, does not hold up in any consistent pattern. Their children, it would seem from the reports, are carrying no special heavy burden. In fact, several persons commented that they were re-united with their families in a special way when the grandchildren were born, or that they were accepted into the neighborhood because the children play together.

The Seattle report concluded by stating that, in general, interracial marriages held up at least as well as racially homogamous marriages. It should be noted, however, that the interracial marriages studied in Seattle included Japanese, Chinese, Koreans, and Indians, as well as Negro-white combinations. Also—once more—the total number was small: 128 individual questionnaires were returned out of which only 57 persons belonged to the Negro-white category.[12]

Three recent studies—all reported in the 1970's and all based on large-scale data—bring the research picture up to date. In Heer's survey, based on U.S. Census data, interracial marriages were found to be "less stable than the racially homogeneous marriages, and marriages involving white husbands and black wives more unstable than those of black husbands and white wives."[13] Unfortunately, the findings were in the form of marital attrition rates and necessarily included death as well as divorce, thus lending a measure of uncertainty to the results.

Two studies by Monahan—based on actual marriage and divorce records—show an entirely different picture. Figures for the state of Kansas revealed that black-white marriages were more stable than racially homogamous unions.[14] For the state of Iowa, Monahan found that the divorce ratio for mixed black-white

---

[12] "People Who Intermarry: Pioneers or Protesters?" *Seattle Urban League Special Report*, Seattle, Washington, April, 1967.

[13] David M. Heer, "The Prevalence of Black-White Marriage in the United States, 1960 and 1970," *Journal of Marriage and the Family*, May, 1974, pp. 246–258.

[14] Thomas P. Monahan, "Interracial Marriage and Divorce in Kansas and the Question of Instability of Mixed Marriages," *Journal of Comparative Family Studies*, Spring, 1971, pp. 107–120.

marriages fell midway between the ratios for white-white and black-black marriages.[15] Specific divorce ratios (per 100 marriages) are as follows:

> white wives—black husbands: 16.8
> white wives—white husbands: 19.4
> black wives—white husbands: 35.1
> black wives—black husbands: 39.1

It was not possible in either the Kansas or the Iowa study to control for migratory divorce, although there is little reason to believe that this factor would have changed the results to any significant degree.

Taken in their entirety, what conclusion can be drawn from all of the above findings? Perhaps the safest generalization would be that black-white marriages are neither as stable as some people have believed, nor as unstable as others—probably a majority—have contended. Intermarrying couples obviously have problems that other couples do not have. Yet, while such problems may be severe, they do not necessarily disrupt the marriage. Perhaps those who marry interracially have a greater determination than most people to make their marriages work.

INTERFAITH AND INTERCLASS MARRIAGES

Interfaith. The Jews have always placed great stress on education and family unity, and while Judaism does not forbid divorce, the practice is generally discouraged. It would not be expected that the Jewish divorce rate would be high, and the various surveys bear out the expectation.[16]

With regard to the intermarriage picture, Heiss—in a matched-sample survey—found that the mixed-Jewish marriages had somewhat lower adjustment scores than nonmixed Jewish marriages.[17] In the Christensen–Barber study, the investigators found that the incidence of divorce for Jewish

---

[15] Thomas P. Monahan, "Are Interracial Marriages Really Less Stable?" *Social Forces*, June, 1970, pp. 461–473.

[16] See, for example, Harold Christensen and Kenneth Barber, "Interfaith Versus Intrafaith Marriages in Indiana," *Journal of Marriage and the Family*, August, 1967, pp. 461–469. For a different approach, see J. Frideres, J. Goldstein, and R. Gilbert, "The Impact of Jewish-Gentile Intermarriages in Canada: An Alternative View," *Journal of Comparative Family Studies*, Autumn, 1971, pp. 268–275.

[17] Jerold Heiss, "Interfaith Marriage and Marital Outcome," *Marriage and Family Living*, August, 1961, pp. 228–233.

intermarriages was the highest of the six intrafaith and interfaith combinations studied.[18] On the other hand, in a related study by Frideres, Goldstein, and Gilbert, it was found that Jewish intermarriage (Jewish husband, Gentile wife) had no appreciable effect on the children, as regards personality factors.

The latter study is of particular interest, since the investigators discovered little relation between a spouse's *nominal* religion and his or her *actual* religious beliefs:

> Recognizing that a person's nominal faith may be just that—nominal—it becomes apparent that spouses who belong to different nominal faiths may in actuality be quite congruent in their religious and ethnic identities, and vice versa. . . .
>
> What is clear (from these figures) is that marriages which were classified as "inter" on the basis of the nominal faith definition, are remarkably similar to those defined as "intra" in terms of the congruence of the spouses' Jewish religious and ethnic identities.[19]

Catholic intermarriage provides an interesting parallel. While the Catholic Church does not necessarily prohibit *civil divorce*, it refuses to recognize such action as breaking the bonds of marriage. Generally speaking, Catholics who have been divorced in a court of law are not eligible, in the eyes of their Church, to remarry. (A Catholic whose marriage has been annulled by the Church, following which she or he procures a civil divorce, would be eligible to marry again.) At any rate, it would be logical for Catholics to evidence a low divorce rate, an expectation that is borne out by all the studies on the subject.[20]

With regard to mixed Protestant-Catholic marriages, all the research studies but one show that such marriages have a relatively high rate of divorce.[21] In a related survey, Haerle investigated the relationship between Catholic intermarriage and membership "leakage." Is it true, he asks, that Catholics who intermarry tend to become lax in such things as church attendance? Findings revealed that a "goodly number of irregularly attending, intermarried Catholics *are continuing a premarital church attendance pattern.*"[22] Stated differently, it was not so much that intermarriage caused a decline in church attendance but, rather, that those who were attending church irregularly tended to intermarry.

The implication of the Frideres–Goldstein–Gilbert and Haerle studies is clear. Those who intermarry seem to have different re-

---

[18] Christensen and Barber, *op. cit.*, pp. 461–469.

[19] Frideres et al., *op. cit.*, p. 272.

[20] See Christensen and Barber, *op. cit.*, pp. 461–469.

[21] *Ibid.*

[22] Rudolf K. Haerle, Jr., "Church Attendance Patterns Among Intermarried Catholics: A Panel Study," *Sociological Analysis*, Winter, 1969, p. 215.

ligious values from those who marry homogamously. In study-ing the divorce rates for interreligious marriages, therefore, a classification based on formal or nominal church membership may be misleading. What is needed is a statistical breakdown that takes into consideration *actual religious values* as well as formal church membership. Until this is done, the entire picture of interreligious marriage will remain out of focus.

Interclass. One of the clearest findings to emerge in recent dec-ades has been the fact that divorce rates increase with *descending* socio-economic status. Irrespective of whether the criterion used is education, occupation, or income, it is apparent that divorce is much more common in the lower than in the upper classes.[23] There are also substantial "horizontal" differences within each class. In a study of the professions, for example, Rosow and Rose found that authors and social scientists had a divorce rate almost twice as high as physicians and natural scientists.[24]

The extent to which lower-class affiliation *causes* divorce is an-other matter. Conceivably, the same kinds of factors that produce low social status might also give rise to divorce, and it is unlikely that a simple causal relationship is involved. At any rate, granted that the divorce rate decreases with increasing socio-economic level, the important question remains: What is the prognosis for cross-class marriages? Four studies—all with similar findings—shed some light on the issue.

In the initial study, Roth and Peck found a definite tendency for same-class marriages to have a better marital adjustment than the cross-class variety. Of those marriages in which the spouses were of the same class, 53.5 percent reported a good adjustment, as compared with 35 percent of those in which the spouses were one class apart, and only 14.3 percent of those in which the hus-band and wife were more than one class apart.[25]

Goode also found a clear tendency for cross-class marriages to be overrepresented in his divorce sample,[26] similar findings being reported by Scanzoni.[27] And finally, in a survey based on

---

[23] See, for example, Phillips Cutright, "Income and Family Events: Marital Stabil-ity," *Journal of Marriage and the Family*, May, 1971, pp. 291–306; and Sally E. Palmer, "Reasons for Marriage Breakdown," *Journal of Comparative Family Studies*, Autumn, 1971, pp. 251–262.

[24] Irving Rosow and K. Daniel Rose, "Divorce Among Doctors," *Journal of Mar-riage and the Family*, November, 1972, pp. 587–598.

[25] Julius Roth and Robert Peck, "Social Class and Social Mobility Factors Related to Marital Adjustment," *American Sociological Review*, August, 1951, pp. 478–487.

[26] William Goode, *After Divorce*, Glencoe, Illinois, The Free Press, 1956, pp. 100 ff.

[27] John Scanzoni, "A Social System Analysis of Dissolved and Existing Mar-riages," *Journal of Marriage and the Family*, August, 1968, pp. 452–487.

Canadian data, it was found that "when 425 divorced couples were compared to a national sample in relation to the similarity in occupational level between the husband and the wife's father, it was found that marriages where there was a similarity contributed less than their share of divorces."[28]

In the absence of contrary evidence, then, it appears that cross-class marriages must be placed in the relatively "high-risk" category.

DESERTION

The emphasis in the present chapter has been on the sociological aspects of divorce. The latter, after all, is a precise term. The occurrence of divorce is a matter of legal record, and data derived from these records have enabled sociologists to compile a fair amount of research material in an effort to come to grips with the problem.

There is another type of marital disruption, however, that also has far-reaching effects, both on the individual and on society. This is the type often referred to as "marital separations." The Census Bureau defines the latter as those couples "with legal separations, those living apart with intentions of obtaining a divorce, and other persons permanently or temporarily estranged from their spouse because of marital discord." Exactly how many couples are separated is not known with any precision, but the number certainly runs into the millions; as a matter of fact, in some cities the separation rate is known to exceed the divorce rate.

While there are various categories of marital separation, perhaps the most prevalent type is that of desertion. In a strict sense, either spouse may desert, but deserting wives are few in number as compared with deserting husbands. At any rate, public and private agencies that handle desertion cases deal with them in terms of deserting husbands, and it is this type of case that is our present concern.

Bryant and Wells write as follows on the subject:

> The husband who does not support his family deviates from the role expectations of marriage, violates the legally established financial responsibility to wife and children, and violates the equilibrium of family order as well as social order. Non-support may occur through the process of the husband physically absenting himself, through willful failure to support his family, by maintaining

---

[28] Cited in Sally E. Palmer, *op. cit.*, p. 259.

irregular work habits, or by drunkenness. In these situations, his actions are legally defined as "desertion," "abandonment," or both.

However, desertion is not always an attempt to evade family financial obligations, as there are many other reasons why men leave their wives and children. Investigators have pointed out that men often desert because of marital strains, in-law problems, unsatisfactory sexual adjustments, incompatibility with the spouse, or feelings of rejection or inadequacy. In general, desertion represents an immature reaction to an unpleasant marital situation.[29]

A Typical Desertion Case. In the usual desertion case the husband reneges on his obligation to support his wife and children. This generally involves a physical departure, though not necessarily so. Many such husbands come and go several times in the course of a year, maintain irregular work habits, drink incessantly, and have little concern for their marital and familial responsibilities. The wife applies to the Domestic Relations Court (called by various names in different cities) and tells her story. The court calls the husband in and listens to his version, after which an attempt is usually made to effect a reconciliation.

Should attempts at reconciliation fail—and in desertion or nonsupport cases this is the rule rather than the exception—the court tries informally to get the party or parties to agree on the amount of financial support to be borne by the husband. If agreement cannot be reached, the court, after a thorough examination of the case, imposes a support order on the husband. Should the latter refuse to pay the stipulated amount, or should he willfully fall behind in his payments, the court will prosecute. Prosecution proceedings, however, are likely to be a last resort, every attempt being made to handle the case in peaceful fashion. Even so, in many of our larger cities, the backlog of "errant husbands" is prohibitively high.

Effects of Desertion on the Individual. A strong argument can be made that, as far as the wife is concerned, desertion has a more deleterious effect than divorce. Whatever may be the traumatic consequences of divorce, the legal proceedings are usually cut and dried. The wife may be awarded alimony by the court, or where the husband is financially well off, she may be able to effect an out-of-court settlement. Whether or not she is able to acquire financial remuneration for herself, the court will see to it that the divorced husband pays for the support of all minor children.

---

[29] Clifton Bryant and J. Gipson Wells, *Deviancy and the Family*, Philadelphia, F. A. Davis Company, 1973, p. 22.

Desertion in some cases can be more painful than divorce. (Philip Jon Bailey)

Moreover, a divorce decree is a legal action permitting the wife to marry if she so chooses. Most divorced wives do remarry—and within a relatively short period. In a fair share of all divorces, therefore, the effects may be more or less temporary.

Desertion cases usually show a different sequence of events. The husband is often a chronic deserter, with the result that the desertion and reconciliation process may drag on for years. It must be remembered also that desertion cases are heavily concentrated in the lowest socio-economic levels; in fact, throughout the sociological literature, desertion has been known as "the poor man's divorce." Financial support by the husband, therefore, is frequently sporadic, and in some cases the wife has no recourse but to apply for public assistance. Moreover, she cannot legally remarry unless she procures a divorce or has her spouse declared dead. Deserted wives often go on for years, never sure whether they are permanently separated or widowed, or whether their husband will return home tomorrow and expect his marital privileges.

The extent to which children are affected by desertion has often been overlooked, although in some ways desertion is also more harmful to children than is divorce. For one thing, there is reason to believe that a larger proportion of desertions than divorces involve minor children, and that the average number of children per desertion is greater than the figure for divorce. Also, most divorcees remarry, which means that the effect on children is only temporary. Deserted wives, to repeat, cannot remarry—at least until they procure a divorce—so that the effects on children are often of long duration. And finally, of course, many deserted children feel, in an emotional sense, that their father has indeed "deserted" them. They may have had close ties to the father, and the feeling of being abandoned may have deep-seated consequences.

And what of the deserting father? How can a man leave his own children without experiencing feelings of remorse, frustration, and guilt? It seems likely that in many cases deserting fathers are plagued not only by feelings of sorrow but by a nagging loss of self-respect. Skarsten writes as follows on the subject:

> Many deserting husbands are inadequate and depressed males who characteristically handle problems by withdrawal. Reared in families where desertion was common, these husbands frequently are rather isolated and not integrated into the appropriate social networks.
>
> The deserting spouse often feels that he is a "refugee." After desertion he is afraid of being found and sees himself as one who must run, yet wishes to go back home. As does his wife, he has mixed and ambivalent feelings—guilt and anger, homesickness, and fear of detection and punishment.[30]

Societal Consequences. There is no way of telling exactly what the yearly public cost is for deserting husbands. In addition to the money paid out by departments of public assistance in the different states, huge sums are required to staff the various Domestic Relations Courts, whose clientele stems largely from desertion cases. Furthermore, it is difficult to assess the financial contribution of private charitable organizations in these cases.

Scattered reports suggest that in the majority of desertions, the father contributes little to the support of his family. The slack must be made up largely out of the public coffers, and the cost is high. In some cases, of course, the husband is sent to jail because

---

[30] Stan Skarsten, "Family Desertion in Canada," *Family Coordinator*, January, 1974, p. 23.

of his familial negligence, and this cost must also be borne by the public.

Under provisions of the Social Security Act, federal grants are made to the states for the support of children in their own homes, where need arises because of the death, unemployment, or absence of a parent. The program is commonly known as AFDC—Aid to Families with Dependent Children. In the nation at large, there are currently millions of AFDC recipients, with the total cost running into billions of dollars annually.

Besides the financial considerations, of course, there are the broader societal implications. For the fact remains that desertion represents failure: failure on the part of the individual to fulfill his marital and familial obligations, and failure on the part of society to impart those values that make for familial responsibility.

MARITAL BREAKUP: THE PROBLEM OF CAUSATION

Over and above the sociological considerations of separation and divorce—discussed in the previous pages—can anything be said regarding causation? What, specifically, is the cause of so much marital breakup? The sociologist is asked this question almost as often as he is asked, "What causes crime?" Neither query, however, is likely to elicit much enthusiasm, for the social scientist does not think in terms of unilateral causation. From the sociological perspective, causes are generally thought of as interrelated links in a sequential chain of events, rather than as single factors. Thus, while the lawyer may state that sexual maladjustment is the chief cause of divorce, and while the social worker may blame juvenile crime on poor housing, the sociologist is quite skeptical of such pat explanations.

If divorce is really caused by sexual maladjustment, why is it that the divorce rate has increased as sex education programs have expanded? And if juvenile delinquency is caused by poor housing, how is it that delinquency has increased as housing conditions have improved? It does not take much deep thinking to realize that phenomena like crime and divorce cannot be explained by simple, isolated causes.

For the sake of convenience, let us examine divorce causation from two points of view, in keeping with the framework of the present volume—namely, the societal and the individual. Societal refers to those conditions associated with social and institutional structure such as economic conditions, technological change, religion, and so on. Individual factors would include the various physical, intellectual, and personality components that come into play whenever two or more people interact.

Societal Factors. Change must be explained by a variation rather than by a constant; or, to put it somewhat differently, one variation must always be explained in terms of another variation. And since divorce and separation rates seem to have risen not only in the United States but in the civilized world at large, it behooves us to list some of the widespread social changes that might be involved.

1. *Changing family functions.* As was explained in Chapter 1, whereas the economic, medical, educational, protective, religious, and recreational functions were once a built-in part of family life, over the years such functions have largely been taken over by outside agencies. The family, as a result, is less of a functional unit than formerly; hence, the reasons for keeping marriages intact are not so compelling as they once were.

2. *Casual marriages.* Parents no longer have the control over mate selection that they used to have. Marriages based on romantic love are more or less taken for granted. Hasty marriages are not infrequent, and youthful marriages are quite common. Some writers feel that this combination of changes has been reflected in a rising rate of marital dissolution.

3. *Jobs for women.* In an age when women were unfairly barred from jobs—and as a consequence were dependent on their husbands for economic support—the prospect of a divorce must have been a rather grim one for wives. With the entrance of large numbers of women into the labor market, an important barrier to divorce was removed.

4. *Decline in moral and religious sanctions.* While the Catholic Church still does not recognize divorce, most of the Protestant denominations have taken a more liberal view of the matter. Also, community opinion no longer represents the barrier of yesteryear. The stigma attached to divorce has largely, if not entirely, disappeared.

5. *The philosophy of happiness.* Whereas marriages were formerly held in place, so to speak, by functional and institutional bonds, modern couples have come to think of happiness as the principal matrimonial goal. If happiness fails to materialize to the degree anticipated, divorce or separation is often resorted to.

Whether or not marital happiness is more widespread today than formerly remains a moot question. However, it is reasonable to suppose that young people today are more concerned with happiness and that, when their aspirations are not achieved, marital breakup is a more likely consequence than it was a century ago.

6. *More liberal divorce laws.* Prior to the Revolutionary War, many of the colonies had little or no provision for divorce. Even during the nineteenth century, divorce was presumed to be granted only for "grave and serious reasons." During the twentieth century, however, more and more new grounds were added, and in recent years some form of no-fault divorce has been adopted by most states. As the legal concept of marital dissolution has changed from "grave and serious reasons" to "divorce on demand," increasing numbers of people availed themselves of the opportunity.

480

Individual Factors. Insofar as individual factors are concerned, the list seems to be interminable: sexual incompatibility, personality problems, infidelity, excessive drinking, financial difficulties, in-law relationships, and so on. In the Levinger study—based on 600 couples who were divorce applicants—it was found that the wives' complaints exceeded the husbands' by a ratio of nearly two to one.

> As to the nature of complaints, wives complained 11 times more frequently than husbands about physical abuse. . . . Wives also complained four times as often about financial problems and about drinking; three times as much about their spouse's verbal abuse. Wives' complaints significantly exceeded husbands' on three other categories—neglect of home and children, lack of love, and mental cruelty—but these ratios were less one-sided.
>
> Husbands' complaints exceeded those of their mates on two counts. They were more apt to mention in-law trouble, by a ratio of five to two; and they more often brought up sexual incompatibility in a ratio of three to two.

Levinger also found that, when the types of complaints were analyzed by social class, it was found that "spouses in the middle-class marriages were more concerned with psychological and emotional interaction, while the lower-class partners saw as most salient in their lives financial problems and the unsubtle physical actions of their partner."[31]

---

[31] George Levinger, "Sources of Marital Dissatisfaction Among Applicants for Divorce," in Paul H. Glasser and Lois N. Glasser, *Families in Crisis,* New York, Harper & Row, 1970, pp. 126–132.

What about the fault-divorce cases themselves? Is there anything in the testimony that might aid in an understanding of divorce causation? Let the readers judge for themselves. The following extract was taken from the writer's study of Philadelphia divorce records and is fairly typical of its kind:

LAWYER: When did your husband start his drinking?

PLAINTIFF: Well, he used to drink right after we were married, but nothing ever came of it . . .

LAWYER: Then what happened?

PLAINTIFF: He took to staying out two or three nights a week. He would come home blind drunk about three or four in the morning, unfit to go to work the next day. Finally he lost his job with the cab company. He got a job as a truck driver, and for a while everything was all right, but then it started all over again.

MASTER: You mean he got drunk two or three times a week?

PLAINTIFF: Never less than that. For a year or so before the separation it seemed like it was almost every night.

MASTER: Where did he get the money?

PLAINTIFF: I'll never know. He was always with a crowd of men. They always seemed to have enough to buy drinks.

LAWYER: Did your husband give you enough to run the house?

PLAINTIFF: He did at first—when he was working, but for the last couple of years he couldn't hold a job. He tried half a dozen different ones but couldn't hold them. We were always moving, too. We lived in seven or eight different houses . . . we couldn't pay the rent . . .

LAWYER: Did he mistreat you in any way?

PLAINTIFF: Well, most of the time he didn't bother me, but I was never sure. Sometimes he would come home and for no reason start punching me. I used to have to lock myself in the children's room. I could hear him downstairs throwing chairs around. Once he threw a clock at me. It hit me in the face and broke my two front teeth off, here [indicating]. I had caps put on at the dentist . . .

LAWYER: Did he mistreat the children?

PLAINTIFF: No, he never went in their room. They were afraid of him, though. We all were. You could never tell what he'd do next.

MASTER: Did he ever harm you when he was sober?

PLAINTIFF: Oh, no, never. When he was sober he used to feel so sorry for what he done when he was drunk. Toward the end he wasn't sober often.

MASTER: Did you ever suggest that he see a doctor?

PLAINTIFF: I used to beg him to go. Once I went with him to our family doctor, but it didn't do any good. He only went once. . . . Honestly, sometimes I didn't know which way to turn. Every time the doorbell rang I thought it was one of the neighbors coming to tell me my husband was lying on the street drunk.

LAWYER: Were you a good wife to him? Did you perform the necessary household duties properly?

481

PLAINTIFF: I certainly tried to . . . I had a hot meal ready every night for him, whether he came home or not . . .

LAWYER: Did you ever refuse to have sex relations with him when he was in a sober condition?

PLAINTIFF: Never, unless I was sick.

MASTER: All right, that will be all.

Although the above case is but one of 1,434 examined by the writer, the complaint of excessive drinking was voiced in 21 percent of all the cases. Before jumping to conclusions, however, the reader should ask a few pertinent questions: (1) Would the case reported above have sounded the same if the husband had been present to testify? (2) Is it possible, from unilateral allegations of the kind found in most fault-divorce cases, to unravel cause and effect? (3) Are the causes alleged in a fault-divorce suit accurate reflections of the real causes?

Most sociologists would answer no to all three questions, for the fact is that grievances voiced in fault-divorce suits tend to be those that fit one of the legal grounds recognized in the particular state. In this connection, the following conclusions were drawn from the Philadelphia study:

In the course of the investigation the writer talked with lawyers who had handled hundreds of divorce cases, clerks of court, judges, experienced masters (lawyers appointed by the judge to hear divorce proceedings), and prothonotary officials. In addition, a number of divorce hearings were attended and upward of 200,000 pages of divorce testimony were examined. For what it is worth, the writer's opinion is as follows:

While in most divorce suits the relationship between real and alleged cause is nebulous, specific incidents as a rule are not fabricated. They are usually exaggerated, both in frequency and intensity, and are sometimes distorted beyond reasonable recognition. Vital aspects of the marital discord are apparently omitted in court hearings. However, in general, incidents that are reported do not spring from thin air; they seem to have some basis in fact. The inflation and distortion that exist appear to be in degree rather than kind. . . .

Even assuming the complaints about drinking to be valid, the problem of cause and effect would still remain. Whether the drinking behavior actually "caused" the marital discord, or whether the reverse was true, or whether, perhaps, deeper personality factors resulted in both excessive drinking and marital troubles, can only be conjectured. Causal intertwinings of this kind are always difficult to unravel, and in this respect it is doubtful whether any new insights are to be gleaned from a perusal of divorce testimony.

By now the reader has probably concluded—and correctly— that causes are perceived differently by different categories of people. That is, the "cause" of a given divorce might be one thing as reported by the wife, something entirely different as reported by the husband, and something still different as viewed by a divorce lawyer. The reasons given during the court proceedings might well have little relationship to any of the foregoing viewpoints. And a marriage counselor or a psychiatrist might unearth certain causative factors that had been overlooked by all concerned. The psychiatrist, especially, is prone to think in such causative terms as ego strength, family equilibrium, stress, and unconscious motivation.

Claims to the contrary notwithstanding, the behavioral sciences have not yet reached the stage where definitive statements can be made regarding specific causes of marital breakup. On the other hand, preventive programs aimed at strengthening marital and familial ties have been making progress, and these will be discussed in the final chapter. Before turning to these programs, however, let us examine some of the "new directions" in American family life styles.

SELECTED READINGS

Andrews, Ernest E., *The Emotionally Disturbed Family*, New York, Jason Aronson Book Publishers, 1974.

Anspach, Donald, "Kinship and Divorce," *Journal of Marriage and the Family*, May, 1976, pp. 323–330.

Bohannan, Paul (ed.), *Divorce and After*, Garden City, New York, Doubleday & Company, Inc. (Anchor Books), 1970.

Bryant, Clifton, and Wells, J. Gipson, *Deviancy and the Family*, Philadelphia, F. A. Davis Company, 1973.

Carter, Hugh, and Glick, Paul, *Marriage and Divorce: A Social and Economic Study*, Cambridge, Massachusetts, Harvard University Press, 1970.

Cutright, Phillips, "Income and Family Events: Marital Stability," *Journal of Marriage and the Family*, May, 1971, pp. 291–306.

England, J. Lynn, and Kunz, Phillip R., "The Application of Age-Specific Rates to Divorce," *Journal of Marriage and the Family*, February, 1975, pp. 40–46.

Glick, Paul C., "A Demographer Looks at American Families," *Journal of Marriage and the Family*, February, 1975, pp. 15–26.

————, and Norton, Arthur J., "Frequency, Duration, and Probability of Marriage and Divorce," *Journal of Marriage and the Family*, May, 1971, pp. 307–317.

Haerle, Rudolf K., Jr., "Church Attendance Patterns Among Intermarried Catholics: A Panel Study," *Sociological Analysis*, Winter, 1969, pp. 204–216.

Heer, David M., "The Prevalence of Black-White Marriage in the United States, 1960 and 1970," *Journal of Marriage and the Family*, May, 1974, pp. 246–258.

Krantzler, Mel, *Creative Divorce*, New York, Signet, New American Library, 1975.

Kuzel, Paul, and Krishnan, P., "Changing Patterns of Remarriage in Canada," *Journal of Comparative Family Studies*, Autumn, 1973, pp. 215–224.

Levinger, George, "Sources of Marital Dissatisfaction Among Applicants for Divorce," in Paul H. Glasser and Lois N. Glasser, *Families in Crisis*, New York, Harper & Row, 1970, pp. 126–132.

Mace, David R. (ed.), "Marriage Enrichment" (series), *Family Coordinator*, April, 1975, pp. 131–173.

Monahan, Thomas P., "Are Interracial Marriages Really Less Stable?" *Social Forces*, June, 1970, pp. 461–473.

———, "Interracial Marriage and Divorce in Kansas and the Question of Instability of Mixed Marriages," *Journal of Comparative Family Studies*, Spring, 1971, pp. 107–120.

———, "An Overview of Statistics on Interracial Marriage in the United States," *Journal of Marriage and the Family*, May, 1976, pp. 223–231.

Palmer, Sally E., "Reasons for Marriage Breakdown," *Journal of Comparative Family Studies*, Autumn, 1971, pp. 251–262.

Plateris, Alexander A., *Children of Divorced Couples: United States, Selected Years*, Public Health Service Publication No. 1000, Series 21, Number 18, February, 1970.

Rausch, Harold; Barry, William; Hertel, Richard; and Swain, Mary Ann, *Communication, Conflict, and Marriage*, San Francisco, Jossey-Bass Publishers, 1974.

Rose, Vicki, and Price-Bonham, Sharon, "Divorce Adjustment: A Woman's Problem?" *Family Coordinator*, July, 1973, pp. 291–297.

Rosenthal, Erich, "Divorce and Religious Intermarriage: The Effect of Previous Marital Status upon Subsequent Marital Behavior," *Journal of Marriage and the Family*, August, 1970, pp. 435–440.

Rosow, Irving, and Rose, K. Daniel, "Divorce Among Doctors," *Journal of Marriage and the Family*, November, 1972, pp. 587–598.

Schlesinger, Benjamin, "Remarriage as Family Reorganization

484

for Divorced Persons—A Canadian Study," *Journal of Comparative Family Studies,* Autumn, 1970, pp. 101–118.

Skarsten, Stan, "Family Desertion in Canada," *Family Coordinator,* January, 1974, pp. 19–25.

Spicer, Jerry W., "Kinship Interaction After Divorce," *Journal of Marriage and the Family,* February, 1975, pp. 113–119.

Washington, Joseph R., *Marriage in Black and White,* Boston, Beacon Press, 1970.

Williams, Kristen M., and Kuhn, Russell P., *Remarriages: United States,* DHEW Publication No. (HRA) 74-1903, Series 21, Number 25, December, 1973.

485

22
Alternative Life Styles

ALTHOUGH AMERICA HAS always been a strongly monogamous society, several "alternative" life styles have made their appearance in recent years. Some of them, such as multilateral marriage—the cohabitation of three or more persons "where each partner considers himself/herself married to at least two other partners"—have never amounted to very much, in terms of numbers.[1] Other alternatives—such as cohabitation and communal living—have involved substantial numbers of people. The present chapter examines some of the more widely publicized life styles, together with their implications for the future.

STAYING SINGLE

Time was when most young people considered the prospect of life without marriage to be a rather grim one. And while to a large extent this is probably still true, there are some signs that the marital image may be changing. More and more, it seems, statements like the following—originally written for the *Atlantic Monthly*—are quoted and re-quoted:

> Parents, teachers, and concerned adults rarely speak the truth about marriage as it really is in modern middle-class America. The truth as I see it is that contemporary marriage is a wretched institution. It spells the end of voluntary affection, of love freely given and joyously received. Beautiful romances are transmuted into dull marriages, and eventually the relationship becomes constricting, corrosive, and destructive.
>
> The basic reason for this sad state of affairs is that marriage was not designed to bear the burdens now being asked of it. It is an

---

[1] See Larry Constantine and Joan Constantine, "Dissolution of Marriage in a Nonconventional Context," *Family Coordinator*, October, 1972, pp. 457–462.

The easing of societal pressures on women to marry early has permitted many women to live satisfying lives outside a marital framework. (Philip Jon Bailey)

institution that evolved over centuries to meet some very specific functional needs of a nonindustrial society. Romantic love was viewed as tragic or merely irrelevant. Today it is the titillating prelude to domestic tragedy. . . .

Marriage was not designed as a mechanism for providing friendship, erotic experience, romantic love, personal fulfillment, continuous lay psychotherapy, or recreation. The family was not designed to carry a lifelong load of highly emotional romantic freight. Given its present structure, it simply has to fail when asked to do so. The very idea of an irrevocable contract obligating the parties concerned to a lifetime of romantic effort is utterly absurd.[2]

Along the same lines, the following article—entitled "More and More People Are Living Alone and Liking It"—recently appeared in a large metropolitan daily:

Whenever Christine Sulat decides to spend a quiet evening at home, she usually cooks herself a few scrambled eggs for dinner,

---

[2] Mervyn Cadwallader, "Marriage as a Wretched Institution," *Atlantic*, Vol. 218, No. 5, pp. 62–68; quoted in Jack R. DeLora and Joan S. DeLora, *Intimate Life Styles: Marriage and Its Alternatives*, Pacific Palisades, California, Goodyear Publishing Company, Inc., 1975, p. 134.

watches television for a while, and then takes a long, leisurely bath before going to bed.

Later, as often as not, she will get up again to listen to records or do some typing, happily oblivious to the fact that it is the middle of the night.

Ms. Sulat, 27, a free-lance writer, is one of a record 13.3 million Americans recently cited by the U.S. Census Bureau as occupants of "single-person households." In other words, she lives alone.

And—contrary to the common but sometimes stereotyped image of live-aloners as miserable and lonely—she loves it.

"I love having my privacy," Ms. Sulat says. "Although it obviously would be cheaper for me to share expenses with a roommate, I just don't think it would be worth it."

Despite the obvious financial disadvantage of maintaining an apartment alone in these troubled economic times, the Census Bureau reported last week that the number of persons living alone has increased by three million in the past five years.

And apparently, unprecedented numbers of people are living in solitude by choice, not chance. . . .[3]

What accounts for this delay in marriage? Since the phenomenon is relatively new, no large-scale motivation studies have been reported. However, Paul Glick, of the U.S. Census Bureau, believes that one reason for the delay among young women is the fact that there are around three times as many women in college as there were in 1960. He goes on to say that:

Another demographic factor is the "marriage squeeze." During recent years this phenomenon has taken the form of an excess of young women at the ages when marriage rates are highest. . . . Other factors include the sharper increase in the employment of women than men, and the amazing decline in the birth rate—both of which signaled expanding roles open to women outside the home.

Among the less tangible factors has been the revival of the women's movement. In fact, the excess of marriageable women in the last few years may have contributed as much to the development of that movement as the ideology of the movement has contributed to the increase in singleness.[4]

It should also be mentioned that at one time a stigma attached to both the never-married and the divorced, but this is no longer true. A young woman today, for example, who prefers a career to marriage is not only not stigmatized but is often envied, particularly if she is successful.

---

[3] Kathy Begley, "More and More People Are Living Alone and Liking It," *Philadelphia Inquirer*, March 4, 1975, pp. 1 ff.

[4] Paul Glick, "A Demographer Looks at American Families," *Journal of Marriage and the Family*, February, 1975, p. 17.

Whatever the reasons, there is no doubt that the nonmarried population is growing. In fact, there are now some 50 million unmarried adults in the United States, although this figure would include the widowed and the divorced as well as the never-married.

While our knowledge of the never-married group is limited, there is a suggestion that the singles tend to migrate to the larger cities. In the Jacoby survey, for instance, one of the respondents replied: "What you value most as a single person is people minding their own business, and you only get that in a big city."[5] The same survey also found that:

Single life seems to satisfy the upper middle class more than any other group. Affluent singles need never choose between a tacky studio apartment and putting up with three roommates. Money is especially useful in combating loneliness, the No. 1 bogeyman of many singles. . . .

Without money, it is difficult to translate the theoretical freedom afforded by the single life into reality. A 36-year-old lawyer emphasized this point as he described his plans to close out a highly successful law practice because he wants to travel and try to write fiction. "I've spent most of my adult life accumulating money," he said; "now I'm going to use it to free myself. I've always wanted to write, and I plan to settle somewhere in Europe and see if I have any talent. If I don't, I can pick up the law practice again. If I were married, I doubt that I would be able to break away. Some of my friends have children who are only a few years away from college. How could I throw over a career in that situation?"

Small but growing numbers of upper middle class women are also enjoying the combination of money, success, and single freedom that was formerly a male preserve. Unlike college-educated men, these women frequently seem surprised by their monetary and professional success. "I've been surprised to find myself making such a good salary," said a 30-year-old Washington woman with a demanding legislative job on Capitol Hill. Rightly or wrongly, I always thought that someone else would provide those things for me, although I was determined to become 'someone' myself."[6]

The Unanswered Question. Before leaving the topic, it should be pointed out that the decline in the marriage rate can mean one of two things: either fewer people are marrying, or else they are postponing marriage to a later period. Perhaps both of these phenomena are occurring. The fact that the average age at marriage

[5] Susan Jacoby, "49 Million Singles Can't Be All Right," *The New York Times Magazine*, February 17, 1974. © 1974 by The New York Times Company. Reprinted by permission.
[6] *Ibid.*

is increasing suggests that many people are merely delaying their marriages. In her interview-survey, Jacoby states that "it is probably too early to tell whether the sharp rise in the singles population indicates a radically new life-style or simply a shift in the timing of marriages. Most of the singles I interviewed, including both the divorced and the never-married, expressed opposition to early and hasty marriages rather than to the idea of marriage itself."[7]

On the other hand, in an address to the National Council on Family Relations, Paul Glick spoke as follows:

490

> A detailed analysis of recent marriage trends has suggested that it is too early to predict with confidence that the recent increase in singleness among the young will lead to an eventual decline in lifetime marriage. However, just as cohorts of young women who have postponed childbearing for an unusually long time seldom make up for the child deficit as they grow older, so also young people who are delaying marriage may never make up for the marriage deficit later on. They may try alternatives to marriage and like them.[8]

Whatever the explanation—that is, whether the dip in the marriage rate is temporary or permanent—the answer will be known within the lifetime of most readers. If the decline should prove to be permanent, the consequences—in terms of the birthrate, the economy, and social behavior would be far-reaching indeed.

COHABITATION

"Cohabitation" is sometimes thought of as a kind of trial marriage, but the two terms actually have different connotations. Trial marriage is a relationship wherein the partners live together for a certain period of time while deciding whether to make the arrangement permanent. Some societies have institutionalized trial marriage,[9] and from time to time the practice has been proposed for our own culture.[10] Cohabitation, according to the dictionary, is simply "living together in a sexual relationship when not legally married."

Although cohabitation occurs in all walks of life, in recent years it has come to be associated particularly with the college

---

[7] Ibid.

[8] Glick, op. cit., p. 18.

[9] See, for example, Richard Price, "Trial Marriage in the Andes," Ethnology, Vol. 4, 1965, pp. 310–322.

[10] For a historical statement see Miriam E. Berger, "Trial Marriage: Harnessing the Trend Constructively," Family Coordinator, January, 1971, pp. 38–43.

population. And, as practiced today on college campuses, cohabitation does not generally signify a trial-marriage arrangement. Thus, when the cohabiting students in Macklin's survey were asked whether they were contemplating marriage, a typical answer was "Heavens, no!"

The same investigator reports that for most cohabitors "marriage might be seen as a possibility for the future, but the distant future. They felt they needed more time to grow and develop before considering marriage, and it was financially impractical. . . . These students do not in general see themselves as even contemplating marriage. Instead, living together seems to be a natural component of a strong, affectionate dating relationship—a living out of 'going steady'—which may grow in time to be something more, but which in the meantime is to be enjoyed and experienced because it is pleasurable in and of itself."[11]

In the Lyness–Lipetz–Davis study, which compared cohabiting couples with going-together couples, the cohabitors were found to have relatively little commitment to marriage, particularly the males. Indeed, only 17 percent of the latter made any mention of marriage. The researchers go on to state that "it would appear that the going-together partners agreed they were headed for marriage. In contrast, living-together couples were found to differ on the question. Whether marriage does, in fact, result from these relationships would appear to depend on which partner's position emerged as stronger."[12]

In the same study, feelings and relationships on the part of going-together couples were compared with those of the cohabiting couples, with the following results:

> Findings make it clear that living-together couples did not reciprocate the kinds of feelings (of need, respect, happiness, involvement, or commitment to marriage) that one would expect to be the basis of a good heterosexual relationship. Whether such a lack of reciprocity is typical of such relationships, and thus reflects the difficulties of bringing off a successful non-normative relationship, or whether it is merely typical of those who volunteered for our research cannot be conclusively answered from these data. Certainly the question calls for additional research, particularly given the apparent popularity and growth of the living-together arrangement in some college communities.[13]

491

---

[11] Eleanor D. Macklin, "Heterosexual Cohabitation Among College Students," *Family Coordinator*, October, 1972, pp. 467, 470. Copyright © 1972 by National Council on Family Relations. Reprinted by permission.
[12] Judith Lyness, Milton Lipetz, and Keith Davis, "Living Together: An Alternative to Marriage," *Journal of Marriage and the Family*, May, 1972, pp. 307, 309.
[13] *Ibid.*, p. 310.

Problems. It is evident that cohabiting couples do have certain problems. In the Macklin survey the chief areas of difficulty were found to be emotional, sexual, and parental. The major emotional problem, for example, was the "tendency to become over-involved, a lack of opportunity to participate in other activities or be with friends, and an over-dependency on the relationship."[14]

In the Henze–Hudson study of college students, cohabitors were compared with noncohabitors in terms of family background, personal characteristics, and so on. Findings revealed that, while there were no differences in family background between the two groups, "cohabitors were less apt to attend church, were more likely to identify with a liberal life style, and were more apt to be drug users (both marijuana and hard drugs)."[15]

Several of the above studies found that cohabiting students had a special problem as far as their parents were concerned. Macklin writes that:

> A major problem area was parents. More than one-fourth indicated that parents had caused "some" or "many" problems: parental disapproval of the boy, fear of discovery, guilt because they were deceiving or hurting their parents, rejection by or ultimatums from parents, and most frequently, sadness at not being able to share this important part of their lives with their parents.
> Because of fear of disapproval, more than two-thirds had tried to conceal the relationship from their parents—by not telling them the truth, and by developing elaborate schemes to prevent discovery.[16]

It is almost self-evident that a real generation gap exists with respect to cohabitation, and public opinion polls simply bear out the obvious. One popular poll asked the question, "Do you approve or disapprove of two people living together before they get married?" In the age group 55-and-over only 12 percent voiced approval, as compared with 41 percent in the under-35 category.[17] The key question, of course, is how the under-35 group will feel when they reach the age where they themselves have children in college.

Positive Features. While cohabiting students do experience certain difficulties, it should not be thought that they live in a sea of

---

[14] Macklin, *op. cit.*, p. 468.

[15] Lura F. Henze and John W. Hudson, "Personal and Family Characteristics of Cohabiting and Noncohabiting College Students," *Journal of Marriage and the Family*, November, 1974, p. 722.

[16] Macklin, *op. cit.*, p. 468.

[17] *A Report on the American Family*, by the editors of *Better Homes and Gardens*, September, 1972, p. 70.

troubles. On the contrary, there seems to be much overall satisfaction. In the Lyness–Lipetz–Davis survey, cohabiting students reported having a high happiness level. They were also found to have a greater satisfaction with sex than the going-together students.[18] In the Macklin study, more than 50 percent of the cohabitors rated their relationship as "very successful," and over 80 percent reported that it was "both maturing and pleasant." The author goes on to say that:

> The benefits seen by the participants included a deeper understanding of themselves and of their needs, expectations, and inadequacies; increased knowledge of what is involved in a relationship; clarification of what they wanted in marriage; increased ability to understand and relate to others. . . .
>
> All persons interviewed indicated that they would not consider marriage without having lived with the person first, and all—while hesitant to say what others should do—felt the move toward cohabitation could only be seen as a healthy trend.[19]

Actual living arrangements may vary somewhat among cohabiting couples, but in most cases the girl moves into the boy's room or vice versa. Macklin reports, however, that in her sample practically all the girls kept their own room in the dormitory or sorority. "Most went back once a day for a few hours to visit, get mail, exchange clothes, shower, or study. Maintaining a separate residence precludes having to explain to parents, ensures a place to live if the relationship is not working well, helps maintain contact with female friends, and provides necessary storage space."[20]

Outlook. What proportion of American college students have cohabited? What is the outlook for the future? Although definitive answers to these questions are not possible at this time, some educated guesses can be made. Questionnaire surveys at Cornell indicated that between 28 and 40 percent of the respondents had practiced cohabitation.[21] At Arizona State, 29 percent of the males and 18 percent of the females reported cohabiting,[22] while at Penn State the corresponding figures were 33 percent for males and 32 percent for females.[23] It is probably safe to say that, at many of the larger universities, somewhere in the area of one-third of the students have practiced cohabitation.

493

---

[18] Lyness et al., *op. cit.*, pp. 307–311.
[19] Macklin, *op. cit.*, pp. 469–470.
[20] *Ibid.*, p. 465.
[21] *Ibid.*, p. 464.
[22] Henze and Hudson, *op. cit.*, p. 724.
[23] *Ibid.*

While the future cannot be predicted with any certainty, there is nothing on the horizon to suggest any reversal of the trend. In no other realm of sex behavior has a permissive trend, once started, been reversed—at least, not in modern times. Most of the researchers mentioned above feel that the trend toward cohabitation will continue, a belief that is also shared by the students themselves. Whether there is a relationship between increasing cohabitation and the declining marriage rate has not been determined.

SWINGING

In essence, swinging is a voluntary and temporary swapping of mates for sexual purposes. The swapping generally involves two or more couples, although occasionally an unattached person —usually a female—is included. But whatever the combinatorial arrangements, the sexual exchange takes place with *the full consent* of all parties concerned. Swinging thus differs from adultery, since the latter ordinarily occurs without spousal agreement.

Swinging usually takes one of two forms. In the first, two couples simply spend a quiet evening together, in the course of which an exchange of mates takes place for sexual purposes. In the second, a number of couples have a party—at which time a whole series of sexual exchanges occurs. Many swingers reportedly begin with the two-couple arrangement, later "graduating" to the group conclave.

After their initial encounter with swinging, some couples never repeat the experience. Others make a veritable career out of swinging. In either case, however, it is difficult to gather valid information since, quite obviously, swingers do not publicize their activities. And, while several studies on swinging have now been undertaken, conclusions based on these studies necessarily contain an unknown margin of error.

Rules of the Game. Estimates of the number of swingers in the United States range from thousands to millions, depending on who does the estimating. Those who indulge, or who are sympathetic to the idea, see swinging as a popular and growing pastime. Others look upon it as little more than a fad, with extremely limited acceptance. Irrespective of the extent of the activity, however, there appear to be certain "ground rules" that are followed.

To begin with, swingers are generally circumspect in their approach to other couples. The nature of the game dictates that they

(Philip Jon Bailey)

procure new partners, yet public opinion is such that they hesitate to make their efforts known to the community at large. The most frequent method of solving the dilemma, according to Bartell, is to utilize advertisements in one of the pertinent magazines or tabloids:

> Florida Marrieds. Attractive, refined, professional marrieds. Would like to hear from similar, liberal-minded marrieds. Complete discretion required, and assured. Can travel southern states. Photo and phone, please. Box number ———.

The same investigator reports three other methods of recruitment: introduction to another couple at a bar, set up specifically for this purpose; personal reference from one couple to another; and actual recruitment, or conversion, of prospective couples. Because of the difficulties involved, this last method reportedly is the least often used.[24]

According to the swingers' philosophy, it is not extramarital sex that is wrong but the lying and deception that usually

---

[24] Gilbert Bartell, "Group Sex Among the Mid-Americans," in Jack R. DeLora and Joann S. DeLora, *Intimate Life Styles*, Pacific Palisades, California, Goodyear Publishing Company, Inc., 1975, pp. 267–279. This article appeared in the *Journal of Sex Research*, Vol. 6, No. 2, May, 1970. Reprinted by permission of the Society for the Scientific Study of Sex.

accompany such activity. For either spouse to have an "affair" without the consent of the other, therefore, would be considered a breach of faith. In fact, irrespective of the amount of extramarital sex they indulge in, swingers contend that there is little or no emotional involvement. Permanent attachments are avoided, sexual contacts with other couples often being limited to a single engagement. By adhering closely to this philosophy, swingers claim that feelings of jealousy seldom arise.

Contrary to what might be supposed, swingers do not engage in typical "wild parties." Bartell reports that there may be closed swingings (couples going to private rooms) or open swingings (couples engaging in open, group sex), but in either case the hilarity and boisterousness associated with the wild party is apparently lacking.

> If the party is a closed party, there are rules, very definitely established and generally reinforced by the organizer as well as the other swingers. These rules may even include clothing restrictions. . . . Most parties are "bring your own bottle" parties, although in a few cases the host supplies the liquor. Food is often prepared by the hostess, but seldom consumed. Stag films are generally not shown. Music is low key fox trot, not infrequently Glenn Miller, and lighting is definitely not psychedelic. Usually nothing more than a few red or blue light bulbs. Marijuana and speed are not permitted. . . . Bizarre costume is not considered proper and clothing is decidedly not "mod," but is very middle class.[25]

Maintaining middle-class respectability seems to be a recurrent theme in the swingers' world. Denfeld and Gordon write that "a common word in the swinging vocabulary is discretion. Swingers desire to keep their sexual play a secret. . . . They want to protect their position in the community, and an effort is made to limit participation to couples of similar status or 'respectability.' Swinging couples consider themselves to be sexually avant-garde, but many retain their puritan attitudes with respect to sex socialization. They hide their swinging publications from their children. Swingers lock their children's bedroom doors during parties or send them to relatives."[26]

Given the rather bizarre nature of the swingers' way of life, it is hardly surprising that ground rules are sometimes broken. Jealousy does occur, and from time to time permanent attachments do develop. Spouses are not always frank and honest with each other, and—more than occasionally—they are not frank with other couples. Some "marrieds," for example, are not married at

---

[25] *Ibid.,* pp. 270–272.

[26] Duane Denfeld and Michael Gordon, "The Sociology of Mate Swapping," in DeLora and DeLora, *op. cit.,* pp. 287–288.

FAMILY DISORGANIZATION AND REORGANIZATION

all but are posing as such in order to be admitted to the swingers' world. According to Bartell, some men have even hired prostitutes to pose as their wives![27] Such cases are exceptional, however, and whether swingers break the ground rules more often than members of other groups is open to question.

Characteristics of Swingers. Who are the swingers? Do they have any distinguishing characteristics? Why do they embark on such a nonnormative way of life? Surveys indicate that swingers come from middle- or upper-middle-class backgrounds, with the most common age group being 25 to 40. Protestants, Catholics, and Jews seem to be proportionately represented, although one study indicated that most of the couples did not attend church regularly.[28] The same study found that 10 percent of the swingers were regular nudists, and that 90 percent of the males read *Playboy*.[29] In fact, Murstein's review of the literature led him to conclude that "the one crystal-clear finding is that swingers possess high sex drives."[30]

Some of the research findings are difficult to interpret. On the one hand, husbands are much more likely than wives to initiate swinging activities. In the Henshel study, swinging was initiated by wives in only 12 percent of the cases, compared with a figure of 59 percent by the husbands. In the remaining cases, the decision was mutual.[31] On the other hand, Bartell found that, once they are involved in swinging, most wives are likely to engage in both homosexual and heterosexual activity, a pattern that is rare among husbands.[32]

Swingers are prone to consider themselves truly "liberated" in the sexual sphere, and it is not uncommon for them to refer to nonswingers as squares. In the Harris survey, for instance, the investigator reports that "some swingers blatantly let you know that their life adjustment is better than yours. They tell you—because they believe it—that unlike you, who out of cowardice are saddled with mental and physical frustrations, they have found the only way of facing life honestly."[33]

---

[27] Bartell, *op. cit.*, p. 274.

[28] *Ibid.*, p. 273.

[29] *Ibid.*

[30] Bernard I. Murstein, *Love, Sex, and Marriage Through the Ages*, New York, Springer Publishing Company, 1974, p. 547.

[31] Anne-Marie Henshel, "Swinging: A Study of Decision-Making in Marriage." *American Journal of Sociology*, January, 1973, pp. 885–891.

[32] Bartell, *op. cit.*, p. 277. Also, by the same author, *Group Sex: A Scientist's Eyewitness Report on the American Way of Swinging*, New York, Peter Wyden, 1971.

[33] Sarah Harris, "Before We Began to Swing," in Clifton Bryant and J. Gipson Wells (eds.), *Deviancy and the Family*, Philadelphia, F. A. Davis Company, 1973, p. 284.

Yet, at the same time, Bartell writes that "only a few in our sample said they would raise their children with the same degree of sexual libertarianism that they themselves espouse, or that they would give the girls the pill at a very early age."[34]

With regard to why they turn to swinging in the first place, the same author writes that:

> What we find in these couples consistently is a boredom with marriage. . . . Swinging may be extremely exciting, inasmuch as it carries elements of danger. Swingers may feel very avant garde in the breaking of cultural and legal taboos. . . .
>
> Also, they can now plan weekend trips together, and take vacations to other parts of the country to meet swingers. . . . They have the opportunity to dress up, make dinner dates, and acquire a full social calendar. They may now feel that they are doing what the "in" people are doing, and living up to their playboy image.[35]

There seems no doubt that, for some couples, swinging has had beneficial results. In addition to the excitement and sociality mentioned above, swinging has in some cases rejuvenated the marriage and enabled the spouses to develop a greater appreciation of each other. In other cases, couples who were sexually maladjusted have found swinging to be the answer to the problem.[36] One review of the literature indicated that "every study reported finding positive contributions in swinging."[37] And compared with having an "affair," as Murstein points out, swinging is less emotionally demanding, less expensive, more educative sexually, more honest and democratic, and is less likely to lead to divorce.[38]

Negative Aspects. Swinging has also been found to have some negative features: guilt and loss of self-esteem, time spent in the never-ending search for new partners, fear of rejection by other couples, threat of venereal disease, prevalence of superficial relationships, and so on. In the Bartell study, the investigator concluded that one of the main difficulties was the "perpetual hazard of discovery."[39]

And while it is doubtless true that swinging has helped some individuals—and some marriages—research has generally

---

[34] Bartell, *op. cit.*, p. 273.

[35] *Ibid.*, pp. 275–276.

[36] *Ibid.*, p. 275.

[37] Duane Denfeld, "Dropouts from Swinging," *Family Coordinator*, January, 1974, p. 45.

[38] Murstein, *op. cit.*, p. 550.

[39] Bartell, *op. cit.*, p. 278.

focused on *those still engaged in swinging*. As Murstein points out, "The difficulty is that no one yet knows much about the attitudes and experiences of those people who try swinging and drop out. How large a number do they constitute, and what is the effect of swinging on their personality and marital adjustment? Rectification of this omission through research will be a major contribution to our ability to predict the viability of swinging marriages."[40]

In order to help rectify this problem, Denfeld sent questionnaires to all members of the American Association of Marriage and Family Counselors. Of those responding, approximately half had counseled at least one swinging "dropout" couple. A total of 1,175 couples had been counseled, and questionnaire responses revealed that the ex-swingers had experienced some serious difficulties.[41]

The three major complaints, in order, were jealousy, guilt, and "threat to the marriage." Jealousy was reported more often by husbands than by wives. Husbands tended to become concerned over their wives' popularity, whereas the wives' feelings were related to "fear of losing their mate." Denfeld states that "these findings suggest the influence of the double standard; the emphasis of the husband is on his pleasure and satisfaction, whereas the emphasis of the wife is on the maintenance of the marital unit."[42]

Commenting further on the prevalence of guilt and jealousy, the same investigator reports that, insofar as the dropout couples were concerned, swinging tended to weaken rather than strengthen the marriage. For example, "fighting and hostilities became more frequent after swinging."[43]

Not all of the results reported by the marriage counselors were negative. Of the 425 dropout couples for whom such information was available, 170 stated that swinging had improved the marital relationship—even though in a number of cases the improvement was only temporary.[44]

---

[40] Murstein, *op. cit.*, p. 551.

[41] Questionnaires were sent to 2,147 marriage counselors, all of those listed in the directories of the American Association and the California Association of Marriage and Family Counselors: 965 questionnaires were returned; 473 counselors had counseled at least one dropout couple; among the remaining counselors who responded, 368 had never counseled a dropout couple and 125 more indicated that they were retired, inactive, or in specialized practice that would give them no opportunity to counsel swinging dropouts. (Duane Denfeld, *op. cit.*, pp. 45–49.)

[42] *Ibid.*, p. 46.

[43] *Ibid.*

[44] *Ibid.*, p. 48.

The major thrust of the Denfeld survey, nevertheless, was to call attention to some of the pitfalls involved in swinging.

> This report from marriage counselors does not allow a rejection of the optimistic view of swinging. It does, however, raise some questions as to the extent of positive outcomes and portrays some of the problems involved. Previously, problems of swinging received little attention because only successful swingers were likely to be included in the research studies. . . .
>
> It is clear, however, that many couples left swinging hurt and psychologically damaged. The positive image previously presented may have encouraged couples to engage in swinging. The indications are that some couples are not emotionally capable of or prepared for swinging. Knowing these things should give pause to anyone who is inclined to recommend or imply that swinging will help a couple's marriage.
>
> The results of the marriage counselors' reports also challenge the argument that swinging demonstrates the realization of equality of the sexes. Husbands often forced wives into swinging, and wives were more dissatisfied with swinging and more frequently initiated the dropping out. Rather than being equalitarian, swinging is more likely to be a truly "sexist" activity.[45]

Even Bartell, whose study of swinging revealed many positive features, concluded that the couples in his sample were not really benefiting themselves because their ideals had not been realized. "Their human relationships outside of the dyad are not good. Their activities with other couples reflect mechanical interaction rather than an intimacy of relationships."[46]

At any rate, the future of swinging remains somewhat clouded. After a rather widely publicized beginning, the practice seems to have tapered off. And while it is certainly possible that the original momentum will be recaptured, at the moment the odds seem to be against it.

COMMUNES

Although communes have existed in the United States since the Colonial era, there have been two peak periods. The first stretched roughly from 1800 to the Civil War and included such well-known groups as Brook Farm, Harmony, Oneida, Amana, Zoar, Bethel, and hundreds of others. Following the Civil War, however, the movement declined, and by 1900 only a handful of communes were left.

---

[45] *Ibid.*, pp. 48–49.
[46] Bartell, *op. cit.*, p. 278.

In the late 1960's there was a resurgence that caught both sociologists and the general public by surprise. Communes of all shapes and sizes seemed to spring up overnight: sacred and secular, urban and rural, structured and unstructured. The variety seemed limitless. Most catered to the younger age groups, and many came to be associated with hippie types. Some, however—such as the groups studied by Ramey—consisted entirely of middle-class members.[47]

Exactly how many communes were formed in the sixties and seventies is unknown, but the number probably ran into the thousands. The rate of failure was also high, however, and it became obvious to all concerned that, while communal living had certain advantages, the problems often proved insurmountable. Let us examine both sides of the coin.

Difficulties Involved. People join communes for any number of reasons, but in most cases the underlying factor relates to a *general dissatisfaction with society*. Commune members contend that their own way of life is superior to the "cutthroat" methods employed on the outside. In an effort to avoid materialistic contamination, therefore, communes tend to become separatist—and the most practicable way to do this is to locate in a rural area.

The catch is that most communes consist of individuals who were reared in an urban or suburban environment. As a consequence, the membership is likely to lack agricultural skills. There is also a lack of equipment, for farm machinery is expensive. Land itself is a problem, for good farm acreage is also expensive. Inadequate plumbing, lack of indoor toilets, poor cooking facilities, insufficient heat—such things tend to aggravate the problem. Everything costs money, and in the culture of the commune the unalterable reality is that money is scarce.

There are urban communes, of course, but they also have economic problems. On the one hand, if members do not work and contribute money the group cannot survive. But, if they do work, they often feel entrapped by the very system they set out to avoid. Heat, light, rent, taxes, maintenance, repairs, food, clothing. Everything costs money. . . .

In the Berger–Hackett–Millar survey, the economic plight of the communes is underscored:

> None of the communes we observed have achieved self-sufficiency. . . . Welfare is a major source of income, a fact which enhances the attractiveness of unattached mothers and their babies.

---

[47] James W. Ramey, "Communes, Group Marriage, and the Upper-Middle Class," *Journal of Marriage and the Family*, November, 1972, pp. 647–655.

"Crazy" people, with disability income from the state for their craziness, is also not uncommon. . . .

The Department of Agriculture's surplus food program is another important source of sustenance. More important is a category we call "windfalls," which would include occasional inheritances, birthday checks, and other unsolicited gifts from relatives and benefactors. . . .[48]

Another problem facing the modern commune is a weakness in social organization and a lack of commitment. Many groups appear to be at loose ends. Goals are often ill-defined, and group loyalties are tenuous. These are extremely important factors, for, as Kanter points out, "the problem of commitment is crucial. Since the commune represents an attempt to establish an ideal social order within the larger society, it must vie with the outside for the members' loyalties. It must ensure high member-involvement despite external competition without sacrificing its distinctiveness or ideals. It must often contravene the earlier socialization of its members in securing obedience to new demands. It must calm internal dissension in order to present a united front to the world. The problem of securing total and complete commitment is central."[49]

In Lamott's study of Morning Star, the following pertinent comments were made:

The daily regime at Morning Star is hard to describe in any convincing detail, for its pure and literal anarchy outrages all one's middle-class bias in favor of order and organization. The style of life here has pushed permissiveness to its outer limits. Work does manage to get done—meals are cooked, dishes are washed, the vegetable garden somehow gets tended—but nobody has been assigned to any particular duty. People sleep, talk, smoke pot, talk, lie in the sun, talk, meditate, talk, sing, and talk.[50]

Leadership presents a special problem in communal living, since the "guru" himself often has no real authority. Lacking both enforcement powers and personal experience, he is nevertheless expected to serve as both guide and beacon. In the present writer's study of communes, the following remarks were

---

[48] Bennett Berger, Bruce Hackett, and R. Mervyn Millar, "Supporting the Communal Family," in Rosabeth Moss Kanter (ed.), *Communes: Creating and Managing the Collective Life*, New York, Harper & Row, 1973, pp. 245–246.

[49] Rosabeth Moss Kanter, *Commitment and Community: Communes and Utopias in Sociological Perspective*, Cambridge, Massachusetts, Harvard University Press, 1972, p. 65.

[50] Kenneth Lamott, "Doing Their Thing at Morning Star," in Kanter, *Communes*, p. 137.

made by a member of Egrad. "Father," in the quoted passage, is a deeply religious young man of about 25.

Father's a good man. If Egrad makes it, it will be because of him. Of course, if we fail, he'll get the blame. Right now, we have problems.

On a personal basis, Father is a natural leader. I guess you could say Egrad is a kind of religious commune. We pray a lot—and I think we've succeeded in reaching God. And Father helps us. He knows the Bible inside out. He knows all about other religions. He reads all the time. And he's sincere. You can tell. You go to him with a problem and I guarantee he'll make you feel better.

The trouble is, he's not so good on practical matters. We're always behind in house rent. He doesn't like to tell people to do things, and as a result things don't get done. Rooms don't get cleaned, toilets don't get fixed. Sometimes the girls don't feel like cooking, and the meals are bad.

A couple of the fellows got mixed up in politics, but Father didn't say anything. He knows we're a religious group and not supposed to do that. Also, he let two girls and two fellows join, and he shouldn't have. They're just not our type. I think one of the girls has a disease. She looks bad.

But what can we do? He's our leader, the best we have. And he understands God. That's the main thing.[51]

Rewards. In spite of the obviously difficult problems faced by communal members, the rewards can also be great. Many members, in fact, look upon their communal experience as being the happiest period in their lives. Yaswen's stay at Sunrise Hill is a case in point:

At Sunrise Hill I was undoubtedly the happiest I had ever been in my entire life. In interpersonal relationships, I could have desired nothing more. . . . In the area of work, I had a far more diverse gamut of roles than I ever incurred elsewhere. It was a good life, intoxicating to work for something I believed in. For the first time in my life I BELONGED somewhere, and that somewhere was on this Earth after all.[52]

In the present writer's study, any number of respondents voiced satisfaction with the communal style of life. For many, life on the outside had been a smothering experience, and now—for the first time—they were feeling an inner peace. For others, the commune proved to be a haven, where one could meet people

[51] William M. Kephart, "Why They Fail: A Socio-Historical Analysis of Religious and Secular Communes," *Journal of Comparative Family Studies*, Autumn, 1974, pp. 130–140.
[52] Gordon Yaswen, "Sunrise Hill Community: Post Mortem," in Kanter, *Communes*, pp. 465–466.

503

with the same outlook on life. Most respondents enjoyed the sociability, the freedom, and the opportunity to "do their own thing." And nearly all appreciated the opportunity to vent their dissatisfaction with society—without adverse repercussions. The following comments are illustrative:

> Oceana may not be perfect, but it's sure an improvement over the way they live out there. Let's face it, society is all fouled up. In their hearts, most people know it, but they're afraid to do anything about it—except talk. . . .
>
> Think about it for a minute. Two hundred million people all complaining. The whole country's broken up into complaint groups. We pick our friends according to whether they have the same complaints. It's crazy.
>
> Well, you won't find much of that nonsense here at Oceana. When you join here, you leave your complaints on the outside.

> . . .

> All the talk about living in a civilized society is a myth. If it were civilized, things would be getting better instead of worse. As it is now, new kinds of problems crop up before the old ones are solved.
>
> Why more people don't flee from the whole mess—like we did—I can't understand. But if that's the way they want to live, let them. Understand, we have some problems here at Zed, but compared to the mess outside, we're living on Treasure Island.

> . . .

> Out there, nobody cares about you. Here at Westover, things are different. We care about each other. Really care. That's what it's all about. Look around you, you'll see what I mean. When you go back to the rat race, think about what I said.

> . . .

> Man is what his environment makes him. As a sociologist, you know that's true. We happen to think society is the wrong environment, and a commune is the right environment. You stay at Kiji for a while, you learn to be a good, considerate person. You stop always trying to be better than the next guy.

> . . .

> Here we say and do what we want, because we have a good relationship. No fancy rules tying you all in knots. We're free. Once you live in a commune, you never want to go back outside. . . . No, I have nothing to do with my parents. They live in a different world. The family is a dying institution.

The Balance Sheet. What has been America's reaction to the modern communal movement—and what does the future hold? Like most other social innovations, communes have provoked

(Cartier Bresson, Magnum Photo)

mixed reactions. The movement as a whole, however, has come
in for some pointed criticism. Communes have been accused of
fostering disrespect for authority, of encouraging licentious liv-

ing, of providing a haven for the shiftless, and of accepting the community's services without a corresponding payment of taxes.

Defenders, on the other hand, point out that communes (1) provide an alternative way of living for those who want it; (2) serve as therapy for certain personality types; (3) help society by absorbing some of the more dissatisfied elements; and (4) create a better understanding of the larger community on the part of those who become disillusioned with group living.

Objectively speaking, both supporters and critics seem to have been wrong. Dire predictions to the contrary, communes have undermined neither the family nor the larger social system. Except in isolated instances, they have not even disrupted the local community. As for licentious living, most communes failed to develop along the free-sex lines that had been predicted.

Conversely, modern communes have certainly not fulfilled the promise originally held out for them. On the contrary, their appeal has often proved illusory, as evidenced by the rapid turnover in membership. Indeed, the most striking thing about the entire communal movement has been the rapidity with which individual communes have folded.

At the present time the communal movement seems to have passed its peak, with some observers predicting that the end is just a matter of time. Others feel that the movement has lost its significance. In what he calls "The Utopian Commune: Birth and Decay of the Counterculture," Murstein contends that the future of the commune "seems largely limited to serving as a developmental stage on the road from adolescence to adulthood."[53]

The present writer would take a somewhat more optimistic approach. Having talked with a fair number of "communitarians," he was impressed with their sincerity. For these people, the commune did indeed offer a much-needed alternative. By providing an alternative life style, furthermore, the movement has perhaps had the effect of making society a little less smug, a little more responsive.

And while many individual communes have become defunct, some remain. It is highly unlikely, furthermore, that the *movement* will die out. More likely, the number of communes will rise and fall depending on certain social conditions. It must be remembered that the basic reason for establishing a commune is a degree of dissatisfaction with society at large. And the fact that these utopian ventures have been a recurrent part of the American scene for some 300 years suggests that the movement will continue—sometimes weak, sometimes strong.

---

[53] Murstein, *op. cit.*, pp. 537–540.

Ald, Roy, *The Youth Communes*, New York, Tower Publications, 1971.

Bartell, Gilbert, "Group Sex Among the Mid-Americans," in Jack R. DeLora and Joann S. DeLora, *Intimate Life Styles*, Pacific Palisades, California, Goodyear Publishing Company, Inc., 1975, pp. 267–279.

Berger, Bennett; Hackett, Bruce; and Millar, R. Mervyn, "Supporting the Communal Family," in Rosabeth Moss Kanter (ed.), *Communes: Creating and Managing the Collective Life*, New York, Harper & Row, 1973, pp. 245–248.

Berger, Miriam E., "Trial Marriage: Harnessing the Trend Constructively," *Family Coordinator*, January, 1971, pp. 38–43.

Bird, Caroline, "Women Should Stay Single," in J. Gipson Wells (ed.), *Current Issues in Marriage and the Family*, New York, Macmillan Publishing Company, Inc., 1975, pp. 32–40.

Cadwallader, Mervyn, "Marriage as a Wretched Institution," *Atlantic*, Vol. 218, No. 5, pp. 62–68.

Casler, Lawrence, *Is Marriage Necessary?*, New York, Human Sciences Press, 1974.

Constantine, Larry, and Constantine, Joan, "Dissolution of Marriage in a Nonconventional Context," *Family Coordinator*, October, 1972, pp. 457–462.

Denfeld, Duane, "Dropouts from Swinging," *Family Coordinator*, January, 1974, pp. 45–49.

Duberman, Lucile, *Marriage and Its Alternatives*, New York, Praeger Publishers, Inc., 1974.

Fairfield, Richard, *Communes U.S.A.*, Baltimore, Penguin Books, Inc., 1971.

Fitzgerald, George R., *Communes: Their Goals, Hopes, Problems*, New York, Paulist Press, 1971.

Glick, Paul, "A Demographer Looks at American Families," *Journal of Marriage and the Family*, February, 1975, pp. 15–26.

Henshel, Anne-Marie, "Swinging: A Study of Decision-Making in Marriage," *American Journal of Sociology*, January, 1973, pp. 885–891.

Henze, Lura F., and Hudson, John W., "Personal and Family Characteristics of Cohabiting and Noncohabiting College Students," *Journal of Marriage and the Family*, November, 1974, pp. 722–727.

Hostetler, John A., *Communitarian Societies*, New York, Holt, Rinehart and Winston, Inc., 1974.

———, *Hutterite Society*, Baltimore, The Johns Hopkins University Press, 1974.

507

Houriet, Robert, "Life and Death of a Commune Called Oz," *The New York Times Magazine,* February 16, 1969, pp. 30 ff.

Kanter, Rosabeth Moss, *Commitment and Community: Communes and Utopias in Sociological Perspective,* Cambridge, Massachusetts, Harvard University Press, 1972.

——— (ed.), *Communes: Creating and Managing the Collective Life,* New York, Harper & Row, 1973.

Kephart, William M., "Why They Fail: A Socio-Historical Analysis of Religious and Secular Communes," *Journal of Comparative Family Studies,* Autumn, 1974, pp. 130–140.

Lamott, Kenneth, "Doing Their Thing at Morning Star," in Rosabeth Moss Kanter (ed.), *Communes: Creating and Managing the Collective Life,* New York, Harper & Row, 1973, pp. 133–141.

Lyness, Judith; Lipetz, Milton; and Davis, Keith, "Living Together: An Alternative to Marriage," *Journal of Marriage and the Family,* May, 1972, pp. 305–311.

Macklin, Eleanor D., "Heterosexual Cohabitation Among College Students," *Family Coordinator,* October, 1972, pp. 463–472.

Melville, Keith, *Communes in the Counter Culture: Origins, Theories, Styles of Life,* New York, William Morrow and Company, 1972.

Musgrove, Frank, *Ecstasy and Holiness: Counter Culture and the Open Society,* Bloomington, Indiana University Press, 1975.

Ramey, James W., "Communes, Group Marriage, and the Upper-Middle Class," *Journal of Marriage and the Family,* November, 1972, pp. 647–655.

Roberts, Ron E., *The New Communes: Coming Together in America,* Englewood Cliffs, New Jersey, Prentice-Hall, 1971.

Smith, James R., and Smith, Lynn G., *Beyond Monogamy,* Baltimore, The Johns Hopkins Press, 1974.

Thamm, Robert, *Beyond Marriage and the Nuclear Family,* San Francisco, Canfield Press, 1975.

Zablocki, Benjamin, *The Joyful Community,* Baltimore, Penguin Books, Inc., 1971.

23

The Future

IN VIEW OF the alternative life styles described in the previous chapter, one could argue that the current American family is not fulfilling the needs of its members. But while this assumption may or may not be true, a fair number of "family strengthening" programs have made their appearance. The nature and effectiveness of these programs—together with their implications for the future—are the subject matter of this, the final, chapter.

THE FAMILY COURT MOVEMENT

In 1899 the first juvenile court was organized in Chicago, Illinois. Less than a half-century later, juvenile courts had been established in every state in the union, and today these courts are an integral part of American jurisprudence. In 1914 the first family court was established in Cincinnati, Ohio; while a number of other cities followed suit, family courts have never received the widespread acceptance accorded juvenile courts. Both types of court, however, have been simultaneously praised and criticized.

As they were originally set up in the various states, juvenile courts operated under the legal philosophy of *parens patriae*. That is to say, the state, acting through the juvenile court, assumed the necessary responsibility for delinquent children—who were presumably being neglected by their real parents. Delinquent children were thus accorded the same protection and guidance as neglected children, and their relation with the state became that of parent and child rather than that of the "Commonwealth v. _____."

Criticism of the above philosophy tended to take two forms. On the one hand, juvenile courts were accused of coddling and pampering youthful delinquents and of fostering an attitude of irresponsibility. Little wonder—so the argument went—that juvenile crime rates rose to such high levels.

On the other hand, juvenile courts have more recently been criticized for violating the constitutional rights of the individual. As Kay points out:

> The first flush of pride in the juvenile court has given way in the United States to serious reappraisals. Indeed, it is now generally conceded that the juvenile court has failed to achieve its goals. . . .
>
> The creation of a therapeutic atmosphere in the juvenile court was thought to require an informal procedure marked by the removal of lawyers, relaxed observance of the technical rules of evidence, and a firm decision that the constitutional rights of adults charged with criminal acts did not apply to the assertedly non-criminal proceedings of the juvenile court. Nearly all of these decisions were set aside by the United States Supreme Court's opinion in the now-famous *Gault* case. . . .
>
> This case has compelled an observance in delinquency proceedings of the child's constitutional rights to representation by counsel, notice, confrontation, and cross-examination of witnesses, and the privilege against self incrimination.[1]

It should be noted that the juvenile court system has not been abolished; indeed, no one has even suggested a return to the old system, wherein youthful delinquents were accorded the same treatment as adult offenders. What has happened is that the procedures have changed, and the goals made more realistic.

The family court has also had its ups and downs. As originally conceived, the family court was to have been to the family what the juvenile court was to the child. Theoretically, at least, it was to be empowered to handle such problems as annulment, legal separation, divorce, alimony, desertion and nonsupport, child custody, adoption, and illegitimacy. Employing a wide range of personnel—probation officers, social workers, psychiatrists, nurses, investigators, marriage counselors—the court was intended to resolve family difficulties, ameliorate interpersonal conflicts, offer professional guidance, and in general preserve family ties.

This was the theory, but in practice a number of difficulties arose. For one thing, personnel costs for social workers, counselors, and the like, were high, and some communities were reluctant to foot the bill. Other communities were unwilling to grant the necessary jurisdictional power to a single court.

---

[1] Herma Hill Kay, "A Family Court: The California Proposal," in Paul Bohannan (ed.), *Divorce and After*, Garden City, New York, Doubleday & Company, Inc. (Anchor Books), 1971, pp. 244 and 247.

510

When families can no longer solve their own problems, they may seek a court-determined solution. (Jerry Berndt, Stock Boston)

In states where family courts were set up, it was often difficult to procure adequate judges. For whereas both juvenile and family court judges should be mature individuals with keen insight into human nature, it is no secret that most judges do not relish such assignments. As Kay points out, "even a six-months stint on the job is more than many judges would like."[2]

And finally, the family courts in existence added to their own problems by neglecting to provide adequate information about the work they were doing. In the area of research, for example, most courts failed to build a solidified, factual body of knowledge that might serve as an aid to understanding and solving the very problems for which the courts were created!

Positive Features.   While it is true that family courts have not fulfilled the promise originally held out for them, they still have many positive features. The economic argument, for example, is probably in their favor. For, while a family court is certainly not cheap to operate, neither are the alternatives. In an integrated family court, all domestic cases are heard under one roof, with a resultant improvement in administrative and economic efficiency. The alternative procedure—still in existence in many of our large cities—is to have three or more different courts assume jurisdiction over family matters.

---

[2] *Ibid.*, p. 246.

Another advantage of the family court is that it provides professional help for those most in need of it. It should be pointed out that domestic relations cases in our large cities are staggering in number, and most of our civil courts are not equipped to handle the daily flow. From this view alone, some sort of family court arrangement is almost inevitable in today's urbanized society.

The research possibilities inherent in the family court system should also be mentioned. After all, solutions to problems such as divorce, desertion, and delinquency hinge on the isolation of the causes that produce these problems, and social scientists devote an immense amount of time to the research area. The point is that a family court, with a small statistical research unit, provides an ideal laboratory for the collection and analysis of information pertaining to family problems.

The fact that many of the existing family courts have not utilized research procedures is largely a budgetary matter. That is, faced with the choice of adding a statistical research unit or of employing additional social workers, many courts have chosen the latter course. And therein lies the vexing cycle. Lacking adequate budgetary provisions, family courts have not been able to fulfill their early promise. And being unable to demonstrate their success, the courts cannot easily make demands for an improved financial base.

In spite of the drawbacks, however, no one has suggested a *better* method for handling the various family-related problems that arise in modern society. Overall, as a matter of fact, family courts have done much good. Hopefully, they will improve their record in the future. To do so, they will need adequate financing—and this in turn means a higher level of public support than has been given in the past.

MARRIAGE COUNSELING

Although marriage counseling is often associated with the family court, the two movements have had quite different histories. Marriage counseling in the United States was originally little more than an informal advisory service, performed in conjunction with the regular duties of the doctor, lawyer, clergyman, or teacher. As the need grew, counseling services came to be an adjunct of family welfare agencies and child guidance clinics. But while the pattern had been set somewhat earlier in Europe, it was not until 1929 that the first formalized American marriage counseling agency was organized: the Marriage Consultation Center in New York City, founded by Drs. Abraham and Hannah Stone. A year later Paul Popenoe organized the American Institute of Family Relations, in Los Angeles. And in 1932 Emily Mudd opened the Marriage Council of Philadelphia.

In the following decades, scores of marriage counseling agencies were organized in various parts of the United States. While not all of them have survived, the counseling movement as a whole has increased in scope, with many of the agencies making substantial contributions to the well-being of the community.

Unfortunately for all concerned, some of the lesser agencies have operated with poorly qualified personnel, and as a consequence the marriage counseling movement has suffered some loss of reputation. To counteract this situation, the American Association of Marriage and Family Counselors was organized in 1942. With the stress on upgrading professional standards, exchanging counseling methods, and otherwise improving services, the organization has achieved an excellent reputation. Shortly after its founding, for example, the Association recommended that every member be required to have a graduate degree from an approved institution, at least three years of professional experience, plus "personal and professional integrity in accordance with accepted ethical standards."

As a result of such formulations, membership in the American Association of Marriage and Family Counselors (AAMFC) has been kept fairly small. There are a limited number of authorized training centers in the United States, and total membership in the AAMFC has never exceeded 3,500. Actually, most AAMFC members are drawn from other professions: medicine, social work, psychology, sociology, and the ministry. Understandably, these individuals are often able to devote but a portion of their time to marriage counseling.

Marriage counseling agencies themselves range from relatively large and complex organizations to small, one-person units. Some of the agencies operate through medical or religious sponsorship, others are under the auspices of civic or educational institutions. Private agencies, however—those run on a profit basis—are few and far between. Most marriage councils are nowhere near the point where they can support themselves solely on the basis of client fees.

Criticisms of Marriage Counseling. A number of criticisms —implicit or explicit—have been directed against marriage counseling activities. Among the more frequently heard allegations are the following:

1. *There are no real qualifying standards for marriage counselors. Practically anyone can become a marriage counselor.* As it happens, this charge is both true and false. Insofar as the AAMFC is concerned, standards are certainly high. The catch is that one does not have to belong to the AAMFC to be a practicing marriage counselor! Believe it or not, only three states—California, New Jersey, and Michigan—have licensing procedures relative to the practice of marriage counseling. Nichols states that:

> Today marriage counseling is an emergent profession, a quasi-profession, and an amateur activity, a field that is populated by highly skilled, clinically sophisticated practitioners at one extreme and by well meaning but incompetent amateurs at the other; by ethically and socially responsible professionals, and by unprincipled charlatans.[3]

From time to time other states have considered procedures for licensing or certification, but so far progress has been slow. Ironically, therefore, one of the major criticisms against marriage counseling is one that qualified counselors themselves have little control over.

2. *Research efforts in the field of marriage counseling have been weak.* The two surveys of marriage counseling research—by Olson[4] and by Goodman[5]—both found this charge to be true. Goodman writes as follows:

> The usual pattern in the sciences is for a subject area to become better defined over time, as investigators increasingly become associated with the field. This has not occurred in marriage counseling research. . . .
>
> It appears that there is no group of persons permanently devoting systematic efforts toward developing techniques for examining the counseling process and producing information which might be used in treatment.[6]

---

[3] William C. Nichols, Jr., "The Field of Marriage Counseling," *Family Coordinator,* January, 1973, p. 5.

[4] David Olson, "Marital and Family Therapy: Integrative Review and Critique," *Journal of Marriage and the Family,* November, 1970, p. 521.

[5] Elizabeth S. Goodman, "Marriage Counseling as Science: Some Research Considerations," *Family Coordinator,* January, 1973, pp. 111–116.

[6] *Ibid.,* pp. 113–114.

The reason for this research weakness probably stems from the fact that marriage counseling is an applied area, and the counselors themselves are "practitioners rather than investigators."[7] At the same time, there is some indication that the research aspect is improving.[8] Within the next few years, furthermore, there is every likelihood that additional gains will be made. It might also be mentioned that other types of advisory service—educational, vocational, financial—have also lagged in the research area, and it would be less than fair to single out marriage councils for special criticism.

3. *Because there is no established body of knowledge to draw on, marriage counseling is largely intuitive—more art than science.* This is related to the previous charge and is largely true. As Olson puts it, "the field has been seriously lacking in empirically tested principles and is without a theoretically derived foundation on which to operate clinically." The same author adds that "only recently are there positive signs that the profession is beginning to expand its empirical and theoretical base."[9]

515

But if marriage counseling is much closer to art than science, are the agencies justified in charging fees for their service? The answer must be in the affirmative. Any number of services in our society—legal, economic, psychiatric—regularly charge for their advice, and there is no reason why that prerogative should be denied to marriage counselors. In fact, marriage counseling agencies are generally organized as nonprofit institutions, and the fees charged are relatively modest.

4. *Marriage counselors themselves do not agree on their goals.* A recent charge, this one is largely false. Counseling is a helping profession, and the goal of counselors is to help those with marital problems. Confusion arises from the fact that in an earlier period the counselors' objective—above all else—was to "save the marriage." Currently, however, most counselors will not hesitate to recommend a divorce if the marriage seems beyond repair. As one counselor put it, "Our job is to help people understand how they are interacting in a relationship. What they choose to do with that understanding is up to them. We are certainly not in the business of gluing them together."[10]

---

[7] *Ibid.*, p. 114.
[8] See Olson, *op. cit.*, p. 503.
[9] *Ibid.*
[10] Quoted in Martha W. Lear, "Save the Spouses, Rather Than the Marriage," *New York Times Magazine*, August 13, 1972, p. 13.

It should be mentioned at this point that marriage counseling agencies routinely handle premarital as well as marital problems. Some agencies—particularly those located near college campuses—report that a fair proportion of their clients are either engaged or soon-to-be-married couples.

Assessment of Marriage Counseling. In Olson's words, "The professions of marital and family therapy have proceeded with a great amount of vigor but without a sufficient amount of rigor."[11] As a result, the field has failed to develop a verified fund of knowledge. Different counselors, therefore, are likely to use different approaches to the handling of marital problems, e.g., psychoanalytic, transactional, behavior modification, eclectic, and so on.

Nevertheless, in spite of some formidable obstacles, the field of marriage counseling has made definite progress. The AAMFC is a vigorous organization, ever on the alert for self-improvement. The number of meaningful articles and books dealing with counseling has been increasing. And with the advent of no-fault divorce procedures, the public has become more aware of counseling facilities.[12]

Marriage counselors as a group, furthermore, are intelligent, hard-working individuals who believe in the efficacy of their work. There is also reason to believe that, compared with most people, counselors' personalities are more in tune with the philosophy of "helping."[13] They are certainly experienced men and women who persevere at a most difficult and trying task. In brief, it would be quite unlikely that a dedicated, qualified group such as this could fail to effect an improvement in the well-being of the community.

Empirical results would seem to bear out the foregoing assumption. A fair number of follow-up studies—designed to ascertain the effectiveness of marriage counseling—have now been undertaken, and for the most part the results have been positive.[14]

---

[11] Olson, *op. cit.*, p. 501.

[12] See Barton Bernstein, "Lawyer and Counselor as an Interdisciplinary Team," *Family Coordinator*, January, 1974, pp. 41–44.

[13] See Clinton Phillips, "A Study of Marriage Counselors' MMPI Profiles," *Journal of Marriage and the Family*, February, 1970, pp. 119–130. See also Vincent Foley and Wayne Dyer, "Timing in Family Therapy," *Family Coordinator*, October, 1974, pp. 373–382.

[14] See Olson, *op. cit.*, pp. 521 ff.; and Meyer Elkin, "Conciliation Courts: The Reintegration of Disintegrating Families," *Family Coordinator*, January, 1973, pp. 63–71.

Finally, it should be pointed out that the marriage council affords problem couples an opportunity to present their case to a professionally trained, objectively oriented person. If the marriage counselor did not exist, where would the couple go for help? Most probably to a friend, relative, family doctor—or to nobody. Well-intentioned though they may be, friends and relatives are likely to have neither the competence nor the objectivity to deal with marital conflict. And, qualifications aside, medical doctors are extremely busy people, with a limited amount of time to devote to marital problems.

In his overview of marriage counseling, Nichols writes as follows: "Stemming from diverse sources, growing at uneven rates, and moving in many different directions, marriage counseling gives no sign of losing its great popularity. . . . It is here to stay."[15]

MARRIAGE ENRICHMENT PROGRAMS

Although there is some overlapping, marriage enrichment programs are basically different from marriage counseling. "Central to the whole marriage enrichment movement," write the Maces, "is a shift from the remedial emphasis of many of our current marital services, to the preventive concept of facilitating positive growth."[16] And while the definition may be somewhat arbitrary, Otto offers the following:

> Marriage enrichment programs are for couples who have what they perceive to be a fairly well functioning marriage and who wish to make their marriage even more mutually satisfying. The programs are *not* designed for people whose marriage is at a point of crisis, or who are seeking counseling help for marital problems.
>
> Marriage enrichment programs are generally concerned with enhancing the couple's communication, emotional life, or sexual relationship, fostering marriage strengths, and developing marriage potentials while maintaining a consistent and *primary focus on the relationship of the couple.*[17]

Whereas marriage counseling in the United States has been in existence for some 50 years, marriage enrichment programs are relatively new. In fact, although they were started in the 1960's, enrichment programs did not really become popular until the

---

[15] Nichols, *op. cit.*, p. 12.

[16] David Mace and Vera Mace, "Marriage Enrichment—Wave of the Future?" *Family Coordinator*, April, 1975, p. 131.

[17] Herbert A. Otto, "Marriage and Family Enrichment Programs in North America," *Family Coordinator*, April, 1975, p. 137.

1970's. They are not a fad, however. On the contrary, the writer would estimate that more than 200,000 couples have already participated in one of the marriage enrichment programs run by various religious, educational, or private agencies.[18] Otto, on the basis of his questionnaire survey, reports a worldwide interest in the movement.[19]

How the Program Functions. Although they are called by different names—Marriage Encounter, Pairing Enrichment, Marriage Diagnosis—marriage enrichment programs operate under a more-or-less common assumption; namely, that while the nature of marriage has changed a great deal, many spouses have not kept pace with the change, and therefore they are not realizing the full benefits from their own marriage.

Regula states that "marriage has suffered a functional loss. A wide variety of functions previously performed by the larger family have been taken over by units outside the family, reducing marriage to its essence—the interpersonal, subjective inner dimension."[20] And the Maces, two of the pioneers in the field, put it as follows:

> The picture now emerges clearly. What we have been calling "the failure of marriage" has rather been the failure of large numbers of individual marriages as they tried to undertake a transition for which the partners concerned simply lacked the basic equipment; namely, training in interpersonal competence. . . .[21]

The basic goal of marriage enrichment, then, is to enhance the interpersonal relationship between husband and wife—and this in turn is believed to hinge on *improved communication*. While no two enrichment programs are exactly alike, most involve small groups of married couples convening for a series of weekend meetings. The meetings themselves—usually held in a church or school building, or in a private residence—are run by a qualified professional person interested in the family field, such as a clergyman, educator, sociologist, or marriage counselor. The fees charged are nominal, though lodging and meals tend to add to the costs.

During the course of the meetings a number of topics are covered, and a variety of pedagogical techniques are used—lectures, filmstrips, reading materials, question-and-answer sessions,

[18] *Ibid.*, p. 141.
[19] *Ibid.*, p. 140.
[20] Ronald R. Regula, "Marriage Encounter: What Makes It Work?" *Family Coordinator*, April, 1975, p. 153.
[21] Mace and Mace, *op. cit.*, p. 133.

and so on. However, since the emphasis is on improving communication between spouses, the enrichment program includes certain concepts not normally found in the classroom. One of these is the concept of "team couples," couples who have already been through the enrichment program. According to Regula:

> The role of the team couples is to drop their masks and to disclose their feelings toward each other to the participating couples. Team couples must initiate the act of self-disclosure, making themselves vulnerable and transparent to the participating couples. This initiatory act has a very powerful impact; it helps the participating couples to discard their anxieties and begin taking the risk of dropping their masks, and of revealing their feelings to their spouse. . . .
>
> Participating couples gradually start to identify, as the team couples reveal their own marriage relationships, going from the romantic stage to the stage of disillusionment. They speak, for example, of how they locked themselves into the roles of "mother of the children" and "provider of the family," growing more distant and less communicative. . . .
>
> After disclosing these personal, "gut-level" experiences, the team couples relate their own approach to Marriage Encounter, including their own initial anxiety and resistance. This is followed by the sharing of their breakthrough, as it actually occurred during their Encounter.[22]

In addition to utilizing the team couple, marriage enrichment programs employ a variety of other concepts—*self-awareness, disclosure, dialogue, reciprocity, esteem-building*—the number and kind depending of the orientation of the person in charge. *Disclosure*, for example, is one of the concepts often employed with participating couples:

> Once a person becomes aware of a particular thought, feeling, or desire, he immediately begins to make a choice. The choice is whether to disclose the content or whether to keep it to himself. There are appropriate times and places for disclosing various types of information, and in order to avoid over or under disclosure, partners must decide for themselves their own set of procedures.[23]

In studying disclosure, Jourard identified what he called the "dyadic effect." That is, he found that if a person revealed an intimate, innermost thought to his or her partner, the partner tended to respond empathetically by also divulging an intimate thought. The reverse was likewise found to be true. If one

---

[22] Regula, *op. cit.*, pp. 154–155.
[23] Sherod Miller, Ramon Corrales, and Daniel Wackman, "Recent Progress in Understanding and Facilitating Marital Communication," *Family Coordinator*, April, 1975, p. 147.

partner was unwilling to divulge personal feelings, the other partner also "blocked." It was Jourard's belief that intimate self-disclosure not only enhanced interpersonal communication but also aided in the process of "really knowing one's self."[24]

Miller, Corrales, and Wackman make the following summary statement, apropos of marital communication:

> When a couple are communicating with dyadic effect operating, they have implicitly agreed to a set of procedures with high levels of disclosure and receptivity. . . .
>
> These advances are truly significant because communication is a central process in marital relationships. By increasing the effectiveness of communication between married partners, the opportunity to take charge of their relationship is greatly enhanced. In short, growth in the relationship need not be only a matter of chance. Rather, it can be directed by the partners themselves.[25]

A Summing Up. There is much more that could be written about marital enrichment, but space precludes further elaboration. Suffice to say that the program holds genuine promise. Thousands of couples have already participated, and thousands more are expected. The reason is basically simple. By stressing positive rather than therapeutic processes, the program literally aims at stopping marital discord before it starts. And by emphasizing improved communication between spouses, the marital enrichment approach—theorectically, at least—gives to the couple the means of at least partially controlling their own marital destiny.

FAMILY-LIFE EDUCATION

Thus far the "preservation" programs discussed, such as marriage counseling and marriage enrichment, have dealt largely with married couples. One of the oldest and largest programs, however—generally referred to as family-life education—involves high school and college students.

High School Courses. Since early records were not always retained, it is difficult to pinpoint the origin of family-life courses

---

[24] See S. M. Jourard, *The Transparent Self: Self-Disclosure and Well-Being*, Princeton, New Jersey, Van Nostrand Company, 1964; and *Self Disclosure*, New York, John Wiley & Sons, Inc., 1971.
[25] Miller et al., *op. cit.*, pp. 148–150.

in American high schools. One of the first courses was offered in Tulsa, Oklahoma, in 1918. However, the big impetus for such courses did not come until after World War II, when family-life offerings were added to the curriculum in response to public demand. Today, high school enrollment in such courses probably runs to well over a million.

There is significant variation in the content of family-life offerings. Some offer instruction in nutrition and family meals, infant training, textiles and clothing, home management, and similar subjects. Other courses center on such topics as dating and courtship, sex education, etiquette, and social relationships. Both types of offering are likely to be under the jurisdiction of the Home Economics department, although the specific names of the courses (Life Adjustment, Social Relations, Personal Relationships, Family Problems) show some ingenious variations.

521

For the most part, family-life courses have been well received, as adjudged by the response of both students and their parents. A well-taught family-life course, rather obviously, can mean a great deal to persons of high school age, beset as they are by a growing awareness of social and sexual relationships. It is little wonder that, over the years, the number of family-life courses has grown.

On the other hand, the courses have not been without their critics, and from time to time there have been headline-capturing statements that family-life offerings are merely frills—snap courses with little academic or utilitarian value. Generally speaking, however, the courses have outlasted their critics. So far as the writer is aware, they have become a permanent part of the educational curriculum.

College Courses. College offerings dealing with the family are generally of two kinds: institutional and functional. The former are concerned with the family as a social institution and normally include such topics as the history of the family, marital customs in other societies, legal aspects, theories and research on mate selection, marital adjustment and maladjustment, and various aspects of sex behavior. Although there is some overlapping, functional family courses concern themselves more with the practical side of premarriage and marriage and generally cover such areas as dating, the engagement, sex education, relations with in-laws, budgeting and insurance, bringing up children, and the like.

Institutional courses in the family were offered in American universities before the turn of the century, and shortly after World War I the first functional courses were introduced. These latter courses proved to be quite popular with the student body, and in a relatively short time functional offerings—often entitled "Preparation for Marriage"—had been adopted at hundreds of colleges. In fact, at present the number of such courses may equal or surpass the institutional offerings.

In an attempt to measure the effectiveness of the functional-type marriage courses, a number of studies have been undertaken wherein (1) attitudes of students are measured before and after taking the course, or (2) attitudes of students who have been exposed to a course are compared with attitudes of a control group who have not been exposed. No matter what method is used to evaluate them, functional marriage courses have consistently been found to have positive value.[26]

Institutional courses in the family have also been exceptionally well received by the student body, and today a large majority of American colleges and universities offer either one type of course or the other. In fact, family courses are among the most widely offered of all sociology courses.

OTHER PROGRAMS

In addition to the programs described in the preceding pages, there are a host of other agencies and services—both governmental and private—that deal with the preservation of American family life. Governmental agencies would include the Bureau of Family Services, the Children's Bureau, the Social Security Administration, the Home Economics Education Service, the Public Housing Administration, as well as a variety of state and local agencies.

Among the private organizations concerned with the family are the National Council on Family Relations, the Groves Conference on Marriage and the Family, the National Congress of Parents and Teachers, the Family Service Association of America, the American Association of Marriage and Family Counselors, and many others.

Special mention should also be made of on-going research, for the family field is fortunate in having a large number of empirical investigators—as the footnotes and bibliographies in the present

---

[26] See Evelyn Duvall, "How Effective Are Marriage Courses? *Journal of Marriage and the Family,* May, 1965, pp. 176–184; and David Olson and Arthur Gravatt, "Attitude Change in a Functional Marriage Course," *Family Coordinator,* April, 1968, pp. 99–104. See also Richard Kerckhoff, Terry Hancock, and panel, "The Family Life Educator of the Future," *Family Coordinator,* October, 1971, pp. 315–325; and Leland Axelson, "Promise or Illusion: The Future of Family Studies," *Family Coordinator,* January, 1975, pp. 3–6.

volume amply attest! Moreover, modern research methods are expensive, and when it is realized that the bulk of family research has involved relatively little money (as compared, say, with the financial outlay for the physical sciences), the record becomes noteworthy indeed.

Research findings and statistics relating to the family are also published by certain government agencies such as the Bureau of the Census, the National Vital Statistics Division, the Women's Bureau, and the Department of Labor. However, the bulk of family-related research has been—and doubtless will continue to be—undertaken by private researchers. At present, most of the work is being done by sociologists, although psychologists, anthropologists, and home economists have also made valuable contributions.

Some idea of the scope of family research can be seen from a partial listing of the professional journals in the field:

Journal of Marriage and the Family
The Family Coordinator
Journal of Comparative Family Studies
Family Process
Journal of Sex Research
Family Law Quarterly
International Journal of Sociology of the Family
Journal of Marriage and Family Counseling
Child Welfare
Journal of Family History
Family Service Highlights
Journal of Youth and Adolescence
Family Therapy
Children Today
Journal of Family Welfare
Family Law Commentator

WHICH DIRECTION?

Twenty-three chapters ago it was pointed out that the American family shows signs of both weakness and strength. In the intervening pages, the pros and cons have been spelled out. On the one hand, certain traditional family functions have been taken over by outside agencies. Sexual gratification, once considered the province of husband and wife, is increasingly being condoned outside the bonds of marriage. In recent years the marriage rate itself has been declining, while —not unexpectedly —the rate of marital breakup has risen sharply. And as the institution of marriage has weakened—at least, so the argument

(Philip Jon Bailey)

goes—a number of alternative life styles have developed, several of which were discussed in the previous chapter.

On the other hand, common observation suggests that our family system is not exactly falling apart. Most Americans not only marry, but—in spite of severe pressures—they manage to stay married. Children are still cherished, and from all indications family life seems to be a genuinely rewarding experience. And while it is true that in recent years a number of alternative life styles have emerged, they do not seem to have had a critical impact on the dominant family system. Indeed, public and professional interest in the family—as evidenced by marriage counseling, family-life education, marriage enrichment programs, and the like—remain high.

And so the question remains—in which direction is the American family heading, up or down? The present writer is inclined to be moderately optimistic on the subject. For one thing, most people seem vitally concerned with their own families. There is no grassroots movement to overthrow the "system." The same is true at the professional level. In fact, despite certain acknowledged weaknesses, all the family-strengthening programs discussed in the previous pages *are substantially stronger today* than they were at the close of World War II.

It is true that the divorce rate has risen, but while this must be considered a negative trend, there is one counterargument;

namely, no-fault procedures may act as a safety valve. That is, with discordant couples finding it much easier to procure a divorce, those marriages that remain intact may well represent a stronger, more solidified marital base than formerly. The same principle can be applied to alternative life styles. Since these provide people in all walks of life with a genuine alternative to marriage, those couples who do choose matrimony probably comprise a better-adjusted, more satisfied group than in the pre-alternative period.

Finally, the writer is optimistic because of the gratifying experience he has had with the thousands of college students who have taken his course in the family. As a group, they have been quick to grasp the institutional significance of the family and the importance of striking a balance between individual and societal needs. They are also aware that their own premarital and marital roles must be evaluated from both perspectives. And, while students do not necessarily agree with the instructor or with each other on what constitutes the optimal point of balance, they are in general accord with the framework in which debate should be held. And so long as the family, society, and the individual can be viewed reciprocally—as interdependent parts of the whole—there is cause for optimism.

Indexes

Index of Names

Brogan, Donna, 232, 299
Bronzaft, Arline, 231, 233
Browne, Henry J., 186
Bruce, Philip, 94
Bryant, Clifton, 475, 483
Buck, Timothy, 438
Bugelski, B. R., 249
Burch, Ernest S., 39
Burchinal, Lee, 241, 245, 247
Burgess, Ernest, 241
Burr, Wesley, 239, 257, 264, 265, 280, 367, 379, 380, 387
Burt, Nathaniel, 412
Byler, Uria, 165
Byrne, Donn, 280, 299

530

Cadwallader, Mervyn, 487, 507
Calhoun, Arthur, 78, 84, 90, 92, 95
Callahan, Parnell, 340, 460
Calverton, Victor, 119
Calvin, John, 65, 66
Campbell, Frederick, 232
Campisi, Paul J., 186
Cannon, Kenneth, 379, 380, 389
Carden, Maren Lockwood, 122, 131, 135, 141
Carmer, Carl, 141
Carns, Donald, 316, 318
Carrera, Michael, 436, 437
Carson, Gerald, 72, 84, 91, 216, 233
Carter, Hugh, 483
Carton, Jacqueline, 437
Carton, John, 437
Casler, Lawrence, 507
Catton, William, 119, 239, 254
Cavan, Ruth, 246, 393, 399
Centers, Richard, 251, 280
Chadwick, Bruce, 412
Chafe, William, 233
Chamberlain, Samuel, 72, 95
Chancellor, Loren, 247
Chaskes, Jay, 316
Chester, Robert, 340
Child, Irvin, 179, 186
Chilman, Catherine, 404, 412
Christensen, Harold, 245, 247, 377, 471, 472
Church, C. C., 141
Clark, Homer, 460
Clarke, Alfred, 290, 299
Clavan, Sylvia, 233
Clayton, Richard, 318
Clignet, Remi, 38, 40
Clore, Gerald, 280

Cochrane, Susan, 367
Cole, Charles L., 379
Coleman, Emily R., 66
Coleman, Richard, 407
Comstock, Anthony, 138
Constantine, Joan, 486, 507
Constantine, Larry, 486, 507
Coolidge, Olivia, 223, 225
Coombs, Robert, 252, 253, 261, 280
Cooper, Clare, 226, 233
Corrales, Ramon, 519, 520
Coser, Rose Laub, 39, 233
Cottrell, Leonard, 241
Covello, Leonard, 186
Crockett, Harry, 244
Cross, Earle, 66
Cross, Whitney, 141
Curtin, Philip D., 211
Cutright, Phillips, 412, 469, 473, 483

Darwin, Charles, 23, 135
Davidson, Karen, 289, 300
Davis, Keith, 265, 266, 315, 318, 491, 493, 508
Davis, Kingsley, 39
Dean, Dwight, 299
Decard, Barbara, 233
De Lora, Jack R., 119, 280, 487, 495, 507
De Lora, Joann S., 119, 280, 487, 495, 507
de Mause, Lloyd, 95, 438
Demos, John, 4, 5, 66, 71, 72, 86, 92, 95, 438
Demos, Virginia, 438
Denfeld, Duane, 496, 498, 499, 500, 507
De Rougemont, Denis, 299
De Sales, Raoul De Roussy, 282, 299
de Tocqueville, Alexis, 416
Devereux, Edward, 431, 438
Dewey, John, 420
Dietrich, Katheryn, 211
Dinitz, Simon, 252
Dinnerstein, Leonard, 186
Ditzion, Sidney, 119, 142
Domhof, G. William, 396, 412
Donald, Henderson H., 202, 204
Dowling, Noel, 164
Duberman, Lucile, 507
Dubin, Murray, 340
Du Bois, W. E. B., 195, 196
Dudley, Donald, R., 66
Duss, John S., 102, 103, 106, 107, 108, 119
Duvall, Evelyn, 522

531

532

533

Mook, Maurice, 166
Moore, Harvey, 438
Moore, John C., 60, 67, 283, 300
Morgan, Edmund, 6, 78, 84, 86, 88, 89, 90, 96, 212
Morgan, Lewis Henry, 19, 23, 24, 40
Morius, Margaret, 368
Morris, Laura Newell, 201, 212
Morris, Naomi, 315, 319
Mortimer, Jeylan, 413
Moynihan, Daniel, 172, 173, 183, 186, 212, 249, 250
Muller, Bernhard, 114
Muncy, Raymond L., 109, 110, 112, 120
Murdock, George, 40
Murstein, Bernard I., 28, 40, 48, 67, 256, 267ff., 271, 281, 377, 497
Musgrove, Frank, 508
Musmanno, Michael, 187
Mutschler, Hildegarde, 109, 112

Nass, Gilbert, 315
Neil, A. S., 430
Nelli, Humbert, 187
Nelson, Harold, 378
Nelson, Lowry, 248
Nelson, Ruth, 378
Newhouse, Sewell, 123, 127, 128
Nichols, William C., 341, 514, 517
Nordhoff, Charles, 103, 108, 111, 113, 118, 120, 142
Norton, Arthur, 241, 483
Noyes, George W., 142
Noyes, Hilda, 142
Noyes, John Humphrey, 120, 121ff., 140, 142
Noyes, Pierrepont, 127, 128, 131, 142
Noyes, Theodore R., 138
Nye, F. Ivan, 10, 241, 281, 422, 438

Oakley, Mary Ann, 363, 368
Ogburn, William F., 4, 9
Olson, David, 514, 515, 516, 522
O'Neill, P. T., 461
Orthner, Dennis, 388
Otto, Herbert, 388, 517, 518
Otto, Luther, 390, 413
Owen, Robert Dale, 365

Palisi, Bartolomeo, 178, 182, 187
Palmer, Sally, 473, 474, 484
Parelius, Ann P., 258, 281

Parker, Robert Allerton, 132, 133, 135, 142
Parkes, A. S., 368
Parrish, John, 229, 230, 233
Pasamanick, Benjamin, 252
Patai, Raphael, 67
Paul, P. W., 394, 397, 398, 412
Pavela, Todd, 469
Peck, Robert, 473
Penn, William, 143
Perkins, Deborah, 438
Peters, John, 40
Petras, John, 389
Phillips, Clinton, 516
Phillips, John, 309, 319
Phillips, Robert, Jr., 424, 438
Pineo, Peter, 378, 389
Pisani, Bartolomeo, 187
Pivar, David, 233
Plateris, Alexander, 484
Platt, Marilyn, 373, 388
Ploscowe, Morris, 341
Polak, A. Laurence, 341
Pomeroy, Wardell, 288, 300, 348, 368
Potts, Anna, 215, 216
Price, Jacob, 67
Price, Richard, 490
Price, T., 38
Price-Bonham, Sharon, 484
Prince, A. J., 246
Procacci, Givliano, 187
Puzo, Mario, 176

Queen, Stuart, 40, 55, 67, 81

Rabb, Theodore, 187
Rainwater, Lee, 212, 406, 407, 408, 410, 413
Ramey, James, 501, 508
Ramsey, Charles, 183, 186
Rapson, Richard, 438
Rausch, Harold, 484
Redekop, Calvin, 166
Redfield, Robert, 166
Reed, Edward, 201
Reed, Sheldon, 252, 257
Regula, Ronald, 518, 519
Reibel, Daniel B., 120
Reik, Theodore, 300
Reimers, David, 186
Reinhard, Anne, 65
Reiss, Ira, 67, 96, 252, 258, 281, 315, 317
Resnicoff, Samuel, 341, 461

534

535

Index of Subjects

Bride-price, 29
'Broad wives (slave), 198
Broken homes, 466
Brook Farm, 500
Budget, Amish newspaper, 151
Bundling
 colonial, 79–81
 Amish, 153
Bureau of the Census, 523

Campus values in mate selection, 279
Cantharidin, 363
Catholic-Protestant marriages, 472
"Cattle Culture," 29
Changes in sex mores, 219 ff.
Changing family functions, 4–9
Changing status of women, 213–234
Child Welfare, 523
Childlessness, 360 ff.
Child-rearing, 414–439
Children
 in colonial period, 86 ff.
 under stirpiculture, 135 ff.
 Amish, 163–164
 and divorce, 466
Chivalry, 60–63
Chukchee, 38
Clinical approach to sexual maladjustment, 382–383
Clitoris, 349
"Close association" theory, 27
"Closed field," in mate selection theory, 270
Code of Hammurabi, 37
Cohabitation
 definition, 490–491
 problems involved in, 492
 positive features of, 492–493
 outlook, 493–494
Coitus interruptus, 367
Coitus reservatus, 136
College, as a factor in mate selection, 252–253
College courses in the family, 521–522
Collusion, as a defense against divorce, 451–452
Colonial family, *see* American family
Common-law marriage
 in Colonial period, 83
 present-day, 335–338
Communes
 history of, 500–501
 difficulties involved, 501–503

rewards, 503–504
 balance sheet, 504–506
 future of, 506
Communication, as an integral part of marriage enrichment, 518 ff.
Companionship, as a reason for marriage, 372
Complementary needs, 263–265
Complex Marriage, 132–135
Computerized (mate-selection) services, 295–296
Concept of childhood, 415
Conception, 354 ff.
Concubines, 43 ff.
Conditioning, Pavlovian, 420
Condonation, as a defense against divorce, 452–453
Conjoint marital-unit therapy, 382
Conjugal courtship, 30
Conjugal family type, 24 ff.
Connivance, as a defense against divorce, 452
Consanguine family type, 24 ff.
Consanguinity, legalities of, 323–324
Contadini, 167 ff.
Contest theory, in U.S. divorce suits, 445 ff.
Contraception, 365–367
Council of Trent, 58
Counterculture, 506
Courtship, *see* Mate selection
Cross-class marriages, 473–474
Cross-cultural survey of family practices, 17 ff.
Cruelty, as a ground for divorce, 450
Cultural enclosure, 125
Culture conflict, 171 ff.
Curvilinear aspects of marital adjustment, 378–380

Dating problems, 272–277
Dating, the American system of, 271 ff.
Death of a Salesman, 400
Decree nisi, 456
Defenses against divorce, 450–455
Delay in marriage, 488
Department of Labor, 523
Desertion
 typical case, 475
 effects on the individual, 475–477
 effects on children, 477
 effects on society, 477–478

538

Detumescence, 348
Dialogue in marriage enrichment, 519
Diploid number, 356
Discipline, child, 416
Disclosure, in marriage enrichment, 519
"Dissolution of marriage," as a substitute for divorce, 448
Divorce, among
   preliterates, 37–39
   Hebrews, 45
   Greeks, 49
   Romans, 52–53
   American colonists, 82
Divorce court dialogue, 445–446
Divorce from bed and board, 455 ff.
Divorce in the U.S.
   rate of divorce, 463–464
   geographic variations, 465
   migratory factor, 465–466
   children involved, 466
   remarriage, 466–468
Divortium a mensa et thoro, 58
Divortium a vinculo matrimonii, 455
Domestic relations court, 475
Dowries, 214
Dropout couples, in swinging, 499
Duration of marriage, 465
Dyadic effect, in marriage enrichment, 519–520

Early American family, *see* American family
Eclectic approach to marriage counseling, 516
Economic communism, Oneida, 126–129
Economic function of the family, 4–6
Economic security, as a reason for marriage, 372
Educational function of the family, 6
Egrad, 503
Endogamy, 242–253, 392
Engagement, *see* Betrothal
Epididymis, 345 ff.
Erection, 348
Errant husbands, 475
Esteem building, in marriage enrichment, 519
Estrogen, 352
Estrous cycle, 351
Eugenics program, Oneida, 135–138
European divorce laws, 460

Evolution of marriage, theories of, 23 ff.
Exchange theory, in mate selection, 261–262
Exogamy, 242 ff.
Extended family, 25
Extramarital sex relations
   among preliterates, 33–34
   in Colonial period, 93
   legalities of, 305
   Roman Catholic view toward, 308
   extent of, 314 ff.
   swinging, 494–500

Fallopian tube, 351
Family Coordinator, 523
Family court
   history of, 509 ff.
   difficulties faced, 510–511
   positive features, 511–512
   future of, 512
Family field approach, 3 ff.
Family functions, changing, 4–9
Family Law Quarterly, 523
Family life education
   high school, 520–521
   college, 521–522
   functional courses, 521–522
   institutional courses, 521–522
Family Service Association of America, 522
Fault system of divorce, 445–446
Federal marriage and divorce law, 339
Female sexual anatomy, 349–351
Feminine attire, 1800's, 216
Feminine Mystique, 228
Fertility, 353, 360 ff.
Fetal development, 358–360
Feudalism, 58 ff.
Fiefs, 59
Filter theory of mate selection, 265–266
Fireplace, colonial, 72–73
Fixation, 418
Folkways, changes in, 219 ff.
Forcible rape, 306
Forestiere, 174
Forms of marriage, 17 ff.
Formulation of divorce policy, 458–460
Fornication, 305
"Four ages" at marriage, 326–327
"Fractional hands," among slaves, 191

Franklin stove, 73
Fraternal twins, 356 ff.
Fraud, marital legalities of, 322
Free love, 132
Free marriage (Roman), 52
Freedmen's Bureau, 203 ff.
Freemen, 59
Frequency of romantic love, 286–288
Freudian theory
  impact on children, 418 ff.
  research findings on, 420
Frieri, 79
Functional courses in the family, 521 ff.
Furnishings, in early colonial houses, 71 ff.

540

Gault case, 510
Generation gap, regarding cohabitation, 492
Geographical variations in divorce, 465
Gestation, 359
Governmental agencies dealing with the family, 522–523
Greek family system, 46–49
Gretna Green marriages, 333–335
"Ground rules" for swingers, 494–497
Grounds for divorce, among preliterates, 38–39
  Hebrews, 45
  Greeks, 49
  Romans, 52–53
Grounds for divorce in the U.S., 449–450
Group marriage, 19–20
Group sex, 496
Groves Conference on Marriage and the Family, 522
Guilt and innocence concept of divorce, 444 ff.

Handfasting, 83
Hard-core families, 411
Harm of inbreeding, 28
Harmony Society, *see* Rappites
Hebrew family life, 42–45
Hetairae, 47
Heterogamy, 255 ff.
High school courses in the family, 520–521
Historical families, 391

Historical perspective
  Hebrews, 42–45
  Greeks, 46–49
  Romans, 49–53
  Early Christians, 53–56
  Middle Ages, 57 ff.
  feudalism, 58–59
  chivalry, 60–63
  Renaissance, 63–64
  Reformation, 64–66
  American colonies, 68–97
History of Childhood Quarterly, 42
Homogamy
  intelligence, 255
  physical traits, 255–256
  social attitudes, 256
  personality, 256–257
  temperament, 256–257
Homosexuality
  among preliterates, 37
  among ancient Greeks, 47–48
Hopi, 38
Housing, colonial, 69 ff.
Husband-wife relationships, 370–389
Hymen, 350
Hyper-romanticism, 291

Idealization, in romantic love, 285–286
Identical twins, 356 ff.
Immediate family, 25
Impermeability of upper class, 391 ff.
Incas, 26
Incest, 323
Incest taboo, 26–30
Increase in singleness, 488
Index of Negro residential segregation, 206–207
Individual-societal perspective, 14–16
Infanticide, 54
Infatuation, 285
Infertility, causes
  age, 360–361
  physicality, 361
  probability, 361–362
  sperm deficiency, 362
Infertility, cures, 363–365
Informal social control, 39, 305
Institute of Family Relations, Los Angeles, 513
Institutional courses in the family, 521 ff.
Interclass marriages, 473–474

Interfaith marriages, 471–473
Interlocking aspects of endogamy, 253–255
Interlocutory decree, 456
Internal sexual contamination, 55
International Journal of Sociology of the Family, 523
Interracial marriage, 468–471
Interreligious and interclass dating, problems of, 274–275
Interstitial cells, 346
Introduction services
  marriage brokers, 293
  lonely hearts clubs, 293–294
  matrimonial agencies, 295
  computerized services, 295–296
  future of, 296–297
"Inveigling," 76
Involuntary childlessness, 361 ff.
Irremediable breakdown, as a ground for divorce, 447 ff.
Italian family
  in Italy, 167–169
  first generation, 169–178
  resistance to change, 173–174
  second generation, 178–182
  third generation, 182–186
Italian foods, 176

Jats, 20
Jealousy, 20–21
Jewish intermarriage, 471–472
Jewish view toward premarital sex, 310–311
Journal of Comparative Family Studies, 523
Journal of Marriage and the Family, 523
Judicial separation, 455–456
Jus primae noctis, 59
Juvenile courts, 509

Kaingang (Brazil), 19
Kaleidoscopic class, 398 ff.
Kinship
  among the Amish, 156–159
  among American upper class, 391 ff.
Kissing, absence of, 30
Krinopathy (Oneida), 131

La Via Vecchia, 169 ff.
Labia majora, 349

Labia minora, 349
Lack of physical attractiveness, as a problem of dating, 275–276
Latency, 418
Legal aspects of marriage
  void and voidable marriages, 321–323
  consanguinity, 323–324
  miscegenation, 325
  legal age at marriage, 325–328
  licensing, 329–330
  blood tests, 330–331
  waiting period, 331–333
  common-law marriage, 335–338
Legal sanctions pertaining to premarital sex, 304–308
Length of marriages that end in divorce, 465
Levirate, 21
Licensing of marriage, 329 ff.
Limited divorce, 455–456
Living alone, 486–490
Log cabin, colonial, 70
Lonely hearts clubs, 293–294
Love, *see* Romantic love
Lower-class family
  classification, 403–404
  courtship, 406
  family life, 407 ff.
  men's view, 408
  women's view, 408
  children, 409
  bright spots, 410–412

"Making out," 219, 309
Male sexual anatomy, 345–349
Mansion House, Oneida, 124 ff.
Manus, 51–52
Marital adjustment, 370–389
Marital breakup, individual factors, 480 ff.
Marital breakup, societal factors
  changing family functions, 479
  casual marriages, 479
  jobs for women, 479
  decline in morality, 479
  philosophy of happiness, 479
  liberal divorce laws, 480
Marital fraud, 322
Marital prediction studies
  method, 375–376
  criticisms, 376–378
Marital separation, 474 ff.

541

Night-running, 79
No-fault system of divorce, 446–449
Nonmarital sex behavior, among pre-literates, 34
Nonmarried population, 489
Norm-interaction theory, 254
Nuclear family, 25
Nuptials, Hebrew, 44

Oceana, 504
Oedipus complex, 418
Old Order Amish, *see* Amish family
One-room school, 88
Oneida Community
    origins, 121 ff.
    social organization, 124–126
    economic communism, 126–129
    mutual criticism, 129–131
    Krinopathy, 131
    Complex Marriage, 132–135
    role of women, 134–135
    eugenics program, 135–138
    breakup, 138–139
    John Humphrey Noyes, 139–141
"Open field," in mate selection theory, 270
Orgasm, female, 350, 383 ff.
Osmosis, 358
Ovaries, 350 ff.
Oviduct, 351

Paesani, 170 ff.
Pantogamy, 132
Parens patriae, 509
Parent-child interaction
    historical statement, 415–418
    Freudian impact, 418–420
    research on Freudian theory, 420–423
    child-rearing pendulum, 423–425
    parent education, 425–428
    permissive school, 429–430
    restrictive school, 430–431
    sex education, 433–437
Parental influence, in dating, 274
Paterfamilias, 43
Patria potestas, 51
Patrilocal residence, 25
Pavlovian conditioning, 420
"Pedestal" system of mate attraction, 214 ff.
Penis, 346 ff.

Perfectionism, 122 ff.
Permissive school of child-rearing, 429–430
Personality testing, 291–292
Petting, 219, 302, 304–305, 309
Physical attraction, 284
Physical examination, as a requirement for marriage, 330–331
Physiological basis of marriage, 345–369
Polyandry, 20–21
Polygamy, 18
Polygyny, 21–23
"Poor man's divorce," 476
Pregnancy, 354 ff.
Preliterate family customs, 17 ff.
Premarital coitus
    in Colonial period, 91
    legal aspects, 305
    extent of, 314–316
Premarital petting, 304–305
Premarital sex codes
    legal sanctions, 304–308
    premarital petting, 304–305
    premarital coitus, 305
    fornication, 305
    rape, 305–306
    seduction, 307
    attitude of churches toward, 308–311
    public opinion, 311–312
Preventive programs, as an approach to marital adjustment, 517 ff.
Primary group, 417
Private agencies dealing with the family, 522–523
Problems of cohabitation, 492
Procedural aspects of marriage, 328–333
Process approach in mate selection, 266–267
Progesterone, 350
Promiscuity, 18
Propinquity, 238–239, 254–255
Prostate gland, 345 ff.
Prostitution, among preliterates, 36
Protestant-Catholic marriages, 472
Protestant Reformation, 64 ff.
Protestant view toward premarital sex, 309–310
Psychoanalytic theory
    in mate selection, 259–260
    in marriage counseling, 516
Ptolemies, 26

543

545

Wife swapping, 494 ff.
Windowing, 79
Witches, in Puritan New England, 85
Woman's rights movement, 221–226
Women as a minority group, 213
Women, role of in American colonies, 83–85

Women's Bureau, 523
Women's liberation, 226 ff.
Working-class family, 403 ff.

Zed, 504
Zoar, 101, 500
Zygote, 351

546

146366

LIBRARY
OF
MOUNT ST. MARY'S
COLLEGE
EMMITSBURG, MARYLAND

ABCDEFGHIJ–H–79876

MAY 2 5 1981